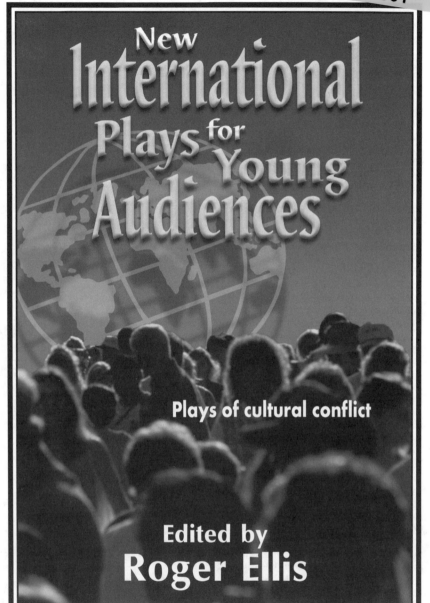

New International Plays for Young Audiences

Plays of cultural conflict

Edited by
Roger Ellis

MERIWETHER PUBLISHING LTD.
Colorado Springs, Colorado

Meriwether Publishing Ltd., Publisher
PO Box 7710
Colorado Springs, CO 80933-7710

Executive editor: Theodore O. Zapel
Cover design: Janice Melvin

Library of Congress Cataloging-in-Publication Data

New international plays for young audiences : plays of cultural conflict
/ edited with a critical introduction by Roger Ellis.
    p. cm.
Summary: An anthology of plays representing various cultures and
societies by playwrights from Croatia, Italy, Argentina, New Zealand,
Australia, the United Kingdom, the United States, and Canada.
Includes bibliographical references
    ISBN 1-56608-081-9
1. Children's plays. 2. Young adult drama. [1. Plays.] I. Ellis,
Roger, 1943 May 18-
  PN6119.9 .N49 2002
    808.82'0083--dc21

                            2002006896

1 2 3 4   02 03 04

Contents

Acknowledgments

Among the many individuals and organizations who lent me their assistance with this book, special recognition should be given to Grand Valley State University which provided me with the much-needed funding and release time from teaching and directing in order to compile and prepare the material. I'm also grateful for the continued support of my editor, Ted Zapel, at Meriwether Publishing.

In addition to the people and groups too numerous to mention who have spread the word about my call for scripts for this anthology, I'd like to thank the following individuals and international organizations which have been instrumental in publicizing my efforts: Association Internationale du Théâtre Amateur/International Amateur Theatre Association (AITA/IATA); Chris Gallagher of the Australian Script Centre; United States Center for the International Association of Theatre for Children and Young People (ASSITEJ/USA); Beatriz Rizk of the International Hispanic Theatre Festival (Miami); Women Playwrights International (Australia); Theatre Playwrights Development Collective (Canada); Priscilla Yates of the Australian Writers Guild; Irish Centre of AITA/IATA; Council of Drama in Education (Canada); Australian Capital Territory Drama Association (ACTDA); North European Amateur Theatre Alliance AITA/IATA (NEATA); Harlekin Theaterverlag (Denmark); May-Brit Akerholt of the Australian National Playwrights Centre; Peter Spencer, editor of *Ideaction*; International Children and Youth Theatre Centre (Netherlands); Dr. Shirley Harbin of the North American Regional Alliance AITA/IATA (NARA), and Dr. Laura Salazar, editor of the *Americas Update* newsletter of NARA; Replay Productions (Ireland); Chris Thompson of the *Drama Australia Newsletter*; Gustavo Ott of the South American Regional Alliance AITA/IATA (SARA); Bernadine Carey, my photo consultant from Grand Valley State University; Fiona Winning of Playworks (Australia); Leonardo Tromp of the Caribbean Regional Alliance AITA/IATA (CARA); and Devanand Misra of the National Institute of Performing Arts (India). And last but not least I owe a debt of gratitude I can never repay to all of the actors and audiences whose performances and responses enabled me to recognize the power and the grace, the subtlety and theatricality of the plays contained in this anthology.

Introduction

International Youth Theatre and Globalization

The growth and continuing vitality of international youth theatre is arguably the most significant feature of global theatrical development that has emerged during the late twentieth and early twenty-first centuries. From Japan to Norway, from Canada to Argentina, in the island nations of Australasia and across the Caribbean — international theatre activity for children and young adults has inspired, involved and empowered millions of young people worldwide. Today youth theatre associations, international networks, festivals, conferences and celebrations of various kinds all testify to this rapidly growing field that annually involves young people and artists or practitioners from hundreds of national and ethnic backgrounds, many different religions, and diverse cultural traditions.

All this impressive activity forms part of a larger social phenomenon that has developed during the same period, that of "global youth culture." Due largely to the planetary impact of communications media, young people the world over share more in common today than was ever the case prior to the 1960s and 1970s. For some time now those in consumer marketing and advertising have been keenly appreciative of this — especially as it pertains to music, fashion and the motion picture industries. Richard Schechner's prophetic observations twenty years ago that cultural boundaries are becoming more relevant than nationalistic political ones[i], seems an apt description of what has been happening with contemporary youth culture, though he certainly failed to envision Marshall McCluhan's "global village" turning into a global mall within his own lifetime. Nonetheless, it is certain that young people all over the planet are now "bonding" in ways their parents could never have foreseen, with consequences still to be determined.

We know, however, that not all of this development in international youth culture has come without cost. Probably the most common issue that concerns critics is that global media imperialism has inculcated pernicious, homogenized tastes in young people the world over: consumer greed, brand-name obsession, slavish idolization of modern (i.e., Western) products and lifestyles. And at bottom, of course, is the widespread fear of questionable "value systems" that are supposedly communicated along with those lifestyles. Sociologists, religious leaders, parents, educators and others wonder if films and television are corrupting the sexual mores of young audiences and eroding respect for bedrock institutions like church and school; while others worry that modern youth's indifference to cultural uniqueness might promote narcissism and self-obsession, or if traditional values such as patriotism, self-sacrifice, tolerance, humility, self-respect and others may soon become quaint and irrelevant to the new generation. Nor are such concerns restricted to developed societies: the anti-Hollywood diatribes of tub-thumping North American evangelists are matched in their fervor by the ferocity of Taliban leaders trashing TV sets, and the brutality of Chinese party officials imprisoning those who download "forbidden" Internet content.

Here in the United States, sociologists have even adopted the sound-bite, media-inspired phrase "Generation X" in an attempt to define a planetary population of young people who often seem indefinable in terms of their values and goals, and who only seem unified by their vague craving for novelty, suspicion of authority and rejection of the past. Listening to such analysts, one might think that the only "shared past" that Generation X — and other "alphabet generations" — possess began with Pink Floyd, marijuana and Nike athletic wear.

But when we regard closely the *theatrical* expressions of international youth, a vastly different picture emerges. In contemporary plays written by and for young people, we confront a repertoire that argues instead on behalf of perspectives and values that are not only shared but fervently held by hundreds of millions of people. And these are not values transmitted by fantasy or escapist works like so many "older" style children's dramas crammed by adult authors with moral meanings and feel-good happy endings. On the contrary, international youth theatre today more often than not looks realistically at painful world problems that baffle policymakers, educators and other leaders. Moreover, the repertoire frequently bristles in outrage at the abuse of human rights that it encounters, struggling to take the moral high ground in seeking solutions.

I have found that among the many concerns addressed by these dramas, one that frequently recurs is that of tolerance and acceptance of cultural diversity. Perhaps this is not so surprising when one recalls that many national educational systems have adopted those two principles as core values within their curricula for at least the last decade. Another explanation for the persistence of this theme in international youth theatre is perhaps the makeup of contemporary society itself: wherever one turns, our global village seems demographically pluralistic, with many national, ethnic, racial, religious and other groups coexisting and intermingling with each other in often unforeseen ways. Or from another standpoint, perhaps it is the all-too-common evidence of intolerance, hatred, prejudice and persecution that has foregrounded this issue in so many plays I have read and seen.

For whatever the reasons, however, we see young people the world over behaving as though they were oblivious to such things as skin color, "foreign" languages, "exotic" foods and other cross-cultural idiosyncrasies when it comes to meeting others, participating in athletics or artistic activities, and — most importantly — forming relationships. And while it is certainly possible to note instances of intolerance, racism and the like among this age group — witness Europe's disillusioned punks and skinheads, the violent thugs inspired by Islamic jihads, the arrogant white supremacists of North America — the young generation as a whole certainly finds it much easier to communicate interculturally and establish relationships with each other than their forbears ever did. One must ask: are young people today really more sensitive to others' needs and feelings than we give them credit for? Are they truly more accepting of cultural differences — in race, gender, age, ethnicity, religion and other areas — than pop media critics realize? And are they as troubled by the consequences of cultural conflict as older generations seem to be?

This anthology is defined by the centrality of that issue in all the plays contained here: the dramas are primarily concerned with conflicts that arise from a breakdown in cultural understanding. By and large, these scripts deal with this issue in three ways: by trying to understand the basis of cultural conflict, by focusing on young people's stakes in such conflict or by devising solutions to the conflict. What is remarkable is that this seems to be the case whether the plays have been written by adults for youth audiences or group-developed by youth performance ensembles themselves. In order to understand how the individual plays accomplish this, however, let's be clear on just what this anthology means by "culture" and the forms of "cultural conflict" that youth theatre addresses.

Cultural Conflict and International Youth Theatre

To begin, we should certainly divest ourselves of some commonly held notions of what exactly the term "culture" signifies. For example, this anthology does not equate "culture" with civilization or education or refinement, in the sense that one nation or person is more "cultured" than another. To speak of culture in this hierarchical way is to use the term as a club in order to elevate some groups and restrict others by beating them "back" or "down" into a kind of second-class social status. Additionally, this view relies upon a very outdated notion of human societies as static, hermetically sealed systems in which intercultural penetration rarely occurs and should be avoided at all costs.

Similarly, the distinction between "highbrow" and "lowbrow" culture that one frequently encounters — the operatic aria versus the folk song, the book versus the motion picture, classical or historical versus avant-garde and contemporary, "pop" versus "elite" — is of little use to us any longer as an inherent measure of quality. Both *The Rise and Fall of the Third Reich* as well as the film version of *Schindler's List* have their positive and negative sides, and who is to say that one will turn out to be more or less influential over the lives of millions of people in the long run? Thus, it may make more sense for us to recognize that Madonna is today more recognizable worldwide (and therefore more influential) than the Pope; and that the value of an artistic work may depend more upon its ability to communicate across cultures with relevance and impact than upon its more or less "formal" adherence to some canon of established work.

Finally, we need also to remind ourselves of the different socio-political developments in recent decades that have resulted in cultural misunderstanding, prejudice and intolerance leveled against groups of people. Such events have given rise to new terminologies that have become household words in the twenty-first century. One thinks immediately, for example, of the horrific incidents of "ethnic cleansing" that were first undertaken in a systematic way in Nazi Germany and that have since recurred with disturbing frequency in Cambodia, the Balkans, the Middle East and in other regions. Another familiar development has been the phenomenon of "population diaspora" — often caused by the political situation just referred to — whereby vast numbers of people have migrated from their home territories to other lands, bringing their values and traditions with them and frequently challenging and clashing with already existing values and traditions in societies that offer them refuge. The repression of "indigenous peoples," the "state terrorism" directed against cultural subgroups within a given society, the "gender discrimination" that feeds so much upon a certain form of stereotyping — all such examples seem not only to occupy much of our understanding of current international events today, but also to define the kind of world in which we are now living.

In researching contemporary plays drawn from the repertoire of international youth theatre, and regarding these kinds of issues that the plays address, I've taken a very broad view of the term "culture" and "cultural conflict." This book understands culture as a notion that encompasses both the social heredity of groups (determined by religion, race, gender, age, ethnicity, etc.) as well as the power relationships and class structures that frequently characterize them (determined by politics, occupation, economics and the like). And so in these plays, cultural conflict assumes the many forms just mentioned: religious persecution, colonial repression, gang violence, racism, age discrimination, to mention but a few. Young audiences and youth ensembles the world over seem to be sensitive to these forms of intolerance and persecution of others, and this anthology aims to provide a sampling of how they deal with these issues in theatrical form.

One group of plays in this collection, for example, addresses itself to the familiar problem of *cultural imperialism*: the assumption that one's own value system is inherently superior to that of others, and the imposition of that "superior" culture upon those who are less powerful and therefore helpless to resist it. Classic examples of this can be readily found in the colonial practices of the 18th and 19th centuries, when technologically developed Western powers occupied foreign real estate and forced less developed peoples to adopt Western forms of government, economic structures, religious practices, educational systems and other social institutions. In this process, key cultural features of the indigenous inhabitants' lives — their language, customs, religion, etc. — were marginalized, suppressed and even eliminated.

William Borden's satirical comedy *Turtle Island Blues* and R.N. Sandberg's *This Land* both examine the legacy of cultural imperialism in the context of the Americas, attempting to rewrite history and "set the record straight" by poignantly identifying what values were lost in that painful process. They are epic in scope, both in their plotting and in their casts of characters, raising many issues as they examine the baffling interplay between human motives, historical necessity and cultural differences on the world stage. By contrast, Claudia Marinelli's one-actor piece, *A Little Monster's Journal*, covers the same ground in a more restricted contemporary context, focusing narrowly upon the cultural arrogance that underlies the responses of a young American student who confronts a truly foreign culture for the first time in her life.

A second group of plays in this book can be broadly understood as dealing with problems that arise today from *cultural stereotyping*, relegating groups and individuals to inferior categories that are mainly based upon outwardly observable features. Stereotyping people (sometimes called "profiling" in legal or political contexts, or just plain "ghettoizing") functions by identifying people according to external characteristics such as skin color, linguistic differences, gender, habits of dress and the like. Once groups have been categorized in this way, they can be separated from "mainstream" society and culture for discriminatory action. This is a very handy and widespread form of cultural prejudice, because stereotyping can be based upon the most superficial features — national origin, economic status, age, etc. — and thus it feeds a longstanding human tendency to privilege oneself over others by dehumanizing them, regarding them as "types" and treating them impersonally.

In this anthology I've selected a group of plays that narrow their focus upon certain cultural values that seem particularly at-risk today of cultural stereotyping. For example, the stories told by Shirley Barrie in *Carrying the Calf* and Susan Battye in *Back Where You Belong* show the difficulty of sustaining new ideas about women's rights, religious customs and gender roles even within multiethnic societies. Shirley Barrie's play is set in contemporary Canada, an "immigrant" nation that prides itself on its "open-door" policy to other immigrants and refugees from many parts of the world. And *Back Where You Belong* locates its cultural conflict within the context of a high school where values of "diversity" and "tolerance" are supposedly being taught. Both writers, however, reveal how cultural stereotyping works to create powerful barriers to understanding and acceptance. While these two plays deal with the *personal* impact of this problem, Neil

Duffield's *Lilford Mill* focuses upon the *political* impact of stereotyping. Duffield finds that English prejudices against the Germans are hardly distinguishable from their prejudices against the Irish; his play thus emphasizes some of the historical consequences upon modern nation-states — in this case the current conflict in Northern Ireland.

A third group of plays that readers will find in this collection deals with the *victimization of cultural groups by oppressive political systems*. Waging war against helpless civilian populations has, of course, become a particularly galling phenomenon of the modern world, and terrorism is perhaps the most ugly manifestation of this. But state terrorism, because it "identifies" its victims by culturally stereotyping them in an official manner, brings the full weight of the political and social system to bear upon the human oppression it carries out, stigmatizing its victims and posing immense legal and diplomatic problems for other nations and international institutions to contend with.

Donna Abela's award-winning drama, *Highest Mountain, Fastest River*, places the reader or spectator alongside the Hmong people in their confused and desperate struggle as they are driven from their village by a brutal government and endure crushing hardships searching for political asylum. The cultural diaspora suffered by the Hmong will certainly remind readers of what many other refugee groups have experienced over the past three decades. Readers will also experience the terror of being one of the "disappeared" victims in contemporary Latin America as they read Bob Mayberry's *A Single Numberless Death*. The way in which young people — intellectuals, students, potential radicals — were singled out and then murdered in Argentina during the seventies and eighties has left its painful mark in many nations of South America where mothers, wives and other family members still gather in public places to remember their loved ones and demand accountability from their governments.

The final group of four plays in this anthology centers upon cultural conflicts that groups encounter by their *replacement of outdated cultural values with more modern ethical choices*. These plays all center upon young characters seeking firm footing on the shifting sands of moral ambiguity in our modern world. The struggles they encounter may arise from different generational, political or religious sources, but all the characters recognize that tolerance and acceptance are now called for, and all have the courage to take risks and explore the future with such fresh outlooks. These are plays that speak to the phenomenon of rapid social change that characterizes so much of our modern world. The plays also validate the importance of values that must underpin all human life. And even if some of those values may eventually turn out to be rooted in humanitarian traditions, nonetheless they must be discovered afresh and affirmed by each new generation.

Riwia Brown's young Maori heroine in *Roimata* typifies this search for meaning and value in contemporary youth culture. The product of a failed marriage, Roimata abandons her rural home with its traditional domestic values in order to adopt an urban lifestyle in the big city and discover what it might offer her; she also consciously rejects the "consolation of religion" offered to her by her boyfriend. In the end, she opts to return to that rural environment, but she does so bearing with her the stamp of the modern age: an extended family, new financial responsibility and an uncertain future as a single parent. Julie Salverson's and Patti Fraser's group-developed piece, *BOOM*, scrutinizes some of the traditional values of Western industrialized nations and finds them insufficient in dealing with new problems of our emerging global village. The issue is land mines, and the culture shock that Roger experiences when he attempts to form a relationship with the Bosnian refugee Ana underscores everyone's need to forge a new ethical system based on social acceptance that can modify and even replace traditional values of isolationism and personal freedom.

Ros Gardner's *Crying for Time* is another group-developed work, one that reminds us of the poignant situation of children victimized by global conflicts that seem far beyond their limited abilities to comprehend and adjust to. As the social system with its traditional institutions collapses under the chaos of civil war, groups of children converge in the play to form a hidden society and hammer-out ways of protecting themselves and accepting each other's differences. Although reminiscent of the classic situation in *Lord of the Flies*, this play takes us directly into the Balkans conflict and examines the purposes that trust, self-sacrifice, courage and other values can serve in war-torn societies. On a much lighter note, Mirjana Buljan's *Mutiny in Crazyland* offers us a topsy-turvy, musical comedy glimpse at the folly of adults and the "wisdom" of children in the twenty-first century. Presented from the perspective of young people, "grown up" values are blown up wholesale under a loony barrage of pop music, TV hype, rollerblades and skateboards. The parents become the children and the kids guide society — the schools, the driver education classes, the banks, the family traditions. The play thus celebrates the absurdity of intolerant and inflexible value systems that rest solely upon generational authority, and scores some well-considered and insightful points for parents and society.

Themes and Issues in International Youth Theatre

The plays contained in this anthology thus present a rich tapestry of characters and situations, themes, settings, dramaturgy and technical challenges. They span historical and contemporary subjects, they utilize large ensembles as well as small casts and even single-character approaches, and their tone is serious, melancholic, lyrical, comedic, satirical and even tragic at times. Their production methods as well reflect a wide range of styles that characterize so much of modern stage practice: Brechtian epic theatre, musical comedy, realism, circus and carnival, multimedia, dance and mime, documentarism, allegory and historical drama.

Among the numerous subjects examined by these plays, I've tried above to describe the major ones in relation to the collection as a whole and to highlight those concerns again in the notes preceding each of the playtexts that follow. There are additional themes, however, that surface more than once — in these plays and in others I've seen — and perhaps it is valuable to single them out here since they throw valuable additional light on the overall field.

As one might expect, the presence of electronic media — television, radio, photography and pop music — is widespread in many plays of the international youth theatre. Sometimes a particular medium becomes a key method of character revelation as in the photo slides of Anstella's foreign tour in *A Little Monster's Journal*. Elsewhere communications media come under direct critical fire as the children make clear to us in *Mutiny in Crazyland* with their satire of TV variety shows. The barrage of information in the form of statistics or "battlefield reporting" that is characteristic of CNN and newspaper articles, and that we find in *Back Where You Belong* (atrocities in Bosnia) or *BOOM* (death and injury from landmines), overwhelms us and the characters in those dramas. Thus, communications media is ever-present in many of these plays, where it functions as a production element communicating "modernity" by its simple presence, a dramatic technique advancing the plot, a device revealing character or an information source provoking more questions than it answers.

A second recurring topic in this body of work is the theme of sexuality, especially in plays written by and for teens and older youth groups. Sexual mores, for example, take center stage in Riwia Brown's *Roimata*, where the central character must formulate her own standards of sexual behavior as she makes the transition from a sheltered rural environment to the fast-track city life that has long aroused her curiosity. The grotesque distortions of sexual abuse and torture are explored in Bob Mayberry's *A Single Numberless Death*, while the problematic sexual relationships among the four women in *Carrying the Calf* serve to underscore that play's focus upon gender roles and stereotyping in modern society. Sometimes the approach to sex is hilariously comic — as Pocahontas beats up a pathetic John Smith when he tries to rape her in *Turtle Island Blues*, or the way the Girls High Netballers mock the relationship between their school principal, Mrs. Towers, and her henpecked husband. At other times, of course, the plays develop tender love relationships and romantic moments, such as those between Cissy and Liam in *Lilford Mill*, Roger and Ana in *BOOM*, or young Owen and the Nisqually girl Onkwo in *This Land*.

Third, there is a surprising amount of historical curiosity expressed today by international plays for youth audiences. Six of the plays contained in this anthology are solidly built upon historical incident, and all are designed to "set the record straight" or otherwise highlight cultural abuses that have been denied, overlooked or falsified by official records. Probably the most disturbing of these is Bob Mayberry's drama on the "disappeared" of Argentina in *A Single Numberless Death* — disturbing because it will continue to be a history without closure until the fates of the murdered victims are finally known and made public to their families and loved ones. But the "rewriting" of history in terms of cultural struggle is also important to several other writers. One thinks immediately of R.N. Sandberg's attempt to redefine the phrase "manifest destiny" in his bittersweet depiction of historical development in the American northwest territories in *This Land*.

Fourth, one must note the optimism these plays demonstrate towards the solution of social problems and societal change. Sometimes optimism takes the form of humor and becomes a defense mechanism to cope with difficult questions — as the "clown chorus" of young students in *Boom* or the embarrassment of Hmong refugees who can't find their bus stop in *Highest Mountain, Fastest River*. In *A Single Numberless Death*, the final chorus of narrators joining together in a song of solidarity seems to reassure us that the "disappeared" will always be remembered, and in that remembrance lies an antidote to the repetition of similar crimes against humanity in the future. The netball trophy finds deserving owners at the end of *Back Where You Belong*, we have little doubt that Roger and Ana will find a meeting ground mutually satisfying to each at the conclusion of *Boom*, and the pregnant Roimata embarks on her new life at the end of the play with confidence and a sense of personal empowerment she has never enjoyed before.

Finally, it is noteworthy to mention the sense of realism these dramas display in their descriptions of cultural conflict and, especially, in the conclusions they reach. The note of optimism just referred to does not seem to discourage playwrights or youth ensembles from dealing with the facts as they find them — indeed, in several cases, the players built the scripts upon factual data in the form of news reports, documentary evidence and the like. *Crying for Time* is especially poignant in this regard since the young actors spent many months researching the experiences of actual children in the war-torn Balkans before using that grim information to develop characters and situations for the play. And Claudia Marinelli generates no false hopes of reforming her heroine at the end of *A Little Monster's Journal*: she knows full well that some people will never change because many cultural attitudes have been ingrained from an early age.

Reflecting the Global Theatrical Scene

To undertake an anthology of contemporary international plays dealing with themes of cultural conflict is to immediately invite criticism of the editor's ability to produce a fair sampling. The present collection, for example, is limited by the sheer logistical problem of gaining global access to a sufficient number of scripts, as well as by my desire to rely only upon plays in English or in English translation. For these reasons, this book does not claim to be a "representative selection" of international work on cultural conflict, but rather an exploratory anthology for English-speaking readers that highlights some of the best that is being thought and said on the subject for young audiences in the theatre.

In selecting these twelve plays I've tried to avoid an over-reliance upon scripts from any one nation. By its very nature, of course, an English-language anthology will tend to be "driven" by authors from English-speaking cultures of North America, the British Isles and Australasia. On the other hand, the collection also contains plays from eastern and southern Europe, South America and the Maori culture of New Zealand; three of them have been translated from original sources. On the whole, therefore, I feel that the collection successfully crosses national lines and avoids partisanship as much as can be expected in a work of this nature.

Apart from my desire to obtain a global sampling of plays for this book, my primary criterion in selecting the dramas has been one of quality. Certainly my own judgment as a theatre scholar, producer and director has counted heavily in my choice of inclusions for the book. I regularly attend international theatre festivals in the United States and abroad in order to gain access to plays in performance and solicit opinions and referrals for work that might be publishable. Playwrights, too, have sent me relevant reviews and criticism to accompany their scripts, and this has helped me in reaching my decisions on plays to include. In this respect, I should point out that all the plays presented here have received stage productions in some form — an essential criterion, I believe, for writing good plays and assessing the worth of any script.

Two other observations should caution readers against regarding this collection as "representative" of global trends in youth theatre. One is the impossibility of adequately describing for general readers of *literature* the wide range of *non-literary performance art* that constitutes so much of global youth theatre nowadays. For example, the theatrical traditions of the Indian subcontinent, the Far East and the southern Americas — while immensely popular with audiences worldwide — are at a distinct disadvantage here. There are so many movement, dance, musical and scenic components to their performances that it is almost impossible for readers to understand how these plays work from a printed scenario alone. Unfortunately, I have had to reject a number of fine plays for the present collection for that very reason. As my mentor, Bill Oliver from Berkeley, once noted in one of his anthologies of Latin American plays: "The folk idiom of the original is so pithy, that one may well wonder if it should be translated at all — it is precisely this sort of value that is lost in almost any translation."[ii]

A second caveat for readers is that whatever international "portrait" this collection may present must also be regarded against a backdrop of international festivals where global youth audiences and ensembles interact in an exciting collaborative context. I regularly attend such events in Asia, South America, Europe and North America, and it is truly impossible to communicate in a literary anthology the inspiring intercultural communication that takes place at these events. In short, a grasp of international *plays* for young audiences is not equivalent to an understanding of the international *theatre activity* for young audiences that is happening today.

Finally, I should also note that I've tried to apply two other selection criteria to this anthology. First, I've concentrated solely upon plays written and produced within the past decade in order to ensure contemporaneity to the collection. And second, I've tried to include only plays specifically written for young audiences or plays with roles that could be performed by young actors. With regard to this latter area, I define "young" as an age group from approximately eight to twenty-four years of age, and part of my reasoning that informed the selection process was the suitability of plays that might be produced well in educational contexts.

All the scripts included here have been personally approved by their authors, and in many cases revised or "updated" specifically for this collection. They are therefore the most current versions of the plays. I have made no editorial changes whatsoever in the writers' playtexts, aside from formatting them in a consistent style. I have, however, written all the introductory sections on the title page of each drama, with the single exception of *Carrying the Calf* by Shirley Barrie.

A Note on Intellectual Property

In all the anthologies I edit, I feel compelled to remind readers that the plays in this collection are intended only for studio exercises or for reading. When it comes to performing them, producing them in public readings, or adapting and reproducing them in any way via the electronic media for other audiences — educational, amateur or professional — then permission must be obtained and royalties paid to the agent or author.

Perhaps this "caution" needs to be restated in this age of the World Wide Web where so much is available online or otherwise reproducible at little or no charge. Readers must remind themselves that plays — like other unique, cultural artifacts — are not equivalent to the bytes and factoids we slug through and digitally manipulate by the thousands every day. They are the intellectual property of human beings who have spent many years earning, and who therefore deserve, proper acknowledgment and compensation for producing and distributing them to the public.

Bear in mind that I'm attempting in this book to highlight and promote the work of a handful of uniquely talented and very highly motivated artists whose worth, importance and cultural value in our world is already deeply discounted, frequently ridiculed and in some cases even despised. Their plays are their honest work, their "products." Pay for them.

If you wish to present any of these plays in public, credits appear at the end of this volume; call, e-mail or write for permission. These artists are not unreasonable in what they expect from us.

---

i   Schechner, Richard. "Intercultural Performance," *The Drama Review,* 26, 2, T94, p. 3 (1982).
ii Oliver, William I., ed. *Voices of Change in the Spanish American Theater* (Austin & London: University of Texas, 1971).

Turtle Island Blues
by William Borden

The genre of the history play has been popular in many societies since the time of the ancient Greeks, but in the United States it has undergone a sea-change over the past two decades. Home-grown authors like David Mamet, Charles Smith, Susan Lori-Parks, David Henry Hwang, Spalding Gray and others have redefined the way we look at history, both our own and that of other people. And this has occurred both on the stage and in motion pictures — witness the popularity of such blockbuster films as *The Right Stuff, All the President's Men, Schindler's List* and others — and as a result we have become simultaneously more conscious and more critical of ourselves as a nation.

What perhaps distinguishes our own American-style history plays from those of other nations, however, is the unique sense of comedy and playfulness that U.S. authors have brought to the genre; *Turtle Island Blues* is certainly indicative of this. On one level, the play is unique in this collection because it's the most "epic" in terms of its sprawling historical scope: it purports to cover the discovery of the new world from the time of Columbus to the present. What is more, it does this in a scrappy, knockabout style full of twists and surprises at every turn, recalling the work of Joan Littlewood or Monty Python. Its highly literate author feels no compunction whatsoever with building powerful scenes that include Leonard Peltier (of F.B.I. fame), Queen Isabella, Pocahontas, Admiral Perry, Sitting Bull, Columbus and many others. Ideas and attitudes carom off each other like billiard balls, and the spectator's familiar understanding of U.S. history is both deepened and enlivened by this brash and upbeat, postmodern reappraisal of the New World, its indigenous inhabitants and how the territory has developed over more than four centuries.

A second noteworthy feature about the play is its theatrical versatility. In the hands of a major professional company, the ten roles (doubling and tripling to more than two dozen scattered through the script) are wonderful challenges for actors who delight in transformations. The presence of song and dance, the need for audio design and scenic flexibility, and costume and property choices are additional artistic challenges that can free the exciting performance potential contained in the script. Alternatively, in the hands of amateur companies, the characters open doors of opportunity for artists of any age or background to learn about U.S. history and have a lot of fun while doing so: researching, parodying, empathizing with and presenting the many characters who "play their parts" upon Bill Borden's stage of the western hemisphere and then are heard no more.

Finally, one needs to also appreciate *Turtle Island Blues* in terms of the exciting emotional adventures it offers readers, spectators and players. For example, there is comedy in abundance here — such as the cross-dressing Queen Isabella, or Sally Hemings writing the Declaration of Independence for her lover, Tom Jefferson. There is also the tragic sense of loss that runs through Sitting Bull's and Caonabo's realization of what is being done to their people and their culture. And there is also the heady outrage of Pocahontas literally kicking the butt of the wannabe-rapist John Smith, the naïveté of the Spanish cleric Father Vickery, the pretentious hypocrisy of F.B.I. agents, the fatuous opportunism of Columbus and so much more. In short, the play offers a rich palette of emotions and ideas to play, to savor and to appreciate.

Characters

Columbus

Isabella

Caonabo

Pocahontas

Leonard Peltier

Sitting Bull

Escobedo

Father Vickery

Bullhead

Sally Hemings

Place
Castile, the Ocean Sea, Turtle Island (sometimes known as America)

Time
1492–present

Production Note
Throughout the play those individuals conventionally called "Indians" will be referred to as "People" — a term which is the equivalent of nearly all tribal names.

1   *(When the house is opened, several PEOPLE are sitting*
2   *around a large drum, drumming and singing traditional*
3   *songs. The drumming and singing fills the theatre,*
4   *reverberates off the walls, and surrounds the audience with*
5   *the heartbeat of Native America. During the play the singers-*
6   *drummers remain in place, from time to time punctuating*
7   *certain moments and scene transitions with drumming and*
8   *singing.*
9   *As the house lights go down, the drumming and singing*
10   *continue for a moment, then abruptly stop. A circle of soft*
11   *light comes up on a wooden table, a large globe, and a*
12   *wooden armchair, all circa 1492. COLUMBUS enters with an*
13   *insolent slouch, as if he might have grown up in a tough*
14   *Italian section of Brooklyn. He wears boots, a puff-sleeved*
15   *blouse open at the neck, a gold neck chain, and a modern sea*
16   *Captain's crisp white cap. He's 41 years of age. He's chewing*
17   *gum. COLUMBUS looks around, as if he's expecting*
18   *someone — indeed, he's been waiting to see her for several*
19   *months. He's been cooling his heels a long time.*
20   *He revolves the globe, tracing a route. He sends the globe*
21   *spinning, falls into the chair, and plops his feet on the table.*
22   *Behind him, unseen by him, ISABELLA appears. She wears*
23   *starched, pressed military pants and blouse. At her throat is*
24   *a splash of bright color — a silk scarf. She wears a military*
25   *beret of the same color. She wears high heels. She, too, is 41*
26   *years of age. She silently watches Columbus.*
27   *He picks up a paper and makes a little boat. He slides the*
28   *boat across the table, playing like a kid, making noises of*
29   *wind and water. He gets up and runs the paper boat around*
30   *the globe. He tries to get the boat to stay on the globe, but it*
31   *keeps falling off. Finally he sticks his gum on the globe and*
32   *the boat to the gum. He falls into the chair again, clomps his*
33   *heels on the table, and shoves another stick of gum into his*
34   *mouth. ISABELLA strolls into the light.)*
35 **ISABELLA: Some challenges may prove greater than others.**

1   *(COLUMBUS jumps, comes to a kind of attention, tries to*
2   *salute and take off his hat at the same time.)*
3 **COLUMBUS: Your majesty!**
4 **ISABELLA: At ease, Captain.** *(She strolls, as insolently as he, into*
5   *the light. He looks around for a way to get rid of his gum.)*
6 **COLUMBUS: Queen Isabella, I –**
7 **ISABELLA: Get rid of the gum, Chris.** *(He sticks the gum to the*
8   *underside of the table. She sits insolently — majestically — in*
9   *the chair and puts her feet on the table.)*
10 **COLUMBUS: I didn't expect you.**
11 **ISABELLA: You've been waiting for me for months.**
12 **COLUMBUS: That's why I didn't expect you.**
13 **ISABELLA: Had you lost faith?**
14 **COLUMBUS: In you?**
15 **ISABELLA: In yourself.**
16 **COLUMBUS: I've never lost faith in myself.**
17 **ISABELLA: Sometimes a little skepticism is in order.**
18 **COLUMBUS:** *(Pointedly)* **I *have* lost faith in others.**
19 **ISABELLA: I've been fighting a war.**
20 **COLUMBUS: I know you've been busy ...**
21 **ISABELLA: I've made Spain safe for Christianity. I've driven**
22   **the Moors into Africa – expelled the Jews – established**
23   **the Inquisition –**
24 **COLUMBUS: You're a heck of a woman!**
25 **ISABELLA: It's not easy!**
26 **COLUMBUS: War is hell!**
27 **ISABELLA: War is exciting! The acrid odor of gunpowder, the**
28   **thunder of cannon, the rumble of hooves, the silvery**
29   **rattle of sword striking sword, the flash of sun reflecting**
30   **from armor – it's ...**
31 **COLUMBUS: Like love?**
32 **ISABELLA: Better.** *(She removes her beret, and, with a shake of*
33   *her head, her long, beautiful hair tumbles sensually down*
34   *her back.)*
35 **COLUMBUS: Sailing is like that.**

1   ISABELLA: Have you sailed far, Captain Columbus?
2   COLUMBUS: The Mediterranean. Africa. England. Iceland.
3   ISABELLA: Sailors tell of seeing monsters and mermaids.
4   COLUMBUS: The sea is full of wonders.
5   ISABELLA: I'm more interested in trade routes.
6   COLUMBUS: In Iceland they tell of sailing only a few days to
7   the west and finding land.
8   ISABELLA: I have no need for ice.
9   COLUMBUS: Gold.
10 ISABELLA: In the ice?
11 COLUMBUS: Farther south. Silver. Spices. Ivory. *(He touches,*
12   *tentatively, her scarf.)* Silk.
13 ISABELLA: The route is long and dangerous.
14 COLUMBUS: By land. But not by sea. *(He takes her to the globe.)*
15   Here is Spain.
16 ISABELLA: I know where Spain is.
17 COLUMBUS: Here is Japan. Here is China. Here is India.
18 ISABELLA: Across the Ocean Sea?
19 COLUMBUS: Exactly.
20 ISABELLA: No one can cross the Ocean Sea. *(He pulls out a map.)*
21 COLUMBUS: It's only this far. *(He holds up his hands to show*
22   *the distance. She measures the distance on the globe and*
23   *holds up her hands.)*
24 ISABELLA: Your ocean is smaller than this one.
25 COLUMBUS: I've calculated the distance using the most
26   reliable sources.
27 ISABELLA: The globe is based on Ptolemy.
28 COLUMBUS: My authority is the Bible. God knows all.
29 ISABELLA: But he's a little fuzzy on geography.
30 COLUMBUS: Come. Look. *(He takes her to a window.)* What do
31   you see?
32 ISABELLA: The Ocean Sea.
33 COLUMBUS: Other men look at the dark blue of the Ocean
34   Sea, and they see only the boundaries to their
35   imagination. But I see — *(He looks into her eyes.)*

1   ISABELLA: What do you see?

2   COLUMBUS: I see the future. Can you see it?

3   ISABELLA: *(Still looking into his eyes)* Yes. I think I can. But

4   only in your fevered imagination.

5   COLUMBUS: *(Pointing to the Ocean Sea)* Empire! Wealth!

6   Glory! *(He jabs at the maps.)* Maps don't lie! *(She looks at*

7   *the maps.)*

8   ISABELLA: *(Reading)* Here monsters be. Here the men with

9   heads below their shoulders. Who makes these maps?

10 COLUMBUS: I do. It pays the rent when I'm not sailing — and

11   when I'm waiting to see people. But the truth lies here,

12   too. I'll bring you gold to mount a new crusade! Capture

13   Jerusalem from the Mohammedans!

14   ISABELLA: Crusades went out with the Middle Ages.

15 COLUMBUS: These *are* the Middle Ages!

16 ISABELLA: We stand at the threshold of the Renaissance.

17 COLUMBUS: What the heck's a Renaissance?

18 ISABELLA: The rise of the nation-state. A flowering of

19   literature, science, reason.

20 COLUMBUS: The end of the world is at hand.

21 ISABELLA: Chris.

22 COLUMBUS: St. Augustine gives us a hundred years.

23 ISABELLA: You're loony tunes.

24 COLUMBUS: All right. Forget Armageddon. Think gold. Think

25   trade. Think power.

26 ISABELLA: Power.

27 COLUMBUS: The Pope will ask your advice. Kings will kiss

28   your feet. Flowers will bloom at your command.

29 ISABELLA: How far? *(COLUMBUS measures on the globe with*

30   *his hands, holds up his hands.)* How far by boat?

31 COLUMBUS: A few days. A week at most. Get the jump on the

32   Portuguese. Sideswipe the English. Roll over France.

33 ISABELLA: Across the Ocean Sea?

34 COLUMBUS: Piece of cake.

35 ISABELLA: Out of sight of land?

1 COLUMBUS: *(At the globe)* **Today, this is Spain. Tomorrow, this**
2 **will be Spain. When I claim these lands in your name.**
3 ISABELLA: **I thought these lands belonged to the Japanese. Or**
4 **Chinese. Someone.**
5 COLUMBUS: **Land is to be conquered. Gold is to be found. Glory**
6 **is to be won. Fame is to be trumpeted through the ages.**
7 ISABELLA: **Whose fame? Whose glory? Whose gold?**
8 **COLUMBUS: Yours! Mine! Ours!**
9 ISABELLA: **Gold, glory, fame aren't everything.**
10 COLUMBUS: **No. No, they're not. There's also the sight of**
11 **mountains never seen before, the melody of birds never**
12 **heard before, the scent of flowers never smelled before,**
13 **the touch of skin never touched before ... There's the fresh**
14 **clean wind of adventure that fills the sails with desire. The**
15 **thrill of discovery that throbs in your bones. The deck that**
16 **pitches and rolls beneath your feet, the timbers that creak**
17 **from the strain as the ship thrusts into the pulsing sea, the**
18 **pounding of the waves, the relentless pounding of the**
19 **waves against the fragile vessel, the exaltation as the ship**
20 **rises on a wave, then plunges deep into a trough – the**
21 **exhilaration when you sight land! The ecstasy of discovery!**
22 ISABELLA: **I wish I could go with you!**
23 COLUMBUS: **I'll need three caravels.**
24 ISABELLA: **Three?**
25 COLUMBUS: **Storms, mishaps ... the unexpected ...**
26 ISABELLA: **They're yours!**
27 **COLUMBUS: Finally!**
28 ISABELLA: **You've won my –**
29 COLUMBUS: **The King of Portugal turned me down. The King**
30 **of England turned me down. But you – !**
31 ISABELLA: **You were going to sail for King John of Portugal?**
32 COLUMBUS: **I petitioned to see you years ago –**
33 ISABELLA: **Or Henry of England?**
34 COLUMBUS: **I just happened to mention something about**
35 **westward expansion ...**

1   ISABELLA: You traitor!
2   COLUMBUS: My dearest – Queen Isabella, I've sought you as a
3   knight seeks his lady, as a lover longs for his beloved – at
4   this moment I'm so excited – !
5   ISABELLA: To be with me?
6   COLUMBUS: That too.
7   ISABELLA: You're nervous?
8   COLUMBUS: I'm a little off balance.
9   ISABELLA: I hope you get your sea legs soon, Captain.
10 COLUMBUS: Admiral.
11 ISABELLA: You've promoted yourself?
12 COLUMBUS: You're not going to send a captain to bring
13   greetings from the Queen of Spain to the Great Khan of
14   China! Now, I'll need men, supplies –
15 ISABELLA: I have no money.
16 COLUMBUS: But you said –
17 ISABELLA: My treasury is depleted. War costs money.
18 COLUMBUS: Then how – ?
19 ISABELLA: Who else did you go to? Did you go to the King of
20   France?
21 COLUMBUS: Never!
22 ISABELLA: The city of Palos owes me money. They'll provide
23   two of the caravels.
24 COLUMBUS: I know Palos. It's full of fine sailors.
25 ISABELLA: To save on salaries, we'll commute the sentences of
26   criminals who volunteer to sail with you.
27 COLUMBUS: Your Highness is too kind.
28 ISABELLA: I want a strict accounting.
29 COLUMBUS: To the penny.
30 ISABELLA: I'll send a secretary to accompany you to keep a
31   record of your expedition, so that we may know the lands
32   we have acquired as a consequence of your courage and
33   navigational acumen.
34 COLUMBUS: My lady. My gratitude is as boundless as the seas,
35   my devotion infinite as the stars, my loyalty –

1   ISABELLA: Cut the bull, Chris.

2   COLUMBUS: Yes, ma'am.

3   ISABELLA: Go to Palos. Ready your ships.

4   COLUMBUS: I'm off. *(He starts to exit.)*

5   ISABELLA: I've often looked out at the Ocean Sea. It's seemed
6   as strange and limitless as the stars, as impossible to cross
7   as the sky itself.

8   COLUMBUS: Faith and a strong wind will take you anywhere
9   you want to go.

10   ISABELLA: Faith? Or obsession?

11   COLUMBUS: Is there a difference?

12   ISABELLA: I've never sailed beyond sight of land.

13   COLUMBUS: You feel like there are only two people in the
14   universe – you and God. But – a woman's place – is in the
15   castle. *(He exits. She thinks a moment.)*

16   ISABELLA: Admiral! *(He returns.)* I'll send you a cabin boy. My
17   personal attendant.

18   COLUMBUS: I prefer no servants.

19   ISABELLA: He'll be my eyes and ears. You must treat him well.

20   COLUMBUS: I'll have enough responsibilities.

21   ISABELLA: He can take care of himself.

22   COLUMBUS: Sailors are a rough bunch.

23   ISABELLA: She's – he's seen war, blood, death, and treachery.

24   COLUMBUS: He's seen too much. *(COLUMBUS exits.)*

25   ISABELLA: Admiral! *(He returns.)* I command it.

26   *(They hold for a moment, then the stage goes black. In the*
27   *darkness, a man screams. Lights up on CAONABO, a Macorix*
28   *People of the time of Columbus's arrival, sitting up from his*
29   *sleep. It is he who screamed. He wears brightly colored boxer*
30   *shorts. Beside him is POCAHONTAS. She wears a nightshirt*
31   *and a flower in her hair. Drumming and singing for a*
32   *moment. Then another scream cuts the darkness, and in*
33   *another part of the stage a light illuminates LEONARD*
34   *PELTIER as he sits up in his prison bunk, his scream waking*
35   *himself from a nightmare. Sound of gunshots. He rolls*

1   *under his bunk for cover. Gunshots continue for several*
2   *moments, then stop. PELTIER climbs out from under the*
3   *bunk. A JUDGE, who will soon play Father Vickery, stands*
4   *before him.)*
5   JUDGE: Leonard Peltier, you are accused of the murder in
6   1975 of two FBI agents near Wounded Knee on the Pine
7   Ridge Reservation. How do you plead?
8   PELTIER: Will I get a fair trial, your honor?
9   JUDGE: This is America, isn't it? How do you plead to the
10   ruthless, cold-blooded murders of those fine, all-
11   American boys?
12   *(Lights down on the JUDGE. A soft light remains on*
13   *PELTIER. Singing and drumming for a moment. Focus on*
14   *CAONABO and POCAHONTAS.)*
15   POCAHONTAS: The dream again?
16   CAONABO: Three great birds coming across the water. White
17   wings fluttering all over, and dark bodies. They skim the
18   water like ducks landing, then they rest, their white wings
19   hanging useless, as if broken.
20   POCAHONTAS: You ate those chilies last night.
21   CAONABO: It's not the chilies.
22   POCAHONTAS: Casava beer.
23   CAONABO: No, no. I was on the back of one of the birds, and its
24   back was flat and hard, like wood. There were creatures
25   living on the bird, two-leggeds.
26   POCAHONTAS: They must have been men.
27   CAONABO: They were like dead men. No color to their skin.
28   Until they stood in the sun. Then their skin turned red.
29   POCAHONTAS: Maybe they're ghosts.
30   CAONABO: There was the smell of blood in the air.
31   POCAHONTAS: Maybe these dreams are from the spirit world.
32   CAONABO: You think so?
33   POCAHONTAS: The old people have talked of dreams like this.
34   CAONABO: The men make loud noises.
35   *(Gunshots sound slowly from far away, as PELTIER crouches*

1   *behind his bunk and returns the fire. Drumming. Rattle.*
2   *The shots fade out.)*
3   POCAHONTAS: The spirits are warning us.
4   CAONABO: Warning us of what?
5   POCAHONTAS: Things are going to change.
6   CAONABO: We haven't done anything.
7   POCAHONTAS: Maybe life is too easy for us. We have plenty to
8   eat and drink. We walk in the woods and swim in the
9   ocean. We collect things from the beach.
10   CAONABO: Everything's in harmony.
11   POCAHONTAS: Sometimes you fight other People.
12   CAONABO: That's just for fun. We don't try to kill each other.
13   POCAHONTAS: Maybe people just aren't allowed to be happy
14   forever.
15   CAONABO: You think it's a kind of grim necessity that's
16   coming down? Or just bad luck?
17   *(Lights up on COLUMBUS, on a platform which represents*
18   *the bow of his ship, taking bearings with a quadrant. Beside*
19   *him are ESCOBEDO, the Queen's Secretary, and ISABELLA,*
20   *dressed as a cabin boy. She adjusts her shirt, trying to*
21   *conceal her breasts. ESCOBEDO writes on a clipboard. The*
22   *three of them sway back and forth and from side to side,*
23   *keeping their balance with the roll of the ship.)*
24   COLUMBUS: *(Dictating to Escobedo)* It's the tenth day.
25   ESCOBEDO: Excuse me, Admiral, it's the fourteenth.
26   COLUMBUS: *(As if amazed)* No!
27   ESCOBEDO: I've kept strict track.
28   COLUMBUS: By the Julian calendar?
29   ESCOBEDO: Gregorian, of course.
30   COLUMBUS: Well, there you go. *(Sighting through the*
31   *quadrant:)* Fourteen degrees ...
32   ESCOBEDO: A day has 24 hours either way.
33   COLUMBUS: ... fifty-six minutes ...
34   ESCOBEDO: The men know how many days they've been at sea!
35   COLUMBUS: *(Slapping the quadrant into Isabella's hand)* Only

1   eighty miles today! We're making no time at all!
2   ESCOBEDO: But the wind's been brisk.
3   COLUMBUS: It's amazing, isn't it, Escobedo?
4   ESCOBEDO: We've sailed at twelve knots all day.
5   COLUMBUS: Are you a licensed navigator, Escobedo?
6   ESCOBEDO: No, sir.
7   COLUMBUS: We've gone sixty miles today.
8   ESCOBEDO: You said eighty.
9   COLUMBUS: I said sixty. Tell the men sixty.
10 ESCOBEDO: Aye, Admiral. *(ESCOBEDO exits.)*
11 ISABELLA: How long can you fool them?
12 COLUMBUS: Until we sight land. It's for their own good!
13   They'd lose heart otherwise!
14   *(Crossfade to POCAHONTAS and CAONABO. Drumming.*
15   *Rattle.)*
16 CAONABO: I dreamed about the strangers again.
17 POCAHONTAS: So did I. Last night.
18 CAONABO: They're getting closer.
19 POCAHONTAS: I don't think they're ghosts.
20 CAONABO: It's not a bird they're on. It's something they made
21   with their hands.
22 POCAHONTAS: There was a woman. But nobody knew she was
23   a woman.
24 CAONABO: How smart can they be?
25 POCAHONTAS: They're never satisfied. A hunger gnaws
26   within them.
27 CAONABO: I get hungry.
28 POCAHONTAS: This is different. It's not their stomachs that
29   are hungry. It's their souls.
30   *(Crossfade to ship as ESCOBEDO joins ISABELLA at the bow.)*
31 ESCOBEDO: Your first voyage, lad?
32 ISABELLA: My first to India. Or Japan. Or wherever we're going.
33 ESCOBEDO: I'm the Queen's secretary.
34 ISABELLA: Do you know your queen well?
35 ESCOBEDO: Isabella? Very well.

1   ISABELLA: You call her Isabella?

2   ESCOBEDO: That's her name.

3   ISABELLA: To her face?

4   ESCOBEDO: Oh, yes. We're very close. And you? Have you ever

5   seen the Queen?

6   ISABELLA: We're close.

7   *(Crossfade to POCAHONTAS and CAONABO. Drumming.*

8   *Rattle.)*

9   POCAHONTAS: Every night now, Caonabo, I dream of the men

10   whose souls are hungry.

11   CAONABO: They don't believe in spirits, these guys. They

12   think the ocean is just water, the wind is just air, the rain

13   is just drops, and the wood under their feet is just a two-

14   by-four to walk on.

15   POCAHONTAS: But everything speaks to us – rocks, trees,

16   animals – wind, water – Father Sky, Mother Earth.

17   Everything has a spirit. We just have to listen.

18   CAONABO: All around them there are spirits, but they can't

19   see them, because they're always throwing light into the

20   darkness, as if the darkness is going to hurt them. But it's

21   in the darkness that we see the mystery.

22   POCAHONTAS: And they don't hear the spirits, because they

23   never stop talking.

24   CAONABO: They think they're all alone in the world.

25   POCAHONTAS: That's why they're so lonely.

26   *(Crossfade to ship, where ISABELLA and FATHER VICKERY*

27   *stand at the bow.)*

28   FATHER VICKERY: Three weeks.

29   ISABELLA: The men are worried.

30   FATHER VICKERY: God holds us in His hand.

31   ISABELLA: What are you here for, Father?

32   FATHER VICKERY: I'm coming to harvest souls. I'm God's

33   farmer. God has sent me. Think of it! Millions of heathens!

34   Who can't wait to be saved! Think of the good I'll do!

35   Millions of souls condemned to the burning pits of hell –

1   saved by me, welcomed to the infinite bliss of Jesus'
2   hacienda in the sky!
3   *(Crossfade to POCAHONTAS and CAONABO. It's night.*
4   *Rattle. Flute. Music under.)*
5   **POCAHONTAS:** They think everything is separate. You there,
6   me here, as if we couldn't walk through the air between
7   us, as if we didn't breathe the same air, you and me and
8   the jaguar and the leaves on the tall trees. I look up at the
9   stars, and I feel them inside me, as well as up there in
10   the sky.
11   *(SITTING BULL, wearing traditional dress, enters, surveys*
12   *the boat, listens to CAONABO and POCAHONTAS.)*
13   **CAONABO:** We're all connected.
14   **POCAHONTAS:** It's like a big spider web, sparkling with dew,
15   and everything's attached – you, me, stars, eagle, the
16   spirits, the old ones, the People not born yet.
17   **CAONABO:** Everybody.
18   **POCAHONTAS:** Even what you can't see. *(Rattle.)*
19   **CAONABO:** But you know it's there. *(Rattle.)*
20   **POCAHONTAS:** The spirit people are chattering, warning us
21   again.
22   **CAONABO:** We've had visitors before. That Viking gang up
23   north. Chinese guys in the west. Africans now and then.
24   **POCAHONTAS:** They didn't stay. They had homes to go back to.
25   **CAONABO:** These guys don't have homes.
26   **POCAHONTAS:** They're lost.
27   **CAONABO:** They're looking for a home.
28   **POCAHONTAS:** They'll always be lost. Until they understand:
29   home is in here. In the heart. Not out there.
30   **CAONABO:** It's an enemy coming. We'd better get ready to fight
31   them.
32   *(SITTING BULL approaches them. CAONABO jumps up,*
33   *ready to fight.)*
34   **SITTING BULL:** Hello, Caonabo.
35   **CAONABO:** How do you know my name?

1 POCAHONTAS: I've seen you in my dreams. You're Sitting Bull.
2 SITTING BULL: I'm a Hunkpapa Lakota. The invaders'll call us
3   Sioux. I'm from up north.
4 CAONABO: Here on vacation? Caribbean getaway?
5 SITTING BULL: I come from the future.
6 CAONABO: You speak a strange tongue, yet I can understand
7   you.
8 SITTING BULL: I wanted to see what it was like back here, at
9   the beginning of the troubles.
10 CAONABO: The strangers?
11 POCAHONTAS: Hungry?
12 SITTING BULL: For power.
13 CAONABO: Lonely?
14 POCAHONTAS: Afraid of the mysteries?
15 SITTING BULL: They're looking for something, but maybe it's
16   the wrong thing.
17 POCAHONTAS: Trying to find the web they can't see.
18 CAONABO: Trying to hear the spirits they won't listen to.
19 POCAHONTAS: Dividing everything up.
20 SITTING BULL: They say the mind is one thing, and
21   everything else is different. And then they try to figure out
22   how they know anything. They call that science.
23   *(Light up on PELTIER and JUDGE. The JUDGE holds up a rifle.)*
24 JUDGE: This is the gun that killed those FBI agents. It was
25   found in your car, Mr. Peltier, weeks later. Conclusive
26   evidence!
27   *(Rattle. Drumming. Crossfade to ship, where ISABELLA,*
28   *holding a compass, looks up at the stars. COLUMBUS joins*
29   *her.)*
30 ISABELLA: The compass is off.
31 COLUMBUS: Impossible.
32 ISABELLA: Either that or the North Star has moved.
33   *(COLUMBUS takes the compass, looks at it, looks at the*
34   *stars.)* The North Star never moves.
35 COLUMBUS: *(Handing back the compass)* It does now.

1   **ISABELLA:** Do you ever look up at the stars and feel
2   insignificant?
3   **COLUMBUS:** No. The stars tell me where I am. They tell me
4   where I'm going.
5   **ISABELLA:** Aren't you afraid?
6   **COLUMBUS:** Of what?
7   **ISABELLA:** Getting lost.
8   **COLUMBUS:** How could I get lost? I have a compass, I have the
9   stars, I watch the waves, the currents, the winds.
10 **ISABELLA:** Do you ever feel small?
11 **COLUMBUS:** God put me here as he put the stars there – to
12   serve a purpose, to have a destiny.
13   *(SALLY HEMINGS, here as a man, an African cook, enters,*
14   *carrying a tray.)*
15 **SALLY HEMINGS:** Here's your late night snack, Admiral.
16 **COLUMBUS:** Not salt pork and dry biscuits again?
17 **SALLY HEMINGS:** I jazzed it up a bit for you.
18 **COLUMBUS:** What are these?
19 **SALLY HEMINGS:** Black-eyed peas. *(COLUMBUS tastes.)*
20 **COLUMBUS:** Hmm. And this?
21 **SALLY HEMINGS:** Chitlin's.
22 **COLUMBUS:** Mmm. *(He tastes something else.)*
23 **SALLY HEMINGS:** Watermelon.
24 **COLUMBUS:** Not bad! And these are from ... ?
25 **SALLY HEMINGS:** Africa.
26 **COLUMBUS:** Africa. Like you.
27 **SALLY HEMINGS:** Like me.
28 **COLUMBUS:** How do you like the clothes, son?
29 **SALLY HEMINGS:** I can't move right. And they scratch.
30 **COLUMBUS:** More civilized, isn't it, wearing clothes?
31 **SALLY HEMINGS:** Is that what you call it?
32 **COLUMBUS:** That's what we call it: civilization.
33 **SALLY HEMINGS:** Civilization scratches.
34 **COLUMBUS:** Civilization: clothes, Christ, and colonization.
35   You're lucky you escaped the heathen life! You wear

1   clothes, you know sin, and you serve the white man.
2   **Congratulations!** *(FATHER VICKERY enters.)*
3   **FATHER VICKERY: Discussing theology?**
4   **COLUMBUS: Politics.**
5   **FATHER VICKERY: Is there a difference?** *(ESCOBEDO joins them.)*
6   **ESCOBEDO: Look at those stars!**
7   *(Light up on PELTIER in his cell. He cranes his neck to see*
8   *the stars.)*
9   **PELTIER: I wish I could see the stars.**
10 *(Lights up on CAONABO, POCAHONTAS, and SITTING*
11 *BULL, as they look over at PELTIER in his cell.)*
12 **CAONABO: Who's that?**
13 **SITTING BULL: That's Leonard. He lives a hundred years after**
14 me. They want to kill him, too, like they killed me. *(They*
15 *walk over to PELTIER's cell.)*
16 **CAONABO: He's in a cage?**
17 **SITTING BULL: Leavenworth Penitentiary.**
18 **CAONABO: Human beings keep other human beings in cages?**
19 **SITTING BULL: They don't belong to the People Nation, as we**
20 do. They belong to the European Tribe.
21 **CAONABO: They must be a primitive tribe.**
22 **SITTING BULL: They speak as if words don't matter, as if**
23 words are the husks of seeds, to be thrown anywhere.
24 *(Crossfade to ship. COLUMBUS and ISABELLA.)*
25 **ISABELLA: Thirty days.**
26 **COLUMBUS: Twenty.**
27 **ISABELLA: It's been twenty days for ten days! The men can**
28 count!
29 **COLUMBUS: Up to twenty! Fingers and toes!**
30 **ISABELLA: You're lying to them!**
31 **COLUMBUS: Did the Queen never lie to you?**
32 **ISABELLA: Sometimes she refused to admit the truth to herself.**
33 **COLUMBUS: That steely-eyed witch? No, lad, you're wrong**
34 there. She had no illusions.
35 **ISABELLA: I know the Queen well, believe me. Steely-eyed — ?**

1   COLUMBUS: Playing war games. Made me cool my heels for
2   years. Not an ounce of romance in her heart.
3   ISABELLA: She loved —
4   COLUMBUS: Power! Control! Making me squirm and plead.
5   ISABELLA: You won her heart!
6   COLUMBUS: Were you there?
7   ISABELLA: She told me.
8   COLUMBUS: Women's wiles.
9   ISABELLA: You seem to forget that I'll return to report to Her
10   Majesty.
11 COLUMBUS: Lad, this is man talk. You'll be a man by the time
12   we get back. You'll understand.
13 ISABELLA: Then you were just telling her what she wanted to
14   hear?
15 COLUMBUS: You don't know much about politics, do you, boy?
16   The ends justify the means. Someone will make that a
17   slogan someday. Escobedo! Write this down!
18   *(He goes off to find ESCOBEDO. ISABELLA looks out over*
19   *the water. Lights up on SITTING BULL, POCAHONTAS, and*
20   *CAONABO.)*
21 SITTING BULL: Once your words go out of your mouth, you
22   can't call them back. *(Drumming. Rattle. Flute music.)*
23 POCAHONTAS: The spirit people are uneasy again.
24 CAONABO: Something going out of balance.
25 POCAHONTAS: Threads breaking.
26 SITTING BULL: As if there were people who thought you could
27   just walk into a place and take things and it wouldn't
28   come back to them.
29 CAONABO: How could anybody be so dumb?
30 SITTING BULL: It's pretty far-fetched, isn't it?
31 CAONABO: You mean they'd be punished?
32 PELTIER: Worse than that. They'd lose their spirit. Lose their
33   soul. Lose their knowledge of what it means to be a People.
34 CAONABO: Who knows what harm they'd do then?
35 SITTING BULL: We'd have to pick up the pieces, try to put the

1   balance back. Do ceremonies, you know, to bring all the
2   parts back into the harmony.
3   CAONABO: But they should have to do that.
4   PELTIER: They don't know how.
5   SITTING BULL: They're like children that way. It'll be a big job.
6   It might take us a long time. But we'll have to do it.
7   Nobody else will do it. It's up to us.
8   *(Lights up on the ship, ISABELLA, ESCOBEDO, and*
9   *COLUMBUS in the bow.)*
10 ISABELLA: Thirty-four days. The men are ready to cut your
11   throat, feed you to the fish, and turn back.
12 COLUMBUS: Look! Birds! Birds atop the sails! Those birds
13   come from somewhere! Look hard, men! Keep your eyes
14   peeled! Keep your noses clean! *(To ISABELLA and*
15   *ESCOBEDO:)* Look at those birds.
16 CAONABO: Look at those birds.
17 POCAHONTAS: What about them?
18 CAONABO: Going out to sea.
19 POCAHONTAS: They do that all the time.
20 CAONABO: They're not coming back. They're staying out there.
21 POCAHONTAS: If they're staying out over the ocean, what are
22   they eating?
23 CAONABO: Good question.
24   *(Dim light on COLUMBUS' boat. ISABELLA, ESCOBEDO,*
25   *and COLUMBUS at the bow, peering into the darkness.)*
26 ESCOBEDO: The men, Admiral, are mutinous.
27 COLUMBUS: Birds are nesting on the yardarms. Tree
28   branches float by all the time. I can smell land!
29 ISABELLA: That's not land. No one on this ship has had a bath
30   for over a month.
31 COLUMBUS: What's unusual about that? I can smell fresh
32   water. I can smell ...
33 ISABELLA: Gold?
34 COLUMBUS: Fame. *(Sound of men grumbling.)*
35 ESCOBEDO: Admiral –

1   **COLUMBUS: What would the Queen think of me if I turned**
2   **back now?**
3   **ISABELLA: That you really needed a bath.** *(Grumbling grows*
4   *louder.)*
5   **COLUMBUS: If we don't find land, cut off my head and sail back**
6   **in peace!** *(Grumbling grows louder.)* **A lifetime pension to**
7   **the first man who sights land! Look lively now!** *(They look*
8   *for land as SITTING BULL prepares for a ceremony.)*
9   **SITTING BULL: Up north, where Leonard and I come from, we**
10   **have a ceremony, a sweat lodge ceremony. We purify**
11   **ourselves that way. We're reborn. We better do that now.**
12   **Let's get in a circle. Come over here, Leonard, you can go**
13   **through space and time, too.** *(SITTING BULL motions to*
14   *BULLHEAD, a young man in the Drumming Circle, wearing*
15   *a suit and tie.)* **You, too, Henry Bullhead, you're part of this**
16   **story.**
17   *(SITTING BULL, CAONABO, POCAHONTAS, PELTIER, and*
18   *BULLHEAD form a circle. Drumming.)*
19   **Build a fire**
20   **over the stones.**
21   **Bring the white hot stones into the lodge,**
22   **the rebirth place.**
23
24   **Make everything dark.**
25   **Pour water on the stones.**
26   **Steam curls around us,**
27   **breath of life**
28   **from the grandfathers.**
29
30   **Offer tobacco,**
31   **sweet grass, sage,**
32   **the sacred plants.**
33   **Rub the sage**
34   **into our sweat.**
35

1   Great Mystery, have pity on us.

2   We pray for all our relations,

3   for the winged ones and the four legged ones

4   and the two legged ones.

5   We pray for our mother the earth.

6   Great Mystery, have pity on us.

7   *(POCAHONTAS takes the flower out of her hair and casts it*

8   *into the sea.)*

9   ISABELLA: Look! A flower.

10   COLUMBUS: We're close! We're close!

11   *(POCAHONTAS and CAONABO look out to sea, sniff the wind.)*

12   POCAHONTAS: What is it, Caonabo?

13   CAONABO: The wind.

14   POCAHONTAS: It blows a funny smell.

15   CAONABO: Like somebody hadn't washed their body for a long

16   time. *(ISABELLA peers into the distance.)*

17   ISABELLA: *(To herself)* Could it be? I think ... no ... Yes! Land!

18   Land ho! *(COLUMBUS rushes up, looks.)*

19   COLUMBUS: I don't see anything.

20   ISABELLA: The pension's mine!

21   COLUMBUS: There's nothing there.

22   ISABELLA: Escobedo! Father Vickery! I saw it first!

23   COLUMBUS: No one but I will see the new world first!

24   ISABELLA: But I saw it.

25   COLUMBUS: Wait! Now – now something's coming into view ...

26   ISABELLA: *Now?*

27   COLUMBUS: I think ... yes ... it wasn't there a moment ago, but

28   now ... I've found it! I've found it! Escobedo! Father

29   Vickery! I saw it first! *(To ISABELLA:)* What would it look

30   like if a cabin boy – or a common sailor – saw land first?

31   What would it look like to history? *(She stares at him.)* Land

32   ho! Land ho! I was the first to sight land!

33   *(Cheers from the men. Crossfade to CAONABO, POCAHONTAS,*

34   *SITTING BULL, BULLHEAD, CAONABO, and PELTIER. As*

35   *the cheers of Columbus' men die away, a profound silence*

1   *fills the air. There is a peacefulness about the silence that*
2   *binds the five People. Finally SITTING BULL speaks.)*
3 **SITTING BULL: When you say a word, you create that thing.**
4   **You walk down the path, and you name things, and you're**
5   **part of them, and they're part of you, and everything is in**
6   **harmony. The Navajo People have a song they sing. I'll**
7   **teach it to you. It goes like this.**
8   *(Gradually the others join SITTING BULL in speaking the*
9   *lines. Gradually the lights brighten on COLUMBUS' boat*
10   *and COLUMBUS, ISABELLA, ESCOBEDO, and FATHER*
11   *VICKERY in the bow, so that as the song of beauty*
12   *progresses, the invaders loom nearer. As they loom nearer,*
13   *PELTIER returns to his cell.)*
14 **SITTING BULL, OTHERS: With beauty before me may I walk**
15   **With beauty behind me may I walk**
16   **With beauty —**
17   *(COLUMBUS throws an anchor off the prow of the caravelle.*
18   *It thuds on the wooden stage.)*
19 **COLUMBUS: Land ho!** *(COLUMBUS jumps onto land.)* **We made**
20   **it!** *(ISABELLA follows, carrying a flag. ESCOBEDO follows,*
21   *carrying his clipboard, pen, and a gun. FATHER VICKERY,*
22   *carrying a Bible, follows.)*
23 **ESCOBEDO, FATHER VICKERY, etc.: We made it!** *(They shake*
24   *hands, etc.)*
25 **COLUMBUS: We're here!**
26 **ESCOBEDO: We're here.**
27 **ISABELLA: We're here.**
28 **FATHER VICKERY: We're here.** *(Several beats, as they look around*
29   *with uncertainty. Meanwhile, SALLY, still as the ship's African*
30   *cook, appears on deck and climbs down onto land.)*
31 **ESCOBEDO: Where are we?**
32 **COLUMBUS: Where we've been headed these thirty-seven**
33   **days.** *(Everyone nods dutifully, then looks questioningly at*
34   *COLUMBUS.)*
35 **CAONABO: They act as if they don't see us.**

1   SITTING BULL: For them, we're not here until they name us.

2   COLUMBUS: We're in China. These are Chinamen.

3   SITTING BULL: This land is not here until they name it.

4   COLUMBUS: Or maybe Japan.

5   CAONABO: Everything already has a name.

6   BULLHEAD: Maybe they're spirits.

7   COLUMBUS: Speak to them, Escobedo.

8   ESCOBEDO: In what language?

9   COLUMBUS: Japanese, of course. What do you think?

10 ESCOBEDO: No one in Europe knows Japanese.

11 COLUMBUS: Well, try Chinese. They may be Chinese, after all.

12   *(ESCOBEDO hesitates.)* **Marco Polo learned Chinese!**

13 ESCOBEDO: *(To Caonabo)* Won ton! Tsing Tao! Chow mein!

14 CAONABO: *(To SITTING BULL)* Sounds a little like Chinese, but

15   the accent's all wrong.

16 BULLHEAD: They must be speaking a spirit language.

17 ESCOBEDO: They must be Japanese.

18 COLUMBUS: Of course they're Japanese. Speak to them in

19   Latin, Escobedo. Everyone knows Latin.

20 ESCOBEDO : E pluribus unum!

21 BULLHEAD: They must be very powerful.

22 COLUMBUS: What'd he say?

23 ESCOBEDO: I'm not sure.

24 COLUMBUS: Talk to them some more.

25 ESCOBEDO: Cogito ergo sum!

26 CAONABO: I think, therefore I am? What kind of nonsense is

27   that?

28 ESCOBEDO: Semper fidelis!

29 CAONABO: I am – therefore I think!

30 COLUMBUS: Well?

31 ESCOBEDO: It seems to be a very rare form of Latin.

32 COLUMBUS: How can it be a rare form of Latin? Latin hasn't

33   changed in fifteen centuries!

34 ESCOBEDO: The Japanese don't know that!

35 ISABELLA: Excuse me, Admiral, but how could the Japanese

1   **know Latin?**

2   **COLUMBUS: Our Lord works in mysterious ways.** *(COLUMBUS*

3   *falls to his knees. ISABELLA, ESCOBEDO, and FATHER*

4   *VICKERY fall to their knees.)*

5   **CAONABO: Are they hurt?** *(BULLHEAD falls to his knees.)*

6   **COLUMBUS: Thank you, Lord, for bringing us safely to ...**

7   **Japan. Or China. Or wherever we are. Thank you, Lord, for**

8   **preventing my cowardly sailors from throwing me**

9   **overboard when they were disheartened and failed in the**

10   **faith that I, your servant, Christopher Columbus, have in**

11   **you.** *(In a low voice, so the others won't hear him:)* **Thank**

12   **you, Lord, for giving me the idea to record fewer miles**

13   **than we actually traveled each day, so these men of little**

14   **faith would not lose heart when we didn't reach land as**

15   **soon as they thought we should.** *(In a loud voice again:)*

16   **And thank you, Lord, for showing these cowardly sailors**

17   **that my vision is true, and that you are behind me, every**

18   **inch of the way!** *(COLUMBUS rises, and the others follow.)* **I**

19   **hereby take possession – write this down, Escobedo – of**

20   **this land!** *(ISABELLA nudges him.)* **In the name of Queen**

21   **Isabella of Castile!**

22   **ISABELLA: Yes!** *(COLUMBUS stares at her.)* **Sir.**

23   **COLUMBUS: I also take possession of this land, from as far**

24   **south as it goes to as far north as it goes – from top to**

25   **bottom! – and as far west as it goes – in the name of**

26   **Western Civilization!**

27   **FATHER VICKERY: And Christ.**

28   **COLUMBUS: And Christ! And I name this land San Salvador!**

29   **ISABELLA: I thought this was Japan.**

30   **COLUMBUS: It's San Salvador now. The Lord saved me, and**

31   **now we can save these ... Japanese. Chinese. Whatever.**

32   *(COLUMBUS steps toward the PEOPLE, hand extended.*

33   *Everybody shakes hands. SALLY greets them with a soul*

34   *handshake — which the People seem to know.)* **Welcome! To**

35   **Spain.**

1 CAONABO: What's he saying, Sitting Bull?
2 SITTING BULL: Beats me.
3 BULLHEAD: We should give them gifts.
4 CAONABO: But who the hell are they?
5 BULLHEAD: Get on their good side.
6 COLUMBUS: *(To ESCOBEDO)* Speak to them in Hebrew. Maybe
7   they're one of the lost tribes.
8 ESCOBEDO: Bar bitzvah! Mazeltov!
9 CAONABO: If they were spirits, they'd know how to speak our
10   language.
11 ESCOBEDO: They don't know Hebrew.
12 FATHER VICKERY: They're savages.
13 POCAHONTAS: Welcome the leader there, the one with the
14   funny hat. *(CAONABO steps forward.)*
15 COLUMBUS: What's he want?
16 ESCOBEDO: Be careful.
17 BULLHEAD: Be careful.
18 ISABELLA: He wants to welcome you.
19 CAONABO: *(Formally)* Welcome — to Turtle Island.
20 ESCOBEDO: He says this land is your land —
21 CAONABO: We've seen you in visions.
22 ESCOBEDO: — This land is my land —
23 CAONABO: You've come a long way.
24 ESCOBEDO: — from California to the —
25 COLUMBUS: We'll take a few back to Spain with us. Show them
26   to Isabella.
27 ISABELLA: Take them prisoner?
28 COLUMBUS: Of course not. Just tie them up and haul them
29   home. Teach them Spanish.
30 BULLHEAD: I wish I knew what they were saying.
31 POCAHONTAS: Maybe we could teach them our language.
32 ISABELLA: Maybe we could learn their language.
33 COLUMBUS: They don't have a language.
34 ISABELLA: What are they speaking?
35 COLUMBUS: Gibberish.

1   BULLHEAD: We should give them gifts. *(BULLHEAD exits.)*
2   CAONABO: Maybe they are spirits. Human beings wouldn't
3   dress that way.
4   FATHER VICKERY: They have no moral sense.
5   ISABELLA: How can you tell?
6   FATHER VICKERY: They're naked!
7   ISABELLA: So are we. Underneath.
8   SITTING BULL: They're ashamed of their bodies.
9   SALLY HEMINGS: They think sex is bad.
10   POCAHONTAS: They're lonelier than I thought.
11   FATHER VICKERY: They have no religion, either.
12   ISABELLA: Are you sure?
13   FATHER VICKERY: Religion means clothes! Besides, do you a
14   see a church?
15   SALLY HEMINGS: They can't dance worth a darn, either.
16   *(ISABELLA holds her head.)*
17   ISABELLA: I have a terrible headache.
18   COLUMBUS: Tough it out. You're a man.
19   SITTING BULL: The boy's head hurts. *(CAONABO pulls out a*
20   *bottle of aspirin.)*
21   CAONABO: Here. Aspirin. From the bark of the willow tree.
22   *(He can't get the cap off.)* I never can get these caps off.
23   *(POCAHONTAS gets the cap off. She hands two aspirin to*
24   *ISABELLA.)*
25   ESCOBEDO: It might be poison!
26   ISABELLA: Get a grip, Escobedo. *(She takes the aspirin.*
27   *CAONABO hands them some leaves.)*
28   CAONABO: Chew these.
29   SITTING BULL: No!
30   CAONABO: Coca leaves. It's a mild stimulant. Pick you up
31   when you're down.
32   SITTING BULL: They won't know when to stop.
33   POCAHONTAS: You mean they have no self-control?
34   *(BULLHEAD enters, carrying bulging grocery bags from a*
35   *local supermarket.)*

1 BULLHEAD: Whether they're spirits or human beings, we
2   should give them presents.
3 CAONABO: I don't know ...
4 SITTING BULL: It's part of our culture to share, you know that.
5   Sometimes a person gives everything away. You start
6   fresh that way.
7 ESCOBEDO: I think they want to trade, Admiral.
8 CAONABO: *(Looks in the bag)* But this is ordinary stuff.
9   Nothing special here. *(CAONABO holds up a tomato.)* A
10   tomato? *(CAONABO tosses the tomato to ESCOBEDO.)*
11 COLUMBUS: Be careful.
12 SITTING BULL: This will revolutionize their eating habits. Can
13   you imagine – they've never had tomato sauce on their
14   spaghetti.
15 COLUMBUS: They're crafty devils. *(SITTING BULL hands*
16   *COLUMBUS potatoes.)*
17 POCAHONTAS: They've never eaten a potato?
18 SITTING BULL: Never even heard of a potato.
19 CAONABO: We've got over three thousand kinds of potatoes.
20 SITTING BULL: News to them.
21 POCAHONTAS: They must be hungry all the time.
22 COLUMBUS: Give them some trinkets. Cheap ones. *(The*
23   *INVADERS pull out trinkets. COLUMBUS gives CAONABO a*
24   *baseball cap.)*
25 SITTING BULL: Mashed potatoes and gravy.
26 COLUMBUS: They won't know the difference.
27 SITTING BULL: Great American dish.
28 CAONABO: What's "American?" *(The INVADERS give the*
29   *PEOPLE trinkets.)*
30 SITTING BULL: Name of an Italian. They're going to call all
31   this land after an Italian guy. Not this one, another one.
32   *(POCAHONTAS pulls packages from the bag and hands*
33   *them to the INVADERS.)*
34 POCAHONTAS: Colors. Dyes. *(SITTING BULL bounces a rubber*
35   *ball to Father Vickery.)*

1 **SITTING BULL: We're going to come dangerously close to**
2   **being called the United States of Vespucci.** *(BULLHEAD*
3   *and POCAHONTAS blow up balloons and hand them to the*
4   *INVADERS.)*
5 **FATHER VICKERY: It's the devil's work.**
6 **CAONABO: They've never heard of rubber? We make raincoats**
7   **and shoes out of this stuff.**
8 **POCAHONTAS:** *(Pulls out a bag of popcorn, passes it around)*
9   **Everybody knows about corn.**
10 **SITTING BULL: Not these guys. Not yet.** *(The PEOPLE pull out*
11   *other things, pass them to the INVADERS.)*
12 **BULLHEAD: Sugar.**
13 **CAONABO: Peanuts.**
14 **POCAHONTAS: Cocoa.**
15 **BULLHEAD: Yams. Squash.**
16 **POCAHONTAS: Mmmm! Tapioca!**
17 **SITTING BULL: Many kinds of beans ...**
18 **POCAHONTAS : Vanilla.**
19 **CAONABO : Maple syrup.**
20 **SITTING BULL: Wild rice.**
21 **BULLHEAD: Berries.**
22 **POCAHONTAS: Avocado.**
23   *(COLUMBUS and ISABELLA wander off by themselves.)*
24 **COLUMBUS: What a beautiful land. Lush, green ...**
25 **ISABELLA: Smell the flowers. A hundred rich fragrances.**
26 **COLUMBUS: Brightly blazoned parrots singing strange songs.**
27 **ISABELLA: Taste this sparkling clear water.**
28 **COLUMBUS: I wish Isabella were here.**
29 **ISABELLA: The witch?**
30 **COLUMBUS: Well, maybe I was a little harsh on her.**
31 **ISABELLA: Maybe you were.**
32 **COLUMBUS: She has to be tough. She's a queen.**
33 **ISABELLA: What would you say to her? If she were here.**
34 **COLUMBUS: I'd say — I'd say, maybe — maybe we've found ...**
35   **paradise.**

1   ISABELLA: It is peaceful.

2   COLUMBUS: And these gentle, naked people ...

3   ISABELLA: Innocent ...

4   COLUMBUS: Generous ...

5   ISABELLA: It's the Garden of Eden.

6   COLUMBUS: It's a new world.

7   ISABELLA: What if we stayed?

8   COLUMBUS: Here?

9   ISABELLA: Forgot about ...

10   COLUMBUS : Empire?

11   ISABELLA : Conquest.

12   COLUMBUS: Forgot about ... ?

13   ISABELLA: War.

14   COLUMBUS: Lived in Paradise?

15   ISABELLA: Took off our clothes? *(They seem on the verge of*

16   *deciding just that, when —)*

17   ESCOBEDO: *(Looking at CAONABO's earring)* Gold! Admiral!

18   COLUMBUS: I knew it! Gold! I promised the Queen we'd bring

19   back gold.

20   ISABELLA: I think she had in mind more than an earring.

21   Admiral, sir.

22   COLUMBUS: *(Making gestures)* That — precious metal — where —

23   do you get? *(ESCOBEDO shines a mirror at POCAHONTAS,*

24   *luring her Off-stage.)*

25   ESCOBEDO: *(To POCAHONTAS)* Come.

26   CAONABO: Does he want my earring?

27   POCAHONTAS: He wants to know where you got it.

28   ESCOBEDO: *(To POCAHONTAS)* For you.

29   CAONABO: *(Yelling at COLUMBUS)* From my sister!

30   SITTING BULL: No, no. Where you got the metal.

31   CAONABO: *(To COLUMBUS, gesturing)* Several islands over!

32   ESCOBEDO: *(To POCAHONTAS)* Come.

33   COLUMBUS: *(To ESCOBEDO)* What's he say?

34   ESCOBEDO: He says back in the jungle a little ways.

35   *(ESCOBEDO lures POCAHONTAS Off-stage.)*

1 COLUMBUS: *(To CAONABO)* I give you heap big trinket for itsy
2   bitsy gold earring.
3 CAONABO: Is he kidding? *(CAONABO gives COLUMBUS the*
4   *earring.)*
5 BULLHEAD: *(To SITTING BULL)* Bring out the pipe and
6   tobacco. We'll smoke the pipe together. We'll be friends
7   forever. *(SITTING BULL brings out a pouch.)*
8 CAONABO: We're giving them all this food and medicine.
9   What are they giving us?
10 PELTIER: Smallpox. Tuberculosis. Malaria. Yellow fever.
11   Bubonic plague. Influenza. Scarlet fever. Typhoid.
12   Cholera. Diphtheria. Gonorrhea. Chicken pox. Measles.
13   Whooping cough. The People had no immunity. In the
14   first hundred years, nine out of every ten native People
15   died of disease brought by the invaders.
16 SITTING BULL: *(To COLUMBUS)* This is a sacred plant. It binds
17   our hearts together, and with it we speak to the Great
18   Mystery. *(ESCOBEDO, clothes awry and face scratched,*
19   *enters.)*
20 COLUMBUS: This'll be your plantation over here, Escobedo.
21   Father, you can put up a church over there. I'll take the
22   rest of the island.
23 BULLHEAD: Maybe they want land.
24 CAONABO: That's ridiculous. No one can own their Mother.
25 COLUMBUS: There must be a gold mine somewhere.
26 ESCOBEDO: We'll need workers to work the plantations.
27 COLUMBUS: And mine the gold.
28 ISABELLA: You'll need thousands of workers.
29 COLUMBUS: *(Points to the PEOPLE.)* They must have friends.
30 ISABELLA: What if they don't want to mine gold or work
31   plantations?
32 COLUMBUS: Is slavery against canon law, Father?
33 FATHeR VICKERY: Slavery? Of course not.
34 ISABELLA: What if they refuse to work?
35 ESCOBEDO: We'll cut off their hands.

1   ISABELLA: I'm sure they'll work hard then.

2   COLUMBUS: Now that that's settled ...

3   ISABELLA: What if they run away? *(COLUMBUS, ESCOBEDO,*

4   *and FATHER VICKERY notice SALLY. They smile.)*

5   COLUMBUS, ESCOBEDO, FATHER VICKERY: There's always

6   Africa.

7   SALLY HEMINGS: Excuse me, sir?

8   COLUMBUS: What is it?

9   SALLY HEMINGS: I was just wondering ...

10   COLUMBUS: Yes, yes, hurry up.

11   SALLY HEMINGS: Well, sir, you've claimed all this land, from

12   the top of the world to the bottom —

13   COLUMBUS: Yes —

14   SALLY HEMINGS: — and as far west as it goes —

15   COLUMBUS: Yes, yes.

16   SALLY HEMINGS: — mountains, rivers, trees, grass, bananas —

17   COLUMBUS: That's right.

18   SALLY HEMINGS: For Western Civilization ...

19   FATHER VICKERY: And Christ.

20   SALLY HEMINGS: But what about these people living here?

21   COLUMBUS: What people?

22   ESCOBEDO: The Chinese.

23   ISABELLA: Japanese.

24   FATHER VICKERY: They don't really look like either one.

25   COLUMBUS: What do you think they are?

26   ISABELLA: Where do you think we are?

27   ESCOBEDO: We might have missed Japan. We were sailing a

28   long time.

29   ISABELLA: We might have sailed past China as well.

30   COLUMBUS: Well, if we passed Japan, and we passed China,

31   that leaves ... *(They look at the PEOPLE.)* **Indians!**

32   ESCOBEDO: Indians ...

33   FATHER VICKERY: Indians!

34   ISABELLA: Indians.

35   BULLHEAD: What are Indians?

1   **COLUMBUS:** *(To PEOPLE)* **You** — **Indians!** **We** — *(He looks*
2   *around for advice)* — **people!**
3   **CAONABO:** These guys are nuts.
4   **SALLY HEMINGS:** But sir —
5   **COLUMBUS:** What!
6   **SALLY HEMINGS:** Isn't it their land?
7   **COLUMBUS:** How could it be their land? I discovered it.
8   **SALLY HEMINGS:** But I mean didn't they discover it first?
9   **COLUMBUS:** You're confused, young man. They don't own this
10   land. They're just ... here.
11   **ESCOBEDO:** That's right. They're just here.
12   **ISABELLA:** *(Thoughtfully)* **Waiting.**
13   **FATHER VICKERY:** Waiting to have their souls saved!
14   **COLUMBUS:** Besides, look around. They're not using this land.
15   **ESCOBEDO:** There are no cities. No farms. No industry.
16   **FATHER VICKERY:** No cathedrals. No monasteries. No
17   Inquisition, poor souls.
18   **COLUMBUS:** They don't even seem to have a king. *(ISABELLA*
19   *kicks him.)* **Or a queen.**
20   **FATHER VICKERY:** Or peasants.
21   **ESCOBEDO:** No sociopolitical hierarchy.
22   **COLUMBUS:** They're anarchists.
23   **ESCOBEDO:** They're democrats.
24   **FATHER VICKERY:** They're savages.
25   **COLUMBUS:** But noble looking, for all that.
26   **ESCOBEDO:** They're noble savages.
27   **FATHER VICKERY:** This land is ...
28   **COLUMBUS:** It's just here.
29   **ESCOBEDO:** *We'll* use the land.
30   **COLUMBUS:** You bet we will!
31   **ESCOBEDO:** We'll clear the trees, plow the soil, build cities,
32   railroads, planes, skyscrapers, computers, satellites,
33   multinational corporations, digital display watches,
34   nuclear power plants, biological warfare canisters, high
35   resolution television — ! *(Everyone stares at him.)* **Maybe I**

1   was getting a little ahead of myself.

2   *(POCAHONTAS enters, clothes torn, limping. She attacks*

3   *ESCOBEDO. The others pull her off.)* **Feisty little thing, isn't**

4   **she? She fought for awhile, but I gave her a good whack or**

5   **two, and then ... well ...**

6   **CAONABO: I say we kill them. Now. Before it's too late.**

7   **POCAHONTAS: I smell death.**

8   **PELTIER: Death for all of us.**

9   **CAONABO: Kill them.**

10 **SITTING BULL: Might not be a bad idea.**

11 **COLUMBUS: Let's go look for that gold!**

12 **POCAHONTAS: Blood runs from their fingers.**

13 **COLUMBUS: I want Isabella's eyes to pop right out of her head**

14   **when she sees all I bring back!**

15 **POCAHONTAS: Sickness lives in their breath.**

16 **PELTIER: They have nothing we need!**

17 **COLUMBUS: Come on, lads! There's gold in them there hills!**

18 *(SITTING BULL, CAONABO, and POCAHONTAS surround*

19 *COLUMBUS, ESCOBEDO, and FATHER VICKERY, and raise*

20 *knives, tomahawks.)*

21 **PELTIER: Kill them!**

22   **END OF ACT ONE**

23

24

25   **ACT TWO**

26

27 *(Lights up on PELTIER and SITTING BULL. At some point*

28   *SITTING BULL puts on PELTIER's cap.)*

29 **PELTIER: You should've killed them!**

30 **SITTING BULL: Maybe we should've.**

31 **PELTIER: Why didn't you?**

32 **SITTING BULL: They were our guests.**

33 **PELTIER: Some guests.**

34 **SITTING BULL: You didn't kill those two FBI agents.**

35 **PELTIER: I was shooting at them.**

1 *(CAONABO appears. He wears jeans. A bandana is tied around*
2 *his head. POCAHONTAS appears. She wears modern dress.)*
3 **SITTING BULL: Columbus and those guys hadn't done**
4 **anything.**
5 **CAONABO: Not yet.** *(COLUMBUS appears.)*
6 **COLUMBUS: We were on the Santa Maria, cruising the coast. It**
7 **was Christmas. Maybe we partied a little too much.** *(Lights*
8 *up on ESCOBEDO and FATHER VICKERY drinking and*
9 *dancing, then collapsing.)* **The boy at the wheel fell asleep.**
10 *(Light on ISABELLA as the Queen.)*
11 **ISABELLA: I did not!**
12 **COLUMBUS: We ran aground. Had to scuttle the Santa Maria.**
13 **POCAHONTAS: We gave the strangers our best houses to live in**
14 **and fed them delicacies of every kind.**
15 **COLUMBUS: We used the timbers from the Santa Maria to**
16 **build a fort.**
17 **POCAHONTAS: Why did you think you needed a fort?**
18 **COLUMBUS: Everywhere we go, we build forts – forts, castles,**
19 **walls – you have to protect yourself.**
20 **POCAHONTAS: We had no forts.**
21 **COLUMBUS: The world's a dangerous place. You can't trust**
22 **people.**
23 **POCAHONTAS: Columbus left behind thirty-nine men.**
24 **CAONABO: Kidnapped seven People.**
25 **COLUMBUS: And sailed back to Spain.**
26 **ISABELLA: Columbus returned with several of the people he**
27 **called Indians. They wanted to bathe every day –**
28 **apparently it was their custom. Our doctors thought that**
29 **was unhealthy, so we forbade it. When they spoke, their**
30 **words were like music. I felt as if I were listening to my**
31 **future. Columbus said –**
32 **COLUMBUS: Look how gentle and docile they are.** *(Pause.)*
33 **They'll make good slaves.**
34 **ISABELLA: I wondered if they might make good friends.**
35 *(Light down on ISABELLA.)*

1 CAONABO: The men Columbus left behind kidnapped our
2   women.
3 POCAHONTAS: Raped us, kept us as slaves, murdered the men
4   who tried to protect us.
5 CAONABO: So we killed them. All of them. What else could
6   we do?
7 PELTIER: We had to fight back. *(To SITTING BULL:)* You fought
8   back. The Caribs fought back.
9 SITTING BULL: The Aztecs.
10 PELTIER: The Incas.
11 SITTING BULL: The Mayans.
12 CAONABO: Cherokee.
13 POCAHONTAS : Iroquois.
14 PELTIER: Shawnee. *(BULLHEAD appears.)*
15 BULLHEAD: Delaware.
16 SITTING BULL: Menominee.
17 PELTIER: Ojibway.
18 CAONABO: During the first hundred years of occupation,
19   three billion dollars in gold was dug out and shipped to
20   Europe.
21 POCAHONTAS: Seminole.
22 SITTING BULL: Creek.
23 BULLHEAD: Chickasaw.
24 SITTING BULL: Lakota.
25 PELTIER: Arikara.
26 POCAHONTAS : Absaroka.
27 CAONABO: Billions of dollars worth of silver, mined by the
28   People under slavery and shipped by the Spaniards to
29   Europe, created the first world economy.
30 BULLHEAD: Ponca.
31 SITTING BULL: Kiowa.
32 CAONABO: Four out of every five People working in the silver
33   mines in the Andes Mountains died.
34 PELTIER: Osage.
35 POCAHONTAS : Iowa.

1 BULLHEAD: Pizzaro, in his lust for gold, killed thousands and
2   destroyed the Incan empire.
3 SITTING BULL: Shoshone.
4 CAONABO: Ute.
5 POCAHONTAS: Cortez and his men murdered the Aztecs and
6   stole their gold.
7 BULLHEAD: Comanche.
8 SITTING BULL: Apache.
9 CAONABO: Arapaho.
10 PELTIER: Wichita.
11 POCAHONTAS: Pawnee.
12 SITTING BULL: Kansa.
13 BULLHEAD: At first the People welcomed the strangers.
14 PELTIER: Cheyenne.
15 POCAHONTAS: Blackfoot.
16 CAONABO: Assiniboine.
17 SITTING BULL: Peoria.
18 PELTIER: Yakima.
19 CAONABO: We let them hunt and fish.
20 BULLHEAD: Modoc.
21 SITTING BULL: Klamath.
22 POCAHONTAS: Flathead.
23 PELTIER: Tlingit.
24 CAONABO: Haida.
25 BULLHEAD: We gave them seeds.
26 SITTING BULL: Kwakiutl.
27 PELTIER: Salish.
28 CAONABO: Tillamook.
29 BULLHEAD: Chehalis.
30 PELTIER: Coos.
31 POCAHONTAS: Of course, they thought the seeds were just
32   seeds. They didn't talk to the seeds.
33 BULLHEAD: Puyallup.
34 SITTING BULL: Nisqually.
35 CAONABO: Clatsop.

1   **BULLHEAD:** Hopi.

2   **SITTING BULL:** More strangers came.

3   **PELTIER:** Navajo.

4   **POCAHONTAS:** Mojave.

5   **CAONABO:** They wanted more land.

6   **SITTING BULL:** Papago.

7   **CAONABO:** Zuni.

8   **BULLHEAD:** Yuma.

9   **PELTIER:** Comanito.

10 **BULLHEAD:** Toboso.

11 **SITTING BULL:** Mohawk.

12 **POCAHONTAS:** In 1637, near what is now New Haven, the
13   Pequot nation was nearly wiped out – women and
14   children burned to death, most of the men killed, the rest
15   sold into slavery.

16 **CAONABO:** Metacom, the Wampanoag sachem, called by the
17   colonialists King Philip, led a resistance a hundred years
18   before their war of independence. Metacom was killed
19   and his body hacked to pieces.

20 **POCAHONTAS:** His wife and son were sold into slavery in the
21   West Indies for thirty shillings each.

22 **BULLHEAD:** Tens of thousands were taken to the West Indies
23   as slaves.

24 **SITTING BULL:** Nimpuc.

25 **PELTIER:** Pensacola.

26 **CAONABO:** Narraganset.

27 **POCAHONTAS:** Tutchone.

28 **SITTING BULL:** Choctaw.

29 **BULLHEAD:** Chitimacha.

30 **CAONABO:** Yurok.

31 **POCAHONTAS:** Miami.

32 **PELTIER:** Illinois.

33 **CAONABO:** In the Southwest, the Acoma, Zuni, Hopi, and
34   others rose up against the Spanish.

35 **SITTING BULL:** Yellowknife.

1   **POCAHONTAS:** Nebesna.

2   **BULLHEAD:** Tecumseh tried to unite all the People to fight

3   against the invaders. He was killed in 1813.

4   **PELTIER:** Ingalik.

5   **CAONABO:** Chawasha.

6   **SITTING BULL:** Natchez.

7   **POCAHONTAS:** Potawatomi.

8   **BULLHEAD:** Biloxi.

9   **PELTIER:** There were many great leaders: Geronimo,

10   Cochise, Satanta ...

11   **CAONABO:** Pontiac, Washakie, Black Hawk.

12   **POCAHONTAS:** Little Crow, Crazy Horse, Kicking Bird.

13   **BULLHEAD:** Seattle, Spotted Tail, Red Cloud.

14   *(Lights down on all but SITTING BULL as COLUMBUS*

15   *approaches him.)*

16   **COLUMBUS:** *(To SITTING BULL)* It's too bad, of course, all

17   those diseases, too bad we had to kill so many – but, hey!

18   Sitting, that's what success is all about! Going all the way!

19   Faint heart never won, give it all you've got, two hundred

20   percent!

21   **SITTING BULL:** One of your elders said –

22   **COLUMBUS:** One of my elders?

23   **SITTING BULL:** Aristotle – said, Moderation in all things.

24   **COLUMBUS:** Aristotle didn't discover America. Aristotle didn't

25   bomb Nagasaki. Aristotle didn't build Trump Towers! You

26   don't get anywhere with moderation! You've got to go all

27   out! You folks live in harmony with the land, right? Kill

28   what you need to eat, ask the forgiveness of the buffalo

29   before you kill him, you're one with nature – am I right,

30   Sitting?

31   **SITTING BULL:** It's a philosophy, Chris, that postulates a

32   harmony throughout the universe.

33   **COLUMBUS:** But I've got the log line, right?

34   **SITTING BULL:** For us, there's no Platonic division between

35   the Ideal and the material worlds.

1   COLUMBUS: That's the pitch, am I right?

2   SITTING BULL: No Cartesian bifurcation between mind and

3   body.

4   COLUMBUS: That's your high concept?

5   SITTING BULL: No Judeo-Christian alienation of the human

6   from the rest of creation.

7   COLUMBUS: All right —

8   SITTING BULL: No Sartrean existential angst in the face of a

9   cosmic loneliness.

10 COLUMBUS: All right —

11 SITTING BULL: None of this mastery over nature nonsense.

12 COLUMBUS: Here's my question. What's it gotten you? What'd

13   it get you before I came? You had nothing. So a few

14   hundred million Indians died. So there are ten buffalo

15   left. So most of your tribes have disappeared from the face

16   of the earth — culture, language, genes — gone. It happens.

17   Right? Am I right? The bottom line, Sitting — do you want

18   the bottom line? The bottom line is this. We invented

19   things. We invented gunpowder —

20 SITTING BULL: The Chinese invented gunpowder.

21 COLUMBUS: We invented the compass —

22 SITTING BULL: The Arabs invented the compass.

23 COLUMBUS: We invented the calendar.

24 SITTING BULL: The Mayans.

25 COLUMBUS: Diplomacy.

26 SITTING BULL: The Iroquois.

27 COLUMBUS: We invented the printing press, horseshoes,

28   double entry bookkeeping, the internal combustion

29   engine, and the fork! We invented Kool Aid! You hadn't

30   even invented the wheel! You live in harmony — that's

31   another word for stagnation. We brought progress.

32   *(SITTING BULL coughs.)* What's the matter?

33 SITTING BULL: Smog.

34 COLUMBUS: Why the cap?

35 SITTING BULL: No ozone.

1 COLUMBUS: Survival of the fittest. Might makes right. Am I
2   right? Sitting? Am I right?
3 *(Lights down on SITTING BULL and COLUMBUS. Lights*
4   *up on ESCOBEDO, who now plays the role of JOHN SMITH,*
5   *as he is thrown to the ground by CAONABO, playing*
6   *WAHUNSONACOCK, or, as the colonists called him,*
7   *POWHATAN. CAONABO brandishes a sword.)*
8 CAONABO: All right, John Smith, you've raided your last
9   People village, killed your last People.
10 ESCOBEDO: We've lived in peace, Powhatan.
11 CAONABO: I'm going to slice you into dog meat.
12 ESCOBEDO: We've traded. We've respected each other.
13 CAONABO: We gave you food when you were starving. This is
14   the thanks we get.
15 ESCOBEDO: One of your Indians killed a white man.
16 CAONABO: And you destroyed an entire village. Killed
17   innocent women and children.
18 ESCOBEDO: They had to be taught a lesson.
19 CAONABO: What kind of lesson does a dead child learn?
20 ESCOBEDO: What're you going to get out of killing me?
21 CAONABO: Satisfaction.
22 ESCOBEDO: Let me go, I'll give you guns. You can fight your
23   Indian enemies.
24 CAONABO: I'd rather kill you, John.
25 ESCOBEDO: What do you think'll happen after you kill me?
26 CAONABO: I'll experience a deep feeling of satisfaction.
27 ESCOBEDO: You'll have a thousand settlers on your ass,
28   Powhatan. Your warriors'll be massacred and scalped.
29   Your women'll be raped and their breasts cut off and
30   they'll be disemboweled in front of their children. The
31   children'll have their heads smashed against rocks. It'll be
32   a typical punitive raid by God-fearing Christians. Don't let
33   a little selfish satisfaction bring about the annihilation of
34   your people. *(POCAHONTAS enters.)*
35 POCAHONTAS: Dad? Have you killed him yet?

1   CAONABO: We've been talking things over.

2   POCAHONTAS: I want the privilege.

3   CAONABO: You want to kill him?

4   POCAHONTAS: Slowly.

5   CAONABO: What did he do to you, Pocahontas?

6   ESCOBEDO: *(To POCAHONTAS)* I never told you I was making

7   a commitment. I told you it was just a fun thing, a mutual

8   attraction, a chance for two lonely people to have a few

9   evenings of good times. I never said I'd marry you,

10   Pocahontas.

11 POCAHONTAS: You think I'd want to marry you, John Smith?

12   That probably isn't even your real name. You're probably

13   on the run from the law. You've probably betrayed other

14   women. Haven't you?

15 ESCOBEDO: You had a good time, didn't you? *(She slaps him.)*

16   Oh, Pocahontas, when I think of your breasts — *(She slaps*

17   *him)* — round and full — *(She kicks him)* — like ripe Indian

18   melons — *(POCAHONTAS grabs the sword from CAONABO*

19   *and puts the sword to ESCOBEDO's throat.)*

20 CAONABO: Go ahead, kill him.

21 POCAHONTAS: He likes to get me mad. He wants me to

22   humiliate him. It makes him excited. Are you excited, John?

23 CAONABO: Use the sword.

24 POCAHONTAS: I will. I'll use the sword.

25 ESCOBEDO: No!

26 POCAHONTAS: You won't mistreat any more women, John

27   Smith.

28 ESCOBEDO: Pocahontas!

29 POCAHONTAS: Oh, John. You're not so excited anymore.

30 ESCOBEDO: Please!

31 POCAHONTAS: Are you trying to hide, John? *(She jerks his*

32   *trousers off. He's wearing ridiculous boxer shorts. He starts*

33   *crying.)*

34 CAONABO: Maybe you'd better let him go. There's no honor in

35   killing someone as pitiful as this.

1 POCAHONTAS: But there'd be satisfaction.
2 CAONABO: We could let him go if he signs a treaty and
3   promises not to bother us ever again.
4 POCAHONTAS: Treaties don't mean anything to them.
5 CAONABO: That's true.
6 POCAHONTAS: They've broken hundreds of treaties.
7 CAONABO: What do you think we should do? *(She aims the*
8   *sword. JOHN screams. She lets him shuffle off, his trousers*
9   *around his ankles.)*
10 POCAHONTAS: Go home, John Smith. Be thankful we're a
11   civilized people.
12 CAONABO: *(Calls after him)* See you next week for
13   Thanksgiving! I'll bring the pumpkin pie!
14 POCAHONTAS: I should've killed him. He'll tell everybody I
15   saved his life because I wanted to marry him.
16   *(Crossfade, to where COLUMBUS, as THOMAS JEFFERSON,*
17   *sits writing.)*
18 COLUMBUS: "We hold these verities to be – " No, "verities"
19   isn't right. "We hold these Ideas"? No. "We hold these
20   hypotheses"? *(SALLY HEMINGS enters with tea tray,*
21   *teacups, etc.)*
22 SALLY HEMINGS: Truths!
23 COLUMBUS: *(As if he had thought of it)* "Truths! To be ...
24   obvious." No. "To be ... clear as day." No.
25 SALLY HEMINGS: Do you want some tea, Tom?
26 COLUMBUS: "We hold these truths to be ... or not to be, that is
27   the ... " Thanks, Sally. "We hold these truths to be – "
28 SALLY HEMINGS: It's self-evident.
29 COLUMBUS: *(Writing)* "Self-evident"! "Self-evident ... that all
30   people – that all *men* ... " *(He looks at her a moment.)*
31 SALLY HEMINGS: Why not all people, Tom?
32 COLUMBUS: Please. I'm busy.
33 SALLY HEMINGS: You said "people," then you changed it to
34   "men." Why?
35 COLUMBUS: Don't you worry your pretty little head about it,

1   Sally Hemings.

2 SALLY HEMINGS: You're writing that Declaration of
3   Independence, aren't you?

4 COLUMBUS: This doesn't concern you.

5 SALLY HEMINGS: It doesn't concern me?

6 COLUMBUS: Sally, I love you. I live with you as my wife, even
7   though it's illegal, even though you have no rights, even
8   though you are inferior to me.

9 SALLY HEMINGS: You find me equal enough when you want
10   somebody to talk to.

11 COLUMBUS: You're a good listener.

12 SALLY HEMINGS: When you want to bounce ideas off somebody.

13 COLUMBUS: You understand me. Madison, Washington,
14   Hamilton – they've all got their own ideas about things –
15   they're not good listeners.

16 SALLY HEMINGS: When you want somebody to cheer you up
17   when you're sad.

18 COLUMBUS: I don't know what I'd do without you, Sally.

19 SALLY HEMINGS: Now what's this word you're looking for?

20 COLUMBUS: I can find my own words!

21 SALLY HEMINGS: Fine! Find your own words!

22 COLUMBUS: Where was I?

23 SALLY HEMINGS: Men.

24 COLUMBUS: "All men are created ... " What shall we say?

25 SALLY HEMINGS: Dumb.

26 COLUMBUS: "The same ... " No.

27 SALLY HEMINGS: Endowed by their Creator ...

28 COLUMBUS: *(Writing)* "Endowed by their Creator ... "

29 SALLY HEMINGS: Whoever She is ...

30 COLUMBUS: *(Writing)* "Whoever She – " No, no. "By their
31   Creator ... with certain ... certain ... " What's a word, Sally,
32   that denotes that which cannot be taken away? *(SALLY is*
33   *silent.)* Come on, Sally. Sal-ly. Saaaallllyyyy. *(She ignores*
34   *him.)* "Certain ... rights?" But what kind of rights? I know
35   there's a word ... Sally? *(She ignores him.)* If I don't finish

1 this tonight, Franklin'll write it, and he'll go down in
2 history instead of me. Is that what you want? *(She ignores*
3 *him. He tries again.)* **Fun rights. Swell rights. Cool —**
4 **SALLY HEMINGS: Oh, for God's sake, Tom! Inalienable rights!**
5 *(He stares at her. Beat. He writes.)* **All men have inalienable**
6 **rights!** *(He writes.)* **All *white* men!** *(He writes, then stops.)*
7 **COLUMBUS: That won't look so good.**
8 **SALLY HEMINGS: It's what you mean.**
9 **COLUMBUS: Of course it's what we mean. What else could we**
10 **mean?**
11 *(Crossfade to ESCOBEDO, as PRESIDENT ANDREW*
12 *JACKSON, and ISABELLA, as his AIDE.)*
13 **ISABELLA: President Jackson, what about the Indians in the**
14 **Southeast?**
15 **ESCOBEDO: Move 'em. Move 'em to ... Oklahoma. Nobody**
16 **lives there.**
17 **ISABELLA: But sir, those Indians've gone to our schools, they**
18 **own farms —**
19 **ESCOBEDO: White people need those farms.** *(Drum.)*
20 **ISABELLA: Sir? Those Indians? The Cherokees? They've**
21 **appealed to the United States Supreme Court.**
22 **ESCOBEDO: What'd the Court say?**
23 **ISABELLA: That the Cherokees could stay on their land.**
24 **What'll we do now, sir?**
25 **ESCOBEDO: Send the army. Never mind the Court.**
26 **ISABELLA: But there are thousands of Indians.**
27 **ESCOBEDO: Send a big army.**
28 **ISABELLA: How will the Indians get to Oklahoma?**
29 **ESCOBEDO: Walk.**
30 **ISABELLA: It's a thousand miles.**
31 **ESCOBEDO: Tell 'em to walk fast.**
32 **ISABELLA: It's winter. They have no blankets. No food. They're**
33 **sick. It'll be a trail of tears.**
34 **ESCOBEDO: They're only Indians!**
35 *(Crossfade to FATHER VICKERY, who plays the JUDGE, at the*

1   *table used at the beginning of Act I. Beside the table, in the*
2   *witness chair, sits COLUMBUS, as an FBI AGENT. PELTIER*
3   *stands in a spotlight. SITTING BULL watches.)*
4   **FATHER VICKERY:** You were one of the FBI agents near
5   Wounded Knee the day the two other agents were
6   murdered?
7   **COLUMBUS:** I was, Your Honor.
8   **FATHER VICKERY:** What was it like out there, Agent?
9   **COLUMBUS:** It was terrific, Judge. FBI, federal marshals, state
10   police, sheriff's deputies, national guard —
11   **FATHER VICKERY:** It must have been —
12   **COLUMBUS:** It was exciting!
13   **FATHER VICKERY:** I wish I'd been there.
14   **COLUMBUS:** We had them surrounded.
15   **FATHER VICKERY:** I played cowboys and Indians when I was a
16   kid.
17   **COLUMBUS:** We had high-powered rifles with night sights.
18   **PELTIER:** All we had was some twenty-twos, a deer rifle or two.
19   **COLUMBUS:** We had bazookas, we had automatic weapons, we
20   had pistols. We had helicopters and armored personnel
21   carriers.
22   **PELTIER:** We thought they were going to kill us all. They just
23   needed an excuse.
24   **COLUMBUS:** We gave each other names. Butch Cassiday.
25   Sundance. Billy the Kid. Wild Bill. Deadeye Dick.
26   **FATHER VICKERY:** I wish I'd been there.
27   **COLUMBUS:** We passed around the Wild Turkey and the Jim
28   Beam.
29   **PELTIER:** They started shooting at us.
30   **COLUMBUS:** We were just having fun.
31   **PELTIER:** We hadn't done anything.
32   **COLUMBUS:** They started shooting back.
33   **FATHER VICKERY:** Savages.
34   **COLUMBUS:** We defended ourselves.
35   **FATHER VICKERY:** I wish I'd been there!

1   COLUMBUS: Two men fell in the line of duty.

2   FATHER VICKERY: And it was Peltier?

3   COLUMBUS: Who else? He was the ring leader. Get the leaders —

4   that's what they teach us in FBI school. Martin Luther

5   King, Malcolm X ...

6   SITTING BULL: They were always trying to figure out who was

7   the chief. We'd try to tell them, we're not like you, we're

8   more democratic. We have to talk things over, reach a

9   consensus. But they'd come up to anybody, give him some

10   whiskey, say, You're a chief, sign here, thanks for the

11   Black Hills.

12   FATHER VICKERY: And the two FBI agents, brutally murdered —

13   COLUMBUS: Their bodies riddled with bullets.

14   PELTIER: Three shots!

15   COLUMBUS: They used guerrilla tactics. They built bunkers —

16   PELTIER: Those were root cellars.

17   FATHER VICKERY: And you saw the accused, Leonard Peltier,

18   cold-bloodedly murder those two fine men?

19   COLUMBUS: I didn't exactly see him, Your Honor.

20   FATHER VICKERY: This is a Court of Law. We have to be fair.

21   We're not going to railroad an innocent man, even if he is

22   a redskin. How do you know it was Leonard Peltier who

23   pulled the trigger?

24   COLUMBUS: We have our sources.

25   FATHER VICKERY: FBI sources?

26   COLUMBUS: Completely reliable and foolproof.

27   FATHER VICKERY: And these sources ... ?

28   COLUMBUS: Prove that Leonard Peltier shot and killed those

29   two FBI agents.

30   FATHER VICKERY: Where are these sources?

31   COLUMBUS: They're not here, Your Honor.

32   FATHER VICKERY: Where are they?

33   COLUMBUS: We can't find them.

34   FATHER VICKERY: But they're reliable?

35   COLUMBUS: Yes sir.

1   FATHER VICKERY: That's enough for me, son. Guilty!

2   *(Drumbeat. Crossfade to CAONABO.)*

3   CAONABO: This is a story the Salish People tell. Long ago, the

4   People had no light. Mink, who was a great thief, heard that

5   on the other side of the world there was something called

6   the Sun. So Mink stole the sun for the People. He stuck it up

7   in the sky so that it would share its light with the people on

8   both sides of the world. *(BULLHEAD appears.)*

9   BULLHEAD: The People praised Mink. He grew proud of

10   himself because of that praise. He said, maybe there's

11   something else I can steal for the People. A long time

12   passed and Mink saw nothing that was worth stealing.

13   Then the Europeans came. They were new people with a

14   lot of power. What do these new people have that we don't

15   have? Mink asked himself. Then he saw what it was. The

16   Europeans had something they called Time. They used it

17   to give them their power. *(POCAHONTAS appears.)*

18   POCAHONTAS: So Mink decided he'd steal Time. He waited

19   until it was dark and sneaked into their house. There, in

20   the biggest room, they kept Time up on a shelf. They kept

21   it in a shiny box which made noises. Two small arrows on

22   the front of the box moved in circles. Mink could see it

23   was a powerful thing. So he carried it off.

24   PELTIER: Now Mink and the People had Time.

25   BULLHEAD: But Mink soon found that it wasn't easy to have

26   Time.

27   POCAHONTAS: He had to watch the hands of that shiny box all

28   of the time to see what the time was.

29   CAONABO: He had to keep three keys tied around his neck so

30   that he could use them to wind up that box full of time so

31   it would keep on ticking.

32   PELTIER: Now that Mink had Time, he no longer had the time

33   to do the things he used to do. There was no time to fish

34   and hunt.

35   POCAHONTAS: He had to get up at a certain time and go to bed

1 at a certain time.

2 BULLHEAD: He had to go to meetings and work when that box
3 full of time told him it was time.

4 PELTIER: Because Mink stole Time, it now owned him and the
5 People.

6 POCAHONTAS: It's been that way ever since.

7 CAONABO: Time owns us the way we used to own the Sun.

8 *(Crossfade to FATHER VICKERY, as JUDGE, and PELTIER.)*

9 FATHER VICKERY: Leonard Peltier, do you have anything to
10 say before I pronounce sentence?

11 PELTIER: Well, Judge, nobody came up here and said they saw
12 who killed those FBI agents. You decided what was to be
13 believed, not the jury. You allowed the prosecutor to say I
14 was a criminal, even though I've never been convicted of
15 a crime until today. And when my lawyers mentioned that
16 everybody else accused of these killings was found not
17 guilty, you wouldn't let the jury hear that. You decided
18 before this trial began that I was guilty, and that you'd
19 sentence me to the maximum penalty under the law. I feel
20 sorry for you, Judge. I feel sorry for you because under
21 your system you're taught greed, racism, and corruption.
22 I'm not the guilty one here, Judge.

23 FATHER VICKERY: Leonard Peltier, you are hereby sentenced
24 to two consecutive terms of life imprisonment!

25 *(Crossfade to ISABELLA, as a PIONEER WOMAN.)*

26 ISABELLA: We came out west by wagon train, me and my
27 husband. There had been trouble with the Indians.
28 Soldiers had wiped out one of their camps, killed women
29 and children. The Indians had killed some homesteaders
30 in retaliation, burned their houses and stolen their
31 horses. We were headed farther west, where we hoped it
32 was more peaceful. Then one morning the Indians
33 attacked. My husband was killed. I was captured. I was
34 scared they were going to torture me and kill me. But the
35 man that carried me off didn't harm me. He treated me

1   with kindness. I learned to make the fire, cook, dress the
2   buffalo hides, find the roots you could eat. I got used to the
3   Indian way. I got used to him. One day, I realized I loved
4   him. One day, I felt like I was an Indian, too. A few years
5   later we were attacked by the army. I was captured again.
6   They thought they had saved me. But their ways were
7   strange to me now. And they didn't like how I'd become
8   Indian. I ran away. I found my tribe again. I found my
9   Indian husband. I lived the rest of my life as an Indian.
10   *(Crossfade to FATHER VICKERY, as FATHER PIERRE DE*
11   *SMET, and SITTING BULL.)*
12 **FATHER VICKERY:** Sitting Bull, I'm Father De Smet. I'd like to
13   give you this cross — it's big medicine — and I'd like you to
14   consider becoming a Christian.
15 **SITTING BULL:** Why?
16 **FATHER VICKERY:** Well, for one thing, it'll help you live a
17   moral life. For example, now, when you get the urge to ...
18   you know ... .
19 **SITTING BULL:** Oh, I do that only with my wife.
20 **FATHER VICKERY:** But don't you get the urge to — you know —
21   wander?
22 **SITTING BULL:** Oh, sure.
23 **FATHER VICKERY:** What do you do then?
24 **SITTING BULL:** Have lots of wives.
25 **FATHER VICKERY:** That's immoral.
26 **SITTING BULL:** We don't have any illegitimate children.
27 **FATHER VICKERY:** Illegitimate children are a sign of
28   civilization. Accept this cross, Sitting Bull. It's the one true
29   faith.
30 **SITTING BULL:** Which Christian faith is it now that's the one
31   true one? I hear the same thing from the Lutherans, the
32   Mormons, the Baptists ...
33 **FATHER VICKERY:** The important thing is that it's Christian.
34 **SITTING BULL:** But I don't feel a need for anything like that,
35   Father.

1   FATHER VICKERY: Ah! There you are! What is it we all need?

2   SITTING BULL: Food. They said if we came in to the

3   reservations, we'd get rations. The government killed all

4   the buffalo, the settlers killed all the game. They promised

5   us cattle, flour – but we haven't gotten anything. And

6   those little biscuits you hand out, Father, that's not

7   enough to feed us.

8   FATHER VICKERY: Those little biscuits are the body of Christ.

9   SITTING BULL: That's his body?

10   FATHER VICKERY: And the wine is his blood.

11   SITTING BULL: And Christ's been dead two thousand years?

12   FATHER VICKERY: It's a miracle, isn't it?

13   SITTING BULL: Let me see if I've got this right, Father. Once

14   upon a time the Great Spirit decided to become a man. He

15   decided to become a man, even though he knew he was

16   going to be killed. He let himself be killed so he could

17   become the Great Spirit again. He did all that so people

18   would live forever. But to live forever, they have to believe

19   this cockamamie story. Why didn't he just tell people they

20   could live forever in the first place?

21   FATHER VICKERY: These are very complicated theological

22   matters, Sitting Bull.

23   SITTING BULL: And now, every time you say "Hocus pocus,"

24   that biscuit turns into his body and that wine turns into

25   his blood, and you eat his body and you drink his blood,

26   but the biscuit still tastes like a biscuit and the wine still

27   tastes like wine. And this dead man wants you to eat him

28   every week. Do I have this right?

29   FATHER VICKERY: Well ...

30   SITTING BULL: That's disgusting.

31   FATHER VICKERY: You're not looking at this in the proper

32   frame of mind.

33   SITTING BULL: I guess I'm just a superstitious savage. I

34   believe that all life is sacred. I believe that the earth is my

35   mother. You better give up on me, Father. I'm just not

1   **sophisticated enough to be a Christian.**

2   *(Crossfade to ESCOBEDO, as PRESIDENT GRANT, who*

3   *presents a document to SITTING BULL.)*

4   **ESCOBEDO: Here, Sitting Bull, you can have the Black Hills.**

5   **SITTING BULL: They're sacred to us.**

6   **ESCOBEDO: The Sioux nation will hold the Black Hills in**

7   **perpetuity.** *(SALLY HEMINGS, as an AIDE, enters and*

8   *whispers into ESCOBEDO's ear as CAONABO approaches*

9   *SITTING BULL.)*

10 **CAONABO: What does "in perpetuity" mean?**

11 **ESCOBEDO: What's that? Gold?** *(ESCOBEDO tears up the*

12   *paper.)* **Get Custer! We've got to keep the Black Hills safe**

13   **for democracy!**

14 **SITTING BULL: It means about two seconds.**

15   *(Crossfade to ISABELLA, as Custer's wife, ELIZABETH.)*

16 **ISABELLA: When the regiment left Fort Lincoln in Dakota**

17   **Territory that summer, I rode beside my husband,**

18   **General George Armstrong Custer, all morning. The**

19   **horses' hooves thudded past us, and the dust blew around**

20   **us. I heard the pans on the cook wagon clanging against**

21   **one another. When it was time for me to return to the Fort,**

22   **I wrapped my arms around his neck and held on, as if by**

23   **mere force of love I could prevent history.** *(Light on*

24   *COLUMBUS, as CUSTER.)*

25 **COLUMBUS: I rode through the Black Hills, the lines of blue-**

26   **coated cavalry stretched behind me, the band playing**

27   **"The Garryowen," my favorite song. At midday we entered**

28   **a meadow, and suddenly the band fell silent. Wildflowers**

29   **stretched before us as far as the eye could see. My battle-**

30   **hardened soldiers, who had waded in blood, reached**

31   **down and picked red and yellow and blue and violet**

32   **blossoms. We rode like that all day, in awed silence, two**

33   **hundred soldiers, carrying armfuls of flowers.**

34   *(Light on CAONABO.)*

35 **CAONABO: Sitting Bull danced the sun dance that summer.**

1   His hands and feet were stained red. Blue stripes were
2   painted across his broad shoulders. Fifty pieces of skin
3   were cut from each arm, from the wrist to the shoulder. As
4   the skin was cut, he sang a song, praying for help for his
5   people. His chest was pierced, and he hung from the
6   center pole, and he danced two days and two nights. He
7   did this as a sacrifice for his people. On the third morning
8   he saw a vision of soldiers falling like grasshoppers into
9   the camp of the People. *(Light on POCAHONTAS.)*
10 **POCAHONTAS:** General Custer told me he loved me, and I
11   loved him. We had a little boy. When Long Hair, as we
12   called General Custer, left that summer, he kissed me
13   hard and said he'd be back soon. My name is Me-o-tzi,
14   which means the Young Grass That Grows in the Spring.
15   *(Light on SITTING BULL.)*
16 **SITTING BULL:** We were camped by the Little Big Horn. I was
17   sitting, talking to my grandchildren, when we heard
18   shots. Crazy Horse organized the counterattack. When the
19   soldiers saw there was no hope, some of them shot each
20   other. Some shot themselves. We thought they'd gone
21   crazy. It was a terrible sight, after it was over. So many
22   dead, both People and invaders. One of the soldiers was
23   just a boy. He had a flower stuck in his cap. The flower was
24   faded, and it was splattered with blood.
25   *(Lights down. Suddenly, gunshots. Lights up. FATHER*
26   *VICKERY, as a SOLDIER, fires at CAONABO and BULLHEAD,*
27   *who fire back. COLUMBUS, as BUFFALO BILL, ESCOBEDO,*
28   *as a SOLDIER, SALLY HEMINGS, as a SOLDIER, and*
29   *ISABELLA, as ANNIE OAKLEY, join the fray. SITTING BULL*
30   *and POCAHONTAS join CAONABO and BULLHEAD,*
31   *fighting back. Yells and war whoops. It's "Buffalo Bill's Wild*
32   *West Show!" The show climaxes — all the Indians are dead.*
33   *The COWBOYS cheer.)*
34 **COLUMBUS:** *(As BUFFALO BILL)* There you are, folks, Buffalo
35   Bill's Wild West Show! Let's hear it for the cowboys and

1   **Indians!** *(Applause.)* **Wild Bill Hickock!** *(ESCOBEDO takes a*
2   *bow.)* **Annie Oakley!** *(ISABELLA takes a bow.)* **And the one**
3   **and only Sitting Bull!** *(SITTING BULL takes a bow.*
4   *EVERYBODY takes a bow. The applause dies down. The show*
5   *is over.)* **Thanks, boys, good show. Tomorrow night, we**
6   **play for the Governor-General of Canada!**

7 **ESCOBEDO, FATHER VICKERY, SALLY HEMINGS, ISABELLA:**
8   **Good night, Bill.**

9 **COLUMBUS: Goodnight.** *(ESCOBEDO, SALLY, ISABELLA, and*
10   *FATHER VICKERY exit. COLUMBUS sits down, pulls off his*
11   *boots.)* **Like the old days, isn't it, Sitting Bull? Gunplay,**
12   **drama, history. Only now nobody dies. That's showbiz.**
13   **Sometimes I wish for the old days, don't you? When we**
14   **really chased the buffalo ...** *(COLUMBUS pretends to ride,*
15   *shoot buffalo.)* **Pow! Pow! Pow pow pow! Powpowpow**
16   **powpow!**

17 **SITTING BULL: That your gatling gun, Bill?**

18 **COLUMBUS: I'd shoot a calf, those steaks would be so tender ...**
19   **Melt in your mouth. There were millions of buffalo! Like**
20   **an ocean!**

21 **SITTING BULL: The buffalo gave us everything – food, clothes,**
22   **shelter ...**

23 **COLUMBUS: Too bad they're all gone.**

24 **SITTING BULL: That's showbiz.**

25 **COLUMBUS:** *(Not catching the irony)* **That's show biz!**
26   *(COLUMBUS exits.)*

27 **CAONABO: Why do the Indians always get killed? Why don't**
28   **the soldiers ever get killed?**

29 **POCAHONTAS: We act out their fantasies.**

30 **SITTING BULL: They're afraid we might really win someday.**

31 **CAONABO: It's demeaning. Where's your dignity, Sitting Bull?**

32 **BULLHEAD: Where's yours?**

33 **CAONABO: I'll show you where mine is. I quit this circus.**

34 **BULLHEAD: You're in Toronto. You going to walk home?**

35 **POCAHONTAS: I'm going to be a stage actress someday.**

1 CAONABO: What are you going play? Pocahontas?

2 POCAHONTAS: Pocahontas might've been different than

3   people think.

4 BULLHEAD: Why are you always so angry?

5 CAONABO: We should all be angry! Everyone of us! All the

6   time!

7 BULLHEAD: Anger just eats you up inside. *(BULLHEAD pulls*

8   *out a bottle of whiskey and takes a swallow.)*

9 POCAHONTAS: We've got to adapt. How else are we going to

10   survive?

11 CAONABO: *(To BULLHEAD)* Is that how you adapt?

12 BULLHEAD: That's how I forget.

13 CAONABO: You forget your heritage.

14 BULLHEAD: I forget my shame.

15 POCAHONTAS: We're all Americans now.

16 CAONABO: You think so? Let me tell you something. We could

17   fight in their armies —

18 BULLHEAD: You think they're going to give you a gun again?

19 CAONABO: — vote in their elections —

20 BULLHEAD: Who're we going to vote for? Sitting Bull?

21 CAONABO: — go to college, even —

22 POCAHONTAS: That's me — Harvard!

23 CAONABO: — but we'll never be Americans, not in their eyes.

24 POCAHONTAS: We can be anything we want to be.

25 BULLHEAD: As long as we're drunk.

26 POCAHONTAS: No, you've got to have pride in yourself.

27 BULLHEAD: As long as we stay in our place.

28 POCAHONTAS: Maybe I'll be a doctor.

29 BULLHEAD: Standing in front of a store holding a bunch of

30   cigars.

31 POCAHONTAS: If I was a lawyer, I could fight for our treaty

32   rights.

33 CAONABO: Why do you do it, Sitting Bull? You fought the white

34   man, you were the last to come in to the rez, you acted with

35   great dignity — I wanted to be like you! But now you shame

1   the people who died in those wars. You used to be a great
2   leader. Now you're a clown. *(CAONABO, POCAHONTAS, and*
3   *BULLHEAD exit, leaving SITTING BULL alone.)*
4   PELTIER: *(To SITTING BULL)* You brought the money back to
5   your people, who were starving. You did it so people
6   would know what we were really like. It wasn't your fault
7   if some of them laughed. *(ISABELLA, as PELTIER's*
8   *LAWYER, enters.)*
9   ISABELLA: We can prove that government witnesses were
10   coerced. We can also prove that the FBI suppressed
11   evidence. Once this evidence is admitted, there's no way
12   they can find you guilty of those two deaths. We're
13   petitioning the judge to grant you a new trial.
14   PELTIER: Same judge?
15   ISABELLA: Same judge.
16   *(Spot on FATHER VICKERY, as JUDGE.)*
17   FATHER VICKERY: Denied!
18   *(Crossfade to SALLY, as another CONVICT, playing the blues*
19   *on a harmonica or guitar, and PELTIER, singing.)*
20   PELTIER: I've got those Turtle Island blues
21   I've got those Turtle Island blues
22   White man come, take the land
23   Turtle Island blues
24
25   *(SITTING BULL joins in.)*
26   I've got those Turtle Island blues
27   I've got those Turtle Island blues
28   Soldiers come, buffalo gone
29   Turtle Island blues
30
31   *(CAONABO, POCAHONTAS, BULLHEAD enter, join in.)*
32   Turtle Island Blues
33   Turtle Island Blues
34   I've got those Turtle Island Blues.
35

1   **Soldiers say, stay on the rez**

2   **Turtle Island Blues**

3   **Soldiers say, stay on the rez,**

4   **I say, Give me Alcatraz**

5   **Turtle Island Blues**

6   **Turtle Island Blues**

7

8   **Government framed Leonard Peltier**

9   **Turtle Island Blues**

10   **Government framed Leonard Peltier**

11   **Turtle Island Blues**

12   **Spirits singing in the air**

13   **Turtle Island Blues.**

14   **Turtle Island Blues.**

15

16   *(FATHER VICKERY, as CAPTAIN PRATT, and ESCOBEDO, as*

17   *a POLITICIAN, enter and shake hands.)*

18   **ESCOBEDO: Captain Richard Henry Pratt. Founder of the first**

19   **Indian School.**

20   **FATHER VICKERY: And now there are hundreds.**

21   **ESCOBEDO: You must be proud.**

22   **FATHER VICKERY: A great general once said, the only good**

23   **Indian is a dead Indian. I agree – in this sense. In these**

24   **schools, we're killing the Indian in the race.**

25   **ESCOBEDO: They have to be civilized.**

26   **FATHER VICKERY: We've been wrong to segregate the Indians**

27   **on reservations. They only keep their own culture then.**

28   **ESCOBEDO: We've outlawed the dances, the pipe, the pagan**

29   **rituals.**

30   **PELTIER: When they took us to boarding schools, hundreds of**

31   **miles from home –**

32   **CAONABO: – sometimes at gunpoint –**

33   **POCAHONTAS: They kidnapped us.**

34   **BULLHEAD: They cut our hair.**

35   **CAONABO: Woke us with ice water, marched us to meals and**

1   classes.

2   POCAHONTAS: Beat us when we spoke our language.

3   BULLHEAD: Made us ashamed of being Indian.

4   CAONABO: If it was another time and place —

5   POCAHONTAS: If it was another government —

6   PELTIER: They'd call it brainwashing.

7   ESCOBEDO: We call it —

8   FATHER VICKERY: Americanizing!

9   *(Blackout. A SPORTS ANNOUNCER'S VOICE comes from*
10   *loudspeakers.)*

11   ANNOUNCER'S VOICE: Here they come, folks, first game of
12   the football season, the Washington Redskins! *(Sounds of*
13   *cheers, etc.)*

14   ANOTHER ANNOUNCER'S VOICE: We're in the seventh game
15   of the world series, and up to bat are the Atlanta Braves!
16   *(Cheers, etc.)*

17   ANOTHER ANNOUNCER'S VOICE: Let's hear it for the
18   Westfield Warriors! *(Cheers.)*

19   ANOTHER ANNOUNCER'S VOICE: Here they come, folks, the
20   Fighting Sioux! *(Cheers. Cheers continue under*
21   *announcements.)*

22   ANOTHER ANNOUNCER'S VOICE: Home run for the
23   Cleveland Indians!

24   ANOTHER ANNOUNCER'S VOICE: Here they come, the Big
25   City Kikes!

26   ANOTHER ANNOUNCER'S VOICE: Let's hear it, folks, for the
27   New York Niggers.

28   *(Silence. Then, from the darkness, SITTING BULL's song. Light*
29   *up on SITTING BULL, barefoot, singing in Lakota. ISABELLA,*
30   *as PIONEER WOMAN, enters and listens until he finishes.)*

31   ISABELLA: That's a sad song, Sitting Bull.

32   SITTING BULL: I'm a sad man.

33   ISABELLA: Is that why you're barefoot?

34   SITTING BULL: I always walk barefoot in the morning, when I
35   welcome the day. Try it. *(ISABELLA takes off her shoes and*

1   *stockings.)*

2   ISABELLA: It's wet!

3   SITTING BULL: The dew washes your feet.

4   ISABELLA: Come, dance with me! *(She skips, whirls. He*

5   *watches. He tries to join her, then stops, limping.)* What's

6   wrong?

7   SITTING BULL: Sometimes I get tired hopping back and forth

8   through time. This foot begins to hurt. A Crow People shot

9   me — just before my spear went into his heart. We were

10   always fighting the Crow. We'd steal their horses, steal

11   their women. That's how you proved you were a man.

12   Here, we'll do a People dance. *(He leads her in a more*

13   *sedate People dance.)*

14   ISABELLA: How did you get your name, Sitting Bull?

15   SITTING BULL: When I was a boy I had a different name. I was

16   called Slow because I always thought about what I was

17   going to say before I said it. Then, when I first counted

18   coup, my father gave me the name I'm called now.

19   Actually "Sitting Bull" means a "buffalo bull who lives

20   among us." Someone strong and with honor. To me it

21   means that I must serve my people. Before that it was my

22   father's name. A buffalo gave the name to my father.

23   ISABELLA: A buffalo spoke to your father?

24   SITTING BULL: Oh, yes.

25   ISABELLA: I've never had a buffalo speak to me.

26   SITTING BULL: Have you ever talked to a buffalo?

27   ISABELLA: No.

28   SITTING BULL: That might explain it.

29   ISABELLA: Why were you singing that sad song?

30   SITTING BULL: General Crook comes today. He brings a new

31   treaty, a treaty I'm afraid the other men will sign.

32   *(ESCOBEDO enters as GENERAL CROOK.)*

33   ESCOBEDO: The only way to make the Indian white is to make

34   him a landowner. We'll divide the reservations into

35   parcels of land, and each Indian man will own his own

1   plot. What's left over, we'll sell to the settlers. And there
2   will be a lot left over.
3 SITTING BULL: I dreamed last night I was hunting again.
4   Buffalo spread across the prairie like a great cloud of
5   black, and the earth shook with the drumming of their
6   hooves. There were no fences, no telegraph wires, no
7   soldiers with repeating rifles. That's what I miss most,
8   Annie – freedom. I can't leave the reservation without
9   permission from the agent, McLaughlin. I can't dance the
10   sun dance. I can't smoke the sacred pipe. Those are our
11   prayers, Annie, our mass and our Christmas and our
12   Easter. A human being's nothing without freedom. Can
13   you understand that?
14 ISABELLA: Yes. Yes, Sitting Bull, I can understand that.
15   *(Light down on ISABELLA as SITTING BULL joins ESCOBEDO,*
16   *as CROOK, CAONABO, as GALL, and BULLHEAD, as JOHN*
17   *GRASS. ESCOBEDO holds official-looking papers.)*
18 ESCOBEDO: When three-fourths of you men sign the treaty,
19   you will receive your land, and money –
20 SITTING BULL: Do you know who I am?
21 ESCOBEDO: Of course I know you.
22 SITTING BULL: Do you recognize me?
23 ESCOBEDO: You're Sitting Bull.
24 SITTING BULL: Do you know what position I hold?
25 ESCOBEDO: You hold no position. You're like all the other
26   Indians at this agency.
27 SITTING BULL: I'm here by the will of the Great Mystery, and
28   by his will I'm a spiritual leader. My heart is red and
29   sweet, because whatever passes near me puts out its
30   tongue to me; and yet you've come here to talk to us, and
31   you say you don't know who I am.
32 ESCOBEDO: *(Ignores SITTING BULL. To CAONABO and*
33   *BULLHEAD)* You know your grandfather, the President in
34   Washington, has given you millions of acres –
35 SITTING BULL: You talk like a man who's drunk!

1   **ESCOBEDO: Sit down!**

2   **SITTING BULL: You stole millions of acres!**

3   **ESCOBEDO: We give you rations —**

4   **SITTING BULL: Our children cry from hunger!**

5   **ESCOBEDO:** *(Pointing to the treaty)* **Three hundred and twenty**

6   **acres a man — !**

7   **SITTING BULL: You stole the Black Hills!**

8   **ESCOBEDO: It's only land!**

9   *(Light down on ESCOBEDO. Drumming, singing. SITTING*

10   *BULL leads CAONABO and BULLHEAD away. SITTING*

11   *BULL sings.)*

12 **SITTING BULL: The Great Mystery**

13   **to him am I related**

14   **The Great Mystery is good**

15   **to him am I related**

16   **from above**

17   **a people**

18   **is my friend**

19   **from above**

20   **an elk**

21   **is my friend**

22   **from above**

23   **a man is my friend.**

24   *(Light fades on SITTING BULL as BULLHEAD, as JOHN*

25   *GRASS, meets with ESCOBEDO, as CROOK.)*

26 **ESCOBEDO: John Grass, we don't officially recognize chiefs**

27   **anymore.**

28 **BULLHEAD: We're not signing the treaty.**

29 **ESCOBEDO: ... but we do recognize leaders.**

30 **BULLHEAD: We're sticking together.**

31 **ESCOBEDO: A leader not only receives respect from his people**

32   **and from the government, he receives extra rations, extra**

33   **gifts.**

34 **BULLHEAD: The land cannot be bought and sold.**

35 **ESCOBEDO: He can reward his friends and punish his**

1   enemies. He can be protected by the soldiers.

2 BULLHEAD: Sitting Bull is a holy man.

3 ESCOBEDO: All he knows are the old ways. You're young, John.

4   You'll get more land than most white men. Land of your

5   own! It's the American Dream! The people will follow you.

6   And, someday, you'll get to vote! Just as soon as you prove

7   yourself. *(ESCOBEDO leaves BULLHEAD and joins*

8   *CAONABO, as GALL.)* Gall, I'm glad you could meet me

9   before the signing tomorrow.

10 CAONABO: We're not signing.

11 ESCOBEDO: I don't want you to be left out.

12 CAONABO: I fought Custer at the Little Big Horn!

13 ESCOBEDO: Gall, the white men are like birds. They're

14   hatching out their eggs every year, and there's not enough

15   room in the East. You've seen them coming. You can't

16   prevent it. The President can't prevent it. They see all this

17   land, and they want it. And they'll have it.

18 CAONABO: Then it doesn't matter if we sign the treaty or not.

19 ESCOBEDO: If you sign, you get something. If you don't, your

20   hands are empty.

21   *(Crossfade to SITTING BULL, putting on war paint and*

22   *singing.)*

23 SITTING BULL: No chance for me to live.

24   Mother Earth, go ahead and mourn.

25 CAONABO: *(As Gall)* Why are you putting on war paint?

26 SITTING BULL: No chance for me to live.

27   Mother Earth, go ahead and mourn.

28 CAONABO: Why are you singing your war song?

29 SITTING BULL: I had a dream.

30 CAONABO: Of battle?

31 SITTING BULL: Of betrayal.

32 CAONABO: Wipe off your war paint.

33 SITTING BULL: The faces were blank, as if the traitors had no

34   character.

35 CAONABO: The wars are over!

1   **SITTING BULL: The war for dignity is never over!**

2   **CAONABO: What dignity is there in fighting for a lost cause?**

3   **SITTING BULL: When everything else is gone – home,**
4   **freedom, the sacred places – when all we have left is**
5   **dignity – what else should we fight for?** *(CAONABO walks*
6   *away from SITTING BULL and joins ESCOBEDO, as CROOK,*
7   *and BULLHEAD. CAONABO takes the pen.)*

8   **SITTING BULL: No!**

9   *(Black. Sound of cold wind. Light up on ISABELLA, as*
10   *JOSEPHINE PEARY.)*

11   **ISABELLA: My husband, Admiral Robert E. Peary, is this**
12   **moment striding bravely across the frozen wastes of the**
13   **Arctic –** *(A cold light comes up on COLUMBUS, as PEARY,*
14   *hidden in furs, staggers on, struggling against an arctic*
15   *blizzard, flounders, falls, gets up.)* **– and will at any moment,**
16   **I'm sure, be the first man to step foot on the north pole.**
17   *(Two other figures in fur enter, battling the blizzard but*
18   *proceeding more methodically. They pull back their hoods to*
19   *reveal SALLY HEMINGS, as MATTHEW HENSON, and*
20   *BULLHEAD, as EGINGWAH, Peary's Inuit guide.)*

21   **SALLY HEMINGS: Peary slipped away from me, took off by**
22   **himself. I've been by his side for eighteen years. Saved his**
23   **life more than once. But he wants to reach the pole by**
24   **himself. He doesn't want me to share in the glory.**

25   **BULLHEAD: What are you going to do, Matthew?**

26   **SALLY HEMINGS: Get there first.** *(SALLY and BULLHEAD pull*
27   *up their hoods and head off.)*

28   **ISABELLA: The Eskimos are a simple and childlike people.**
29   **The one night I spent in an igloo, I was surprised to find**
30   **that, because of the warmth, the women had removed all**
31   **of their furs and were stark naked, wearing nothing but**
32   **their jewelry. Robert had been gone for three years. I**
33   **missed him so much, I arranged to sail to meet him, to**
34   **surprise him. When I arrived, the Eskimos talked freely to**
35   **me about my husband's – friend – Aleqasina.**

1   *(Light up on POCAHONTAS, as ALEQASINA.)*

2   **POCAHONTAS:** I had two sons with Peary. Peary first noticed

3   me when I was ten. He was taking photos. He made us take

4   our clothes off. He said this was the scientific way. When I

5   was fifteen my husband offered to let me sleep with Peary.

6   Peary said he loved me. But he never came back. We call

7   ourselves Inuit. It means "the People."

8   *(SALLY and BULLHEAD stop, pull back their hoods.)*

9   **BULLHEAD:** What's so special about the north pole? There're

10   no seals here, no musk ox, no polar bears – nothing to eat.

11   **SALLY HEMINGS:** It's the idea of being first, Egingwah. Like

12   Columbus was the first to reach America.

13   **BULLHEAD:** So you're first? So what?

14   **SALLY HEMINGS:** It seems to be a white thing. But we might as

15   well get credit where credit's due. Here?

16   **BULLHEAD:** Anywhere. It doesn't matter.

17   **SALLY HEMINGS:** We have to be sure.

18   **BULLHEAD:** He doesn't know the difference.

19   **SALLY HEMINGS:** Here?

20   **BULLHEAD:** Here.

21   **SALLY HEMINGS:** On the dot?

22   **BULLHEAD:** Smack on the pole.

23   **SALLY HEMINGS:** Admiral! Admiral Peary!

24   **COLUMBUS:** Matthew! Egingwah!

25   **SALLY HEMINGS:** We found it.

26   **COLUMBUS:** What? What did you find?

27   **SALLY HEMINGS:** The north pole!

28   **COLUMBUS:** You?

29   **SALLY HEMINGS:** Right here! Where I'm standing.

30   **BULLHEAD:** I found it, too. Right here.

31   **COLUMBUS:** You're sure?

32   **BULLHEAD:** I'm an Inuit. We have a mystic sense.

33   **COLUMBUS:** Matthew?

34   **SALLY HEMINGS:** We have a mystic sense, too.

35   **COLUMBUS:** That would mean that you were first. No. No, the

1   North Pole is ... *(He takes a few steps.)* **Here! I found it! I**
2   **found the North pole! I was the first! I was the first, I was**
3   **the first, I was the first** ... *(COLUMBUS skips off, singing "I*
4   *was the first." SALLY and BULLHEAD walk away.)*
5   **POCAHONTAS:** *(As ALEQASINA)* **Peary took six Inuit people to**
6   **New York. Within months four of the six died of**
7   **tuberculosis.**
8   *(FATHER VICKERY, as a MUSEUM SUPERINTENDENT,*
9   *enters, carrying a large box.)*
10 **FATHER VICKERY: Here at the Museum of Natural History we**
11 **collect things. That's what a museum is for – collecting**
12 **things. One of the things we collect are bones.** *(He drops*
13 *the box on the floor. Bones rattle inside.)*
14 **POCAHONTAS : One of the men who died was Qisuk.**
15 **FATHER VICKERY: We have dinosaur bones.**
16 **POCAHONTAS: Qisuk's son, Minik, was one of the two who**
17 **survived.**
18 **FATHER VICKERY: We have the bones of lions, elephants,**
19 **vultures, camels ...**
20 **POCAHONTAS: When Qisuk and the other three Inuit died,**
21 **they were taken to Bellevue Hospital, where medical**
22 **students dissected their bodies.**
23 **FATHER VICKERY: All kinds of bones.**
24 **POCAHONTAS: After their bodies were dissected, they were**
25 **taken to a macerating plant and placed in acid until only**
26 **the bones were left.**
27 **FATHER VICKERY: Indian bones. Many tribes, from all over.**
28 **POCAHONTAS: Several years later, Minik, Qisuk's son,**
29 **discovered where his father's bones were.**
30 **FATHER VICKERY: We're a museum.**
31 **POCAHONTAS: He asked for his father's bones.**
32 **FATHER VICKERY: We collect bones.**
33 **POCAHONTAS: He wanted to take the bones home to bury**
34 **them.**
35 **FATHER VICKERY: They're our bones.**

1 POCAHONTAS: Minik had been adopted by William Wallace.
2   Minik was given the name Minik Peary Wallace.
3 FATHER VICKERY: To keep.
4 POCAHONTAS: William Wallace owned a macerating plant.
5 FATHER VICKERY: Forever.
6 PELTIER: The Museum of Natural History still has Qisuk's
7   bones. And the bones of many of our grandfathers and
8   grandmothers. Other museums, too.
9 FATHER VICKERY: For scientific purposes.
10   *(Crossfade to BULLHEAD, as another CONVICT,*
11   *approaching PELTIER.)*
12 BULLHEAD: Leonard?
13 PELTIER: Yes, Bob.
14 BULLHEAD: You know, I've never taken myself seriously, as an
15   Indian, I mean, never was interested in the old ways, but I
16   have to tell you something. Some guys want me to kill you.
17   They took me to the warden's office. This guy was there,
18   blond, brown suit, striped tie, said he'd see to it I'd get
19   paroled, and I wouldn't have to stand trial for shooting
20   that cop in Oklahoma City. All I'd have to do, he said, is
21   neutralize you – that's the word he used. Neutralize you.
22   Said if I didn't cooperate, some accident would happen to
23   me on the way to Oklahoma City. I just thought I'd tell you.
24   *(Crossfade to ESCOBEDO, as a MODERN MARRIED MAN,*
25   *and ISABELLA, as his WIFE.)*
26 ISABELLA: You're restless.
27 ESCOBEDO: I want to wander. I want to shoot some bad guys.
28   Guys that smile and have a gold tooth, and their spurs
29   jingle jangle as they walk down the muddy street, fingers
30   itching for the cold steel of the Colt 45. I want to roam.
31 ISABELLA: But, dear, you're needed here at home.
32 ESCOBEDO: I want to be a ramblin' man! *(He strides away from*
33   *a bewildered wife. He picks up a cowboy hat, he buckles on*
34   *a gunbelt. He comes up to CAONABO, who's lying on a*
35   *couch.)* Come on, let's go right some wrongs.

1 CAONABO: Who, me?

2 ESCOBEDO: We'll roam. The schoolmarm'll fall in love with

3   me, but I'll have to ride on. There'll be other bullies in

4   other towns. Other guys with spurs that jingle jangle.

5   Other pretty schoolmarms. We'll ramble.

6 CAONABO: You can ramble by yourself.

7 ESCOBEDO: You're right. Of course I can ramble by myself.

8   *(ESCOBEDO starts off, Comes back.)*

9 CAONABO: Now what?

10 ESCOBEDO: I can't do it by myself.

11 CAONABO: Of course you can.

12 ESCOBEDO: Of course I can. *(ESCOBEDO starts off, returns.)*

13   No, I can't. See, I'm not going out there just to leave pretty

14   schoolmarms pining for me. *(ESCOBEDO lies on the couch.*

15   *CAONABO sits in a chair at ESCOBEDO's head, taking notes*

16   *like a psychoanalyst.)* I'm talking about the frontier of the

17   psyche. I'm talking about the psyche of America as

18   manifested in its recurring myths and motifs. I'm only

19   half a man, Caonabo.

20 CAONABO: Which half are you?

21 ESCOBEDO: The head. Reason.

22 CAONABO: You don't reason all that well.

23 ESCOBEDO: I'm lacking ... intuition.

24 CAONABO: You're all ego.

25 ESCOBEDO: Yes ...

26 CAONABO: The lines are down between your ego and your

27   superego ...

28 ESCOBEDO: That's why I rape and pillage, murder and enslave.

29 CAONABO: And the elevator's out between your ego and your id.

30 ESCOBEDO: I have no spontaneity.

31 CAONABO: On the other hand —

32 ESCOBEDO: I'm feeling a lot better to get this off my chest.

33 CAONABO: You're afraid of women.

34 ESCOBEDO: I am?

35 CAONABO: You left your wife.

1   ESCOBEDO: I'm a ramblin' man.

2   CAONABO: Because you can't face adult responsibilities.

3   ESCOBEDO: You think outdrawing outlaws isn't an adult

4   responsibility?

5   CAONABO: It's infantile escapism.

6   ESCOBEDO: I'm civilizing the frontier.

7   CAONABO: A real woman threatens your manhood.

8   *(ESCOBEDO draws his sixguns.)*

9   ESCOBEDO: My manhood's in my fists! All twelve shots!

10 *(ESCOBEDO shoots his pistols in the air — all twelve shots.)*

11 CAONABO: Feel better?

12 ESCOBEDO: I feel kind of depleted.

13 CAONABO: You deny your dark side.

14 ESCOBEDO: That's why I need you! You're dark! You and my

15   trusty servant, the black man. Huck had Jim. Ishmael had

16   Queequeg. Peary had Matthew Henson and Egingwah.

17   Jack Benny had Rochester. I need someone dark beside

18   me. He's my sexual potency – which I must forbid. He's

19   my physical prowess, which I've never developed. He's my

20   sinfulness, which I can't admit, because I believe I'm

21   chosen by God. He's my stupidity – which I can't admit,

22   either.

23 CAONABO: Very good, Kemo sabe.

24 ESCOBEDO: I'm alienated from Nature, too! That's another

25   reason I need you, Tonto. *(ESCOBEDO puts on a Lone*

26   *Ranger's mask.)* I need you to go with me. Into the West.

27   Into the Frontier. You're my link with Nature. You *are*

28   Nature!

29 CAONABO: What's the mask for?

30 ESCOBEDO: I'm not sure.

31 CAONABO: What are you hiding?

32 ESCOBEDO: I don't know.

33 CAONABO: Your true self?

34 ESCOBEDO: I don't know.

35 CAONABO: What are you hiding from?

1   **ESCOBEDO:** I don't know.

2   **CAONABO:** Responsibility?

3   **ESCOBEDO:** I —

4   **CAONABO:** Guilt?

5   **ESCOBEDO:** I —

6   **CAONABO:** You're not self-actualized! *(ESCOBEDO draws his*

7   *guns.)*

8   **ESCOBEDO:** Come on, Tonto! We're gonna kill!

9   **CAONABO:** Kill what, Kemo Sabe?

10   **ESCOBEDO:** Bullies! Outlaws! Sheepherders! Bears! Bad

11   Indians!

12   **CAONABO:** Kemo sabe....

13   **ESCOBEDO:** Yes, Tonto?

14   **CAONABO:** I *am* a bad Indian.

15   *(CAONABO puts on the mask. Light down on ESCOBEDO as*

16   *CAONABO turns and has a microphone thrust at him by*

17   *SALLY HEMINGS as a REPORTER.)*

18   **SALLY HEMINGS:** You're calling yourself Mr. X?

19   **CAONABO:** That's right.

20   **SALLY HEMINGS:** And you were there near Wounded Knee in

21   1975 when the two FBI agents were shot and killed?

22   **CAONABO:** I was there.

23   **SALLY HEMINGS:** Did Leonard Peltier kill the agents?

24   **CAONABO:** No. Leonard didn't kill anybody.

25   **SALLY HEMINGS:** How do you know that?

26   **CAONABO:** Because I killed them. I shot them both. I drove up,

27   shot them, and drove away. Drove past the roadblocks. Got

28   away.

29   **SALLY HEMINGS:** And you're admitting this today on national

30   television.

31   **CAONABO:** That's right. They started shooting. We defended

32   ourselves. But Leonard Peltier didn't kill them.

33   *(Crossfade to FATHER VICKERY, as JAMES McLAUGHLIN,*

34   *Indian Agent.)*

35   **FATHER VICKERY:** James McClaughlin's the name. Indian

1   Agent at Standing Rock. I'm a friend of the Indian. I'm

2   married to an Indian woman. I know Sitting Bull well.

3   He's a liar, a thief, a polygamist, and a coward. At the end

4   he got mixed up with the Ghost Dance. *(Drumming.*

5   *CAONABO appears.)*

6 CAONABO: If we danced long enough, we saw visions of our

7   ancestors. They told us the buffalo were coming back, and

8   the white men would be destroyed because of their evil

9   ways. *(POCAHONTAS appears.)*

10 POCAHONTAS: We sewed shirts, and on the backs were

11   painted eagles in blue, and in the front suns and moons in

12   red. We thought the shirts would stop the white man's

13   bullets.

14 FATHER VICKERY: It was getting out of hand. There was talk

15   of killing all the whites.

16   *(SITTING BULL is in the cell with PELTIER. POCAHONTAS,*

17   *as one of Sitting Bull's wives, and ISABELLA, as a friend, are*

18   *also in the cell.)*

19 SITTING BULL: *(To PELTIER)* I knew the buffalo were gone. I

20   knew the shirts were only cloth. But it was a way for the

21   People to live in the spirit world. It gave them hope. I tried

22   to focus that energy that was flying all around, with the

23   dancing and the visions and the wild talk. I didn't want

24   anybody to get hurt.

25 FATHER VICKERY: I sent the Indian Police to arrest Sitting

26   Bull. He was the ringleader. He was the one in charge.

27   Then Bill Cody stuck his nose into things.

28 COLUMBUS: *(As Buffalo Bill)* If he'd come with me on my next

29   tour, nothing would've happened. Sitting Bull, I said,

30   you're a natural showman. You're famous. You have

31   charisma. I even offered him more money. But he said his

32   people needed him. When I heard McLaughlin was going

33   to arrest him, I was afraid there'd be trouble. I

34   remembered Crazy Horse, how they killed him when they

35   tried to arrest him. So I headed out to Dakota. I rode all

1   night, trying to find my old friend.

2   **FATHER VICKERY:** All Cody wanted was more headlines. We

3   gave him dinner, got him drunk, headed him the wrong

4   way.

5   **COLUMBUS:** But I got lost.

6   **BULLHEAD:** Sitting Bull! Come out! You're under arrest!

7   **PELTIER:** What are you going to do?

8   **SITTING BULL:** He's my brother. I'll talk to him. Come on in,

9   Bullhead! *(BULLHEAD comes into the cell.)*

10 **BULLHEAD:** I've got to take you in, Sitting Bull.

11 **SITTING BULL:** I'm an old man. I can't do any harm.

12 **BULLHEAD:** The people still follow you.

13 **SITTING BULL:** That McLaughlin is worried over nothing.

14 **BULLHEAD:** There's talk of killing the whites.

15 **SITTING BULL:** Those days are over.

16 **POCAHONTAS:** He's done nothing!

17 **ISABELLA:** If it weren't for him, you *would* have killing!

18 **BULLHEAD:** *(To Sitting Bull)* You sleep with white women now?

19 **PELTIER:** He's old, he's not dead.

20 **BULLHEAD:** Come on, Sitting Bull. I've got to take you to jail.

21 **ISABELLA:** Don't go!

22 **POCAHONTAS:** Remember Crazy Horse!

23 **SITTING BULL:** Better to avoid bloodshed.

24   *(He leaves the cell with BULLHEAD. CAONABO appears,*

25   *shoots BULLHEAD. As BULLHEAD falls, he shoots SITTING*

26   *BULL. Screams, gunshots, drumming. Then, slowly,*

27   *CAONABO and BULLHEAD get up. They and PELTIER and*

28   *POCAHONTAS put the dead SITTING BULL on a stretcher*

29   *and bear him, as in a funeral procession, as they speak.)*

30 **POCAHONTAS:** After Sitting Bull was killed, the army went

31   after Big Foot and his people.

32 **BULLHEAD:** The army was afraid the People were going to

33   spread the Ghost Dance farther.

34   *(Drumming, softly, in the background.)*

35 **PELTIER:** All the People wanted to do was get away from

1   the army.

2 CAONABO: We camped at Wounded Knee Creek.

3 POCAHONTAS: It was cold. Everybody was hungry. Mostly
4   there were women and children.

5 BULLHEAD: The soldiers rode up, all around us there where
6   we were camping in the snow, five hundred of them, and
7   they had four cannons.

8 CAONABO: The soldiers came in to take the rifles from the
9   men.

10 POCAHONTAS: Sitting Bull's adopted son was with us. He was
11   deaf. He didn't understand the soldier.

12 PELTIER: Someone fired a shot. *(In the distance, a shot.)*

13 BULLHEAD: The soldiers opened fire. *(In the distance, ghostly*
14   *shots echo.)*

15 POCAHONTAS: They kept shooting and shooting and shooting.

16 BULLHEAD: The People tried to run.

17 CAONABO: The soldiers rode after them.

18 POCAHONTAS: Shooting.

19 BULLHEAD: They ran for three miles.

20 CAONABO: The soldiers rode after them.

21 POCAHONTAS: Shooting.

22 BULLHEAD: A baby crawled in the snow.

23 POCAHONTAS: Trying to nurse from the breast of her dead
24   mother. *(They exit with SITTING BULL's body.)*

25 ISABELLA: Bodies were buried in silence and snow, and the
26   puddles of blood froze in the trampled grass. *(COLUMBUS*
27   *wanders in. He's wearing his old sea captain's cap. ISABELLA*
28   *doesn't see him yet.)* Sitting Bull's cabin was taken apart
29   and shipped to Chicago, where it was reassembled and put
30   on display at the Exposition of 1892, celebrating the four
31   hundredth anniversary of the arrival of Columbus. *(She*
32   *sees COLUMBUS.)* What's the matter, Chris?

33 COLUMBUS: I don't know where I am.

34 ISABELLA: This is the spirit world.

35 COLUMBUS: Whatever it is, I thought it'd be more stable. Stay

1   in one place.
2   ISABELLA: I thought you liked to travel.
3   COLUMBUS: I do. But I never seem to get anywhere. *(SITTING*
4   *BULL enters.)*
5   SITTING BULL: Where you been, Chris? You look upset about
6   something. *(POCAHONTAS, CAONABO, BULLHEAD, SALLY*
7   *HEMINGS enter.)*
8   COLUMBUS: I ran into a bunch of other spirits. Your people.
9   They died of smallpox from the blankets we gave them.
10   They died at Sand Creek. They died at Blue Water. They
11   died at Wounded Knee.
12   SITTING BULL: We had our wars. But we never mutilated
13   women and children. We never wiped out whole nations.
14   POCAHONTAS: I think the white people were scared.
15   SALLY HEMINGS: They killed what they feared.
16   BULLHEAD: Whatever was different — that was the enemy.
17   CAONABO: There were too many of them. There wasn't
18   enough room for us all.
19   SITTING BULL: There was room. There was room for us, for
20   them, for the buffalo. How much room does a human
21   being need? How fast does he have to go? You have to do
22   things differently, that's all. *(ESCOBEDO and FATHER*
23   *VICKERY enter.)*
24   ESCOBEDO: We have so much now! Space travel,
25   supercomputers, fax machines, microwaves, antibiotics —
26   FATHER VICKERY: Electronic mass, instant confession, fast-
27   salvation at the drive-in McChurch!
28   COLUMBUS: They died so many places. Five hundred years
29   after I came here, Sitting Bull, I see them still dying, of
30   tuberculosis, of diabetes, of alcohol, of suicide. My heart
31   weeps, Sitting Bull. I should have stayed in Spain. I should
32   have just continued to make maps, and I should have
33   written on the maps: This land is People land.
34   SITTING BULL: Turtle Island.
35   COLUMBUS: Turtle Island. People live there.

1 SITTING BULL: Well, I guess if it hadn't been you, it would've
2   been somebody else.
3 PELTIER: We can't go back.
4 SALLY HEMINGS: We've got to go forward.
5 BULLHEAD: One person can make a difference.
6 ISABELLA: We can turn guilt into action.
7 POCAHONTAS: Every act is spiritual.
8 SITTING BULL: A ceremony is a spiritual journey.
9 PELTIER: In a ceremony you're not alone. All your relations
10   are there, human and other. *(Drumming. SITTING BULL*
11   *begins the chant. POCAHONTAS, PELTIER, CAONABO,*
12   *BULLHEAD, SALLY HEMINGS, ISABELLA, join in.)*
13 SITTING BULL: With beauty before me may I walk
14   With beauty behind me may I walk
15 ESCOBEDO: I won't be made a fool of!
16 CAONABO: Too late for that.
17   *(POCAHONTAS draws ESCOBEDO into the circle.)*
18 SITTING BULL: With beauty above me may I walk –
19 COLUMBUS: We've spent ten thousand years pulling ourselves
20   out of superstition!
21 ISABELLA: Isn't it lonely out there? *(ISABELLA pulls*
22   *COLUMBUS into the circle.)*
23 SITTING BULL: With beauty below me may I walk
24   With beauty all around me may I walk
25 FATHER VICKERY: This is pagan worship!
26 BULLHEAD: Chill out, Father. *(BULLHEAD brings FATHER*
27   *VICKERY into the circle.)*
28 SITTING BULL: As one who is long life and happiness may I
29   walk
30 SITTING BULL and OTHERS: In beauty it is finished
31   In beauty it is finished.
32   *(SITTING BULL turns to the audience.)*
33 SITTING BULL: Everybody who wants to join us, you stand up,
34   say the words with us. See what power we have. See what
35   it feels like to all be related.

1   ALL: With beauty before me may I walk
2   With beauty behind me may I walk
3   With beauty above me may I walk
4   With beauty below me may I walk
5   With beauty all around me may I walk
6   As one who is long life and happiness may I walk
7   In beauty it is finished
8   In beauty it is finished.
9   *(Lights down on all but PELTIER in his cell. Then that light*
10   *down and out.)*
11
12   **END OF PLAY**
13
14
15
16
17
18
19
20
21
22
23
24
25
26
27
28
29
30
31
32
33
34
35

Highest Mountain, Fastest River
by Donna Abela
with Salamanca Theatre Company

Refugees, displaced persons, boat people, population diaspora — these terms became household words in the last half of the twentieth-century, defining the momentous demographic shifts in human migratory patterns occasioned by worldwide political upheavals. Civil war, foreign invasion, state terrorism, ethnic cleansing, grinding poverty — the culprits were many, and they are all too familiar to us even today, creating financial, social and political burdens on a regular basis. Among the intractable problems generated by such phenomena, certainly the psychological dislocation suffered by those abandoning their homeland is one of the most painful, and the most resistant to financial, institutional or legislative amelioration. Nothing can ultimately replace the sense of being culturally adrift in a new society of strangers, friendly and sympathetic though they may be.

This play looks at three critical stages in the lives of refugees: the intolerable conditions that drive people to flee their neighborhoods and villages, the desperate and dangerous journey to freedom and safety, and the initial period of adjustment to the customs, language and social groups in their new sanctuaries. Perhaps the last situation — the arrival of the refugees in Hobart — receives the sharpest focus in Donna Abela's play because today the issue of cultural assimilation affects societies worldwide, and hence touches us all. In her play the grafting of Hmong refugees on to modern Australian society during the 1980s and 1990s succeeds in revealing problems as well as joys that this process will always occasion.

Highest Mountain, Fastest River poses strong challenges to producers on several levels. First, its large multiracial cast tests any group's ability to create believable characters who range from urban teens to simple peasants to cruel and brutal military oppressors. In this regard, the play requires research in the background of the cultural groups represented onstage: the Australians, the Hmong people, and the various ethnic and age-determined subgroups within those two camps.

A second powerful challenge in the play that directors, designers and others should exploit is certainly the creative design choices the story requires: sound effects, music, costumes, choreography, sets and lighting. These nonverbal elements tell as much or more of Donna Abela's story as the language does, and no production can succeed without careful decisions being made about them. Together with the poignancy of the human lives depicted in the drama, these technical and design aspects establish locales, create the cultural contexts, and control the mood and tempi of the dramatic action at many points.

Highest Mountain, Fastest River is unique in this collection not only because of its subject of the cultural conflicts affecting political asylum-seekers, but also because of its east Asian performance style. By knitting its tale of Hmong refugees to a production approach grounded in movement, music and sound effects, Donna Abela brings to the world stage a work thoroughly Asian in its character and universally compelling in its dramatic action.

Characters

Ker's Mother
Australian Children
Hmong Children
Scott – *a ten-year-old Australian boy in Hobart*
Villagers
Yang – *ten-year-old Hmong boy in his village in Laos*
Yang's Friend
Yang's Sister
Yang's Other Sister
Yang's Brother
Yang's Grandmother
Koa – *Tong's sister*
Villager One
Villager Two
Tong – *ten-year-old Hmong boy living in an occupied village in Laos*
Village Child
Latecomer
Ge

Dua
Father
Aunt
Villager Three
Villager Four
Mee — *Koa's friend*
Koa's Husband
Attacked Villagers
Moua — *guerilla fighter who lives in the jungle*
Girl with a Baby
Wife
Man
Husband
Refugees
Refugee Child — *ten-year-old in a Thai refugee camp*
Fiancé — *young man in a Thai refugee camp*
Traveller — *young person preparing to leave a Thai refugee camp*
Ker — *ten-year-old Hmong girl living in Hobart*
Ker's Uncle
Ker's Relatives
Ker's Cousin
Ker's Father
Ker's Brother
Hmong Teacher — *teaches at weekend Hmong school in Hobart*

Highest Mountain, Fastest River was originally devised by Donna Abela and Salamanca Theatre Company in 1991. The play toured schools in Tasmania and went on to win the 1992 Human Rights and Equal Opportunities Award for Drama. In 1993, the play was revised for a larger cast and toured across South Eastern Australia. This is the revised version.

Original Devising Team

Director .... Annette Downs
Writer .... Donna Abela
Actors .... .Lian Tanner, Kym Tonkin, David Williamson

Original Creative Personnel and Crew

Hmong song teacher .... Neng Lue
Qeej musician .... Phia Yang
Composer .... Imogen Lidgett
Sound Designer .... David Gurney
Sound Engineer .... Sandy Campbell
Stage Manager .... Sandy Campbell
Costumes .... Kate Stephens-Lewincamp
Fabric Construction .... Sara Lindsay
Sound Operator .... Annette Downs
Photography .... Tony Ryan

1993 Team

Director .... Annette Downs
Writer .... Donna Abela
Actors .... Franz Docherty, Jordana Langridge,
Consuelo Torrealba, Michael Newbold

This play would not have been possible without the support of the Hmong community in Hobart. We wish to thank them for their enormous generosity in sharing their stories, inviting us into their homes, and devoting many hours to the development and rehearsal of this play. We would also like to thank Margaret Eldridge from the Adult Migrant Education Service, Darrelyn Gunzberg, Mary Hickson, Liz Marshall, Margaret Horton, Peter Bansel, Ruth Hadlow, Karl Underwood, and Christine Best.

Production Notes

Highest Mountain, Fastest River aims to evoke, rather than literally portray, the refugee experiences of the Hmong people. Disconnected character journeys and stylised movement were used in order to avoid sensationalism and melodrama. In our production, four actors continually transformed into new characters. However, the play can be performed by a larger cast.

1   ***PRE-SHOW:*** A Hmong tune can be heard as the actors seat the
2   audience. The tune is played on the qeej, and is from a
3   selection of music known as "Fingers" which is played by
4   Hmong musicians as they warm up.
5   ***PROLOGUE:*** The qeej music fades as KER'S MOTHER enters
6   singing "At War and Living In Another Country" in the
7   Hmong language. The other actors become AUSTRALIAN
8   CHILDREN playing a make believe war game. They kill each
9   other repeatedly with guns, grenades, bombs, mines or
10   swords.
11
12   **AUSTRALIAN CHILDREN:** *(Ad libbing)* **Bang! ... You're dead!**
13   **I'm not! You are! ... Argh ... You got me ... You're dead**
14   **you're dead you're dead! ... Blood. Blood. Guts. Blood ...**
15   **I'm the Terminator. You can't kill me ...**
16   *(Sound effects: gunfire, then a warplane tearing across the*
17   *sky. The actors become HMONG CHILDREN huddling in*
18   *fear, watching the warplane pass overhead and disappear in*
19   *the distance.)*
20   **ACTORS:** *(In canon)* **This is a story, but a true story. It is not our**
21   **story but it was told to us. It is not our story, but it is a true**
22   **story.**
23
24   **SCENE ONE: SALAMANCA MARKETS**
25
26   *(At the markets KER'S MOTHER sings and sets up her stall.*
27   *She unfolds embroidered cloth panels that depict the*
28   *Hmong's escape from Laos. She does this as SCOTT speaks.)*
29   **SCOTT: This is Salamanca Market in Hobart. My mum wants**
30   **me to buy her a pillowcase from them people over there**
31   **because she's right into this ethnic stuff. I reckon they**
32   **might be from China and my dad reckons they might be**
33   **Catholic because they've got all these kids. They're here**
34   **every Saturday, but mainly just women. Don't know what**
35   **the blokes do on Saturdays. Probably wash their cars, hey?**

1   They sell stuff like veggies and coriander and parsley. And
2   pillowcases with pictures of animals and trees and
3   brightly coloured people. Some pillowcases even have
4   soldiers on them. Like it's some sort of story.
5   KER'S MOTHER: This is a story. But a true story. It is the story
6   of my people, the Hmong people, and we lived in the
7   highest mountains of Laos. But the years brought fighting
8   between many countries. We lost the fight. Soldiers took
9   our homes, our mountains and our country. The winners
10 of the fighting wanted us dead. So we ran for our lives
11 through the jungle, towards a new life which lay on the
12 other side of the fastest, fastest river.
13 SCOTT: Yeah. The pillowcases look alright I reckon, but my
14 doona cover's better because it's got Batman all over it.
15 And I don't believe that stuff about the soldiers. Soldiers
16 don't take things from people. They just shoot things.
17 Pretty exciting, I reckon. BANG! You're dead! *(Freeze.)*
18
19
20   **SCENE TWO: THE VILLAGE**
21
22 *(The ACTORS slowly, almost ritually, tie indigo sashes*
23 *around the waist of their loose black clothing. They become*
24 *Hmong VILLAGERS calling and gathering their animals for*
25 *the morning feed.)*
26 VILLAGERS : Aiyee! Aiyee ... ! Kuru kuru Kuru kuru ... ! Bou
27 bou bou bou bou ... *(Having fed their animals, they walk to*
28 *their fields.)*
29 YANG: The sun is up and it's called us to work, so we walk to
30 our fields that have been slashed and burnt and fertilised
31 with ash. After two hours of walking, we'll plant rice seeds
32 in the rain-soaked clay. The fields will ripen into a golden
33 harvest that we'll gather handful by handful. *(They plant*
34 *and hoe their field. They resume this action when not*
35 *portraying village life.)*

1   YANG: Since my father was killed in the war, my brother is
2   head of our household, and he looks after us. I've been
3   working in these fields for hours! I wish it was time for the
4   New Year Festival. Then I could play games. Like tops! Or
5   hopscotch!
6   YANG'S FRIEND: No! Let's play n'dua paa! *(They play this game*
7   *with sticks, ad libbing.)*
8   YANG: At the New Year Festival, my sister will play games too.
9   She'll play catch with her boyfriend. He sometimes comes
10   to our house at night and sings and whispers to her
11   through the walls. Really quietly, so my mother can't hear.
12   But I listen. Sometimes I laugh. I can't help it. I bet she
13   can't wait to play catch!
14   YANG'S SISTER: I made this ball myself, and I'm going to
15   throw it to Pierre. If he likes me he'll catch it, and agree to
16   play. Each time he drops the ball, he has to give me a piece
17   of his clothing. If he doesn't win back all the clothing he
18   lost, he'll have to come to my house and collect them by
19   singing me love songs. If his singing is good, everyone will
20   crowd around and listen. I hope his voice is beautiful.
21   YANG: One of my other sisters is in grade two at a school in the
22   next village. I went to grade three, but I don't go anymore.
23   I might finish grade four if my family can save enough
24   money for books. That's if I don't get married first.
25   YANG'S OTHER SISTER: This is my doll, Jue. Her boyfriend is
26   taking her to his village a long way away. She's going to
27   live with his family until they get married. She's very shy.
28   I can hear her crying. I think she misses her family.
29   YANG: My brother was married last year. The festivities began
30   at our house and lasted nearly all night. We had two pigs,
31   four chickens, and ten bottles of liquor! Our father would
32   be proud of my brother, because he has just become a
33   father too.
34   YANG'S BROTHER: This is my new son. In three days an elder
35   will hold a ceremony, and invite your soul to live inside

1   you. He will show you to the household spirits who will
2   promise to keep you safe. But now you must grow strong
3   and sleep, so I can take care of your mother.

4 YANG: My grandmother lives with me and my mother and my
5   other brothers and sisters. She's very old. I like working
6   with her because she tells me stories. She says our people
7   are brave and that I will be brave too. Everyone loves
8   listening when our grandmother speaks.

9 YANG'S GRANDMOTHER: These are my burial clothes. I
10   began sewing them when I was twenty, and spent many
11   years making them beautiful with my finest stitches. Now
12   you are twenty, it is time for you to begin making your
13   burial clothes. When we wear these in the world of our
14   ancestors, our souls will be proud and prosper.

15 YANG: When our family gather for a ceremony, there are so
16   many people that we hardly fit inside our house. We eat
17   the best food we have. My favourite part is catching the pig.
18   *(They chase after the pig. They catch it and kill it. Freeze.)*

19 YANG: My father was a soldier. I want to be brave like he was
20   and fight the enemy who killed him. The enemy are
21   soldiers too. They hurt us, burn our crops, and scare us
22   when they walk through our village.

23 VILLAGERS: *(In canon)* Che's plough hit a landmine. It was
24   hidden in his field. He is dead. ... Shh. The soldier is
25   watching us. Be quiet and careful. ... Grind your rice and
26   hope for peace. That's all we can do. ... Shh. He's coming.

27

28   **SCENE THREE: THE OPTIONS,**
29   **AND THE OCCUPATION OF THE VILLAGE**

30

31   *(Sound effects: A haunting reverberation: "1975. The*
32   *Hmong people will not obey the government. We must*
33   *eradicate the Hmong to their very roots." The VILLAGERS*
34   *are working in the field.)*

35 KOA: Is it true?

1 VILLAGER ONE: Yes. Fong brought the news last night. The
2   enemy is now the government.
3 VILLAGER TWO: We can't call them the enemy. If we do,
4   they'll kill us.
5 KOA: It's a rumour.
6 VILLAGER ONE: It's not a rumour. Fong's family have fled to
7   the jungle. I think we should do the same.
8 VILLAGER TWO: Yes. Run to the jungle and fight.
9 VILLAGER ONE: We have been fighting for years. Our country
10   is finished. Fong is escaping to Thailand. We should follow.
11 VILLAGER TWO: We must get weapons.
12 KOA: We should stay here. Where we belong. Now that the
13   enemy have power they might leave our people alone. We
14   should try and live with them.
15 VILLAGER TWO: How can I live with them? They killed my
16   father.
17 VILLAGER ONE: They can't be trusted. We must hide in the
18   jungle.
19 KOA: And run like scared chickens? Eat nothing but leaves?
20   What kind of life is that for your children?
21 VILLAGER ONE: If you stay here the village will be bombed.
22 VILLAGER TWO: And if you go to the jungle they'll chase you
23   with bullets. We have no choice. We must fight.
24 VILLAGER ONE: With what?
25 VILLAGER TWO: We'll get weapons from Thailand.
26 VILLAGER ONE: No. We'll go to Thailand and wait until it's
27   safe to return.
28 VILLAGER TWO: What good is waiting while they take our
29   land? If you leave, you may never see Laos again.
30 KOA: I just want to farm. Not leave or fight. Things might be
31   fine if we co-operate. Running might provoke them.
32 VILLAGER ONE: Don't you see? They're coming to kill us.
33 KOA: But this land is our future.
34 VILLAGER ONE: The enemy has stolen our future. We must
35   escape to Thailand.

1   VILLAGER TWO: In Thailand, you will grow old and useless.

2   KOA: I don't want to live in someone else's country.

3   VILLAGER ONE: At least you'd be alive.

4   KOA: But how do we cross the Mekong River? None of us can
5   swim. And what about my grandmother? How can she run
6   through the jungle? Or my children? The journey would
7   kill them.

8   VILLAGER TWO: If you stay, you will be killed. If you submit,
9   you will be destroyed. I will not live here under someone
10   else's rules. I'm going to fight!

11   VILLAGER ONE: I'm going to escape!

12   KOA: I'm going to stay and hope you're both wrong!

13   *(Time lapses.)*

14   KOA: Tong! Where is the chicken? Find the chicken. Quickly.

15   TONG: Kurukuruk! Kurukuruk! One of our chickens is
16   missing. If we don't find it, we'll get in trouble.
17   Everything's different now. There are strange rules, and
18   our leaders are missing. The new government surrounded
19   us with hundreds of soldiers. "Don't be afraid. We're here
20   to help you. We'll give you a better education, improve your
21   country, and secure a brighter future. We are your
22   friends." But they don't seem like friends. They ask
23   questions all the time. Especially about our men. "Hello,
24   little child. Did your father go away for a long time before
25   the government came?"

26   VILLAGE CHILD: No.

27   TONG: "Did he wear a green uniform? Did he carry a gun?"

28   VILLAGE CHILD: No. I don't know. I can't remember.

29   TONG: "Did his friends wear green? Did they carry a gun? Do
30   you think they were soldiers? Do you?"

31   VILLAGE CHILD: I can't remember!

32   TONG: The government count our people to make sure no one
33   is missing. They come to our houses twice a day for roll
34   call. If you're late, they get suspicious and say "Where
35   were you? You were with the rebel fighters, weren't you?"

1   LATECOMER: No.

2   TONG: "Then why are you late for roll call?"

3   LATECOMER: I had to take the rice to the warehouse. The bag

4   broke. I had to pick up the rice with my hands. The guards

5   stood over me with a gun. I wasn't with the rebels!

6   TONG: "You are coming with us."

7   LATECOMER : No!

8   TONG: "Move! Ge!"

9   GE: Here.

10 TONG: "Were you a rebel soldier during the war?"

11 GE: No.

12 TONG: "Dua!"

13 DUA: Here.

14 TONG: "Were you a rebel soldier during the war?"

15 DUA: No.

16 TONG: "You were a rebel. You oppose the government. We

17   must take you away for training." They've taken many of

18   our men, including my father.

19 FATHER: Where are you taking me?

20 TONG: "To a school. To be re-educated."

21 FATHER: I have a family. And fields. I can't go with you.

22 TONG: "You must come and learn to take pride in your country."

23 FATHER: I have pride in my country. I won't go with you.

24 TONG: "You have no choice. Come!" Many of our men have

25   disappeared. None have come back yet. We don't know

26   what to believe anymore. We're afraid and confused, and

27   we get in trouble for reasons we don't understand.

28 AUNT: My sister is ill. I'm here to help her.

29 TONG: "Where is your visitor's permit?"

30 AUNT: Visitor's permit? I only live next door.

31 TONG: "Where is your visitor's permit?"

32 AUNT: I don't have one.

33 TONG: "Then you are here illegally. You are disobeying the

34   government. You must learn to obey." They take away our

35   people, and they take half of everything we own. "You will

1   share everything you have."

2 VILLAGER THREE: But we do share. We share with our own

3   people.

4 TONG: "Now you will share with the whole country. Give us

5   half of your animals."

6 VILLAGER THREE: I only have twelve chickens. But I need

7   some for my daughter's wedding.

8 TONG: "Only twelve?"

9 VILLAGER THREE: Yes. Twelve. That's all I have.

10 TONG: "Where are your animals?"

11 VILLAGER FOUR: There. Two pigs.

12 TONG: "Only two?"

13 VILLAGER FOUR: Yes. That's all. Don't take one of them.

14   Please. That's food for our family.

15 TONG: Kuru kuru kuru kuru! The government knows we've

16   got seven chickens. If they come and see there are only six,

17   they will say, "One of your chickens is missing. You used it

18   to feed the rebel fighters, didn't you?" I have to find my

19   chicken, or we'll get in trouble.

20 KOA: Tong! Tong! The soldiers are going. They're leaving our

21   village tonight. Decorate the village. The soldiers are

22   leaving forever.

23 TONG: They're probably lying.

24 KOA: No. This time it's true. Look. They're packing their

25   belongings. Everyone who went to the re-education camp

26   will be back tomorrow. They promised. My husband will

27   be back tomorrow. So tonight we're having a party.

28 TONG: It won't be a real party. They'll just give us more rules.

29 KOA: It will be a real party. Go and kill the biggest pig.

30   Decorate the village. Hurry. *(TONG exits.)*

31 MEE: Koa. Come here. Quickly.

32 KOA: What is it?

33 MEE: Go quietly to the edge of the village. Your husband is

34   waiting.

35 KOA: My husband? But he's not due back until tomorrow.

1   **MEE:** Shh. He's hiding.

2   **KOA:** Hiding? Why?

3   **MEE:** Go! *(KOA finds her husband on the edge of the village.)*

4   **KOA:** You can't be my husband. My husband was a strong man.

5   A farmer. A builder. He could do anything.

6   **KOA'S HUSBAND:** Koa. I've escaped.

7   **KOA:** You're so frail.

8   **KOA'S HUSBAND:** Listen. The re-education centre wasn't a

9   school, it was a prison. They called us criminals.

10   **KOA:** But they took you for training.

11   **KOA'S HUSBAND:** The word "training" is like the word "killing."

12   **KOA:** What did they do to you?

13   **KOA'S HUSBAND:** They blamed us for the fighting. Made us

14   confess to things we hadn't done. Used us like animals to

15   plough their fields. We'd drop with hunger, but they'd

16   never let us stop. And they tortured us. I've seen things I

17   never want to speak about.

18   **KOA:** My husband –

19   **KOA'S HUSBAND:** I bribed one of the guards. He let me escape.

20   You must escape too. Come!

21   **KOA:** No. The soldiers are leaving our village tomorrow. We're

22   having a party to say farewell. It's true.

23   **KOA'S HUSBAND:** The soldiers are in the jungle, preparing

24   their ammunition. They are coming to kill you.

25   **KOA:** No.

26   **KOA'S HUSBAND:** I've seen them. They're surrounding the

27   village. We must escape to Thailand.

28   **KOA:** But my family –

29   **KOA'S HUSBAND:** There's no time. They're closing in. You

30   must leave. Now! *(KOA and KOA'S HUSBAND flee. MEE and*

31   *TONG are decorating the village.)*

32   **TONG:** The soldiers don't deserve a party.

33   **MEE:** Tong. The decorations aren't straight.

34   **TONG:** I don't care.

35   **MEE:** You must care … The soldiers. They're surrounding the

1   village.

2   **VILLAGERS:** *(Entering, in canon)* **The soldiers are surrounding**

3   **us.... They're pointing their guns ... The soldiers are**

4   **surrounding us ... with flaming torches ... The soldiers are**

5   **surrounding us ... To destroy the village ... The soldiers**

6   **are surrounding us!**

7

8

9   **SCENE FOUR: THE SURPRISE ATTACK**

10

11   *(The village is attacked. Sound effects of gunshots,*

12   *screaming, crying, burning, running, and breathing.*

13   *VILLAGERS flee into the jungle. They run and hide and fall*

14   *when they are shot. SOME PEOPLE survive, but collapse,*

15   *exhausted.)*

16

17

18   **SCENE FIVE: LIVING IN THE JUNGLE**

19

20   *(MOUA comes to inspect what he thinks are dead bodies.*

21   *KOA, KOA'S HUSBAND, and a GIRL WITH A BABY wake in*

22   *fright, ready to kill. MOUA recognises them. The scene is*

23   *whispered.)*

24 **MOUA: Don't speak. Keep low and follow me.** *(They follow,*

25   *helping each other because they are wounded.)* **Keep the**

26   **child quiet. If she cries, they'll shoot us. Tread softly.**

27   **Hurry.** *(They journey to the guerilla camp.)* **Sit here and**

28   **rest. We're safe for the moment. We have spotters keeping**

29   **watch around the camp.**

30 **KOA'S HUSBAND: Where are the others from our village?**

31 **MOUA: Dead. Now rest. Recover your strength.**

32 **KOA: What happens now?**

33 **MOUA: You learn to survive. You sleep fully dressed and ready**

34   **to run. You keep watch when it's your turn. You listen for**

35   **every noise. And you never make a sound.**

1   GIRL WITH A BABY: My brother's been killed —

2   MOUA: Stifle your grief. If you don't, you will get us killed.

3   *(Time lapses.)*

4   KOA'S HUSBAND: Here are the guns stolen from the dead.

5   Others are watching over abandoned supplies and will

6   bring more weapons as soon as it's safe.

7   MOUA: Good. But the enemy will know we have more guns.

8   Their soldiers will follow us. We'll break camp tonight and

9   move on. Koa!

10   KOA: Yes?

11   MOUA: Take one of these guns.

12   KOA: No. I won't fire a gun.

13   MOUA: You will when you have to. So it's time to learn. Your

14   husband will teach you. Our bullets are few, so learn not

15   to miss. Go with him. You must become a sky soldier.

16   *(Time lapses.)*

17   GIRL WITH A BABY: Moua. There are fish in the river!

18   MOUA: Don't touch them.

19   GIRL WITH A BABY: Why not?

20   MOUA: They've been poisoned by the yellow rain.

21   GIRL WITH A BABY: They can't be. The bananas aren't ripe.

22   The sugar cane is empty. There are no wild potatoes.

23   There's no food anywhere. Our people are weak and

24   there's nothing to feed them. We need food.

25   MOUA: We'll keep eating leaves.

26   GIRL WITH A BABY: No. The fish can't be poisoned. I'll get

27   some and —

28   MOUA: If you eat them, you'll bleed inside and die within

29   minutes.

30   GIRL WITH A BABY: But there's no food ...

31   MOUA: Then we'll just have to keep looking.

32   *(Time lapses.)*

33   KOA: We're shooting our own people!

34   MOUA: The enemy capture our men and force them to fight us.

35   GIRL WITH A BABY: They are using them like shields.

1 **MOUA:** If they don't fight us, they are tortured to death. They
2   have no choice.
3 **KOA:** We're shooting our own people ...
4 **KOA'S HUSBAND:** Listen. Planes. Rockets are exploding.
5 **MOUA:** They're bombing us with yellow rain. Close your eyes.
6   It will burn your eyes!
7 **GIRL WITH A BABY:** Even the sky is against us.
8 **MOUA:** We can't win. Run to the dam. Run!
9   *(They run to the dam. The dam is in sight. They stop suddenly.)*
10 **KOA:** Before us is a huge dam. Soldiers are separating the
11   women from the men. The women, pinned by the guns,
12   watch helplessly as the men are shot and killed. The
13   soldiers walk towards the women. They reach and say,
14   "give us your babies." The women resist and shield the
15   children with their bodies. The soldiers shoot. The
16   women fall. Life slumps away. Babies are crying. There
17   are hands dumping the babies in the dam. The dead
18   babies. The many dead. Long dead and newly dead,
19   everywhere. *(They walk slowly among the bodies, reaching*
20   *out to some of them. Their grief builds to fury.)*
21
22
23 **SCENE SIX: THROUGH THE JUNGLE TO THE MEKONG RIVER**
24
25   *(They run through dense jungle, towards the river.)*
26 **ALL:** Running and running and running for days.
27   Pulling leeches from my swollen legs
28   Clothes rip from my back
29   My feet are sliced to pieces
30
31   Running and running and running for days
32   Dead people are everywhere
33   Starved and shot
34   One of us is killed
35   No time to bury

1

2   **Running and running and running for days**

3   **Fleeing day and night**

4   **Dragging children too scared to run**

5   **Eating anything we can swallow**

6   **Never safe to stop**

7

8   **Running and running and running for days**

9   **For ten whole days we followed the sun**

10   *(They collapse.)*

11

12

13   **SCENE SEVEN: CROSSING THE MEKONG RIVER**

14

15   WIFE: Look!

16   MAN: The river.

17   HUSBAND: On the other side. Bikes and cars and buildings.

18   It's Thailand.

19   WIFE: We're nearly free!

20   WOMAN: Shh! Guards are everywhere.

21   HUSBAND: Start cutting bamboo. Slowly and silently. We'll

22   cross in the middle of the night. Hurry.

23   *(They prepare to cross.)*

24   WIFE: Will Thailand be good or bad?

25   HUSBAND: I don't know. But we have no choice. We must

26   cross.

27   WIFE: I'll tie our valuables to my back.

28   HUSBAND: I'll tie myself to you. *(They embrace and walk together*

29   *to the edge of the river. They enter and fight the river, freezing*

30   *as the words are spoken. The river is represented by fabric*

31   *that is manipulated by two actors who also speak the*

32   *following speeches. Sound effects of water and drums.)*

33   ACTOR 1: My heart screams when the riverbed leaves my feet.

34   I bite my lip to stay quiet. The river drags me from its bank

35   into a black night that blinds me. So I breathe and listen

1 and bite my lip until it bleeds.

2 ACTOR 2: My children, you mustn't cry. Your tears are too
3 heavy. Give them to the cold river who will wash them
4 away. You must hold your heads high and help me, so that
5 tomorrow you will be warm and safe.

6 ACTOR 1: I struggle to float and not choke on my fear. I dread
7 the sound of bullets, or the pirates that may wait with no
8 heart. I am pulled into the unknown, but I have no choice
9 but to give this river my trust.

10 ACTOR 2: My wife is tied to me. I'm swimming for both of us,
11 but she no longer speaks. My arms are weak, my legs like
12 ribbons, but I must go on swimming. When freedom is
13 ours, maybe she will speak to me again.

14 ACTOR 1: My brother has drowned. His little fingers have
15 stopped squeezing my neck. I will drown too if he stays on
16 my back. So I untie the rope and watch him float away
17 without me.

18 ACTOR 2: There is sand beneath my feet. A little further and I
19 will tread soil not water. I will fall on the Thai riverbank
20 and sleep. When daylight wakes me, I will be free.

21 *(Reaching Thailand, they collapse. They slowly stand.)*

22 REFUGEE 1: Kind villagers bring me food and care for me.

23 REFUGEE 2: Guards punch me to the ground.

24 REFUGEE 3: Pirates steal everything I have.

25 REFUGEE 4: Officers from the UN protect me.

26

27

28 **SCENE NINE: THE REFUGEE CAMP**

29

30 *(They are taken to the refugee camp.)*

31 REFUGEES: *(In canon)* There are thousands of people. How
32 many in the camp? ... How long will we be here? Will we be
33 safe? ... Have you seen my family? How can I find them?
34 Did they get here alive? ... When can we go back to Laos?
35 When? ... There are thousands and thousands of people.

1   *(The gates to the refugee camp close.)*

2   **REFUGEE CHILD:** I've been in this refugee camp for two
3   months. Last night the guards beat me and put me in
4   prison. They found me outside the camp. I didn't want to
5   escape. I just wanted water. It's summer, and there's no
6   water in the camp, so I had to do something. They said if
7   I'd been older they would have shot me. I was only looking
8   for water. Life here is difficult. I can't get used to things
9   and I keep making mistakes. When I arrived in the camp,
10   the guards put rice in a trough, then blew a whistle.
11   Hundreds of people rushed and grabbed some food. I was
12   shy. I thought we ate with a spoon. I didn't eat for three
13   days. That's when my cousin found me, and told me to
14   grab food too. He took me to live in his hut so I could get
15   used to things. But it's difficult. I keep remembering what
16   we have lost. We all remember what we have lost and
17   sometimes our room is full of crying. We can't forget our
18   people who have vanished like the wind. But we forget the
19   rules of the camp. We forget them easily. The guards hate
20   it when we forget. This is the first time I've been in prison.
21   My cousin will come in the morning, and bribe the guards
22   to let me out. He always helps me, because I can't get used
23   to things and I keep making mistakes. So I keep getting
24   beaten. I wish I could just get used to things, and forget.

25   **FIANCÉ:** I've been in this refugee camp for six years. When I
26   arrived I found my mother. I was overjoyed. Then I cried
27   as she told me the story of her escape. It's an awful story.
28   Now, she spends her day sitting on the floor, sewing her
29   story onto pillows. After six years of sewing, tears still fall
30   onto her stitches. I used to be a teacher. I taught grade four
31   and grade six, then I became a head teacher and prepared
32   lessons for all the schools in the camp. But then they said
33   teachers couldn't be paid anymore, so I had to stop
34   teaching. I need work that will bring in money, so that one
35   day we can leave for a new country. My girlfriend looks

1 around the camp and sees the orphans and cries for them.
2 She says this is no place to raise children. So we have to
3 leave. Then we'll get married, and have children who will
4 be happy and free. So now I sit with my mother and
5 girlfriend and sew my story onto pillows. We send them to
6 our relatives in Hobart, who sell them at a market and
7 send us the money. Sometimes we use our money for food
8 or medicine, and sometimes it's taken by the guards. But
9 we keep sewing. We have to, because one day it will buy us
10 a new life.
11 TRAVELLER: I've been in this refugee camp all my life. I was
12 born here ten years ago, after my parents crossed the
13 Mekong. We're packing our things so we can live in
14 Australia. We've had interviews and medical checks and
15 we leave on an aeroplane tomorrow. But my father is sad.
16 He wanted to go back to Laos. But my mum kept saying
17 you can't go back. She misses Laos deeply, but in her heart
18 she knows that we must go forward and find a life that is
19 free and safe. So we're leaving this camp and its
20 thousands of people, to make a home in a country where
21 we will be strangers. I'm excited and scared. And sorry to
22 say goodbye to my friends and cousins and aunts and
23 uncles. The hardest part is leaving my grandmother. She
24 refuses to come with us because she wants her body
25 buried in Laos. She will stay here to die and I know I will
26 never see her again. I can't imagine what our new life will
27 be like. I can't imagine life in Laos either. It's my country
28 but I've never lived there. Maybe one day I'll see Laos for
29 the very first time. But now we must move forward. Have
30 you ever packed your life into a suitcase?
31 *(Sound effects: Airport announcements and airport sounds.*
32 *The TRAVELLER and other REFUGEES board the plane for*
33 *their journey to Australia. Everything is unfamiliar. They sing*
34 *the following song, "At War and Living In Another Country,"*
35 *in English. The audience should recognise the tune as the one*

1   *sung by KER'S MOTHER at the beginning of the play.)*

2 **REFUGEES: In the past our country was stable**

3   **We lived in our village together**

4   **Now our country is at war**

5   **We have to leave our village behind**

6

7   **Because our country is heavily at war**

8   **We are leaving to live in another man's country**

9   **Because our country is heavily at war**

10   **That is why we are leaving to live with you now.**

11

12   **We are truly going step by step by road**

13   **We are leaving our village behind**

14   **We are truly going step by step by road**

15   **We are leaving our village behind**

16

17   **We climb onto an airship that races across the sky**

18   **leaving brothers and sisters and friends behind**

19   **We climb onto an airship that races into the distance**

20   **to live an isolated life with unknown different people**

21

22   **Leaving behind our faded village**

23   **to live in a different country; we will miss each other**

24   **Leaving behind our faded village**

25   **to live with different people; we must learn to love**

26   **each other**

27

28

29   **SCENE TEN: HOBART**

30

31 **KER: I'm Ker. My friends call me Kerry. When we arrived in**

32   **Hobart two years ago, my uncle met us at the airport.**

33   *(At the airport:)*

34 **KER'S UNCLE: When I saw you last, you were just a baby!**

35 **KER: Yes, uncle.**

1   **KER'S UNCLE:** You're not happy. Why?

2   **KER:** I feel so strange. People are staring. We're the only ones

3   with black hair, and we're very thin. We look different.

4   **KER'S UNCLE:** Don't worry. We'll be different together.

5   **KER:** When he drove us to his house, the lights from the city

6   looked like stars that were too close. I thought this new

7   country must be crazy.

8   *(At the party:)*

9   **KER'S RELATIVES:** Hello. Welcome! My cousin. Welcome! etc.

10   *(Ad lib.)*

11   **KER:** Our relatives held a party and talked to us all night. They

12   gave us clothes. They were being kind, and at the time we

13   thought the clothes were great, but when I look at the

14   photos I think, how embarrassing. They were really daggy.

15   Then they let us sleep in real beds. I'd never slept in a bed

16   before. I didn't like it. It was too soft. So I slept on the floor

17   until I got used to it. We had to get used to other things too.

18   Like when my mother went to the supermarket.

19   *(At the supermarket:)*

20   **KER'S COUSIN:** Then you get one of these shopping trolley

21   things —

22   **KER'S MOTHER:** It doesn't seem to work properly.

23   **KER'S COUSIN:** They never do. Now you can push the trolley

24   down the aisles, and choose the food you want.

25   **KER'S MOTHER:** Where do they keep the pigs and chickens?

26   **KER'S COUSIN:** Well. You can get bacon over there, and

27   drumsticks over there —

28   **KER'S MOTHER:** No. I mean live pigs and chickens.

29   **KER'S COUSIN:** There are none. Everything's already killed

30   and wrapped.

31   **KER'S MOTHER:** How can I see what I'm buying?

32   **KER'S COUSIN:** You read the label.

33   **KER'S MOTHER:** But I can't read English yet!

34   **KER'S COUSIN:** Don't worry. If you get stuck, just do what I do.

35   **KER'S MOTHER:** What's that?

1   KER'S COUSIN: Buy a pizza!

2   KER : We ate lots of pizzas. And we eventually learned English,

3   too. When I went to school I didn't know any English, so I

4   was given an Australian friend who helped me. And one of

5   my teachers taught me how to say cool things so I could

6   stick up for myself. It's hard when there's no one to help

7   you. You get so scared. Especially getting around the city.

8   *(On the bus:)*

9   KER'S FATHER: Now children, watch carefully for the bus

10   stop. Uncle says it's just past the shops.

11   KER'S BROTHER: I wish he was with us.

12   KER'S FATHER: We'll be alright. Australian children catch

13   buses by themselves. So we can, too. We mustn't be

14   frightened just because things are new.

15   KER'S BROTHER: I still wish he was with us.

16   KER: There's our bus stop!

17   KER'S FATHER: Why isn't the bus stopping?

18   KER'S BROTHER: I don't know.

19   KER: How do we make it stop?

20   KER'S FATHER: Let us off! Stop! Stop!

21   KER'S BROTHER: Stop the bus! Let us go home!

22   KER'S: Please. Don't let us get lost!

23   KER'S FATHER: They can't understand us! STOP!

24   KER: Eventually we learned to stop the bus by pushing the right

25   button. We made lots of mistakes like that. Some things

26   they told us about in Thailand, like how to flush a toilet, but

27   other things we had to find out for ourselves. It was hard at

28   first, but soon we learned how to stop a bus, wash clothes in

29   a machine, and use the hot water tap without getting

30   burned. We've learned many new things. We also go to

31   Hmong school and learn things about our people.

32   *(At Hmong School:)*

33   HMONG TEACHER: Our people now live in many parts of the

34   world. It's very difficult to describe the terrible things we

35   have suffered, but the more we explain them, the less

1   painful it will feel.

2   KER: My parents go to language school to learn English, and I go

3   to high school, where they used to call me Chinagirl. But

4   that's stopped now because we're studying Thailand and

5   Laos and my teacher gets me to do the dances I learned in

6   the refugee camp. My friends like my dances and want me

7   to teach them. But I want them to teach me about rock

8   music. *(KER'S BROTHER strums a few chords of "Smoke on*

9   *the Water." KER rolls her eyes.)* My brother wants to be a rock

10   star. Don't tell him, but he's not very good. Michael Jackson

11   is heaps better. I don't know what I want to be yet. Maybe an

12   air hostess. But my uncle says I'd be away from my family

13   too much. I'll finish school first, and then decide. My father

14   used to be a doctor when we were in Thailand, but now he

15   goes to our people's farm. He grows spring onions and

16   coriander and cabbages for me and my mother to sell at

17   Salamanca markets. We also sell embroideries made by

18   other Hmong people in refugee camps, and then we send

19   them the money. Someone did the same for us once. Now

20   it's our turn to help someone else.

21   *(At Salamanca Markets. SCOTT enters stalking and playing*

22   *his shoot out game.)*

23   KER: Oh. And this is Scott.

24   SCOTT: G'day. How are ya?

25   KER: He goes to my school.

26   KER'S MOTHER: This is a story. But a true story. A story of the

27   Hmong people, who were born into a war. We ran for our

28   lives towards a new life which lay on the other side of the

29   fastest river. Now our people live in many countries, and

30   my family is here in Australia. Our new home is Hobart,

31   among very different mountains.

32   SCOTT: BANG ! You're dead. *(Pause.)*

33   KER: No, we're not. *(Pause. The actors exit singing "At War and*

34   *Living In Another Country" in the Hmong language.)*

35   **END OF PLAY**

Mutiny in Crazyland
A Play for Little and Old Children

by Mirjana Buljan
Translated from the Croatian by
Nina Antoljak and Mirjana Buljan

At first glance, readers might find this musical play a strange inclusion in an anthology that seems seriously devoted to more painful examples of cultural conflict: war, ethnic cleansing, state terrorism and other subjects. In fact, the play is unique in that it's the only example of outright comedy in this collection — and an oddly familiar form of comedy, too. It seems to belong to that age-old genre of "generational comedy" that has amused audiences since the time of the ancient Greeks: children struggling against their parents, lampooning reactionary and conservative mores and strictures that are too rigid and uncompromising to permit a free expression of life, freedom and progress.

But beneath the surface of the play readers can detect something else at work that is very modern, speaking to us in a uniquely contemporary fashion. The issues that are singled out here — buying and selling in today's society, the obsession with technology and the influence of pop media — should raise red flags among parents, teachers and counselors. Of course, such issues not only confound adults but perplex our children as well; and when youth and adults come into conflict over the values embedded in those themes, then we have more than simple "generational conflict."

Today the "generation gap" continues to widen between adult and youth culture, and most painfully between parents and children. Increasingly we see in industrialized societies the disastrous effects upon children of the breakdown in domestic and institutional values as a result of increasing pressure from commerce and worldwide, media-propelled cultural entertainment — not to mention a host of other pernicious influences such as crime, drugs, social upheavals and the like. Mirjana Buljan's play takes a lighthearted, fantastical glance at all this from the unique perspective of the children who, in *Mutiny in Crazyland*, actually take over adult society and remake it according to their standards: no more money, no more reckless skateboarding and bike-riding, no more sarcastic "attitudes" flaunted at parents. Just respect. Just plain "crazyland."

It is noteworthy to point out that when the play was originally produced in 1981 at the Zagreb Youth Theater, the author had to change the title from *Mutiny in Crazyland* to *Crazy Days in the Crazyland*, in order to avoid censorship and political interference with the production. "Mutiny" was a very conspiratorial and dangerous word in eastern Europe prior to the early 1990s, and artists in Zagreb — especially at the struggling Youth Theater — had no wish to be branded as political satirists. But even the suffocating atmosphere of an academic round table that was created with prominent child psychologists and pedagogues and others to accompany the premiere, could not stifle the success of this play which held the stage for a number of years and is frequently considered for revivals.

Characters

Charley *(a puppet)*
Alka, *a Crazyhead*
Dara, *a Crazyhead*
Miki, *a Crazyhead*
Kiki, *a Crazyhead*
Tiny
Mom & Dad Kiki
Mom & Dad Miki
Grandma
Grandpa
Little Girl 1
Little Girl 2
Boy
Whitejoy *(a Western boy)*

Ebony *(a boy from Africa)*
Pong-ping *(a girl from Asia)*
TV Presenter

Character Notes

CHARLEY is a stylized child, comical and even ugly but in an attractive way. He and the TV PRESENTER wear similar costumes: a suit and a cap in bright checks, a tie with large spots or stripes, also in the appropriately lively colors.

The CRAZY HEADS: ALKA, DARA, KIKI AND MIKI are children aged ten to twelve. KIKI is a smarty-pants and wears eyeglasses. The CRAZY HEADS wear garish disco costumes and have punk hairdos.

MOM and DAD KIKI are a plump couple, Mom is sexy, while Dad has a big, fat tummy. Mom is flirty, while Dad is always trying to get something for nothing.

MOM and DAD MIKI are slim.

GRANDPA and GRANDMA: GRANDPA is a youngish oldster, he wears youthful clothes, blue jeans, and is covered in chains, pendants and earrings, he has a gray beard and is balding. GRANDMA fits the old concept of grandmothers, her hair is in a bun and she dresses in black.

TINY is a small boy who sometimes still uses baby-style talking.

WHITEJOY is a fair-haired boy who wears a safari suit, while EBONY wears an African toga.

PONG-PING is a raven-haired little girl from Asia.

TV PRESENTER is there at the beginning, present but unconscious until the end, when he helps to set to rights the topsy-turvy world of Crazyland.

1   **SCENE ONE**

2

3   *(On the stage a television set stands to the side. The TV*
4   *PRESENTER comes onstage with a microphone around his*
5   *neck. The lights come on, illuminating him. He stands*
6   *beside the TV set, adjusts his hair, and then his tie. He looks*
7   *for his eyeglasses, and pulls out the text he will be reading.*
8   *He looks towards the audience and gives a few test smiles.)*
9   **TV PRESENTER:** *(Testing the microphone)* **Testing, one, two,**
10   **three.** *(He looks at the audience again, smiles again.)* **Dear**
11   **Viewers, a sensational piece of news is coming in from all**
12   **the world agencies** — *(He is interrupted by a ball coming*
13   *from the audience, knocking him down. In his place,*
14   *CHARLEY enters in the same outfit.)*
15   **CHARLEY: Hi there, everybody! Dear viewers, dear friends,**
16   **welcome from your always crazy Charley Bang-bang! This**
17   **is Crazyland Radio & Television. Crazyville Associated**
18   **Press has announced that there has been a children's**
19   **coup in Crazyland! All power is now in the hands of the**
20   **children led by the craziest Crazy Heads, known for their**
21   **crazy hit, "We're All Crazy ... "** *(The CRAZY HEADS appear*
22   *on the screen, waving to the audience.)* **... and here they**
23   **are ... the four great Crazy Heads: Alka Roller ...** *(ALKA*
24   *comes out onto the stage on her rollers, and bows to the*
25   *audience.)* **... Dara Guitar ...** *(DARA appears with her guitar*
26   *and strikes a few chords. And KIKI and MIKI, the greatest*
27   *experts on everything else, join them.)*
28   **EVERYONE:** *(Singing)* **Crazy you, crazy me,**
29   **And you and he and you and me,**
30   **Come on now, one, two, three**
31   **Crazy things are what you'll see ...** *(From the screen,*
32   *CHARLEY holds out the microphone to ALKA who is barely*
33   *able to maintain her balance in one place.)*
34   **CHARLEY: You all know Alka Roller! She's the famous contestant**
35   **from the great international Golden Roller Skates**

1   competition, where no one had a hope of beating her

2   coming in last ... *(ALKA waves to the audience and almost*

3   *topples over.)* ... because with extraordinary effort she

4   managed to remain for the entire race on the starting line.

5 ALKA: It was really hard, but I gave it all I had.

6 CHARLEY: Alka, the folks are asking about the new trends in

7   children's politics? *(ALKA rushes around the stage on her*

8   *roller-skates, while CHARLEY and the TV screen run after her.)*

9 ALKA: From now on, we're banning payment of fares in city

10   busses and trams. Everyone has the right to ride for free!

11   Since public transportation will be free, the use of all

12   other vehicles is banned — apart from rollers, scooters,

13   skateboards, bicycles, sleds and ice skates! The streets

14   may be used for walking, playing, hopscotch and things

15   like that. Many adults will be delighted with these

16   changes. For those of them who didn't have a chance

17   when they were kids to learn how to use the means of

18   transport mentioned, we're setting up courses in riding a

19   skate board, scooter, roller-skating, sledding, ice skating,

20   and bike riding. *(ALKA exits.)*

21 CHARLEY: Our second guest is another celebrity, Dara Guitar,

22   a former member of the "Hot Steam" group! Hi there,

23   Dara!

24 DARA: Hello, Charley! Do you have any idea how cute you are

25   on the screen?

26 CHARLEY: *(Embarrassed but pleased)* All the girls say that. And

27   now I have to ask you something, and you have to give me

28   a straight answer here in front of everybody – that's

29   what's called an interview, in case you didn't know.

30 DARA: Of course I know that. And I know even more ... I'm

31   opening a school.

32 CHARLEY: You are? What sort of school?

33 DARA: A rock school giving advanced training to moms and

34   dads, and grandpas and grandmas. Tuition will be free

35   and comprehensive! Kids, make it possible for grown-ups

1   to make up for the gaps in their knowledge. Help them to
2   gain a modern education! Give them everything you can
3   now, it'll be worth it in the future! Think of their
4   happiness! Enroll them in our rock school where I am the
5   principal – me, Dara Guitar, formerly from the "Hot
6   Steam" band, and now one of the Crazy Heads Four!
7   *(DARA returns the microphone to CHARLEY. She leaves,*
8   *waving to the audience.)*
9
10

11 **SCENE TWO**
12
13   *(MIKI and KIKI draw closer. They are exchanging something*
14   *between themselves, poking around in their pockets, and*
15   *near the front of the stage. CHARLEY comes over to them*
16   *with the TV "screen".)*
17 **CHARLEY:** *(Pushes the microphone in front of KIKI)* **And you**
18   **are ...**
19 **KIKI:** I'm Kiki.
20 **CHARLEY:** And you?
21 **MIKI:** I'm Miki.
22 **CHARLEY:** What are you doing?
23 **KIKI:** *(Nonchalantly)* You can see, swaps.
24 **CHARLEY:** *(Turning to the audience)* **Dear viewers, in the**
25   **Crazyland language that means exchanging.**
26 **KIKI:** We've abolished money as the means of payment and
27   have introduced swaps instead.
28 **MIKI:** In any case, money was one of the stupidest things ever
29   invented by grown-ups. First of all you sell something for
30   money, and then you give that same money to buy
31   something else – instead of just swapping things!
32 **KIKI:** I give you a rabbit, you give me a lion.
33 **MIKI:** Or – I give you a needle, you give me a fiddle!
34 **CHARLEY:** Guys – I'm all for swaps! I'll give you some
35   matches, you'll give me a flashlight!

1   *(CHARLEY hands them a box of matches, They put a small*
2   *flashlight into his hand. MIKI and KIKI put up a sign that*
3   *reads "SWAP SHOP." They stack all sorts of things at the side.*
4   *The CRAZY HEADS appear on the screen.)*
5   **CRAZY HEADS:** *(Singing)* **You had a lion, a lion, a lion**
6   **A terrible king of the jungle.**
7   **We had a mace, a mace, a mace**
8   **The terrible mighty kings the ace**
9   **Diddle, diddle, doo.**
10   **A lion for us, a mace for you,**
11   **The ace for us, the king for you,**
12   **Diddle, diddle, doo.**
13   **If you want a king**
14   **Give us your lion,**
15   **If you want the mace**
16   **Give us your ace**
17   **Diddle, diddle, doo.**
18   **CHARLEY: Isn't that wonderful, dear viewers! A whole lion for**
19   **some sort of king, a whole cat for just a hat! I think that**
20   **clears up any misunderstandings about the children's**
21   **economic reform program. It's just come in from**
22   **Crazyland Associated Press that the first Swap Shop has**
23   **been opened in the capital, Crazyville. You can swap**
24   **anything at all, and values will depend on supply and**
25   **demand. Our leading bank, Crazybank Savings and Loan,**
26   **will be publishing an exchange list every day. We're sure**
27   **that folks will be delighted with this news that will**
28   **improve the standard of living of the smallest buyer, the**
29   **so-called average kid.** *(The potential SWAPPERS start*
30   *gathering on the stage. MOM KIKI and MOM MIKI arm in*
31   *arm, then GRANDMA and GRANDPA, DAD KIKI and DAD*
32   *MIKI, and some CHILDREN, KIKI and MIKI, are putting up*
33   *a large notice board with a sign reading: "CRAZYBANK*
34   *SAVINGS & LOAN — EXCHANGE LIST." The GROWNUPS and*
35   *the KIDS gather around the notice board. EVERYONE is*

1   *carrying something. A fairground atmosphere. They press*
2   *around the notice board and the benches.)*
3   **MOM MIKI:** Ms. Kiki, just think, one cat for only ten mice, and
4   two at a discount for only fifteen!
5   **KIKI:** We have a lot of cats on sale.
6   **GRANDPA:** I can't see very well so could someone please tell
7   me the going rate for small white buttons? My pension
8   was paid out in small white buttons.
9   **DAD MIKI:** Disgusting. Why didn't they at least give you large
10   black ones? Surely you've earned that much!
11   **GRANDMA:** They offered us beautiful small green frogs, but
12   what would we do when they started hopping around the
13   house? At our age we could hardly run around after them.
14   **DAD KIKI:** Look, white buttons are holding their own. Ten for
15   one frog.
16   **GRANDPA:** I always say: keep your white buttons for black
17   days.
18   **GRANDMA:** And black days for white crows.
19   **SMALL BOY:** *(Waving his lollipop)* Anyone want a lollipop? A
20   lollipop for some hip-hop!
21   **DAD KIKI:** *(Importantly)* I think we should invest in frogs.
22   **DAD MIKI:** Have you heard something?
23   **DAD KIKI:** *(In a lower voice)* The storks have arrived and their
24   numbers will go down. Maybe there'll be a shortage of
25   frogs, but there'll be plenty of stork eggs.
26   **LITTLE GIRL 1:** I'm swapping chocolate for jelly!
27   **MOM KIKI:** Ms. Miki, what a lovely handbag! *(They both walk*
28   *over to the bench.)*
29   **MIKI:** That's real crocodile skin.
30   **MOM MIKI:** I'd even give ten cats for that.
31   **KIKI:** Out of the question. We're swapping it for an alligator.
32   **MOM MIKI:** Oh, for an alligator exactly?
33   **MIKI:** Or for some other tough guy.
34   **MOM MIKI:** Some tough guy?
35   **MOM KIKI:** Ms. Miki, what do you think, would my husband,

1   Mr. Kiki, be enough?

2   MOM MIKI: Ms. Kiki, I wouldn't do anything rash, it's better to

3   wait awhile, maybe you could get a better price – excuse

4   me, I meant to say – a better swap.

5   SMALL BOY I: Anyone want some marbles? I'm looking for

6   fishing hooks.

7   LITTLE GIRL 2: Do you have a big piece of chalk? I'll swap it

8   for my soft teddy bear. *(SMALL BOY 1 looks through his*

9   *pockets. He walks over to LITTLE GIRL 1. TINY joins them.)*

10   LITTLE GIRL 1: What we'd really like is to swap a sister for a

11   brother.

12   TINY: *(Tapping LITTLE BOY 1 on the shoulder)* What about it,

13   bro? I don't think there are many offers like that. *(The*

14   *small BOYS AND GIRLS seal their deal by shaking hands*

15   *with their arms crossed.)*

16   LITTLE GIRL 1: And now ... break it through! *(They break each*

17   *other's grasp, each BOY hugs one of the LITTLE GIRLS, and*

18   *then each COUPLE holds hands and mixes in with the others.)*

19   GRANDMA: Ah, what a good thing that we've saved a lot of

20   white buttons all our lives. Now perhaps we'll have a

21   chance to swap them.

22   GRANDPA: For a real, live granddaughter!

23   GRANDMA: I'd even give my right arm for a granddaughter!

24   DARA: *(Running over to them and hugging them)* And I wanted

25   to give all my books, all my toys and all my CDs, even my

26   guitar, for a real Grandma and Grandpa.

27   GRANDPA: Well then, what are we waiting for? Let's get down

28   to business.

29   GRANDMA: We'll take you, Dara Guitar, and you'll take us as

30   your Grandma and Grandpa! *(They, too, shake hands the way*

31   *they do at country fairs and then break each others' grasps.)*

32   CRAZY HEADS: *(Singing)* Isn't it better to swap things

33   Than to buy and sell.

34   'Cause this world is all ours

35   And the lion could be yours.

1   **As for the great lion**

2   **The one they call the king,**

3   **What's a king, what's a mace**

4   **When we hold the ace,**

5   **Diddle, doodle, diddle.**

6   *(ALL of them are swapping things to the rhythm of the song,*

7   *and this gradually develops into a choreographed dance.*

8   *The SWAPPERS alter the stage setting, take down the signs,*

9   *close the counters.)*

10

11

12   **SCENE THREE**

13

14   *(A new sign above the counter: "DRIVING LICENSES." A*

15   *queue of people holding rollers, ice skates, tricycles or*

16   *pulling along sleds, pushing bicycles, skate boards, are all*

17   *lined up in front of the counter. There is a space for parking*

18   *to the side. Various "vehicles" are parked there. Among*

19   *them, a luxurious scooter with a radio antenna stands out. It*

20   *is all shiny chrome and has a host of extras. TINY is standing*

21   *at the center of the stage doing the work of a traffic*

22   *policeman. KIKI and ALKA are giving out driving licenses at*

23   *the counter. The people stand patiently in line holding their*

24   *various "vehicles" under their arms. ALKA examines each*

25   *"vehicle" while MIKI is stamping the driving licenses.)*

26   **KIKI: Please keep moving. Next, please!**

27   **ALKA: Yes, of course. All right!**

28   **KIKI: Next!**

29   **ALKA: All right!**

30   **MIKI:** *(Joining them)* **How's everything going?**

31   **ALKA:** *(She is examining a pair of rollers when one of the wheels*

32   *comes off in her hands)* **These rollers are excluded from**

33   **traffic for the moment.** *(DAD MIKI and DAD KIKI arrive.*

34   *They are both carrying their "vehicles," a second-hand*

35   *tricycle and an old scooter, under their arms. They stop*

1   *beside the parking area, admiring the luxurious scooter.*

2   *They circle around it.)*

3   **DAD MIKI:** *(With amazement)* **Well, Mr. Kiki, what do you have**

4   **to say?**

5   **DAD KIKI: A Harley Pinocchio automatic!**

6   **DAD MIKI: The last word in technology.**

7   **DAD KIKI: What would you say, Mr. Miki? How much would**

8   **this little beauty be worth?**

9   **DAD MIKI: Man to man – I'd say at least ten of these scooters**

10   **of mine!**

11   **DAD KIKI: If I only knew whose son bought this crazy bauble**

12   **for his dad.**

13   **DAD MIKI: And I'm interested in the jerk who's going to ride it!**

14   **DAD KIKI: Ah, he's surely some son's silly, spoiled dad!**

15   **DAD MIKI: Yeah, some eager beaver and snitch.**

16   **DAD KIKI: But still, all the girls will be crazy about him!**

17   **DAD MIKI:** *(Almost crying)* **And even though we're the coolest,**

18   **so strong and muscular ...** *(He pokes out his chest and flexes*

19   *his biceps)* **... the girls don't even look at us with these**

20   **wrecks!** *(He kicks out angrily at his scooter. DARA and*

21   *GRANDPA join them. They approach the new scooter. DARA*

22   *hands GRANDPA his permit.)*

23   **DARA: Here you are, Grandpa. Here's your scooter and here's**

24   **your permit.**

25   **GRANDPA:** *(Delighted, overjoyed)* **Dara, are you giving this to**

26   **me as a present? How did you know that this was just the**

27   **vehicle I've wanted ever since I was a kid?** *(DARA wraps a*

28   *scarf around GRANDPA's neck, adjusts his tie, behaving like*

29   *a grandmother fussing over her grandchild, kisses his*

30   *forehead, takes out a handkerchief and wipes his nose.)*

31   **DARA: You take care now, don't go too fast ...**

32   **DAD MIKI:** *(Surprised)* **It's just not possible, Dara, that you gave**

33   **this to such a ...**

34   **DAD KIKI:** *(Taking his head in his hands)* **... to such an old**

35   **bungler?**

1   **GRANDPA:** *(Angrily)* **That dad of yours is a bungler!**

2   **DARA: Why shouldn't I give it to him? He's my only**

3   **grandfather! I'd give him everything I could.**

4   **DAD MIKI: So is it any wonder that our grandmothers and**

5   **grandfathers are so childish and spoiled!**

6   **GRANDPA: Your dad is childish and spoiled!**

7   **DARA: Isn't he cute? He always has the last word! That's the**

8   **way, Gramps, you show them, let them see what a cool guy**

9   **you are!**

10 **GRANDPA:** *(Shouting)* **Yoo-hoo!** *(He races off on the scooter and*

11   *does a few turns around the stage.)*

12 **DARA: No one can ever understand the love of a grandchild,**

13   **until they experience it themselves ...**

14 **DAD KIKI:** *(To DAD MIKI as they go towards the counter)* **My son**

15   **told me that grandchildren are to blame that their**

16   **grandfathers sometimes grow down into rowdies, but I**

17   **can't believe it ...** *(In front of the counter. DAD KIKI joins*

18   *the queue, standing in line after a couple of children. ALKA*

19   *checks his three-wheeler.)*

20 **KIKI: Alka, check it out, see if the old fella knows how to ride!**

21 **ALKA: Get on, please ...** *(DAD KIKI is confused.)* **Now then, one**

22   **leg right, one left ...** *(ALKA shows him how to hold the*

23   *handlebars.)* **You hold on here ...**

24 **DAD KIKI:** *(To KIKI)* **Come on, Kiki, what is all this about? You**

25   **know what a whiz I am on a three-wheeler! I taught you**

26   **how to ride one, for goodness sake!**

27 **KIKI: When was that? Those were different times! You hardly**

28   **ever saw a three-wheeler in the street then. But look now!**

29   **A real traffic jam! You can't step out into the street, there**

30   **are so many three-wheelers, scooters, toy cars and skate**

31   **boards!**

32 **TINY:** *(Standing next to DAD KIKI and DAD MIKI)* **Move along**

33   **there, you're holding everybody up! The regulations are**

34   **the same for everyone! No preferential treatment!** *(DAD*

35   *KIKI sits angrily on his three-wheeler, and jangles his bell.)*

1 **DAD KIKI: I'll show you how to ride!** *(DAD KIKI starts off*
2 *towards MIKI and runs into GRANDPA coming from the*
3 *opposite direction. They both fall, get to their feet, roll up*
4 *their sleeves and approach each other threateningly.)*
5 **DAD KIKI: You idiot, you moron! What fool gave you a license!**
6 **GRANDPA: You weren't even born when I was riding a**
7 **skateboard! But I'd bet anything you're riding that three-**
8 **wheeler without a license, you clown!** *(They attack each*
9 *other and start punching. The PASSERS-BY make a ring*
10 *around them like a boxing ring and start cheering them on.*
11 *TINY, the traffic cop, plays the role of the referee.)*
12 **GRANDMA: Let him have it under the right rib, Grandpa!**
13 **MOM MIKI: Right on the chin!**
14 **MOM KIKI: Don't baby him, set into him like Tyson!** *(TINY, the*
15 *traffic cop, makes sure the fight is fair. He separates the*
16 *boxers, blows his whistle at fouls, writes out fines, hands*
17 *them out, calls the end of the rounds. GRANDMA and MOM*
18 *KIKI cool off the boxers, rubbing them down with towels,*
19 *giving them instructions, lightly slapping their cheeks.)*
20 **GRANDMA: Watch out for his left, he's a southpaw! Keep your**
21 **guard lower ...**
22 **MOM KIKI: Do something with your legwork! Did you see how**
23 **he hops around? Get the lead out ...** *(TINY signals with his*
24 *whistle that the next round is starting. The BOXERS rush at*
25 *each other.)*
26 **CHARLEY:** *(From the screen, in an excited voice)* **Dear viewers!**
27 **The traffic police have announced that traffic is blocked at**
28 **the Main Street intersection because of a collision between**
29 **Dad Kiki and Dara's grandpa. A fight has broken out**
30 **between the parties and they're trying to solve it in a**
31 **sporting way. You're watching the third deciding round of**
32 **this exceptionally interesting fight. Grandpa is on the left,**
33 **one hundred and eighty centimeters tall ...** *(CHARLEY sizes*
34 *him up)* **... seventy kilograms. Dad Kiki is on the right, one**
35 **hundred and seventy-five centimeters tall, weighing in at**

1   **about one hundred kilograms. The first two rounds were a**
2   **draw. There, look at Grandpa's killing left hook, even Ali**
3   **would envy it. I have just heard that EUROVISION has asked**
4   **to tune in and has offered a huge amount for the rights to**
5   **broadcast this exciting sporting event. Dad Kiki is now**
6   **trying to hit Grandpa's chin – and all of Europe is watching!**
7   **A great fight, folks! Fantastic. The referee, Tiny the traffic**
8   **cop, is doing a fine, conscientious job. Now an uppercut**
9   **from Grandpa! Dad Kiki is tottering. He's down! Tiny gives**
10   **the count.** *(TINY blows his whistle and starts counting,*
11   *marking each count with a wave of his arm. DAD KIKI gets to*
12   *his feet on "three" and punches GRANDPA with a shattering*
13   *blow. GRANDPA goes down. TINY counts as far as "three"*
14   *again, and GRANDPA straightens up as TINY blows the signal*
15   *for the end of the fight, taking a hand of each of the fighters*
16   *and lifting them together.)* **We're waiting for the judges'**
17   **decision. It's a draw! Look at that, dear viewers, the**
18   **opponents are shaking hands, congratulating each other,**
19   **hugging each other, and there's a kiss on the cheek!**
20   *(GRANDMA and MOM KIKI are clapping with delight. The*
21   *EUROVISION signal sounds. The ONLOOKERS start to leave.*
22   *DAD KIKI and GRANDPA pick up the pieces of their "vehicles."*
23   *They tip their hats to each other and go their separate ways,*
24   *arm-in-arm with their respective wives. The onlookers pick up*
25   *their "vehicles" from the parking lot and depart. Only a few*
26   *which have parked in the NO PARKING zone are left. TINY*
27   *writes out their tickets and sticks them on the "vehicles." The*
28   *TOWING SERVICE arrives, hooks up the offending "vehicles"*
29   *and tows them away with a great deal of noise.)*
30
31
32   **SCENE FOUR**
33
34   *(School. The STUDENTS are dancing in a disco atmosphere.*
35   *A light show. GRANDPA is banging away at the drums. All*

1   *the ADULTS are dressed as children. DARA GUITAR is*
2   *making her way from the back of the stage through the*
3   *throng of dancers. She is holding a microphone and moving*
4   *to the rhythm of the music.)*
5   **DARA: Good evening, dear parents, good evening, dear**
6   **viewers! Welcome to our newly-opened rock-music school!**
7   *(The DANCERS move apart. We can see the child-sized desks.*
8   *The PARENTS sit at them. GRANDPA is still sitting in front of*
9   *the drums. GRANDMA throws a paper plane at him. He*
10 *throws it at DARA's back. DARA turns around.)*
11 **DARA: Grandpa, sit in the front row this minute!** *(GRANDPA*
12 *sheepishly does as he is told. Behind DARA's back, the whole*
13 *CLASS is throwing things all over the place. Some of the*
14 *STUDENTS poke out their feet so that they fall over them.*
15 *The general atmosphere is that of a restless classroom. KIKI*
16 *is the worst of the lot.)*
17 **DARA: The first thing I want to make clear is that we're having**
18 **minor misunderstandings from time to time, because it's**
19 **still not clear to all of you that relations between students**
20 **and teachers have changed, but there are still those**
21 **among you who are trying to maintain things as they**
22 **were. However, I want to inform you that a new rule**
23 **comes into force today, and telling tales is strictly**
24 **forbidden! Copying from the student next to you and**
25 **whispering the answers to questions is not only allowed, it**
26 **is desirable! Little parents, we want you to become one**
27 **with the class without any of you standing out, and that**
28 **with fraternal concern towards the majority who know**
29 **hardly anything at all, you all remain as you have been –**
30 **likable blockheads! The first is always last and only the**
31 **last shall be first! And now – settle down! Quiet! We're**
32 **live!** *(A red signal lights up high above the middle of the*
33 *stage, and all of them stay motionless in the same position.)*
34 **CHARLEY:** *(From the TV screen)* **Dear viewers, dear studio**
35 **guests, dear students of the rock school!** *(He strikes the pose*

129

1   *of a quiz master.)* **We are happy to be able to welcome you to**
2   **the first broadcast of our rock-music education series for**
3   **school radio-television!** *(They all come alive again.)*
4   **CRAZY HEADS:** *(Singing)* **Everyone's crazy, except us,**
5   **Here's a lion, here's a mace,**
6   **The king too, but not the ace,**
7   **Not even for a hundred cakes —**
8   **Just for all the fun it makes!**
9   **DARA: You've just heard a quaint little song, a wonderful**
10   **example of simplicity, no deep message, sure to be what**
11   **we call a hit! Now then, I want someone to tell me in their**
12   **own words with the others helping what "hit" actually**
13   **means!** *(A bell rings just like in a TV quiz marking the time,*
14   *and the clock starts ticking. The sound of whispering and*
15   *fidgeting.)* **Anyone like to try? Let's see ... I have to warn**
16   **you about the time ...** *(Again the sound of whispering as the*
17   *STUDENTS try to agree among themselves. GRANDPA*
18   *nudges DAD MIKI to stand up. DAD MIKI hesitates but*
19   *stands up and goes towards the audio cabin. He puts on the*
20   *earphones.)*
21   **CHARLEY: There, dear viewers, we have our first candidate!**
22   **DAD MIKI:** *(Triumphantly and with self-assurance)* **"Hit" means**
23   **when you hit a ball!**
24   **DARA: What do you mean? Could you please explain!** *(Audible*
25   *murmuring among DAD KIKI's helpers, we can pick up*
26   *someone saying "hit parade," and "the latest hit.")*
27   **DAD MIKI:** *(Slowly, guessing)* **Well, as in ... well, hit parade!**
28   **DARA: Wonderful, Dad Miki! And now if you will just explain**
29   **what "hit parade" means?**
30   **DAD MIKI: That's simple enough!** *(Importantly:)* **A parade of hits!**
31   **You know ... soccer. Let's say goals made by the head, from**
32   **the right lower corner to the left upper corner of the goal!**
33   **DARA:** *(Confused)* **There seems to have been a small**
34   **misunderstanding. We're talking about music. Your**
35   **answer is not quite clear. How do we stand on points,**

1   **Charley?**

2   **CHARLEY:** I have to ask viewers to be patient. The jury is still

3   counting. *(CHARLEY bends his head, disappears for a*

4   *moment and then appears again with a piece of paper.)* **The**

5   **jury has decided that the answer can be accepted.**

6   **DARA:** Charley, did you tell them that this is not a quiz about

7   soccer? *(CHARLEY disappears again and reappears.)*

8   **CHARLEY:** Folks, please excuse this brief interruption to the

9   broadcast while the jury make their decision on the

10   similarity and differences between soccer and rock-music

11   education! In the meantime, let's listen to one of the

12   possible correct answers to the question:

13   **CRAZY HEADS:** *(Singing)* **Not all chocolate,**

14   **Not all marmalade,**

15   **Makes a real hit parade!**

16   **If you want to feel fit**

17   **Then go out and buy the Hit,**

18   **Even just a piece of it**

19   **Makes you smile and benefit!**

20   **CHARLEY:** Chocolate-marmalade cake! Hittiest of all the hits!

21   **DARA:** Well now, dear little parents, can anyone tell me what is

22   the most essential element in this song, the most

23   important idea, the essence of it? A real hit parade, or

24   feeling OK, or maybe the hittiest of all the hits? *(The bell*

25   *rings, the clock starts clicking. Again we hear the murmurs*

26   *and the whispering.)* **Anyone?**

27   **GRANDPA:** *(Putting his hand up)* I know, I know!

28   **DARA:** Go ahead, Grandpa, the microphone is yours!

29   *(GRANDPA rushes into the audio cabin and puts on the*

30   *earphones. He shouts.)* **The cake!** *(Wild applause)*

31   **DARA:** There you are, that's the way to answer! Grandpa, are

32   you staying on?

33   **GRANDPA:** Only if you give me Hit, even just a piece of it!! I

34   love cakes, especially hittiest of all the hits!

35   **DARA:** I don't have any —

1 GRANDPA: I want the cake!

2 DARA: Be patient, Grandpa! You'll get one when you answer all
3   the questions.

4 GRANDPA: *(Sulking)* I want one now! If you don't give me one, I
5   won't play any more! *(He defiantly puts down the earphones*
6   *and goes back to his place. He thumbs his nose at DARA.)*

7 CHARLEY: You can see what sort of misunderstandings arise
8   because of a lack of a real understanding of what
9   education is all about! That's why we've sent out an urgent
10   call for assistance. We've heard that a package with the
11   cake Hit is on its way to the rock-music school and other
12   cultural institutions of particular importance. *(The AID*
13   *WORKERS arrive. They put down their cartons full of cookies*
14   *and hand out one to everybody present. DARA takes more*
15   *than one as befits her role and fills her mouth with them.)*

16 DARA: *(Speaking with her mouth full)* And now, back to
17   business! Dear little parents, who can tell me who wrote
18   the inspired song hit about the Hit cake? *(Whispering*
19   *between the parents: "The Blue Butcher-Birds," "No, the*
20   *Black Buttons" "No, no, the Stoning Rolls." DAD KIKI raises*
21   *his hand.)*

22 DARA: Dad Kiki? This is a surprise! Your son Kiki will be very
23   proud! Go ahead! *(The bell rings, the clock starts clicking.)*

24 DAD KIKI: May I please be excused!

25 DARA: What did you say? Don't you want to answer?

26 DAD KIKI: *(Fidgeting like someone who needs urgently to go to*
27   *the little boys' room)* I can't, I really must be excused! Now!

28 DARA: Haven't you already been ... *(She is embarrassed now.)* ...
29   there?

30 MOM KIKI: Dara, can't you see he's kidding you? Be excused,
31   indeed! He wants to go outside and smoke! He only waited
32   to get his cake, and now he'd like to cut class!

33 DAD KIKI: Snitch! *(He gives MOM KIKI a shove.)*

34 ALL THE CLASS: Yuck! Boo!

35   Mom Kiki is a snitch

1   Let her go to see a witch

2   And ask there for a cake

3   She will give her just a snake

4   Or a monster from the lake

5   And a slimy homeless snail

6   To bring her the daily mail

7   'Cause even an ugly witch

8   Hates the tell-tale and the snitch!

9 MOM KIKI: I am not a snitch! It's not true! Our son Kiki told

10   me that I had to keep an eye on my husband because he

11   had strictly forbidden him to smoke. And you should

12   listen to your children, shouldn't you, Dara? *(MOM KIKI*

13   *starts sobbing, DARA strokes her hair.)*

14 DARA: There now, it's all right, Mom Kiki!

15 MOM KIKI: I suppose you'll give her a candy now!

16 GRANDPA: And you said that snitches would be thrown out of

17   school!

18 DARA: You have to see the difference between telling tales and

19   friendly, helpful informing.

20 GRANDMA: How do we know which is which?

21 DARA: That will be my problem! All you have to do is let me

22   know everything that's going on. There can't be any

23   secrets between us. We must have full trust. Parents

24   mustn't hide anything from their children! Because –

25   remember this – your children are your best friends.

26 MOM KIKI: *(Sniffling)* I keep telling that to my husband, Mr.

27   Kiki – but he's very naughty and just pulls my hair!

28 DARA: Dad Kiki? Is that true?

29 DAD KIKI: I'm not the only one! All the boys pull the girls' hair.

30 THE GIRLS: That's true, that's true!

31 DARA: *(Going over to GRANDPA)* Grandpa, you too?

32 GRANDPA: *(Confused)* Well ...

33 DARA: Do you pull Grandma's hair?

34 GRANDPA: Not just hers ...

35 GRANDMA: *(Jumping to her feet as if she has sat on a stinging*

1   *nettle)* **Who else's hair do you pull, you big oaf? How**
2   **dare you pull another gal's hair? Just you wait ...** *(Tugging*
3   *at his ears:)* **... I'll show you when we get out of class!**
4   **Behind my back, eh?** *(GRANDPA and GRANDMA start in the*
5   *way kids do.)*
6   **DARA:** *(Pounding on the desk with her fist)* **Stop that now!** *(She*
7   *separates them.)* **Shame on you! You two are supposed to**
8   **give an example to the others! I can't believe my eyes! Both**
9   **of you will have to stand in the corner. Grandpa, you in**
10   **that one, and you Grandma, over there!** *(She points to the*
11   *corners on opposite sides.)* **And now I think I'll have to move**
12   **Mom Miki because she's a bad influence on Mom Kiki,**
13   **who would surely be an exemplary last in the class, if she**
14   **had a different husband, Dad Miki, for instance ... Well,**
15   **Dad Miki, collect your things and move over to Mom Kiki's**
16   **desk. Dad Kiki, you go and sit next to Mom Miki.**
17   *(DAD KIKI makes a Dumbo ears gesture with his hands at*
18   *MOM MIKI. As DAD MIKI goes past him, DAD KIKI tries to*
19   *trip him with his outstretched leg, and doesn't notice that*
20   *DAD MIKI has hung something on his back. MOM KIKI*
21   *strokes DAD MIKI's cheek, while MOM MIKI bangs her guitar*
22   *on DAD KIKI's head as he sits down beside her at her desk.)*
23 **DARA:** **I hope your behavior will improve now, otherwise I**
24   **shall have to call in your children to a Children Teacher**
25   **Association meeting!**
26 **THE CLASS:** *(Disappointed)* **No, not that, we'll be good!**
27 **DAD KIKI:** *(Getting to his feet)* **I solemnly promise that we will**
28   **do our very best to learn as little as possible and earn the**
29   **very best failing marks!**
30 **DAD MIKI:** *(He starts rapping, and the others join in)* **The less**
31   **you know, the better off you are.**
32 **MOM MIKI:** **"A's" spoil easily, F's are the best, so not to worry,**
33   **if you're worse than all the rest!**
34 **GRANDPA:** **When you know a lot, happy you're not.**
35 **GRANDMA:** **No gain, no pain.**

1 **DAD KIKI: A diligent man has everything, a lazybones even**
2 **more, if he knows the score.**
3 **DARA:** *(Surprised)* **Where did you learn all this? Who's been**
4 **filling your sweet little ears with such pieces of wisdom?**
5 *(All of them hold up a little book of the same format.)*
6 **MOM KIKI: It's all in here!**
7 **DAD MIKI: The wise words of the Crazy Heads!**
8 **GRANDMA: Compiled and adapted by Kiki and Miki.**
9 **DARA:** *(Taking one of the books and reading from it)* **For**
10 **children up to the age of fourteen only!** *(She holds up the*
11 *book and cries out in a strict voice.)* **Forbidden reading for**
12 **adults! So as a punishment you will all get a special merit!**
13 **THE CLASS:** *(Disappointed and saddened)* **No, Dara, why? What**
14 **did we do?**
15 **DARA: Because wise words are not planned for in our classes!**
16 **You are here to learn rock-music which will make it**
17 **possible for you to live a carefree life and to have a good**
18 **time. Don't you realize, little parents, that it's all for your**
19 **own good! All we want is for you to be happy and carefree ...**
20 **CRAZY HEADS:** *(Singing)* **The wise men are all dead**
21 **So play the fool instead**
22 **And be a crazy head.**
23 **Crazy you, crazy me,**
24 **And you and he and you and me,**
25 **Come on now, one, two, three**
26 **Crazy things are what you'll see ...**
27 *(The CLASS becomes restless, they throw around pieces of*
28 *paper, use their sling-shots, the BOYS pull the GIRLS' hair,*
29 *peep under their skirts, trip each other ... and leave.)*
30
31
32 **SCENE FIVE**
33
34 *(MOM KIKI and MOM MIKI run in out of breath. They are*
35 *pushing a doll's pram. They stop and look around. Then they*

1   *start taking make-up out of the pram, powder their noses,*

2   *comb their hair, make themselves pretty, straighten their*

3   *skirts, tuck in their blouses. It is obvious they have been in*

4   *some sort of skirmish. A bench in the park)*

5   **MOM MIKI: Ms. Kiki, how long are we supposed to let our guys**

6   **beat us and pull our hair like this?**

7   **MOM KIKI: Ms. Miki, that gang will be the end of us!**

8   *(GRANDMA enters, She is also disheveled and untidy — and*

9   *angry, too. She is also pushing a pram with two dolls in it.*

10   *She stops beside MOM KIKI and MOM MIKI.)*

11   **GRANDMA: Oh, girls, this is terrible! I don't even dare go**

12   **home ...**

13   **MOM KIKI: We'll have to tell our children.**

14   **MOM MIKI: If my Miki knew about this!**

15   **GRANDMA: Dara heard about it and she let Alka know.**

16   **MOM KIKI: Just wait until my Kiki gets hold of them!**

17   *(ALL three of them sit on a bench. They take the dolls out of the*

18   *pram and start playing with them. MOM KIKI and MOM MIKI*

19   *have dolls dressed like little boys [Miki and Kiki] while*

20   *GRANDMA has two little girl dolls [Dara and Alka]. They dress*

21   *the dolls, give them their bottles, comb their hair, rock them in*

22   *their arms and show what they are saying with their gestures.)*

23   **MOM MIKI: My Miki, too!** *(She lifts her doll and makes a*

24   *threatening gesture with its arm.)*

25   **GRANDMA: Dara's not just a hot guitar player, she also**

26   **bankrolled some projects.**

27   **MOM KIKI: But still, Kiki's the strongest one. He could even**

28   **wrestle an elephant to the ground.**

29   **MOM MIKI: But my Miki is building Kon-Tiki.**

30   **GRANDMA: No wonder, when Dara put up all our buttons! And**

31   **everyone knows only Alka can win the Golden Rollers.**

32   *(ALL three start to sing and play dancing.)*

33   **MOM KIKI:** *(Cunningly and curiously)* **Where is little Miki,**

34   **sailing on Kon-Tiki?**

35   **MOM MIKI: Along a great crazy river, across a great crazy sea ...**

1   GRANDMA: *(Mockingly)* **Over a crazy mountain, maybe ...**

2   MOM KIKI: *(Importantly)* **My Kiki is destined for the heights!**

3   GRANDMA: **From the ups to the downs!** *(She gestures a fall with*

4   *her hand.)*

5   MOM KIKI: **Better that way than not at all.**

6   MOM MIKI: **Is something worrying you, Grandma old?**

7   GRANDMA: **Perhaps I'm old and crazy, but Dara is worth more**

8   **than a crazy river, or a crazy sea, or two crazy mountains!**

9   MOM MIKI: **So is my Miki ...**

10   MOM KIKI: **And my Kiki ...**

11   MOM MIKI: **They have an elephant, they have a raft ...**

12   MOM KIKI: **They have a river, they have a sea ...**

13   MOM MIKI: **They have two crazy mountains ...**

14   MOM KIKI: **And the uplands and the lowlands ...**

15   GRANDMA: **So what, who cares! One day, in a year or two, my**

16   **little girls will have all that and them, too.**

17   *(On all sides, the sounds of KIKI, MIKI, ALKA and DARA*

18   *calling their family members to lunch. "Mom Miki, lunch!"*

19   *"Grandpa, it's time to wash your hands!" "Dad Kiki, come*

20   *home at once!" "Lunch is on the table!")*

21

22

23   **SCENE SIX**

24

25   *(The dining-room at the Kiki household. MOM and DAD*

26   *KIKI and little TINY are sitting on small chairs at a small*

27   *children's table. The table is set for lunch. KIKI comes in and*

28   *puts chocolate on each of their plates.)*

29   DAD KIKI: *(With a grimace of disgust)* **Phooey, chocolate again?**

30   MOM KIKI: **We had chocolate yesterday!**

31   KIKI: *(To TINY)* **You see, little one, how they try to shame me in**

32   **front of you!** *(He turns to the parents.)* **Aren't you ashamed**

33   **of yourselves, we have a guest and you behave like this.**

34   TINY: **Kiki, please don't get upset, that's the way parents are.**

35   **We have to be patient. One day when they grow down it**

1   **will be easier with them.** *(KIKI sits with them at the table.*
2   *DAD KIKI unwraps the chocolate and makes an airplane of*
3   *the silver paper, throwing it at MOM KIKI's head.)*
4 **MOM KIKI: Kiki, Dad Kiki won't leave me alone! He threw a**
5   **plane at my head!**
6 **DAD KIKI: She poked me with a knitting needle!**
7 **MOM KIKI: That's not true, that's a lie! Kiki, you can see I don't**
8   **have a knitting needle.** *(She shows him her empty hands.)*
9 **DAD KIKI: You did it yesterday!**
10 **MOM KIKI: Yesterday! Are you crazy? Making things up ...**
11 **DAD KIKI: Yesterday, during lunch, but I'm not a tattle-tale!**
12 **KIKI:** *(Banging his fist on the table)* **That's enough! Does there**
13   **have to be an argument during lunch every day? It spoils**
14   **every mouthful! I have told you a hundred times that**
15   **when you're at the table, you eat and keep quiet!**
16 **TINY: This chocolate with walnuts, dried grapes and marzipan**
17   **is absolutely lovely. Why don't you eat, dear little parents?**
18   **Why are you bothering poor Kiki?**
19 **KIKI: There, even my guest has to quiet you down! Mom, how**
20   **long are you going to play with that chocolate? Dad, you**
21   **haven't even touched yours! What are the two of you**
22   **thinking?**
23 **DAD KIKI: I can't even stand the sight of chocolate any more!**
24   **It's the same thing every day: chocolate, candy, cookies! I**
25   **want a good steak! I'd give my life for some roast pork!**
26 **MOM KIKI: I'd like some southern-fried chicken with spinach —**
27   **mmm. I wouldn't even say no to a Vienna schnitzel.** *(She*
28   *clicks her tongue.)* **Tender and juicy ...**
29 **TINY: You have to eat what's on your plate! All good, obedient**
30   **parents eat what they're given. My Mom and my Dad**
31   **wouldn't ever dream of complaining. They tried to once,**
32   **you know, and they didn't get anything to eat for three**
33   **days. Now I never have any trouble with them.**
34 **KIKI: No picking and choosing, you say?**
35 **TINY: Picking and choosing? Out of the question!**

1 KIKI: As you can see, I'm gentle and indulgent with them and
2   now I have to blush at the way they're behaving in front of
3   you. I try to talk them round in a friendly way – I've told
4   them, my greatest concern is their health ... *(The TV set*
5   *comes in.)*
6 CRAZY HEADS: *(Singing in an advertising style)*
7   Chocolate makes you strong and big
8   It's better than an egg and meat ...
9   Sugar, milk and vitamins
10   Cocoa and proteins
11   Chocolate is a real hit
12 CHARLEY: *(Shouting)* High calorie, tasty and healthy! So, dear
13   parents, not even a day without chocolate! Kids, make
14   your parents happy! Buy them candy, cookies and rolls –
15   all made of chocolate!
16 KIKI: You heard Charley! Surely you believe me now?
17 MOM KIKI: If Charley says so – I'll have some more!
18 TINY: Why do you all listen to Charley! My Mom's crazy about
19   him, too!
20 MOM KIKI: Because he's so sweet and on the TV and TV never
21   lies.
22 DAD KIKI: They just repeat what other people say to them ...
23 CHARLEY: *(Going on in the same tone)* Our fathers are
24   sometimes wild, our mummies always mild. They're
25   gracious and sweet, tidy, gentle and obedient.
26 MOM KIKI: I've eaten my chocolate, aha! I've eaten my
27   chocolate!
28 KIKI: *(Stroking her hair)* Son's good little Mom! You see, she
29   can be really good when she wants to. Isn't she a sweetie?
30 TINY: As sweet as honey ... *(He strokes MOM KIKI's cheek.)* ... as
31   a piece of candy!
32 CHARLEY: *(Continuing in the advertising style)* So, you guys, be
33   good to them. Make them happy with small presents and
34   large presents. Our department store has everything for
35   your wife, your sister, your grandma and your aunt.

1   **KIKI: Since you've been such a good girl, you can make a wish!**

2   **MOM KIKI:** *(Clapping her hands)* **I'd like a new dress! I need a**

3   **new dress!**

4

5

6   **SCENE SEVEN**

7

8   *(The sound of the low, gentle music played for fashion*

9   *shows. The lights go down, except on the side where a*

10   *"runway" passes by the table. A model LITTLE GIRL in a*

11   *stylized dog costume appears on the "runway.")*

12 **CHARLEY: Our unbeatable designer, the great Coco Spaniel,**

13   **shows her newest high fashion collection. For this season,**

14   **she foresees her typical dark rings around the eyes which**

15   **give such a sad, secretive and feminine appearance. This**

16   **year ears are silky and down to the floor. The fur of the**

17   **coat must be long, curly and soft. This wonderfully**

18   **refined little lady, winner of so many international**

19   **awards, has created a completely new collection,**

20   **unknown until now, for care of the ears without washing,**

21   **using her enchanting perfume "Coco Spaniel 5."**

22   *(MOM KIKI gives a rapturous sigh and sneezes loudly. The*

23   *MODEL looks down on her, and then goes over to her and*

24   *wipes her nose with a handkerchief. Then she lifts MOM*

25   *KIKI's hair and examines her ears. She also looks at the ears*

26   *of DAD KIKI and those of the others at the table. She puts*

27   *some bottles on the table, one smaller than the others, bows*

28   *and leaves the stage with her model's walk. They all take a*

29   *bottle, dampen their index fingers and rub their ears.)*

30 **CHARLEY:** *(With emphasis)* **No more ear washing in the cold**

31   **sleepy mornings! A collection for the whole family! Peace**

32   **in the house, no tears and no arguments – and the lovely**

33   **smell of perfume everywhere ...**

34 **MOM, DAD, KIKI and TINY: Coco Spaniel 5 – at six every**

35   **morning and throughout the day ...**

1   **KIKI:** *(Banging his fist on the table)* **But you can forget about the**
2   **dress!**
3   **MOM KIKI: Why, Kiki?**
4   **KIKI: Because they're useless and superfluous, because you**
5   **have closets full of them! Because you wear everything**
6   **once and then you aren't interested in them any more ...**
7   **But then we don't know what to do with them! They're all**
8   **around the house.**
9   **TINY: Although there are many moms in the world who have**
10   **nothing to wear ... and they'd be happy if they had at least**
11   **one change of clothes ...**
12   **KIKI: Dear Mummy, I'd like to give you something useful and**
13   **healthy. For instance, roller skates.**
14   **MOM KIKI:** *(Surprised and disappointed)* **Roller skates?**
15   **KIKI: You don't get enough exercise, you need to do some**
16   **jogging or something! So you'd be able to wear some**
17   **beautiful old dresses that don't fit now.**
18   **DAD KIKI: You've started to put on weight!**
19   **KIKI: You keep out of this, no one asked for your opinion!**
20   **TINY: My dad's the same. He interferes in everything.**
21   **KIKI: So he has to have the last word, too?**
22   **TINY: Oh no, as far as that's concerned ...** *(Proudly and in a*
23   *strict tone:)* **... what I say goes.**
24   **KIKI: Did you hear that, you two? Other parents aren't treated**
25   **with kid gloves ... It's time that I woke up! So there it is,**
26   **Mom, you're getting roller skates and that's the end of it!**
27   **MOM KIKI: But, Son, what if I fall?**
28   **DAD KIKI:** *(Mockingly)* **Perhaps you'll break your nose and bite**
29   **the tip off your tongue!**
30   **MOM KIKI: Did you hear that? That's the way he makes fun of**
31   **me, even in front of guests ...**
32   **DAD KIKI: I was only joking. Surely you don't think I mind**
33   **that you'll be getting roller skates! Kiki can buy you two**
34   **pair as far as I care, I don't envy anyone, especially not**
35   **you! You really need them anyway. You're beginning to**

1   look like a barrel!

2   **MOM KIKI:** *(She starts yelling, hitting her fists on the table and*

3   *banging her feet on the floor)* **Like a barrel – he dares to**

4   **say that to me, and he looks like a wineskin with that**

5   **paunch!** *(She hurls a plate at his head.)* **It's finished**

6   **between us! Over! I'll never play with you again! Never,**

7   **ever! From now on, I'll play with Mr. Miki! So there!**

8   **DAD KIKI:** **What did you say?** *(Leaping angrily to his feet*

9   *and grabbing her shoulders:)* **Say that one more time!**

10 **MOM KIKI:** **Kiki – Dad Kiki is hitting me!** *(KIKI jumps to his*

11   *feet and separates them. He pulls at their ears.)*

12 **MOM KIKI:** **It's not my fault ... he started it!**

13 **KIKI:** **Silence! I don't want to hear another word! You'll both**

14   **get roller skates because you've been so naughty! And now**

15   **pick up the guitar and put on the CDs, and until you learn**

16   **to play you're both grounded!** *(MOM and DAD KIKI are*

17   *subdued and leave. KIKI sits down and rests his head in his*

18   *hands.)* **They both have to get the same gifts, or there's no**

19   **peace in the house.**

20 **TINY:** **Don't upset yourself, Kiki! Mine are just the same ... they**

21   **fight over nothing at all, because of ridiculous parental**

22   **things. Then they make up, but we're left with the**

23   **headache ...**

24 **CRAZY HEADS:** *(Singing)* **You'll be happy just like me,**

25   **Never tears or sorrow see.**

26   **Choose an armchair comfortably**

27   **Then find Charley on TV.**

28   **Charley gives advice for free**

29   **If it's happy you would be,**

30   **Never tears or sorrow see.**

31

32

33   **SCENE EIGHT**

34

35   *(GRANDPA is singing the song and accompanying himself*

1   *on the drums. At the other end of the stage, GRANDMA is*
2   *recording with headphones on her ears.)*
3   **GRANDPA:** *(Singing)* **Charley gives advice for free**
4   **If it's happy you would be,**
5   **Never tears or sorrow see.**
6   *(DAD MIKI comes in with his guitar over his shoulder. He is*
7   *carrying a basket.)*
8   **DAD MIKI: Sorry, I'm a bit late ...**
9   **GRANDPA: Where have you been?**
10 **DAD MIKI: Over seven crazy mountains, across seven crazy**
11   **seas, where a crazy lake is ... and your dear Dara lives,**
12   **that's where the secret is ...** *(GRANDMA puts aside the*
13   *earphones and goes over to the basket.)*
14 **GRANDMA: Our Dara told you?**
15 **DAD MIKI:** *(Rubbing his hands together with satisfaction)* **She**
16   **told me ...**
17 **GRANDPA: But what did she tell you?**
18 **DAD MIKI:** *(Secretively)* **Did you ask about the stork's eggs?**
19 **GRANDMA:** *(Surprised)* **Did we ask about what?**
20 **GRANDPA:** *(Secretively)* **Grandma doesn't know anything yet.**
21   *(He draws DAD MIKI aside. GRANDMA looks at the basket.)*
22   **I would like ... to talk alone with you ... to start with.**
23 **DAD MIKI: Of course ...** *(GRANDMA stands there in two minds.*
24   *She is trying to hear what they're saying, and she'd also like*
25   *to know what is in the basket.)*
26 **GRANDPA: The thing is that Grandma and I would like to have**
27   **more grandchildren, not just Dara. At least a little**
28   **grandson.** *(GRANDMA goes after them and listens to what*
29   *they're saying.)* **Do you maybe know how children are**
30   **made, and where we could get some?**
31 **DAD MIKI:** *(Confused)* **Well now ... you really have surprised**
32   **me. Your question isn't an easy one ... I don't know what to**
33   **tell you ...**
34 **GRANDPA:** *(Insistently)* **The truth, of course, just tell me the**
35   **truth.** *(GRANDMA is close by, eavesdropping on their*

1 *conversation.)* **Don't hide anything from me. Surely I'm**
2 **old enough ...**
3 **DAD MIKI: Still ... it's a sensitive matter ...**
4 **GRANDPA: You don't have to worry! I won't tell anyone, not**
5 **even Grandma.**
6 **DAD MIKI: Actually, my father told me, and his father told**
7 **him, while we were still small, that the stork brought us in**
8 **a basket like that one ...** *(DAD MIKI points at the basket.)*
9 **GRANDPA: They told me that when I was small, too. However —**
10 **you know Mr. Kiki — well, when we were talking about it,**
11 **he swore that babies were lowered down into the house**
12 **through the chimney.**
13 **DAD MIKI: Look, I wouldn't take everything Mr. Kiki says at**
14 **face value. He makes things up sometimes, he likes to joke**
15 **around ... or just mix the things up. Through the chimney**
16 **comes Santa Claus.**
17 **GRANDPA: Well, yes, I thought it was fairly unconvincing. And**
18 **beside that, these new houses often don't have chimneys**
19 **so it would be quite impractical for babies.**
20 **DAD MIKI: And for Santa Claus.**
21 **GRANDMA:** *(Going near to them)* **I was told —**
22 **GRANDPA: Have you been listening?**
23 **GRANDMA: Oh!** *(She is embarrassed.)* **Please don't be angry, I**
24 **know it's not nice, but I've always been interested in**
25 **everything, ever since I was a little girl.**
26 **GRANDPA: What was it that they told you?**
27 **GRANDMA: That in olden times babies grew in the garden.**
28 **But you know I'm not as young as I used to be — I can't**
29 **remember if they grew under the cabbages or under the**
30 **lettuce.**
31 **DAD MIKI: Interesting, an interesting theory — however, it still**
32 **hasn't been scientifically proven.**
33 **GRANDPA: Does that mean that you go with the stork story?**
34 **DAD MIKI: That depends ...**
35 **GRANDMA: Are storks good layers?**

1   **GRANDPA: And even more importantly, are they good sitters?**

2   **DAD MIKI: Well, now ... would you like to see some stork eggs?**

3   *(He jumps over towards the basket.)* **Exactly ten eggs, just**

4   **what you asked for.**

5   **GRANDMA: And how much do you want for them?**

6   **DAD MIKI: Well ... seeing it's you ... and because of Dara ... I'd**

7   **swap them for a good pair of scissors.**

8   **GRANDPA: You're sure they're fresh?**

9   **DAD MIKI: I took them directly from the nest.** *(GRANDMA*

10   *takes an egg from the basket and gently shakes it, and then*

11   *goes on to do the same with the remaining eggs, and then*

12   *returns them all to the basket. She takes a large pair of*

13   *scissors from her pocket and hands them to DAD MIKI.)*

14   **DAD MIKI:** *(Examining the scissors)* **Thank you, that was a**

15   **really equitable swap.**

16   **GRANDMA: Good luck to you then!**

17   **DAD MIKI: Whenever you need anything, just let me know!**

18   **Maybe some other eggs if we're wrong about the storks?**

19   *(DAD MIKI leaves. GRANDMA and GRANDPA look with*

20   *delight into the basket.)*

21   **GRANDMA: Just as well you didn't tell him how storks make**

22   **babies out of their eggs. Just think, if everybody heard**

23   **about it, there would be a real rush for their eggs!**

24   *(GRANDMA settles herself on the eggs.)*

25   **GRANDPA:** *(Helping Grandma to sit carefully on the eggs)* **Then**

26   **we wouldn't get them for less than ten pairs of scissors.**

27   *(GRANDPA brings a skein of wool and sits down in front of*

28   *GRANDMA. They start to wind the wool into a ball.)* **Only**

29   **one thing bothers me. How long do you have to sit here for**

30   **the babies to be born, and how long for little storks?** *(They*

31   *both think about the problem.)*

32   **GRANDMA: Didn't your father tell you when you were small?**

33   **GRANDPA: My father thought I should know as little as**

34   **possible about it.**

35   **GRANDMA: Just like my Mom ...**

1 GRANDPA: **Perhaps we should tell Dara to teach us in her**
2   **school about sitting on stork eggs, and not just about rock**
3   **music.** *(There is a ring on the front doorbell.)*
4 GRANDMA: *(Excitedly)* **That must be Dara. What should I do**
5   **now? I should give her lunch ...**
6 GRANDPA: *(Helping Grandma to her feet)* **You go ahead, don't**
7   **worry about anything. Whenever it's necessary, I'll always**
8   **sit in for you.** *(GRANDMA leaves, while GRANDPA settles*
9   *down on the basket. Instead of sitting on it, he falls into the*
10   *basket and his face takes on a agonized expression. He slowly*
11   *stands up, turning his back to the audience. The seat of his*
12   *trousers is bright yellow from the broken eggs.)*
13 GRANDPA: **I didn't know that babies were so breakable.**
14
15
16   **SCENE NINE**
17
18   *(At the Miki house. DAD MIKI has a punk hair-do and color*
19   *and he is dressed in the disco dancer style. But he is having*
20   *trouble dancing to the disco music. One moment his ankle*
21   *gives way, the next, his back hurts and he freezes in an*
22   *impossible position. MIKI is sitting next to the stereo putting*
23   *on the CDs, and illuminating DAD MIKI in various colors,*
24   *using a flashlight. MIKI beats out the rhythm with his hand.*
25   *DAD MIKI stops dancing, his body in a twisted position.)*
26 DAD MIKI: **Son, that's it, I'm finished!**
27 MIKI: **You MUST go on! At least four hours a day! You'll only**
28   **become a well-known disco dancer if you practice.**
29 DAD MIKI: **Who told you I wanted to become a well-known**
30   **disco dancer? That's the last thing I want!**
31 MIKI: **It's not important what you want, but what I want! And**
32   **I think it's a great profession for a cool dad.**
33 DAD MIKI: **I'd rather look for birds' eggs and frogs.**
34 MIKI: **Aren't you ashamed of yourself? You, my dad, the father**
35   **of such a well-known son?**

1   **DAD MIKI: When I was small, they told me that all work is**
2   **equally honorable and worthwhile!**
3   **MIKI: We say that now, too, but ask the girls what they think**
4   **about it.**
5   **DAD MIKI: You want me – a real cool dad – to ask girls for**
6   **their opinion?** *(MOM KIKI comes in, looks at DAD MIKI who*
7   *is still in his unusual pose, and stops in her tracks,*
8   *enchanted with him.)*
9   **MOM KIKI: Oh, my dear Mr. Miki – you really are wonderful!**
10   *(DAD MIKI is flattered and to impress her even more, he*
11   *ventures a couple of additional dance figures.)* **Simply**
12   **fantastic ... unbelievable!** *(These new attempts have left*
13   *DAD MIKI frozen in an even stranger position.)*
14   **DAD MIKI: Yow!**
15   **MOM KIKI: Don't stop now, please!** *(Very slowly, to the sound of*
16   *moaning, DAD MIKI tries to untwist his body.)* **What**
17   **perfection of movement ...** *(DAD MIKI has managed to*
18   *unravel himself and stands proudly upright. MIKI turns off*
19   *the music.)*
20   **MIKI: Did you hear that? Perfection of movement! If you only**
21   **knew, Ms. Kiki, if you only knew how much effort I've put**
22   **into making a man of him, and he threatens me with**
23   **collecting birds' eggs and frogs!**
24   **MOM KIKI: Mr. Miki, to waste such talent and good looks!**
25   **Instead of being grateful to your son for everything he's**
26   **doing for you! Do you think our children are so**
27   **demanding of us because of some silly ideas they have?**
28   **MIKI: Our only wish is to offer you a happy life in the new**
29   **world that we're building. Parents have never had it as**
30   **good as today! We've bought you electric guitars, stereo**
31   **systems, CDs, you have the very best rock-music**
32   **education! Your tummies are full of cream cakes, candy,**
33   **chocolate and sweets – puddings, custards, ice-cream,**
34   **honey ...** *(DAD MIKI is tottering from exhaustion.)* **... while**
35   **in other parts of the world parents are hungry and have to**

1   **wage war for their rights!** *(DAD MIKI finally collapses.)*

2 **DAD MIKI:** *(Weakly)* **If I could only have a sausage or a bit of**

3   **ham ...**

4 **MIKI: Sorry about that, all I have is chocolate – some people**

5   **are just never satisfied!** *(MOM MIKI runs over to DAD MIKI.)*

6 **MOM KIKI:** *(She takes DAD MIKI's limp hand in hers and he*

7   *moans)* **Can I play with him now?**

8 **MIKI:** *(Stroking her head)* **All right – but be quiet and nice, so I**

9   **don't have trouble with the neighbors later.**

10 **MOM KIKI:** *(Joyfully)* **Thank you, Miki, we'll be good! Don't**

11   **worry!**

12 **MIKI:** *(He starts to leave and then pauses)* **Be careful, don't**

13   **overdo it ...**

14 **MOM KIKI: Of course we'll be careful, Miki.**

15 **MIKI: Watch yourselves ...** *(MIKI goes to the edge of the stage*

16   *and lounges in a rocking chair. He picks up a telephone that*

17   *stands on a small table and starts dialing a number.)*

18 **MIKI: Alka, is that you ... ?** *(He sighs deeply.)* **Yes, I'm finally**

19   **alone. What a day ... The old folks? Mom has gone to town,**

20   **she's swapping around, while Dad Miki is playing with**

21   **Ms. Kiki ... Can I come over ... ? In ten minutes ... Ciao!**

22   *(MIKI leaves.)*

23

24

25   **SCENE TEN**

26

27 **DAD MIKI: Ow!***(MOM KIKI has taken a large syringe, a huge*

28   *bandage, a stethoscope out of her bag, followed by a white scarf*

29   *with a red cross on the front, which she ties around her head.)*

30 **MOM KIKI:** *(In a sweet tone)* **There, now ... we'll play hospitals.**

31   **Mr. Miki, keep still and be patient, because you are very,**

32   **very ill.** *(MOM KIKI takes DAD MIKI's pulse, places her hand*

33   *on his forehead, listens to his heart-beat, and then starts*

34   *straightening his twisted limbs. At each of MOM KIKI's*

35   *interventions, DAD MIKI moans. She picks up the syringe.)*

1   **MOM KIKI:** **Since this is hurting so much, I think I'll have to give**

2   **you some curative salts in curative water ...** *(DAD MIKI*

3   *suddenly straightens up and moves away from the syringe.)*

4   **DAD MIKI:** *(Agitated and frightened)* **Madame Kiki, I've had**

5   **enough of playing hospitals. I'd rather play company**

6   **directors and secretaries.**

7   **MOM KIKI:** **But we haven't got the toys for that game.**

8   **DAD MIKI:** **What about playing mummies and daddies?**

9   **MOM KIKI:** **We'd need other clothes for that.** *(She removes the*

10   *registered nurse scarf from her head and takes out a*

11   *wedding dress from her bag. She hands DAD MIKI a top hat.*

12   *He doesn't take it, but moves away from her.)*

13   **DAD MIKI:** *(Confused)* **Weddings was not what I meant.**

14   **MOM KIKI:** **What else is there?** *(She picks up the syringe.)* **Or we**

15   **could go on playing hospitals.**

16   **DAD MIKI:** *(With alarm)* **But no injections?**

17   **MOM KIKI:** **We have to have injections ...**

18   **DAD MIKI:** **All right then – I give in.** *(He puts the top hat on his*

19   *head. MOM KIKI puts on the wedding dress and a long white*

20   *veil. She stands up and with difficulty straightens up DAD*

21   *MIKI. She puts her arms through his. GRANDMA and*

22   *GRANDPA come in. They stop in astonishment.)*

23   **GRANDMA:** **What does this mean?**

24   **MOM KIKI:** **We're playing weddings. Do you want to be our**

25   **witnesses?**

26   **GRANDPA:** *(Cheerfully)* **I've always loved weddings and funerals!**

27   **GRANDMA:** **Because of plenty of good food and drink!**

28   *(GRANDMA and GRANDPA pick up the end of the bride's*

29   *veil. The procession starts moving, although DAD MIKI is*

30   *walking shakily.)*

31   **GRANDMA:** **Mom Kiki and Dad Miki ...**

32   **GRANDPA:** **A couple in love ...**

33   **GRANDMA & GRANDPA:** **We'll swap them a present. A pot for**

34   **a dove!** *(MOM MIKI arrives back from town and stands there*

35   *frozen, holding a ham in her hand.)*

1   **MOM MIKI:** *(Stuttering)* **Mm ... mm ... Madame ... K ... K ... Kiki**
2   **... and m ... my ... hus ... husband ...**
3   **GRANDMA & GRANDPA:** *(Cheerfully)* **A couple in love!**
4   **MOM KIKI: Miki said it was all right but he told us to be**
5   **careful because of the neighbors.**
6   **MOM MIKI: Whaat?**
7   **GRANDMA & GRANDPA: We'll swap them a present. A pot for**
8   **a dove!** *(MOM MIKI rushes angrily at MOM KIKI and throws*
9   *the ham in her face. DAD MIKI grabs the ham, hugs it to him*
10   *lovingly, and runs away.)*
11   **MOM KIKI: You cow, you coarse, bad-mannered cow!** *(MOM*
12   *MIKI defiantly pokes her tongue out at MOM KIKI.)*
13   **MOM KIKI: Witnesses. Did you see that? She poked out her**
14   **tongue at me! She dares to make fun of me ...**
15   **MOM MIKI:** *(In a fighting mood)* **Oh, really? You're breaking**
16   **my heart!** *(She attacks MOM KIKI. GRANDMA and*
17   *GRANDPA try to separate them. KIKI and MIKI arrive. They*
18   *each catch hold of their mothers' ears and separate them.*
19   *MIKI takes his mom and dad off the stage.)*
20
21
22   **SCENE ELEVEN**
23
24   *(At the Kiki home. MOM and DAD KIKI rush in, stumbling as*
25   *if someone has pushed them from behind. KIKI follows*
26   *them in and he doesn't look at all pleased.)*
27   **KIKI:** *(Angrily)* **Who would ever have thought that I would**
28   **experience something like that from my own parents!**
29   **Simply shameful! Mom, how could you fight with Mom**
30   **Miki ... ?**
31   **MOM KIKI:** *(Interrupting him in a tearful voice)* **She started it,**
32   **she hit me first!** *(In tears)* **Ask Grandma and Grandpa!**
33   **KIKI:** *(In a thundering voice)* **Silence! I'm speaking now!** *(He*
34   *turns to DAD KIKI.)* **And what about you? Do you know**
35   **where I just was?**

1   **DAD KIKI:** *(Fearfully)* **No, I don't ... how would I know that ... ?**

2   **KIKI: You don't know, eh? From the children-teacher association**

3   **meeting at the rock-music school!**

4   **DAD KIKI:** *(Stalling)* **Oh, yes ... I forgot to tell you ... that Dara was**

5   **asking all the children to come ... to that CTA meeting ...**

6   **KIKI: You forgot that Dara had asked the children to come in**

7   **for that meeting? That didn't surprise me when I heard**

8   **what your grades were like! A disaster! The very worst last**

9   **in the class! Who do you think I collect marbles and**

10   **buttons for, who do I climb trees for looking for birds'**

11   **eggs, and wade through the pond for, looking for frogs ...**

12   **and what do I get in return? All I ask from you is that you**

13   **study, study, study, and I've taken over all the worry and**

14   **responsibility for everything so that you two can have a**

15   **carefree parenthood. Just so you know, we're turning a**

16   **new leaf, and I'm going to be much stricter with you!**

17   **Here, you'll find a quiz in this magazine about the best**

18   **Crazy Heads over the last ten years ...**

19   **DAD KIKI: Ten?**

20   **KIKI: That's right, ten! And until you solve the quiz, there's no**

21   **playing outside, no television. You're grounded!** *(KIKI*

22   *gives each of them a copy of the magazine.)* **And now I don't**

23   **want to hear another word from either of you!**

24   **MOM KIKI: My son, do you smoke?**

25   **KIKI: Yes, I smoke – and what of it?**

26   **DAD KIKI: Why don't you let me smoke then?**

27   **KIKI: Of course I don't let you. Cigarettes are not for adults,**

28   **they can even be very harmful for you, your lungs are all**

29   **damaged, you all have chronic bronchitis, pharingitis,**

30   **laryngitis, not to mention the state of your heart and your**

31   **blood pressure! The only thing that can save you is that**

32   **you stop smoking before it's too late. And anyway, why are**

33   **we having this conversation? I don't have to explain to**

34   **you. Surely it's enough that I say you must not smoke!**

35   **MOM KIKI:** *(Timorously)* **But ... don't you think it's harmful ...**

1   for your lungs, too?

2 **KIKI:** Please Mom, I've had a very hard day. The meeting and

3   arranging the welcome ceremony for our dear guests, the

4   Children's World Delegation, who are going to visit us, the

5   press conference, and finally that damned meeting at the

6   school, which finished me right off! *(Suddenly shouting:)*

7   And why am I explaining all this to you? Surely you're the

8   one to talk to me about smoking! *(He looks at his watch.)*

9   Pick up your things, go to your room, and don't let me

10   hear a sound out of you!

11 **DAD KIKI:** Why not?

12 **KIKI:** I have guests coming. Come on, hurry up and tidy this

13   mess! Mom, you put away that knitting, and Dad, take out

14   the newspapers.

15 **MOM KIKI:** Who's coming?

16 **KIKI:** My friends ... and when children come to visit their

17   friends, parents have no business there. When Miki has

18   guests, his parents are as quiet as mice. You don't see

19   them and you don't hear them ... that's what I call good

20   upbringing! *(MOM KIKI pulls at DAD KIKI's arm, but he*

21   *stands there defiantly. The sound of the front-door bell*

22   *ringing.)* What are you standing there for? *(In an irritated*

23   *tone:)* Off you go ... they're here!

24 **DAD KIKI:** I'm not moving ... *(MOM KIKI rushes about picking up*

25   *her things and DAD KIKI's newspapers. KIKI goes to open the*

26   *door. DAD KIKI stamps on the floor in protest. The GUESTS*

27   *come in — the children's delegation: KIKI, ALKA and DARA.)*

28 **THE GUESTS:** Good evening! Hello! *(The GUESTS say their*

29   *greetings in foreign languages.)*

30 **DARA:** Good evening, little parents!

31 **DAD KIKI:** My deepest respects! *(ALKA strokes his head.*

32   *EBONY, a boy from Africa, goes over to MOM KIKI and*

33   *pinches her cheek.)*

34 **EBONY:** Oh, Kiki, you have such sweet parents ...

35 **DARA:** If they'd only try harder at the rock school.

1   **KIKI:** But they've promised to do better. We just had a very
2   serious talk, and I told them that they're grounded until
3   they improve their grades.
4   **PONG-PING:** Your mom is a real sweetie. *(She gives MOM KIKI a*
5   *resounding kiss.)* **Such pink cheeks.** *(As PONG-PING speaks,*
6   *she pronounces separately the syllables in the words.)*
7   **KIKI:** It's all make-up, you have no idea how much it all cost
8   me! But our parents are everything in the world to us, so
9   no sacrifice is too great.
10   **MIKI:** But these little golden curls. *(He runs his fingers through*
11   *her hair.)* **Just like a little angel!**
12   **KIKI:** That's Hair Highlight Number Ten.
13   **DARA:** Well, at least Dad Kiki's red nose is completely natural,
14   isn't that so? *(DARA squeezes his nose.)*
15   **DAD KIKI:** *(In pain)* **Gently, Dara, gently!**
16   **DARA:** Sorry, but I just love fat red noses! They're made to be
17   pinched.
18   **ALKA:** Your old folk really look wonderful, Kiki. If you look at
19   the parents, you can see what the children are like. But do
20   they mind you?
21   **KIKI:** What can I say, you know what parents are like!
22   **DARA:** Dear little parents, I've brought you a small present. I
23   know what you like – roast pork, crackling, not greasy,
24   but juicy!
25   **PONG-PING:** Peking duck! *(She hands them a package.)*
26   **EBONY:** Grilled locusts! *(He hands them a bag.)*
27   **WHITEJOY:** Potato chips and salad ... *(He gives them a picnic*
28   *box. DAD and MOM KIKI are beside themselves with joy,*
29   *they hug each other and jump about hugging their presents,*
30   *and then filling their mouths with these delicacies.)*
31   **MOM & DAD KIKI:** This is our craziest day in Crazyland!
32   You're simply wonderful children! Long live the children
33   of the whole world!
34   **KIKI:** Did I hear someone say thank you? You forgot to say
35   thank you!

1   **MOM & DAD KIKI:** **Thank you! Thanks! Danke! Merci!**

2   **KIKI:** **They've set to as if they never see food! You make me**

3   **blush in front of my guests!** *(He turns to the guests.)*

4   **They're always eating, sweets, puddings, ice-cream, honey.**

5   **But it seems that what they're given by others is always**

6   **sweeter. Every time they're asked to somebody's place for**

7   **a meal, they always eat too much and have tummy trouble**

8   **the next day. Instead of leaving something for later.** *(KIKI*

9   *turns back to MOM KIKI and DAD KIKI.)* **Leave something**

10   **for later! Our friends will think you're starving ...**

11   **ALKA:** **Please don't talk like that, Kiki. You can see how Mom's**

12   **blushing, this time for real and not from rouge ...** *(MOM*

13   *KIKI chokes on a mouthful, DAD KIKI thumps her on the*

14   *back.)* **You see, she almost choked!**

15   **KIKI:** **Alka, you know I believe in discipline, and our parents**

16   **are terribly spoiled ...**

17   **EBONY:** **Your parent very advanced! Our parent not so**

18   **advanced ...**

19   **PONG-PING:** *(Separating her syllables)* **In Asia, Mom hungry and**

20   **love cake. Not difficult with food, but have other problem.**

21   **WHITEJOY:** *(Striking a wise pose with his hands in his pockets*

22   *and his tummy poked out, speaking with a British accent)*

23   **It's completely up to us what the parents of the world are**

24   **like. The tree does not fall far from the apple. Developed**

25   **children who are not hungry must help the undeveloped**

26   **and hungry kids!**

27   **EBONY:** **With potato chips?**

28   **PONG-PING:** **And salad?**

29   **KIKI:** **Dear friends.** *(He tries diplomatically to change the*

30   *subject.)* **My little parents would like to say good-night.** *(He*

31   *turns to MOM and DAD KIKI.)* **Come on, old folks, say**

32   **"good-night" nicely to everyone.**

33   **MOM & DAD KIKI:** **Good-night!**

34   **THE GUESTS:** **Bye-bye, Adios, good-night!**

35   **KIKI:** **And now into the bathroom, off with that make-up and**

1   **under the shower! Mom, don't forget your night cream**
2   **and your neck-cream!**
3 **ALKA: Sweet dreams, little parents!** *(The PARENTS leave, and the*
4   *CHILDREN sit down at a large table, facing the audience. TINY*
5   *arrives with his MARINES. Other GUESTS come in: CHARLEY,*
6   *GRANDMA and GRANDPA, MIKI with his parents.)*
7
8
9   **SCENE TWELVE**
10
11   *(The GUESTS start decorating the stage for a ceremonial*
12   *welcome to a foreign delegation. They hang up garlands of*
13   *candy, gingerbread men, and write on a banner, "LONG*
14   *LIFE TO THE CHILDREN OF THE WORLD." The sounds of*
15   *march music issues from the loud speakers.)*
16 **CHARLEY:** *(Happily, and then with solemnity)* **Crazyland, our**
17   **guests will soon be here, friends from all four corners of**
18   **our planet, Earth! People of Crazyland, let's all decorate our**
19   **capital, Crazyville! Let's all give a real Crazyland welcome**
20   **to our guests! Crazyland Associated Press has announced**
21   **that the first international children's delegation will soon**
22   **be arriving in our country! This is one of the most**
23   **important and significant moments in our history, the first**
24   **international recognition of life as we live it!** *(The*
25   *CRAZYLANDIANS roll out a red carpet. The CRAZY HEADS*
26   *arrive, led by ALKA on her rollerblades. MOM KIKI, MOM*
27   *MIKI and DAD MIKI are waiting at the end of the red carpet,*
28   *holding huge ice cream cones. DAD KIKI is photographing the*
29   *CRAZY HEADS. Then the PARENTS arrive, and the HONOR*
30   *GUARD OF MARINES, with TINY leading them. The*
31   *MARINES are wearing caps made of newspaper. Beside them*
32   *are the HONOR GUARD DRUMMERS — two little girls — with*
33   *their tin drums at the ready.)*
34 **CHARLEY: Well folks, as you can see, all of Crazyland is on its**
35   **feet! Everyone has come to welcome the delegation from**

1   **abroad.** *(CHARLEY is very excited.)* **They'll be here any**
2   **minute and they're arriving on a giant one hundred-miler**
3   **skateboard.** *(The sound of applause and shouts of "Hurrah!"*
4   *The DELEGATION: EBONY, WHITEJOY and PONG-PING*
5   *arrive on the stage on a huge skateboard. The DRUMMERS*
6   *give a roll on their drums. The PARENTS hand them their*
7   *giant ice cream cones, come down from the bench and*
8   *mingle with the Crazy Foursome.)*
9 **CHARLEY:** *(Who can't hide his delight)* **The first children's**
10   **delegation to visit our country is now arriving on its giant**
11   **skateboard. The parents, Moms Kiki and Miki and Dads**
12   **Miki and Kiki, are presenting them with their ice creams.**
13   **Our great Crazy Heads are greeting their friends!**
14 **CRAZY HEADS:** *(Singing in a ceremonial rhythm, as everyone*
15   *stands to attention)* **Dear Crazyland, we sing to Thee**
16   **Land of the happy and the free**
17   **With power in the hands of kids**
18   **Who all eat candy and play in the streets**
19   **And if anyone doesn't like sweets**
20   **He better keep quiet about this.**
21   **In our land only the bad guys and mice**
22   **Like savories but don't like sweets**
23   **And that's why this Crazyland happy and nice**
24   **Is loved by everyone, not just by kids**
25   *(Applause and shouts of approval.)*
26 **TINY: Honor guard! Attenshun!!! Quick march!** *(The HONOR*
27   *GUARD marches pass the GUESTS and the CRAZY HEADS.*
28   *The CRAZY HEADS together climb up onto the giant*
29   *skateboard and move off, while the HONOR GUARD take*
30   *their skate boards and stand to the side accompanying them.*
31   *The CROWD showers the delegation and the CRAZY HEADS*
32   *with candies, cakes and sweets.)*
33 **CHARLEY: Dear viewers! As you can see, all of Crazyland is on**
34   **its feet! Everyone has come to welcome these**
35   **distinguished guests! They're being showered by the**

1 **crowd with all sorts of candies. The world has never seen**
2 **a welcome like this one!** *(The procession moves off as all of*
3 *them on the skateboard wipe away from their faces the signs*
4 *of the welcoming candies and cakes.)*
5 **CHARLEY: After this welcoming ceremony, the guests and**
6 **their hosts will be coming together at a conference where**
7 **the main theme of their official discussion will be the**
8 **advancement of swapping and borrowing in international**
9 **co-operation and the children's rights all over the world.**
10 *(The band plays the Crazyland anthem.)*
11
12
13 **SCENE THIRTEEN**
14
15 *(TINY's MARINES put four chairs behind and four on one*
16 *side of the large table, and two at the opposite side. TINY*
17 *comes in leading MOM and DAD MIKI, and MOM and DAD*
18 *KIKI. They sit on the four side chairs. GRANDMA and*
19 *GRANDPA follow them in and sit on the two chairs at the*
20 *other side. A courtroom. Judges: the CRAZY HEADS. The*
21 *accused: MOM and DAD MIKI, and MOM and DAD KIKI. The*
22 *witnesses: GRANDPA and GRANDMA. CHARLEY, the*
23 *CHILDREN'S DELEGATION, CRAZYVILLE CITIZENS.)*
24 **CHARLEY: Hey there, guys! We're at the Crazyland Supreme**
25 **Court in the capital, Crazyville. This is a public trial**
26 **coming to you live! As you can see, the courtroom is full of**
27 **curious Crazylandians who expect to see real Crazyland**
28 **justice. The members of the first international children's**
29 **delegation to our country are guests at the trial, and**
30 **they'll be taking home the experience they gain here.**
31 **Order in the Court! The trial is about to begin!** *(CHARLEY*
32 *blows his whistle. ALKA gets to her feet.)*
33 **ALKA: Dear accused!**
34 **TINY: The accused cannot be "dear!"**
35 **DARA: The parents are dear even if they are accused.**

1 **MIKI:** All right, let them be "dear."

2 **ALKA:** Dear accused, you must be very sad because fate has

3   brought you to court, accused of fighting and being bad.

4   How do you plead?

5 **KIKI:** *(Whispering)* It was Tiny who brought them to court, not

6   fate!

7 **ALKA:** *(Whispering back)* But it's fate and what they ate that

8   brought them to trial! *(Loudly to the parents:)* Do you

9   confess?

10 **MOM KIKI:** Confess what?

11 **ALKA:** That you are sad.

12 **THE ACCUSED:** *(Sadly)* We confess. It's better to be sad than to

13   be bad.

14 **ALKA:** What say the witnesses?

15 **THE WITNESSES:** It's true.

16 **ALKA:** Thank you. That's an unmitigating circumstance.

17 **DAD KIKI:** Why?

18 **ALKA:** You're not only guilty, but also sad and not mad of being

19   guilty. So I ask the judges to issue a judgment on the final

20   justice in this trial. *(ALKA sits down.)*

21 **KIKI:** The accused Mom and Dad Kiki will now rise! *(MOM and*

22   *DAD KIKI stand up.)* Dad Kiki, is it true that you started

23   first?

24 **DAD KIKI:** Mom Kiki didn't want to play with me!

25 **MOM KIKI:** Because he said I was a tattle-tale, and a fat barrel

26   and my son's spoiled mummy.

27 **KIKI:** What say the witnesses?

28 **GRANDMA:** All boys say that to women.

29 **GRANDPA:** And girls like to be pets.

30 **THE CRAZYLANDIANS:** That's right!

31 **CHARLEY:** Silence! This is a crazy courtroom and not a crazy

32   court ballroom! *(A bell rings.)*

33 **KIKI:** That's a mitigating circumstance. So I would ask the

34   Court to ignore it!

35 **MOM KIKI:** Why?

1   **KIKI: Because others are like that. Thank you.** *(He sits down.)*

2   **MIKI:** *(Getting to his feet)* **Let the accused rise.** *(MOM and DAD*

3   *MIKI stand up.)* **Mom Miki, is it true that you beat Mom**

4   **Kiki?**

5   **MOM MIKI: She was playing with my husband, Mr. Miki!**

6   **DAD MIKI: Because you were wandering around town,**

7   **swapping jam for a ham!**

8   **MIKI: What say the witnesses?**

9   **GRANDMA: It's better to eat marmalade than to wander along**

10   **the promenade, and swap jam for a ham.**

11   **GRANDPA: Punish the ham! The ham is guilty!**

12   **THE CRAZYLANDIANS: That's just! Where's the ham?**

13   **CHARLEY: Come on, guys, louder!**

14   **THE CRAZYLANDIANS:** *(Even more loudly)* **The ham is guilty!**

15   **Sentence the ham!**

16   **MIKI:** *(Raising his hand for silence)* **I would ask the Court to**

17   **take this into account! The witnesses are loud and clear,**

18   **no namby-pamby here! Thank you.** *(He takes his seat. The*

19   *CRAZY HEADS put their heads together and whisper.)*

20   **DARA:** *(Standing up)* **The Supreme Court of Crazyland sitting**

21   **in the capital Crazyville has weighed and unweighed all**

22   **the circus-stances in this case and has judged that the**

23   **guilty ham that was swapped by the accused Mom Miki,**

24   **shall be sliced, cut and minced by the accused Dad Miki**

25   **and mixed by the accused Mom Kiki and as hamburgers**

26   **grilled by the accused Dad Kiki. All the accused are hereby**

27   **ordered to eat them for lunch sentenced by this Court to**

28   **wash the dishes afterwards. All – not just mums!** *(DARA*

29   *sits down and ALKA gets to her feet.)*

30   **ALKA: The trial is over! You are all free to go!** *(Murmuring*

31   *sounds in the courtroom. MOM and DAD KIKI hug each*

32   *other and congratulate each other, and then the CRAZY*

33   *HEADS join them and there are congratulations all round.*

34   *The others join them and there is hugging and shaking*

35   *hands all round.)*

1   **THE CRAZY HEADS:** *(Singing)* **If you've been naughty and bad**

2   **and angry at your mom and dad**

3   **Come to our Crazyland**

4   **Join our crazy band.**

5   **'Cause if you like to fight**

6   **not to go to bed at night**

7   **And brushing hair and baths you hate**

8   **Here can you sleep till late**

9   **and always get a cake.**

10   *(To the last bars of the song, DAD MIKI hands out the*

11   *hamburgers. The TV PRESENTER, who has been unconscious*

12   *all this time, starts to come around. He rubs his eyes, stands*

13   *up and comes close to them. DAD MIKI gives him a*

14   *hamburger, too.)*

15   **TV PRESENTER: What's going on here? What are those**

16   **children doing?** *(ALKA catches sight of him, and recognizes*

17   *him. She gets a fright.)*

18   **ALKA: That's my Dad! He's awake! What will happen now?** *(The*

19   *CHILDREN'S DELEGATION hides under the table and*

20   *creeps away off the stage.)*

21   **TV PRESENTER:** *(Seeing ALKA)* **Why aren't you in bed?** *(He*

22   *looks at his watch.)* **Do you know what time it is?** *(He sizes*

23   *up all the children.)* **Which one of you threw that ball at**

24   **me?** *(The CHILDREN start fidgeting and moving away from*

25   *him, as he looks questioningly in turn at each one of them.*

26   *The ADULTS slowly take their places in front of the*

27   *television set and chew on their hamburgers.)*

28   **MOM MIKI: Come on, children, that's enough now, off you go!**

29   **DAD KIKI: Leave us in peace!**

30   **GRANDMA: Isn't it enough that you've been nagging us all day**

31   **long, at least give us a rest in the evening!**

32   **DAD MIKI: What are you waiting for? You've got your**

33   **hamburgers already!**

34   **MOM MIKI: Did you pick up your things?**

35   **GRANDPA: To the bathroom, wash your teeth, don't forget**

1   **your neck and your ears, and straight to bed!** *(The*
2   *CHILDREN leave.)*
3 **CHARLEY: This is Crazyland Radio and Television, Crazyland**
4   **Studio ...** *(The TV PRESENTER goes over to the TV set and*
5   *bangs it at the side. CHARLEY disappears inside and there is*
6   *an atonal buzzing. The TV PRESENTER enters the TV set.*
7   *Only his head can be seen. He gives a professional smile and*
8   *moves his lips, but not a word can be heard. DAD KIKI goes*
9   *over to the TV set and he, too, gives it a bang at the side.)*
10 **TV PRESENTER:** *(Suddenly the sound comes on)* **... all our**
11   **viewers a very good-night!**
12 **THE CRAZY HEADS:** *(Singing)* **Where on earth does Kiki go,**
13   **Where on earth does Miki go,**
14   **And what about Alka,**
15   **And Dara Guitar?**
16   **To the great crazy river,**
17   **To the great crazy sea,**
18   **All the folks are crazy there,**
19   **Even you and me.**
20   **Crazy you, crazy me,**
21   **And you and he and you and me,**
22   **Come on now, one, two, three,**
23   **It's all crazy, as you see ...**
24
25
26   **THE END**
27
28
29
30
31
32
33
34
35

3 - Song Crazy You, Crazy Me!

LUD SAM JA, LUD SI TI I TI I ON

I VI I MI AJ-MO SAD JEN, DVA, TRI, LU-DO, LU-DO, LU-DO, LU-DO

LU-DI-TI, LU-DI-TI.

FINE

DA CAPO
DEL FINE

(c) 2001. Edicija Tulac

162

This Land
by R.N. Sandberg

On one level this play seems to focus on the racial conflicts between whites, African-Americans and indigenous Americans in the nineteenth century American northwest. Certainly the ethnic cleansing of the Native American populations and the enslavement of African peoples in the United States have been well documented and received much commentary over the years. *This Land*, however, sheds new light on these themes because it focuses narrowly upon how these issues played out in the region of the Oregon territory, and also because it associates the plight of the Africans with that of the indigenous peoples in the westward settlement and agrarian-industrial development of the North American continent during those years. Indeed, the linkage that Robert Sandberg establishes between Native Americans and African Americans as marginalized populations, both of whom shared some common values and encountered a similar foe, encourages us to reconsider some widely held stereotypes that govern our understanding of this historical period.

On a second and more profound level, however, the play develops an insightful commentary upon the development of the natural environment of nineteenth-century America — and indeed upon the emerging nation that we now know as the United States. As Robert Sandberg has remarked: "The historical events seemed to me to capture essential elements of the conflicts, perseverance, destructiveness, and ultimate accomplishments not only for the Northwest but for the country as a whole." We stand today at the brink of the twenty-first century and painfully confront the environmental degradation that has already occurred in our land, knowing full well how much more still threatens. It is difficult for us to travel back to the time when policies were first established in order to see how it all went wrong. It is painful to consider the beauty of virgin forests, wild waterways and so many other natural wonders that are now forever lost to us. It is sad to recognize the betrayal of human hopes, desires, ideals and values that has occurred in this regard over the past two centuries. And it is certainly frustrating and paradoxical that we should have come so far and achieved so much in developing "this land," when we pause to think of what it has all cost.

If this were all that Robert Sandberg's play accomplished, it would certainly deserve recognition here and even wider recognition on our country's stages. But of course, there is more to this drama than a bittersweet history lesson that hopefully will set the record straight once and forever. There is also the moving tale of the all too compelling characters — many of whom are historical. The courage, perseverance and resourcefulness of George Bush and his wife Isabella, striking out from an overcrowded and racially prejudiced eastern white America to make a new life for themselves. The growing love between young Owen, Bush's son, for Onkwo, a teenager from the Nisqually tribe, who dies so tragically when her people are exiled by the whites. And the struggle of Onkwo's brother, Leschi, chief of the Nisqually, who realizes how hopelessly he is trapped between the forces of settlers, politicians and warring tribes — all of whom are caught up in the historical movement of what we now call the "manifest destiny" of the nineteenth century United States of America.

The play was originally commissioned for the Washington State Centennial and designed to be performed in a rustic amphitheater, the Snoqualmie Falls Forest Theater, about a quarter mile's hike into the woods, with a huge waterfall off in the distance. It was produced there in four different summers: 1980, 1981, 1985, 1987. As the author has remarked: "The theater no longer exists — but the woods and falls do."

Characters

George Bush — a robust, brown-skinned man in his fifties
Isabella — his wife, white, in her thirties
Owen — their son, in his teens
Leschi — leader of the Nisqually, in his twenties
Onkwo — his sister, Nisqually, in her teens
Governor Isaac Stevens — short, powerful, white man, wears a military uniform
Mike Simmons — white, in his thirties
Mary McCalister — matronly white woman
Joe Meek — hearty, good old boy, in his thirties

Helen Meek — his daughter, no more than ten
Narcissa Whitman — physically worn white woman, in her thirties
Marcus Whitman — a missionary, white
Kanasket — leader of the Stkamish
Sealth — leader of the Duwamish
Lieutenant Kautz — regular army, white

Indians, trappers, settlers, soldiers

(With doubling, the play may be performed by 8 men, 4 women, 1 girl plus extras)

A large open space.

The play is set in what is now called the Northwestern United States.

The main action spans approximately thirteen years, from 1844 to 1857.

The major events of the play actually happened. The characters are based upon real people.

ACT I

PROLOGUE

(A clearing in the woods. A robust, brown-skinned man in his fifties, GEORGE BUSH, pokes out from behind the trees. He looks around cautiously, is startled to see the audience, and immediately snaps his rifle to ready.)

LESCHI: *(From behind the audience)* **Do not let him frighten you. He is a gentle man.** *(LESCHI comes through the audience. He is a strong, vibrant Nisqually man in his twenties. BUSH does not hear, see or refer to LESCHI — or to ISAAC STEVENS, a short, powerful white man in his thirties, who is entering from behind the other side of the audience.)*

BUSH: I was expectin' Cayuse. Nice t' see some friendly faces.

STEVENS: We're all friends.

BUSH: I'm George Bush. No relation t' the ones you know. This here's beautiful country, isn't it? Used t' be full o' animals in my trappin' days.

LESCHI: Back then.

BUSH: Beaver, elk, so many deer it was like pickin' blackberries.

STEVENS: A land of immense resources.

BUSH: This land. Most comfortin' thing there is, peaceful, little plot ya can call yer own.

LESCHI: The land belongs to no one.

BUSH: Which is why I've come back. Ya see, me and my family, we had a real nice farm in Missouri. But – well, these days, folks in Missouri are more interested in black folks bein' property rather than ownin' it.

STEVENS: We must concentrate on the positive. Move forward, improve, develop.

BUSH: So you can understand when the government started talkin' about free land, land where there wasn't a bunch o' people rippin' things apart, well, we decided t' head out. T' this peaceful, beautiful place – Oregon Territory.

1   STEVENS: The West!

2   BUSH: The Willamette Valley!

3   STEVENS: The land of opportunity!

4   LESCHI: Our home.

5   BUSH: We're gonna make us a home nobody's gonna take

6   away. And as soon as Congress passes the Land Act —

7   STEVENS: Which they will.

8   BUSH: We'll have claim to six hundred and forty beautiful

9   acres ... ! That is, if we make it through this here eastern

10   part of the Territory. This is Cayuse country, ya see. *(He*

11   *exits.)*

12 LESCHI: It belongs to no one. It is home for all.

13

14

15   **SCENE ONE**

16

17 *(Cayuse Country. Eastern Oregon Territory.)*

18 ISABELLA: *(Off)* Owen? Owen?! Owen!! *(OWEN rushes on. He's a*

19   *teenager with skin the fairest possible shade of brown.*

20   *ISABELLA, his mother, enters. She's a tall, strong, white*

21   *woman in her thirties. She carries a rifle.)*

22 ISABELLA: You come on back, now.

23 OWEN: No.

24 ISABELLA: Owen.

25 OWEN: I can miss one group social. Billin' and cooin' about

26   the promised land. *(With disgust:)* The Willamette Valley.

27 ISABELLA: Owen, it's getting dark.

28 OWEN: Good.

29 ISABELLA: We don't know what's out here. Your father said

30   there's —

31 OWEN: You think anybody could really live in this place? We're

32   carryin' provisions and we're starvin' — eatin' roots and

33   blackbirds. Practically nothin' t' drink. Oregon Territory?

34   More like Oregon cemetery. Why couldn't you let us stay in

35   Missouri?

1   **ISABELLA:** You don't remember.

2   **OWEN:** We had enough to eat and drink. We didn't have t' pull

3   wagons through knee deep mud. We didn't spend months

4   walkin' in freezin' mountains and blazin' deserts.

5   **ISABELLA:** What about walkin' down streets afraid we'd be

6   attacked? What about worryin' you or your father'd be

7   snatched up, called slave and nobody'd do a thing about

8   it? When we get to the Willamette –

9   **OWEN:** We're never gonna get to the Willamette. We're gonna

10   die in this desert.

11   **ISABELLA:** Owen. Owen, we'll make it.

12   **OWEN:** I'm so hungry, mama, so thirsty.

13   **ISABELLA:** I know. *(She holds him. There is some movement in*

14   *the background. THREE CAYUSE enter surreptitiously. They*

15   *start to move slowly forward when a booming voice makes*

16   *them jump.)*

17   **SIMMONS:** *(Off)* George! George! *(MIKE SIMMONS enters. He's*

18   *a barrel-chested, white man in his thirties. He has a short*

19   *fuse, but a good heart. He carries a rifle.)*

20   **SIMMONS:** Where is he? It gets later and later every day.

21   **ISABELLA:** He's doin' his job, Mike.

22   **SIMMONS:** We're practically outa water.

23   **ISABELLA:** He said it can't be far, now.

24   **SIMMONS:** Two weeks ago, he said it'd be ten days.

25   **ISABELLA:** We've had wagons t' fix.

26   **SIMMONS:** Two weeks! He's the guide. He's supposed to know.

27   **ISABELLA:** How's he supposed to know about the wagons?

28   **SIMMONS:** He's not here all day long. He don't hear the

29   complainin'. How'm I supposed t' know where the next

30   water is? I know wagons and farmin'. I never been out

31   here before. Just cause we organized this thing together

32   don't mean I know what he does.

33   **OWEN:** Mama, I'm hungry.

34   **ISABELLA:** All right, Owen. Come on. *(The CAYUSE start to*

35   *advance again.)*

1   SIMMONS: Whatta we gotta stop at this Whitman mission for,
2   any way? Let's just head for the Columbia.
3   ISABELLA: George told you it's cause of the Indians.
4   SIMMONS: Aw, Indians. We ain't even seen any Indians. It's
5   water we need.
6   OWEN: Mama, I want to go back to the wagon.
7   SIMMONS: Yeah, sure, go back and rest. I don't get no rest, but
8   everybody else might as well get some. *(The CAYUSE,*
9   *hearing something, duck back. BUSH enters.)*
10   OWEN: Papa!
11   BUSH: Isabella, what are you doin' out here? You know I said —
12   ISABELLA: One of his fits. I'm gettin' him back fast as I can.
13   BUSH: Son, you know —
14   SIMMONS: George, whadya find?
15   BUSH: Springs're no more than four miles up ahead.
16   SIMMONS: Water! Hah! Water!
17   BUSH: Let's all get back to the circle, now.
18   SIMMONS: Dang, George, you always come through. I don't
19   know why I get so worked up. You always come through.
20   Hah! Water!
21   BUSH: Come on, now. Everything's gonna be fine. Can't be
22   more than two days to the Whitmans from those springs.
23   OWEN: Ya mean we're really gonna get outa this place?
24   BUSH: Less than a week to the Columbia.
25   OWEN: All right! Willamette, here we come!
26   BUSH: Let's get back to now —
27   SIMMONS: Hold on a minute, George, I been thinkin'. We all
28   feel the way the boy does. The Willamette's where we
29   wanna get. No sense wastin' time at this mission. After
30   that spring, we should head due west for the river.
31   BUSH: Mike, we agreed we needed —
32   SIMMONS: George, we ain't on schedule any more.
33   BUSH: The Cayuse in this area and further on, the Yakimas,
34   we don't know how they'll react to us. The Whitmans are
35   on good terms with these people.

1   **SIMMONS: Have we seen any Indians, had any trouble so far?**

2   *(There is some noise off. The BUSHES and SIMMONS jump*

3   *to ready.)*

4   **MCCALISTER:** *(Off)* **George, Isabel, Mike?!** *(MARY MCCALISTER*

5   *enters. She's a round faced, matronly white woman.)* **The**

6   **whole circle's waitin on you. You gonna spend all night**

7   **out here arguin'?**

8   **ISABELLA: You're right, Mary.**

9   **BUSH: Come on.**

10   **SIMMONS: Oh, and it's my fault, I suppose. I'm always wrong,**

11   **and George is always right. Always right, always so danged —**

12   **ISABELLA: Don't you ever stop?!**

13   **BUSH: Mike. Back at the circle, you ask folks which they want.**

14   **You tell 'em we're at the springs and —**

15   **MCCALISTER: The springs.**

16   **SIMMONS: Yep, tomorrow.**

17   **MCCALISTER: Hallelujah.**

18   **SIMMONS: I told ya all not t' worry.**

19   **BUSH: I'll abide by whatever folks want. Come on, now.**

20   *(They start to go. ONE of the CAYUSE goes towards them.*

21   *ANOTHER restrains him. The CAYUSE whisper together as*

22   *the SETTLERS exit.)*

23

24

25   **SCENE TWO**

26

27   *(The Whitman Mission. A few days later. From Off-stage,*

28   *children's voices are heard singing the "ABC's" in a hesitant*

29   *manner. From the other side of the stage, a young GIRL runs*

30   *on, yelling. She is dressed as an Indian but has white features.)*

31   **GIRL: Mrs. Whitman! Mrs. Whitman! They're here!** *(NARCISSA*

32   *WHITMAN, a slender, haggard white woman in her thirties,*

33   *enters.)* **The Bostons are here, Mrs. Whitman!**

34   **NARCISSA: Americans, Helen. You wouldn't call your father a**

35   **Boston, would you?**

1   HELEN: He's a trapper.

2   NARCISSA: He's an American, from Virginia. Just as these

3   people are Americans – wherever they've come from.

4   *(BUSH, ISABELLA, OWEN and SIMMONS enter.)*

5   HELEN: I'll get Dr. Whitman. *(She runs off.)*

6   NARCISSA: Welcome, friends.

7   BUSH: George Bush, Mrs. Whitman. My wife Isabella and son

8   Owen.

9   SIMMONS : Mike Simmons.

10   NARCISSA : You must be exhausted. Come up to the house.

11   There's shade, and water –

12   SIMMONS: We don't need no water now. Just point the way to

13   the promised land and tell those Indians to let us pass.

14   BUSH: Take it easy, Mike.

15   ISABELLA: We've heard so much about your work.

16   NARCISSA: Nobody knows what it's really like till they're here.

17   OWEN: Well, we know the Willamette's gotta be better than

18   this stinkin' desert.

19   ISABELLA: Owen.

20   BUSH: We're all kinda beyond ourselves, Mrs. Whitman. Trip's

21   been more than a little rough, and now that the end's in

22   sight –

23   SIMMONS: Eden, ho!

24   ISABELLA: It's a dream come true, Mrs. Whitman, a sweet,

25   sweet dream.

26   SIMMONS: Amen.

27   NARCISSA : I'm sorry to have to tell you this but – here, the

28   Willamette, the whole Territory, it's not what you think.

29   It's not the promised land.

30   BUSH: When you're comin' from Missouri – or Mississippi or

31   New York or any o' the places I've been, this land looks as

32   good as Eden.

33   *(From off there is whooping and shouting. The BUSHES and*

34   *SIMMONS throw themselves to ground, prepared for an*

35   *attack. JOE MEEK and a couple TRAPPERS burst on.)*

1   **MEEK:** *(Trying to hug her)* **Narcissa, you goddess!** *(She breaks*
2   *away from him.)* **How's my Helen, how's my little girl?**
3   *(SIMMONS and the BUSHES get up.)* **Well, I'll be, more**
4   **white faces. What a day, boys!** *(Shaking SIMMONS' hand:)*
5   **Joe Meek's the name. Ain't seen a white woman in nearly**
6   **a year. Hope ya don't mind if I give yer wife a squeeze.**
7   *(He's going for ISABELLA. BUSH starts towards him, but*
8   *before he can get there, ISABELLA has stuck a rifle in*
9   *MEEK's chest.)* **Now, there's a woman for ya, boys.** *(They're*
10   *laughing.)*
11 **BUSH: Still haven't learned any manners, have ya, Meek?**
12 **MEEK: Mind yer business, boy.**
13 **BUSH: This is my business.**
14 **ISABELLA: He's my husband.**
15 **OWEN: And I'm their son.**
16 **MEEK: Well, I'll be —**
17 **BUSH: Most likely you will, Joeboy.**
18 **MEEK:** *(Stops and looks hard at BUSH. It comes to him)* **Bush.**
19   **Old Black Bush.**
20 **BUSH: George Bush.**
21 **MEEK: I thought you were dead and settled in Missouri.**
22 **BUSH: Too many Virginians there, these days.**
23 **MEEK: Plenty of us here, too.**
24 **ONE OF THE TRAPPERS: Just a matter o' time till we turn it**
25   **into slave territory.**
26 **MEEK: Now, come on, Ben. Bush here's a good old boy. Taught**
27   **me plenty o' lessons when I first came t' the mountains.**
28 **BUSH: That's not the way I remember it.**
29 **MEEK: Snot-nose kid never lets on what he appreciates.**
30 **THE OTHER TRAPPER:** *(With a laugh)* **Now, maybe, it's yer**
31   **turn t' teach him, ey Joe?**
32 **MEEK:** *(Playfully pushing him)* **Teach anybody if I can teach**
33   **you, hambone.**
34 **BEN, THE FIRST TRAPPER:** *(Staring at Bush)* **Somehow, I don't**
35   **think he looks real eager t' learn.**

1   OWEN: You don't watch out, he'll lay you flat on your back,
2   mister.
3   ISABELLA: Owen.
4   BUSH: *(Laughing)* When have you ever seen me lay anybody
5   out flat?
6   MEEK: Those days are gone, huh, George?
7   BUSH: I got some sense, Joeboy. If your head ever comes down
8   outa the mountain air, maybe you'll get some, too.
9   MEEK: The mellow voice of advice once again. Welcome back
10   t' the Territory, George. You and yer family. *(HELEN runs*
11   *on, followed by WHITMAN and a few CAYUSE, the same who*
12   *stalked the settlers in scene one.)*
13   HELEN: Daddy!
14   MEEK: Darlin'! You been learnin' yer lessons, sweetheart?
15   HELEN: Ah, daddy.
16   WHITMAN: Mrs. Whitman, do you think children have the
17   patience to wait ten minutes for their teacher?
18   NARCISSA: Marcus, these good people —
19   WHITMAN: These heathens have little enough interest in
20   learning. They need no example of sloth from us. *(She*
21   *turns to go. He stops her.)* You needn't rush back. I have
22   given them their lesson. *(To the CAYUSE:)* Go and watch
23   over the children. And sit in the chairs, not the dirt. *(They*
24   *stare at him for a moment, then exit. Shaking SIMMONS'*
25   *hand:)* I'm Marcus Whitman.
26   SIMMONS: Mike Simmons.
27   BUSH: George Bush.
28   MEEK: Ain't been sick or anything, have ya, sweetheart?
29   HELEN: I been fine, daddy.
30   WHITMAN: *(Extending his hand to ISABELLA)* I hope your
31   journey hasn't been too arduous, Mrs. Simmons.
32   ISABELLA: Bush. Isabella Bush.
33   WHITMAN: Forgive me.
34   ISABELLA: Our son Owen.
35   MEEK: We both got us families, now, huh, Bush?

1 **WHITMAN: Living with a squaw does not make a family, Mr.**
2   **Meek.** *(To SIMMONS and the BUSHES:)* **You'll find life out**
3   **here quite different. We are trying to civilize the country.**
4   **People like Meek — they outsavage the savages.**
5 **MEEK: Indians got civilization, too, Marcus. Bush here taught**
6   **me that. Just a shame you never learned t' appreciate it.**
7 **WHITMAN: I am not here to learn from them, Mr. Meek.**
8   *(Motioning for SIMMONS and the BUSHES to leave:)* **I don't**
9   **think we need to spend any more time in this company.**
10 **MEEK: Narcissa, before you go — I just wanna thank you for all**
11   **you done for Helen. I'll be takin' her with me, this time.**
12 **HELEN: But, daddy —**
13 **MEEK: We ain't gone back t' the mountains, sweetheart.**
14   **Beaver's almost played out up there. We're gonna make**
15   **ourselves a real home. We're gonna live on a farm t'gether.**
16 **HELEN: But I like it here, daddy.**
17 **MEEK: You'll like it better with me and yer mama on a farm.**
18   **Just like a real family. Just like that boy there. Ain't that**
19   **right, Bush? Make our families some real nice farms in**
20   **the Willamette.**
21 **HELEN: No, I wanna stay with Mrs. Whitman! I wanna stay**
22   **here!**
23 **MEEK: We got to do it, sweetheart. The animals just ain't up**
24   **there no more.** *(She runs off. NARCISSA follows her. MEEK*
25   *is crushed. He wants to go after her, but doesn't let himself.)*
26 **MEEK: Well, boys, we came down here t' celebrate, didn't we?**
27   **Come on and let's do some celebratin'.**
28 **HAMBONE, THE SECOND TRAPPER:** *(With a sly laugh, to BUSH)*
29   **See ya real soon, friends.** *(MEEK and the TRAPPERS exit.)*
30 **ISABELLA: I thought it would be different.**
31 **BUSH: We're not there yet.**
32 **OWEN: I'm not afraid of 'em.**
33 **BUSH: Fightin' doesn't solve a thing, son.**
34 **SIMMONS: That's right. This territory's a big place. When we**
35   **get to the Willamette, everything'll be fine.**

1   WHITMAN: I admire your optimism, Mr. Simmons, but I'm
2   afraid the Willamette's as full as the mountains with
3   those of Mr. Meek's ilk. I suspect that you, like Mr. Meek
4   and his cohorts, are unaware that the Territory's passed a
5   new law. Any Negro trying to stay in Oregon can be
6   publicly whipped. *(They're all shocked.)*
7   BUSH: We come all this way.
8   SIMMONS: Now, George, hold on a minute. We'll just about
9   double the population when we get to the Willamette.
10   We'll change the law.
11 BUSH: I've been hearing about laws since I was ten years old.
12   What this one's gonna do, how that one's gonna change and
13   no matter what happened, no matter where I went, it was
14   always the same. You're colored, you got trouble. Unless it
15   was just you and the land. You and nobody else. It's people
16   who make laws, people who enforce 'em. White people.
17 SIMMONS: Now, wait a minute, George. Take a look at me.
18   Take a look at Isabella.
19 BUSH: You gonna be whipped, Mike?
20 ISABELLA: I'm not makin' my home with people like that.
21 SIMMONS: Well, what're we supposed to do, turn around and
22   go back? Spend four more months to get where? Missouri?
23   Virginia?
24 WHITMAN: You're of course welcome to stay with us as long as
25   you desire.
26 OWEN: Rot here in the desert?!
27 WHITMAN: If I might make a suggestion? The Willamette's the
28   only place in the Territory anyone could attempt
29   enforcing the law. You might consider going further
30   north. Above the Columbia, near the Sound, for example.
31   There aren't even any Americans there and it's supposed
32   to be good land.
33 BUSH: I was there once.
34 SIMMONS: George, you think folks're gonna travel further?
35   We don't have the supplies. We don't know what the

1   Indians'll be like.

2   **ISABELLA:** I'm not going to the Willamette.

3   **BUSH:** Mike, I know I promised to –

4   **SIMMONS:** George –

5   **BUSH:** I promised and I'll take you.

6   **ISABELLA:** *(Simultaneously, with OWEN)* **No, George**

7   **OWEN:** *(Simultaneously, with ISABELLA)* **No, Pa.**

8   **BUSH:** But only to the head of the valley. When you all head

9   south, we're gonna go north – to the Sound.

10   **OWEN:** All right! Sound, here we come! *(ISABELLA and BUSH*

11   *nod at each other, resolved but not happy.)*

12   **SIMMONS:** You been there before, huh?

13   **BUSH:** Long time ago.

14   **SIMMONS:** And the land's good?

15   **BUSH:** The Nisqually, all the Indians there, they lived off it

16   without ever plantin'.

17   **SIMMONS:** All right then. We came out together. We stick

18   together. The Sound it is.

19   **STEVENS:** *(Who has remained off to the side watching*

20   *throughout)* The American spirit – miraculous, isn't it?

21   You meet adversity – you push on. You help your neighbor.

22   **SIMMONS:** More than one Eden in this territory, I reckon.

23   **BUSH:** Let's just get on with it.

24   **STEVENS:** We are a people of destiny. We move ourselves and

25   our country ever forward.

26

27

28   **SCENE THREE**

29

30   *(Nisqually country, east of lower Puget Sound. Oregon*

31   *Territory. LESCHI is in a clearing surrounded by some trees.*

32   *His sister ONKWO runs on to him. They are dressed totally*

33   *different from the Cayuse. He playfully starts to chase her,*

34   *making animal sounds. They collapse laughing. When their*

35   *laughter subsides, They look around and become serious.*

1   *LESCHI takes something from his pouch and begins to hang*
2   *it on a tree. Voices are heard from Off-stage. LESCHI and*
3   *ONKWO quickly conceal themselves. OWEN enters. He*
4   *surveys the clearing.)*
5   **OWEN: Perfect. Just perfect.** *(Yelling back)* **Ma! Pa! Look at this!**
6   *(BUSH and ISABELLA enter.)*
7   **OWEN: I think this is it. The river's over there. The meadow**
8   **stretches out forever for plantin'. And this clearing's**
9   **perfect for the house.**
10 **ISABELLA: I don't like it.**
11 **OWEN: Whadaya mean?**
12 **ISABELLA: I don't like it.**
13 **BUSH: Soil's good, both in the meadow and here.**
14 **ISABELLA: I think we oughta head further north.**
15 **OWEN: You're crazy. It's the first place I've seen that I like.**
16 **BUSH: Lotta clearin' to do.**
17 **ISABELLA: Yes, too many trees.**
18 **OWEN: Whadaya think we're gonna make the house outa?**
19 **ISABELLA: We don't need an entire forest.**
20 **OWEN: We could build a sawmill.**
21 **BUSH: Let's stick to the house first.**
22 **OWEN: Ya mean we're gonna stay?**
23 **BUSH: Could be a good place to stake a claim.**
24 **OWEN: All right!** *(He dashes off.)*
25 **ISABELLA: George —**
26 **BUSH: Isabella, the McCallisters, Mike, all the others've found**
27   **land around here. This could make a good farm.**
28 **ISABELLA: George, that fort back there —**
29 **BUSH: They're Hudson Bay Company. British. They don't care**
30   **about some law the Americans passed. We're a hundred**
31   **miles from the Willamette. That's far enough north of the**
32   **Columbia, don't you think?** *(OWEN returns with an axe.)*
33   **What are you doin'?**
34 **OWEN: Gonna make it official. Gonna clear the first tree.**
35   *(He starts to chop. ONKWO charges out, wielding a knife.*

1   *She heads straight for OWEN. LESCHI catches her and*
2   *knocks the knife from her hand.)*

3 **ONKWO:** Murderer! Murderer!

4 **OWEN:** What's she talkin' about? Wha'd I do?

5 **ONKWO:** You tear at my mother! You hack at her limbs!

6 **OWEN:** I was just clearin' a tree. We're gonna make our –

7 **ONKWO:** No!

8 **OWEN:** We gotta right to stake a claim just like anybody else.

9 **BUSH:** *(Who has his rifle trained on ONKWO and LESCHI)* **Hush,**
10   **Owen.**

11 **OWEN:** Let her stake her own claim if she wants it so bad.

12 **BUSH:** Hush, I said. *(To ONKWO:)* **If this place is sacred to you,**
13   **we'll find another.**

14 **LESCHI:** Every place is sacred. Every tree, every rock, every
15   piece of earth. This clearing we first came to with our
16   parents when we were children.

17 **BUSH:** There's enough land for us to leave you what you care
18   about.

19 **ISABELLA:** Yes, let's go.

20 **OWEN:** But, Pa, he said it's all sacred. It's all the same to them.

21 **ISABELLA:** We don't need trouble, Owen.

22 **OWEN:** No, I'm stayin'. This is our land.

23 **LESCHI:** The land belongs to no one. It is we who belong to the
24   land. This land is everyone's home.

25 **OWEN:** Then there's no reason we can't settle here.

26 **LESCHI:** You may make your home where you choose – but do
27   not harm the earth.

28 **ONKWO:** No, let them go somewhere else. They will destroy this
29   place. Then how will we remember our mother and father?

30 **LESCHI:** Do our mother and our father live only in this
31   clearing? Is this land like your knife that you would call it
32   yours and carry it with you?

33 **ONKWO:** They will call it theirs.

34 **LESCHI:** That is their way, not ours, Onkwo. You would tear at
35   their bodies just as they tear at the earth's. They are

1 ignorant. They do not know the harm they commit. Let
2 our mother, the earth, punish them if she is offended. Let
3 us show them how Nisqually live. *(Pause. He picks up her*
4 *knife and gives it to her.)*
5 BUSH: You're Nisqually.
6 LESCHI: Yes.
7 BUSH: *(Starting to lower his rifle)* **Many years ago, I was a friend**
8 **of the Nisqually. Even gave a knife something like that to**
9 **the Yakima bride of one. I'm George Bush.**
10 LESCHI: George Bush? George Bush. The dark trapper,
11 Onkwo. The gentle bear.
12 OWEN: Gentle bear?
13 ONKWO: Our mother named him for his strength and
14 kindness.
15 LESCHI: And for his brown fur. *(They laugh.)*
16 ISABELLA: I used to call him that, too.
17 LESCHI : I'm Leschi. This is Onkwo. You were the friend of our
18 parents. Perhaps, now, we may claim your friendship, too.
19 BUSH: I hope our whole families may be joined in friendship.
20 How are your parents?
21 LESCHI: Our father was killed in a raid from the mountains by
22 the Snoqualmie.
23 ONKWO: Our mother died after the white men came, of their
24 spotted disease.
25 OWEN: *(To ISABELLA)* Measles?
26 ISABELLA: Or smallpox.
27 BUSH: I'm sorry.
28 LESCHI: They have gone on to another world.
29 ONKWO: Perhaps in their new world, the people are all wise
30 and do not tear at the earth.
31 BUSH: Our ways may be different from yours, Onkwo. But we
32 don't mean to harm the land. We'll look elsewhere to
33 make our home.
34 OWEN: No, Pa! I don't want to go no further. This is the place
35 we've been lookin' for.

1   ISABELLA: Didn't you hear what these people have been
2   saying?
3   OWEN: We can leave all these trees. We can leave this clearing
4   just as it is. We can keep this place special for them, but we
5   don't have to give it up. Do we pa?
6   ISABELLA: We're not wanted here.
7   BUSH: We're not wanted most anywhere.
8   LESCHI: We do not tell you where to make your home.
9   ISABELLA: Your sister does.
10 LESCHI: We offer our friendship to you wherever you rest.
11   *(He takes some dried berries from his pouch and offers them*
12   *to ISABELLA.)*
13 ISABELLA: Thank you. *(He offers some to BUSH.)*
14 BUSH: Thanks.
15   *(LESCHI turns to ONKWO and motions for her to give some*
16   *berries to OWEN. She hesitates.)*
17 OWEN: *(Tentatively)* If we make our home here, you can still
18   come around. This place can belong to both of you as
19   much as to us.
20 ONKWO: The land belongs to no one.
21 BUSH: Your parents brought you here, Onkwo, and you loved
22   this place. Now, I have brought my child and he loves it.
23   We've traveled far to find a place to rest, because there's so
24   many people who've hated us because we're different. Do
25   you think we might rest here and not be hated because
26   we're different?
27 ONKWO: I think the Snoqualmie, the Stkamish, many others
28   hate what is different, and they will not let you rest. For
29   me, I think, if you are kind to the earth, she will return the
30   favor and you will find rest here. *(She goes to OWEN and*
31   *offers the berries. He takes them and turns to BUSH.)*
32 OWEN: So Pa?
33 BUSH: Aren't you going to thank her?
34 OWEN: Thanks, Onkwo. *(To BUSH:)* Does this mean? *(BUSH*
35   *turns to ISABELLA.)*

ISABELLA: I suppose so.

OWEN: **All right!** *(Indian drumming starts as OWEN jumps for joy. BUSH, ISABELLA and OWEN exit as LESCHI and ONKWO move off to the side. MEEK enters carrying HELEN in his arms. As he speaks, the Indian Council meeting — scene 4 — forms.)*

MEEK: **Why'd they do it? Why didn't they just kill Whitman? He was pushin' on 'em, askin' for it. But why kill my Helen? Why kill my pretty little baby? If I'd a taken her outa here, if I'd a ... Well, I'm gonna get out, now. I'm gonna leave this place and never come back. But I'm gonna take a few of them gutless butchers before I go. Gonna carve up every Cayuse face I can.** *(The council starts as MEEK exits.)*

SCENE FOUR

(Indian Council Grounds, Whidbey Island. Oregon Territory. LESCHI sits with KANASKET, chief of the Stkamish, and SEALTH, chief of the Duwamish. Other MEN sit near them. ONKWO sits with the women, off to one side.)

KANASKET: **These white people are evil. They bring disease, make our people sick. Stkamish, Nisqually, Duwamish must join together and drive these people away.** *(He looks at LESCHI.)* **And let us start with the Bostons at Tumwater.**

SEALTH: **If we go to war, Kanasket, we shall lose all. These Bostons are like the leaves on the trees. Their wagons stretch endlessly beyond the mountains.**

KANASKET: **They take our land, Sealth. At Tumwater, already they have built their houses, dug up the earth. Soon they will believe this land has always been their home. We should not embrace these dogs. We should tear out the insides of this George Bush and his people just as they've torn apart our mother, the earth.**

1   SEALTH: I do not like talk of spilling blood in our land.

2   KANASKET: Woman! We should make the earth burn with the

3   heat of their blood, like our brothers the Cayuse did to the

4   Whitmans.

5   ONKWO: Yes, what great fighters the Cayuse were. Twenty

6   warriors to slaughter two men, two women and some

7   children. How brave.

8   KANASKET: Let this woman know her place at the council.

9   ONKWO: Is Kanasket afraid to hear a woman speak? He would

10   fight the Bostons, yet he is afraid of a woman's voice. The

11   Boston men have no such fear; they listen to a woman's

12   heart.

13   KANASKET: Then perhaps Onkwo should go live among the

14   brave Bostons, who are so wise they take council from

15   women. *(Laughter.)*

16   LESCHI: A foolish man laughs at what he does not understand.

17   A foolish warrior enters a fight he cannot win. The Cayuse

18   thought Whitman was evil. They killed him. The Bostons

19   punished the Cayuse. They won nothing.

20   KANASKET: Whitman was dead.

21   SEALTH: Yes, and many Cayuse, too.

22   LESCHI: A wise warrior fights the battle he can win. If we kill

23   all the Bostons here, ten times the number will come to

24   take their place. Do we want our people to die or to

25   prosper? If we fight, many will die. If we make the Bostons

26   our allies, we will have peace and prosper.

27   KANASKET: Why is it that Leschi talks of nothing but peace? Is

28   it because the Nisqually have become slaves to the Bostons

29   at Tumwater? Is it because he loves big brown Bush and his

30   pretty white woman more than he loves his own people?

31   LESCHI: I love no people more than the Nisqually. I love many

32   people more than Kanasket.

33   KANASKET: You fear me because I do not hesitate to draw my

34   knife. You hide your face when a warrior should lift his arm.

35   LESCHI: *(Drawing his knife)* My face is not hidden. My arm is

1   **ready.** *(KANASKET draws his knife. SEALTH jumps between*

2   *them.)*

3   **SEALTH: Brothers must not spill each other's blood. This**

4   **council was meant to join us.**

5   **KANASKET: In war.**

6   **LESCHI: It takes little hate to begin a war. It takes much love to**

7   **make a peace. We will not fight each other, and we will not**

8   **fight the Bostons.**

9   **KANASKET: The Nisqually will not fight the Bostons. Some of**

10   **us will follow our hearts.** *(He goes. The council breaks up.*

11   *On the other side of the stage, a Hudson Bay Company MAN*

12   *enters, whistling a tune. He is pacing, on guard duty at the*

13   *fort. He hears something.)*

14   **HBC MAN: Who goes there? I say, who goes. Declare yourself.**

15   **Declare your** — *(A shot rings out. Another. He yells Off-*

16   *stage.)* **Sound the alarm! Sound the alarm bell!** *(More shots,*

17   *yelling, the alarm bell ringing.)* **Board the fort! Board up**

18   **the gate! It's an attack!** *(He fires his rifle, then is wounded*

19   *and staggers Off-stage. The gunshots and hubbub continue.*

20   *After a few moments, the sounds of the attack fade.)*

21   **STEVENS: If they attack the Hudson Bay fort, they surely will**

22   **have no fear to attack our citizens' farms. How can we**

23   **expect our people to make their homes if they live in this**

24   **kind of fear? They have only themselves, and though they**

25   **are strong, it is obvious that by themselves they cannot**

26   **survive. There can be no progress. We must help them.**

27   **Not merely by sending the army to protect them, but by**

28   **bringing out civilization, by bringing out a government**

29   **that will shape this raw land into a developed nation.**

30

31

32   **SCENE FIVE**

33

34   *(Tumwater. Oregon Territory. OWEN, slightly older, is*

35   *splitting shakes — wood shingles.)*

1　OWEN: Get the wood, Owen. Split the shakes, Owen. Got t' have
2　　　　a new roof for the shed, don't we? Don't want us t' be
3　　　　starvin' like everybody else this winter, do ya? *(He stops.)*
4　　　　How're we gonna starve with all the grain we got? Just
5　　　　stupid. Darn old roof's only four years old. It's not gonna
6　　　　leak. If he's so worried, why don't he do it himself insteada
7　　　　runnin' off to the HBC. Everybody's so scared of an attack
8　　　　they won't budge from their beds, but no not him. I hope he
9　　　　gets ambushed on the way back; that'd serve him right.
10　　　*(ISABELLA enters with MARY MCCALISTER, who carries a*
11　　　*sack of grain and a rifle.)*
12　MCCALISTER: I don't know how we'll repay ya, Isabel.
13　ISABELLA: Some day, we'll need help. We're just lucky we're
14　　　　by the river. Otherwise, the drought woulda got us too.
15　MCCALISTER: If next year's like the last two, I don't know
16　　　　what we're gonna do.
17　ISABELLA: Just keep rememberin' those first years, Mary – so
18　　　　much rain we couldn't tell the shore from the Sound.
19　MCCALISTER: You tell George thanks from me when he gets
20　　　　back.
21　ISABELLA: *(Suddenly much quieter)* Yes, I will.
22　MCCALISTER: You want me to stay till he gets here?
23　ISABELLA: No, you go on. Jim and the kids'll be waitin'. *(A sound*
24　　　　*off in the distance. OWEN stops chopping. MARY raises her*
25　　　　*rifle. All three are edgy.)* Maybe, Owen oughta go with you.
26　MCCALISTER: And leave you here alone?
27　ISABELLA: Mary –
28　MCCALISTER: Isabel, we got more important things to worry
29　　　　about than a few riled up Indians. If he doesn't get that
30　　　　roof on and your crops get soaked, we'll all be done for,
31　　　　Indian attack or no. And anyway, nobody's gonna stop me
32　　　　from getting this back to my kids. God bless you and
33　　　　George. You too, Owen. *(She exits.)*
34　OWEN: You gave Mrs. McCalister grain.
35　ISABELLA: Yes.

1 OWEN: You think we got enough for two families?

2 ISABELLA: We've got more than anybody else. That means

3   we've got enough to share.

4 OWEN: Does Pa know you're doin' this?

5 ISABELLA: Your father's never turned away a person in need.

6 OWEN: Yeah, but —

7 ISABELLA: Owen, you're doin' the shakes. I'm takin' care of the

8   grain. You do your chores; let me take care of mine.

9   *(SIMMONS enters. He carries an empty grain sack and a rifle.)*

10 SIMMONS: Isabel, Owen.

11 ISABELLA: Hello, Mike. Thought you'd still be in the fields.

12 SIMMONS: Yeah, well, ain't that much t' do out there, this

13   harvest, ya know ... George around?

14 ISABELLA: He's at the fort. Took over some peas and potatoes

15   to repay 'em for the help they gave us those first years.

16 SIMMONS: You got enough for Hudson Bay and we can't even

17   feed ourselves.

18 ISABELLA: Mike —

19 SIMMONS: I'm sorry, Isabel, but you know how it feels seein'

20   your —

21 ISABELLA: Mike, don't. You just come on down to the grain

22   shed.

23 SIMMONS: I — I don't feel right doin' this.

24 ISABELLA: We're neighbors. You come on, now.

25 SIMMONS: I thank you. *(They start to go.)*

26 OWEN: Ma-ah? *(She points emphatically towards the shakes. She*

27   *and SIMMONS exit.)*

28 OWEN: We're gonna be the only family with nothin' to eat this

29   winter. *(He begins chopping furiously. There is some*

30   *movement in the bushes. ONKWO enters. She watches him*

31   *for a moment.)*

32 ONKWO: You chop as if the wood were your enemy.

33 OWEN: *(On guard, then seeing who it is)* **Onkwo!** *(They look at*

34   *each other for a moment.)*

35 ONKWO: I like to watch your arms when you work.

1   OWEN: Do you really?

2   ONKWO: Yes.

3   OWEN: You've got nice arms too. *(Pause.)*

4   ONKWO: I must pick the last of the berries.

5   OWEN: Oh.

6   ONKWO: I thought, perhaps, you might walk with me.

7   OWEN: Really?

8   ONKWO: The berries are very sweet now.

9   OWEN: I – I can't Onkwo. I gotta get a new roof on the shed.

10   ONKWO: You should live like the Nisqually. When the food
11   leaves a place, we leave.

12   OWEN: Yeah, well, I'd rather have a home.

13   ONKWO: Than food? You're very funny. You take a piece of
14   land, call it home and then must never leave it. You must
15   plant the crops, work the fields, harvest the grain, fix the
16   roof. You're a slave, I think, Owen. A slave to the land.

17   OWEN: Look, I told ya I don't have time t' wander around the
18   woods pickin' berries. So why don't you just go.

19   ONKWO: Our way is enjoyable and yours is not, so you're
20   angry.

21   OWEN: It's just that I wasn't cut out to be lazy like an Indian.

22   ONKWO: No, you were made like a white man, to hate
23   whatever is Indian. *(She turns to go.)*

24   OWEN: Onkwo! ... I ... I'm sorry. That was stupid ... I want to
25   walk with you. I kinda been thinkin' for a while myself
26   about askin' ya t' go pick some flowers or somethin'. But I
27   never quite, well – ya know.

28   ONKWO: This makes me happy, Owen. *(She offers her hand.)*

29   OWEN: I've gotta have these cut when Pa gets back.

30   ONKWO: At the sun's rise, we leave for our winter grounds.

31   OWEN: Leave?

32   ONKWO: The food is gone, here.

33   OWEN: If you need food, you could have some of our grain.

34   ONKWO: *(Laughing)* What would we do with grain? *(They share*
35   *the laugh. It subsides and they're quiet for a moment.)*

1   **ONKWO: We shall meet again in the next season.** *(She turns to*
2   *go.)*
3   **OWEN: Onkwo** — *(She turns back. Pause.)*
4   **OWEN: You think I can pick enough berries in one afternoon**
5   **to last a whole winter?**
6   **ONKWO: Together, perhaps, we can.** *(They clasp hands and run*
7   *off.)*
8   **BUSH:** *(Off. Calling weakly)* **Isabella? Owen?** *(He enters limping,*
9   *holding his side. He moves slowly, painfully across the*
10   *clearing. He collapses.)*
11   **ISABELLA:** *(Off)* **Now, don't you worry yourself about taking**
12   **that. Folks gotta stick together.** *(ISABELLA and SIMMONS*
13   *enter. He carries a large sack of grain.)*
14   **SIMMONS: That's the truth it is.**
15   **ISABELLA: George! George, are you all right?**
16   **SIMMONS: Did they attack the fort again?**
17   **BUSH: No, no, it was** — *(He looks at SIMMONS and hesitates,*
18   *then:)* **You're not gonna believe this, Isabella** — **but** — **I fell**
19   **off the wagon. It was late, and I knew you'd be worried, so**
20   **I was going faster than I should have. Hit this rut and**
21   **before I knew it** — **bam!** — **wagon practically ran me over.**
22   **SIMMONS: Dang but ya can't turn around without some kinda**
23   **trouble out here.**
24   **BUSH: One trouble's over, anyway. Indians brought in a**
25   **Snoqualmie named Kussass. Said he'd been the one**
26   **responsible for the raid. Said there'd be no more problems.**
27   **ISABELLA: Thank goodness.**
28   **SIMMONS: If ya can believe 'em. String the savages up is the**
29   **only way ya can be sure**
30   **BUSH: Joe Meek's holdin' him for trial. Guess someone found**
31   **a way to stop himself from killin' "the savage."**
32   **SIMMONS: Ah look, George, you know I'm as good a friend as**
33   **you to Leschi and the peaceful Indians. All I'm sayin' is I**
34   **don't want no more attacks.**
35   **BUSH: Maybe if you were marshal like Meek, you'd be more**

1   civilized about it.

2   SIMMONS: It's just I got enough trouble feedin' my family

3   without worryin' about that.

4   BUSH: Yeah, well, it looks like you got part of your problem

5   solved, any way.

6   ISABELLA: George, I gave Mike some grain. Gave some to

7   Mary, too.

8   BUSH: I don't begrudge it to anyone. Just don't take more than

9   you need.

10   SIMMONS: You think I got more than I need?

11   BUSH: I just mean other folks may need some, too. Leave

12   enough for them.

13   SIMMONS: You got a whole barn full. Whadayou worried

14   about?

15   BUSH: I'm gonna clean up.

16   SIMMONS: Always so dang righteous, so high and mighty. Easy

17   for you, isn't it, with your barn full and your family –

18   ISABELLA: Mike –

19   SIMMONS: No. It's because of him we're here. We were comin'

20   out to a garden o' Eden, a place where we woulda had no

21   problems. But because o' you, because o' your color, we

22   ended up in this miserable – We're starvin' and beggin'

23   and scared to death and everything's just hog full up

24   perfect for you.

25   BUSH: I'll tell ya what's perfect. My leg that boots been kickin'

26   and my ribs that a rifle butt's slammed in. That's what's

27   perfect.

28   ISABELLA: George?

29   BUSH: There wasn't any wagon accident. When they brought

30   in that Kussass, a few of the good citizens, the civilized

31   white citizens, tried to string him up. When I stepped in,

32   Chapman offered that "An Indian's got no more rights

33   than a nigger." And they started swingin'.

34   SIMMONS: George, I'm sorry. I'm a dang fool. It's just all this –

35   I shoot my mouth off. You know I don't mean it. I'm sorry.

1   Anything I can do — anything.
2   BUSH: Yeah.
3   SIMMONS: You need any help, you let me know. You let me
4   know, Isabel; he won't. It's just a few of 'em, George. When
5   that Land Act passes and this place is all yours, they'll let
6   up. They won't have no way t' drive ya out then.
7   BUSH: Nobody is going to drive us out. *(Silence)*
8   SIMMONS: Yeah. Well. I guess our Indian worries are over, any
9   way. That's somethin'. I'd better let the McCalisters know.
10   BUSH: Mike. Forgot your grain.
11   SIMMONS: Yeah. Thanks. *(He exits.)*
12   ISABELLA: Was it just Chapman?
13   BUSH: A few others.
14   ISABELLA: It's never going to end.
15   BUSH: People were scared by the attack, and we're friends with
16   the Nisqually. Crops're bad, and we had a good harvest.
17   ISABELLA: And you just happen to be —
18   BUSH: You think you have to tell me what I happen to be ... ?
19   We are making a good home here. The Land Act will pass.
20   Things will change.
21   STEVENS: *(To the audience)* And lo, the United States Congress,
22   knowing the plight of its many poor citizens, passes the
23   Donation Land Act, taking an historic step towards
24   developing this western wilderness into a great nation. But
25   a law, my friends, is not enough. There must always be
26   men. Men of vision, of authority, men capable of shaping
27   this wilderness with a firm but just hand. I, Isaac Stevens,
28   am such a man. And my time is fast approaching. My
29   friends in Congress are looking for the right place for me
30   to make my contribution, for I am determined to make a
31   contribution. You see, although I have never seen the west,
32   I have a vision of what it may become. It is my destiny.
33
34
35

SCENE SIX

(Tumwater. Oregon Territory. LESCHI is examining BUSH's cultivator.)

BUSH: I woulda thought you'd take hold of Kanasket's hand before you'd take hold of that.

LESCHI: What is it for?

BUSH: Plantin'.

LESCHI: It digs the earth?

BUSH: Yeah.

LESCHI: Show me.

BUSH: What for?

LESCHI: I want to learn.

BUSH: To plant?

LESCHI: To do everything you do.

BUSH: You been talkin' to a missionary?

LESCHI: I am Nisqually, Bush, and will always remain so. But, in this land, now, there are more of your people than mine. Each season, more come. Each year, there are fewer trees, fewer salmon, fewer places we may go.

BUSH: There's still a lotta space.

LESCHI: For how long? Your Land Act has passed. You rejoice, but I am sad. Your people will come and take land until nothing is left.

BUSH: Our government can put a limit on how much land can be claimed.

LESCHI: But will they? Do they understand how we live? My people must be able to protect the land themselves. If we learn your ways and farm the land, then your people will not be able to claim it. When you came here, we taught you which roots to dig, which berries to pick, which places to catch the salmon.

BUSH: We wouldn't've made it if you hadn't.

LESCHI: Now, we will learn from you. Show me.

BUSH: I can't quite picture you as a farmer.

1   LESCHI: If I change my clothes, perhaps.

2   BUSH: Yeah, a pair of overalls, a shovel and some hogslop.

3   LESCHI: I'll wear your clothes and use your tools, but hogslop,

4   I think, is only for your people. *(JOE MEEK enters. He is*

5   *somehow changed.)*

6   MEEK: Be careful, Leschi, ya hold on to that cultivator too

7   long, ya might turn into a white farmer. Or if you're really

8   lucky, a black one.

9   BUSH: What can we do for you, Marshal?

10   MEEK: Had another good harvest I heard, Bush. Startin' ta

11   turn into a real farm here, isn't it? Wish I could say the

12   same o' my place.

13   BUSH: Still plenty to be done, but we know it's ours, now.

14   MEEK: Yeah, well, uh, I'll tell ya. I wouldn't count on that.

15   BUSH: I've filed the claim forms, Marshal.

16   MEEK: You're gonna have t' resubmit.

17   BUSH: What's wrong with it?

18   MEEK: Nothin'. Letter perfect. Everyone knows ya read and

19   write better than most white men in the Territory.

20   BUSH: Why do I have to re-file?

21   MEEK: Well, it's like this. I'm here today in an official capacity.

22   With the Land Act passin', we gotta have a record of every

23   man, woman and child; and I'm the census taker. Now, you

24   and Isabella and Owen livin' here, that right?

25   BUSH: Yes.

26   MEEK: Right. Well, the census also puts folks into categories.

27   We got white, slave and free colored. Now, Isabella, I'd say

28   is white. But you and Owen – and Leschi here while we're

29   countin' – you're all what I'd call free colored. *(No longer*

30   *playing:)* According to the Land Act, only a white man is

31   entitled to stake a claim.

32   BUSH: I am claiming this land.

33   MEEK: No claim can be recorded. That's the law.

34   BUSH: We worked five years to build this farm. It's our land.

35   Nobody's gonna throw us off it.

1   **MEEK: Nobody's tryin' t' throw ya off, George. I'm just tellin'**
2   **ya, that legally ya can't call it yours.**
3   **LESCHI: And if another American comes, a white American,**
4   **and claims this land as his?**
5   **MEEK:** *(Putting on the good ole boy manner again)* **Well, that'd**
6   **be a sticky situation, now, wouldn't it? Get us into a**
7   **question of law enforcement. I tell ya though, I got so**
8   **much enforcin' to do south of the Columbia that who**
9   **knows when I'd get up here t' straighten it out. Nobody**
10   **cares what goes on north of the Columbia, anyway. Except**
11   **you people who live here, I guess.**
12   **BUSH: Are you tellin' me I oughta just throw off anybody who**
13   **tries to move in here?**
14   **MEEK: I just don't think there's any worry about somebody**
15   **tryin' t' work land that's already bein' farmed. There's**
16   **plenty of land.**
17   **LESCHI: For how long?**
18   **MEEK: Well, ya know what I always say, Leschi, drink up today**
19   **for tomorrow the barrel might spring a leak. Look,**
20   **George, ya got a good farm. Enjoy it while ya can and don't**
21   **worry about what's down the road. For all you know a**
22   **bear could come outa those woods and gobble ya down**
23   **before ya slept another night. A bear could, that is, if we**
24   **hadn't killed 'em all off.** *(He laughs. Music starts, joyous*
25   *American folk dancing music. The crowd of dancers and*
26   *guests for scene 7 sweeps onto the stage.)*
27
28
29   **SCENE SEVEN**
30
31   *(Tumwater. Washington Territory. Thanksgiving. Music,*
32   *dancing, celebration — American and Indian. OWEN, dressed*
33   *partially as Nisqually, dances with ONKWO. STEVENS enters.*
34   *The crowd freezes as he speaks to the audience.)*
35   **STEVENS: My time has come. A new territory has been created —**

1   Washington Territory – this land. And Congress, in all its

2   wisdom, has seen fit to give me the task of governing it, of

3   joining it to the rest of our great country. I have plans, my

4   friends. *(The dance resumes. STEVENS stands apart.*

5   *ISABELLA goes to BUSH.)*

6   ISABELLA: George? George, we have company.

7   BUSH: I know.

8   ISABELLA: George Bush – it's Thanksgiving and you'd darn

9   well better get yourself in hand. God knows you've got

10   plenty to be thankful for.

11   BUSH: Yeah.

12   ISABELLA: You've got a good family, fine friends, a home –

13   BUSH: No, Isabella. We don't have a home. We're not on the

14   fringe of Oregon, now. We're smack in the heart of

15   Washington. The law's gonna be enforced.

16   ISABELLA: George, Jim McCalister told you –

17   BUSH: I know. When the first territorial legislature meets,

18   they'll grant me an exemption.

19   ISABELLA: Well, if the legislature –

20   BUSH: They don't have the power. It's just sentiment, Isabella.

21   The federal government's the only one who can give us

22   the land.

23   ISABELLA: If the territory does, the federal government will.

24   BUSH: You think Virginians and Georgians will? Say fine, let

25   that darkie own some land?

26   ISABELLA: You're a free man.

27   BUSH: Of color. You know what's goin' on back there.

28   ISABELLA: I know.

29   BUSH: Slave, free, north, south. People ready t' kill for –

30   ISABELLA: We came here to get away from all that.

31   BUSH: We came here t' make a home.

32   ISABELLA: Which is what we've done.

33   BUSH: No. I'm worse off than I was in Missouri. No better than

34   a slave. I can't even own the land I live on.

35   ISABELLA: Neither can I. Neither can Leschi – or Onkwo.

1   None of us can own any land. Even if I weren't married to
2   you, I couldn't. All a woman's good for is givin' her
3   husband the right to claim 320 extra acres.
4 BUSH: A white husband.
5 ISABELLA: I swear men can't think of anything but
6   themselves.
7 BUSH: If I were white —
8 ISABELLA: If you were white, you wouldn't be here. That
9   wouldn't be your boy. This farm wouldn't exist ... *(The*
10   *dance ends. An Indian dance begins as MEEK brings*
11   *STEVENS the BUSHES.)*
12 MEEK: George and Isabella Bush, Governor Isaac Stevens.
13 STEVENS: Mr. Bush, Mrs. Bush, my pleasure.
14 ISABELLA: Ours, Governor. I hope you'll be able to join us for
15   Thanksgiving dinner.
16 STEVENS: I'd be delighted. Just a word with Mr. Bush first, if I
17   may. *(He takes GEORGE aside.)* Mr. Meek's been telling me
18   about you. I want you to know the bills that go before the
19   legislature will have my full support, both here and back
20   east in Washington, D.C. And you should know, I have
21   many friends in Congress, Mr. Bush.
22 BUSH: Governor, you don't know what it'd mean.
23 STEVENS: I think it's important that a man of your caliber get
24   not merely an exemption to own his land, but that he be
25   given full citizenship as well. You didn't know there'd be a
26   proposal to make you a citizen.
27 BUSH: No.
28 STEVENS: What you've done to this land is an example for
29   every person in the territory. In the country. I admire you
30   greatly, Mr. Bush.
31 BUSH: Thank you, governor.
32 STEVENS: There is something else. I hesitate to bring it up,
33   now. I thought we might have a meeting – but perhaps
34   you and I don't need to be so formal.
35 BUSH: I'm not much for politics, governor.

1   STEVENS: This concerns you directly, Mr. Bush. You see, we
2   can't legally claim any of this land until the Indians have
3   signed it over to us. Mr. Meek tells me you're quite close to
4   one of the tribes.
5   BUSH: The Nisqually.
6   STEVENS: You might do a great service to the country and
7   yourself by helping get the Nisqually to sign a treaty.
8   BUSH: I don't think you'll need my help, governor. If the
9   treaty's fair – well, the Nisqually are reasonable people.
10   STEVENS: Good. Excellent. Let's hope all the tribes are.
11   *(The dance ends.)*
12   MEEK: Gather round, folks. It's my pleasure to introduce to
13   you a man come here direct from Washington, D. C. and
14   the U. S. army – Major Isaac Stevens, first governor of
15   Washington Territory. *(Applause)*
16   STEVENS: Thank you, friends. First of all, let me apologize for
17   interrupting your holiday. I was just too eager to meet all
18   my new citizens. And besides, since everybody within
19   thirty miles seems to be here, there wasn't any place else
20   I could get Thanksgiving dinner. *(Laughter)* You people
21   came out here to stake your claims, to make this land
22   yours and America's. Well, we're a territory, now; but
23   we're still not truly part of America. On my way out here
24   though, I plotted the northern route of the Trans-
25   continental railroad. That route is through Washington
26   Territory, right through our own Snoqualmie pass. In five
27   years time, Walla Walla will be linked to Tumwater, New
28   York to Olympia. The railroad will make us a truly great
29   territory, truly a united nation.
30   MARY MCCALISTER: And when we came out, all I thought we
31   were doin' was startin' a farm.
32   SIMMONS: Well, I knew I was comin' out for America. I staked
33   my claim for the good old U. S. of A.
34   ISABELLA: That what it says at the claims office, Mike? Land
35   owned by the U. S. of A.? *(Laughter)*

1   **SIMMONS: I just meant I came out to do my bit to make this**
2   **land American.**
3   **LT. KAUTZ: I thought you came out to get away from that horse**
4   **thievin' charge.** *(Laughter)*
5   **STEVENS: We understand what you mean — Mr. — Simmons,**
6   **is it?**
7   **SIMMONS: Used to be Colonel Simmons, governor.**
8   **LT. KAUTZ: Till he stole that horse.**
9   **STEVENS: People like you and Mr. Bush, you make this**
10   **country what it is, colonel. And I appreciate that. There's**
11   **no greater good we can do for this wild land than bring it**
12   **freedom and civilization, make it part of the United**
13   **States. But before we can officially do that, we must sign**
14   **treaties with our red brethren. I see we have some of our**
15   **red brethren here today, helping us celebrate our**
16   **Thanksgiving. My welcome to you.**
17   **ONKWO: I am not his red brethren.**
18   **OWEN: Give him a chance, Onkwo.**
19   **STEVENS: The President of the United States, the great White**
20   **Chief beyond the mountains, told me to say to you that he**
21   **loves you, his red children, like he loves his white**
22   **children. Because he loves you, he offers to give you**
23   **money so that his white children, like the Bush family**
24   **here, may live on this land.**
25   **ONKWO: This family has lived here for many years. Your**
26   **people have lived all over this land for many years.**
27   **STEVENS: That's true, young lady. But the President doesn't**
28   **want there to be any fighting among his children. He**
29   **wants to be generous to you. He wants to give you schools**
30   **and doctors and, best of all, a place to live that will never**
31   **be taken away from you. The Great White Chief — and I**
32   **and Mr. Bush here — we want our children to live in peace**
33   **and prosperity. Isn't that right, Mr. Bush?**
34   **BUSH: If what you say about schools and doctors and such can**
35   **really be done, well, I'm sure —** *(LESCHI steps forward.)*

1   This is Leschi, governor, of the Nisqually.

2 STEVENS: I'm honored.

3 LESCHI: You mean your words to be kind. But we are not the

4   children of your President. We are the children of our

5   parents and of the earth. Children of this land which you

6   seek to buy from us.

7 STEVENS: We will give you much in return.

8 LESCHI: Our eyes do not see this land in the same way. To you,

9   it is property, something to be bought and sold. When it is

10   bought, one must stay; when it is sold, one must leave.

11 BUSH: Leschi, he doesn't —

12 LESCHI: I know he does not understand. But this is the man

13   we must bargain with. If he does not understand, how will

14   we make a treaty between us? Will he let us live our way as

15   we learn yours? Will you ever be able to make him

16   understand that this land is sacred? *(To STEVENS:)* Every

17   forest, every clearing, every mountain and valley — for the

18   earth is our mother and the ashes of our ancestors cover

19   her body. And even if my people should perish, you would

20   still not be able to make this land your sole "property." For

21   my people, though not visible to your eyes, will always

22   inhabit this land. You will never be alone here.

23 BUSH: We don't want to live alone. You know that. We want to

24   share this land with you, like we always have.

25 STEVENS: That's right, Mr. Bush. Exactly. We want to share

26   this land. And that's just what we are going to do. *(Turning*

27   *to the settlers with a laugh:)* But I believe I've kept you from

28   your Thanksgiving dinner long enough. I don't want to

29   make those hungry appetites wait one minute more. So

30   folks, shall we get to it? *(Agreement, relief, some laughter.*

31   *STEVENS and the settlers, except for BUSH and OWEN, exit*

32   *for the house. The INDIANS stand apart. As the settlers exit,*

33   *ISABELLA turns back for BUSH and OWEN. They are caught*

34   *between following the hungry settlers and remaining with*

35   *the steadfast Indians. The lights fade.)*

1   **END ACT I**

2

3

4   **ACT II**

5

6   **SCENE EIGHT**

7

8   *(Medicine Creek. Washington Territory. OWEN and ONKWO.)*

9 **OWEN:** We should be able to see the falls from here. I was

10   thinking, Onkwo, it's at the falls that tribes bound

11   themselves to each other.

12 **ONKWO:** The falls – soon to be the "property" of the Great

13   White Chief.

14 **OWEN:** Can't you forget the treaty for a minute?

15 **ONKWO:** No. I see land that was ours, and that when the sun

16   dies today will be yours.

17 **OWEN:** It won't be mine.

18 **ONKWO:** It will be white man's land. You're a white man.

19 **OWEN:** Depends on who's doin' the lookin' ... You know, when

20   I hear those falls, it makes me think how beautiful your

21   language is. Waterfall: tum-chuk. Like the sound of a

22   heart beating. My heart's beating right now. Today, our

23   people are going to be joined together, and I was –

24 **ONKWO:** This treaty will not join our people. It is your way of

25   taking the land.

26 **OWEN:** Onkwo, I'm –

27 **ONKWO:** Why don't you go back to your own home?

28 **OWEN:** This is my home.

29 **ONKWO:** This is Nisqually, not American land. But you

30   Americans think you can take everything because it is

31   your destiny.

32 **OWEN:** I don't care about any American destiny.

33 **ONKWO:** But you're American and so you'll take.

34 **OWEN:** I'm about as American as I can be – born on July

35   fourth, parents married on July fourth – but I'm not

1   tryin' to steal anything. I see what they're tryin' to do. We
2   don't have t' let 'em. We can make our own way. We can
3   share the land. We can share our lives. Onkwo — *(He gets*
4   *down on one knee.)* **I want to ask** — *(She stares strangely at*
5   *him.)* **This is stupid.** *(He gets up. STEVENS, MEEK,*
6   *SIMMONS, BUSH and a few others enter.)*

7 STEVENS: A grand day for it, gentlemen.

8 SIMMONS: Ain't rainin' yet, anyways.

9 STEVENS: The first Indian treaty in Washington Territory. An
10   historic occasion. Mark it down for your memoirs. Well,
11   where are our red brethren? This isn't the only business
12   on my agenda.

13 MEEK: They'll be here, governor. They're holdin' their final
14   council. It's a big decision they gotta make.

15 STEVENS: Really, Mr. Meek? Thank you for that unique
16   perspective. *(Taking SIMMONS aside:)* I am depending on
17   you, Mr. Simmons. I made you Indian agent for a reason.

18 SIMMONS: Don't you worry, governor. They trust me almost as
19   much as Bush. I'll get 'em to sign their death warrants.

20 STEVENS: This is a treaty with the United States government
21   we're talking about, colonel.

22 SIMMONS: Yes, sir.

23 BUSH: Governor.

24 STEVENS: Mr. Bush, we've included your suggestions. They've
25   got to free their slaves. They're getting twenty years of free
26   schooling.

27 BUSH: But, governor, the land in the treaty — well, for
28   example, Leschi's got his own farm. Why couldn't that be
29   included in the reservation?

30 STEVENS: Think about it. His farm and now we give it to all of
31   them. There'd be fighting tooth and nail over it.

32 BUSH: You're gonna have fightin' anyway with what you're
33   doin'. Puttin' tribes that hate each other together on those
34   tiny tracts of land.

35 STEVENS: If they fight, Mr. Bush, that is their problem. My

1   concern is for America and American citizens.

2 BUSH: But, governor, these people, this land —

3 STEVENS: Mr. Bush. I've listened to you patiently throughout

4   this process. The treaty is now final.

5 BUSH: They won't sign it.

6 STEVENS: That kind of talk is why you're not Indian agent, Mr.

7   Bush.

8 BUSH: I thought it was 'cause an Indian agent's got t' be a citizen

9   and the legislature just happened t' refuse me that one. We

10   know how fond you are of people who aren't citizens.

11 STEVENS: I deny that accusa —

12 MEEK: Governor. *(The Indians are entering — LESCHI,*

13   *KANASKET, SEALTH, others.)*

14 STEVENS: My friends, this is a great day for you and for us, a

15   day of peace and friendship between you and the whites

16   for all time to come ... The Great Father wishes to make

17   this bargain with you. You will be paid $32,500 for your

18   land, the amount to be paid partially or wholly in goods to

19   be determined by the United States Government. You will

20   retain the rights to fish, hunt, gather food and pasture

21   your horses on any land unclaimed by United States

22   citizens. You will be given two tracts of land, each of 1280

23   acres, for your permanent homes. You will move to these

24   new homes within a year's time; but the President of the

25   United States retains the right to consolidate the

26   reservations or select alternative sites at some future date.

27   These things and the rest of our agreement are written on

28   this paper, which I read to you in full yesterday. If it is

29   good, you will sign it, and I will send it to the great White

30   Father. Shall we agree upon it?

31 SEALTH: Your people are many, like the grass that covers the

32   prairies; while my people are few, like the scattered trees

33   of the storm swept plain. I will sign your treaty because I

34   have no choice. I must put my trust in your paper and

35   your promises.

1 STEVENS: My heart and the heart of the Great White Father
2   smile to hear the wisdom of Sealth. I let you pledge
3   yourself first to our friendship.
4 SIMMONS: All you gotta do is make your mark there. I'll write
5   down your names, so as we know whose mark's whose.
6 STEVENS: *(To BUSH and MEEK)* Not sign it? You see, this was
7   not such a difficult decision. They're happy with it.
8 MEEK: I wouldn't exactly call it happy.
9 LESCHI: I should be the next to make my mark. But my heart
10   stops me. Not because it is filled with anger toward you. I
11   have always been the friend of the white man. My heart is
12   filled with sadness. I do not want to leave my home. I do not
13   want to leave the salmon and berries for food that will not
14   grow. How am I to farm this land that you give me? A plow
15   cannot dig in a mountain. Wheat cannot grow in rocks.
16 STEVENS: I have read to you that the President may move your
17   reservations.
18 LESCHI: Yes, but will the land be good land if we are moved?
19   Will you give the Indians good land and take the bad for
20   yourselves?
21 STEVENS: We will make the decisions.
22 LESCHI: In your treaty, we are told to free our slaves; yet, you
23   would make slaves of us.
24 SIMMONS: If he don't sign, I'll do it for 'em.
25 LESCHI: Our tribes are given two plots of 1280 acres. A married
26   white man may claim half that himself. Hundreds of
27   Indians to live on the land of two white families.
28 STEVENS: Others are satisfied. Will you sign?
29 LESCHI: I love this land more than my life.
30 STEVENS: Then you will just have to love the land the United
31   States gives you.
32 LESCHI: You do not give me anything.
33 STEVENS: You wouldn't even be here if it weren't for me. Who
34   do you think made you chief of the Nisqually? It's by my
35   authorization that you're even allowed to sign the treaty.

1   **LESCHI:** *(Taking out a piece of paper)* **Then I shall return your**
2   **gift. This authorization! It is my people who make me**
3   **their leader not you.** *(He tears the paper and throws it on*
4   *the ground.)*
5   **STEVENS: You impudent son of a — Get out! Go on back to your**
6   **mud shack and squaws, you Ignorant —**
7   **MEEK: Governor —**
8   **STEVENS: I'm in charge here!**
9   **MEEK: Of course you are. But we're tryin' t' make an**
10   **agreement.**
11   **STEVENS: When I want your opinion, I will ask for it. When I**
12   **require any form of assistance, I will request it. Have I**
13   **made myself clear?**
14   **MEEK: Yes, sir.**
15   **STEVENS:** *(Turning back to the Indians)* **Friends, we were**
16   **sealing our friendship —**
17   **LESCHI: There can be no friendship —**
18   **STEVENS: You have had your chance, Leschi. You are finished.**
19   **LESCHI: I will speak.** *(Pause)*
20   **STEVENS: You will speak — because I allow you to. You will say**
21   **all you have to say and then you will be silent. Now, speak.**
22   **LESCHI: When the white men came to this land, I embraced**
23   **them with an open heart. We lived like brothers, learning**
24   **one another's ways. My heart longs to keep this new**
25   **brother. But we are promised land to farm, and we are**
26   **given no farm land. We are promised the right to fish,**
27   **hunt and pasture our horses, and we are told to do this on**
28   **land you do not claim. Only the fool would believe such**
29   **land will go unclaimed. All that I desire is what has been**
30   **promised: a plot of lowland to fish and farm, a plot of high**
31   **pastureland for my horses, a small piece to join the two. Is**
32   **this too much to ask for those who have lived here since**
33   **the day raven and coyote came? Is this too much to ask in**
34   **a land of such bounty? If my people wish to choose**
35   **another chief, if they wish to bend themselves to the white**

1   chief's words, then they will. But I will not sell my people's

2   trust for sadness. I will die in a place of my own choosing.

3   *(He exits, followed by ONKWO then OWEN.)*

4   STEVENS: This arrogant man, this proud Leschi, thinks of

5   himself though he talks of his people. It is you who sign —

6   BUSH: He's only asking for what you said, governor.

7   STEVENS: Mr. Bush, are you deaf that you did not hear my

8   statement about interruptions?

9   BUSH: I'm not one of your subordinates, major.

10   STEVENS: I'm the governor of this territory, Bush.

11   BUSH: Is there a territory if the Nisqually won't sell their land?

12   STEVENS: Does the earth belong to those who first find it, Mr.

13   Bush, or to those who best use it? Shall a great country

14   with many resources be turned over to a few Indians to

15   roam over, making no use of the soil or timber and other

16   resources? Or should it be for civilized man to develop, to

17   make the abiding place of millions of people instead of

18   just a few?

19   BUSH: So you're gonna just take it from them? *(Pause)*

20   STEVENS: Perhaps, Mr. Bush, since you disagree with

21   government policy — in fact, since you're not even a

22   citizen of this country — you should leave here. After all,

23   you don't even have claim to the land you live on, do you?

24   And should some loyal citizen decide he wants that land ...

25   *(STEVENS smiles, then turns and exits. The OTHERS follow,*

26   *leaving BUSH alone.)*

27   BUSH: I know there are good people in this world. I see

28   kindness everyday. I know there must be good people in

29   our government. Why is it then that this man is the one

30   who's been sent here? Lord, there's just no rest is there?

31   Well, I'm not runnin' any more. This is my land. They're

32   gonna learn that.

33

34

35

1   **SCENE NINE**

2

3   *(Tumwater. Washington Territory.)*

4   **MEEK:** This is some farm, Bush.

5   **BUSH:** Whadayou want?

6   **MEEK:** Ya know, my land's been my own now for five years, but

7   ya think I got somethin' t' compare to this? I spend all my

8   time workin' for the government, travellin' the territory —

9   and whadaya think happens to the farm? Can't harvest if

10   ya don't plant, can't plant if ya ain't around. And even if I

11   do get somethin' planted and growin', I'm never there t'

12   take proper care of it. But this place —

13   **BUSH:** Did Stevens send you?

14   **MEEK:** I'm here 'cause I wanna be.

15   **BUSH:** You're aimin' t' take it yourself, aren't you?

16   **MEEK:** He's got you on the run, ain't he?

17   **ISABELLA:** *(Off)* George?! George?!

18   **OWEN:** *(Off)* Let's just set it here.

19   **ISABELLA:** *(Off)* A little further, Owen. Come on now. *(They*

20   *enter carrying a large wooden crate.)*

21   **ISABELLA:** Here it is. First reaper in Washington Territory.

22   Get something to open it with.

23   **OWEN:** I've had enough of this for one day.

24   **ISABELLA:** When harvest comes and you don't have to cut by

25   hand, you'll appreciate it.

26   **MEEK:** A reaper, huh? You just keep on goin', don't ya, Bush?

27   **BUSH:** That's right. I was thinkin' we might even clear those

28   trees up by the north meadow.

29   **OWEN:** Haven't you cleared enough already?

30   **BUSH:** That'd give us twenty more acres t' plant.

31   **OWEN:** Just like Stevens, use up the land.

32   **BUSH:** This is gonna be the best place anyone's seen. They're

33   gonna say that's the Bush family did that, that's their land.

34   **MEEK:** All right, Bush. You worked for it, you fight for it. You got

35   what I only wish I had. I envy you. Admire ya, too. That's

1   why I come. Wanted t' be the one t' tell ya. We just got word

2   from back east. Congress passed the bill. This is your land,

3   now. Legally. Congratulations. On the reaper, too.

4 OWEN: It's not his yet. Nobody owns the land till the treaty's

5   signed.

6 MEEK: Well, signed or not, Congress is gonna be spittin' that

7   one out, any day now, too.

8 BUSH: Has Stevens requested any changes?

9 MEEK: Nope, just like ya heard it.

10 BUSH: He's gonna force Leschi into a war.

11 MEEK: Man's a fool. Kanasket and some of the others, they've

12   just been lookin' for the chance. *(He exits.)*

13 ISABELLA: You used to think building this farm was

14   important.

15 OWEN: I used to think a lot of things.

16 BUSH: You'll be able to do what you want with it when it's

17   yours.

18 OWEN: It's not gonna be mine. Onkwo and I are getting

19   married and we're not gonna waste our time here.

20 BUSH: You can marry who you choose if she and her people'll

21   have you. But you better be darn sure you can make a life

22   together – and this farm is the best life the two of ya could

23   ever have.

24 OWEN: We don't think so.

25 BUSH: Then you're fools.

26 ISABELLA: George.

27 OWEN: I'm not gonna be slave to this land.

28 ISABELLA: This is your home.

29 OWEN: No more. *(LESCHI and ONKWO enter. OWEN runs to*

30   *ONKWO. LESCHI comes to the BUSHES, who are still by the*

31   *crate.)*

32 LESCHI: The reaper?

33 BUSH: Yeah.

34 LESCHI: I think I shall never have a chance to use such a thing

35   on my farm.

1 ISABELLA: Something will be done. They can't just throw
2   people outa their homes.
3 LESCHI: Your government thinks they can do as they will. But
4   if they pass the treaty, our council will meet. I have come
5   to tell you that I will never raise a hand against you or
6   yours. But if you join the army, I cannot be responsible for
7   what others may do – for our people are going to fight.
8 BUSH: A war can do no good.
9 LESCHI: I will not let your government force us from our
10   homes. I will fight until I have won what was promised or
11   until I die.
12 ISABELLA: A lot of your people will die, too.
13 LESCHI: If we do not fight, shall we escape dying?
14 BUSH: You know the value of peace and you choose to fight.
15   This is just like Stevens.
16 LESCHI: Shall I jump into my grave without a fight?
17 BUSH: How many warriors will you have? Thirty? To fight
18   hundreds of Americans?
19 LESCHI: You would have me bend my knee and say, "Oh, Great
20   White Chief, take this land." I will not. I will not submit to
21   this, Stevens.
22 BUSH: I would have you find a way to change him.
23 LESCHI: There is no way. This Stevens thinks he's more than a
24   man. Let him see his blood and then call himself God.
25 BUSH: Your heart runs away with your head and makes you
26   foolish.
27 LESCHI: My heart rages for my people and guides me.
28 BUSH: Your people will suffer.
29 LESCHI: Will you tell me what is best for my people? You are an
30   American, Bush. Whether your skin is brown or white, you
31   are an American. Till now, you have been my friend – but
32   still, you are an American. *(He exits. ONKWO starts to follow.)*
33 OWEN: I'm comin' with you.
34 ONKWO: No.
35 OWEN: This is my fight, too.

1   ONKWO: You want to fight your own people?

2   OWEN: I won't let them take your land.

3   BUSH: You could do more good by staying here.

4   OWEN: Don't tell me what to do! I'm gonna fight.

5   BUSH: You think you're gonna make the difference beatin'
6   the U.S. Army? The only chance the Nisqually have is
7   for enough Americans to support their fight. Loyal
8   Americans to force Stevens to change the treaty.

9   ONKWO: Owen — I want you to come with me. But your father,
10   I think, is wise. You may help more by staying.

11 OWEN: No, Onkwo.

12 ONKWO: When we have won, we will be together. *(She exits.*
13   *Indian drumming starts.)*

14

15

16   **SCENE TEN**

17

18   *(Indian Council Grounds. Slow drumming. From one side of*
19   *the clearing, LESCHI and some NISQUALLY enter. From the*
20   *other, KANASKET and some STKAMISH. They are prepared*
21   *for war.)*

22 KANASKET: Now, you are ready to fight.

23 LESCHI: Yes.

24 KANASKET: Good. You will go to the Yakimas and get them to
25   join us?

26 LESCHI: I will go to my mother's people. I will ask them to join
27   us.

28 KANASKET: We will be strong even without Sealth and the
29   Duwamish. When we kill all the whites, they will have no
30   one to serve.

31 LESCHI: We fight for homes, not to kill whites. We fight only
32   the American government.

33 KANASKET: We fight only the government. *(They seal their*
34   *bond. LESCHI moves off. To one of the Stkamish:)* **Which**
35   **means we will kill every American who walks this land.**

1   *(They exit to rapid drumming. STEVENS enters and speaks*
2   *to the audience.)*
3   STEVENS: I'm made out to be the villain, but do you know
4   what these People have now done? They have murdered
5   McCalister. They have massacred five families at the
6   White River. Are any of us safe? The army was out after the
7   massacre, but now they claim there's no danger. General
8   Wool has ordered them to ignore my commands and only
9   respond to him. Well, I will not leave my citizens
10   unprotected.
11
12
13   **SCENE ELEVEN**
14
15   *(Tumwater. Washington Territory. Christmas. From the*
16   *house, the sound of "Silent Night" being sung. OWEN enters*
17   *from the woods with a freshly cut fir. STEVENS moves*
18   *towards him. OWEN, startled by STEVENS, turns ready to*
19   *fight, then sees who it is.)*
20   OWEN: You're lucky I didn't have a gun, governor. I mighta
21   shot.
22   STEVENS: Christmas eve's a time for generosity, boy, not
23   hostility.
24   OWEN: You gonna just take a free dinner tonight, then,
25   insteada grabbin' some land?
26   STEVENS: What I do is for the people of this territory. I have
27   gained nothing personally from any transaction with the
28   Indians.
29   OWEN: They just have a lot to lose.
30   STEVENS: There's a war going on, boy. We didn't start it.
31   OWEN: There was no war before you came.
32   STEVENS: Ninety percent of the Indians are still at peace with
33   us. It's only a few who choose defiance.
34   OWEN: And you'll exterminate them in no time, right? Merry
35   Christmas, governor. I'm sure we'll have peace on earth

by New Year's. *(ISABELLA enters, followed at intervals by BUSH and their guests.)*

ISABELLA: You do enjoy spending holidays down here, don't you, governor? That's a beautiful tree, Owen.

STEVENS: I'm afraid it's business that's brought me, Mrs. Bush. I'm sorry to intrude on your holiday, but under the powers invested in me as Governor, I have the right to organize civilian military forces. I am now doing so to combat the hostile Indians.

BUSH: Leschi has made you a peace offer.

STEVENS: Yes, to be pardoned. But they've killed American citizens. I won't negotiate with renegades. You people want to make a home here. You want title to this land. I'm trying to help you.

OWEN: Like a fox in a henhouse.

MARY MCCALISTER: I don't know, Owen. Leschi and the Nisqually were always good to us. But when my Jim went out to talk peace, somebody shot him. I don't know if any of us can feel safe till the whole thing's settled.

STEVENS: That's right, Mrs. McCalister. In fact, Leschi himself has gone across the mountains to bring the Yakimas into this war. If they come over, we'll need more than the army. We've got to protect ourselves. My plan is to get three hundred volunteers to finish this war up before planting time. That way, you'll all be able to go into your fields with peace of mind.

SIMMONS: Sounds good to me. I'll sign up.

A SETTLER: Me, too. *(About half the SETTLERS go over to STEVENS' side.)*

STEVENS: *(To BUSH and OWEN)* What about you?

OWEN: We're not gonna join our enemies to fight our friends.

MARY MCCALISTER: Are we your enemies, Owen?

ISABELLA: Of course, you're not.

OWEN: The Nisqually's enemies are my enemies.

STEVENS: Treason's a serious crime, boy.

1 OWEN: You're the traitor. You're the one destroyin' the
2   country.
3 STEVENS: I am enforcing the laws of this territory. We had five
4   families butchered up at White River.
5 OWEN: They shoulda done their butcherin' in Olympia.
6 BUSH: Now, you hush, boy.
7 MARY MCCALISTER: I can't believe what I hear from you,
8   Owen. You want more killin'? You wanna see your Pa
9   carried in cold and bleeding? Watch your Ma wipe the
10   blood off the table, clutchin' the rag to stop herself from
11   screamin'? That what you want?
12 OWEN: If it'd do some good, I'd see the lot of ya dead.
13 ISABELLA: Owen! That's enough. We don't want any more
14   killing. Not any of us, not any of the Nisqually. The
15   Nisqually are our friends, but these folks are too.
16 STEVENS: You can't have it both ways. You've got to choose.
17   You're either American or Indian.
18 BUSH: We're just people, governor, just plain people.
19 SIMMONS: That wasn't one of the choices, George.
20 ISABELLA: We're Americans, of course. But that doesn't mean
21   we can't see wrong being done to others.
22 MARY MCCALISTER: You'd better stop worryin' about others
23   and start worryin' about your own, Isabella. You got one
24   sick boy there. Take care of the hate in your own house
25   fore you try curin' the rest of us. *(She tosses a small*
26   *wrapped package on the ground. She exits as ISABELLA*
27   *picks up the package.)*
28 STEVENS: So, Mr. Bush, what will it be?
29 BUSH: We'll take our chances on our own.
30 SETTLER ON THE BUSH SIDE: That's right. We don't gotta
31   choose sides just cause he says so.
32 STEVENS: No? You try tellin' Kanasket you're an American
33   friend of his when he shows up. *(STEVENS and the*
34   *SETTLERS on his side exit. Silence. ISABELLA moves off by*
35   *herself. OWEN follows.)*

1 OWEN: Ma, I'm sorry. But those people —
2 ISABELLA: Owen. You know how much hate I've seen in my
3   life? Since the day I married your father, everywhere
4   we've gone. And now, to see it in one of my own.
5 OWEN: I wasn't the one to start it, ma.
6 ISABELLA: And it looks like you won't be the one to put an end
7   to it, either.
8 BUSH: It breeds on itself, son. And you're becomin' part of it.
9   (*Noises off in the woods. The SETTLERS tense, rifles ready.*
10   *All still, listening.*)
11 A SETTLER: Kanasket?
12 BUSH: Don't know. (*Warily, they move back into the house.*
13   *OWEN stands apart and speaks to himself.*)
14 OWEN: Kanasket is out to kill us. Stevens is out to kill the
15   Nisqually. Leschi's killed some too, probably. And I'm
16   ready to see more.
17
18
19   **SCENE TWELVE**
20
21   (*Tumwater. Washington Territory. Early spring.*)
22 BUSH: Time to plant, son.
23 OWEN: What's wrong with me, Pa?
24 BUSH: Nothin'. Nothin's wrong with you, son.
25 OWEN: I'm just so — mad. I'm mad at everything.
26 BUSH: There's plenty to be mad about in this world. Ya either
27   let it eat ya up, or ya push through it. You'll be all right.
28   Just takes time.
29 OWEN: I feel like runnin' far away.
30 BUSH: Yeah. I know the feeling. But we can't now. We got
31   plantin' t' do. (*STEVENS, SIMMONS, MEEK and some of the*
32   *civilian force enter.*)
33 STEVENS: George Bush, you and your family are to
34   immediately pack your belongings and come with us.
35 BUSH: What for?

1 STEVENS: We are moving all foreign born and non-citizen
2   settlers into the fort for reasons of safety.
3 BUSH: We've got a blockhouse, here. We can take care of
4   ourselves.
5 STEVENS: Are you coming peacefully?
6 BUSH: We're not comin' at all.
7 STEVENS: Then, you force us to take you.
8 SIMMONS: If they don't wanna go —
9 STEVENS: They're collaborators. Why do you think they
10   haven't been attacked?
11 OWEN: Mike's place hasn't been attacked. Maybe, he's helpin'
12   Leschi, too.
13 STEVENS: You've made clear whose side you're on. You're
14   traitors.
15 BUSH: We're not traitors, governor — and if you want us to
16   come into the fort, we will.
17 OWEN: No, Pa!
18 BUSH: But you said you wanted folks to be able to plant their
19   crops. Let us plant, then we'll come.
20 STEVENS: It's planting time for Americans, not you.
21 BUSH: We'll come after we've done our planting.
22 STEVENS: Not only are you coming now, but I'm confiscating
23   this farm.
24 MEEK: We got a war with the Indians. You want a war between
25   Americans, too?
26 STEVENS: If you choose to obstruct justice, Mr. Meek, we will
27   take you in as well. I have the legal right to confiscate
28   property of enemies of the territory, and I'm going to do it.
29 BUSH: I got a field to plow.
30 STEVENS: Seize them. *(There is a scuffle. SIMMONS stands*
31   *apart. MEEK tries to intervene to help BUSH and OWEN, but*
32   *is thrown out of the way. STEVENS and the VOLUNTEERS*
33   *gain control of BUSH and OWEN.)*
34 STEVENS: I declare this land forfeit to the government of the
35   United States of America. Maybe, you'll have some respect

1   for authority, now, Bush. *(Lieutenant KAUTZ and a few*

2   *regular ARMY TROOPS enter.)*

3 KAUTZ: What's the problem here, governor?

4 STEVENS: Just trying to maintain some law and order,

5   Lieutenant.

6 KAUTZ: Are you arresting these people?

7 STEVENS: Exactly.

8 KAUTZ: On what charge, sir?

9 STEVENS: Treason.

10 KAUTZ: I'm afraid that's out of your jurisdiction, sir.

11 STEVENS: I'm the Governor of this territory, Lieutenant.

12 KAUTZ: You've got no authority to arrest anyone on a charge of

13   treason, sir.

14 STEVENS: I've got the authority to arrest anyone on any

15   charge I please.

16 KAUTZ: I'm afraid you don't, sir.

17 STEVENS: Are you telling me how to run this territory?

18 KAUTZ: No, sir. I'm just telling you you can't arrest these folks.

19 STEVENS: And I'm telling you I will arrest them, right now.

20   Take them away.

21 KAUTZ: Governor, I don't want there to be any bloodshed,

22   here. But if I have to, I'll order my men to shoot.

23 STEVENS: I'm ordering you to get out of my way.

24 KAUTZ: I'm sorry, sir, but I don't take orders from you.

25   General Wool is my superior.

26 STEVENS: This is your last warning, Kautz.

27 KAUTZ: *(To his men)* Prepare to fire. *(They lift their rifles.)*

28 STEVENS: I order you to put those rifles down.

29 KAUTZ: Aim. *(They aim their rifles.)*

30 STEVENS: Do you hear me?! I order you! I'm governor of this

31   territory! *(A long pause. The SOLDIERS do not flinch. KAUTZ*

32   *stares directly at STEVENS.)* I'll have you court-martialed.

33 KAUTZ: You can try sir.

34 STEVENS: Release them.

35 KAUTZ: Stand easy. *(STEVENS starts to exit.)*

1   BUSH: Governor! You claim you want law and order, but —

2   STEVENS: I don't need a lecture from you, Bush.

3   BUSH: For once you're gonna listen! You're always so busy

4   talkin' you can't hear anybody but yourself. People don't

5   care about laws — or progress. People care about havin' a

6   home. That's all we want. That's all Leschi wants.

7   STEVENS: There are many people in the United States

8   Government, Bush, many people, who would exterminate

9   every Indian in this land. There are people who would

10   enslave all Negroes and deport all those of the yellow race. I

11   don't support these policies. I believe in letting people live.

12 BUSH: On your terms. Would you want me always layin' down

13   the rules for you? Everyone's got to give a little sometime.

14   Give a little, governor. Compromise. Make peace.

15 KAUTZ: You ought to be able to now, governor. I came by to

16   deliver this dispatch: Kanasket's Dead — and Leschi's

17   turned himself in.

18 BUSH: It's over.

19 STEVENS: Not till he's punished.

20 OWEN: Is Onkwo with him?

21 KAUTZ: Dispatch only mentioned Leschi.

22 STEVENS: But, Bush, I can make peace, now. If the Nisqually are

23   really no longer at war, then I may be able to give them what

24   they want. Do you want to know what might be good land for

25   their reservations? This farm. With your agreement, of

26   course. It would be a just compromise, don't you think?

27   *(He turns and goes. SIMMONS wants to say something but*

28   *he can't. He follows STEVENS. MEEK goes to BUSH.)*

29 MEEK: George.

30 BUSH: Go on, get outa here.

31 MEEK: George.

32 BUSH: Go lick his boots.

33 MEEK: George, I'm not on his side. I'm up t' here with 'em. I

34   seen my fill o' vengeance and hate. I'm gonna try and stop

35   'em. If I can't, I'll resign. *(He exits.)*

1   OWEN: Pa ... ? Pa? *(BUSH is numb. Slow drumming as LESCHI*
2   *enters. He turns to the audience. He holds up his chains.)*
3   LESCHI: Where do they think I will run? I chose to come here.
4   They have tried me once already and found me innocent.
5   That was a mistake, of course. So now, they are trying me
6   again. With a new judge. A judge chosen by the governor.
7   A judge who would not let Lieutenant Kautz testify,
8   because the Lieutenant's map proved I could not have
9   killed the men they claim I did. It is silly. I know my fate.
10
11
12   **SCENE THIRTEEN**
13
14   *(Fort Steilacoom. Washington Territory. LESCHI, chained,*
15   *guarded by a soldier. BUSH and OWEN, sadly downcast, go*
16   *to him.)*
17   LESCHI: You should not look like it's the hundredth day of
18   rain, Bush. It's planting time, a time for hope.
19   OWEN: Pa's not real eager to plant, this year. I was thinkin' we
20   might try to get a sawmill goin'.
21   LESCHI: I sometimes wonder if there will come a day when
22   there will be no more trees. The trees will disappear like
23   the beaver, and then the water will follow. The red men
24   will vanish and the white men will be left with nothing
25   but dust. *(He laughs. KAUTZ enters with a blanket.)*
26   KAUTZ: My wife thought you could use this.
27   LESCHI: She is kind.
28   KAUTZ: It's cold for this time of year.
29   LESCHI: The spring will come.
30   KAUTZ: They've called the court back. They must have
31   reached a verdict. Are you ready?
32   LESCHI: I would rather breathe clean air.
33   KAUTZ: You don't have to be afraid. There's no way they're
34   gonna find you guilty.
35   LESCHI: Kautz, my friend, I am not afraid to hear your court's

1   words. I have no need to hear them. You go. You be my
2   ears. *(KAUTZ is hesitant. He looks at BUSH.)*
3 BUSH: We'll stay.
4 KAUTZ: *(Aside to BUSH)* I'm not gonna allow them to execute
5   that man in this fort. *(He exits. A silence.)*
6 OWEN: *(With difficulty)* Leschi, I haven't heard a thing from
7   Onkwo since that first note saying she hadda rest east of
8   the mountains. Why haven't I heard from her?
9 LESCHI: When we fled our land and walked through the
10   mountains, the journey was hard. We crossed back and
11   forth through the icy river, many times, more times than
12   there are nights of the moon. Even when we reached the
13   plain, the cold of the waters would not leave Onkwo. So
14   she rested. She tried to warm her body; and she seemed to
15   grow strong. But the cold returned. Now, she will remain
16   east of the mountains in her mother's land.
17 OWEN: But for how long?
18 LESCHI: When her soul is strong enough, it will walk her
19   father's land, too.
20 OWEN: Her soul?
21 BUSH: She's dead, Owen.
22 LESCHI: There is no death, only a change of worlds.
23 OWEN: *(Trying to hold back his sobs)* Why didn't I go with her?
24 LESCHI: I am the one who led Onkwo across the mountains.
25 BUSH: You're not to blame.
26 LESCHI: I helped bring about many deaths. So did Stevens —
27   and many others. Soon we will all cease to live this life.
28   Your court is announcing my fate, now.
29 BUSH: Everybody knows you didn't kill those men.
30 LESCHI: All that is important is I killed some Americans.
31 BUSH: It was wartime. They can't convict for murder during a
32   war.
33 LESCHI: To many, the person who begins the war is nothing
34   but a murderer.
35 BUSH: When we fought the British, nobody called us murderers.

1 LESCHI: I think you are wrong. I think the British called you
2   murderers. But you won your war. I have lost mine. Still, I
3   have no regrets. I would fight again. I am sad for my
4   people, not for myself. *(Pause)*
5 BUSH: Your people may yet win. Stevens has offered the
6   possibility of new reservations ... If I give up the farm,
7   Stevens will make it a reservation.
8 LESCHI: And you will do this?
9 BUSH: He can take the farm even without my agreeing.
10 LESCHI: You will give up your home without a fight?
11 BUSH: What kind of home is it? It's mine by "special
12   exemption" not by citizenship. Half the people follow
13   leaders like Stevens. They persecute people like you. I've
14   been fighting my whole life. I'm tired of it.
15 LESCHI: And where will you find another home?
16 BUSH: Look, sooner or later, they're gonna do to me and mine
17   what they're doin' to you.
18 LESCHI: They kill my body not my spirit. And my spirit, having
19   fought for this land, is strong. It will find a home in another
20   world. Will you find a home if you give this one up? *(Pause.*
21   *KAUTZ enters. He goes to LESCHI. He drops his head. Indian*
22   *drumming. LESCHI sings a strong, vibrant chant as he is led*
23   *off. BUSH picks up the blanket. He wraps it around the*
24   *sobbing OWEN and holds him close.)*
25
26
27   **SCENE FOURTEEN**
28
29   *(Tumwater. Washington Territory. Bright American music*
30   *and a festive atmosphere. Some NEIGHBORS are putting a*
31   *red, white and blue bunting on a fence. ISABELLA is*
32   *greeting arriving GUESTS.)*
33 ISABELLA: Happy fourth, friends.
34 A SETTLER: Happy anniversary, dear.
35 ANOTHER SETTLER: A special one, it is, too. No more war.

1   **THE FIRST SETTLER: And no more Isaac Stevens! Everything's**
2   **gonna be fine, now. All of us together sharin' the good times.**
3   **ISABELLA: George is inside. Go on and get yourselves something**
4   **to eat.** *(They exit.)* **All of us together.** *(MARY MCCALISTER*
5   *enters, moving tentatively towards ISABELLA.)*
6   **MCCALISTER: Isabella?**
7   **ISABELLA: Mary!**
8   **MCCALISTER: I didn't know if —**
9   **ISABELLA: Yes. Yes, I'm glad you're here. I've missed you.**
10   **MCCALISTER: Holidays just haven't seemed right. This is for**
11   **you and George. And this one's for Owen, for his birthday.**
12   **ISABELLA: Mary — Mary, thank you ... Do you know that boy is**
13   **still up there trying to get that darned mill working? On a**
14   **day like this. Fiddling with that mill and watching the**
15   **waterfall. Seems he doesn't even eat any more. But you're**
16   **here. That's good. That's good.**
17   **MCCALISTER: I'm so sorry, Isabel.**
18   **ISABELLA: You did what you thought was right. We all did.**
19   *(They embrace.)*
20   **MCCALISTER: I heard the government's puttin' up Leschi's**
21   **farm for auction. Maybe, you and George could buy that.**
22   **ISABELLA: Why would we want to buy Leschi's farm?**
23   **MCCALISTER: You haven't heard what he's done?**
24   **ISABELLA: We refused, Mary. George and I refused to give up**
25   **the farm.**
26   **STEVENS:** *(Entering)* **Happy Independence Day, Mrs. Bush. I**
27   **hope I'm not intruding. I just wanted to pay my respects**
28   **before I go off to Washington.**
29   **ISABELLA: Sorry you'll be leaving us.**
30   **STEVENS: Yes, you're happy to be rid of me, but I'm equally**
31   **happy to be going. I believe in this territory, and being**
32   **your representative to Congress —**
33   **ISABELLA: You won't be representing me, governor.**
34   **STEVENS: I represent everyone, you as well as the majority of**
35   **people in this territory, who as you know voted to send me**

1   to Congress.

2 ISABELLA: Maybe, they just wanted to get you back east. You'll

3   excuse us. I've got guests to attend to. *(During STEVENS'*

4   *speech, BUSH and others come out of the house and some*

5   *NISQUALLY enter from the same direction as STEVENS did.)*

6 STEVENS: You may despise me as much as you like, Mrs. Bush,

7   but you can't deny what I've done for this territory. I've

8   gotten roads built, mail service started, land authorized

9   for a university. I've made sure single women could stake

10   land claims. I haven't done these things for myself. I've

11   done them for the people.

12 ISABELLA: Governor, I don't think you give a lick about

13   people. *(Going to the NISQUALLY, who are extremely*

14   *somber:)* Good to see you, friends. Come right on in.

15 STEVENS: Yes, come in. I'm glad —

16 BUSH: We can welcome our own guests. *(He clasps hands with*

17   *a few of the NISQUALLY.)*

18 STEVENS: I came here to tell you this personally before I leave

19   tomorrow. Because I believe in serving the people of this

20   territory, because I believe we've all got to live together, I

21   went to the Nisqually last night and gave them new

22   reservations. I gave them the best farmland available. I

23   gave them, despite your refusal to agree, your farm.

24 ISABELLA: No, you can't. He can't do it, George.

25 BUSH: He's got the power.

26 STEVENS: These people, unlike Leschi, have remained loyal to

27   our government. They deserve a good reservation.

28 ISABELLA: This is our land.

29 STEVENS: You'd deny the Nisqually the farmland that's their

30   due? You'd fight Leschi's people?

31 MCCALISTER: There's no proper Christian word to describe you.

32 ISABELLA: We're not going to let you take it.

33 STEVENS: It was their home long before you came, Mrs. Bush.

34 BUSH: Are you trying to tell us about the Nisqually? I'm a

35   peacable man, but I swear I could rip your head right off

1   your shoulders.

2   STEVENS: Just like an ape, ey, Bush? *(BUSH charges at*

3   *STEVENS. Some SETTLERS pull him off and throw him*

4   *back. BUSH draws his pistol.)*

5   BUSH: Every part of my body's sayin' kill that man. Kill 'im

6   and hold onto this land. Why is it the only way you can do

7   justice to people of color is by taking from other people of

8   color? *(He lowers the gun.)* I'm not gonna let you turn me

9   against the Nisqually. Whether they fought with Leschi or

10   not, they deserve this land. *(To ISABELLA:)* We'll do what

11   we shoulda done a dozen years ago. We'll go further north

12   like you wanted when we came. We'll try another country.

13   SETTLERS: No. No. No, George, you can't.

14   BUSH: There isn't a soul alive who loves this land more than

15   me. But we're one family, and this is a whole people.

16   There's been enough fightin'. Let there be a little peace

17   now and some justice – even if it's not for all of us. *(Pause.)*

18   ONE OF THE NISQUALLY: We came here today to talk to you,

19   Bush. But we do not need to hear any more. This is the paper

20   the governor gave us. *(Tears it.)* We will not take your farm.

21   STEVENS: This is the land I gave you.

22   ANOTHER NISQUALLY: We will have Leschi's farm as our

23   home or nothing.

24   SETTLERS: Yes. That's right. It's only fair.

25   SIMMONS: There's no reason why they can't, governor.

26   There's no Americans on it, and they've got a real tie to it.

27   *(STEVENS gives him a scorching look. SIMMONS just smiles.)*

28   STEVENS: You don't want the best land available? You want

29   Leschi's farm? I give it to you. And another two thousand

30   acres on top of that. *I* give it to them. By my choice.

31   Because what is done in this territory is my responsibility

32   and is done by my power. And when this new reservation

33   is approved by Congress, and when the railroad comes

34   through and brings prosperity to this territory – a

35   prosperity you all want – that will be my doing as well.

1   You people will reap the benefits of what I've done for
2   years to come, and you had better remember who was
3   responsible. *(He exits. OWEN runs on.)*
4 OWEN: Pa! Pa! I did it! I did it! The mill's goin'! I just moved the
5   wheel up a little higher to catch the falls sooner. The
6   falls're pushin' the wheel around and that blade is just
7   buzzin' away. We got the first mill in the territory.
8 BUSH: That's great, son, great. *(OWEN notices everyone*
9   *gathered around, staring. He looks at his father.)* Stevens
10   was here. He gave the Nisqually new reservations.
11 ISABELLA: He tried to give them our land, but they'd only take
12   Leschi's. *(OWEN rushes to the NISQUALLY, clasping hands*
13   *with them. BUSH and ISABELLA embrace. Music,*
14   *celebration starts. OWEN rushes back to his parents and*
15   *hugs them. The music stops, the crowd freezes. LESCHI and*
16   *ONKWO slowly walk toward the family.)*
17 OWEN: *(To his parents with determination)* **I'm gonna work.**
18   *(ONKWO lays a hand on his shoulder. He doesn't*
19   *acknowledge her presence but a lightness fills him.)* **And I'm**
20   **gonna take care of this land.**
21 BUSH & LESCHI: And it will take care of you.
22 ISABELLA: We're gonna be all right now.
23 OWEN: *(Hugging his parents)* I love you. *(STEVENS has come*
24   *slowly On-stage. He speaks gently with feeling to the audience.)*
25 STEVENS: And I love all of you, my friends. That's why I have
26   done this. *(Simultaneously, STEVENS, LESCHI and BUSH*
27   *each scoops up a handful of earth and turns to the audience.)*
28 STEVENS: *(The earth clenched tightly in his fist, speaking*
29   *passionately but without harshness)* **For you!** *(LESCHI*
30   *smiles, holding his hand in the air, and lets the earth fall*
31   *freely.)*
32 BUSH: *(Kisses the earth he holds)* **We got a home. Woooo!** *(He*
33   *throws the dirt high in the air as He turns back to the crowd*
34   *On-stage)* **We got a home! A home!!** *(People shout for joy. The*
35   *dance swings into full motion. The music rises. As the lights*

1   *and music fade, BUSH, STEVENS and LESCHI walk toward*
2   *the audience.)*
3   BUSH: George Bush died peacefully on his farm in 1863.
4   STEVENS: Isaac Stevens was killed leading a Union Army charge
5   at the Second Battle of Bull Run during the Civil War.
6   BUSH: And when Washington became a state in 1889, Owen
7   Bush was elected to the first State Legislature.
8   LESCHI: On July 4th, 1895, he led a procession of a thousand
9   celebrants as they carried Leschi's body from its initial
10   resting place to a more fitting burial site among the
11   forests and waters of the land of Leschi's ancestors.
12   STEVENS: They made the journey on the railroad Isaac
13   Stevens brought to this land.
14   LESCHI: This land.
15   STEVENS: Our country.
16   BUSH: Our home.
17
18
19   **CURTAIN**
20
21
22
23
24
25
26
27
28
29
30
31
32
33
34
35

Julie Salverson

Patti Fraser

BOOM
by Julie Salverson and Patti Fraser

One of the most distinguished public figures of the late twentieth-century was certainly Princess Diana of the United Kingdom, and she earned distinction by her efforts devoted to the terrible global scourge caused by the use of land mines. Raising funds for international organizations dealing with their eradication, visiting the tragic victims of land mines—especially injured children—militating against the use and manufacture of mines and calling for their banishment as a legitimate weapon of war, Diana did much by her speeches, public appearances and other measures to heighten public awareness of the dangers and the shame that otherwise civilized nations had caused by the use of this insidious military device.

Far from being a polemical, didactic scenario treating this issue, Julie Salverson and Patti Fraser's play offers a highly dramatic yet wonderfully interactive performance opportunity for young students. Developed with Canadian students and teachers, and refined in public performances, the play engages the issue from the perspective of young adults in first-world nations struggling to come to grips with a problem that seems remote and irrelevant to them personally, as well as unclear to them intellectually and historically. The play, that is, provides information and statistics but also puts a human face on the problem in a way that the dramatic arts can best accomplish.

Two special features of the play bear special mention. The first is the plot focus on the relationship between the high school students Roger, from Canada, and Ana, a Bosnian refugee. Roger would like to date Ana, but she resists because she's so focused on her own work and scholarship. By the end of the play, however, they both realize that building a relationship requires a willingness to really learn what drives the other person, and both are ready to do just that. This relationship forms the emotional core of the play: Roger's struggle as a first-world teenager to become more informed about this seemingly overwhelming and remote issue that consumes Ana, and Ana's struggle to communicate her experience of familial and social tragedy to her schoolmates; and their mutual attempt to build a meaningful personal relationship. Their situation thus provides a strong sense of development and a powerful point of identification between spectators and characters that is relevant and engaging for young audiences.

The second noteworthy feature of *BOOM* is its performance style: mainly that of a clown show. Rather than wrestle with the all-too-familiar problem of representing (more or less realistically) violence and human suffering onstage, the writers chose to portray these issues metaphorically. To this end, the cast of characters takes the form of a "clown chorus" who portray the thirteen-plus roles, with the exception of the principal parts of Roger and Ana. This strategy presents an enormous opportunity for group-developed student creativity and humor (particularly satire) in presenting painful, shocking and occasionally brutal situations that are often difficult for younger actors to play. Certainly humor can always serve as a "coping mechanism" for engaging serious issues, but in *BOOM* it becomes the bedrock for organizing rehearsals, casting the roles, improvising scenes, and relating the story to the audience in a frank and unabashed way.

Perhaps the best way to "explain" this play to a new reader is to remind one to bear in mind the words of the clown chorus, frequently repeated throughout the drama: "this is a show from beginning to end, so don't take things so seriously!"

Characters:

Roger: a high school student
Ana: a high school student
Class Clowns: (doubling or expanding roles is possible)
    Clown Queen
    Teacher
    Don: Roger's friend
    Mother
    Son
    Daughter
    Game Show Host
    Maria
    Billy
    Tour Guide
    Passenger
    Speaker
    Musicians

Music: A music tape accompanies the script, and live music can also be combined with it. Music is important to give the feeling or reality of a band. For example, the Clown Chorus is often introduced and punctuated by drumbeats, played live by the band.

Setting: The main feature of the set is a large, pale blue screen on which cutout images appear through shadow-puppets and/or overhead projections. When the audience enters, the title BOOM is projected on the screen in handwritten letters. In front of the screen are a number of blocks which, when piled together, present the image of a field and trees. When the blocks are separated and used throughout the play, the image is also separated. There is a border on either side of the screen that presents an image of nature similar to that on the blocks, but not identical. Stage Right is a computer terminal and screen where Ana works on her experiment. The play takes place within the classroom that takes on several locales, all of which are progressively distorted from scene to scene. Musicians double as clowns and their band area sits Stage Left. This is all one world. All actors remain On-stage for the entirety of the play.

    BOOM is intended for a wide audience, but in particular young people from the ages of ten and up. It is intended to be performed by young people ages thirteen to twenty-four. The play was developed through a workshop process with a class of teachers in training at the University of British Columbia in the summer of 1996. It was then commissioned by The Canadian Red Cross, and co-produced by Flying Blind Theatre Events in Toronto for its premiere on December 1, 1997, at the YMCA of Greater Toronto. The thirteen performers were from Medway High School, Middlesex County, Ontario. The director was drama teacher Toni Wilson. The designer was Ruth Howard, with Medway students courtesy of the Ontario Arts Council Artists in Education program. Consulting director was Aleksandar Lukac.

1	<div align="center">**SCENE ONE**</div>
2	
3	*(The sound of a drum flourish. CLASS CLOWNS enter.)*
4	**CLOWNS:** *(Whispering)* **This is a play from beginning to end**
5	**So don't take things too seriously**
6	**This is a play from beginning to end**
7	**So don't take things too seriously**
8	**CLOWN QUEEN:** **We've all gone mad, it's all gone bad, so**
9	**What should we, what could we, what should we do?**
10	**CLOWNS:** **What should we, what could we, what should we do?**
11	**CLOWNS:** *(Spoken)* **Don't take things too seriously!**
12	*(ROGER and ANA enter.)*
13	**ROGER:** **She's hard to explain. I mean, Ana's different. Keeps**
14	**to herself, doesn't go to parties n' stuff. She's only been in**
15	**the school about a year. We just started talkin' on the field**
16	**trip last spring, I got stuck at the front of the bus but it**
17	**turned out okay. 'Cause I got to sit with her, eh? Then she**
18	**won this big prize, like the best science student for all**
19	**Canada. But she's still okay. I told her she should date or**
20	**she'd look like too much of a brainer. She laughed, kinda.**
21	**ANA:** **Scientific equipment is so fantastic. Clean, measurable,**
22	**predictable. Mostly I like to be alone and work on my**
23	**invention. It takes hours of work and it's going to make**
24	**me world famous. I'm not going out with Roger, he's a**
25	**friend. I kinda like him, though. He's funny and sort of**
26	**weird, like if he wanted to, he could care about things.**
27	**ANA:** *(To Roger)* **Did you hear, we had a test yesterday in English?**
28	**ROGER:** **No way! I was at hockey practice, she knew I was**
29	**missing class.**
30	**ANA:** **Totally unfair. She has to let you make it up. Hey, tell her**
31	**you'll write her a story about the finals. Like, from an eye**
32	**witness point of view.**
33	**ROGER:** **I can't write like that.**
34	**ANA:** **You can, just do it like a diary or something. I'll be your**
35	**editor.** *(Drum beat. TEACHER enters. ANA and ROGER sit,*

1   with CLOWNS *as classmates. During the following ANA and*
2   *ROGER remain seated together.)*

3   **TEACHER: Class ...** *(The class comes to attention.)* ... **What would**
4   **you do? If I was to tell you something you didn't want to**
5   **hear?**

6   **ANA:** *(To ROGER)* **I would ask myself, how do you know I don't**
7   **want to hear it?**

8   **ROGER:** *(Joking to ANA)* **I'd keep my mouth shut!**

9   **CLOWN: I'd wonder if it's about me?**

10 **CLOWN:** *(Puts up hand)* **Is it about what happened in the**
11 **newspaper yesterday?**

12 **CLOWN: Which things? The horrible made-up ones or the**
13 **horrible ones that are true?**

14 **CLOWN: Did you hear about ...** *(CLOWNS say three or four lines*
15 *about the horrible things that might have happened, e.g. "Ten-*
16 *Car Pile-Up," "Terrorist Attack," etc. These are to be chosen by*
17 *each cast. The TEACHER is trying to get the class's attention.)*

18 **CLOWN:** *(Whistles, gets attention, the song stops)* **I guess it**
19 **kinda depends on what happens after you hear a bad**
20 **story. I mean, does it mean you have to feel BAD about it?**

21 **CLOWN QUEEN: Oh, you'll feel bad when you hear this.**

22 **CLOWNS: Shhhhhhh.**

23 **TEACHER: Today we are studying the humanitarian crisis**
24 **caused by antipersonnel landmines. That means, mines**
25 **that hurt people. Imagine millions of acres of green**
26 **farmland you couldn't walk across because it was filled**
27 **with explosives. Couldn't walk to gather food, or get fresh**
28 **water, or visit friends, or play. In Ottawa this December an**
29 **historic occasion will be taking place.**

30 **CLOWNS: Ahhhhhh.**

31 **TEACHER: Over 100 countries ...**

32 **CLOWNS: Maybe Russia, not China, not the United States.**

33 **TEACHER: ... will be signing a ban on the production and use**
34 **of landmines.** *(Screen: words with facts the teacher is*
35 *speaking, or others, are scribbled on to an overhead*

1 *projection.)* **The signing countries will have to destroy**
2 **their stockpiles and begin the honorable and difficult**
3 **work of de-mining the over 100 million landmines in the**
4 **world today, and finding funds to help with the enormous**
5 **costs to mine-affected countries. I would like each of you**
6 **to write a report about what you might do.** *(CLOWNS start*
7 *to cheer, then stop. CLOWN puts up hand.)*
8 **CLOWN: Did you say ... 100 million?**
9 **TEACHER:** *(Becomes automaton-like. During the following*
10 *speech handwriting appears on the overhead, the scribbling*
11 *of students trying to keep up, crossing out one figure,*
12 *adding another.)* **There are an estimated 110 million active**
13 **landmines scattered over 70 countries, one for every 52**
14 **people in our world. A further 110 million have been**
15 **stockpiled. 2,000 people are involved in accidents every**
16 **month. Landmines are left from really old wars and put**
17 **in every day from brand new ones. Every year 26,000**
18 **people are maimed or killed. One goes off every twenty**
19 **minutes.** *(CLOWN goes to screen, hangs a clock on it, sits*
20 *under it and watches it.)*
21 **CLOWN: Statistics make my brain hurt.**
22 **CLOWN: What brain?** *(Drum beat. Screen goes dark.)*
23 **CLOWNS:** *(Chanting and marching)*
24 **Only the bold, forward please!**
25 **Only the bold, forward please!**
26 **Only the bold, should stay in their beds**
27 **Only the bold, should stay in their heads**
28 **Only the bold ... come forward!**
29 **TEACHER:** *(Starting to look slightly mad)* **Doctors say the**
30 **injuries from landmines are more horrible than**
31 **anything. Most people injured are just going about their**
32 **daily lives. Most are too poor to pay for medical help,**
33 **artificial limbs, or even anesthetic.**
34 *(Holds up pictures facing Upstage.)* **These are the**
35 **pictures that I will not show you because you would not**

1   **sleep at night.** *(CLOWNS rush up and crowd TEACHER,*
2   *looking at the picture.)*
3   **ROGER: Why should I listen to this? Why? I'm not even**
4   **finished grade twelve. I didn't put them there. There are a**
5   **lot of problems right here in this town that need sorting**
6   **out. Landmines aren't my problem.**
7   **ANA: Problem: something hard to understand. Doubtful or**
8   **difficult matter requiring a solution.** *(She stands and crosses*
9   *to her experiment.)* **I'll find the solution. It's my invention.**
10   **ROGER: What invention?**
11   **ANA: A probe. A kind of probe that doesn't rely on human**
12   **hands at the end of it. That's what they do now, use**
13   **bayonets, and metal poles inch by inch over the surface of**
14   **a mined area. Real people hold the probes. Now if —**
15   **ROGER: Just a sec. There were landmines in your country**
16   **right? I mean the country you came from. Serbia.**
17   **ANA: Bosnia. I mean, we went to Croatia but I'm from Bosnia.**
18   **ROGER: So you're Bosnian?**
19   **ANA: I'm Croatian.**
20   **ROGER: Oh.**
21   **ANA: It's like being French Canadian and not living in Quebec.**
22   **My mother says people are French all through Canada.**
23   **Isn't that why you take French?**
24   **TEACHER: A landmine goes off every 20 minutes, stepped on in**
25   **a field or on a road, by a child playing, a woman going to**
26   **market.** *(CLOWN at clock makes sound of explosion,*
27   *occasionally looking up at it and moving it from five to ten to*
28   *fifteen etc. minutes.)* **Weapons of mass destruction in slow**
29   **motion, they lie waiting for years. Landmines don't know**
30   **the war is over. If you step on one, they don't know you're**
31   **not a soldier. Just a kid. Or a farmer. Or a Canadian tourist.**
32   **CLOWNS:** *(Slow blues song)* **Mines are the stars of this show**
33   **They don't sleep, and they never go**
34   **They wait forever and ever**
35   **They never let you know**

1   Just when the whole thing will blow
2   CLOWN: How long is forever?
3   CLOWN: As long as it takes!
4
5
6   SCENE TWO
7
8   ROGER: When you lived in Croatia, did you see any?
9   ANA: Of course.
10   ROGER: What was it like?
11   ANA: What do you think?
12   ROGER: I don't know.
13   ANA: You must know. You get good marks in this class. What
14   do you think?
15   ROGER: Scary. Lonely?
16   ANA: Lonely, why? I had my whole family then.
17   ROGER: But when I'm scared it's like there's nobody. Even if
18   there is, you know.
19   ANA: What are you scared of? The math test? Your father
20   chewin' you out? Really scary stuff.
21   ROGER: Don't act like I'm a jerk just cause I'm askin'
22   questions. Don't think I'm stupid. Bosnia or Serbia, it's
23   like this mine thing, why should I have to know? I'm sorry.
24   I just know that you're from Europe and there was a war.
25   ANA: Your life's here, maybe nobody tells you anything. You
26   want me to make you feel better about that?
27   ROGER: No.
28   ANA: You want to know about my country, read about it.
29   You've got a million TV channels, do you watch them?
30   ROGER: But it's just TV. You know, you were there.
31   ANA: You see this experiment I'm designing? The molecules
32   have a strong attraction, polarized by the water and the
33   magnets. I have to learn what these instruments do, put
34   my hands on the cold metal, feel the tension in my body
35   waiting to balance the magnetic force. Carefully, so

1 carefully. A wrong move and it dissipates or explodes. My
2 breath learns to move with the water sliding down the
3 tube. I shut out the other noises in the room, I listen to the
4 crystals, the tiny particles moving. But first ... before I can
5 try the experiment, I have to read. Everything, all the
6 scientists. I learn how much the container can hold, I
7 respect the instruments, the delicate balance I must
8 achieve. The molecules are alive, they breathe, I know this
9 before I use them in my experiment. It's my life you're
10 asking about, Roger. Go find out something. Anything.
11 ROGER: Okay. Um, what about Saturday night? To work on the
12 story? I mean, my finals story.
13 ANA: I don't know. I have to babysit. I'm too busy.
14 ROGER: Busy doin' what? All you do is play around with
15 experiments, wanting to be a hero.
16 ANA: And what's wrong with that? *(ANA goes back to the computer*
17 *terminal Stage Right where she works on her experiment.)*
18 ROGER: What'd I do? Just asked a question? What's the big
19 deal about a question? So the world's a lousy place, I'm not
20 blaming her! I don't care.
21
22
23 **SCENE THREE**
24
25 *(Drum beat. CLOWNS enter.)*
26 CLOWNS: Care about this! care about that!
27 My head's so full of caring
28 I'm falling flat!
29 ROGER: I thought she liked me. Maybe she hates me. Why are
30 women so complicated?
31 DON: Hey man, you're startin' to get too serious. Take my
32 advice. Chill. *(DON hands ROGER a Coke. ROGER sits with*
33 *him and turns on the TV. Sitcom music introduces the*
34 *scene: Marge, Bart and Lisa Simpson.)*
35 MARGE: My goodness, you children are early for dinner!

1   Homer isn't even here yet. Is something wrong?

2   LISA: In an emergency, it is best to remain calm.

3   MARGE: My goodness, an emergency? How exciting.

4   LISA: Mr. Mitchell down the street is mildly upset.

5   BART: He's gonna kill us for accidentally breaking his window!

6   MARGE: *What did you say????* Another broken window?

7   LISA: Technically it's not our fault. We were simply playing in

8   front of Russell's house and then – BOOM! – the whole

9   thing kind of blew up.

10   BART: ... and Mr. Mitchell's windows broke, and there's this

11   big hole with dirt everywhere on Russell's front yard, and

12   I lost my hand, and Mrs. Mosca's roses blew over ...

13   LISA: What civilized person would leave bombs lying around,

14   *this* is my question.

15   MOTHER: Didn't I tell you, didn't I tell you not to walk

16   anywhere except on the sidewalk! Now what are we going

17   to do, just wait till I tell Homer. And who am I going to

18   send to the store for the dessert? What if I told you it's 90

19   percent safe? OK, 95 percent safe. Who wants to go?

20

21

22   SCENE FOUR

23

24   *(ROGER flicks the TV game show on. Sound of game show.*

25   *Enter HOST, MARIA and BILLY. BILLY is dressed as a First*

26   *World western power, MARIA as smaller Third World nation.)*

27   TV HOST: Welcome to North meets South, the quiz show that

28   asks the question, who knows what, and how come? My

29   guests Maria and Billy are about to win bonus points up to

30   50,000 dollars. Are you ready for the next round of quick-

31   fire questions?

32   BILLY: Born ready!

33   MARIA: Raised ready!

34   HOST: Question one. What has caused more death and injury

35   over the last decade? Chemical weapons, nuclear

1   **weapons, or landmines?**

2   **ROGER:** *(Who can't believe what he's heard)* **Landmines?**

3   *(Audience cheers. MARIA and BILLY look at each other like*

4   *they don't know who answered, and keep going.)*

5   **HOST: You're right! Points to both of you!** *(Audience cheers.*

6   *MARIA and BILLY look happy but confused.)*

7   **HOST: Question Two. How many active landmines are there**

8   **estimated to be in the world? Nine thousand, Nineteen**

9   **thousand, or 119 million?**

10 **MARIA AND BILLY: Umm.**

11 **HOST: Come on Billy, your team made most of them, you**

12   **should know!**

13 **BILLY: Nineteen thousand?**

14 **HOST: Nope. How about you Maria, your team steps on them,**

15   **you should know.** *(She shakes her head, confused.)* **The**

16   **correct answer is 119 million.** *(Audience groans.)*

17 **HOST: How were most American soldiers in Vietnam injured?**

18   **Enemy bullets, enemy bombs, landmines?**

19 **ROGER: Landmines?**

20 **HOST: You are right! And most important ...**

21 **BILLY: This is embarrassing.**

22 **HOST: Their own landmines! Bonus points to both sides!**

23   *(BILLY and MARIA look astonished at each other, then clap*

24   *wildly with the audience. They still don't know where the*

25   *voice is coming from.)*

26 **HOST: In 1995 the United Nations estimated that 70,000**

27   **people in Angola had limbs amputated. True or false?**

28   *(MARIA and BILLY get poised to hit the bell.)*

29 **ROGER: True.**

30 **HOST: In 1997, most people watching this on television can't**

31   **believe their ears and want to switch us off. True or false?**

32 **ROGER: True.** *(ROGER switches off TV. It doesn't work.)*

33 **HOST: But you can't switch off the landmines. Sorry, terribly**

34   **sorry, they don't switch off. Maria and Billy are now**

35   **willing to risk all their points in ... the minefield!**

1   *(Audience cheers. MARIA and BILLY clap wildly.)*

2   **HOST: Are you ready? Put on your blindfold!** *(Audience cheers*

3   *while BILLY blindfolds Maria.)* **What happens here is Billy**

4   **tells Maria what steps to take in the minefield while**

5   **Maria has to be careful not to step on any mines. Are you**

6   **two ready?**

7   **BILLY: Ready!** *(He starts to give MARIA directions through field.)*

8   **BILLY: One step forward, good, good.** *(Counts on his fingers.)*

9   **Three steps forward ... one to the side ... four big ones and**

10   **you're out. You'll make it. Just a little ways.**

11 **MARIA:** *(Cheating by lifting the blindfold to see her way)* **That's**

12   **not a little ways, you're cheating.**

13 **BILLY: Says who?**

14 **MARIA: It's not fair, you can see and I can't!** *(MARIA and BILLY*

15   *start to argue. ROGER goes into the field to see if he can get*

16   *through it while they argue. SCREEN: He gets part way*

17   *through, hits a mine and lights go up on the shadow screen.*

18   *We see shadows of two people, one handing water to the other.*

19   *One of these figures stops and points at the ground. They move*

20   *toward it. ROGER starts to speak and knocks down another*

21   *mine. On screen, mine explodes, silently. The lights on shadow*

22   *screen go out. Then lights come on again and a hand is*

23   *reaching out. ROGER holds out his hand towards the hand on*

24   *the screen. He turns to the audience, looking at his hand.)*

25 **ROGER: Ana says there are molecules of DNA right on the**

26   **palms of our hands. And so everywhere we go, and**

27   **everything we touch, we leave the molecules of life**

28   **behind. And the atoms that make up every person who**

29   **ever lived are still here on the planet.** *(Audience cheers,*

30   *game show is cleared as ROGER flicks the TV and another*

31   *comes up with TEACHER on it.)*

32 **TEACHER: It would take 20 people working eight hours a day**

33   **for one month to clear a football field of mines. If the world**

34   **was cleared at one foot at a time, it would take ... 20 people**

35   **... eight hours a day ... carefully trained ...** *(TEACHER repeats*

1   *last two phrases until game show is clear.)*

2   **ROGER:** *(Switches off screen when game show is clear)* **I'm**

3   **really losing it, man, I'm seeing things. This landmine**

4   **thing is starting to make me crazy! I can't believe Ana**

5   **never told me about this. It's horrible.**

6   **DON: Maybe she thought it was a turn-off.**

7   **ROGER: Why would she think that?**

8   **DON: Isn't it?**

9

10

11   **SCENE FIVE**

12

13   *(Lights on other side of the stage, on ANA with her experiment.)*

14 **ANA: Mine clearance is properly done in phases: verification,**

15   **using sniffer dogs, metal detectors, ground penetrating**

16   **radar. What a joke. As if any of the countries with mines**

17   **could afford mine penetrating radar! That's why my**

18   **invention is going to be so good. An electronic probe for**

19   **the local people, that's what I'm going to figure out. It's**

20   **only by training local people that you know it's going to be**

21   **a reliable job. Lots of de-miners are people who've been**

22   **injured by mines and then get trained to clear them. Make**

23   **more money than most people in their countries see in a**

24   **year. And man, do they deserve it. They wear a flak jacket**

25   **and visored helmet, and these weird big shoes. And that's**

26   **it, the only protection against the blast. Lying on your**

27   **belly, hands out in front, feeling nice and slow through**

28   **the long grass. It's a slow process, inch by inch. The**

29   **ground gives way to the 30 centimetre steel probe with a**

30   **sudden jolt. They say you never forget the fear, the**

31   **adrenalin surge and the tightening of your stomach the**

32   **first time you slide the slender metal probe into the**

33   **ground and locate a live antipersonnel land mine. I'm**

34   **gonna invent something that can probe the earth at a safe**

35   **distance and detonate at the same time. I'll save**

1   thousands of lives, millions of dollars. I'm gonna –

2   *(ROGER enters her part of the stage.)*

3 ROGER: Ana?

4 ANA: How'd you get here?

5 ROGER: Your mum said it was OK. You've been in here too long.

6   Look, come on, come out with me. My story's due Monday.

7 ANA: It's an eye witness account. Maybe it'd be better if you

8   write it all yourself. At first, anyway.

9 ROGER: I don't know where to start. Anyway, you're not

10   babysitting, your mum's home.

11 ANA: She might go out. Look, I want to help you. But not now.

12 ROGER: Come on. How come you're always hiding out,

13   working on weird experiments for science prizes?

14 ANA: This is more than an experiment, it's an invention. It

15   isn't just theory, it's applied. My prize was for something

16   different, a theoretical abstraction.

17 ROGER: Speaking of theoretical abstractions maybe you could

18   help me with this little problem I'm having.

19 ANA: What's that?

20 ROGER: Landmines, I can't get them out of my head. I didn't

21   even go to baseball today because I think the bases will

22   blow up. When I walk down the street I look to see how

23   many legs people have. It's like, everywhere I go, everything

24   I see turns into some weird thing about landmines.

25 ANA: Lighten up Roger. I mean it, go see a movie or something.

26   I'm sorry if I got mad at you before. It isn't your problem.

27 ROGER: Can't I worry about landmines too? Why else did they

28   give us that stupid class on it? Anyway, it's too late, I don't

29   even sleep or anything. We could both see a movie?

30 ANA: See this? These molecules have to be balanced perfectly.

31   Think of the crystals under the light, it's like they're

32   dancing. Responsibility. The ability to respond. We are

33   innately free to respond however we want. Depending.

34   You wanna take a look?

35 ROGER: What's this got to do with my problem!

1 ANA: Everything! What I'm trying to do here, with this
2   invention, I'm trying —
3 ROGER: No, not about your stupid invention, about what was
4   it like to live among landmines? What did you do? Did you
5   hide, did you stay inside?
6 ANA: Forget it. Just forget it. *(Drum beat.)*
7 CLOWN QUEEN: Roger, we want to tell you a story. There's this
8   soccer field in Mozambique, outside the town of Mamba.
9   Surrounded by a crumbling wall. During the war children
10   didn't play there because it was known to be mined.
11 CLOWN: When peace came a helicopter landed in the field and
12   nothing happened. No explosions. So the local children
13   decided to cut the grass on the field. When they were
14   cutting, a little kid was bitten by a snake.
15 CLOWN: Once the grass was cut they played every day for two
16   weeks. Then a young girl stepped on a landmine. For a few
17   weeks they stayed out of the field, but then they started to
18   play again. It was several weeks before someone stepped
19   on another mine. Now months have passed and there
20   have been no accidents.
21 ROGER: Why aren't they afraid to play on the field?
22 ANA: Why should they worry about landmines when they
23   never worry about stepping on poisonous snakes?
24 ROGER: Is that how it was for you Ana? *(She doesn't answer,*
25   *goes back to experiment.)* Why don't you ever give me one
26   straight answer? *(ROGER leaves experiment and ANA.)*
27 ROGER: I bet she'd answer me if I invented some kind of land
28   clearance tool. She'd want to talk to me then!
29   *(SOUND: Music theme.)*
30 CLOWN: By day you're Roger MacKenzie. By night, special
31   captain R.M of the Laser Probe, the landmine detector
32   orbiting station. On board the station first mate Borg has
33   detected a landmine sighting. A mine lies hidden in a
34   mango tree. A woman and her children are coming to pick
35   fruit. You tell all crew to stay on board and beam down

1   into a nasty and terrifying landmine site. Suited in full

2   body metallic suit ...

3 CLOWN QUEEN: Every morning for twenty years that woman

4   walked with her children into that orchard to get food.

5   How come it's him that's the hero?

6 ROGER: *(To ANA)* Isn't that what you want to be? Some kind of

7   hero, some kind of saviour? Isn't that what we all want to be?

8 ANA: Yeah, well, for you to be a hero, what does that make me?

9   The helpless victim, right? You all want it to be so simple.

10   Some crazy war in one of those countries over there. Like

11   it would never happen in Canada. Listen, it's not your

12   fault, but you don't know. You just weren't there and you

13   don't know anything.

14 ROGER: Then tell me! Show me! Give me something.

15

16

17   **SCENE SIX**

18

19   *(ANA exits. CLOWNS converge on ROGER. They aim the*

20   *following lines at him with increased intensity, eventually*

21   *overlapping, pushing him.)*

22 CLOWNS: Roger's a hero, grab a camera

23   Roger's a hero, grab a camera

24   put him on the evening news

25   put him on the evening news

26

27   our man on the spot

28   boy, is he ever on the spot.

29   how's it feel, Roger? whatcha gonna do?

30   *(CLOWNS form images of Zagreb. CLOWN enters dressed as*

31   *a TOUR GUIDE. He gives ROGER a large cartoon tour guide*

32   *book, that ROGER refers to.)*

33 TOUR GUIDE: Welcome to Zagreb, our beautiful city which has

34   been the capital of Croatia since 1557. Spread out over the

35   Sava River, much of the medieval city remains today.

1   There are many fine parks, galleries and museums and
2   Zagreb is Croatia's main centre for culture and art. As you
3   can see, Zagreb hardly appears to be the capital of a
4   country that was at war. Visitors will see unarmed soldiers
5   going about their business. People are well dressed and
6   smiling, but watch out for offers on the black market.
7   *(CLOWNS turn towards ROGER and click cameras at him.*
8   *They freeze.)*
9 CLOWN QUEEN: Is this how you want him to learn about your
10   country, Ana? Is this how you want him to know you? What
11   do you think, Ana? *(ANA appears behind shadow screen.)*
12 ANA: Between my village in northern Bosnia and a border town
13   in Croatia there was a beautiful bridge and a river the colour
14   of emeralds. We would go swimming on vacations, and see
15   beautiful birds in the spring. One morning men who had
16   been our neighbours came to the door and told my father we
17   had ten minutes to leave the village. It was like they were
18   warning us we were Croatian and no longer welcome. My
19   mother took me and my sisters. My father and brothers
20   stayed to fight. We crossed the bridge with only what we
21   could carry in paper bags. It was Easter, 1992, the birds were
22   beautiful and the river was green. More than 10,000 people
23   crossed the bridge that day.
24 TOUR GUIDE: Remember Zagreb is only 50 kilometres north
25   of the front. But don't worry, the biggest problem you'll
26   encounter is finding a cheap place to stay.
27 ANA: A few weeks after we crossed the bridge was blown up. It
28   was early morning, and everyone still crossing fell to the
29   river below. April is the most beautiful month. It was the
30   start of spring, our whole class would go for picnics.
31   *(CLOWNS form a line of smiling faces and waving hands.*
32   *They freeze.)*
33 GUIDE: You might expect Croatia to be a depressing place? Not
34   so! As you can see life goes on as always, seemingly
35   unaffected by the nearby destruction. Let me give you a

1   little warning, it's only when you talk to people.

2   ROGER: What do you mean? Talk to people?

3   GUIDE: It's only when you talk to people, you find out the real

4   price, ya hear the sad stories.

5   ROGER: But I tried to talk. To my friend.

6   GUIDE: Like relatives in other areas killed or forced to flee

7   their homes, or shortages, or children coming back

8   wounded. Or dead. Such insights bring you closer to the

9   human component behind the headlines, which is what

10   real travel is all about!

11   ANA: *(Behind screen)* Sorry. Pardon. Dobar dan. Can you show

12   me? Can you show me?

13   ROGER: Can you show me? Can you show me? *(Drum beats.*

14   *Line of smiling faces parts to reveal image formed by clowns,*

15   *showing loss caused by the war. This image is chosen by each*

16   *cast. Other CLOWNS turn cameras towards the image.)*

17   CLOWNS: Click! *(Lights down on ANA behind screen.)*

18   CLOWNS CHANT: Oh, oh, what have we here?

19   Don't take things so seriously?

20   Care about this! Care about that!

21   Don't take things too seriously

22   *(Chant sounds distorted, stranger and stranger.)*

23   My head's so full of caring

24   I care so much and I care so often

25   My head's so full of caring

26   I care so much and I care so often

27   TOUR GUIDE: *(Blowing whistle)* Sdravo, come this way. All

28   aboard. All aboard. *(EVERYONE gets on the bus.)*

29   CLOWNS: Only the bold, only the bold

30   only the bold step forward *(CLOWNS sit on invisible bus,*

31   *ALL go to sleep except for PASSENGER and ROGER. TOUR*

32   *GUIDE observes from above on blocks.)*

33   PASSENGER: Are you English?

34   ROGER: Oh, ah ... I'm Canadian.

35   PASSENGER: You have a nationality? That's good. Over here

1   **we have so many we have to pick which part of us comes**
2   **first. Serbian, Croatian, really the same language** *(Whistle*
3   *blows, PASSENGER looks around.)* **But, ah, I'm not**
4   **supposed to say that anymore.** *(CLOWNS on bus wake up.*
5   *As they say the following lines they join hands.)*
6 **CLOWNS: Muslims Croats, Serbs, Macedonians**
7   **We loved each other!**
8   **We married each other!**
9   **We all swam in the same river.**
10 **PASSENGER: Ah, but times change.** *(CLOWNS drop hands and*
11   *go back to sleep.)*
12 **ROGER: I don't understand this war. I never studied anything**
13   **about it.**
14 **GUIDE: My dear Canadian friend! I didn't study it either! I eat**
15   **it, and drink it, and shit it out, but I didn't study it. What**
16   **is it exactly that you are here for?**
17 **ROGER: Ana ... no, I, landmines ... I** – *(QUEEN taps ROGER on*
18   *the shoulder, takes him from the bus Downstage.)*
19 **CLOWN QUEEN: You're on your own here, Roger. How are you**
20   **going to understand it? From books, TV, movies. How can**
21   **you know? Really know? What do you need to know, Roger?**
22 **ROGER: You see, I don't think this tour book is accurate, about**
23   **the war and everything.** *(GUIDE jumps down from sitting*
24   *above on blocks, joins them.)*
25 **TOUR GUIDE: So, my dear student, what does the good book say?**
26 **ROGER:** *(Reading)* **Although the coast is as enchanting as ever,**
27   **be prepared for inconveniences such as hotels used for**
28   **emergency housing for refugees or museums closed with**
29   **exhibits in storage for safekeeping. Areas near the 'front'**
30   **are only for the adventurous traveler as there is extensive**
31   **damage and slight chance of being exposed to war activity.**
32   *(Stops reading.)* **But that sounds like the danger is guns**
33   **and stuff. It doesn't say anything about landmines.**
34 **QUEEN: That's because landmines don't know when the war is**
35   **over and therefore are not to be considered as war activity.**

1   **TOUR GUIDE:** As you can see, there are many beautiful fields
2   and forests. Please under no circumstances walk through
3   them, they are filled with mines. In some areas you will
4   see mined areas surrounded by orange string.
5   **PASSENGER:** Could we stop? I have to take a leak.
6   *(Drum beat.)*
7   **TOUR GUIDE:** Going to the bathroom is permitted ...
8   *(CLOWNS jump up and try to leave the bus, but bump against*
9   *each other inside the confines of the invisible bus.)*
10   **TOUR GUIDE:** ... but you must stay on the road beside the bus.
11   **DO NOT LEAVE THE PAVEMENT. Men at the front of the**
12   **bus – women out back.** *(Whistles.)* **Everyone out!**
13   *(CLOWNS break from the bus. They whisper menacingly*
14   *through the following action.)*
15   **CLOWNS:** This is a play from beginning to end
16   So don't take things too seriously
17   This is a play from beginning to end
18   So don't take things too seriously
19   *(CLOWNS slowly begin to march around the stage, trying to*
20   *find their way off, but bumping into each other. ANA enters*
21   *by her experiment and watches. They turn to ROGER, pick*
22   *him up, pass him around, higher and higher in the air. ANA*
23   *watches. Finally ROGER almost falls.)*
24   **ROGER:** What the hell are you doing? This is craziness. What
25   do you want, to totally confuse me? Scare me? Guilt me
26   out? I'm doing everything I can to try to understand you,
27   Ana, and you push me away every bloody time. I can't do
28   anything about your war, or your silence, or your family or
29   any of it. I don't know what happened to you, cause you
30   won't bloody tell me. I wish you would. I like you, I want
31   to be friends. But you gotta tell me something. You gotta
32   give a little. Oh, forget it, you don't care anyway, what
33   some dumb guy thinks. Maybe I just can't take a hint.
34   Fine, I won't bug you again. But whatever your big secret
35   is, maybe you better just get over it. You live here now, this

1   is Canada, so get a life.

2

3

4   **SCENE SEVEN**

5

6 **CLOWNS:** *(Song from earlier in the play, sung as they resume*

7   *places in the classroom)* **Mines are the stars of this show**

8   **They don't sleep, and they never go**

9   **they wait forever and ever, they never let you know**

10   **just when the whole thing will blow.**

11   *(Overhead screen comes on. TEACHER points to a map*

12   *showing shapes of landmines, poison signs. Drawing of tree*

13   *with mines in it. ANA sits apart at her experiment.)*

14 **TEACHER: Now line up children and pay attention to this**

15   **morning's drill. These are the many different ways mines**

16   **look. Pay attention. Some fall from helicopters like**

17   **butterflies. Many are made to look like children's toys.**

18   **Landmines don't know we aren't soldiers, they don't**

19   **know who we are but they can hurt us. It is important to**

20   **always look where you are walking. So when you cross the**

21   **schoolyard ...**

22 **CLOWNS: When you cross the schoolyard ...**

23 **TEACHER: ... when you go to the fields to gather straw for your**

24   **buffalo to eat ...**

25 **CLOWNS: ... when you gather firewood ...**

26 **TEACHER: ... when you go to the river for water for your**

27   **mother ...**

28 **CLOWNS: ... when you go to the fields ...**

29 **TEACHER: ... when you go to the Seven-Eleven for chips, Coke,**

30   **video games ...**

31 **CLOWNS: ... when you go ...**

32 **TEACHER: ... when you meet your friends on the corner ...**

33   *(Points at map.)* **This string indicates a mine field, do you**

34   **understand? Do not walk anywhere where there is this**

35   **orange string, it means de-miners are working. Clearing.**

1   Do you understand? Don't walk. Don't walk. Always look.
2   Or else you could end up hurt, blinded, wounded, dead.
3   *(STUDENTS turn Upstage to look at screen. TEACHER flashes*
4   *blank pictures in a series of lights on the screen. STUDENTS*
5   *breathe together the soft sound of "auuuuuuu." When ANA*
6   *begins speaking, the sounds stop but the blank flashes*
7   *continue.)*
8   TEACHER: So remember. Don't walk anywhere where there is
9   this orange string.
10 ROGER: But ... what do you do when there are no orange strings?
11 ANA: *(To ROGER)* What do you do when there are no orange
12   strings? Just roses. My father was desperate to see home.
13   When the war ended, we went back to the village just to see.
14   Just to see the roses in his garden. There were so many that
15   year, it was as if the plants knew something. There was
16   something else planted in his garden too. In the end they
17   found 45 mines in our garden alone. That was after my
18   father found the first one. "Ana. Ana, look see, I told you
19   they are still here, still blooming." That's when it happened.
20 ROGER: Ana. Ana, I didn't know. I'm so sorry.
21 ANA: It was a mine nicknamed "Bouncing Betty", it's designed
22   to bounce up to the abdomen area and severely maim a
23   person. Due to its large explosive charge it can kill and is
24   designed to be almost impossible to neutralize.
25   *(ANA goes to work, absorbed in her experiment. ROGER*
26   *stays separate from ANA, perhaps at band area Stage Left.*
27   *Someone, if possible ROGER, sings the following.)*
28 ***SONG:*** A NIGHT IN YOUR GARDEN
29   You say anybody can walk your walk, but you do it with so
30   much style
31   I'm all clumsy and full of talk, but my legs go weak every
32   time you smile
33   There's a sadness behind those eyes, they're hiding a big
34   surprise
35   that goes back to your country and back to your home

1   and back to a night in your garden

2

3   You say anybody can walk your walk, but you do it with so

4   much grace

5   I keep trying to make you talk but I get stupid and out of

6   place

7   There's a sadness behind those eyes, they're hiding a big

8   surprise

9   that goes back to your family and back to your father

10 and back to a night in your garden

11

12 Well I heard that he was bending, to pick for you a flower

13 when the whole world exploded in blood as red as roses

14 and right before your eyes, he disappeared in light

15 a blast that pushed your memory and your dreaming out

16   of sight

17

18 You say anybody can walk your walk, but I wonder where

19   that step goes

20 is your bravado just so much talk, can't you tell me what

21   your heart knows

22 won't you take me behind those eyes, show me the big

23   surprise

24 that goes back to your country and back to your father

25 and back to a night in your garden

26

27 I know I'm no one special, but maybe I could listen

28 maybe you could trust me, maybe I could know you

29 I wish I could be bending to pick for you a flower

30 cause everybody has to leave the darkness sometime

31

32

33   **SCENE EIGHT**

34

35 *(CLASS turns to face forward. ROGER and ANA take the same*

1   *positions. They watch shadow play. SPEAKER can be a boy or*
2   *a girl. It is best if the narration is spoken over a microphone,*
3   *from behind band area, so that speaker can see the screen.*
4   *What is seen on the screen are images, words that tell the*
5   *following story. How they are assembled, possible different*
6   *puppets for shadow play, created by each group that does the*
7   *show. The following are the suggested places for images.)*
8   **TEACHER: Sharbat Khan sells scrap metal in Pakistan.**
9   **SPEAKER: In my country there is a plant where sometimes it**
10   **grows everywhere. It has one stalk and many many**
11   **branches of flowers that grow white and purple like a**
12   **midnight sky.**
13   *(IMAGE.)*
14   **SPEAKER: My family is like that plant, it has roots, and a stalk,**
15   **and many branches with leaves of spun out feathers.**
16   *(IMAGE.)*
17   **SPEAKER: Like the flowers, I too, know I am part of my family.**
18   *(IMAGE.)*
19   **SPEAKER: One day my sister and I were excited to find a round**
20   **piece of metal the colour of sand. It was a lucky day, we'd**
21   **collected enough to have them weighed by the shop keeper.**
22   *(IMAGE.)*
23   **SPEAKER: Something fell off his scale. The earth broke up**
24   **and I fell down and there was dust everywhere.**
25   *(IMAGE.)*
26   **SPEAKER: After a few minutes I saw my right hand and the two**
27   **fingers of my left hand were cut off. I remember thinking,**
28   **"Is it mine?" My sister was calling me. Then I fainted.**
29   *(IMAGE.)*
30   **SPEAKER: I know I am like the plant, I am a branch of my**
31   **family.**
32   *(IMAGE.)*
33   **SPEAKER: The next day my father borrowed some money and**
34   **rented a car to bring me to Pakistan. All that time my**
35   **father drove me, I lay beside him.**

1   *(IMAGE.)*

2   **SPEAKER:** It took three days and three nights to reach the

3   hospital. I told myself to stay alive, stay alive because this

4   is so far for my father to go.

5   *(IMAGE.)*

6   **SPEAKER:** For my family it has been very hard. We are very

7   poor. And all the people and relatives had the impression

8   I would die before we got to Quetta.

9   *(IMAGE.)*

10 **SPEAKER:** But I stayed alive. I, like my family, am flowers of

11   one stalk and many branches.

12 **TEACHER:** This story comes from the testimony of ten year old

13   Sharbat Khan at a hospital run by the International

14   Committee of the Red Cross. *(Lights down on shadow play.*

15   *CLASS are whispering to themselves.)*

16 **TEACHER:** Class ... Class! *(They stop whispering and look at the*

17   *TEACHER.)* What would you do, if I was to tell you

18   something you didn't want to hear?

19 **ANA:** *(To ROGER)* I would ask myself how do I KNOW you don't

20   want to hear it? Maybe I should give you a chance.

21 **ROGER:** *(To ANA)* I'd say to myself, go ahead and try me.

22 **CLOWNS:** *(Repeating and building, they overlap the following*

23   *line, ending in a grotesque tableau)* We'd say, this is a show

24   from beginning to end, so don't take things too seriously!

25   *(Light change to open white light.)*

26

27   **THE END**

28

29

30

31

32

33

34

35

Crying for Time
by Ros Gardner

Perhaps of all the shocks endured by societies convulsed by cultural conflict, nothing is more tragic than the impact upon children. In fact, children suffer from cultural conflict in two ways, physical and spiritual. Not only are they, like everyone else, victims of death and injury, malnutrition, disease, abuse and enslavement; they are also crippled by the loss of parents or caretakers, by the destruction of their homes, by the collapse of supportive social institutions and by witnessing horrible forms of violence in their everyday environment. And most tragic of all, they are the ones who are most vulnerable to disillusionment, cynicism and despair. Adults, we may feel, are better equipped to cope with social upheavals: they can rationalize the suffering, harden themselves to emotional shocks, take a long-range view of adversity or adapt somehow to rebuilding anew. But it is not so with our children: their sense of loss is far more keen, far more painful, far more mindful of that betrayal of their childhood into a living nightmare.

It is perhaps the knowledge of this desperation in children that wrings our souls most painfully when we contemplate the bleak effects of war, ethnic and racial conflicts, and outbreaks of cultural hostility in the contemporary world that have created so many casualties and refugees. One stands speechless and largely helpless before a child's loss of innocence, for we know that innocence is the one thing that can never be restored once it is torn violently from a child's soul.

Of course, images of thousands of displaced, vagabond children wandering helplessly across the land have been seared into our modern consciousness since perhaps the time of the Russian "besprizornikis" of 1900, uprooted by the October Revolution. Since then, the many social upheavals of the twentieth century have only added to their numbers in all corners of the globe. Today we find them in huge numbers in the Balkans, in South America, in the Mideast and in Asia; these dislocated bands of children in the third world have their eerie counterparts in the gangs and bands of homeless, cast-off and disillusioned youth who also populate the urban jungles of the industrialized West.

This play is set in a no-man's-land on the edge of a modern "war zone." A group of young people, between the ages of ten and nineteen, seek shelter in an old deserted warehouse. The story, told in simple flashback by one of the characters, explores alienation and loss as they struggle to cope with the day-to-day losses they've experienced. The action centers on the last couple of weeks they are together, and the events that push them into running away — again. As the playwright describes her work with the students who first presented the play: "The play is one small story — but the young actors found that the image stayed as they learned with difficulty, determination and laughter to hold up the mirror."

Crying for Time was developed with young actors in a workshop process for Auckland's Performing Arts School Youth Company, and performed for a season in July 1999. During rehearsals, the actors were exposed to TV and newspaper images of the situation in Kosovo, of young people the same age as the actors who were caught in circumstances not of their making and outside their control. Each actor created his or her own name and created a story behind their journey in the play. The group rehearsed in very confined spaces and in very open spaces, exploring the intensity of proximity. Most of all they used the voices of the characters, their thoughts in action, to explore who they were and what they wanted. The show was remounted for the New Zealand International Peace Conference in 2000, was most recently performed for Arts Alive in Auckland City and has been touring the secondary schools in Auckland.

Characters, ages ten to nineteen:

First group —
Musso, a young boy, the narrator, a resourceful leader, discovered the shelter with Fish
Fish, a boy, discovered the shelter with Musso
Zeth, a young boy
Phayne, a young girl
Rafe, a young girl
Xadhe, a young girl
Mattie, a young girl
Pai, a young girl
Jix, a young boy

Second Group —
Cwynne, a very young girl with a doll, saved by Dreus
Dreus, young boy, the leader of the second group
Tesse, a young girl
Ginny, a young girl
Baye, a young boy
Quey, a young boy

Late Arrivals —
Ellie, a young girl
Mole, a very young girl, she was alone in the shelter before
    anyone

Setting

An abandoned warehouse in no-man's-land, on the edge of a war zone. The setting created for the original production was claustrophobic, designed to evoke the inside of a deserted warehouse turned into living quarters. The designer created the oppressive atmosphere using cardboard boxes, different levels with rostra, ramps, chain link fencing, all touched by grime of age and ill use. The shape of the space meant that some hiding places were situated between blocks of audience, which drew them directly into the action.

On tour, the show was pared down to some flats and a few large boxes that could be used for hiding. The director worked in traverse, which maintained the intensity of the stage production. The play works effectively with either naturalistic or stylised settings — the only requirement is that the actors can conceal themselves and their belongings. What is important is the sense of containment — claustrophobia — that builds with the assistance of the lighting throughout the play.

1   **ACT ONE**

2

3   *(CHARACTERS enter without light. Voice sounds.)*

4   **MUSSO:** *(To audience)* **Six months ago this was home. Six**

5   **months – or a lifetime.** *(Torch light on)* **It didn't look so**

6   **different a lifetime ago. Funny, how after a while, things**

7   **can't get dirtier. There were only a small group of us at first.**

8   *(Dim light on group Upstage Right, eating.)*

9   **FISH: It's not even hot!**

10   **ZETH: I ran out of wood – the fire won't burn forever.**

11   **PHAYNE: The fires haven't stopped for two years. Why do you**

12   **think they'll stop now?**

13   **ZETH: What will the generals do? Invade the places they've**

14   **already invaded? They won't.** *(Pause)* **Anyway, they run out**

15   **of people to kill. No war can go on forever.**

16   **PHAYNE: Don't make jokes.**

17   **ZETH: It wasn't a joke.**

18   **FISH: It wasn't funny.**

19   **RAFE: Maybe this is forever – for some of us.**

20   **FISH: Maybe. It's a word, that's all, meaning alive. That's what**

21   **I am, and that equals forever.**

22   **RAFE: What do you mean?** *(RAFE and FISH bicker good-*

23   *naturedly.)*

24   **PHAYNE: These potatoes are delicious. We haven't had any**

25   **since Musso left ... nearly two months now ... because the**

26   **rats got into our supplies – so, thanks.**

27   **XADHE: It's okay.**

28   **PHAYNE: Is your bed all right? Not too draughty? Dry?**

29   **RAFE:** *(To XADHE)* **Don't tell if you've found a dry place. We'll**

30   **all want it.**

31   **XADHE: Not dry – not really.**

32   *(Light fades as MUSSO speaks again.)*

33   **MUSSO: Other groups arrived. Sometimes they were looking**

34   **for us particularly, but sometimes, it was other things that**

35   **led them.**

1   *(Lights down. Torch light goes off. There is the sound of*
2   *scrabbling, then a GROUP enters cautiously.)*
3   **CWYNNE: I can smell food.**
4   **DREUS: You're always smelling food. You expect it to drop**
5   **from the skies into your lap.**
6   **TESSE: She's right. I can smell it too** – like potatoes, and
7   spice ...
8   **GINNY: What about gravy? Savoury and thick ...**
9   **TESSE: And chicken, to dip in the gravy, and roll up in the**
10   **crusty bread. Oh** – **I can smell all that! Where is it?**
11   **DREUS: There's nothing. Just the air.** *(Pause)*
12   **GINNY: Well, at least we won't be changing our diet.**
13   **BAYE: Weren't there meant to be others here? That we could**
14   **join up with? You promised!**
15   **DREUS: I didn't promise. It was maybe. May-be! Anyway, it was**
16   **just a rumour.**
17   **TESSE: But that man we met back in the little town.**
18   **GINNY: In that burnt-out church.**
19   **TESSE: Yes. He said there would be people here.** *(Pause)*
20   **GINNY: Would he send us here on purpose?**
21   **BAYE: You mean** – **a trap?**
22   **TESSE: And the smell of cooked potatoes to lure us in** – **like**
23   **rats.** *(The GROUP murmur unhappily.)*
24   **DREUS: Be quiet! Why would they trap us? We are waste. If we**
25   **float away, no one would care. We've already been flushed**
26   **out this far. We're on the edge of nowhere. We own**
27   **nothing, we are no one** – **the only thing I've got are my**
28   **secrets and who would want them?** *(During this speech*
29   *BAYE has moved away, investigating.)*
30   **BAYE: People have been here, though. This is a sort of bed ...**
31   **PHAYNE:** *(From the shadows)* **That's my bed.** *(Panic as the*
32   *STRANGERS try to escape. Eventually, they are stopped and*
33   *huddle together as the first GROUP checks them out.)*
34   **ZETH: They're all right.** *(He grabs doll that CWYNNE is*
35   *carrying.)* **And what could they do to us?** *(Shakes doll.)* **Very**

1   frightening.

2 XADHE: They're carrying weapons!

3 DREUS: To protect ourselves, not to attack.

4 GINNY: And these weapons are only big sticks — that's all.

5 TESSE: We don't want to fight.

6 ZETH: Neither do we.

7 MATTIE: We've been here for three months and no one

8   appears.

9 PAI: Are they selling maps out there?

10 PHAYNE: Why are you here?

11 BAYE: Some old man told us to come here — you remember?

12   Half his nose was all hairy ...

13 RAFE: There's your map seller.

14 FISH: That's my grandfather! And it's not his nose that's hairy,

15   stupid. It's his eyebrow. You should try living as long —

16 RAFE: Quiet Fish, sssh!

17 PHAYNE: Enough!

18 DREUS: Can we stay?

19 PHAYNE: I don't know. I think —

20 DREUS: Please. At least until it's warmer? For the shelter.

21 ZETH: We haven't got much food ...

22 BAYE: We've got some flour — and sugar.

23 PAI: Not much room ...

24 DREUS: We're small! We'll help out. We'll stay out of your way.

25 TESSE: We'll do what we need to. Can we stay?

26 PHAYNE: Yes! Yes! *(The tension releases and GROUPS settle*

27   *together. Food is shared, etc.)*

28 XADHE: You'd let these people in — just like that?

29 ZETH: If they're human, they're hungry. Let them eat.

30 XADHE: But there's not enough.

31 ZETH: There's never enough. What we have we share.

32 XADHE: But they might be the enemy.

33 RAFE: So might you. Where we come from a wink could turn

34   us into good friends one day, killers the next. Go and look

35   for enemies there if you want — not here. *(To DREUS:)*

1   Where are you going?

2   DREUS: Anywhere. Away. Taking our time.

3   FISH: Well, this is forever! Take some of that.

4   RAFE: Don't listen. *(To FISH:)* You're a fool.

5   FISH: You've said that before.

6   RAFE: If you'd listened then, I wouldn't need to repeat it.

7   FISH: What have I done now? What's wrong with you?

8   PHAYNE: They're eating. Let's be civilised!

9   RAFE: That's a lost word.

10 PAI: A lost cause. *(MUSSO has entered.)*

11 MUSSO: So we'll find it again. *(Excitement from FIRST GROUP.*

12   *SECOND GROUP are wary.)*

13 ZETH: We wondered if you would return.

14 MUSSO: I said I would.

15 ZETH: We were waiting.

16 MUSSO: But not watching. It could have been anyone walking

17   in.

18 JIX: Sorry, Musso. *(MUSSO passes bags etc. to RAFE and ZETH.)*

19 MUSSO: Here, can you sort this stuff out? I need some help.

20   There's a sick girl hidden about half a mile away – I

21   wasn't quite sure what I'd find here. Phayne? Fish? Let's

22   go quickly, before it gets dark. *(They leave, as OTHERS take*

23   *bags and investigate.)*

24 XADHE: Who is Musso? Who does he know to get stuff like

25   this?

26 ZETH: What do you mean, who does he know?

27 RAFE: He isn't a traitor. He bargains. Finds things.

28 ZETH: He found us this place.

29 RAFE: He goes away – comes back with food. Sometimes he

30   brings other people to hide for a while.

31 XADHE: To hide here? It's not safe.

32 ZETH: We're hiding here.

33 XADHE: But we're not being chased. *(Silence.)* Are you? Are you

34   wanted? Are you being followed?

35 ZETH: What do you want us to say?

1   **DREUS:** We've all escaped something. *(Pause)* Is that the right
2   answer?
3   **JIX:** Everyone's running away. I suppose that means there's
4   someone running after. *(Pause)*
5   **ZETH:** Musso has had this place for two years. He looks after it,
6   and us. Finds things; brings back the news. You'll see. We
7   can trust him. We need him.
8   **XADHE:** All right. I'm sorry. It's just ... I remember things.
9   **RAFE:** We all have things we remember. Forget them.
10   *(MUSSO, PHAYNE and FISH enter with ELLIE, noisily.)*
11   **PHAYNE:** Go on! Kick something else over! In case someone
12   out there hasn't heard you.
13   **FISH:** No one is left out there! They're all in here now!
14   **RAFE:** Thanks to you. It was your grandfather who sent them
15   here.
16   **ZETH:** Bring her here — it's warmer.
17   **PHAYNE:** Get some water. She's so dry her lips are sticking
18   together. Is there something she can lie on? Come on! Find
19   something! Do something! *(Pause)*
20   **MUSSO:** Phayne. Take this.
21   **PHAYNE:** Thanks. *(There is some activity as settling in occurs.)*
22   **MUSSO:** *(To FISH)* Looks as though your grandfather has been
23   busy. Did he send all of these people?
24   **FISH:** Some of them. Not all. *(Pause)* Did you see him this time?
25   **MUSSO:** He's all right. Still hiding in his church. Still
26   frightening the locals and saving strangers.
27   **PAI:** Saved us.
28   **TESSE:** And us.
29   **GINNY:** Although I nearly died of fright when I first saw him.
30   What an eyebrow! I thought he was an old witch.
31   **TESSE:** He was a good angel.
32   **PAI:** Funny looking angel.
33   **GINNY:** How did his nose — his eyebrow — get like that?
34   **FISH:** It was an explosion.
35   **JIX:** In his face?

1 FISH: No. In the street. We were walking and suddenly, BOOM!

2 JIX: *(Whispers)* BOOM!

3 FISH: And there was flame and smoke, everything – bits of
4   brick and glass flying ... and a bit of glass sliced off my
5   grandpa's eyebrow.

6 MATTIE: And it grew back like that? Down his nose?

7 FISH: No, no, no, of course not. It was much too messy. I sewed
8   it back on – grandad made me. Tapestry needle and
9   thread ... but I couldn't keep it still ...

10 MATTIE: His head?

11 FISH: My hand. It just kept shaking and shaking ... he was
12   quiet but still I was shaking and I didn't want to hurt him,
13   and I was dripping sweat, or tears and I couldn't see ...
14   When I finished I'd sewn his eyebrow in a curve, down his
15   nose.

16 GINNY: It suits him.

17 FISH: Just because my hand was shaking so much. *(Pause)*

18 TESSE: And he pretends – I think it's pretend – anyway, he
19   squeals as the bombs drop, and he carries a stick which he
20   shoots at fighters.

21 BAYE: He makes a good gun sound.

22 MATTIE: And he throws rocks at the planes, and dances in the
23   bomb craters ...

24 GINNY: So none of the soldiers go near him. They think he's
25   just another madman.

26 FISH: He's my grandfather! And he saved you didn't he?
27   Rescued you and sent you here?

28 GINNY: Yes.

29 FISH: He's clever!

30 PAI: I liked the way he danced in the craters.

31 QUEY: Why doesn't he come here, with you?

32 FISH: He won't leave his home. *(ZETH gives MUSSO a hot drink.)*

33 MUSSO: Thanks. It's freezing out there – you should build up
34   the fire.

35 PHAYNE: We don't want to be seen.

1 MUSSO: It's a cold foggy night on the edge of nowhere. Let's
2   find some warmth for a while.
3 PHAYNE: *(Indicating ELLIE)* She's warmer now. Who is she,
4   Musso? Where's she from?
5 MUSSO: Well, I was working in a factory —
6 RAFE: The chocolate story!
7 JIX: Chocolate?
8 PHAYNE: Oh, Musso!
9 BAYE: Is there some chocolate?
10 RAFE: In the story.
11 JIX: Let's have it.
12 MUSSO: It was only a short while ago. I managed to find work
13   in a chocolate factory.
14 FISH: Hey — these ginger bits have not been dipped properly.
15 RAFE: I don't believe you. I did them myself.
16 FISH: It's true though. *(Holds up ginger.)* Look!
17 RAFE: It is true — but you know what? It seems as though the
18   chocolate has been licked off the side.
19 ZETH: Revolting! And how can we sell chocolates with all that
20   mixture missing?
21 FISH: We're going to be fired!
22 ZETH: Half the chocolate gone! We'll be done!
23 RAFE: We could dip again.
24 ZETH: All of them? *(MUSSO whispers in MATTIE's ear.)*
25 RAFE: It would only take a little while.
26 MUSSO: But they've been licked. Someone's tongue has
27   dragged across this chocolate, leaving a little tongue trail ...
28   think of all that spit. *(ZETH drops chocolate.)*
29 RAFE: Who?
30 FISH: Huh?
31 RAFE: Who is the licker?
32 ZETH: Well, not me.
33 RAFE: Nor me. I hate chocolate. Like everyone here.
34 FISH: Wasn't me. *(Others variously deny licking. ALL look at*
35   *MATTIE.)*

1   MATTIE: Hey. Don't look at me like that!

2   ZETH: Well, can you explain what all that is around your mouth?

3   MATTIE: No, let me guess. Is it chocolate?

4   RAFE: You admit it!

5   MATTIE: I do not! The chocolate flicks up, or ... okay, okay, I do

6   lick my fingers now and then. Especially when it's

7   caramel. It's caramel I like, not chocolate. Is that so bad?

8   FISH: It's worse. It's our livelihood.

9   ZETH: Our lives.

10   RAFE: What do you think will happen to us? Redundancy? No,

11   we'll be punished.

12   ZETH: Death maybe.

13   MATTIE: But it wasn't me!

14   RAFE: And who else?

15   MUSSO: There's only one thing we can do. We will punish you.

16   ZETH: Is that necessary? Couldn't we just hide the evidence?

17   RAFE: No! That wouldn't work. We have to show them that

18   we're not going to give trouble. Show we'll toe the line.

19   FISH: We don't want to die, do we? *(Pause)* Let's dip her.

20   RAFE: In the full milk chocolate?

21   ZETH: Yes! But just half way.

22   RAFE: Seems a waste.

23   FISH: We have to punish? Let's punish!

24   MATTIE: But I didn't do it! I'm innocent! *(Riot breaks out: They*

25   *grab MATTIE and dip. Unfortunately they drop her into the*

26   *chocolate. Eventually they get her out — she hardens in the*

27   *cold air.)*

28   RAFE: That's a lot of chocolate.

29   FISH: She deserved it.

30   ZETH: It was punishment, wasn't it.

31   FISH: What shall we do with ... ?

32   MUSSO: Leave her. It will be a reminder to any others who

33   think they can put us at risk. *(Dips finger in "chocolate*

34   *figure" and licks it sadly.)*

35   JIX: What a waste of chocolate.

1   MUSSO: Have some. *(MATTIE reacts to that, defrosting. GROUP*
2   *disperses.)*
3   JIX: She said she didn't do it, but they still dipped her.
4   DREUS: They were frightened.
5   JIX: She was innocent.
6   BAYE: If I had been there, I would have stopped them. Nobody
7   would have dipped an innocent person like that. How did
8   she escape?
9   MUSSO: The chocolate was hot.
10 RAFE: But she had been sucking a lifesaver peppermint when
11   she was dipped.
12 MUSSO: The hole in the peppermint allowed her to breathe.
13 FISH: The chocolate hardened quickly, so she cracked her way
14   free, and escaped ...
15 ZETH: Taking enough chocolate to sustain her for days ...
16 PHAYNE: While she laid low, and waited for her burns to heal.
17   Enough chocolate story, Musso, enough. There's no need.
18 MUSSO: Maybe, maybe not. *(Pause)* Zeth, we must block up
19   that hole on the northern side, it will snow later. *(Talk and*
20   *activity as ZETH, MUSSO, DREUS and MATTIE leave to*
21   *repair building.)*
22 XADHE: What was that about? That story? Is he mad, telling us
23   fairy tales?
24 RAFE: Fairy tale! Eh, Phayne, she thinks that was a fairy tale!
25 PHAYNE: Good. Maybe that way it won't give her nightmares.
26 TESSE: I understand. If any of us step out of line ...
27 GINNY: Or put the others at risk ...
28 TESSE: Then we are in danger.
29 CWYNNE: But Mattie was innocent. She didn't do anything.
30 PHAYNE: In today's story she was. Usually I play her part, and
31   then, I am guilty. I did lick the chocolate.
32 XADHE: Usually?
33 RAFE: Musso always tells that story to newcomers.
34 BAYE: It's a warning.
35 RAFE: Yes, it is. *(To XADHE, TESSE, GINNY etc:)* Be careful.

1   PAI: Careful! We don't need to be told that.

2   XADHE: You give us that warning without knowing anything

3   about us.

4   PHAYNE: We know something.

5   XADHE: What is that?

6   RAFE: We know you are desperate – and alone.

7   GINNY: Oh, and that takes some guessing. We're all on our

8   own here.

9   TESSE: And I can't breathe now without being careful. Or

10   cunning. Or selfish. Or afraid – you all know. What's it

11   like to do an everyday thing, simply, normally –

12   something like waking up? I can't remember.

13   JIX: I can remember chocolate.

14   XADHE: We just need to be strong.

15   GINNY: She knows more about strength than most. If you

16   knew what had happened –

17   TESSE: Ginny!

18   XADHE: How is her story different to any here?

19   GINNY: *(Pause)* Not different. Another escape.

20   PHAYNE: We'll hear it.

21   TESSE: I don't need to tell it.

22   PHAYNE: We will hear it. Every tale of escape, we must hear.

23   It's like ...

24   RAFE: Hope. It gives hope.

25   PAI: Please?

26   TESSE: It's simple. My father was taken, and my mother and I

27   waited. He didn't return. My mother was sick, since way

28   before the fighting, but there was no medicine. I came

29   home with food one afternoon, but she didn't want it. The

30   next morning I couldn't wake her. I don't know when she

31   died – maybe while I slept – maybe when I went to find

32   help. I waited for three days for someone to come to

33   arrange the funeral. No one came. *(Pause)* The guns were

34   louder – much nearer than they had been. Those

35   neighbours who had remained were leaving. When I

1   looked out the window, or the door, they looked through
2   me, already gone. So I took my old spade, you know the
3   sort. It was lucky I could find it. And I dug a place in the
4   back garden. I couldn't dig deep, because the ground was
5   so frozen, but – deep enough. I wrapped Mum in some
6   soft things, then her bedding, then – some rubbish bags.
7   Then I buried her. I piled the rubble high on top, and
8   wrote her name on a stick, and then I left. Out through my
9   front door.
10 GINNY: Right into the arms of the enemy.
11 CWYNNE: What? What happened?
12 TESSE: A soldier. Coming to take me and my mother to my
13   father, or that's what he said.
14 CWYNNE: You found your father?
15 TESSE: No! Why would I trust a soldier? I took off!
16 GINNY: And screamed! Loud!
17 TESSE: It felt good, but he kept following, and so I was
18   throwing things, then suddenly ... *(To FISH:)* ... your
19   grandfather was there, screaming as loudly as me, and
20   throwing things, and the soldier turned and ran.
21 GINNY: And I had to scream and throw things at the both of
22   them to make them be quiet.
23 PHAYNE: An escape.
24 XADHE: No different.
25 RAFE: No different. You got away.
26 BAYE: I was sitting on my doorstep, playing, and I didn't even
27   hear the sound the missile makes. You know that sound?
28   When I woke up, my whole street had disappeared.
29   Flattened. Gone. My mother and my sister underneath the
30   house. Just me and the doorstep left whole.
31 PHAYNE: Musso and I found this place – ages ago, and we
32   staked our claim. The edge of nowhere! Away from
33   everything. We made it part of our let's-pretend-there's-
34   no-fighting game. A refuge. A sort of doorway to the past,
35   which we could just fall through and be brother and sister

1   again. And when we let others in — it was like letting in the
2   future. We've all escaped together. *(Noise of argument as*
3   *MUSSO, ZETH, DREUS and MATTIE enter.)*
4 **DREUS:** It wasn't my fault! *(To MATTIE:)* **You were holding the**
5   other end!
6 **MATTIE:** I didn't let go!
7 **DREUS:** You say.
8 **ZETH:** It's lost, now! Leave it.
9 **PHAYNE:** What happened?
10 **MUSSO:** We climbed up on the fire escape. These two were
11   holding the boards and Dreus let go.
12 **ZETH:** The hammer flew out of my hand — I didn't even hear it
13   hit the ground.
14 **MATTIE:** Maybe we can find it tomorrow — if the fog clears.
15 **DREUS:** You should find it — yes.
16 **MATTIE:** It wasn't my fault!
17 **FISH:** Accept it, Dreus. You did it.
18 **DREUS:** I did nothing.
19 **FISH:** So you'll have to be punished.
20 **JIX:** In chocolate?
21 **MATTIE:** Would you be quiet about the chocolate!
22 **JIX:** But that's all I remember.
23 **FISH:** *(To DREUS, ominously)* If I were you I would hide.
24 **RAFE:** Or run?
25 **XADHE:** Maybe it's not so safe here.
26 **PAI:** I like his coat. *(MATTIE has grabbed DREUS's bag of*
27   *belongings.)*
28 **MATTIE:** I like his trousers.
29 **FISH:** Have them.
30 **DREUS:** What?
31 **FISH:** Take them.
32 **DREUS:** Wait on — *(MATTIE tosses bag to PAI and a cruel game of*
33   *catch proceeds, with DREUS desperate to get it back. Only*
34   *MUSSO, PHAYNE and XADHE don't join in.)*
35 **FISH:** Well, take them. Go on — they're yours, go on, go on,

1   don't hold back, he deserves to lose them.

2 **DREUS:** *(Yells at Fish as he gets the bag)* **Give it back!** *(Pause)*

3 **FISH:** He's punished.

4 **DREUS:** You're as mad as your grandfather.

5 **FISH:** Don't forget it.

6 **MUSSO:** Enough. *(DREUS moves away.)*

7 **PHAYNE:** You shouldn't let that happen.

8 **MUSSO:** I don't let anything happen. They do what they want.

9 **XADHE:** But one word from you stops them.

10 **MUSSO:** Luck.

11 **XADHE:** Fear.

12 **MUSSO:** Friendship.

13 **XADHE:** Need. *(MUSSO moves over to DREUS.)*

14 **PHAYNE:** There's nothing wrong with need.

15 **XADHE:** It's a risk. *(Pause)*

16 **PHAYNE:** You don't trust much.

17 **XADHE:** Nothing.

18 **PHAYNE:** Then you'll have nothing to lose, I suppose. *(She sees*

19   *somebody at entrance.)* **She's here.**

20 **CWYNNE:** I didn't hear anyone. Who?

21 **XADHE:** More visitors?

22 **PHAYNE:** Sssh. Be still. *(A young girl, MOLE, enters — dirty,*

23   *matted hair. She steps a little way into the space. GROUPS*

24   *are either at ease or curious. ZETH moves down quietly.)*

25 **ZETH:** We didn't hear your whistle. The fog softens the sound,

26   and we missed it. These are new people, but they're safe.

27   It's all right. You're all right. Feel your heart beat.

28 **MATTIE:** He's treating her like an animal.

29 **PHAYNE:** She has been treated like that, but not by him.

30   *(MOLE moves in, "checks" everyone, then moves in and*

31   *takes a crayon from her pocket and begins drawing on*

32   *cardboard on the floor, ignoring everyone.)*

33 **CWYNNE:** Where is she from?

34 **PHAYNE:** She was already here, when we came. *(ZETH gives*

35   *her some bread.)*

1 PHAYNE: It's all right now. She's settled.

2 JIX: In our town, we called children like that ghosts, because

3 they had no one to care for them, or help them, and we

4 knew they would soon die.

5 CWYNNE: They had someone, once.

6 DREUS: A long time ago. It doesn't matter now.

7 CWYNNE: It does! A mother and a father were real! The father

8 pushed me on my swing, and the mother read me stories.

9 And she gave me a bath, and cleaned me, and he played —

10 it was real! It was real!

11 DREUS: He ran away when the guns got too near — remember

12 how fast he could run? And she ran too — for the booze —

13 and I saved you when she tried to drown you in the bath!

14 Not the mother or the father! ME!

15 CWYNNE: It doesn't matter now.

16 DREUS : Cwynne, listen!

17 CWYNNE: I will not listen!

18 BAYE: I was a ghost.

19 DREUS: You? You're a frog.

20 MATTIE: We were at school. We saw the trucks coming.

21 PAI: We heard everything on the loudspeakers. Work detail

22 one! Work detail two! We heard them crashing through

23 the classrooms.

24 MATTIE: But we hid in the toilets and no one checked.

25 PAI: We were on our way to find our families. We were the only

26 ones in the village left behind. *(Muted conversation breaks*

27 *out around this revelation. MOLE suddenly stops playing, and*

28 *stands up, listening. She moves cautiously to door, then turns*

29 *and scurries to box and hides.)*

30 PHAYNE: What out there would frighten her? *(Realisation.)*

31 Musso!

32 MUSSO: *(Quietly)* Fish. You and Rafe go and check the

33 blackouts. The rest of you, stay quiet. And don't tell stories

34 to pass the time. We want time to stand still just now.

35 *(MUSSO, FISH and RAFE exit, the group waits.)*

1 GINNY: I know this feeling.

2 TESSE: Sssh, Ginny. We'll be all right.

3 GINNY: It's the same taste in my mouth. And my head is going

4   to burst. And my heart. My heart feels like it's breaking.

5 TESSE: Think about something else. *(FISH and RAFE enter.)*

6 FISH: We could see nothing from that side of the building –

7   but it only looks down to the river.

8 RAFE: Except the fog has lifted – and the moon's bright.

9   *(MUSSO enters slowly.)*

10 MUSSO: It's them.

11 FISH: How many?

12 MUSSO: Six, and so many weapons ...

13 PHAYNE: Tell us what to do, Musso. *(The GROUP moves in to*

14   *MUSSO, wanting an answer.)*

15 MUSSO: I don't know. I don't know! They've settled for the

16   night – they've lit a fire, put up the tents – right outside

17   our main gates.

18 FISH: We can't get out without walking past them. What do we

19   do?

20 MUSSO: Wait! Just wait.

21

22

23   **ACT TWO**

24

25   *(The room is dimly lit. It is nighttime. BAYE is keeping watch*

26   *through top window. The OTHERS are waiting and*

27   *watching. There are boxes piled in front of the entranceway.)*

28 BAYE: The lamps have gone out. They're going to sleep.

29 QUEY: At last! What do they do all that time?

30 FISH: They drink. Sing. It's a regular party.

31 QUEY: It's a long party.

32 CWYNNE: What's going to happen, Musso? One week has gone

33   and they're still out there – we're still trapped and we

34   don't know what they want. What do they want?

35 DREUS: They're on holiday.

1   ELLIE: What?

2   DREUS: Look at them. They've got warm tents, food, drink.

3   They're away from the fighting. They can do what they want.

4   RAFE: Well, I wouldn't choose this as a holiday spot.

5   BAYE: I'd like to go somewhere warm.

6   ELLIE: With restaurants and cafes, and lots of bread

7   everywhere ... paving the streets ...

8   CWYNNE: And a gingerbread house.

9   XADHE: Baked in the sun ...

10 JIX: Give me a bit.

11 XADHE: What?

12 JIX: Of the gingerbread house? *(MOLE watches intensely. She*

13   *has CWYNNE'S doll. CWYNNE watches her.)*

14 XADHE: Your stomach is full of rubbish! Chocolate ...

15 JIX: Only in my dreams. I won't die from that.

16 ELLIE: She makes me uncomfortable. The soldiers watch

17   from outside, and she watches us inside.

18 ZETH: She's good luck. She warned us, didn't she?

19 CWYNNE: *(Watching child play with doll)* You play with her

20   now, but I'm taking her back when we go.

21 FISH: When will that be?

22 CWYNNE: In the morning, when I've had my breakfast. My

23   brother's going to take me home.

24 DREUS: Cwynne, be quiet!

25 FISH: Good! Go! You can lead those guys away from our front

26   gate!

27 TESSE: They must leave soon. What would they want here?

28 RAFE: *(Interrupting.)* Who's on watch?

29 FISH: Mattie. Why?

30 RAFE: She should be back by now. *(Pause)*

31 MUSSO: *(Sighs.)* Jix, you come with me. *(The doorway is*

32   *uncovered and JIX and MUSSO leave.)*

33 PHAYNE: Be careful.

34 GINNY: Why go and look? Mattie'll come back.

35 TESSE: I agree. We're safer staying together. Just think – all of

1   us against those six. What could they do?

2   PHAYNE: Guns. *(Pause)*

3   GINNY: When is it spring?

4   FISH: Next year.

5   RAFE: Last year.

6   ZETH: Why?

7   GINNY: Because when Tesse and I were on watch yesterday, we

8   saw a little patch of tulips, over the bridge.

9   ELLIE: You saw tulips?

10 TESSE: Well, we couldn't exactly see ... but it was red ...

11 GINNY: And the sort of place tulips would grow.

12 ELLIE: Spring is two, maybe three months away.

13 XADHE: It wasn't tulips you saw.

14 GINNY: But we saw –

15 XADHE: It wasn't. *(There is a slight noise outside. BAYE is still on*

16   *watch.)*

17 BAYE: Here they come! *(Relief as MUSSO, JIX and MATTIE enter.)*

18 MUSSO: *(Pushing MATTIE in)* You're stupid! Stupid! What were

19   you doing?

20 MATTIE: I just wanted to find some –

21 MUSSO: Nothing is worth the risk! It's a threat to us all!

22 MATTIE: I didn't do anything!

23 MUSSO: You need to be punished!

24 MATTIE: No!

25 ZETH: Wouldn't a warning do?

26 XADHE: Your fairy tale's come back to haunt you, Musso.

27 MUSSO: She put all of us in danger!

28 PHAYNE: Stop! *(To FISH and DREUS who are holding MATTIE:)*

29   Let her go. And tell us what she did. *(MUSSO is silent;*

30   *furious.)*

31 JIX: We found her crawling around their camp.

32 MATTIE: I was crawling away!

33 JIX: You might have been caught!

34 MATTIE: And endangered myself. Not you. Anyway, they're

35   drunk.

1 JIX: They would be curious. They'd start to look around.

2 PHAYNE: Why did you do that, Mattie?

3 MATTIE: I went too near. I was stupid, but I could smell coffee ...

4 MUSSO: We'll punish you!

5 XADHE: How? Dipped? To be saved by a peppermint?

6 MUSSO: That's just a game.

7 TESSE: And this is not. So don't use game rules for real life.

8 PHAYNE: Even if we can understand why, you were wrong.

9   Musso – let it go. There's nothing we can do now.

10 MATTIE: But I –

11 MUSSO: No excuses.

12 MATTIE: I found some things. *(She takes out a small bag.*

13   *CWYNNE pounces on it.)*

14 CWYNNE: That's mine. I thought I'd lost it, miles away.

15 PHAYNE: What is it?

16 CWYNNE: Just – personal things.

17 PHAYNE: What?

18 MATTIE: But I found it. *(She grabs it back.)* We share

19   everything here. It's a rule, isn't it?

20 CWYNNE: *(Trying to grab bag back)* This isn't part of that rule!

21   *(The bag spills open, scattering things on the floor. The*

22   *CHILDREN dive and grab.)*

23 TESSE: *(Holds up soap)* You thought to bring soap. *(They gather*

24   *around to touch it and smell it.)*

25 BAYE: It's like – spice.

26 ELLIE: No, it's flowers.

27 JIX: Like roses – those big pink ones.

28 TESSE: I get lavender.

29 RAFE: I get – the bathroom at home.

30 BAYE: The bathroom?

31 RAFE: Bath time at six o'clock. After play. Before dinner. We

32   used to run deep baths – and put bubbles in. And the water

33   was never too hot, but the room would fill up with steam.

34 XADHE: Did you make steam pictures?

35 RAFE: On the mirrors? Takes soap.

1 TESSE: And on the tiles around the bath? It smells like
2   freesias.
3 RAFE: It's called "Delight" – see? I loved being clean. *(To*
4   *CWYNNE:)* Please, could we ... use it?
5 CWYNNE: *(Grabs soap)* No! This might last me for ages, forever.
6   All of you would go through it too fast. There'd be none left.
7 FISH: *(Taking soap)* You have to share. Zeth! Bring some water.
8   *(ZETH brings the water. FISH soaps his hands and puts the*
9   *soap carefully down beside the bucket of water. Then he*
10   *holds out his hands to RAFE. She moves over and takes his*
11   *hands. He gently soaps her hands, watching her.)*
12 FISH: *(To RAFE)* Everyone is allowed to be clean.
13 RAFE: *(Holding up her hands, whispering)* Like flowers.
14 JIX: Me too! *(Soon EVERYONE is wandering around with soapy*
15   *hands, slapping them together, making bubbles, writing*
16   *with them, printing them on boxes.)*
17 TESSE: I close my eyes, and I'm taken out of here.
18 RAFE: I haven't been so clean since ...
19 FISH: Forever! *(Laughter)*
20 PHAYNE: Zeth, look. *(MOLE is sitting beside bowl, washing her*
21   *hands.)*
22 MATTIE: I found something else. *(Takes out another wallet.)* On
23   the road.
24 PAI: Good! To share?
25 MATTIE: No. For Musso. *(MUSSO grabs wallet.)*
26 MUSSO: Now we're really in trouble. Why did you pick this up?
27   This is a soldier's pouch. It's where he keeps his orders.
28 ZETH: Then open it.
29 MUSSO: When he finds this is gone ...
30 ZETH: Open it up and let's find out what they are doing here.
31 MUSSO: *(Opens and tries to read; hands it to PHAYNE)* I'm not
32   very fluent. You read it.
33 PHAYNE: *(Trying)* I can't make out – the dialect's too hard.
34 XADHE: I'll try to read ...
35 ZETH: Let me see it.

1 PAI: **So many volunteers! Give it to me.** *(Takes and reads. To*
2 *ZETH:)* **You're right. Now we know why they're here.**
3 **They're looking for us!**
4 MUSSO: **For you?**
5 PAI: **Us – all of us – or ...** *(She keeps reading)* **... or at least, all**
6 **the females.**
7 RAFE: **No!**
8 PAI: **All females between the ages of ...** *(She checks)* **... ten and**
9 **eighteen.**
10 PHAYNE: **Why?**
11 PAI: **It says that small "bands" of youths have been sighted**
12 **traveling north, and are known to have settled in –**
13 **surprise – this town – ha! – in the old warehouses on the**
14 **river. Good hiding place, Musso.**
15 PHAYNE: **But why? Why would they want young women to the**
16 **point of taking time out from fighting to find them?**
17 PAI: *(Still reading)* **Not all young women – just two. One ... I**
18 **can't make out her name, and a seventeen year old, Lena.**
19 **Oh, and photos are supplied ...** *(She searches the wallet.)*
20 **But not here.**
21 MUSSO: *(Bitter)* **Good. Now we know all of nothing.**
22 PAI: **They know we're in here.**
23 MUSSO: **How?**
24 PAI: *(Reads)* **"Maintain presence outside building where**
25 **sighting occurred. Do not search. Keep surveillance**
26 **unobtrusive, until signal."**
27 BAYE: **What does that mean?**
28 FISH: **It means, "don't let us see them see us."**
29 CWYNNE: **But we haven't done anything!**
30 FISH: **We don't have to.**
31 PAI: *(Reads.)* **"Transportation to camps will be provided."**
32 MATTIE: **I'm not going to a camp!**
33 FISH: **They haven't asked us yet.**
34 MUSSO: **Is that all the information?**
35 DREUS: **Yes.**

1 **MUSSO: Then put it back in the wallet.** *(To MATTIE:)* **You have**
2 **to return it to where you found it.**
3 **MATTIE: I can't do that.**
4 **CWYNNE: You crawled around before.**
5 **MATTIE: I didn't know anything then. I can't by myself ...**
6 **MUSSO: Sssh – so, someone will go with you. Jix.**
7 **JIX: Why me? I already risked my life getting her back here!**
8 **MUSSO: It's dark, Jix, and you'll be fast. Just put it where she**
9 **says, and come back.**
10 **JIX: If I don't come back ...**
11 **PHAYNE: We don't say things like that here.**
12 **JIX: Sorry.** *(Angrily:)* **Even my mother couldn't make me do**
13 **this.**
14 **MUSSO: Jix!**
15 **JIX:** *(Snaps.)* **I'm going!** *(JIX and MATTIE leave.)*
16 **FISH: Will it be all right?**
17 **MUSSO: She's fast, and she's sneaky. She'll do it.**
18 **PAI: It's true. She's a scrounger, a little rat. She can get into**
19 **anything, anywhere.**
20 **TESSE: Even knowing what they want, what can we do?**
21 **MUSSO: I think ... Be ready to leave.** *(MUSSO's words push people*
22 *into action, and they gather up their belongings. Pause)*
23 **RAFE: What would happen if I walked right out, through the**
24 **door, over the bridge ...**
25 **ELLIE: Into the arms of the enemy?**
26 **RAFE: Maybe I could distract them and the rest of you could just**
27 **slip down the bank, into the river. They wouldn't see you.**
28 **FISH: Yes, they would.**
29 **GINNY: I can't swim.**
30 **BAYE: Neither can I.**
31 **FISH: And there are great hunks of ice floating around. We'd**
32 **freeze.**
33 **DREUS: Why do you want to be a hero?**
34 **RAFE: I want to do something. I'm thinking – I've made it this**
35 **far, and I start to imagine, maybe I'm a real person again,**

1   with food, and tomorrow – and clean hands. So I think –

2   maybe what I want, counts, but then, then ...

3   XADHE: It all goes. It disappears. You're back at that place,

4   always, where you can't do anything.

5   RAFE: And I would be doing something, wouldn't I, if I just

6   went out there ...

7   FISH: You're not Lena!

8   RAFE: It won't matter to them. There are reasons for wanting

9   a sixteen year-old female.

10   PHAYNE: You don't need to do that. *(Pause)*

11   CWYNNE: What we have to do, is find who they're looking for,

12   and send her out, don't we, Dreus?

13   TESSE: And which "her" are you talking about? There is no

14   Lena here.

15   MUSSO: Perhaps we should make sure of that. *(Enter MATTIE*

16   *and JIX.)*

17   XADHE: You would hand over one of us?

18   JIX: Who are you handing over?

19   XADHE: No one.

20   DREUS: Maybe not. *(There is a huge furor as the GIRLS realize*

21   *the threat is serious.)*

22   XADHE: What happens if it's your sister?

23   DREUS: She's been with me, always. No one wants us.

24   MUSSO: Some of us can account for each other. Let's hear it.

25   TESSE: Are you judge now too, Musso?

26   MUSSO: We need to do this fairly.

27   XADHE: And what happens if it is one of us? What will you do

28   then?

29   MUSSO: *(Ignores XADHE)* I'll speak for Phayne.

30   PHAYNE: You don't need to. I came –

31   MATTIE: I was split from my family in the convoys. I joined

32   these others a while ago. It's not me!

33   PAI: You know our story. Why would they want us?

34   MUSSO: Tesse?

35   TESSE: This is wrong.

1   **MUSSO:** But?

2   **TESSE:** You know about me.

3   **MUSSO:** We need to know –

4   **TESSE:** What? Details of how lost I am? No! We should be

5   keeping each other safe, not opening the door for the

6   enemy. You're doing a wrong thing.

7   **FISH:** It's making a choice. Between living and dying.

8   **XADHE:** It might be living for only one minute more if they

9   decide to take you, too.

10   **FISH:** It might be forever!

11   **MUSSO:** Ginny?

12   **TESSE:** She's with me.

13   **MUSSO:** Since when?

14   **TESSE:** For a long time now. Remember, she screamed at us –

15   at the church, with the soldier ... I told you.

16   **MUSSO:** And what about before?

17   **GINNY:** There was no before. Before I screamed, I was ... *(She*

18   *goes to MOLE.)* I know what she's doing. You live inside an

19   egg, and silence is the shell. You keep your mouth shut

20   and don't speak and it's safe. Because it's only your voice

21   that will crack the silence. I am not Lena.

22   **CWYNNE:** *(Pointing to MOLE)* What about her? Dreus? Dreus,

23   what about her?

24   **PHAYNE:** She's been here forever.

25   **ZETH:** Nobody wants her.

26   **MUSSO:** So, who is left? Rafe?

27   **FISH:** It's not Rafe. They aren't looking for her!

28   **RAFE:** They might.

29   **ELLIE:** That's why she was willing to give herself up. She's

30   guilty.

31   **FISH:** She's not. She stole some clothes, that's all.

32   **RAFE:** I burnt down their house ...

33   **PHAYNE:** You burnt ... ?

34   **RAFE:** Where they kept all of the girls they used. I burnt it

35   down, by accident, and then I ran, to escape them – but

1   here they are again.

2 **FISH: It's not you they want. That was just another burnt**

3   **building.**

4 **BAYE: I would have burnt it down too.**

5 **MUSSO: I brought Ellie here. She needed help. She'd been left**

6   **for dead. If they were looking, it would be to bury her.**

7 **XADHE: Would you stop this!**

8 **TESSE: Stop it before it goes further.**

9   *(JIX is high up on the top lookout with BAYE.)*

10 **JIX: Musso! Musso, they're lighting fires.** *(OTHERS get where*

11   *they can see out.)*

12 **FISH: They've lit the building down at the far end, and those**

13   **funny sheds right on the edge of the river.**

14 **RAFE: They must have heard me!**

15 **DREUS:** *(To JIX and MATTIE)* **They must have seen you two.**

16 **ZETH: They'll smoke us out.**

17 **PAI: They want to burn us out.**

18   *(MUSSO is tying a large piece of white fabric around his staff.)*

19 **PHAYNE: What are you doing that for? These aren't those tame**

20   **soldiers you bargain with. You're not making a deal for**

21   **food. They won't listen!**

22 **MUSSO: We would be dead now, if that's what they wanted. I**

23   **need to find out exactly what they do want.** *(MOLE gives*

24   *ZETH a notebook which has fallen from XADHE's bag.)*

25 **DREUS: Who they want. Lena.**

26 **MUSSO: Then I'll tell them she isn't here.**

27 **ZETH: You can't say that. This is Lena's.**

28 **MUSSO:** *(He holds up the notebook.)* **Who?** *(There is a moment of*

29   *accusation; guilt.)*

30 **XADHE: Maybe it's me. The last one on your "let's play fair"**

31   **list.**

32 **ELLIE: We would have found out.**

33 **XADHE: How? Not from me. What would you do? Turn me over**

34   **to the enemy?**

35 **MUSSO: Yes.**

1   XADHE: And if you do that, won't you feel like you're turning
2   yourself in? *(Pause)*
3   TESSE: It's me. I'm Lena.
4   GINNY: No. It's all right. I'm Lena.
5   RAFE: It's me.
6   CWYNNE: I'm not.
7   PAI: I think, maybe I'm Lena.
8   MATTIE: My name's ...
9   MUSSO: Quiet. *(Pause)* Is this funny? How can it be? Six
10   soldiers are out there, quietly, calmly, waiting to take us. It
11   would be easier if they were shouting and screaming, but
12   they're not. They don't care enough to do that! We're so
13   much nothing. Like something else on their shopping list.
14   So you watched your father shot, and you buried your
15   mother. They don't care. Not when it comes to the choice
16   between what they've been told to do, and our survival.
17   They don't care.
18   TESSE: Like you don't care about Lena.
19   MUSSO: Not when I can care about Phayne.
20   PHAYNE: We can't give her away – whoever she is, Musso. We
21   can't just hand her over, maybe to die.
22   XADHE: You won't need to. She's already dead. *(Pause. To*
23   *GINNY:)* Funny you talking about tulips. I thought you
24   must have found her. I couldn't bury her, because the
25   ground's hard, and I didn't have a spade. In the end, she
26   was so red, like autumn leaves, and I left her by the
27   bridge, slightly hidden. But then a little snow fell, and she
28   must have coloured the snow, and you thought she was
29   tulips.
30   RAFE: Who was she?
31   XADHE: She was ...
32   MATTIE: Why is she wanted?
33   XADHE: They aren't looking for her! They're looking for me.
34   *(Suddenly loud, distorted voices and sirens through*
35   *loudspeakers, are heard ordering, threatening.)*

1   DREUS: Then they've found you! Isn't that your call?

2   PHAYNE: Why you, Xadhe?

3   XADHE: My stepfather is the colonel who gave the orders to

4   wipe out Susdow. Your houses. Your homes.

5   ELLIE: So, why are you here? You could be safe, at home, with

6   the enemy.

7   XADHE: Safe? *(Pause)* My stepfather is a soldier. Lena's father

8   was a fighter. She used to leave messages, for him,

9   secretly. My mother found out I went with Lena to deliver

10   them. She told my stepfather. They laid a trap, Lena's

11   father was caught. *(Pause)* And that night, my stepfather

12   told my mother they were going to take Lena's whole

13   family in. For questioning. So I went to her place –

14   sneaked out past curfew – but I'd just got there when the

15   soldiers came. Lena and I climbed out her window – but

16   her mother answered the door ... *(She stops.)* Then – you

17   know the vegetables I brought in on the first day? We were

18   stealing them from a barn, miles from anywhere, and an

19   old man appeared and shot at us. Again and again. Lena

20   was behind – she fell on me. I crawled for ages with her,

21   and when I stopped – I was still carrying the potatoes.

22   PHAYNE: How do they know you're with Lena?

23   XADHE: I rang my mother! To tell her I couldn't go home!

24   *(Loudspeakers blast out again.)*

25   DREUS: They're not listening.

26   XADHE: I just want to keep running.

27   RAFE: How can you escape?

28   CWYNNE: It seems to me that you could be our escape. You

29   could do what Rafe suggested. Distract them.

30   FISH: We'd freeze in the river.

31   MUSSO: We're trapped, whatever we do. Six years, surviving,

32   growing clever, for nothing.

33   *(MOLE has been pulling at the wallboards/cartons upstage,*

34   *and disappeared. JIX notices and investigates.)*

35   JIX: I think ... there might be a way out. *(BAYE joins JIX.)*

1   **PAI:** Don't, Jix. This isn't the time for your stupid ideas.

2   **BAYE:** It's not stupid. I'm going to do it. I'm going to get out.

3   **MUSSO:** How, Jix?

4   **JIX:** Here. You can see into the gap between the inside and the
5   outside wall. And it's really, really wide. And I can look
6   right down, and see the earth. You could climb down the
7   wall – like a ladder, then outside.

8   *(FISH crawls through to look and emerges triumphant.)*

9   **FISH:** That's it – come on, Rafe. That's what we'll do.

10   *(They start pulling boards away. PEOPLE begin to disappear*
11   *into the wall. JIX climbs high to keep watch on soldiers.)*

12   **GINNY:** I can't, Tesse. I can't do this again. *(She climbs in,*
13   *protesting the whole time.)*

14   **TESSE:** You have to. I'll throw down my bundle when you're at
15   the bottom.

16   **RAFE:** Fish – I can't find my rug.

17   **FISH:** Leave your rug. We've got to go! While they're busy.
18   Quickly! *(The lights and noise burst through again. This*
19   *time there is the sound of running feet and shouting.)*

20   **MUSSO:** If they're seen – they'll be shot.

21   **PHAYNE:** Shall we go? What shall we do?

22   **TESSE:** We've got to keep together. Please – hurry.

23   **MUSSO:** *(Pulls out a torch from his stash)* Now's the time. Let's
24   stick close.

25   **PHAYNE:** Who's left? Us, Zeth, Mattie – are you there?

26   **MUSSO:** She's gone already.

27   **PHAYNE:** Xadhe – where's she?

28   **JIX:** *(From high up)* She's being the distraction.

29   **MUSSO:** Jix, what did you say?

30   **JIX:** Xadhe's being the distraction! She's just walked out –
31   going down to the bridge. There is shouting, footsteps and
32   more lights from outside. They're aiming at her. *(Pause)*
33   She's stopped. *(Pause)* They've got her. *(Pause. JIX climbs*
34   *down.)*

35   **PHAYNE:** She could have stayed with us. *(MUSSO watches*

PHAYNE and JIX exeunt. He turns to look at the space. The lights shift to the state of the opening scene. Torchlight passes over MOLE, lying on stomach, crayoning. MUSSO shines torch around warehouse, brushing over MOLE.)

MUSSO: A lifetime, passed. *(The torch light flicks out. In background, very faintly, comes the sound of children playing or singing "game" songs.)*

THE END

Carrying the Calf
by Shirley Barrie

This is a play about women having problems with men in their lives, each of whom takes an initial step towards standing up for herself — a step that is right for them. There is now a general public recognition that violence against women is a major problem in societies the world over, but the steps towards changing our behaviour sometimes seem painful and slow. We should not conclude from this that the situation is hopeless, however. Rather, having acknowledged the problem, we must understand that there is still much for both men and women to learn about relating to each other. If we want to bridge the gap, we must find a way to do it. Fetneh, after all, didn't work for six years in order to reject Bahram-Gur but to have a positive relationship with him.

The drama develops the metaphor of a self-defence class for women, led by the instructor Firoza. As each of the three other women gradually master the kata, a series of combative postures and movements, their personalities change and they become more self-assertive and aware of their personal situations. On one level, the drama deals with the cultural conflict of gender discrimination in personal relationships, family situations, work roles and societal expectations. On a much deeper level, however, the playwright connects this external conflict to each of the character's own self-conflicts.

This provocative play is outwardly realistic in style, developing the action chronologically in four scenes spanning several weeks of karate lessons. It presents unique challenges, however, to the actors who must convincingly perform the combative exercises described in the stage directions. These movements reflect their dramatic development from the starting point of "raw beginners" to the final scene where they've become more skilled both athletically and in their personal lives. The movements also communicate a great deal of the subtext between the four women, at various times becoming disguised hostility, affection, competition, uncertainty and so forth. The play is thus highly physical, despite the realistic dialog.

Thus *Carrying the Calf* is rich in visual as well as verbal imagery, developing a story that is at once both very modern and very classical. And the ethnic backgrounds of the four characters — Asian, Indian, African, Caucasian — provide a subtle commentary on the universality of the drama's theme and the notion of cultural diversity that infuses many societies today.

The story of Fetneh, Bahram-Gur and the Calf that Firoza tells in the play is an ancient Persian tale contained in a book published by the Metropolitan Museum of Art in New York, *Mirror of the Invisible World: Tales of the Khamseh of Nizami* by Peter J. Chelkowski.

The playwright would like to thank all of the people and organizations involved in the original commissioning and development of the play: Alby James, Artistic Director of Temba, the Black Theatre Company in London, England; Susan Seagrove, Don Bouzek, and the Mayworks Festival of Working People and the Arts; Jane Dingle, Malika Mendez, Rachel Crawford, Arthi Sambasivan, Mishu Vellani, Catherine Bruhier, Jeneanne Smith, the Ontario Arts Council and the City of Toronto through the Toronto Arts Council. Special thanks to Zulaikha Van Patter and Ken Chubb. The playwright acknowledges the assistance of the 1991 Banff Centre for the Arts Playwrights' Colony.

Characters:

Indira, 17, of South Asian extraction, has lived in Canada from the age of 5.

Sharon, 17, born in Canada of West Indian parents

Ann, pushing 40, white, divorced, mother of 4

Firoza, mid-late 20's, Ugandan of South Asian extraction, university educated.

Setting:

The play takes place in an empty room in a community center. There are gym mats and a couple of benches. The four scenes span the eight weeks of a self-defence class for women.

Production Notes:

In staging *Carrying the Calf* it is important to find a physicalization for each of the characters that shows the evolution of their physical confidence and their skills. This should be a part of the performance throughout and not just in the moments where physical action is scripted. While there is a measure of "acting" involved in making some of the physical moves in the play read effectively, it proved invaluable to have a good self-defence teacher/trainer as a part of the production team. Concern for safety and adequate warm-ups are important when undertaking this kind of work, particularly when performers are coming into physical contact with one another. Having actors of different heights playing Indira and Sharon in the remount of the production showed us that breaks from holds and throws must be adapted to the size and the physical agility of the actors.

The scripted physical moves in the play are of two types: generally taught self-defence tactics (such as locating the vulnerable spots on an attacker, and breaking from holds) and the "kata." A kata is an integral part of karate training. It is a carefully orchestrated series of moves against imaginary attackers, moves that look very much like a choreographed dance. We chose a beginner's kata that visually revealed the grace, control, strength and confidence that the women develop over the weeks of the course.

The play was first produced by Straight Stitching Productions in association with Prologue to the Performing Arts. The first performance was sponsored by the Bickford Centre on February 4, 1992 at the Central High School of Commerce in Toronto. A four-week tour followed with the following cast:

Indira .... Catherine Bruhier
Sharon .... Michelle Moffatt
Ann .... Mary Durkan
Firoza .... Helen-Claire Tingling

The production was directed by Lib Spry, set and costumes by Chris Bryden, stage management by Nancy Katsof and music performed by by the Groupo Gekko (formerly Urban Pygmies). Combatives director was Julie Busch of the Toronto Academy of Karate, and Denise Fujiwara was choreographic consultant. The Teacher's Guide was written by Sue Daniel, and production graphics were by Rudolf Stussi. The production was remounted and toured in October 1992 with the following changes:

Indira .... Sharon M. Lewis
Sharon .... Melanie Nicholls-King

1   **SCENE 1**

2

3   **INDIRA:** *(From off)* **201. This is it.**

4   **SHARON:** *(From off)* **I can't go in like this.**

5   **INDIRA:** *(Off)* **We're late. Come on.** *(She enters. She wears a dark*

6   *skirt and white blouse — almost like a school uniform. She*

7   *carries a school bag. She's a bit breathless.)* **Nobody's here!**

8   **SHARON:** *(Entering)* **Good.** *(She's very stylishly dressed,*

9   *including dress shoes — but she only wears one shoe. The*

10   *other is in her hand. She limps to the bench and sits down,*

11   *rubbing her ankle.)*

12   **INDIRA: Are you all right?**

13   **SHARON: I twisted my ankle on those stupid stairs and broke**

14   **the heel on my best shoes. I'm terrific.**

15   **INDIRA: Sorry.**

16   **SHARON: And I'm all sweaty from running through the park.**

17   **Yuk. If you'd a been on time we could've walked around.**

18   **INDIRA: I couldn't help it, could I? My brother was going out**

19   **and my dad said he had to walk me to the library.**

20   **SHARON: The library! Is that where you told them you were**

21   **going? What if they find out?**

22   **INDIRA: They won't.**

23   **SHARON:** *(Trying to walk on one shoe, but the heel collapses)*

24   **Chuh! I can't wear this!**

25   **INDIRA: They were kinda dumb shoes to wear here anyway.**

26   **SHARON: My running shoes are in my bag. Anyway you're a**

27   **great one to talk.** *(Gesturing to the skirt:)* **I mean, wearing**

28   **that here, now that's dumb.**

29   **INDIRA: I'm gonna change. Anyways, my Mum and Dad don't**

30   **ask so many questions if I dress like this. You're lucky**

31   **your parents don't tell you what to wear.**

32   **SHARON: They tell me. I just don't pay no attention. It's okay**

33   **though. You expect that kinda thing from parents. But**

34   **when teachers ... D'you know what that witch Turnovski**

35   **had the nerve to tell me last week? That I —**

1   **INDIRA:** That you wouldn't have come down with a cold if you
2   dressed properly.
3   **SHARON:** Yeah, well I can't wait to get out of that dump. I'm
4   gonna get a job downtown in one of those fashion places.
5   You get a discount on the clothes, you know. Hey – we
6   could look for a job together.
7   **INDIRA:** I'm staying at school.
8   **SHARON:** With what's happening to you? It's your funeral. I
9   can't wear runners with this.
10 **INDIRA:** So it'll be dark when we finish. Nobody'll see you but
11   me. And I won't tell. *(Pause)*
12 **SHARON:** Uhh, Calvin's meeting me.
13 **INDIRA:** You never told me that!
14 **SHARON:** I never got a chance, did I?
15 **INDIRA:** But you said you never go out with him on Tuesdays.
16 **SHARON:** I don't. Usually. But he called me after school and ...
17   You know.
18 **INDIRA:** No. *(She doesn't know.)*
19 **SHARON:** Give me a break, eh? I told him I couldn't till after.
20 **INDIRA:** But how am I gonna get home?
21 **SHARON:** I'll ask Calvin if he'd mind ... driving around by your
22   place.
23 **INDIRA:** Oh, great. It's bad enough I hang around with you. If
24   my parents see me with you and Calvin, it'll be the end.
25 **SHARON:** So we'll drop you on the corner. *(She's been fiddling*
26   *with the shoe again. The heel falls off.)* This'll never stay on.
27   I'm gonna haveta go home.
28 **INDIRA:** You can't. You promised!
29 **SHARON:** Look, why don't you just open your stupid big
30   mouth and tell somebody about Jakey Barnes?
31 **INDIRA:** Cause if it got back to my dad he'd take me out of
32   school. You don't know him, Shar. *(Pause)*
33 **SHARON:** It's not easy being your friend, you know. I mean,
34   what am I gonna tell Calvin?
35 **INDIRA:** I thought you already talked to him.

1 **SHARON:** I said I'd promised to come here for a class with you.
2   I didn't tell him what class.
3 **INDIRA:** Why not? Are you gonna lie?
4 **SHARON:** You're a great one to talk about lying! *(INDIRA is*
5   *destroyed.)* Hey — I never said it. Indie, forget I said it, all
6   right? I don't want you going all guilty on me.
7 **INDIRA:** I don't want to lie. I didn't. Not exactly. But they
8   wouldn't understand ...
9 **SHARON:** Yeah, well, it's the same with guys. You don't lie. You
10   just have to ... figure out a way to say it. Anyway, it's no big
11   deal. It'll be over by then.
12 **INDIRA:** Sharon!!
13 **SHARON:** I only promised to come once. *(ANN enters. She is out*
14   *of breath. There is a sudden silence.)*
15 **ANN:** Hi. *(Pause)* Those stairs are killers. Am I late?
16 **SHARON:** For what?
17 **ANN:** The class.
18 **SHARON:** You got the wrong room.
19 **ANN:** This is 201 isn't it?
20 **SHARON:** God, you've stuck us in the wrong room, Indira.
21   They'll have started already and we'll have to walk in in
22   front of everybody.
23 **INDIRA:** I checked after school, Shar. It was this room.
24 **ANN:** Maybe we've signed up for the same class.
25 **SHARON:** Huh?
26 **ANN:** It is possible. *(SHARON and INDIRA giggle.)*
27 **SHARON:** I don't think so.
28 **ANN:** This is supposed to be self-defence for women.
29 **SHARON:** Chuh! You've really dumped us in it now, Indie. Let's
30   go.
31 **INDIRA:** No.
32 **ANN:** What're you signed up for? *(Embarrassed pause)*
33 **INDIRA:** The ... defence thing.
34 **ANN:** Well that's all right then.
35 **SHARON:** *(Muttering)* This is gonna be terrific!

1   ANN: *(To INDIRA)* Aren't very many of us, are there? I almost
2   didn't come myself. Well ... it's hard to get out with the
3   kids'n all.
4   SHARON: I can't believe it. She's gotta be as old as my Mom.
5   INDIRA: Shhh.
6   SHARON: I mean — what's she here for?
7   ANN: D'you know if we're supposed to bring anything special
8   for this class?
9   INDIRA: No. Sorry.
10 ANN: You've never come to anything like this before then?
11 SHARON: No way. Let's go, Indie.
12 INDIRA: No.
13 ANN: Is this all they give us to sit on? Oh well. *(She sits on the*
14   *bench, moving INDIRA's bag and jacket to make room for her*
15   *own things.)* It's quieter'n home. Kids fighting over the TV.
16 SHARON: God, she's taking over the whole place.
17 INDIRA: *(Pulling SHARON aside)* Why d'you have to be so rude?
18 SHARON: Why d'you have to be so polite? I mean, I wouldn't be
19   stuck here with you if you didn't let people walk all over
20   you, would I?
21 INDIRA: It's not the same thing.
22 SHARON: Isn't it? *(Pause)* And have you thought about the kind
23   of person who's gonna be teaching this class then?
24 INDIRA: Yeah.
25 SHARON: What if it's a guy — huh? And if it's a woman, she's
26   probably some big butch man-hater, muscles out to here.
27   Yuk!! *(Silence)* Ah, c'mon, Indie. Let's go. I came, didn't I?
28 INDIRA: Yeah. *(INDIRA goes to get her bag. SHARON sighs with*
29   *relief. FIROZA enters. She's slim, very pretty, East Indian.*
30   *She has a computerized printout.)*
31 FIROZA: Hi, everybody. Thanks so much for waiting. My name
32   is Firoza, and I'm your instructor.
33 SHARON: Ohhhh no.
34 FIROZA: Is something wrong, Sharon? Or is it Ann?
35 ANN: I'm Ann.

1 INDIRA: She just got a bit tired of waiting. That's all.

2 FIROZA: I'm really sorry about that.

3 SHARON: You're going to teach us?

4 FIROZA: Well, that depends on you.

5 SHARON: On me! Hey – I didn't do nothing.

6 FIROZA: I didn't mean just you, Sharon. I meant all of you.

7 *(Pause)* You see, usually they won't run a class with a

8   registration of three ...

9 SHARON: Oh. Too bad.

10 FIROZA: But – since this course is something the community

11   centre says it really wants started, I've managed to

12   persuade Phil to let us carry on. But he'll only agree if all

13   three of you are really committed to the course and plan

14   to keep coming.

15 SHARON: Chuh!

16 FIROZA: I know it's laying a lot on you, and ...

17 INDIRA: I'll come.

18 SHARON: Indie! *(INDIRA glares at her. To FIROZA:)* But what if

19   we're sick or something?

20 FIROZA: Well, I don't think Phil will pull the plug if you're in

21   bed with the flu one week, but ...

22 SHARON: What if somebody can't do it?

23 FIROZA: Oh, I'm sure you won't have any problems, Sharon.

24 ANN: *(She's not going to be put down by SHARON.)* I'll come.

25 SHARON: Gawd!! Look. You gotta understand. It wasn't my

26   idea, coming here. She talked me into it.

27 FIROZA: Oh.

28 SHARON: It was a favour like ...

29 FIROZA: I see ... Well, you don't have to decide right now. You

30   don't even know what you're getting into. Right? Tell you

31   what. Why don't we go ahead with this class and then we

32   can talk at the end when you've got a better idea of what

33   it's all about.

34 INDIRA: All right. *(ANN nods. SHARON shrugs.)*

35 FIROZA: I'll show you something we'll be learning. *(She*

1   demonstrates a beautiful and powerful *kata — a*
2   *choreographed series of movements used in karate.*
3   *SHARON is impressed in spite of herself. ANN is skeptical*
4   *about what she's let herself in for. INDIRA is enthralled.)*
5
6
7   **SCENE 2**
8
9   *(It's halfway through the third class. FIROZA is working with*
10   *ANN.)*
11 **FIROZA: Let's go back to the Cross Arm Grab.**
12 **ANN: Oh, gawd.**
13 **FIROZA: Do you remember?**
14 **ANN: I ... think so.**
15 **FIROZA: Ready?** *(FIROZA grabs her.)*
16 **ANN:** *(Fluffs it.)* **Sorry.**
17 **FIROZA: That's okay. I'll go over it again.** *(She waits.)*
18 **ANN: Oh. I'm the aggressor now. Right.** *(She grabs FIROZA.*
19   *FIROZA cleanly breaks the hold, perhaps describing in*
20   *words the sequence of moves that leaves ANN on her knees.)*
21   **Got it ... I think.**
22 **FIROZA: So ...** *(She grabs ANN. ANN breaks the hold, not*
23   *smoothly but effectively and with relish.)* **Good.** *(INDIRA*
24   *enters. She's wearing more appropriate clothes — closer in*
25   *style to FIROZA's than SHARON's.)*
26 **FIROZA:** *(Breaking off with ANN)* **Well?**
27 **INDIRA: No answer.**
28 **ANN:** *(Breathing heavily)* **Is it time for a break yet?**
29 **FIROZA: Why not.**
30 **ANN: Thank god.** *(She collapses on the bench.)*
31 **FIROZA: She seemed to be catching on to things so quickly last**
32   **week. I thought. ...**
33 **INDIRA: She said she was coming.**
34 **FIROZA: Did I say something to upset her?**
35 **INDIRA: Noooo.**

1 ANN: Something probably just came up.

2 INDIRA: Or someone.

3 FIROZA: With my luck Phil will pick tonight to do a spot check.

4 INDIRA: He wouldn't, would he? *(FIROZA shrugs.)*

5 ANN: No. Don't worry so much, Indira. I don't suppose Firoza

6   pays the rent by doing stuff like this, eh?

7 FIROZA: No.

8 INDIRA: What do you do?

9 FIROZA: *(Laughs.)* Ah well ...

10 INDIRA: I'm sorry. It's none of my —

11 FIROZA: No, Indira. It's okay. I used to be a government

12   researcher.

13 ANN: Hooo. That sounds like a pretty good job. D'ya get laid

14   off?

15 FIROZA: I hated it. I quit.

16 ANN: Must be nice.

17 FIROZA: I wanted to be a writer.

18 INDIRA: Wow!

19 FIROZA: Well, not exactly a writer. I wanted to edit a book.

20 INDIRA: What about?

21 FIROZA: It's a collection of stories that women tell. Women

22   who've come here from all over the world.

23 ANN: Who's gonna pay you for doing that?

24 FIROZA: That's exactly what my mother said. "After all I went

25   through to send you to university, Firoza. I should have let

26   your uncles marry you off like they wanted to." Well, you

27   know what families can be like, eh, Indira?

28 ANN: Yeah well she's got a point, don't you think? I mean —

29   who's going to read something like that?

30 FIROZA: I'd hoped — people like Indira and you.

31 ANN: You're wasting your time on me. No offence, but when I

32   finally get everything cleaned up in the evening, all I

33   wanna do is sit down, maybe have a bit of a laugh at

34   something on the TV and crawl into bed.

35 INDIRA: I'd read it. I'd really like to.

1 FIROZA: Thanks, but you're not going to have the chance. I
2   just got a rejection letter from the publisher this morning.
3   He agrees with Ann.
4 INDIRA: Oh.
5 FIROZA: So it really hasn't been my day.
6 INDIRA: I'm sorry.
7 FIROZA: It's not your fault.
8 INDIRA: I'm gonna kill her. She said she was coming.
9 FIROZA: I guess this class is really important to you, Indira.
10 INDIRA: Yeah.
11 FIROZA: Why?
12 INDIRA: Oh well ... I don't know ... you hear a lot these days
13   about how dangerous it can be for women, don't you? I
14   just thought, you know, it's better to be prepared ... And
15   I'm really getting a lot out of it.
16 FIROZA: You're lucky, you know.
17 INDIRA: How?
18 FIROZA: Being able to do something like this while you're still
19   young and at home. You must have a very supportive
20   family.
21 INDIRA: Oh...yeah, they're great.
22 FIROZA: What about you, Ann?
23 ANN: What?
24 FIROZA: What made you come?
25 ANN: Me? *(Pause)* Uhh ... masochism. *(FIROZA laughs.)*
26 ANN: Isn't that the right word?
27 FIROZA: Yes. I guess so. *(SHARON enters.)*
28 SHARON: Hi everybody.
29 INDIRA: Where have you been?
30 SHARON: *(To everybody)* Something came up.
31 INDIRA: I bet.
32 FIROZA: Don't worry about it. We're just glad you're here now.
33 INDIRA: What were you doing?
34 ANN: See. All that worry for nothing. *(ANN and FIROZA begin*
35   *laying out the mats.)*

1 SHARON: I couldn't get away.

2 INDIRA: From what?

3 SHARON: Calvin wanted me to meet his cousin, Roy.

4 INDIRA: Why now?

5 SHARON: 'Cause he was driving back to Sarnia tonight, wasn't

6   he?

7 INDIRA: Firoza was really worried. The whole class could've

8   been cancelled. You let her down, not turning up.

9 SHARON: Is that why you're coming now, Indie?

10 INDIRA: What d'ya mean?

11 SHARON: *(Sarcastic)* You don't want Firoza to lose her precious

12   class. Well – I don't care that for Firoza. *(Snapping her*

13   *fingers)*

14 INDIRA: Sharon!

15 SHARON: It's you I was coming for.

16 INDIRA: Just cause I like Firoza doesn't mean I don't care

17   about the class.

18 SHARON: Yeah? Well, I'll tell you Indie. I'm not gonna lose

19   Calvin over this class. Not even for you. Got it? *(She is trying*

20   *to get off a new pair of strapped shoes and get on her running*

21   *shoes. INDIRA goes off on her own and practices a kata.)*

22 ANN: *(Getting up from placing a mat)* Ohhh. I seem to be full of

23   muscles I never knew I had.

24 FIROZA: It'll get better.

25 ANN: Yeah. Sure. Last week I only ached for two days. First

26   week it was seven. I was crippled.

27 FIROZA: *(Jokingly)* You haven't been getting enough exercise,

28   Ann.

29 ANN: I'm a cleaner for god's sake.

30 FIROZA: Well, we are using different muscles here.

31 ANN: You don't have to tell me. I can feel every one of them.

32 SHARON: Doesn't bother me.

33 ANN: Yeah, well you're ...

34 SHARON: Black!

35 ANN: I wasn't going to say that!

1   SHARON: Sure.

2   ANN: I was going to say young. Probably take gym or whatever

3   they call it now.

4   SHARON: Not for long. Thank god.

5   FIROZA: My goodness, Sharon, you make it sound like you're

6   leaving.

7   SHARON: Yeah. So.

8   FIROZA: Oh. Well ... *(Pause)* Have you got a job?

9   SHARON: Haven't found the right thing yet.

10 FIROZA: Maybe you'd have more choice if you stayed on.

11 SHARON: What planet's she living on?

12 ANN: I don't think she wants to stay on.

13 SHARON: Wouldn't make any difference if I did.

14 FIROZA: But if she had a graduation diploma ...

15 SHARON: When's the last time you talked to a guidance officer?

16 INDIRA: Do we have to talk about this?

17 SHARON: I didn't start it. Last month I went to see the

18   Guidance. About what courses to take. I told Mrs. Gorman

19   what I wanted and she spent half an hour trying to talk

20   me out of it. Very subtle, like, you know. But I'm not

21   stupid. I knew what she was doing. Going on about how

22   good it was to be ambitious, but needing to be realistic

23   and how important it was to have something to fall back

24   on, if things didn't work out.

25 FIROZA: If you understood what she was doing, why'd you pay

26   any attention to her?

27 SHARON: I ain't finished yet. Richard Bates goes in right after

28   me, see. Now, I'm no brain, but he's a real dweeb. Stu ...

29   pid. And there was old Gorman, just slobbering with the

30   effort to get him to take the same courses she'd been

31   talking me out of because she couldn't bear to have him

32   sell himself short on his potential.

33 INDIRA: How d'you know she said that?

34 SHARON: There wasn't nobody else around so I listened

35   outside the door.

1   FIROZA: The important thing is why Mrs. Gorman did it.

2   SHARON: S'obvious. Richard's white, isn't he?

3   ANN: He's also a guy.

4   FIROZA: Sharon, we can't let other people's prejudices stop us

5   from doing what we want. Indira's staying on at school.

6   She'd be there to support you.

7   SHARON: Is that what she told you?

8   INDIRA: *(Tries to shut SHARON up)* Isn't it time to get back to

9   work?

10 FIROZA: Yes. *(Pause)* Well — Sharon's story has shown us pretty

11   clearly that society still has lots of ways of making us think

12   that we're inadequate. It doesn't mean we are. That's one

13   of the things we're learning here.

14 SHARON: All we're learning is how to do rolls and falls an' hit

15   the air an' stuff. That's nothing.

16 ANN: It is if you're not used to it.

17 FIROZA: Let's move on then. *(She grabs SHARON's wrist.)*

18 SHARON: Heyyyy!!! *(She's really panicked. She can't break away.)*

19 FIROZA: *(Lets her go)* I'm sorry, Sharon. I didn't mean to

20   frighten you. But that's how suddenly it could happen.

21   Let's say ... I'm an aggressor. *(She moves to INDIRA.)* And I

22   grab hold of you. *(She grabs INDIRA's wrist.)* What do you

23   feel?

24 INDIRA: Scared?

25 FIROZA: What do you want to do about it?

26 INDIRA: I don't know.

27 FIROZA: Do you want to break away?

28 INDIRA: I suppose so.

29 FIROZA: Well, you must decide. If you're uncertain you give

30   your opponent the advantage.

31 SHARON: Well, he's got the advantage, hasn't he? I mean, he

32   wouldn't have grabbed her in the first place if he wasn't

33   stronger than her, would he?

34 FIROZA: I guess we'd better review the old oriental recipe for

35   victory in battle. First — Ann?

1   ANN: Oh, gawd. Um – uhh – eyes.

2   FIROZA: That's right. Be aware of your opponent. Two –

3   INDIRA: Legs.

4   FIROZA: For balance. Maybe even just to run away.

5   ANN: Guts.

6   FIROZA: Yes. Strength of will. You want to defend yourself.

7   And what comes right at the bottom of the list, Sharon?

8   SHARON: *(Pause)* Strength.

9   FIROZA: Right.

10 SHARON: Why're you picking on me? This whole thing is just

11   dumb. I don't need to learn all this stupid stuff.

12 FIROZA: Why not?

13 SHARON: 'Cause I can stick up for myself. Me 'n my friends.

14   It's like I keep telling Indie, us West Indians, we stick up

15   for each other. Your trouble is you don't help each other

16   out. You're scared.

17 FIROZA: You know, you're partly right, Sharon. But only

18   partly. South Asians have been taught that it's shameful to

19   fight in public. That's not quite the same thing as being

20   scared.

21 ANN: Could look the same.

22 SHARON: So what're you doing this for?

23 FIROZA: Because girls and women from whatever culture, are

24   scared. And we limit ourselves because of that fear. I think

25   it's important to know how to avoid dangerous situations

26   and get out of them if they arise. Even you, Sharon – you

27   can't go everywhere with a gang of friends, can you?

28 SHARON: Yeah – well I've got someone lookin' out for me.

29 FIROZA: A special guardian angel?

30 INDIRA: That's one way of describing Calvin.

31 FIROZA: A boyfriend!

32 SHARON: Yeah. And nobody gives me no trouble when he's

33   around.

34 FIROZA: And when he's not?

35 SHARON: What're you getting at?

1   FIROZA: You sound a bit like my old uncle...

2   SHARON: Wha — !

3   FIROZA: ... when he found out I was taking self-defence. I
4   should not be doing such a thing, he said. I should be
5   content not to go out, especially at night, unless I had a
6   man to protect me. What about coming home after
7   working late, I asked? You should get married, he said.

8   SHARON: Yeah, well, it's different for me.

9   FIROZA: What would you do if Calvin wasn't around?

10 SHARON: Look — that's not going to happen. I'm not gonna let
11 it.

12 FIROZA: He could, by chance, get run over by a bus.

13 SHARON: That's really sick!

14 FIROZA: All I'm saying is people change. Circumstances
15 change.

16 SHARON: You're just saying that 'cause you can't get anybody.

17 FIROZA: I don't want a man to have to look after me.

18 SHARON: Well, you're weird!

19 INDIRA She didn't really mean that. You didn't, did you,
20 Sharon?

21 ANN: I wanted somebody to look after me. Well, why not? I was
22 working in a factory when I was 15. I nearly died of the
23 boredom and my ears hummed all the time from the
24 noise. Seemed to me it'd be heaven to get married, stay at
25 home, have somebody look after me.

26 SHARON: See!

27 ANN: Trouble was it didn't last. I was home with the kids. He
28 never was. Then he started getting laid off every job he
29 got. Drank too much. I was cleaning out toilets to make
30 ends meet.

31 SHARON: Yuk!

32 ANN: Smell, noise. What the hell? Life was shit whichever way
33 you looked at it.

34 FIROZA: So doesn't it make sense to be able to look after
35 yourself as well as you can?

1 SHARON: You don't give up, do ya? Hey – I'm not the brightest
2   person in the world, but even I can figure out that some
3   stupid piece of paper isn't gonna get me a job.
4 FIROZA: That isn't true. There are jobs.
5 SHARON: Yeah – well you won't catch me cleaning out
6   somebody else's toilets. I'd rather get married and take
7   my chances.
8 ANN: This Calvin got a good job then?
9 SHARON: He's self employed. He makes good money. And he's
10   generous. He bought me those shoes.
11 ANN: I bet he's sexy too.
12 SHARON: Yeah.
13 INDIRA: Yeah. He is. And cool. *(INDIRA begins to "play out"*
14   *Calvin. She does it very well. The walk, the gestures, the*
15   *monopolization of space. The intention of play acting at the*
16   *beginning is to release the tension, but it turns into*
17   *something more serious. Even FIROZA gets out of her way.*
18   *But then both she and ANN take it as a joke at first.)*
19 INDIRA: Hey, man. *(Imaginary handshakes)* **Getting' through?**
20   **Magic. That little business, man. Soon come. No worries,**
21   **man. Soon come. Trust me, brother. Yeah.** *(She moves*
22   *around the area, full of masculinity, enjoying the power she is*
23   *finding. SHARON giggles INDIRA goes to her.)* **Looking good,**
24   **woman. Yes, man. That's one good looking babe fer me to go**
25   **out walking with. Get rid of your friend now.** *(SHARON*
26   *laughs.)* **Three's too many for what I got in mind. Hey, Indira,**
27   **your books're waiting for you, girl. They're about the only**
28   **hard thing you'll come in contact with.** *(She laughs.)* **Hey – ey**
29   **– loosen up, woman. Too much up here ain't good fer you.**
30   **Chuh! Can't take a joke, that girl. So –** *(She puts her arm*
31   *around SHARON's shoulder and in a very sexy fashion runs it*
32   *across her shoulder and down her arm. She stops at her wrist,*
33   *grabs it viciously and twists it up her back.)* **– what d'ya say?**
34 SHARON: Please, Calvin, don't do that. You're hurting me.
35   Please.

1   **INDIRA:** *(Lets her go.)* **Thass nice. Hey, let's see a big smile, now.**
2   *(Strokes her cheek.)* **I'm walkin' out with my woman.**
3   **FIROZA: Indira. That's enough. Are you alright, Sharon?**
4   **SHARON: Yeah, yeah. She was just fooling around.** *(INDIRA is*
5   *very surprised and horrified at what she has done.)*
6   **FIROZA: Was she?**
7   **SHARON: Calvin said you'd be trying to turn me against him.**
8   **FIROZA: I'm not.**
9   **SHARON: Well, you're not going to. You don't even know him.**
10   **You don't know nothing.**
11   **FIROZA: So explain it to me.**
12   **SHARON: I can't. Why should I! Look — it's just the way things**
13   **are.**
14   **FIROZA: It's not the way they have to be.**
15   **SHARON: Chuh! I knew I shoulda stayed at MacDonalds with**
16   **Calvin and Roy. At least we were having a few laughs.** *(She*
17   *goes to her coat and starts out.)*
18   **ANN: Sharon.**
19   **SHARON: What?**
20   **ANN: Harry — that's my ex-husband, you know. Well, he come**
21   **round to the house a few weeks ago. He was drunk as a**
22   **skunk. Pushed his way in saying it was his place. He**
23   **smashed Mikey's model. That kid spent hours building**
24   **that plane and Harry... I just stood there. I was terrified.**
25   **My older boy finally shoved the jerk out the door. But I**
26   **can't depend on him all my life, can I? In a couple of years**
27   **he'll be gone and there's the little ones to think about ...**
28   *(Silence. SHARON puts her coat down.)*
29   **ANN: So maybe we can get back to work.**
30   **FIROZA: Right. Partners.** *(She goes toward SHARON, but*
31   *SHARON turns toward INDIRA.)*
32   **ANN: Looks like you're stuck with me.**
33   **FIROZA: Let's review what we did last week. Front choke hold.**
34   *(SHARON does a sudden grab and throw-down of INDIRA*
35   *who lands heavily. She's paying INDIRA back. Not daring to*

1 *directly reprove SHARON, FIROZA pointedly repeats the*
2 *correct instruction.)*
3 **FIROZA: Front choke hold.** *(Pause)* **Remember all the open**
4 **spots you've got to choose from.** *(To ANN:)* **Grab me.** *(She*
5 *demonstrates.)* **Hair, ear, floating ribs, solar plexus, groin,**
6 **knee, instep, break away.** *(SHARON and INDIRA practice*
7 *while FIROZA works with ANN. SHARON is very good at it*
8 *and there is a growing enjoyment between the two girls.)*
9 **FIROZA:** *(To ANN)* **Ready?**
10 **ANN: Yeah.**
11 **FIROZA:** *(Grabs her.)* **Remember you've got seven places to**
12 **choose from.** *(ANN begins.)* **Good.** *(ANN pauses.)* **Solar plexus?**
13 **ANN: Where's that again?** *(She points.)*
14 **FIROZA: Yes.**
15 **ANN:** *(Carries on.)* **And the top of the foot.**
16 **FIROZA: Good. Now push the attacker away.** *(ANN does.)* **That's**
17 **really coming, Ann.** *(Turns to see SHARON doing a very*
18 *strong but aggressive sequence ending with a break away.)*
19 **That's really ... coming. Let's finish now.** *(She goes into a*
20 *formal bow. SHARON barely bobs her head and is out of*
21 *there, INDIRA following.)*
22 **FIROZA: See you next week?** *(No reply. ANN begins to gather up*
23 *her things.)* **You're doing really well, Ann.**
24 **ANN: Yeah. I didn't know I had it in me.**
25 **FIROZA: I ... wanted to say thanks. For helping me out earlier.**
26 **You know ... with Sharon.**
27 **ANN: Oh. That's okay.**
28 **FIROZA: She's so ... difficult.**
29 **ANN: Oh, I don't know. I wouldn't wanna be her mum, but I**
30 **kinda like her spunk.**
31 **FIROZA: You think I was too heavy.**
32 **ANN: You're the teacher.**
33 **FIROZA: That doesn't mean I'm always right.**
34 **ANN: So you were too heavy.**
35 **FIROZA:** *(Pause)* **D'you think they won't come back?**

1 ANN: Hard to say.

2 FIROZA: I'm just not getting through to them.

3 ANN: I think what you mean is, you're not getting them to

4   agree with you.

5 FIROZA: No! *(Pause)* I just want them to understand ...

6 ANN: Yeah, well ... maybe it's you that don't understand.

7 FIROZA: What?

8 ANN: Ah, forget it.

9 FIROZA: No. You want the class to continue, so help me out

10   here. Please.

11 ANN: You're just different from us. Even from Indira. You got

12   answers to questions we ain't even asked yet. But I don't

13   think you got a clue about how things are. Look, you come

14   down here once a week with all these "facts" and "ideas."

15   Most women have to work. Be strong. Well, you might be

16   right. But you can't ignore love ... and sex. You know the

17   kind of stuff kids read. "How can Amanda get Kevin to

18   notice her?"

19 FIROZA: But they can't take that kind of thing seriously.

20 ANN: Why not? D'you expect something like "How can Amanda

21   get top marks in her OAC's?" to turn them on?

22 FIROZA: Come on, Ann. You told Sharon the story about Harry

23   coming back to your house. You know all this romantic

24   stuff's a myth.

25 ANN: Some people think God's a myth. But plenty of them still

26   believe in him anyway – especially when the chips are

27   down. Haven't you ever been in love?

28 FIROZA: Well, yes, I suppose so, but –

29 ANN: No. I don't think you have. Well, it's wonderful! I may be

30   getting fat and pushing forty and divorced, but I haven't

31   forgotten how fantastic it felt. Somebody loves you in spite

32   of the fact that you don't look like Raquel Welch. You're

33   the centre of his life. You count. And you relax because

34   someone else is in charge now. *(Pause)* But then you wake

35   up one morning and you realize that he might be the

1   centre of your life, but he's not there when you need him,
2   and feeding your kids is more or less up to you, and ...
3 FIROZA: So the old myth's a fake.
4 ANN: It sucks you in.
5 FIROZA: You got out.
6 ANN: Yeah. But I'm not proud of it, Firoza. I'm not looking
7   forward to spending the rest of my life on my own. But I
8   haven't figured out what having a good relationship with
9   a man really means. I don't think they know either.
10 FIROZA: How could they? They're too young.
11 ANN: Men I mean. The old myth whammies them too, don't it?
12   They're supposed to be always in control. Never show
13   they're weak. Well, that's impossible. Maybe that's why
14   Harry drinks. I don't know. Gawd! I gotta go. I left the two
15   youngest on their own. They're probably tearing the place
16   apart. *(She leaves. FIROZA is left on her own.)*
17
18
19   **SCENE 3**
20
21 *(INDIRA enters obviously upset. She puts down her school*
22 *bag. The skirt and blouse she's just changed out of are stuffed*
23 *any old how in the top. She begins to practice the kata with*
24 *aggression, but she can't get it right and keeps breaking off in*
25 *frustration. SHARON enters. Watches INDIRA.)*
26 SHARON: No, Indie. Look. *(She demonstrates. She can do it*
27   *really well.)*
28 INDIRA: I did that.
29 SHARON: And forward.
30 INDIRA: Oh.
31 SHARON: And then ... *(She finishes.)* **Do it again.** *(INDIRA starts.*
32   *SHARON begins to warm up.)* **I saw your dad today.**
33 INDIRA: Where?
34 SHARON: In the store, stupid. Where d'you think? My Mum
35   made me go down for some vacuum cleaner bags. Right

1 before video hits ... Usually your old man doesn't say
2 more'n two words to me. But today, when I'm trying to get
3 back for the number two song, he starts giving me the
4 third degree. *(INDIRA stops the kata.)* Wants to know how
5 we're getting on with the big project.

6 INDIRA: He suspects something. I'm dead. What'd you say?

7 SHARON: What could I say? I couldn't even remember what
8 you said we were supposed to be doing!

9 INDIRA: "The benefits of physical exercise on the learning
10 process."

11 SHARON: Oh.

12 INDIRA: What'd you tell him, Shar ... ?

13 SHARON: Nothing too ... specific. It was a lot of hard work. You
14 know. Stuff like that. Don't worry. I think he bought it.

15 INDIRA: *(Relief)* You do that real well.

16 SHARON: What?

17 INDIRA: Talking a lot to cover up the fact you don't know
18 nothing.

19 SHARON: *(Goes after INDIRA, semi-playfully hitting/tickling
20 her)* Very funny, Miss Know-It-All, Do-Nothing.

21 INDIRA: I was just teasing.

22 SHARON: I waited for you for two buses after school. Where
23 were you? *(No reply)* Indie?

24 INDIRA: I was ... in the washroom.

25 SHARON: *(Pause)* Jakey Barnes.

26 INDIRA: Why is he picking on me?

27 SHARON: Don't be so dumb, Indie. You're smart, and you
28 wouldn't go out with him and you're brown. You should
29 just tell him to screw off.

30 INDIRA: I can't, Sharon. Every time I see him I get so scared.

31 SHARON: All these weeks you been dragging me out here ...
32 Haven't you learned anything?

33 INDIRA: Yeah. But ...

34 SHARON: Did you think if you came out to this class for a
35 couple of months, all your problems would just – go

1   away? Poof!!

2   INDIRA: I guess I wish they would. Yeah.

3   SHARON: Daydreams! Bullies are real, Indie.

4   INDIRA: I know that.

5   SHARON: You're gonna have to tell somebody.

6   INDIRA No! Look – I told you already, Shar, it'd get back to my

7   dad. I know it would. And he'd take me right out of school.

8   He'd send me back to India.

9   SHARON: Come on.

10   INDIRA: He's already talking about it.

11   SHARON: Why?

12   INDIRA: Because ... *(Mimicking her father:)* ... "there are no

13   moral standards in this country." There's no sex or drugs

14   in India.

15   SHARON: Yeah?

16   INDIRA: That's what he thinks. I've lived here since I was five

17   years old, Sharon. This is where I want to be.

18   SHARON: Well he can't make you go.

19   INDIRA: Oh no? And even if he didn't, he wouldn't let me stay

20   at school. I'd be working in the store. I've got to sort it out

21   on my own.

22   SHARON: So what'd you tell him about the rip in your jacket

23   the other day?

24   INDIRA: I said I caught it on my locker.

25   SHARON: Yeah, well just remember, I won't be around to get

26   you out of trouble next year.

27   INDIRA: You got the job!

28   SHARON: No.

29   INDIRA: Maybe you will end up back at school.

30   SHARON: I'm not that desperate. But my parents're getting

31   really mean. If I'm not at school they're gonna make me

32   pay a fortune in rent.

33   INDIRA: So why don't you stay in school?

34   SHARON: Thank you, Firoza.

35   INDIRA: This doesn't have anything to do with her. For four

1   years all you've talked about is going to college and being

2   a fashion designer. And now it's like you're giving it all up

3   cause some stupid counsellor gets up your nose.

4   **SHARON:** Just bug off, alright? *(Pause)* God, I'm glad this

5   stupid course is nearly finished.

6   **INDIRA:** I thought you were enjoying it.

7   **SHARON:** Huh!

8   **INDIRA:** You're the best one of all of us.

9   **SHARON:** Yeah. I know. But it makes me feel funny.

10   **INDIRA:** What d'you mean?

11   **SHARON:** I don't know. Just funny. I don't like it.

12   **INDIRA:** You mean Calvin doesn't like it? *(SHARON looks at*

13   *her.)* Are you gonna wait while I change tonight?

14   **SHARON:** You were taking too long.

15   **INDIRA:** Firoza was loaning me the calendar for her

16   university. And I wasn't that long!

17   **SHARON:** Calvin was getting restless. You know what he's like.

18   It's weird, eh? All this time we've been going out he was

19   always busy on Tuesdays. All of a sudden he's free – every

20   damn Tuesday he's waiting for me, and I'm all hot and

21   smelling like the school changing room. Chuh! *(She looks*

22   *in her bag.)* I knew it! I forgot my deodorant. Have you got

23   any, Indie?

24   **INDIRA:** I'm not meeting anybody after, am I? Anyways I use

25   the smell to keep people away when I have to walk home

26   on my own. *(She goes after SHARON, arm up. They play out*

27   *a smell/repel routine.)* I scare off attackers.

28   **SHARON:** Nooo. Help! It's an offensive weapon.

29   **INDIRA:** But legal. Ha, ha. *(She surprises SHARON with a hold*

30   *and flip.)*

31   **SHARON:** *(Leaps up, on the attack. Then she softens)* That was

32   pretty good, Indie. *(They laugh.)* You'll do.

33   **INDIRA:** No I won't ...

34   **SHARON:** Indira!

35   **INDIRA:** I'm not scared of you. I just can't imagine getting

1   close enough to somebody I'm scared of to do that.

2 SHARON: Hey – those goons at school weren't six feet away
3   when your jacket got "caught on your locker," were they?

4 INDIRA: No. But ...

5 FIROZA: *(Entering)* Hi, girls.

6 SHARON/INDIRA: Hi.

7 FIROZA: How's things?

8 INDIRA: Great! *(SHARON looks at her. Sucks her teeth. Turns*
9   *away. INDIRA helps FIROZA get rid of the mats.)*

10 ANN: *(Entering. She's very down)* Sorry I'm late.

11 FIROZA: Is something the matter?

12 ANN: No. I just come from a meeting with my social worker.
13   That's always depressing.

14 FIROZA: Well then ... If we're all ready, we'll do some warm
15   ups. *(They're going to begin with a stretching exercise in*
16   *pairs. INDIRA moves to SHARON, but SHARON turns to*
17   *FIROZA. A first. ANN moves to work with INDIRA, and they*
18   *begin the exercise.)*

19 SHARON: *(Doesn't take FIROZA's outstretched hands)* Does this
20   stuff really work? I mean it's one thing playing around in
21   here. But out there – is it gonna work? *(INDIRA is worried:*
22   *what is SHARON up to?)*

23 FIROZA: If we want it to. *(Offers her hands again. SHARON*
24   *snorts.)* Let's be honest, Sharon. Learning the right moves
25   isn't some magic formula that's going to somehow make
26   everything all right out there. *(SHARON looks knowingly at*
27   *INDIRA.)* I know someone who has a black belt in judo, but
28   wilts in any kind of aggressive situation. And there are
29   people who've stood up to intimidation without having a
30   self-defense class in their lives.

31 ANN: Are you telling us – after all this pain – that we don't
32   need this?!

33 FIROZA: No. But what we need as well as the ability, is
34   confidence. We have to believe that what we want matters.
35   *(She's not getting through.)* I remember trying to tell my

1   mother I wanted to quit my job and be a writer. Well, my
2   mother is barely five feet tall and she's never raised a hand
3   to anyone in her life. I'd been taking self-defence for a year
4   and for six months I was too scared to open my mouth.
5 SHARON: Yeah, but being scared of telling somebody
6   something ... That's a lot different than somebody trying
7   to – well – beat up on you or something.
8 FIROZA: Yes. But in both cases you have to deal with your fear.
9   And fear isn't a bad thing.
10 INDIRA: It isn't?
11 FIROZA: Hey – if we were never scared, we'd probably all be
12   dead before we were five. Fear warns us of danger. It
13   releases adrenalin which gives us extra energy. Now, we
14   can use that energy to do something about the situation,
15   or we can let it all seep away by shaking in our boots. It's
16   our choice.
17 ANN: Choice!
18 FIROZA: Yes.
19 ANN: That's rich, that is. How many of us ever get a choice?
20 FIROZA: We all have choices.
21 ANN: Yeah, but you can stand your ground and still get hurt.
22 FIROZA: Yes. But you've got a chance ...
23 ANN: Only in your dreams. In the real world most choices are
24   between bad and bad.
25 FIROZA: So give me an example.
26 ANN: Okay. I've just been talking to my social worker, okay?
27   About quitting work and going on Mother's Allowance. I'd
28   actually be better off.
29 SHARON: Sounds good to me.
30 ANN: I don't wanna quit. I don't want those bastards prying
31   into my life.
32 FIROZA: Well, if you've managed so far, Ann ...
33 ANN: And as for work ... I can be touched up or quit.
34 INDIRA: But that's a choice, isn't it?
35 ANN: Oh, for –

1   FIROZA: Are you saying you're being sexually harassed, Ann?

2   ANN: I don't know about that. All I know is that ever since we

3   got this new supervisor – well, you never know where the

4   slimy bastard's hands are gonna end up. *(To SHARON:)*

5   And if you laugh, so help me, I'll belt you.

6   SHARON: I ain't laughin'.

7   FIROZA: But you don't have to take that, Ann.

8   ANN: Yeah. I know. I can quit. Go on Mother's Allowance. Or

9   get a job cleaning offices at night and leave the kids on

10   their own to run wild.

11   FIROZA: You can report him.

12   ANN: Hah! If that's all you've got to offer –

13   FIROZA: There are laws –

14   SHARON: Chuh!

15   ANN: I don't know what world you live in. His word against

16   mine? You gotta be joking.

17   FIROZA: But –

18   ANN: They got all kinds of ways to make your life miserable if

19   you rock the boat. You got no idea how long it took me to

20   get my hours increased. They could cut me back just like

21   that. *(Silence. They wait for FIROZA.)*

22   FIROZA: All right. I accept it's hard. *(INDIRA is crushed. The*

23   *miracle hasn't happened.)* But there must be something we

24   can do.

25   ANN: So tell me something. *(Pause)* Can't. Can you?

26   FIROZA: I can tell you about a woman who found herself in a

27   very difficult position, and found a way out of it. It's a very

28   old story ...

29   ANN: Oh great. A story!

30   FIROZA: ... about a woman called Fetneh, and the King of

31   Persia, whose name was Bahram-Gur.

32   SHARON: Weird names!

33   INDIRA: Shh.

34   FIROZA: Bahram-Gur means wild ass. He was a crack shot

35   with a bow and arrow and killed a lot of wild asses. Fetneh

1   would play beautiful music on her harp while he hunted.
2 SHARON: Typical.
3 FIROZA: I suppose so. But she was a very good musician. One
4   day, after a large kill, Fetneh didn't praise the king for his
5   skill. Bahram-Gur got very angry. "Tell me then, Fetneh,
6   how should I have killed the ass?" he said. Now Fetneh was
7   fed up with praising him all the time for what he could do
8   so easily. So she said, "You should have pinned its hoof to
9   its ear." Bahram-Gur sighted a wild ass, and taking careful
10   aim, just grazed its ear. And as the ass raised its hoof to
11   rub the scratch, Bahram-Gur let fly with a second arrow
12   and pinned its hoof to its ear!
13 ANN: I bet she felt pretty stupid.
14 FIROZA: Well, she still wouldn't praise him. "You do this
15   through practice," she teased him. "In everything, my
16   King, practice makes possible." Bahram-Gur was furious,
17   and he ordered her to be put to death.
18 INDIRA: So she shouldn't have talked back.
19 FIROZA: Well, I don't know about that. What I do know is that
20   she refused to accept that there was no way to save
21   herself. First of all, she persuaded her guard to spare her
22   life for one week.
23 ANN: That's just putting off the agony.
24 FIROZA: Not quite. She had a plan. You see, she knew that
25   Bahram-Gur was angry because his pride had been hurt,
26   but that he probably wouldn't stay angry for long. At the
27   end of the week, the guard would go to Bahram-Gur and
28   tell him that Fetneh was dead. If the King was pleased
29   then the guard would return and kill her. But if he cried,
30   the guard would let her live.
31 ANN: Risky.
32 FIROZA: The alternative was certain death. When the guard
33   went to the King a week later and said that Fetneh was
34   dead, the King —
35 INDIRA: The King cried!

1 FIROZA: Yes. He did.

2 INDIRA: So her life was saved. So if Fetneh could outwit a king,

3   you gotta be able to get round your supervisor, Ann.

4 ANN: It's just a story.

5 SHARON: Strike to maim! *(She goes through an imaginary*

6   *attack. A few hard jabs, a trip, ending up stomping on his*

7   *fingers.)* Break the bastard's fingers!

8 ANN: And get charged with assault!

9 SHARON: Disguise yourself. And jump out at him when he's

10   not expecting it.

11 FIROZA: That's definitely assault.

12 INDIRA: And anyway, he wouldn't know who'd done it. He'd

13   probably just carry on ... you know – at work.

14 SHARON: But only when he got out of hospital.

15 ANN: Hasn't solved my problem, though.

16 INDIRA: We gotta think of something more – ingenious.

17 SHARON: Ohhhh. Aren't we using the words now.

18 INDIRA: Shut up, Shar. Look. He's gotta get the message, right?

19   But in a way that he can't pin anything on you.

20 ANN: Yeah. *(She doesn't believe it.)*

21 SHARON: So what's he like?

22 ANN: Huh?

23 SHARON: We're supposed to know the enemy. Right?

24 ANN: Right. Well ... *(She thinks. Gives up.)* He's a real slime ball.

25 SHARON: Yeah, we know that, Ann. C'mon. C'mon. The details.

26 ANN: Five foot ten. Fortyish.

27 SHARON: This isn't helping.

28 INDIRA: What's he like?

29 SHARON: What's he do?

30 ANN: All right. Picture it. Him. Monday. Back from his package

31   holiday to Florida. He comes swaggering in like he's God's

32   gift – know what I mean? And you should've seen him.

33   Suntanned – and dressed – whoooo! Off-white pants, one

34   of those wild Hawaiian shirts, open down to here.

35 INDIRA/SHARON: Yuk!

1   ANN: And snakeskin shoes!

2   SHARON: Ohhhh. This man is too much.

3   ANN: He's supposed to wear his uniform to work.

4   SHARON: And what're you doing?

5   ANN: I'm down on my hands 'n knees with a bucket, trying to
6   clean the legs of a desk. You wouldn't believe what those
7   kids get on the table legs.

8   INDIRA: Yuk!!

9   SHARON: So – Slime Ball sleazes his way over for a feel and
10   you – *(Sudden inspiration:)* – throw the pail of water all
11   over him. Haaaa!!

12 INDIRA: No. That's not good enough, Shar.

13 SHARON: Why not?

14 INDIRA: He's still gonna know you did it on purpose. Do it
15   again. I'll be Ann. *(She gets down.)*

16 SHARON: And I'm the Slime Ball. Stickin' out my hollow chest,
17   trying to make like I'm a "real" man. I reach out to grab a
18   feel of this great behind.

19 ANN: Get away!

20 INDIRA: I know he's coming. I can sort of sense it. Usually I'd
21   move, stand up or something. But this time I stay where
22   I am.

23 SHARON: She hasn't heard me. I reach out.

24 INDIRA: My hand's on the pail. Just as he touches me ... *(In*
25   *surprise:)* Ohhhh! I dump the pail of filthy water all over
26   him – accidental, like. *(They all yelp with delight.)*

27 ANN: But I don't crack a smile. "Mr. Saunders," I say, "I'm so
28   sorry. But you gave me a real scare, sneaking up on me
29   like that." *(THEY laugh and do a victory hand clap. SHARON*
30   *begins to do the kata exuberantly. The OTHER TWO follow.*
31   *FIROZA watches. They finish with a strong vocalization,*
32   *then break out of it, laughing.)*

33

34

35

1   **SCENE 4**

2

3   *(INDIRA and SHARON. INDIRA is glum. SHARON has a bag*

4   *of chips.)*

5 **SHARON:** He never turned up last week, you know. I nearly

6   froze my toes off standing out there in those stupid shoes

7   he gave me, and he never showed. "Something came up,"

8   he said. Something's always turning up for him. For me,

9   it's a big zero. And my parents are really starting to bug

10   me. *(She opens the bag.)* D'you think I should get him to

11   marry me?

12 **INDIRA:** What?

13 **SHARON:** You think I couldn't?

14 **INDIRA:** Sharon, I don't think Calvin's ready to settle down.

15 **SHARON:** Chuh! When did you get these?

16 **INDIRA:** I went downstairs at the beginning of the break.

17 **SHARON:** You don't know nothing, do you? They always put

18   old ones in machines in places like this. *(She gives the bag*

19   *back to INDIRA.)* Great last class, eh?

20 **INDIRA:** Thought you'd be thrilled. It's over.

21 **SHARON:** Thought you'd be Wonder Woman. Wha-Booom.

22   *(She does a Wonder Woman routine.)* Specially after last

23   week. *(She carries on, deflecting bullets.)*

24 **INDIRA:** That was dumb.

25 **SHARON:** Excuse me. I been watching reruns with my little

26   sister, okay?

27 **INDIRA:** I mean us, Sharon.

28 **SHARON:** Huh?

29 **INDIRA:** Getting all worked up over that stupid story.

30 **SHARON:** It wasn't that stupid.

31 **INDIRA:** Think about it, Shar. So this Fetneh saved her life. So

32   what? She couldn't go back home, could she? That

33   Bahram-Gur guy — he'd be so angry at being tricked he'd

34   probably kill her himself, and the guard. And Ann didn't

35   show up.

1   **SHARON:** What?

2   **INDIRA:** She's probably too embarrassed.

3   **SHARON:** She's probably sick. Had to work late or something.

4   You and Firoza're making too big a deal about this, Indie.

5   **INDIRA:** It'd be a lot easier to just do what people expect

6   you to.

7   **SHARON:** Alright. So tell your dad what's going on at school.

8   Get sent off to live in India till they marry you off.

9   **INDIRA:** I don't want to.

10 **SHARON:** Then why're you talking about it?

11 **INDIRA:** Forget it.

12 **SHARON:** Oh no. For eight weeks now you've been dragging

13   me out to this class. You got my brain all screwed around

14   so I don't know what I think half the time. I'm not

15   forgetting it. You tell me.

16 **INDIRA:** *(Long pause)* I'm scared.

17 **SHARON:** Not good enough. Firoza talked about that,

18   remember. I made myself look like a real jerk so she'd talk

19   about it. Remember?

20 **INDIRA:** What I'm talking about is different. *(Pause)* Like, what

21   if I'm not good enough?

22 **SHARON:** Come on!

23 **INDIRA:** Let's say I do – somehow – sort it out at school. And I

24   do well in my OAC's ...

25 **SHARON:** Yeah.

26 **INDIRA:** Well, then there's university.

27 **SHARON:** So?

28 **INDIRA:** The science programme at Firoza's university is

29   exactly what I'm looking for.

30 **SHARON:** This is a problem?

31 **INDIRA:** I couldn't commute, Sharon. I'd have to live away

32   from home.

33 **SHARON:** Sounds good to me.

34 **INDIRA:** They'd have a fit. You can't imagine how upset my

35   father would be. And what if – after all that – what if I

1   don't make it?

2   SHARON: Indie, you'll make it. If you want to.

3   INDIRA: Yeah, but even if I do — I could end up all on my own.

4   My family won't understand. I know they won't.

5   SHARON: *(Pause)* What's Firoza say about all this?

6   INDIRA: She doesn't know about it.

7   SHARON: Well, don't you think you better talk to her?

8   INDIRA: No.

9   SHARON: Why not? *(Silence:)* What's happened to the big

10   friendship of the decade then?

11 INDIRA: Nothing's happened to it. And nothing's going to,

12   okay? Things are fine just the way they are.

13 SHARON: Oh sure! All this moaning means everything's just

14   great.

15 INDIRA: With Firoza and me, dummy. *(Pause)* She thinks I'm

16   all set to finish my OAC's. Maybe even go to her university.

17 SHARON: Where'd she get that idea then? What's she gonna

18   think when she finds out you're a wimp?

19 INDIRA: She's not going to. This is the last class. I'll never see

20   her again.

21 SHARON: I don't get this. You're talking about giving up on

22   your future, and you won't ask for help.

23 INDIRA: She can't help me.

24 SHARON: Maybe she could talk to your dad.

25 INDIRA: You crazy?

26 SHARON: What?

27 INDIRA: She's Ugandan. She's not married. And she's a Muslim!

28 SHARON: So!

29 INDIRA: Look ... I can't explain it. It's like — I don't know. It

30   wouldn't work. All right?

31 SHARON: No!

32 FIROZA: *(Enters with ANN.)* Look who I found downstairs.

33 ANN: Sorry I'm late. I know — I say that every week.

34 SHARON: See?

35 ANN: I was telling Firoza — I was having a drink with a few of

1   the women from work, and I sort of lost track of the time.

2   **INDIRA:** You forgot about our last class!

3   **FIROZA:** Not exactly. Tell them, Ann.

4   **ANN:** Well, after last week — you remember — well, I finally got
5   up the nerve ...

6   **SHARON:** You did it! You dumped a bucket on the sleaze!

7   **ANN:** No. Nothing as dramatic as that! But I talked to a couple
8   of the women I work with and they've been getting it too.
9   We've worked out some signals, ways of letting each other
10   know he's coming and then they can like — come in and
11   ask me for something — you know.

12 **INDIRA:** Is that all?

13 **FIROZA:** Indira!

14 **SHARON:** It's a start, Indie. At least some people try.

15 **INDIRA:** You're a great one to talk! *(INDIRA turns away.)*

16 **FIROZA:** *(Silence)* Well, I think what Ann did is important. It's
17   not going to solve the problem tomorrow, but it's one step.
18   It's better than running away.

19 **INDIRA:** Fetneh ran away.

20 **ANN:** No she didn't.

21 **FIROZA:** Well, I think what Indira means is that she couldn't
22   go back home. You can imagine why. *(ANN makes a throat-
23   cutting gesture.)* But that wasn't the end of the story. She
24   went to live at the country home of the guard who'd
25   helped her. And on this estate there was a beautiful high
26   pavilion that you could only reach by climbing sixty steps.
27   Soon after Fetneh arrived, a calf was born, and she picked
28   it up and walked up the sixty steps to the pavilion.

29 **SHARON:** Why'd she want to do that?

30 **FIROZA:** Every day for six years, she climbed the stairs to the
31   pavilion, carrying the calf, which, of course, grew and grew
32   until it was a great ox. But she could still carry it easily.
33   Then she asked the guard to invite Bahram-Gur to the
34   country estate and give a feast for him in the pavilion.
35   When the King had climbed the stairs he said to the guard,

1   "Tell me, my friend, how will you climb these sixty stairs

2   when you are sixty years old?" "Easily," said the guard.

3   "Why, there is a woman in the house who carries an ox up

4   these stairs as if it was a feather." Bahram-Gur, of course,

5   demanded to see this. So Fetneh covered her face with a

6   veil, picked up the ox, carried it up the sixty steps and

7   placed it at the feet of Bahram-Gur. "How do you suppose I

8   performed this feat?' she asked him. "The secret must be

9   practice," he said. "You see, my King," said Fetneh, lowering

10   her veil, "in everything, practice makes possible."

11 INDIRA: But that's what she said when he shot the ass.

12 SHARON: What happened?

13 FIROZA: Bahram-Gur cried with joy when he recognized her

14   and understood what she had done. He accepted her as

15   she was and they laughed together, and returned to the

16   palace. Friends.

17 ANN: Is that one of the stories in your book?

18 FIROZA: Yeah. *(She shrugs.)*

19 ANN: Well, don't you think you better practice what you

20   preach?

21 FIROZA: Pardon?

22 ANN: Send the book to another publisher. It's a great story.

23 INDIRA: Yeah. But that's all it is. It's just a story.

24 FIROZA: But ... stories can be examples of how people deal

25   with problems, Indira.

26 INDIRA: Oh, sure. Carrying a great big ox is really gonna help

27   me.

28 FIROZA: She started with a calf.

29 INDIRA: Oh, great.

30 FIROZA: Indira, what's wrong?

31 INDIRA: Nothing!

32 FIROZA: Maybe we can talk on the way up to the university

33   next week? And my friend has found someone who'll show

34   you around the science building.

35 INDIRA: *(Caught)* I ... don't know if I can go. I ... think I'll be too

1   busy. Studying. You know. *(Pause)*

2 SHARON: Hey! I've got an idea! Let's celebrate making it

3   through the course together. We could order a pizza. Yeah?

4 ANN: I'd love to, Sharon. But I haven't been home since work.

5   The kids'll probably be fighting World War III. *(SHARON is*

6   *trying to signal to ANN that INDIRA needs to talk to*

7   *FIROZA.)* You could all come to my place, though. It's just

8   a couple of blocks away.

9 SHARON: Great!

10 INDIRA: Sharon ...

11 SHARON: *(To FIROZA)* How about it?

12 FIROZA: All right.

13 INDIRA: You can't, Sharon.

14 SHARON: Why not?

15 INDIRA: What about Calvin?

16 SHARON: What about him?

17 INDIRA: He's meeting you here, isn't he?

18 SHARON: Oh, yeah. *(Pause. A challenge between them)* I ...

19   well ... I'll phone him. Tell him something came up.

20 ANN: Don't tell him it was a calf. He'll never believe you.

21 SHARON: I ... don't think I've got a quarter.

22 ANN: I've got one. Here. *(She hands it over.)*

23 SHARON: Oh. Well ... here goes.

24 ANN: I'll phone for pizza.

25 SHARON: What're you gonna do, Indie?

26 INDIRA: *(Silence)* Firoza ?

27 FIROZA: Yes?

28 INDIRA: I need your help. *(The FOUR WOMEN in unison do the*

29   *kata.)*

30

31   **THE END**

32

33

34

35

Back Where You Belong
by Susan Battye

The presence of political refugees in many societies today is no longer the exception but the rule. Social upheavals of the late twentieth and early twenty-first centuries have generated a worldwide migration of populations, both of groups and individuals that is unlikely to abate in the foreseeable future. Civil war, economic distress, state terrorism, pestilence, religious discrimination — the causes are manifold and seem to be universal. And we are still only beginning to come to grips with the disturbing and dislocating personal, psychological and cultural issues raised by this phenomenon.

Another play in this collection deals with this same problem, *Highest Mountain, Fastest River* by Donna Abela. The following drama by Susan Battye, however, differs from that work because it addresses more narrowly the problem of cultural assimilation, and it does so by focusing upon only one person's situation rather than that of an entire population. The teenager Zaria, sent by her Montenegran parents to live with relatives in New Zealand, struggles to perform well in her school where institutional and peer group misunderstandings challenge her ability to adapt to her new host culture.

What makes this play particularly suitable for young audiences is the way in which Susan Battye links Zaria's cultural difficulties with coming-of-age problems that teens experience in every society. Zaria seeks peer group acceptance in social, athletic and academically competitive situations; and her cultural "difference" as an immigrant only intensifies — rather than provokes — her difficulties as a teenager. This situation makes the play easy for young actors to relate to, whether as performers or spectators. Absent are the ideological and political conflicts, or military and police threats that are so much a part of the geopolitical immigration scene. Instead, the play foregrounds day-to-day activities in an all-girls school, and especially the athletic competition that forms the backdrop to the central conflict.

A second remarkable feature of this play that makes it accessible to young audiences is its "stageability" for young performers. Susan Battye has captured so well the distinctive features of young people: their everyday speech patterns, their humor, their trends and fads, their competitiveness and the different personality types that constitute that unique community we call "the school environment." Interestingly, most of the roles — and all the best ones — in this play are for young women, although several parts for males are also called for. And the pretentious, silly and at times downright incompetent school administrators provide a rollicking comic undercurrent that adds much to the play's upbeat mood and pace.

At the same time, however, the poignancy of the central character's situation is foregrounded, as well as the cultural differences that separate her from her more fortunate and affluent friends. The play's central conflict, in fact, centers on Zaria's misunderstanding of her fellow students' intentions in discarding their unwanted clothing: are they carelessly leaving pullovers and scarves behind when they walk off the ball courts and out of the locker rooms? Or do they expect the garments will somehow be returned to them? Unthinkingly, Zaria collects the items to send home to destitute children in her war-torn homeland, and in so doing, she is accused of theft. The way in which the author finally resolves this issue, both on a personal as well as a social level, makes this play an engaging study of peer group relationships in a school setting, as well as a fascinating commentary on the humanitarian responsibilities that are called for in modern times.

Characters

Jess, Eastern team netballer, 14
Erin Perkins, 15
Zaria, Recent immigrant from Montenegro, in the Balkans, (former Yugoslavia), 15
Megan Carter, Captain of the Eastern netball team, 15
Netballer 1, Eastern College netball player, 15
Sheena, Eastern College netball player, 14
Pearl, Eastern College netball player, 15
Phina, Girls' High Netballer, 14
Daz, Girls' High Netballer, 15

Mickey, Girls' High Netballer 14
Girls' High Supporter 1
Girls' High Supporter 2
Girls' High Supporter 3
Jan Carter, Mother of Megan, 40's
Robin, Jan's partner, 40's
Mrs. Towers, Deputy-Principal of Eastern College, 50's, ambitious.
Brian Towers, House husband, 50's.
Felicity, Mrs. Tower's loyal secretary, 30's.
Detective Sidebottom, 30's
Tuck Shop Operator
Mr./Mrs. Patel, the Indian Dairy Owner
Aunty, Zaria's Aunt
Uncle, Zaria's Uncle

Note on Casting

It is possible to double several parts as the original cast discovered when actors were absent. The following parts may be played as either male or female, depending on production decisions:
The Tuck Shop Operator
Robin
Mr./Mrs. Patel
Detective Sidebottom
Girls' High Supporter 1
Girls' High Supporter 2
Girls' High Supporter 3

Playwright's Note

I wrote this play for my Year 10 drama class after reading something on a website run by Education International, which talked about the plight of Albanian students in Montenegro. Since that time the conflict has worsened, and not only are young people being denied education, but also denied their native language by groups trying to ban Albanian from official recognition. I am grateful to Moana Taylor, a student of Albanian extraction at Epsom Girls Grammar School for her advice in writing this play.

Production Notes

Staging

The play can be staged very simply with one stand which can be reversed and can be either the Tuck shop or hold the Fruit shop billboards and fruit selection. A fancy desk and chair will create Mrs. Towers' office, while two chairs and a couple of large cushions will create the effect of Megan's living room. The corridor lockers can be unseen "downstage." The final knitting scene may be best staged with classroom chairs.

Sound

A soundscape can be created simply on an electric guitar played live and the BBC commentary may work best pre-recorded with a recognisable jingle from the TV or radio news. The guitar riffs can bridge scenes and serve to create atmosphere.

Costume

Mrs. Towers might wear white gloves and pearls throughout the play. The students all wear mufti.

Lighting

Various lighting states can suggest the locations of the netball courts, Megan's house, Zaria's bedroom, Mrs Tower's office, the school corridor, the tuck shop, Patel's dairy and outside Mrs Tower's office and the two detention classrooms.

Glossary

"Netball" — a little like basketball except that you can't run with the ball. It's a game that girls traditionally play. The positions are Goal Shoot (GS), Goal Attack (GA), Centre (C), Wing Defence (WD), Wing Attack (WA), Goal Defence (GD), Goal Keep (GK). The game is played widely in British Commonwealth countries; and New Zealand's Silver Ferns rival Australia and Jamaica periodically for the World Cup.

"Haka" a Maori dance that often expresses a challenge. Seen before Rugby games.

"Jersey" — a sweater made of wool.

"Dairy" — a New Zealand Drug store which sells milk shakes, cigarettes, fruit, magazines and other items.

"Mufti" — ordinary street clothes, not school uniform.

"Fawlty Towers" — a British television comedy programme starring John Cleese as Basil Fawlty. Everything goes wrong at his hotel, Fawlty Towers.

"Tuck Shop" — School shop or canteen that sells pre-packaged food to students.

"Colonel Bogey" — a marching tune whistled by soldiers who built the Bridge over the River Kwai in Thailand during the Second World War.

"Montenegro" — formerly part of Yugoslavia. A wild, mountainous state found between Albania and Herzegovina. The Albanian migrants who live there are mainly Muslim. The circumstances recorded in this play concerning their situation were true at the time the play was written in September, 2000, according to Education International, a teachers' umbrella union.

In New Zealand it is illegal to sell cigarettes to people under 18 years of age. The first performance of *Back Where You Belong* was in the Epsom Girls' Grammar School Drama Room in Auckland, New Zealand, on November 8, 2000 with the following cast:

Girls' High Supporter 1	Naomi Diack
Megan	Olivia Ewen
Erin Perkins	Charlotte Gordon
Pearl	Talia Harvey
Jess/Robin	Jessica Jouning
Phina	Parisa-Mohummed-Jafari
Uncle/Daz	Sherie Muys
Aunty	Micha O'Connor
Deborah Towers	Morgan O'Reilly
Mickey	Natalie Mosca
Felicity/Girls High Supporter 2	Melissa Parke
Sheena	Alex Parker
Tuck Shop Operator	Rachel Pattenden
Zaria	Iana Podrouaeva
Brian Towers	Sarah Rushton
Detective Sidebottom	Lizzie Stanyer
Mrs. Patel	Kohe Tocker
Jan	Pip Walter

Original music provided by Julia Vahry. Lighting by Naomi Diack and Crystal Carroll.

1 **SCENE ONE**

2

3 *(A winter's afternoon, the present, Auckland. New Zealand.*

4 *The netball courts at Girls' High School. A series of three*

5 *freeze frames accompanied by live electric guitar riffs.*

6 *In the blackout a whistle blows off. Lights up on JESS,*

7 *ERIN, ZARIA and MEGAN together with NETBALLER 1,*

8 *SHEENA, and PEARL playing a game of netball for the*

9 *Eastern College team. The opposing Girls' High team*

10 *consists of PHINA, DAZ, and MICKEY and other PLAYERS as*

11 *available. THEY wear netball bibs distinguishing the two*

12 *teams with the positions marked on them, e.g. GA for Goal*

13 *attack. Every player is "marked" by an opposing player.*

14 *Girls' High are winning. Between each "frame" PLAYERS*

15 *reposition. Lights up. Guitar music expresses excitement.*

16 *Frame 1. PHINA is about to throw the ball to DAZ but*

17 *ZARIA comes between them.*

18 *Blackout. Lights up. Guitar music expresses suspense.*

19 *Frame 2. ZARIA has the ball and is about to be ankle*

20 *tapped.*

21 *Blackout. Lights up. Guitar music expresses pain.*

22 *Frame 3. PHINA from the Girls' High team foot-trips*

23 *ZARIA as she goes to defend a goal. The scene comes to life as*

24 *ZARIA falls over in agony, hugging her ankle.)*

25 **GIRLS HIGH SUPPORTER 1:** *(From the sidelines)* **What a**

26 **Hollywood!**

27 **GIRLS HIGH SUPPORTER 2:** *(From the sidelines, to ZARIA)*

28 **Why dontcha go back where ya come from?**

29 **GIRLS HIGH SUPPORTER 3:** *(From the sidelines)* **Yeah, go back**

30 **where you belong!** *(The Eastern TEAM surround ZARIA.)*

31 **GIRLS HIGH SUPPORTER 2:** *(From the sidelines)* **She's not**

32 **hurt.** *(The Eastern TEAM help ZARIA to stand. She is*

33 *obviously in pain.)*

34 **GIRLS HIGH SUPPORTER 3:** *(From the sidelines)* **Wog face! Get**

35 **off the court!**

1   *(ERIN makes as if she is going to fight the Girls' High*
2   *SUPPORTERS. Her TEAM MATES pull her back. The Eastern*
3   *SUPPORTERS boo from the other side of the stage. JAN*
4   *moves to offer ZARIA help.)*
5 **JESS:** *(To PHINA)* **Talk about bad sports! You did that**
6   **deliberately. Apologise!**
7 **PHINA: Make me!**
8 **JAN:** *(Loudly)* **The ref's blind!**
9 **GIRLS' HIGH SUPPORTER 2: She's faking!** *(A freeze. Blackout.)*
10
11
12   **SCENE TWO**
13
14   *(The netball courts. The final whistle blows Off-stage in the*
15   *blackout. Lights up. JESS, ERIN and MEGAN are on stage,*
16   *puffing from the exertion of finishing the netball game.*
17   *NETBALLER 1, PEARL and SHEENA stand with them. PHINA,*
18   *DAZ and MICKEY stand Upstage eyeing them warily.)*
19 **JESS:** *(Grudgingly)* **Three cheers for Girls' High.**
20 **THE EASTERN TEAM: Hip-ray! Hip-ray! Hip-ray!**
21 **JESS: And one for the ref.**
22 **ALL:** *(Grudgingly)* **Hip-ray!**
23 **DAZ, PHINA AND MICKEY:** *(Grudgingly)* **Three cheers for**
24   **Eastern. Hip-ray, Hip-ray, Hip-ray.**
25 **NETBALLER 1: Tough game, Jess. Better luck for Eastern next**
26   **time eh?** *(She exits.)*
27 **JESS:** *(Calling after her)* **Yeah! Pity about the crowd and that**
28   **Phina chick!**
29 **PHINA: Whadidya say?**
30 **JESS: I said you lot make me sick.**
31 **DAZ: You Eastern chicks are so up yourselves!**
32 **ERIN: Yeah, well, at least we play the ball and not the girl!**
33 **DAZ: What's that supposed to mean?**
34 **ERIN: Deerr!**
35 **MICKEY: Ignore them, Daz. Hey, Megan, put someone in your**

1   team who doesn't have two left feet, will ya? That girlie
2   couldn't defend for crap. Thought this was supposed to be
3   first grade netball.
4   **JESS:** *(To ERIN, aside)* Do you think she's got permanent PMT?
5   **ERIN:** *(Laughing)* For sure!
6   **MICKEY:** What's so funny?
7   **ERIN:** Nothing.
8   **DAZ:** Aw, come on, Mickey. Let's split. *(They go to exit.)*
9   **PEARL:** *(To Girls' High team as they leave)* That was harsh.
10 **SHEENA:** It was so bad what they did to Zaria. *(Loud to the*
11   *Girls' High girls, off:)* The foot tripper deserves to go down!
12   *(ZARIA enters limping, one foot bandaged.)*
13 **PEARL:** *(Loud to the Girls High team)* That was a dirty trick!
14 **JESS:** Forget it. We'll get them in the semis.
15 **SHEENA:** *(To ZARIA)* You okay?
16 **ZARIA:** *(Standing on one leg)* It nothing, Sheena, really. We
17   won? No?
18 **ALL:** No!
19 **MEGAN:** *(Offering an arm)* Here, lean on me.
20 **ZARIA:** *(Grateful)* Sorry I let team down.
21 **JESS:** You did not.
22 **ERIN:** *(To ZARIA)* You okay, Zaria? They said some nasty things.
23 **ZARIA:** Happen all the time.
24 **MEGAN:** It'll be totally different when we make the Silver
25   Ferns and play for New Zealand, right?
26 **ALL:** Right! *(MEGAN puts out her hand and they all pile their*
27   *hands on top.)*
28 **MEGAN:** One for all and all for one!
29 **ALL:** One for all and all for one! E.A.S.T.E.R.N. Who are we?
30   *(Leaping in the air:)* We're Eastern!
31 **ZARIA:** Ow!
32 **MEGAN:** Careful!
33 **PEARL:** *(Leaving)* Bye! Look after yourself, Zaria.
34 **SHEENA:** *(Leaving)* See you tomorrow!
35 **PEARL:** See you at Studley Dudley's party!

1   SHEENA: Bring the vodka! *(SHEENA and PEARL exeunt.)*

2   MEGAN: They're off the planet, those two. Anyone need a ride?

3   My Mum's doing a haka boogie on the side line. *(Waving to*

4   *JAN, off:)* **Hang on a mo!**

5   ZARIA: Umm aunty, he does not drive. No car. Bus went away.

6   I walk home.

7   MEGAN: *(Correcting her English)* **She** doesn't drive. And you're

8   not walking. Be my guest. Hope you can stand the smell of

9   our dog and my little step-brother!

10 JESS: What is it with third form boys that they stink like

11   mouldy cheese?

12 MEGAN: Hey, Zaria, you can come for lunch. Mum'll put an ice

13   pack on that ankle.

14 ZARIA: You sure?

15 MEGAN: Course I'm sure. *(They all laugh. JESS exits.)*

16 JAN: *(Yelling, off)* **Megan, if you don't come now you'll be**

17   walking the dog home.

18 MEGAN: Coming, Mum!

19 ERIN: *(Picking a jersey up off the netball court)* **Whose is this?**

20 MEGAN: I'll scrape the dog fur off the back seat for you, Zaria.

21   *(MEGAN exits.)*

22 ZARIA: That girl Daz, she wear it. I take.

23 ERIN: You sure?

24 ZARIA: We see them at semis. No?

25 ERIN: Yeah. Unfortunately. What are you going to do? Stick

26   pins into it?

27 ZARIA: Excuse?

28 ERIN: You know. Black Magic! *(Pause)*

29 ZARIA: No! Erin, can I ask question?

30 ERIN: Yup.

31 ZARIA: Am I really useless?

32 ERIN: Look, for someone who saw her first netball four

33   months ago, I'd say you're playing like a professional.

34   *(A freeze. Crossfade.)*

35

1   **SCENE THREE**

2

3   *(Half an hour later. MEGAN's lounge in a middle class*

4   *suburb of Auckland. MEGAN enters, cushion in hand. She*

5   *helps ZARIA to sit on a chair that JAN provides. JAN hands*

6   *ZARIA an ice pack wrapped in a tea towel. ROBIN pushes a*

7   *desk and chair on stage. ROBIN enters and hands ZARIA an*

8   *ice pack wrapped in a tea towel.)*

9   ZARIA: Thank you. You have nice house. We had house like

10   this when I was little.

11   JAN: You're welcome. Make yourself at home. Zaria, this is my

12   partner, Robin.

13   ZARIA: Pleased to meet you, Robin. *(JAN and ROBIN exeunt.*

14   *The sound of the BBC-TV news theme plays from the TV*

15   *Downstage. MEGAN immediately switches channels. JAN*

16   *enters with a basket of washing that she places on the floor*

17   *close to MEGAN.)*

18   JAN: I was watching that! Switch it back.

19   MEGAN: Aw, Mum!

20   JAN: Don't aw Mum me! The BBC news is very educational.

21   You might learn something. How long till lunch, Robin?

22   ROBIN: *(Off)* Not long.

23   MEGAN: What's for lunch?

24   ROBIN: *(Off)* Pork Chow Mein.

25   ZARIA: Pork?

26   ROBIN: *(Entering)* Is there a problem?

27   ZARIA: I don't eat pork.

28   ROBIN: These girls and their diets.

29   JAN: *(To ROBIN)* Maybe it's not a diet! Zaria, how does

30   macaroni cheese sound?

31   ZARIA: Macaroni?

32   JAN: Pasta and cheese sauce?

33   ZARIA: Yes, thank you. I don't want trouble.

34   JAN: It's no trouble, is it, Robin?

35   ROBIN: What? Oh yes, no trouble at all. *(MEGAN changes the*

1   *channel with the remote back to the news programme.)*

2   **ROBIN:** *(Reading a letter)* **We got the loan, Jan.**

3   **MEGAN:** *(To ROBIN as she starts sorting some washing)* **How**

4   **come YOUR SON never gets to sort the washing?**

5   **ROBIN: Because he's cunning and lazy. And he makes like the**

6   **Invisible Man when it comes to chores.**

7   **MEGAN: That's not fair! What loan?**

8   **NEWS READER:** *(Over)* **And in Montenegro today, the leader of**

9   **the Yugoslav army said that recent road and shipping**

10   **blockades were provoked by Albanian separatists.**

11   **JAN: Robin, that's great! Does that mean we can afford to**

12   **extend the house?**

13   **ZARIA: What is this about?**

14   **NEWS READER:** *(Over)* **With fifty per cent unemployment in**

15   **the region and winter fast approaching, people are**

16   **joining ever increasing food queues.**

17   **ROBIN:** *(To JAN)* **It sure does. Except we'll be working for the**

18   **rest of our lives to pay it off.**

19   **MEGAN:** *(To ZARIA)* **It's just some dumb programme about a war.**

20   **ZARIA: They are calling Albanians troublemakers.**

21   **MEGAN: So?**

22   **ZARIA: I am Albanian. Always someone blames us for something.**

23   **JAN: Turn it down, Megan.** *(MEGAN turns the TV down low.)*

24   **Zaria, what happened on the courts today?**

25   **ROBIN: Ahh! Netball. Didya win?**

26   **MEGAN: No!**

27   **ROBIN: How come?**

28   **MEGAN: Those bitches from Girls' High took Zaria out.**

29   **ROBIN: What, like the Mafiosa?** *(Like a machine gun sound:)*

30   **Brrrrrr?**

31   **MEGAN: No, you know, ankle tapping.**

32   **ROBIN: Standard tactic. In my day —**

33   **MEGAN: Yeah, but this was different. It was like they were**

34   **targeting her or something.**

35   **ZARIA: Is not first time.** *(A pause. They all look at ZARIA.)*

1   **JAN: I bet it's not.**

2   **ROBIN: How come you're in New Zealand, Zaria? You're**

3   **Albanian, right?** *(ZARIA looks at MEGAN who nods at her,*

4   *encouraging her to talk. The lights change to focus in on the*

5   *group.)*

6   **ZARIA: You know Kosovo?**

7   **JAN: Used to be part of Yugoslavia, north of Albania?**

8   **ROBIN: There was a major conflict going on between the local**

9   **people and —**

10 **ZARIA: Albanian. When I was seven we crossed border. At first**

11   **was okay. Then ethnic cleansing. You know what is ethnic**

12   **cleansing? In our village all men go first. My father goes.**

13   **In middle of night. In pyjamas. To camp. With barb wire.**

14   **Is very cold winter.**

15 **MEGAN: Your father? Why? How come?**

16 **ZARIA: Maybe someone says he is Muslim? But neighbour is**

17   **good person. I play with children. Teach songs in**

18   **Albanian. They give cake on Christian festival. Everybody**

19   **friends. Before. Then bombing starts.** *(Sound of distant*

20   *bombing from the TV. They all look disturbed at the TV.)*

21 **JAN: Go on.**

22 **ZARIA: No one sleeps. Everyone is frightened. They say the**

23   **men in camp are tortured. I kiss photograph of my father**

24   **and I pray. No one can work. No work, no money, no**

25   **school. No money, no petrol, no food.** *(The sound of a*

26   *Brahms piano piece is faintly heard.)* **My grandmother has**

27   **a beautiful white grand piano. I play piano for one last**

28   **time. Her sixtieth birthday.**

29 **MEGAN: You should hear Zaria play the piano in the hall at**

30   **school, Mum.** *(JAN puts her arms around her daughter to*

31   *keep her quiet.)*

32 **ZARIA: Then chicken man comes to door with truck.**

33   **Grandmother cries. She puts white piano in dirty truck.**

34   **Gives grandmother eggs.** *(Music stops.)*

35 **MEGAN: Eggs?**

1   **ZARIA:** Four dozen.

2   **ROBIN:** For a grand piano?

3   **ZARIA:** My mother, he never smiles. One day beautiful clown

4   stands among broken buildings. Clown is from Peace Bus.

5   It miracle! She blows up red balloons. So big! Makes a

6   rude noise. I laugh. My mother, he laughs. Then everyone

7   laughs until they cry. Clown comes from "Down Under"

8   they say. Peace Bus goes. Square is empty. I pick up

9   something. Mother thinks I am bleeding. She screams.

10   *(ZARIA pulls a red balloon from her pocket and shows them.*

11   *She puts the balloon back in her pocket for safekeeping.)* I

12   keep it. To remind me of home, of hope.

13   **MEGAN:** Down Under? That's —

14   **ZARIA:** New Zealand. After, we go to Montenegro with

15   grandmother and Albanian cousins. At school Albanian

16   children are not welcome. People have nothing. Winter is

17   very cold in Montenegro. Children need woollen things.

18   Here is never cold. Not really.

19   **JAN:** And now you are here. But your mother and father?

20   **ZARIA:** Mother says, "Make us proud, Zaria. Go to New

21   Zealand with Aunty and Uncle. Here is passport for Zaria,

22   Uncle. Go. Now. Go while you can. Work hard. Don't look

23   back. Go where you belong. Here is no future."

24   **JAN:** So your mother waits for news. *(She moves closer to ROBIN.)*

25   **MEGAN:** Will your mother come too, Zaria?

26   **ZARIA:** Only when we find my father.

27   **ROBIN:** You must let us know if there is anything we can do to

28   help.

29   **ZARIA:** You are kind people. One day you will come to my

30   home for a feast. *(The lights change.)*

31   **ROBIN:** Food! Our apologies. You must be starving.

32   **MEGAN:** *(Jumping up)* I'll make the macaroni cheese pie!

33   **JAN:** Wonders will never cease! *(Crossfade)*

34

35

1   **SCENE FOUR**

2

3   *(Flashback. The week before. ZARIA stands in a school*

4   *corridor after school, she has two scarves around her neck.*

5   *She has a rubbish bin and is doing detention picking up*

6   *rubbish. She finds a woollen jersey, looks around then ties it*

7   *round her waist. She keeps moving, picking up the rubbish*

8   *and as she salvages another jersey she shakes her head in*

9   *disbelief. She surveys the corridor for one last time and*

10   *exits. The lights fade.)*

11

12

13   **SCENE FIVE**

14

15   *(The same day. ZARIA's bedroom. ZARIA sits in the centre as*

16   *she puts jerseys and scarves into a box. She reacts to UNCLE*

17   *and AUNTY's words as she works. The sound of an Albanian*

18   *folk song is heard through the following dialogue. AUNTY*

19   *appears in a spotlight on one side of the stage.)*

20 **AUNTY: Zaria, can you find a job? We need to send more**

21   **money back home. You have time to work after school and**

22   **you need to speak good English. For us is hard.** *(UNCLE*

23   *appears in a spotlight on the other side of the stage.)*

24 **UNCLE:** *(Reading from the newspaper)* **"Car wash-ing atten-**

25   **dant wanted." Think a man with an engineering degree**

26   **can do that job? Think Uncle could be a car washer?**

27 **AUNTY: This place is so stupid. I know computer programming.**

28   **Is easy! But no English, an accent on the phone, and they**

29   **leave us to rot. Suddenly the position is already filled.**

30   **Unbelievable!**

31 **UNCLE: No, Zaria, you cannot go on the school trip to the**

32   **ballet. How can you be enjoying yourself when our people**

33   **are dying and living on the bread of the tyrant? Your**

34   **mother has no support now. You are her support. You**

35   **have to learn to fight, fight for your life, Zaria, to save**

1   others. And —

2 **ZARIA and UNCLE:** *(Together)* **Be careful who you talk to at**

3   **school, Zaria.**

4 **UNCLE: Our enemies are everywhere!**

5 **AUNTY and ZARIA:** *(Together)* **Try to make friends, Zaria.**

6 **AUNTY: Your mother wants you to settle here so that she can**

7   **come as soon as your father returns.**

8 **UNCLE: These people have no culture, Zaria. We had**

9   **everything. Your grandmother was a concert pianist.**

10 **ZARIA: When she played the piano, the world smiled.**

11 **AUNTY: Here is your passport, Zaria. You must take it to the toilet**

12   **on the plane and rip it into a hundred pieces. Then watch it**

13   **flush down. That is how it will be when we arrive in New**

14   **Zealand. That is how they will know who we really are.**

15 **ZARIA: Children need books and pens, hats and gloves.**

16   **Children have nothing. They will die in snow when**

17   **soldiers come to the house looking. You can help, Zaria.**

18   **New Zealand is rich. Go to school and build a bridge for all**

19   **your family.** *(She finishes fixing the parcel and stands up.*

20   *The lights change so that the whole stage is lit.)*

21 **AUNTY: Zaria! We need you to come to the Benefit Office and**

22   **translate for us.**

23 **ZARIA: Coming, Aunty! Aunty, I have a parcel to send home.**

24   **I've got the money. I saved it from my newspaper round.**

25 *(Crossfade)*

26

27

28   **SCENE SIX**

29

30 *(Friday morning. Mrs. Towers' office at Eastern College.*

31   *MRS. TOWERS stands in front of her desk. Her husband,*

32   *BRIAN, waits for instructions, pad and pencil in hand. He*

33   *wears a raincoat, a backpack and old motorbike helmet.)*

34 **MRS. TOWERS: So that's the groceries, the dog licence, and**

35   **the Play Station for our dearest son's twenty-second**

1   birthday. Any sign of him leaving home?

2 BRIAN: His bed's been slept in three times this week.

3 MRS. TOWERS: Pity.

4 BRIAN: Yes, Deborah. May I –

5 MRS. TOWERS: I'll be home at five. Lay out my black crepe for

6   the Girls' High Ball.

7 BRIAN: *(Writing it down)* Black crepe – . Pardon me but didn't

8   we do the Eastern Ball last week, my dove?

9 MRS. TOWERS: We did. This ball is quite a different kettle of fish.

10   This is the Girls' High Ball and God willing, if we get the

11   netball cup in the bag, this little appearance could clinch the

12   deal. *(Pause)* Your dinner suit needs pressing. Clear?

13 BRIAN: Clear. What deal, my little daisy?

14 MRS. TOWERS: *The* deal, Brian. Principal of Girls' High! That

15   will put a shine on your scooter hooter! It's a great pity you

16   know ...

17 BRIAN: What?

18 MRS. TOWERS: That gap in the display cabinet. That's where

19   the netball cup sits. Or used to sit. Now. My holiday.

20 BRIAN: Do you want me to ... ?

21 MRS. TOWERS: Yes, cancel the papers, book Tibbles into the

22   Dogs' Hotel and Poopsie in the Sunset Lodge.

23 BRIAN: Are you sure?

24 MRS TOWERS: Yes. Now run along, Brian, there's a love. Don't

25   forget to feed Tibbles, will you?

26 BRIAN: *(Writing it down)* Feed Tibbles. I never forget to feed

27   your mother. Scrambled egg for lunch today.

28 MRS. TOWERS: You do a fine scrambled egg, if I say so myself.

29 BRIAN: I do.

30 MRS. TOWERS: You could get a learning credit for those

31   scrambled eggs.

32 BRIAN: *(Unsure)* I could? *(MRS. TOWERS gives him a little wave.)*

33 MRS. TOWERS: Au revoir, Brian.

34 BRIAN: *(Forlornly)* Bye-Bye Deborah! *(He exits. MRS. TOWERS sits.)*

35 MRS TOWERS: Take me to the tropics! *(She turns on a tape*

1   *recorder. A Tahitian hula dance plays on the tape. MRS.*
2   *TOWERS produces a plastic lei from behind her desk. She*
3   *stands and practices the hula. The music stops abruptly.)*
4   **TAPED VOICE:** *(Over)* **Voulez-vous couchez avec moi ce soir?**
5   **MRS. TOWERS: Voulez-vous couchez avec moi ce soir. Now, does**
6   **that mean, "Can I have a hot bath please?"** *(FELICITY knocks*
7   *on the door and MRS. TOWERS stops the tape and hurriedly*
8   *removes her lei, putting it back in the drawer. Loudly:)* **Enter!**
9   **FELICITY: Your mail, Mrs. Towers.** *(She deposits a huge stack of*
10   *packages.)* **There's these from the Ministry of Education**
11   **and there's this from your travel agent.**
12   **MRS. TOWERS:** *(Pushing the Ministry pile to one side, grabbing*
13   *the envelope)* **Gimme, gimme!** *(Ripping open the envelope:)*
14   **Due to unforeseen circumstances, the Sundowner resort**
15   **will not be able to offer you its usual luxury class**
16   **accommodation. All correspondence should be addressed**
17   **to coup leader Monsieur ... what is this?** *(Looks in the*
18   *envelope.)* **No tickets. What's happened to my tickets?**
19   **FELICITY: Up the spout?**
20   **MRS. TOWERS: This is ridiculous. Ring the Ministry.**
21   **FELICITY: Yes, Mrs. Towers.**
22   **MRS. TOWERS: No, ring Foreign Affairs.**
23   **FELICITY: Foreign Affairs. For?**
24   **MRS. TOWERS: To get them to send a battleship and stop the**
25   **coup so that I can go on holiday, of course. Better still, ring**
26   **the police.**
27   **FELICITY: The police are here.**
28   **MRS. TOWERS: That was quick.**
29   **FELICITY: I'll show them in, shall I?**
30   **MRS. TOWERS: Yes, do.** *(FELICITY exits.)*
31   **FELICITY:** *(Off)* **You can go in now, Detective Sidebottom!**
32   *(DETECTIVE SIDEBOTTOM enters and holds out a hand to*
33   *MRS. TOWERS who shakes it heartily.)*
34   **MRS. TOWERS:** *(Impressed)* **You people have certainly taken**
35   **the new broom philosophy to heart! Shall I show you my**

1   letter, Detective Sidebottom?

2   DETECTIVE: That's Sid-e-bo-tom.

3   MRS. TOWERS: Quite.

4   DETECTIVE: Look, Mrs. Towers —

5   MRS. TOWERS: Call me De-borah.

6   DETECTIVE: De-borah. We're both busy people so I won't beat

7   about the bush. I'm here to talk about crime.

8   MRS. TOWERS: I'm all ears, Detective-Sergeant.

9   DETECTIVE: Detective.

10   MRS. TOWERS: I should warn you, however, that the Privacy

11   Act is very powerful. The days of body searches are well

12   and truly over.

13   DETECTIVE: The police appreciate that. But, to make "in

14   roads" on this problem we need concrete information.

15   There are sweatshops operating in this area.

16   MRS. TOWERS: Sounds nasty.

17   DETECTIVE: Very. There's a flood of cheap jeans on the

18   market. They're coming from overseas.

19   MRS. TOWERS: I think you'll find there's no "cheap genes"

20   among my girls. Quite brilliant some of them, take —

21   DETECTIVE: Watch for signs of abuse, tired kids,

22   malnourishment, that sort of thing.

23   MRS. TOWERS: If I had a bob for every tired student I've found

24   lurking in the library, Detective-Inspector, I'd be a rich

25   woman. Are we talking about people making these

26   garments for next to nothing?

27   DETECTIVE: Precisely.

28   MRS. TOWERS: Can't they just go?

29   DETECTIVE: Go where? No passport, no status.

30   MRS. TOWERS: Surely there are fenced in places ... ?

31   DETECTIVE: They've been told this is the land of Milk and

32   Honey. Their families are depending on them to get a good

33   job. They speak little English and have no reason to trust

34   the police.

35   MRS. TOWERS: I'll keep an ear to the ground.

1   **DETECTIVE: We'd appreciate that.** *(MRS. TOWERS goes to the*
2   *"window" Downstage with a bullhorn.)*
3   **MRS. TOWERS:** *(Through the bullhorn)* **Erin Perkins report to**
4   **the office at three-thirty for detention. Bubble gum on my**
5   **BMW is a hanging offence!** *(To the DETECTIVE:)* **I speak**
6   **metaphorically, of course.**
7   **DETECTIVE: I was hoping so.**
8   **MRS. TOWERS: Now if you'll excuse me, I've some petty theft**
9   **to attend to.**
10 **DETECTIVE: Petty theft?**
11 **MRS. TOWERS: Yes, I know, shocking isn't it? But even in a**
12 **"good school" we have our little probs. Maybe my meeting**
13 **with the "Gifted and Talented" student committee will**
14 **shed some light on the matter. They're always good for a**
15 **theory or two.**
16 **DETECTIVE:** *(Shaking hands)* **Of course. Let me know if there's**
17 **anything you think we can do.**
18 **MRS. TOWERS: Mon plaisir, Superintendent! Oh, if you come**
19 **across a small man in the car park trying to start a scooter,**
20 **would you mind giving him a push? His spark gives out.**
21 **DETECTIVE: Not a problem.** *(Star Wars style:)* **May the Force be**
22 **with you.** *(The DETECTIVE goes to exit. There is a knock.*
23 *ZARIA enters limping in mufti wearing DAZ's jersey. They*
24 *almost bump into each other.)*
25 **DETECTIVE: Sorry.**
26 **ZARIA: My fault.** *(DETECTIVE takes a hard look at ZARIA before*
27 *he/she leaves.)*
28 **MRS. TOWERS: Come in, Zaria.**
29 **ZARIA: You wanted to see me, miss?**
30 **MRS. TOWERS:** *(Opens a file)* **I've got a letter here from ... what**
31 **happened to your leg?**
32 **ZARIA: Netball. We lost. Bad.**
33 **MRS. TOWERS: So I gather. Any chance of a fight back?**
34 **ZARIA: I fix.**
35 **MRS. TOWERS: You can fix a game? I'm impressed. You need**

1   to see a doctor, Zaria.

2 ZARIA: Is expensive.

3 MRS. TOWERS: You need money to fix the game?

4 ZARIA: No – doctor is expensive.

5 MRS. TOWERS: Go and find the Nurse when I've finished with

6   you. Incidentally, why are you here?

7 ZARIA: You want passport?

8 MRS. TOWERS: Ah, yes. Zaria, bring me a photocopy of your

9   documents. Ministry's gone mad!

10 ZARIA: Yes, miss. I am not sure that I can –

11 MRS TOWERS: Your passport, Zaria.

12 ZARIA: Yes Miss. *(Pause)* Who is Ministry?

13 MRS. TOWERS: Bureaucracy. How do you like it here? Getting

14   ready for final exams? Off to Uni next year, eh?

15 ZARIA: I am fifteen.

16 MRS. TOWERS: Ah, yes. Settling into year ten, then? Enjoying

17   the cut and thrust of the classroom? Bit different from

18   what you're used to I expect? Hmm?

19 ZARIA: Yes, miss.

20 MRS. TOWERS: It's good to see you joining in.

21 ZARIA: Yes, miss.

22 MRS. TOWERS: So, no problems?

23 Zaria: Yes, miss.

24 MRS. TOWERS: Good. What?

25 ZARIA: No, miss.

26 MRS. TOWERS: On Ethnic Day you'll be wearing your national

27   costume? The press is coming.

28 ZARIA: Miss?

29 MRS. TOWERS: Ethnic Day.

30 ZARIA: What is ethnic?

31 MRS. TOWERS: You are ethnic. For-eign. A-li-en.

32 ZARIA: Alien?

33 MRS. TOWERS: From abroad.

34 ZARIA: Yes, miss.

35 MRS. TOWERS: So glad to have had this little chat. Your

1   English is improving by leaps and bounds.

2   ZARIA: Miss?

3   MRS. TOWERS: YOUR ENGLISH ... Oh, never mind. Make sure

4   you beat those Girls' High girls in the semi-finals, won't you?

5   ZARIA: Yes, Miss.

6   MRS. TOWERS: The school's honour is at stake.

7   ZARIA: I will win for Eastern.

8   MRS. TOWERS: That's the spirit. Close the door on the way

9   out. *(ZARIA turns to go.)* Oh – and Zaria?

10 ZARIA: Yes, Miss?

11 MRS. TOWERS: Get a uniform pass.

12 ZARIA: Miss?

13 MRS. TOWERS: Yes?

14 ZARIA: It is mufti day!

15 MRS. TOWERS: Ah! *(Crossfade)*

16

17

18   **SCENE SEVEN**

19

20 *(Ten minutes later. The Eastern school tuck shop. As MRS.*

21 *TOWERS and ZARIA exit, the TUCK SHOP OPERATOR*

22 *organises her tuck shop stand. He/she puts out a bag of chips*

23 *and sandwiches including a wholemeal sandwich.*

24 *NETBALLER 1 and SHEENA stand in front of her. The TUCK*

25 *SHOP OPERATOR is serving them. JESS and ERIN dance*

26 *around MEGAN who is in the queue.)*

27 ERIN: *(Together)* **A pie, a pie, a pie, I want a chicken pie.**

28   **Chippies, chippies, chippies! Now. Food. Feed me!**

29 JESS: *(Together)* **Lemonade, no Coke, no lemonade, no an**

30   **orange and chocolate! Hit me with caffeine, no a cookie!**

31 MEGAN: If you think I'm buying you a chicken pie, Erin,

32   you've got another think coming.

33 TUCK SHOP OPERATOR: *(To NETBALLER 1 and SHEENA)* **Sure**

34   **I can't sell you a nice wholemeal sandwich?**

35 ERIN: So who is he?

1 **NETBALLER 1: Doughnuts.** *(Hands over money.)*
2 **MEGAN:** Don't you ever give up?
3 **TUCK SHOP OPERATOR:** Doughnuts what?
4 **ERIN:** Have you done it yet?
5 **MEGAN:** Don't be sick.
6 **SHEENA:** Doughnuts and bubble gum.
7 **JESS:** Erin! You'll have them married next.
8 **TUCK SHOP OPERATOR:** We don't do bubble gum. Have an
9   apple.
10 **SHEENA:** Don't want your mouldy old apple.
11 **TUCK SHOP OPERATOR:** That's it. *(She shuts up shop.)*
12 **NETBALLER 1:** Oy! I want my change. *(NETBALLER 1 and*
13   *SHEENA leave, muttering.)*
14 **ERIN:** Aw, come on. I told you about Jase Duncan.
15 **MEGAN:** Like what a good kisser he is.
16 **ERIN:** Well, he is.
17 **MEGAN:** That kiss doesn't count. It was a fake one.
18 **ERIN:** What do you mean?
19 **MEGAN:** It was in front of four hundred people.
20 **ERIN:** So?
21 **MEGAN:** It was in the script!
22 **ERIN:** It does so count. There was tongue and everything.
23 **JESS:** Ooh, yuk. Can we talk about something else? I'm still
24   waiting to eat my lunch.
25 **ERIN:** Don't make out like you don't want to know.
26 **TESS:** It's probably her long lost cousin from Taupo that she
27   keeps talking about.
28 **MEGAN:** *(Dreamy)* The one that plays bass guitar.
29 **JESS:** That's the one. Is it him?
30 **MEGAN:** Uh, No! *(ZARIA enters wearing DAZ's jersey. She has a*
31   *bandage on her leg and walks with the aid of a crutch,*
32   *limping.)*
33 **MEGAN:** Hi, Zaria. You been to see Fawlty?
34 **ZARIA:** Miss Towers – is she a bit funny? *(She indicates "in the*
35   *head.")*

1   JESS: She's not called Fawlty Towers for nothing. What did she
2   want? To give detentions to innocent bystanders on the
3   last day of term?
4   ZARIA: I not know. He —
5   ERIN: She ...
6   ZARIA: She talks fast. She told me I am alien.
7   ERIN: Told.
8   ZARIA: Told.
9   MEGAN: Alien?
10 JESS: What, like in the *X-Files*? She can't do that! You've got
11   rights.
12 MEGAN: Are you sure?
13 ZARIA: I must put on costume for the special day. I not have
14   costume.
15 ERIN: Fawlty's really lost the plot.
16 MEGAN: Anything else?
17 ZARIA: And win the game.
18 MEGAN: Oh, great. She asks a new girl with a crook foot to
19   retrieve the cup. How's that for logic? Hey what happened
20   to the Tuck Shop?
21 ERIN: They closed.
22 MEGAN: Was it something I said? Now I'm really dying of
23   hunger. *(ZARIA starts laughing.)* What's so funny?
24 ZARIA: *(Laughing)* You saying you're dying of hunger. I have
25   seen people who almost die of hunger. They don't look
26   like you. *(They all look at ZARIA intently.)*
27 MEGAN: Well, perhaps not.
28 ZARIA: You can see their ribs and they stare without speaking.
29   *(A pause. MEGAN, ERIN and JESS look embarrassed.)*
30 JESS: Let's go to Patel's dairy.
31 MEGAN: What about the prefects on the gate?
32 JESS: They're bribeable. A hokey pokey ice cream will do the
33   trick. *(MEGAN and JESS exit. ZARIA goes to leave. ERIN*
34   *grabs ZARIA by the arm.)*
35 ERIN: Hey, you're taking your life in your hands. Aren'tcha?

1   ZARIA: What you mean?

2   ERIN: Wearing Daz's jersey. She'll do you.

3   ZARIA: It good jersey.

4   ERIN: I know it's a good jersey. That's the point. *(Beat)* **Zaria,**

5   **you're not in some sort of trouble are you?**

6   ZARIA: No trouble.

7   ERIN: Because if you are, we're your mates, right?

8   ZARIA: Mates. Kiwi word for friends.

9   ERIN: That's right. *(Beat)* **Oh, come on!** *(Crossfade)*

10

11

12   **SCENE EIGHT**

13

14   *(An Eastern College School Corridor. MRS. TOWERS, walkie-*

15   *talkie in her hand, crouches on one side of the stage and*

16   *FELICITY crouches at the other side of the stage, also with*

17   *walkie-talkie.)*

18   MRS. TOWERS: *(To the walkie-talkie)* **Big Momma to Good**

19   **Buddy. Do you read me? Over.**

20   FELICITY: *(To the walkie-talkie)* **Good Buddy to Big Momma. I**

21   **read you.**

22   MRS TOWERS: *(To the walkie-talkie)* **Any sign of pilfering down**

23   **your end of the lockers, over?**

24   FELICITY: *(To the walkie-talkie as she looks through a pair of*

25   *binoculars at the lockers)* **No sign. Over. Corridor is quiet.**

26   **Over. Usual pile of litter from lunch. Over. All lockers are**

27   **closed. Over.**

28   MRS. TOWERS: Felicity?

29   FELICITY: Yes?

30   MRS. TOWERS: Stop saying "over." Over.

31   FELICITY: Roger, Mrs. Towers. *(FELICITY's cell phone rings and*

32   *she answers it.)* **Good afternoon. Eastern College. May I**

33   **help you?** *(Listens. TUCK SHOP OPERATOR enters.)*

34   TUCK SHOP OPERATOR: Oh, there you are Mrs. Fawlty!

35   MRS. TOWERS: It's Towers, you fool. Keep your voice down.

1 TUCK SHOP OPERATOR: **Sorry, Mrs Towersyuful, Force of**
2   **habit. Why are we whispering?**
3 MRS. TOWERS: **We're on patrol.**
4 TUCK SHOP OPERATOR: **Oh, I see. Look, I won't keep you. Only**
5   **I wanted to give you this in person.** *(Hands over an envelope.)*
6 MRS. TOWERS: *(Stage whisper)* **What's this?**
7 TUCK SHOP OPERATOR: **My resignation. Find yourself**
8   **another lackey. I won't stand there and be insulted any**
9   **more. Cheerio!**
10 MRS. TOWERS: *(Wailing)* **But what about the contract?**
11 TUCK SHOP OPERATOR: **I don't give a fig for your contract.**
12   **Goodbye.** *(Exits.)*
13 MRS. TOWERS: **Come back!** *(NETBALLER 1 enters and looking*
14   *behind her cautiously goes Downstage toward her "locker."*
15   *She crouches down and puts her hand out towards the locker.)*
16 MRS. TOWERS: *(To the walkie-talkie)* **Red alert! We have a**
17   **target, Good Buddy, at three o'clock! All systems go!**
18 FELICITY: *(Calling out to MRS. TOWERS)* **It's Foreign Affairs.**
19   **They're advising you to cancel your holiday until further**
20   **notice.** *(Simultaneous action with NETBALLER 1 and MRS.*
21   *TOWERS:)*
22 NETBALLER 1: *(Leaping up nervously)* **Arrgh!**
23 MRS. TOWERS: **Damn! All right, you little thief!** *(Pointing the*
24   *walkie-talkie like a gun:)* **Stop right there!** *(NETBALLER 1*
25   *puts her hands in the air.)* **Caught you red handed! Give!**
26   **Felicity! Specimen bag!** *(FELICITY holds open a plastic bag.*
27   *NETBALLER 1 holds out the tampon by the string then*
28   *drops it in the plastic bag. FELICITY hands it to MRS.*
29   *TOWERS who is looking directly at NETBALLER 1. MRS.*
30   *TOWERS looks at the bag and groans. NETBALLER 1 looks at*
31   *both women in disbelief. The cell phone rings.)*
32 FELICITY: **Hello?** *(Listens. Offers the phone to MRS TOWERS.)*
33   **It's your husband. He wants to know if you have a recipe**
34   **for removing scorch marks from a little black dress.**
35 MRS TOWERS: **Sacre Bleu!**

1 NETBALLER 1: Can I call my lawyer? *(Freeze. Crossfade.)*

2

3

4 **SCENE NINE**

5

6 *(Friday lunchtime. Outside Patel's Dairy. MR./MRS. PATEL*
7 *brings on the fruit stand. The New Zealand Herald*
8 *newspaper billboard reads: "Children Will Suffer European*
9 *Winter." Alongside it is a women's magazine billboard. DAZ,*
10 *PHINA and MICKEY enter and stand outside the dairy*
11 *counting their money. PHINA looks at the magazine*
12 *billboard of a glamorous model.)*

13 DAZ: *(Holding a coin in her hand)* Heads we smoke, tails we eat.

14 MICKEY: Have we got enough for a chocolate milk shake?

15 DAZ: I've got enough for a shake. You've got enough for a jube.
16   The point is, do you wanna smoke?

17 PHINA: *(Looking at the billboard)* Do you think if I got one of
18   those new push up bras I could look like that?

19 MICKEY: Forget the bras. *(Flips the coin.)* Smokes.

20 PHINA: You're lucky, Mickey, your boyfriend likes you "just
21   the way you are."

22 DAZ: Why is it we always end up talking about weight?

23 PHINA: We're not talking about weight, Daz. We're talking
24   about personality.

25 DAZ: Coulda fooled me.

26 MICKEY: Yeah, well let's get on with it. I don't want to run into
27   any of those Eastern chicks. Why did we have to come to
28   this side of town anyway?

29 DAZ: Because all the local dairies have satellite spy dishes.

30 MICKEY: Really?

31 DAZ: They spot Girls' High girls immediately. "We don't serve
32   minors."

33 PHINA: *(Reading the billboard)* "Children Will Suffer European
34   Winter". What do you think that's about, Mickey?

35 MICKEY: Phina, I'm not a clairvoyant. Take Media if you want

1   to ask twenty questions. Hey, Daz, did you find your jersey
2   when you went back to the courts?

3   DAZ: Nuh, but one of our Girls' High supporters said she saw
4   that scuzzie Zaria chick pick it up after the game.

5   PHINA: Yeah? She deserved to go down, I reckon. We've gotta
6   get that back. Team honour an' all that.

7   DAZ: I paid good money for that jersey, or rather Dad did. So
8   who's going to buy the ciggies?

9   MICKEY AND PHINA: Bags not!

10 DAZ: Chicken. Do you see a policeman? No. I don't think so!
11   What are you worried about?

12 PHINA AND MICKEY: We're under age!

13 PHINA: Gotta be eighteen.

14 DAZ: Sssh! Patel will sell them to you, Mickey. You look old
15   enough.

16 MICKEY: Me? I'm not going in. She/He looked at me all funny
17   through the window.

18 DAZ: Probably thought Phina was going to run away with their
19   billboard. Anyway who cares what they think? She/He's
20   only a dirty foreigner. *(PHINA and MICKEY look at DAZ*
21   *expectantly.)*

22 DAZ: Oh, all right, I'll go! Give us your money. *(They hand over*
23   *the money.)*

24 MICKEY: And don't come back with no menthols. *(DAZ enters*
25   *the shop. SHEENA and PEARL enter stage left. They*
26   *recognise MICKEY and PHINA.)*

27 SHEENA AND PEARL: *(Mocking)* A bit outa your way, aren'tcha?
28   *(Blackout.)*

29
30
31   **SCENE TEN**
32
33   *(The Eastern College corridor. MRS. TOWERS and FELICITY*
34   *confer over the tally on FELICITY's clipboard. They still have*
35   *their walkie-talkies, binoculars and cell phones.)*

1 **MRS. TOWERS:** I still say we could've held her on possession.

2 **FELICITY:** Of what?

3 **MRS. TOWERS:** Incriminating evidence. What's the tally so far

4   in Block A?

5 **FELICITY:** From this corridor alone, three jerseys, two jackets,

6   and six scarves.

7 **MRS. TOWERS:** Felicity. Help me! I have to solve this before

8   three-fifteen or they'll all be gone and that will be that for

9   the term.

10 **FELICITY:** Tried the Op Shops?

11 **MRS. TOWERS:** Do you mind?

12 **FELICITY:** Flea markets? *(The cell phone goes. FELICITY*

13   *answers it. Sweetly:)* **Mrs. Tower's office. Can I help you?**

14   *(Listens. She mouths "Upstairs.")*

15 **MRS. TOWERS:** *(Takes the phone. Sweetly)* **Cassandra! We're**

16   **just ...** *(Listens.)* **Right.** *(Listens.)* **Right.** *(Listens.)* **Of course.**

17   *(Listens. Looks at FELICITY and rolls her eyes.)* **Immediately!**

18   *(Punches the phone.)* **We're off to the dairy. Upstairs'**

19   **orders. The widower next to Patel's dairy has spotted our**

20   **girls out of bounds on a spree. This will have to wait.**

21   *(MRS. TOWERS whistles the Colonel Bogey tune as they*

22   *march off. Crossfade.)*

23

24

25   **SCENE ELEVEN**

26

27   *(Outside Patel's dairy. DAZ is walking backwards out of the*

28   *dairy. SHEENA and PEARL stand on the footpath arms*

29   *folded in a stand off with MICKEY and PHINA.)*

30 **DAZ:** *(Yelling back into the shop and waving the cigarettes in the*

31   *air)* **Yah stupid nong! Fooled ya! Woohoo! Why don't you**

32   **curry munchers go back where you belong!** *(DAZ walks*

33   *into the arms of SHEENA and PEARL.)*

34 **SHEENA:** Going somewhere?

35 **PEARL:** Aren't you the loud mouth from the game the other day?

1   DAZ: What the ... ?

2   PEARL: Wha'doya reckon, Sheena?

3   MICKEY: No luck?

4   SHEENA: I reckon she's cruising for a bruising. No one pushes

5   our team mates around and gets away with it.

6   PHINA: You're making a big mistake here.

7   PEARL: *(Grabbing the packet of cigarettes)* **What have we here?**

8   *(The GIRLS' HIGH SUPPORTERS 1,2, 3 enter.)*

9   SHEENA: *(Seeing the Girls' High Supporters)* **Pearl. Pass it!**

10 GIRLS' HIGH SUPPORTERS 1,2,3: *(Mocking)* **Pass it, Pearl!**

11   *(PEARL throws the cigarette packet in SHEENA's direction. It is*

12   *intercepted by GIRLS' HIGH SUPPORTER 1 who throws it to*

13   *GIRLS' HIGH SUPPORTER 2 who throws it to GIRLS' HIGH*

14   *SUPPORTER 3 who throws it to a surprised BRIAN as he walks*

15   *out of the shop with a pack on his back and helmet on his head.)*

16 BRIAN: I gave up smoking two years ago, sorry. Whose are these?

17   *(They all come to a halt. Then DAZ, MICKEY and PHINA*

18   *launch themselves at him.)*

19 DAZ, MICKEY AND PHINA: Mine! *(A siren and flashing lights. The*

20   *DETECTIVE enters and takes the cigarette packet from DAZ's*

21   *hands. Then MR./MRS. PATEL comes out from the shop.)*

22 DETECTIVE: *(To the shop keeper)* **I'm Detective Sid-e-bo-ttom.**

23   *(There is a collective in-drawn breath from the GIRLS HIGH*

24   *SUPPORTERS and the NETBALLERS.)* **Did you sell this**

25   **person a packet of cigarettes?**

26 SHOPKEEPER: Yes, I did. But she shouted racist things at me.

27 DETECTIVE: *(To DAZ)* **How old are you?**

28 DAZ: Eighteen.

29 SHEENA AND PEARL: Liar! She's fifteen.

30 DETECTIVE: Did you see this person buy the cigarettes?

31 PEARL: No, but we know her. She's lying. She's supposed to be

32   at school and so are yous! *(Indicates MICKEY and PHINA.*

33   *and the GIRLS' HIGH SUPPORTERS.)*

34 GIRLS' HIGH SUPPORTER 1: Yeah? And what about yous?

35   You're the Eastern waggers.

1　**DETECTIVE:** *(To BRIAN who stands near DAZ and MICKEY and*
2　　　*PHINA)* **Are you wagging too?**
3　**BRIAN: Well, in a way I am. I'm running away. The Nifty Fifty's**
4　　　**full of juice and I'm off.** *(They all look at BRIAN in disbelief*
5　　　*and then turn back to resume the argument. JESS , ERIN,*
6　　　*ZARIA and MEGAN enter. ERIN and JESS, hooked into a CD*
7　　　*player, dance their way towards the group, blissfully unaware*
8　　　*of what is going on.)*
9　**PHINA: Hey Daz, look what the cat just dragged in.**
10　**DAZ: That's my jersey! Officer, I demand that you arrest that**
11　　　**girl for stealing my jersey!**
12　**ZARIA: I do not steal. I find.** *(Goes to take it off.)* **Here. I keep**
13　　　**safe for you. See you in semis.**
14　**DAZ : She's a thief. That's my jersey.**
15　**MICKEY AND PHINA: Thief! Thief! Thief!**
16　**MEGAN:** *(To DAZ)* **You're wrong and anyone who calls her a**
17　　　**thief will have me to answer to!**
18　**DETECTIVE: Whoa! Stop right there!** *(To ZARIA:)* **Young**
19　　　**woman, why don't we go down to the station and discuss**
20　　　**this? You do not have to say anything but anything you do**
21　　　**say may be used in evidence against you. Is that clear?**
22　**ZARIA: I don't steal.**
23　**DETECTIVE:** *(To ZARIA and DAZ:)* **Now, you two and I are going**
24　　　**to have a little chat and I want the rest of you to clear off.**
25　　　*(Nobody moves.)* **Now!** *(To ZARIA and DAZ:)* **Get in the car,**
26　　　**you two.**
27　**SHOPKEEPER: What about my complaint?**
28　**DETECTIVE: We'll come to that later.**
29　**BRIAN: This is the most excitement I've had all week. Perhaps**
30　　　**I'll stay after all.**
31　**MEGAN: Where are you taking her?**
32　**DETECTIVE: To the station, of course.**
33　**ZARIA: Megan don't leave me!**
34　**DAZ: You're in the crap now!** *(MEGAN joins ZARIA.)*
35　**DETECTIVE:** *(To DAZ)* **In the car, you, and clear off the rest of**

1   you before I arrest you for obstruction! *(DAZ exits.)*

2   MEGAN: I'll get my mother onto you! Then you'll be sorry!

3   *(MRS. TOWERS enters followed by FELICITY.)*

4   MRS. TOWERS: We're bound to find some of the girls here!

5   SHEENA, PEARL, JESS, PHINA, ERIN, NETBALLERS 1, 2, 3:

6   Sprung! *(They all run away Off-stage.)*

7   BRIAN: Ooops! *(He goes to leave on tiptoe.)*

8   MRS. TOWERS: I could've sworn I saw some of our girls just

9   then. Wasn't that Erin Perkins? Brian Towers, what are

10   you doing here?

11   BRIAN: Shopping?

12   MRS. TOWERS: *(To MEGAN and ZARIA)* Girls, I want you back

13   at school now! *(To BRIAN:)* I'll deal with you later.

14   DETECTIVE: I'm sorry, Mrs. Towers, that won't be possible.

15   MRS. TOWERS: Oh, Detective, why not?

16   DETECTIVE: Because I'm taking this one in for questioning.

17   MRS. TOWERS: *(Incredulous)* For wagging?

18   DETECTIVE: Theft, I'm afraid. But this one's free. *(Looks at*

19   *MEGAN.)*

20   MRS. TOWERS: No, she's not! *(DETECTIVE leads ZARIA off the*

21   *stage.)*

22   MEGAN: *(Calling)* Don't worry, Zaria. I'll sort it out. *(She turns*

23   *to find MRS. TOWERS facing her.)*

24   MRS. TOWERS: Well, well, well. And here was I thinking she

25   was a deserving cause. Just goes to show you can't judge a

26   book by its cover. *(To MEGAN:)* Now, young lady –

27   MEGAN: See you. *(She exits.)*

28   MRS. TOWERS: *(After her)* And I want to see you in my office ...

29   BRIAN: *(As he goes to leave)* By the way, Deborah. Your

30   mother's at Dog's Hotel and the dog's entertaining the

31   Golden Oldies at Sunset Lodge, and there's a TV dinner in

32   the microwave. Au revoir!

33   MRS. TOWERS: Au revoir?

34   BRIAN: I've had a gutsful running after you. I'm off.

35   MRS. TOWERS: Off? Off where? What about Tibbles and

1   Poopsie? What about the ball?

2   BRIAN: I'm going to see the world. You'll have to make other

3   arrangements. Ring an escort agency. *(He exits)*

4   MEGAN, FELICITY, AND SHOPKEEPER: Yes! Yow! Good one!

5   *(MEGAN exits.)*

6   MRS. TOWERS: *(Shocked)* Felicity! Water! I need water! *(To*

7   *MEGAN as she exits:)* And I want you in my office ... bother.

8   PHINA: *(To MICKEY)* Who's that?

9   MICKEY: The Eastern principal. They call her Fawlty ...

10   PHINA: Excuse me, Mrs Fawlty —

11   MRS. TOWERS: I beg your pardon. The name is Towers.

12   PHINA: Mrs. Towers. We'd like to speak to you.

13   MRS. TOWERS: Felicity will make you an appointment. I'm a

14   bit busy at the moment.

15   MICKEY: No, it's about all this girl, Zaria.

16   MRS. TOWERS: In that case I'll see you in my office now. *(She*

17   *turns to leave.)*

18   SHOPKEEPER: Mrs. Towers, about your students, we cannot

19   sell cigarette to underage student —

20   MRS. TOWERS: Put it in writing! *(Blackout.)*

21

22

23   SCENE TWELVE

24

25   *(ZARIA's room later that day. The DETECTIVE examines*

26   *AUNTY and UNCLE's papers.)*

27   DETECTIVE: These immigration papers seem to be in order. I

28   see your refugee status has been confirmed.

29   AUNTY: We are good people, officer.

30   UNCLE: No trouble, please. Zaria, tell the officer you have

31   done nothing wrong. *(DETECTIVE sees the box ZARIA has*

32   *behind her.)*

33   DETECTIVE: Uh-uh. What have we here? *(He pulls out the box*

34   *and opens it. It is full of jerseys and scarves.)* Whose are

35   these? Zaria, are these your jerseys?

1   ZARIA: They are nobody's.

2   UNCLE AND AUNTY: Zaria!

3   DETECTIVE: How can they be nobody's? *(The doorbell rings.*

4   *Nobody moves. It rings again.)*

5   UNCLE: I will go. *(UNCLE exits.)*

6   DETECTIVE: Zaria, I had a call from Mrs. Towers. She had

7   information from some girls that they have seen you

8   stealing clothes on a regular basis.

9   ZARIA: No!

10   AUNTY: How can you bring this shame on the family, Zaria?

11   JAN: *(Off)* We want to see Zaria!

12   UNCLE: *(Off)* Is not possible. *(JAN enters with ROBIN and*

13   *MEGAN.)*

14   ZARIA: Megan!

15   JAN: Sorry to barge in, officer.

16   DETECTICE: And you would be?

17   JAN: Jan Carter. Megan's my daughter and Zaria is her friend.

18   Megan's explained to me what's happening here and I

19   think there's a simple explanation.

20   DETECTIVE: Which is?

21   MEGAN: Zaria's not a thief. She's a collector.

22   DETECTIVE: Meaning?

23   MEGAN: It's for the children.

24   ZARIA: Yes. The children.

25   DETECTIVE: What children?

26   MEGAN: Kids leave jerseys behind all the time. In class. She

27   thought they didn't want or need them.

28   AUNTY: Is this true, Zaria?

29   ZARIA: Is very cold in winter in Montenegro. My relatives –

30   they could die.

31   UNCLE: Oh, Zaria! We thought you find these things in street.

32   ZARIA: New Zealand students are rich. My mother she says,

33   "Make us proud!" How can I make her proud if there is no

34   money to send home? I know what to do. I find warm

35   things. They like this back home.

1 ROBIN: We're here to vouch for these people, officer. And I'm
2   here to offer them jobs if they want them in my coffee shop.
3 AUNTY: Job? You say job?
4 ROBIN: I can't pay much but it will be a start for you. Can you
5   wash dishes?
6 AUNTY AND UNCLE: Of course!
7 DETECTIVE: Well, I can't promise anything. We'll have to see
8   what the judge says. I guess the last thing you want is to be
9   deported.
10 AUNTY: Zaria, you must give these things back immediately to
11   the school.
12 UNCLE: This has never happened to us before! Zaria! How
13   could you do this to us?
14 JAN: Don't be angry. Please. She thought she was doing the
15   right thing.
16 AUNTY: This is hard for us.
17 UNCLE: But we understand why you have done this, Zaria.
18   *(MEGAN gives ZARIA a hug.)*
19 MEGAN: I told you it was going to be all right.
20   *(Crossfade.)*
21
22
23   **SCENE THIRTEEN**
24
25   *(MRS. TOWERS' office. Saturday morning. FELICITY hands*
26   *MRS. TOWERS a list.)*
27 FELICITY: You wanted the list of girls to be "stood down," Mrs.
28   Towers?
29 MRS. TOWERS: *(Examining the list)* Right. Wheel them in.
30 FELICITY: *(At the door)* You may come in now. *(ERIN, JESS,*
31   *MEGAN and ZARIA enter followed by PEARL, SHEENA, and*
32   *NETBALLER 1)*
33 MRS. TOWERS: Do you know what day this is? Do you?
34 ERIN: The first day of the holidays, Miss?
35 MRS. TOWERS: That's right, Erin Perkins. The first day of the

1   holidays. And where am I?

2 NETBALLER 1. In your office?

3 MRS. TOWERS: Correct. And where would I rather be?

4 JESS: In a library?

5 MRS. TOWERS: Wrong. On a Pacific Island. And whose fault is

6   it that I'm not there?

7 ERIN, JESS. MEGAN, ZARIA, PEARL, SHEENA, NETBALLER 1:

8   Ours?

9 MRS. TOWERS: Correct. You see this piece of paper? Hmm?

10   What is it?

11 SHEENA: A letter to our parents?

12 MRS. TOWERS: A black mark. That's what it is. A black mark

13   on your records.

14 ERIN, JESS, PEARL, SHEENA: But we haven't done ...

15 NETBALLER 1: ... anything!

16 MRS. TOWERS: Haven't done anything? That's not what I've

17   heard. Smuggling!

18 ALL: Smuggling?

19 MEGAN: Who says?

20 MRS. TOWERS: Some little birdies from Girls' High tell me

21   you're deep into a smuggling ring.

22 JESS: Phina, Mickey and Daz!

23 MRS. TOWERS: There is, of course, one way I might overlook

24   this whole thing.

25 MEGAN: And that would be?

26 MRS. TOWERS: If we get the cup back! *(ERIN, JESS, MEGAN,*

27   *PEARL, ZARIA, SHEENA and NETBALLER 1 look at each*

28   *other. Blackout.)*

29

30

31   **SCENE FOURTEEN**

32

33 *(Later that morning. On the Sideline. JAN, ROBIN, AUNTY*

34 *and UNCLE, GIRLS' HIGH SUPPORTERS 1, 2, and 3 are on*

35 *the sidelines. We don't see the game. A whistle blows.)*

1   **JAN AND ROBIN: Go, Eastern!**

2   **GIRLS' HIGH SUPPORTERS 1,2,3: Girls' High! Girls' High!**

3   **Girls' High!**

4   **AUNTY AND UNCLE: Go, Easter!**

5   **JAN: Eastern.**

6   **AUNTY AND UNCLE:** *(They look at her and turn back to the*

7   *game)* **Go, Zaria!**

8   **GIRLS' HIGH SUPPORTERS 1,2,3: Girls' High! Girls' High!**

9   **Girls' High!**

10   **JAN: That's it, Megan! Go for it!**

11   **ROBIN: Goal!** *(The whistle blows "full time.")*

12   **JAN AND ROBIN:** *(Jumping up and down)* **We did it! We did it!**

13   **We won the cup!** *(A freeze. Blackout.)*

14

15

16   **SCENE FIFTEEN**

17

18   *(That afternoon. Two classrooms, side by side. On one side*

19   *of the stage in a spotlight MICKEY, DAZ and PHINA sit in a*

20   *row knitting scarves.)*

21   **MICKEY: I still don't think it's fair.**

22   **PHINA: If you hadn't said all those things to the Patels we'd be**

23   **sweet.**

24   **DAZ: Well, it's too bad. How long until the first ciggie break?**

25   **PHINA AND MICKEY: Daz!** *(On the other side of the stage in*

26   *another spotlight knitting scarves sit ZARIA, MEGAN, JESS,*

27   *PHINA and ERIN.)*

28   **JESS: It's not fair.**

29   **ERIN: What's not fair?**

30   **PHINA: Why are we here?**

31   **MEGAN: Hullo! We're here for wagging and Zaria's here for**

32   **collecting.** *(JAN and ROBIN enter on MEGAN's side.)* **Mum!**

33   **How come you're here?**

34   **JAN: We've done some negotiating. You can all come home**

35   **when you've finished a scarf. Those kids in Montenegro**

1 will be very grateful. Zaria, we've managed to find some
2 more warm clothes to add to the collection.
3 MEGAN: What about Mrs. T?
4 JAN: Your Mrs. Towers has changed her tune since you won the
5 cup back.
6 ZARIA: Maybe this is where I belong after all. *(MRS. TOWERS*
7 *enters in a flurry on MEGAN's side followed by FELICITY.)*
8 MRS. TOWERS: Girls! Girls! Terrible news, I'm afraid! You're
9 the only ones here! I had to tell someone!
10 ALL: What?
11 MRS. TOWERS: The cup!
12 MEGAN: What about the cup?
13 MRS. TOWERS: The cup's been stolen! I've been robbed!
14 Cheated of my glory!
15 JAN: Serves you right.
16 MRS. TOWERS: I beg your pardon!
17 JAN: There is such a thing as karma, Mrs. Towers, and
18 sometimes we get what we deserve. Come on, Zaria, we're
19 taking you home, where you belong.
20 MRS. TOWERS: Hold me, Felicity! *(They all freeze. The lights*
21 *change to focus Downstage. BRIAN scoots onto the stage on*
22 *foot powered scooter dressed as before with his backpack on*
23 *and carrying the large netball cup. BRIAN holds the netball*
24 *cup aloft in victory.)*
25
26 **THE END**
27
28
29
30
31
32
33
34
35

A Little Monster's Journal
by Claudia Marinelli

This solo performance piece for a young actress was originally written as a short story and later adapted by the author for the stage. On the surface, it seems a satirical piece that is deeply suspicious of American youth pop culture, but upon closer examination the play can be seen to direct its sharpest criticism at universal attitudes of cultural discrimination that are widespread today among youth culture in many parts of the industrialized world.

Anstella, the central character, is certainly a product of modern American society, but so are her parents, as the author takes pains to reveal at key moments throughout the script. Although one can only speculate on the extent to which Anstella's mother years ago developed a cross-cultural relationship with her college friend from Italy (with whom Anstella and her girlfriend are staying), it's certain that her parenting of Anstella left much to be desired in the way of teaching tolerance, acceptance, and respect for foreign cultures and different value systems.

It is in this sense that Anstella becomes a very complex character. Her insensitivity to her Italian relations, her indifference to Italy's cultural heritage, her condescension towards her Italian peers (especially young men), her superior attitude that springs from her wealth and upbringing — all these traits are more than just the product of her social milieu, contemporary United States society. They arise instead from a complex set of circumstances that affect young people today all over the world: from the privileges deriving from their socio-economic class, from media influences that have inculcated in them the importance of brand names and "image," from the trendy self-obsession and hedonism dominating modern youth culture of which Anstella is a part, and perhaps also from Anstella's own natural personality traits of ignorance, indifference and complacency.

Anstella doesn't change during her monolog, although she certainly comes near to doing so because she does entertain doubts about her experiences and some of the conclusions she draws. The sad fact is, however, that like many people we encounter, Anstella is so self-centered that she's incapable of feeling anything for anyone besides herself. This is what truly prevents her from reconsidering her attitudes in any substantive way, because that would mean reconsidering her values towards life and understanding the world around her beyond appearances. As the author describes it: "That's very monstrous, and that's an attitude many people have in our 'civilized' and wealthy world (Italy is not different from the rest of the world) ... It seems that, as long as the appearances are satisfactory, who wants to care about the real meaning of attitudes and actions, and even words? And that also is a very common monstrous attitude of our world."

The monolog presents several important challenges for a young actor in order to be most effective. For one thing, Anstella should not be caricatured: though she is certainly a "type," it is her vulnerable and uncertain qualities that will make her more human and sympathetic to the audience. As the author declares: "It's important that Anstella looks and talks like a 'normal' teenager, somebody you would easily meet in a mall, and that you could admire for her beauty."

A second important challenge for the actor is the performance style of direct address to the audience. There is really "nowhere to hide" on Claudia Marinelli's stage: the actor must drive the piece forward by herself, at her own pace, developing confidence alone onstage and learning to "work the crowd" in a very skilful way for the play to function successfully. Indeed, the actor cannot "hide behind a mask" in the traditional sense of portraying a character, because the play showcases raw emotions — Anstella's impatience, surprise, pride, irritation, condescension, disbelief, tedium, etc. In short, *A Little Monster's Journal* demands that the actor risk herself onstage in this way — a hallmark of good acting in all historical periods and in all dramatic media.

Characters

Anstella is a seventeen-year-old girl. She is tall and slender, very pretty, with long dark hair and a few highlights. She wears black shoes with high heels, a black slit skirt, a fashionable expensive black or grey jersey with a brand name printed on it (it could be "Valentino," or "Les Copains," or "Versace"). The brand name should be visible to the audience, it could even shine. She wears grey tights and ambles in a swanky way as models do on runways.

Setting

The stage is a family room. The audience should feel in the room with Anstella as if sitting on the couches of the family room. There are a projector, a cordless telephone, a couple of magazines and a remote control on a coffee table up front in the middle of the stage. A big, nice-looking wooden bookcase/entertainment center fills the Upstage. There are books on the shelves, picture frames, a couple of knick-knacks, and a few plants with falling leaves (pothos, ground ivy, or croton). The bottom shelves are closed with little cabinets. In the middle of the bookshelf, just over the small cabinets, there is a big expensive TV that seems part of the furniture. On Stage Left very nice French doors are closed. On Stage Right there is a beautiful French window with daylight coming through. There are dark blue or brown drapes hanging on the two sides of the window. A few pictures could hang from the walls next to the door or the window. A big screen, where Anstella will project her slides, is also onstage. As she talks, Anstella will show pictures of her trip, so she will make the slides appear on the screen with the remote control, but the light from the projector should never prevent the public from clearly seeing her on the stage.

1   *(ANSTELLA enters Stage Left and looks at the audience. She*
2   *smiles as she calmly reaches, over her high heels with calculated*
3   *swanky paces, the center of the stage just behind the coffee table.*
4   *Then she faces the audience.)*

5   **Hi there! My name is Anstella Stone, my mom will soon be**
6   **back from work. I know it's not polite to leave our guests by**
7   **themselves, so I thought you might be entertained by hearing**
8   **about my trip. And ...** *(She ponders for a few seconds, she frowns*
9   *and touches her chin with a hand)* **... maybe you'll be able to give**
10   **me some advice.**

11   **I went to Italy with my friend Caitlyn over the Spring break**
12   **to visit some Italian friends of my mom. My mom was so excited**
13   **for me. She said that trip was going to be ... the greatest ... the**
14   **funniest ... most exiting opportunity for me ... Such a vacation!**
15   **Well ...** *(She shrugs with a sigh.)* **A vacation for me is a time to rest,**
16   **sleep all day long, have fun with new guys ...** *(She puts a hand at*
17   *her waist.)* **I really went over there to meet attractive boys, seduce**
18   **them or at least, make them fall for me because, as you can see ...**
19   *(She lets her hands slide down her body as if to show it better to the*
20   *audience)* **... I'm very pretty and ... there aren't many girls as**
21   **pretty as me. Caitlyn is cute, of course, but only a few girls can**
22   **compete with me. Well, let's start.** *(ANSTELLA walks to the*
23   *window, closes the drapes. Then she walks next to the projector and*
24   *takes the remote control. Her paces are always calculated and*
25   *elegant. She turns the projector on, and the screen becomes bright.)*

26   **We arrived over there on Wednesday, and Clara, my**
27   **mom's friend, picked us up at the airport. Nino, Clara's son,**
28   **was there too.** *(ANSTELLA lights up the first slide. On the screen*
29   *a forty year old, dark haired, woman appears. She's smiling.)*

30   **She was fluent in English, as was her son and her**
31   **husband, Ugo. Her car was so small, though! A ... a ...**
32   **ridiculous car!** *(With an amused tone of voice:)* **We held**
33   **ourselves not to laugh out loud: it was so funny and comical to**
34   **watch that woman Clara and her son Nino fix one of our**
35   **suitcases on the top of the roof rack!**

1   *(Slide: an Italian Fiat Panda — or another kind of small car —*
2 *CLARA and NINO are lifting one suitcase to put it on the roof rack.*
3 *Next to the car ANSTELLA and CAITLYN are watching with*
4 *amused expressions.)*

5   **She drove us to her house right away, in a village near**
6 **Rome. The house was not that great, they didn't have designer**
7 **furniture, not even a black microwave.** *(Obvious and self-*
8 *confident tone of voice:)* **These people were like ... old-**
9 **fashioned, you know!**

10   *(Slide: an Italian house from the outside, it's made out of*
11 *concrete.)*

12   **We got Nino's bedroom.**

13   *(Slide of a boy's nice bedroom with a trundle bed. ANSTELLA*
14 *faces the audience with the remote control in her hand.)*

15   **Can you believe it? They wanted to show us the village's**
16 **castle as soon as we got settled! But we said NO, NO!** *(She shakes*
17 *one hand as to reinforce the negation.)* **A castle! And the beds**
18 **seemed so tempting!** *(She gestures to the slide with the beds.)* **We**
19 **locked ourselves up in our room and had a nice, good nap.**
20 **After dinner we went to a party at Nino's friend's house. Of**
21 **course I was the prettiest girl there, and the most smartly**
22 **dressed with my stylish slit skirt, and my black silk tight top.**
23 *(She slides a hand through her hair from the neck.)* **Besides my**
24 **hair and my make-up were perfect.**

25   *(Slide of ANSTELLA sitting in an armchair, leaning against*
26 *its back, crossed legs, with many teenage boys around her.)*

27   **Everybody was looking at me, only me. I was so unique and**
28 **so beautiful that all the boys talked to me, let out remarks ... in**
29 **Italian, of course ...**

30   *(Slide of ANSTELLA standing near a table covered with food,*
31 *a glass in her hand with many boys around her, many of them*
32 *openly making sexy advances.)*

33   **I wonder what they said?** *(She ponders for a couple of*
34 *seconds with a hand at her chin looking at the slide, then she*
35 *turns to the audience.)* **Well ... of course they congratulated me!**

1   But they were teenagers, kids ... none of them was older than
2   seventeen. Just not worthy of notice. As you can see ... *(She*
3   *slides her hands down her body again)* ... **I look like I'm twenty!**
4   **Thursday Clara woke us up at 1:30 p.m.**
5   *(Slide of ANSTELLA and CAITLYN in a very bad mood under*
6   *the sheets.)*
7   **Just unbelievable! We had to eat with the rest of the**
8   **family.** *(She turns her eyes to the ceiling, and lightly touches her*
9   *forehead with her fingers.)* **An agony! After lunch we had to go to**
10   **Rome with Nino and his friend Alex. Before leaving, that**
11   **woman started telling us about monuments, and places, and**
12   **churches we would visit** ... *(A little louder:)* **She EVEN**
13   **DRAGGED A MAP OUT OF A DRAWER!**
14   *(Slide of CLARA and ANSTELLA. CLARA is holding a map of*
15   *Rome in her hand, ANSTELLA has a very bored expression.)*
16   **I didn't listen to such boring stuff. Rome is okay, it's**
17   **shabby though ... and tiring! We walked and walked, really**
18   **exhausting!** *(Slide of ANSTELLA and CAITLYN walking with*
19   *bored expressions behind the two boys.)* **Nino and Alex wanted to**
20   **show us the Coliseum, but we said "NO, NO!" The Coliseum!**
21   **What's the fuss about it? It's all over the pictures. We didn't**
22   **want to miss our shopping!** *(Slide of ANSTELLA and CAITLYN*
23   *shopping.)* **I got so many things, it was fun! We arrived in a**
24   **place with some white steps and a fountain** ...
25   *(Slide of the Spanish Steps, badly taken.)*
26   **... and McDonald's.**
27   *(Slide of McDonald's at the Spanish Steps in Rome, very well*
28   *taken.)*
29   *(ANSTELLA faces the audience and asks:)* **What's better**
30   **than McDonald's for a nice fast dinner? After dinner there was**
31   **that planned concert Nino had bought tickets for.**
32   *(Slide: teenagers at a rock concert with the hands up,*
33   *ANSTELLA and CAITLYN in the middle of the crowd with a very*
34   *bored and condescending attitude.)*
35   **Such a stupid concert!** *(She moves her head slightly as to*

1   *say "no."*) **In Italian! Compared to our shows it was just ... crap!**
2   **They're so backwards over there! Friday the day started off a**
3   **little better. Clara woke us up at two thirty in the afternoon**
4   **because lunch was ready!**
5   *(Slide of ANSTELLA and CAITLYN sitting at a table with a*
6   *very sleepy and bored attitude.)*
7   **Even if we didn't care at all about lunch, because we could**
8   **have slept more ...** *(She sighs)* **...we ate with the Italians. Then**
9   **we fixed ourselves up and joined Nino at Alex's place, a couple**
10 **of houses down the road. There we met Fabio.**
11   *(Slide of a classical "Guido" guy next to his scooter.)*
12   **He asked us if we wanted to go to a play fun park. "Of**
13 **course!" we said. Why didn't they tell us about that park before?**
14 **We went there with Alex and Fabio, because Fabio was so**
15 **attracted to me right away! I rode on his scooter and he stopped**
16 **for a few minutes and we ... kissed. An Italian kiss ... you know!**
17   *(Slide of ANSTELLA and FABIO on a bumper-car.)*
18   **The bumper-cars were pure fun! Everybody wanted to**
19 **bump my bumper-car, our screams in English really worked**
20 **out as magnets for these Italian guys. They even shouted "I**
21 **LOVE YOU!!!!" to me.**
22   *(ANSTELLA's bumper car is surrounded by other similar cars*
23 *with shouting boys. ANSTELLA turns to the audience and then*
24 *paces the stage, she can twirl once if the actress will find it good for*
25 *her acting as she says:)* **Everybody stared at me because I was the**
26 **prettiest, the most attractive, the most beautiful girl there!** *(She*
27 *stops, faces the audience and opens her hands with a little shrug,*
28 *her expression means "it's obvious" and says:)* **What can I say? As**
29 **always all over the world, boys fall for me easily! It's obvious.**
30 **After dinner we went to see something really weird. It was**
31 **called "The Passion of Christ" and it was ... SPOOKY! The village**
32 **was crowded with people and there was like a show going on in**
33 **the narrow streets with men and women in costumes.**
34   *(Slide of ANSTELLA and CAITLYN walking on a narrow street*
35 *with stone houses with bored expressions. The street is crowded*

1   *with people and actors in costumes, it could be Roman*
2   *Centurions, Jewish women as they were dressed at the beginning*
3   *of the first millennium.)* **They crucified a man on a castle's walls.**

4   *(Slide of a crucifixion on top of a 15th-century wall, that*
5   *could be a very interesting slide but very badly taken.)*

6   **Well, it was Good Friday! I don't know how that man**
7   **didn't freeze! They are really insane in Italy, I'm telling you!**
8   *(ANSTELLA looks straight at the audience, she seems to ponder*
9   *for a couple of seconds.)* **Don't you think so too? Finally on**
10   **Saturday they left us alone! We slept till four thirty!** *(Slide of the*
11   *girls sleeping under the sheets.)* **We took our showers but, like**
12   **at five thirty Clara came to our room and asked us if we**
13   **were okay. "Of course," we answered. But she insisted and was**
14   **going ... like: "Are you sure you're okay?"**

15   *(Slide of ANSTELLA and CAITLYN standing in front of*
16   *CLARA with jeering expressions.)*

17   **And I went. "Yeah, yeah ... we're okay!"** *(ANSTELLA*
18   *snickers.)* **I was like ... cracking up, but Caitlyn and I held**
19   **ourselves till she left the room. We couldn't believe it! They just**
20   **don't sleep in Italy. Like an hour later my mom called up from**
21   **New York, she was upset and angry. She, she just made such a**
22   **fuss because Clara sent her an e-mail telling that we were**
23   **sleeping and she couldn't bring us anywhere as planned!**
24   *(ANSTELLA sighs.)* **That woman Clara was ... just unbelievable!**
25   **Would you have done something like that? No American would**
26   **have acted like this! Is sleeping a problem in Italy? And mom**
27   **was going like ...**

28   *(Slide of ANSTELLA on the phone with a bored expression.)*

29   **"You're missing such an opportunity, you have to grow up,**
30   **interest yourself to a new country, to the culture, to the art, to**
31   **the language ... and blah, blah, blah ... "** *(She puts the remote to*
32   *her ear as if it was a receiver.)* **I said, "Yeah, yeah ... " and "okay,**
33   **okay...." Anyways, my mom is very understanding and, soon as**
34   **I told her that I was going to see the Pope the next day, she**
35   **forgot about the whole thing and became so excited! But ... we**

1 were cross! At dinner time, Caitlyn and I hardly spoke.

2 *(Slide: ANSTELLA and CAITLYN sitting at a dinner table*
3 *with cross attitudes. Pasta is on the table.)*

4 **Of course we said...** *(Very polite tone of voice:)* **"Thank you"**
5 **or "grazie," that means thank you, when they held out food to**
6 **us. We ARE very polite, and VERY well mannered, we even**
7 **helped with the dishes. After dinner Clara brought us to an**
8 **Italian Mass. My mom had recommended her that we don't**
9 **miss Masses. We took Communion, Clara didn't.** *(She faces the*
10 *audience to ask her question.)* **What's the use of going to Mass if**
11 **you don't take Communion?** *(She ponders for a couple of*
12 *seconds.)* **Can you answer that? I really can't. She's a queer**
13 **woman. Anyways ... here comes the good part ... something**
14 **really awesome came up! We went to a disco after Mass, a COOL**
15 **disco with Nino and Alex.**

16 *(Slide: the four teenagers in front of a disco entrance)*

17 **Nino knew the owners, and talked to them a lot, but the**
18 **boys had to pay. We didn't because ...** *(Snooty again:)* **... I guess**
19 **we were so pretty that these people didn't dare to ask us money**
20 **to get in!** *(She now faces out, the picture of the disco entrance is*
21 *still on the screen. She talks with an enthusiastic tone of voice.)*

22 **That disco was COOL, AWESOME, TOTALLY RAD! They**
23 **played only American music. The place was huge, packed with**
24 **people, there were three levels to it, lots of separate rooms, two**
25 **huge dance floors, black lights throughout the place, couches**
26 **everywhere and lots, lots of fast, loud music! There were so**
27 **many good-looking, sexy guys. Real hunks.**

28 *(Slide: inside of the disco as described by ANSTELLA)*

29 **Could we just stay with Nino and Alex?** *(Pause)* **Of course**
30 **not! So we said we had to go to the bathroom and dumped**
31 **them! Finally, we had FUN. It was easy to pick up a couple of**
32 **hunk guys and dance with them throughout the night.**

33 *(Slide: ANSTELLA and CAITLYN dancing with two Guidos*
34 *very, very close to each other.)*

35 **At last we could find out how Italian guys kiss, at night! We**

had heard so much about it back home! *(She turns towards the slide, considers it for a couple of seconds, puts a hand at her chin.)* I'm going to tell Sam, my boyfriend, about this disco, but ... not about the guy I met! *(She turns to the audience.)* By the way ... I didn't even ask him his name ... well ... *(She shrugs.)* ... he didn't ask mine either! But ... *(She sighs deeply and with pleasure bending her head a little backwards)* ... he kissed thoroughly, and he ... *(She looks out and smiles)* ... Well ... you don't need to know about that ... What a night! *(She turns to the projector again.)* On Easter Sunday we had to get up at 8 a.m.!!!!

(Slide: ANSTELLA and CAITLYN in their pyjamas with very sleepy and bored expressions)

We were not in a good mood, considering that we went to bed around five a.m. Nino didn't even say "hi!" or "good morning" to us. *(ANSTELLA ponders)* Oh! He might have been upset because of the night before. Well ... we didn't like him, we couldn't help it, so ... Anyways, we showered and got into our Easter outfits, and left Rome with Clara to see the Pope while he was saying Mass. He was in a big, big place, and we saw him from a distance and took pics.

(Slide: ANSTELLA taking pictures, St. Peter's Square is in the background.)

Mom will be ... overwhelmed about it. Don't you think it's a nice picture? *(To the audience:)* You know what? There were more than half a million people in that place that day! And everybody, everybody turned to watch us as we walked. Of course, they didn't watch Clara!

(Slide: ANSTELLA taking off her jacket. She's dressed in a slit skirt, and a tight top without sleeves.)

I took off my jacket, it was hot and then ... why should I cover my pretty body? I told Caitlyn: "Watch, watch! Everybody, everybody is looking at us!" Clara heard me, but ... she didn't congratulate me! She seemed ... *(She ponders with a hand at her chin)* ... annoyed. I wonder why? *(Out:)* Do you think I shouldn't have taken off my jacket? And why? I like to be looked at, and

1 there's nothing wrong about it, is there? Well ... I just think that
2 Clara was jealous! Besides she's what? Like forty? But ... when
3 we went back to the car I said: *(Very polite tone of voice:)* "Thank
4 you for bringing us to see the Pope." She didn't even answer ...
5 she's weird, and impolite! After displaying myself for those
6 people (what a great experience!) we went to Clara's relatives
7 for Easter lunch where we met Nino and Ugo again. Everybody
8 talked English but ... who wanted to consider all these people?
9 Luckily we found something like a porch, with nice couches
10 where we fell asleep cozily!
11   *(Slide: the two girls sleeping on a couch under a nice porch.)*
12   We were so tired, and had nothing to say to all these
13 Italian people ... *(She opens her arms)* ... so, we fell asleep.
14 What's wrong with that? The following day we went to
15 Florence, as planned by Clara and Mom, with Ugo and Nino. We
16 had to wake up so early! It was like ... in the army ...
17   *(An Italian car riding on a highway. It's bigger than the Fiat*
18 *Panda.)*
19   **Florence!**
20   *(Slide: Florence from a distance, the picture is badly taken.)*
21   What can I say? It's cramped and small, it's okay. But that
22 woman was just going to spoil everything, she wanted to tell us
23 about the monuments AGAIN! *(She turns out and lightly shakes*
24 *her head.)* She's not that smart, really! Couldn't she understand
25 that we just didn't give a damn? So every time she started to
26 talk to us, I would turn to Caitlyn and talk to her. I had to do
27 that three times ... *(She shows the number 3 with her hand.)* ...
28 before she figured it out: WE DON'T WANT TO KNOW
29 ANYTHING ABOUT SILLY MONUMENTS!
30   *(Slide: CLARA next to the girls with a very upset expression.*
31 *The girls don't look at her.)*
32   We walked to a place with a dark brown building and a
33 tower.
34   *(Slide: Florence, Piazza della Signoria where the*
35 *reproduction of Michelangelo's David is located.)*

1 *(Amazed:)* **And in front of that building there was a statue**
2 **of a naked man! And everybody was taking pics under that**
3 **naked statue! Even Clara, Nino, and Ugo did that! Just**
4 **unbelievable! So we were curious and asked what it was. Clara**
5 **said: "Michelangelo's David."**

6 *(Slide: CLARA, NINO and UGO under the statue of*
7 *Michelangelo's David. You can only see up to the knees of the*
8 *statue)*

9 **I don't understand ...** *(ANSTELLA turns out)* **... it's so ugly!**
10 **Really disgusting, obnoxious, and ... shameful.** *(Pause)* **Italians**
11 **ARE weird! We went to McDonald's for lunch.**

12 *(Slide: McDonald's)*

13 **The place was crowded so, as Ugo and Nino got in line for**
14 **food, we went downstairs with Clara to get a table. After a few**
15 **minutes Clara found two seats for us, but when Ugo and Nino**
16 **came down, she called us because they found a big table that**
17 **sat six. Well ... who wanted to have lunch with them? I got up**
18 **and told them that we wanted to eat by ourselves. I was very**
19 **polite though, I said:** *(Politely:)* **"If you don't mind." They gave**
20 **us our food without even uttering a word.**

21 *(Slide: McDonald's, a table with ANSTELLA and CAITLYN*
22 *alone and, in the background, another table with CLARA, NINO,*
23 *and UGO.)*

24 **Do you think we were impolite ... ? Should we have sat**
25 **with them ... ? Well, they paid for our food! But ... we tried to**
26 **give them back the money, they didn't want it! We couldn't**
27 **figure out why ... ? If they didn't want the money back, we**
28 **couldn't force them!** *(Her tone of voice is very self-confident, she*
29 *opens her arms and then drops them.)* **We tried our best!**

30 *(Slide: the five people walking in the streets of Florence in*
31 *two separate groups.)*

32 **We were fine for the rest of the afternoon, and just**
33 **followed the Italians that, luckily didn't talk to us anymore.**
34 **The ride back was so boring!**

35 *(Slide: Italian car on a highway.)*

1   And Clara even tried to start a conversation with us ...
2   "OH, NO!" I thought. So Caitlyn and I began to laugh, to tell
3   each other funny stories, we even stamped our feet on the car
4   floor ... I really didn't understand why Ugo got upset. He said
5   out loud: "Enough now, I have a headache!" That was not nice!
6   *(Slide: in front of the house, next to the car the five people*
7   *are standing as if they just got out of it.)*
8   But, WE were very polite. As soon as we got out of the car
9   I said: *(Politely:)* "Thank you for bringing us to Florence."
10   Again, they didn't even pretend to say "you're welcome."
11   *(ANSTELLA lightly shakes her head.)* So ... so rude! On Tuesday
12   Clara came into our room, it was six p.m., we were up like ...
13   what? An hour or so. Well, she closed the door behind her and
14   asked: "Did we do anything wrong to you?"
15   *(Slide: CLARA standing in the girls' room in front of them*
16   *with a questioning expression. The girls have indifferent*
17   *expressions.)*
18   We said: "No." Then she goes: "Did we offend you? Or said
19   something that you didn't like?" And we said again: "No." And
20   then she goes on: "Then you have to explain to me your
21   attitude." Caitlyn and I looked at each other: "What attitude?"
22   we asked.
23   *(Slide: the TWO GIRLS looking at each other with*
24   *wondering expressions.)*
25   And then she says: "You really misbehaved, you behaved
26   as if we didn't exist. Yesterday, every time I started to talk to
27   you, Anstella you started to speak to Caitlyn." Don't you want to
28   know anything about what you're seeing?" Oh my! I thought.
29   *(She sighs.)* That was just unbelievable. I promptly answered:
30   *(Sweetly:)* "Oh, I'm sorry, I didn't notice you were talking to
31   Caitlyn." *(Her tone of voice is lower and lightly grumpy.)* And she
32   goes: "Really? Three times you didn't notice?" And I said:
33   *(Mannered, nice tone of voice:)* "Oh, yes! I didn't notice. I
34   wouldn't have interrupted you. I'm sorry."
35   *(Slide: ANSTELLA with a very sorry face.)*

1   She looked at me in a very weird way. Then she went: "OK,
2   I can accept this explanation, then you have to tell me why you
3   didn't want to eat with us." *(ANSTELLA opens her arms and*
4   *drops them right away.)* What a pain in the neck she was. I felt
5   annoyed, so I told her what we felt, that's it. I said: *(Nice tone of*
6   *voice:)* "Well, that's because we're very conservative and want
7   to be left alone." Do you think she understood us?
8   *(Slide: CLARA in front of the girls with a very angry face.)*
9   She wasn't happy, actually she turned out to be very upset,
10   and cross, and started to say that our behaviour was not nice,
11   that she was deeply offended by our attitude, that my mom had
12   been such a nice friend she couldn't believe her daughter would
13   act like this, and blah, blah, blah ... *(ANSTELLA turns to the*
14   *audience questioningly.)* Do you think our attitude was offensive?
15   I really can't figure out why. We DID want to pay for our food!
16   THEY didn't want the money. Should we have eaten with them
17   just because of that? We really didn't like them, so should we
18   have forced ourselves? *(Pause)* We asked them if they didn't
19   mind! We were very polite! No, these people are weird, that's it.
20   But that evening we went down for dinner and talked to the rest
21   of the family. We didn't want to take any chances. After all Clara
22   could call my mom up or e-mail another letter to her! *(ANSTELLA*
23   *sighs and lightly shrugs)* Our trip was really boring after that. The
24   next interesting thing we did was going to a pub with Nino and
25   his friend Charles. We had a B-52, I lit up into a fire, and fire, and
26   fire ... A fantastic, awesome experience!
27   *(Slide: ANSTELLA drinking in a pub and laughing.)*
28   Oh! This is nice in Italy: everybody can drink, they don't
29   ask for your ID. But ... those boys over there are really stupid ...
30   they don't drink! *(ANSTELLA turns to the audience.)* Don't you
31   think it's weird for teenagers? Oh! I have to be fair, though.
32   Free drinking is not the only cool think over there, as I said
33   there are those nice discos and ... *(With a sensual tone of voice:)*
34   ... ice cream! Right! Italian ice cream is excellent, so creamy,
35   and soft ... ummmmmmm! Worth a whole trip there!

1   *(She paces the stage, always in a swanky way.)* **I have very**
2 **little left to tell you. The remaining days we really had a**
3 **terrible time. That family just asked us if we wanted to visit**
4 **castles, monuments, old cities ... They don't know how to have**
5 **fun over there! We thought we'd go crazy. We just locked**
6 **ourselves in our room and drank wine.** *(She goes to the*
7 *projector.)* **What else could we do?**
8   *(Slide: the GIRLS drinking a bottle of wine in their room.)*
9   **Can you believe that Caitlyn actually read a book? We were**
10 **like ...** *(She lightly shakes her head, touching it with a hand.)* **...**
11 **going out of our minds. We sank to a new low ... and started to**
12 **smoke! Nobody even talked to us! The day before we left we**
13 **went with an organized tour to see "Rome by Night." That was**
14 **planned from America. That family just brought us in front of**
15 **the agency and then left us there. They made sure we took the**
16 **right tourist bus but ... not even one word.** *(She faces the*
17 *audience.)* **Well, what can you expect from weird people? That**
18 **tour was OK. We had to suffer through a lot of illuminated**
19 **monuments ...**
20   *(Slides of lighted monuments like the Coliseum, Venice*
21 *Square, Spanish steps ... very badly taken.)*
22   **But at the end ... came a nice dinner with lots of food, and**
23 **lots and lots of nice wine ... hee-hee-hee-hee-hee-hee!**
24   *(Slide: the two GIRLS drinking in a restaurant.)*
25   **We felt like ... drunk ... it was such a great experience! So**
26 **funny! So exciting ... that compensated a little for all the boring**
27 **time we spent locked in our rooms!** *(ANSTELLA sighs.)* **Finally on**
28 **Sunday we left for home. I was ... like ... so happy, I couldn't wait.**
29   *(Slide: Fiumicino airport.)*
30   **Clara drove us to the airport. Before saying goodbye, I**
31 **took 200,000 Lire from my purse and handed the money to her.**
32 **That's like 100 dollars.**
33   *(Slide: ANSTELLA handing some money to CLARA who has*
34 *a very angry and offended expression.)*
35   **I said:** *(Politely.)* **"Thank you for driving us around and to**

1 Florence, I hope this money is enough!" *(Normal tone of voice)*
2 She just looked at me and said: *(Offended:)* **"Keep your money,**
3 **your behaviour is just unbelievable, you're insulting me!" She**
4 **turned around ... like that, and left. She didn't even say good-bye,**
5 **nothing, she didn't shake our hands, not even ... a little kiss ... or**
6 **... a little hug! So ... so ... RUDE!** *(She slowly paces the stage.)*
7   **Why? Why? Why did she act like that? What did we do that**
8 **was unbelievable?** *(She thinks.)* **Was it because we didn't talk to**
9 **them that much during our stay? Well ... we had nothing to say!**
10 **We didn't like them, that's it, what could we do about it? They**
11 **are not interesting people, old fashioned, they ride in small**
12 **cars, they're not that good looking ... they wanted us to see**
13 **monuments ... They didn't know how to have fun ...** *(She thinks*
14 *again)* **We did want to pay them, though. They must have spent**
15 **some money to drive us around ... ! But THEY did not want our**
16 **money, so ...** *(She slightly shakes her head.)* **I don't understand ...**
17 **Not even a little hug when we left! THAT'S unbelievable! I**
18 **really can't figure out Italian people. They're just ... nonsense!**
19   *(ANSTELLA turns to the audience.)*
20   **Really, who cares?** *(She shrugs.)* **But ... what do you**
21 **suggest? What should I tell my mom?** *(She thinks with a hand at*
22 *her chin.)* **You know what? I'm just going to tell her the truth:**
23 **how hard to believe Italian people are, and how rude was that**
24 **friend of hers after all!**
25
26   **THE END**
27
28
29
30
31
32
33
34
35

Lilford Mill
by Neil Duffield

Although the plot of this epic drama focuses upon Britain's "Irish problem" in the context of World War One, this play is more than an historical study. In one sense, of course, the "Irish problem" is still with us, continuing today to generate painful conflict, interminable discussion and negotiations, and a bitter and frustrated feeling among all the participants. In another sense, however, Neil Duffield reveals other important issues bound-up with the history of this small Lancashire town called Lilford Mill: European socialism, gender discrimination, pacifism, patriotism, racism and the slaughter of war.

The strength of this play in weaving so many themes together accounts for its extraordinarily moving impact upon audiences. It was commissioned and first performed by the Pit Prop Theatre Company in Leigh, an ensemble widely recognized in the United Kingdom as one of the leading Theatre-in-Education companies in the country, where Mr. Duffield is the resident writer. The drama played to packed houses for months when it premiered in 1987 for audiences sixteen years and upwards.

One of the play's strongest points is its historical underpinnings since it is based on a true story. Indeed, it presents numerous opportunities for Theatre-in-Education companies to connect with schools and public institutions in researching and re-creating the historical context surrounding the play. The original production was replete with turn-of-the-century photographs, posters, news clippings and other historical materials that helped to inspire the audience's imaginations, and stimulated thought and commentary long after the curtain went down. And in the design of properties and costumes, as well as in the language challenges — German, Irish, English dialects — the drama is replete with historical and cultural layers that add extraordinary interest.

In addition, Neil Duffield's dramaturgy is refreshingly contemporary and presents strong challenges to producers, directors, designers and performers who would present the piece. Using a variety of theatrical styles — Brechtian epic theatre, music hall, realism, dream play, improvisation and actor/character transformations — the drama shifts the audience's attention both in time and space. It takes us, for example, from the north of England to Ireland and then to France; and it moves, not necessarily in chronological order, from the years before and during World War One to the late 1960s and up to the present day. *Lilford Mill* is thus not at all a "boring" history lesson but a stimulating and unpredictable journey in the magical context of the playhouse where audiences encounter history with tears, with romance, with humor, love and friendship.

But perhaps most challenging of all for theatre groups are the acting skills the play requires. Although the drama includes more than two dozen separate characters, these roles can all be played by only five young actors (or more, as the production ensemble desires). Additionally, Neil Duffield has carefully and clearly scored the mechanics of these role transformations into the script so that they become not just a convenient way to mount a play with only a small number of actors who might be available; they are crucial to one of the most central and recurring themes in the contemporary theatre: the interchangeability of human roles and the role-playing nature of all human experience.

Characters:

The play is written for five actors — 3 male, 2 female

Ghost of Liam Mulcahey, Dubliner in WWI British Army
Ghost of Friedrich Schmidt, a young WWI German POW
Ghost of Thomas Bekaan, a young WWI German POW
Nuala Mulcahey, young Dubliner, Liam's younger sister
Cissy Collins, young British labor union organizer

All other characters are played by these five, sometimes using cross-gender doubling.

Doubling:

Friedrich: Mrs. Harrison, Building Worker, Prison Governor, Anglo-Irish Lady, Englishman, Mr. Holroyd, Lad 1

Thomas: Mayor of Leigh, Building Worker, Prison Officer, Cathal, Magistrate, Lad 2, Soldier 2

Liam: Building Worker, Stonemason, Mrs. Standish, Gravedigger. Female Farmer, Picket

Nuala: Child Skipping, English Officer, Woman in Cemetery, Sentry

Cissy: Child Skipping, Maggie, German Officer, Soldier 1

Setting:

A multi-location set giving the overall impression of a P.O.W. camp

1   **ACT ONE**

2

3   *(Dim light, the two WOMEN sing gently Off-stage.)*

4   **WOMEN: It's a long way to Tipperary**

5   **It's a long way to go**

6   **It's a long way to Tipperary**

7   **To the sweetest girl I know**

8   **Goodbye Picadilly**

9   **Farewell Leicester Square**

10   **It's a long long way to Tipperary**

11   **But my heart's right there.**

12   *(During the song LIAM, THOMAS and FRIEDRICH march*

13   *On-stage. LIAM wears the uniform of a WWI British soldier*

14   *and carries a rifle. THOMAS and FRIEDRICH wear German*

15   *uniforms. The song ends. They stand to attention.)*

16   **THOMAS:** *(German accent)* **Thomas Bekaan. Corporal. 9th**

17   **Bavarian Infantry.**

18   **FRIEDRICH: Friedrich Wilhelm Karl Schmidt. Fusilier.**

19   **Funfunddreisigste Infanterie Regiment.**

20   **LIAM:** *(Dublin accent)* **All prisoners present and correct.**

21   *(Lights come up to full. Two young CHILDREN run in,*

22   *modern dress, laughing and playing. Start to turn a skipping*

23   *rope and chant.)*

24   **CHILDREN: England Ireland Germany**

25   **England Ireland Germany**

26   **England Ireland Germany ...**

27   *(The SOLDIERS relax. FRIEDRICH approaches the children,*

28   *indicates to the others he's going to skip. Jumps in. Starts*

29   *to skip.)*

30   **In the year of nineteen fifteen**

31   **Into the town of Leigh**

32   **Two thousand German prisoners**

33   **Crossed the Irish sea.**

34   **They came from Tipperary**

35   **A long long way to go**

1   **But why they were all brought here**
2   **No one seems to know.**
3   **In Lilford Mill they put them**
4   **With sentries all about**
5   **And big barbed wire fences**
6   **To stop them getting OUT!**
7   *(FRIEDRICH tries to get out. Fails. The CHILDREN run*
8   *around him laughing and coiling him in the rope. They run*
9   *to the first of four furled up flags on the set and start a hand-*
10   *clapping game.)*
11   **England Ireland Germany**
12   **Which flag is it going to be?**
13   **England Ireland Germany**
14   **Which flag is it going to be?**
15   *(The CHILDREN stop, look to FRIEDRICH. He consults*
16   *THOMAS.)*
17   **FRIEDRICH: Welches ist es?** *(THOMAS shrugs. Guessing:)*
18   **Deutschland!** *(The CHILDREN unfurl the flag. It's the union*
19   *jack. They chant and clap football style.)*
20   **CHILDREN: Engla-and** *(Clap-Clap-Clap)*
21   **Engla-and** *(Clap-Clap-Clap)*
22   **Engla-and** *(Clap-Clap-Clap)*
23   *(They exit, chanting and laughing. FRIEDRICH finishes*
24   *untangling himself from the rope. LIAM addresses the*
25   *audience.)*
26   **LIAM: So it's Lilford Mill you've come to hear about then? I**
27   **expect there'll be those of you who've never even heard of**
28   **it ... Who could blame you? You've come to the right place,**
29   **mind. There isn't much about Lilford Mill myself or the**
30   **Corporal can't tell you ... or Private Schmidt for that**
31   **matter – if there's any of yous can manage to understand**
32   **what he says.**
33   **FRIEDRICH: Was?** *(THOMAS motions him to be quiet.)*
34   **THOMAS: The mill stood in the town of Leigh. Beside the**
35   **canal. A few years ago you would have been able to see it**

1   for yourselves. It was nothing very impressive, you
2   understand. An ordinary weaving shed. In those days the
3   towns of Lancashire were full of such mills. Now of course
4   it is gone. All you can see of Lilford Mill is the ground on
5   which it stood ... children play games on it. *(He picks up*
6   *the skipping rope and tosses it Off-stage.)*
7 **LIAM:** But if you'd'a happened along on the morning of the
8   twentieth o' January, nineteen fourteen, you'd'a found the
9   exact same piece of empty ground ... and standing on it ...
10   the Mayor of Leigh ... *(Places a mayoral chain around*
11   *THOMAS' neck)* ... together with Mrs. T.D. Harrison ... *(Puts*
12   *a hat and fur on FRIEDRICH)* ... and assorted members of
13   the public. *(Indicates the audience.)*
14 **MAYOR:** *(Reading from prepared speech)* Ladies and
15   Gentlemen. It is my proud pleasure as Mayor of this
16   borough to welcome you all to this ceremony and to
17   extend my thanks to the directors and shareholders of the
18   Lilford Weaving Company for inviting me to officiate. I'm
19   sure I've no need to remind those present that the land on
20   which we are now standing has been purchased by the
21   Lilford Weaving Company for the construction of a
22   weaving shed. You'll be pleased to know that building
23   work is to commence immediately and the contractors are
24   confident the mill will be completed by the end of the
25   year. So without further ado, I shall call on our good lady
26   ... *(Indicates FRIEDRICH)* ... Mrs. T.D. Harrison, wife of the
27   Chairman to perform the ceremony. *(LIAM claps. Pushes*
28   *FRIEDRICH forward. THOMAS produces a spade.)* On
29   behalf of the Directors, it is my honour to present you,
30   Ma'am, with this engraved silver spade. I'm sure it will
31   remind you for many years to come of the day you used it
32   to cut the first sod at Lilford Mill. *(THOMAS hands the*
33   *spade to FRIEDRICH. FRIEDRICH doesn't know what to do.)*
34 **LIAM:** Cut the flaming sod, will you?
35 **FRIEDRICH:** Was?

1   **LIAM: Jesus! Will you never get it right?** *(THOMAS motions*
2   *FRIEDRICH to dig. He puts the spade against the earth.*
3   *Exasperated, LIAM grabs it from him.)*
4   **THOMAS: Irish temper perhaps?** *(LIAM doesn't like the remark.)*
5   **LIAM: Prisoners prepare for body search!** *(THOMAS and*
6   *FRIEDRICH take off their military jackets and caps. Dressed*
7   *in trousers and vests they spread their arms ready for body*
8   *search. LIAM starts to frisk FRIEDRICH.)*
9   **THOMAS: So ... The building of Lilford Mill began. Scaffolders,**
10   **bricklayers, plumbers, joiners ...**
11 **LIAM: I thought we agreed it was me who'd tell this part o' the**
12   **story.** *(THOMAS shuts up. LIAM finishes frisking*
13   *FRIEDRICH and starts on THOMAS.)* **So ... The building of**
14   **Lilford Mill began. Scaffolders, bricklayers, plumbers,**
15   **joiners ...**
16 **FRIEDRICH:** *(Enthusiastically to the audience)* **Vor dem Kreig**
17   **war ich Bauarbeiter.**
18 **THOMAS:** *(Translating)* **Friedrich was a building worker –**
19   **before the war.**
20 **LIAM: Will the two of yous kindly allow me to –**
21 **FRIEDRICH:** *(Continuing)* **Ich war Handlangar! Zugleich zwolf**
22   **Zieglen in meinem Morteltrog!**
23 **THOMAS: A hod carrier. Friedrich could carry twelve bricks at**
24   **a time in his hod.**
25 **LIAM: This has nothing whatever to do with –**
26 **FRIEDRICH: Die Leiter hinauf und am Baugerust entlang.**
27 **THOMAS: Up ladders. Along scaffolding.** *(LIAM throws off his*
28   *cap in frustration.)*
29 **FRIEDRICH: Starke Arme und Beine.**
30 **THOMAS: Strong arms and legs.**
31 **LIAM: I'm trying to tell these people about the building of**
32   **Lilford Mill!**
33 **FRIEDRICH: Ich war in der Bauarbeitergewerkschaft!**
34 **THOMAS: A member of the building workers' trade union!**
35   *(FRIEDRICH starts to sing the "Internationale" in German.)*

1   **LIAM:** Prisoner will remain silent!

2   **FRIEDRICH:** Was?

3   **THOMAS:** *(Laughing)* **Shhhh.** *(In despair LIAM pulls off his*

4   *military jacket and sits down. Lighting change. CISSY and*

5   *NUALA appear at a distance from the three men whom they*

6   *see as building workers. The two WOMEN are dressed in*

7   *1914 period costume. NUALA has a Dublin accent.)*

8   **CISSY:** We've come at a good time. It looks like they're on

9   dinner.

10 **NUALA:** You're not just going to walk in there, are you?

11 **CISSY:** Well I can't see me being able talk to them from here.

12 **NUALA:** Will they join?

13 **CISSY:** I don't know. I've never tried recruiting men before.

14 **NUALA:** You never told me that.

15 **CISSY:** Don't let 'em rattle you. Look 'em straight in the eye.

16 **NUALA:** What if they won't listen?

17 **CISSY:** Look. Why don't you go home? I'll be fine on my own.

18   I'm used to this.

19 **NUALA:** No.... No. I said I'd help and I will.

20 **CISSY:** Unfurl the flag then.

21 **NUALA:** What?

22 **CISSY:** The banner. *(NUALA unfurls the second of the four flags*

23   *on the set. A large red banner. They start to move over to the*

24   *three building workers.)*

25 **WORKER 1:** What the?

26 **WORKER 2:** Will you look at this.

27 **WORKER 3:** *(Whistles)* I wouldn't say no to a handful of that.

28 **WORKER 2:** Over here, darling. Looking for a job are you?

29 **WORKER 3:** I'll give her one. No trouble. *(They laugh.)*

30 **NUALA:** What're we going to do?

31 **CISSY:** Leave it to me. *(She approaches them.)* **This the Lilford**

32   **Mill site, is it?**

33 **WORKER 3:** No, sweetheart. It's Buckingham Palace. *(They all*

34   *laugh.)*

35 **CISSY:** Oh, I'm very sorry. I didn't realise. We've come to the

1   wrong place clearly.

2   WORKER 3: That's alright. We're just starting the tea-party,

3   aren't we. Lads? Come and join us.

4   CISSY: No, thanks. I'm not a great one for royalty. Anyway

5   there's a thief to catch. Come on, Nuala. *(She turns to leave.)*

6   WORKER 2: What? Hey, no. Hang on. Don't go ... What thief?

7   CISSY: You haven't heard? There's a pickpocket on the Lilford

8   Mill site. They say he's stealing from every man on the job.

9   Enjoy your party.

10   WORKER 3: Hey. Wait. What is this? Who are you? What're you

11   on about?

12   CISSY: I told you. We're after a thief.

13   WORKER 2: What thief? Where?

14   CISSY: Have a look in your pocket. You're just the sort he'd

15   rob. Check how much you've lost. *(The three MEN share*

16   *perplexed glances.)*

17   WORKER 2: Is this some sort of joke?

18   CISSY: It is for him. I should imagine he's laughing all the way

19   to the bank.

20   WORKER 3: Well, he'll not die laughing with what he finds

21   in these pockets. *(Pulls them out to reveal nothing. They all*

22   *laugh.)*

23   CISSY: Oh, don't underestimate him, friend. This thief is no

24   ordinary pickpocket. He's cleverer than you think. He

25   steals your money even before you get it.

26   WORKER 1: She's a bible thumper. Pound to a penny. There's no

27   chapel lovers here, darling. You're wasting your breath.

28   CISSY: God won't punish the thief I'm talking about, brother.

29   You'll have to catch this one for yourselves.

30   WORKER 3: A suffragette. That's what she is. A bloody

31   suffragette.

32   CISSY: You're getting closer. How much do you get paid?

33   WORKER 3: What?

34   CISSY: How much? Eightpence an hour?

35   WORKER 2: Eightpence an hour. You must be joking.

1   CISSY: How much then? Come on. Seven ... ? Six ... ? Six. I was
2   right then, wasn't I? You are being robbed. Every one of
3   you. Tuppence for every hour you spend here. And guess
4   who's doing the robbing. *(The penny drops.)*
5   WORKER 1: Oh ... Clever. Very clever ... You had me fooled for
6   a minute there.
7   WORKER 2: So you know all about building workers' wages
8   then, do you?
9   CISSY: I know the union minimum is eightpence an hour.
10 WORKER 3: If there's owt worse than a suffragette it's a bloody
11   socialist. Look, luv, I don't want to be rude or anything but
12   you might as well clear off. You're wasting your time here.
13   Nobody wants to join a union and there's nothing you can
14   tell us about it we haven't heard before.
15 CISSY: So you're happy being robbed every day? Is that what
16   you're saying?
17 WORKER 2: There's no way this lot'll ever pay eightpence an
18   hour. Not in a million years.
19 CISSY: Funny you should say that. It's exactly what they said in
20   Wigan – till they joined the union. Do you know what
21   they're on now?
22 WORKER 1: She knows her stuff, I'll give her that.
23 WORKER 3: She's talking rubbish ... So it's strikers you're
24   after making of us, is it? Like that lot in Wigan? Well just
25   answer me this, Miss Whatever-your-name-is ... after we've
26   all joined this union of yours and all downed tools, what's
27   to stop the bosses sacking the lot of us and bringing in a
28   fresh gang? You think there aren't enough men out there
29   who'd do it?
30 CISSY: How many of you are there? Fifty? Sixty ... ? You picket.
31   You stand outside the gates and you picket.
32 WORKER 3: Oh, picket! Now I see! Now I get it! It's easy then,
33   isn't it! We just stand outside the gates and stop the others
34   coming in! No problem ... ! So answer me this, comrade ...
35   when three van loads of coppers arrive with truncheons

1   swinging, where will you and your friend be? You'll just

2   breeze along with some of your fancy patter and talk 'em

3   into leaving us alone, will you? Is that the plan?

4 CISSY: It isn't forced to happen like that.

5 WORKER 3: Oh, isn't it? Well you must know something about

6   the police I don't. Got inside information have you?

7   They'll just stand around and watch will they? Nice cosy

8   chat?

9 CISSY: It doesn't have to end in violence.

10 WORKER 3: Oh that's reassuring. Well, let's just say for a

11   moment you're wrong. What's the plan then? What do you

12   and your not-very-talkative friend here intend doing to

13   stop us getting our heads smashed in?

14 CISSY: Strikes can be organised peacefully. Violence doesn't

15   come into it.

16 WORKER 3: Don't give me that. I've seen it. I know. Just tell us

17   where the two of you will be when the punches start flying.

18 CISSY: You don't understand what I'm saying to you. It's a

19   matter of –

20 NUALA: Here! We'll be here! We'll both be here!

21 CISSY: What?

22 NUALA: You're frightened of truncheons? I don't blame you!

23   I've seen 'em! And he's right, Cissy! They'll come! They

24   always come. Big men in helmets. Blue uniforms.

25   Running. Swinging. Kicking. Hitting. Swearing at you.

26   Dragging at your hair. Tearing your clothes. Ripping the

27   buttons from your coat. I've seen it. I've seen it like he has.

28   And if you think the policemen in Dublin are any

29   different to the ones here you're wrong. You're wrong!

30 CISSY: Nuala, what are you saying? You don't understand.

31   Leave it to me, will you?

32 NUALA: I don't understand ... ? No. I don't suppose I do. I don't

33   understand any of it. I never did ... One minute it's quiet.

34   Peaceful. Just standing there listening to the speakers.

35   The next minute it's like some kind of nightmare. *(Pause.*

1 *She looks round. The MEN watch her, stunned by her*
2 *sudden outburst.)* **Things scattered around in the street. A**
3 **green purse. A silver watch. A pair of spectacles. A bag of**
4 **shopping.   A boy running, clutching his bundle of**
5 **newspapers. A woman. Grey hair. Trying to get out of the**
6 **way. I saw this policeman behind her. His truncheon**
7 **raised. Filthy words pouring out of his mouth. I saw the**
8 **woman turn ... There was this little book. It dropped from**
9 **her hand as she fell. I wanted to pick it up. Save it for her.**
10 **But I couldn't. I couldn't move. There was nowhere to go,**
11 **you see. No way out. People pushed. Screamed. They**
12 **yelled for mercy. It was all useless. There was nothing**
13 **anybody could do. And the truncheons just kept on.**
14 **Battering. Battering. On and on. I huddled down inside a**
15 **shop doorway. I didn't look. I watched that little book as it**
16 **was gradually ripped to pieces. I wasn't part of it, you see.**
17 **I wasn't a striker. I wasn't even in a union. I'd only stopped**
18 **to listen for a minute. I was out shopping for Madam.**
19 *(Pause)*
20 **WORKER 1: It's alright, lass. Just take it easy, eh.**
21 **NUALA: I will be here when the police arrive ... I will. And so**
22 **will she.**
23 **WORKER 1: Aye. Aye, that's alright.** *(Lighting change. WORKER*
24 *2 puts his uniform back on and becomes LIAM.)*
25 **LIAM: Inspection of prisoners' equipment!** *(CISSY and NUALA*
26 *exit. THOMAS and FRIEDRICH put their jackets back on and*
27 *start to lay out their equipment.)*
28 **LIAM:** *(To the audience)* **So there you have it. Socialism. Some**
29 **say that's what it was all about. Oh, don't sneer. It wasn't**
30 **the same then. Socialism was a word you could use. Not**
31 **the dreary old-fashioned conversation-stopper it's**
32 **become now. Strikes, trade unions, even revolution.**
33 **That's the sort of stuff people talked about in those days.**
34 **They still had hope then, God love 'em.**
35 **THOMAS: In Germany it was the same. We had the largest**

1   socialist party in the world.

2   **FRIEDRICH:** Eine socialisten ich war.

3   **THOMAS:** Friedrich himself was a member.

4   **FRIEDRICH:** Socialisten Party von Deutschland.

5   **LIAM:** I think we've had enough interruptions for one day,

6   comrade. *(THOMAS stifles a giggle.)* **Where's your spoon?**

7   **FRIEDRICH:** Was?

8   **LIAM:** Your spoon! Where's your bloody spoon? *(FRIEDRICH*

9   *searches for his spoon as lights crossfade to Cissy's house.*

10   *Small working-class interior with some evidence of her work*

11   *as a trade union organizer. NUALA is sitting at a table putting*

12   *a letter into an envelope. CISSY enters, takes off her coat.)*

13 **CISSY:** Letters home, is it?

14 **NUALA:** My mother ... I promised her I'd write once I'd found a

15   job and somewhere to stay. I'd not got round to it till now.

16   How was your day?

17 **CISSY:** Oh, alright ... I've just come from Lilford Mill.

18 **NUALA:** How are they doing? Still holding out, are they?

19 **CISSY:** No. No, they're not ... As a matter of fact it's over.

20 **NUALA:** What?

21 **CISSY:** It's all finished. They're back at work.

22 **NUALA:** But they can't be ... What? You mean all of them?

23 **CISSY:** Not a one left out.

24 **NUALA:** I don't believe it. How can they? They've only been out a

25   week. Didn't you try and stop them? Didn't you talk to them?

26 **CISSY:** What was the point? They'd already taken the vote. It

27   was unanimous.

28 **NUALA:** And after all you've done. All the time you spent there.

29   Recruiting. Organising. And they hadn't even the guts to

30   stick it out for a few –

31 **CISSY:** Nuala, they won.

32 **NUALA:** What?

33 **CISSY:** They won.

34 **NUALA:** Won?

35 **CISSY:** The company's agreed to give them the minimum.

1 NUALA: What? ... Oh, you rotten ... Cissy! You rotten tease! Why
2   did you let me —
3 CISSY: Eightpence an hour! A shilling overtime! And full
4   recognition for the union!
5 NUALA: No police?
6 CISSY: No police. No truncheons. No riots. The men are all
7   asking after you.
8 NUALA: Me?
9 CISSY: You were the reason they joined. You must go, Nuala, go
10   and see them. They can't believe it. They're over the moon.
11   Oh, wait till the word gets round. Wait till people hear.
12   Every building site in the town'll want to join after this!
13 NUALA: That's wonderful news. I'd say you were going to be
14   kept busy then.
15 CISSY: You too! It was you they listened to. You who gave them
16   the courage ... Something's in the air, Nuala. Not just
17   round here. It's everywhere. Even the bosses can sense it.
18   The great sleeping giant of the working class is beginning
19   to stir. And when that begins to happen nothing on earth
20   will stand in its way. The railwaymen, the transport men,
21   the miners. At long last they're coming together. Wait till
22   the autumn. You'll see something then. A general strike
23   yes ... but that'll just be the beginning – the spark that
24   lights the flame. It'll grow into a struggle the like of which
25   the world has never seen.
26 NUALA: I'd better get down to the post office.
27 CISSY: The end of capitalism. That's what we're talking about,
28   Nuala. That's what we're witnessing. The final agony. And
29   after that who knows what life will be like? A chance to
30   build the sort of world people could only ever dream
31   about. Oh, think of all those generations of men and
32   women who've fought and battled and lost...and now here
33   we are, us, on the very verge of victory.
34 NUALA: I'm happy for you Cissy.
35 CISSY: It'll need work. We can't afford to be complacent.

1   Nothing's inevitable, not even socialism ... You'll help
2   won't you? You'll be part of it?

3 NUALA: I don't know.

4 CISSY: But you can't keep out of it! You're too valuable. That
5   day at the building site —

6 NUALA: You're the socialist, Cissy.

7 CISSY: But you're with us. I know you are. We're going to need
8   everyone we can get, Nuala. It's our one chance to change
9   everything. Not just work. Not just wages. Everything.
10   Every aspect of our lives. A few months, that's all I'm
11   talking about. The autumn. That's when it'll happen.

12 NUALA: I might not be here in the autumn.

13 CISSY: What ... ? What do you mean?

14 NUALA: I mean I might have to leave.

15 CISSY: But you've only been here a few months ... What is it ... ?
16   The rent? Look, Nuala, if you're finding it too much I can
17   always —

18 NUALA: The rent's fine. I'm very grateful to you for taking me
19   in. You've been very kind.

20 CISSY: Then what? What is it?

21 NUALA: I may have to go home.

22 CISSY: Has something happened? Your family? It's not ... ?

23 NUALA: No. Nothing like that.

24 CISSY: What then? Talk to me, Nuala ... .What's the matter?
25   What's happened?

26 NUALA: Nothing. I'm Irish, Cissy, that's all that's happened.

27 CISSY: I don't understand. What do you mean Irish?

28 NUALA: I knew I wouldn't be able to explain it to you.

29 CISSY: You mean you're homesick? Nuala, you're bound to feel
30   that. Everybody feels like that when they first —

31 NUALA: *(Sharply)* I'm not homesick! *(Pause)*

32 CISSY: Nuala, it doesn't matter where you come from.
33   Nationality isn't what counts.

34 NUALA: Isn't it?

35 CISSY: You're a woman. A working class woman. That's all that

1   matters. The same as me. Stay. Give yourself more time.

2 NUALA: And what about what's happening in Ireland?

3 CISSY: It's not that is it ... ? Catholics against Protestants?

4 NUALA: *(Suddenly angry)* It's not religion! It's never been

5   about religion!

6 CISSY: What is it about then ... ? People killing each other!

7 NUALA: Oh, fine ... ! I have a brother the same as you. No

8   violence. Peaceful means ... The English locked him away

9   for eight years for a crime he didn't commit! *(Pause)*

10 CISSY: Nuala ... let's not fall out with each other. It's been such

11   a lovely day and ...

12 NUALA: ... and Ireland's not worth falling out over, is it? *(She*

13   *exits.)*

14 LIAM: *(To the audience)* Now at this point in the proceedings

15   there'll be those of yous who may be wondering just what

16   in the name of Jesus have the troubles in Ireland to do

17   with a weaving shed in Lancashire ...

18 THOMAS: A great deal. As you will eventually see.

19 LIAM: The corporal considers himself a bit of an expert on the

20   history of Anglo-Irish relations.

21 THOMAS: Of course. You British robbed the Irish of their

22   land, turned them out of their homes, starved them,

23   drove them into exile, locked them in your pri –

24 LIAM: Alright. They've heard it ... Get on with the story, Corporal.

25 THOMAS: It is August, 1914. With Lilford Mill only half built ...

26 LIAM: ... and the country about to be engulfed in socialist

27   revolution ... *(FRIEDRICH unfurls the German flag.)*

28 FRIEDRICH: Deutschland! *(Applause)*

29   Deutschland! *(Applause)*

30   Deutschland! *(Applause)*

31 THOMAS: War changed everything, of course – as wars

32   usually do. People very quickly forgot about Lilford Mill.

33 LIAM: Socialist revolution, too.

34 THOMAS: The war, of course, you all know about. We need

35   only say that several months after it began, the British

1   discovered they had a problem — they had nowhere to put
2   their German prisoners.

3   **LIAM:** And that was when some bright spark remembered
4   Lilford Mill.

5   **THOMAS:** So you see what happened.

6   **LIAM:** *(Indicating the set)* Fences. Barbed wire. Sentry towers.
7   And a brand new name — *(Opens his mouth to announce it.*
8   *FRIEDRICH beats him to it.)*

9   **FRIEDRICH:** Kriegsgefangenenlager — Leigh!

10   **LIAM:** Inspection of prisoners' bedding! *(FRIEDRICH and*
11   *THOMAS unroll blankets.)*

12   **THOMAS:** It was the month of February when we arrived at
13   Lilford Mill.

14   **FRIEDRICH:** Sehr kalt!

15   **THOMAS:** Two thousand of us. One blanket for each prisoner.
16   The regulations said two, but we had only one ... *(He stops*
17   *and looks to LIAM to continue, but LIAM appears to be*
18   *obsessed with FRIEDRICH's blanket. THOMAS gives him a*
19   *prompt.)* ... but we had only one.

20   **LIAM:** *(Holding up the blanket)* Will you look at the state o' this!

21   **THOMAS:** *(Making the decision to carry on regardless)* They
22   brought us from Ireland where we had spent the last
23   three months.

24   **LIAM:** This is disgusting! *(Hurls the blanket to the floor. Eyes*
25   *FRIEDRICH.)*

26   **THOMAS:** *(Departing from the agreed story)* We could not
27   understand why Irishmen saw us as their enemies ...

28   **LIAM:** I can see I'm going to have to give you something of an
29   education, Fritz.

30   **THOMAS:** ... or why they chose to wear the uniform of the
31   British!

32   **LIAM:** We agreed there'd be no mention of any of that!

33   **THOMAS:** And fight on the side of their greatest enemy.

34   **LIAM:** Prisoners to report for Roll Call! Attention! Corporal
35   Bekaan!

1   THOMAS: *(Steps forward a pace)* **Thomas Bekaan. Corporal.**
2   **9th Bavarian Infantry.**
3   LIAM: **Tell the audience what happened to you, Corporal.**
4   THOMAS: **I am sorry?**
5   LIAM: **I'm sure they'd all be very interested.**
6   THOMAS: **We agreed there'd be no mention of —**
7   LIAM: **We agreed? Oh, we agreed, did we?** *(Pause. THOMAS*
8   *begins.)*
9   THOMAS: **I was captured during the first few weeks of the war**
10   **at La Fere in France.**
11   LIAM: **Go on.**
12   THOMAS: **The British took us to Ireland. To a place called**
13   **Templemore.**
14   LIAM: **For those of you who aren't familiar, that's in Tipperary.**
15   THOMAS: **They kept us in an old army barracks ... This is not**
16   **what we agreed!**
17   LIAM: **Continue, Corporal.** *(Slight pause. He continues.)*
18   THOMAS: **After several months the British decided to transfer**
19   **us from Ireland to Lilford Mill. They told us it was because**
20   **of the lavatories ... Why are you doing this?**
21   LIAM: **And when you arrived ...**
22   THOMAS: **I stayed here at Lilford Mill for almost four years ...**
23   **until the war ended.**
24   LIAM: **And then?**
25   THOMAS: **Two weeks after Armistice Day ...**
26   LIAM: **Just as you were about to be sent home to Germany ...**
27   **Go on ... Tell them.**
28   THOMAS: **Thomas Bekaan. Corporal. 9th Bavarian Infantry.**
29   **Died of influenza. Buried with full military honours.**
30   **Leigh Cemetery.**
31   LIAM: **Survived four years of war and died o' flu. Now**
32   **wouldn't you say that was the worst kind o' luck a man**
33   **could ever have?**
34   THOMAS: **Why don't you tell them what happened to Friedrich!**
35   FRIEDRICH: *(Stepping forward)* **Friedrich Wilhelm Karl**

1   Schmidt. Fusilier. Funfunddreisigste Infanterie Regiment.

2   LIAM: What happened to him had nothing to do with me!

3   THOMAS: Ah.

4   LIAM: You know damn fine it didn't!

5   THOMAS: In that case, tell them what happened to yourself.

6   LIAM: I'm the one who gives the orders around here, Corporal!

7   THOMAS: And why should that be?

8   LIAM: Because I'm the one with the ... *(He realises he's left the*

9   *rifle leaning against the set. FRIEDRICH beats him to it,*

10   *grabs it, and immediately levels it at LIAM. The situation*

11   *visibly changes.)*

12   THOMAS: Prisoner will report for Roll Call.

13   LIAM: I hope you aren't being serious.

14   FRIEDRICH: Achtung! Schnell! *(LIAM stands to attention.)*

15   LIAM: Private Liam Mulcahey. Infantryman. 35th Leinster

16   Regiment.

17   THOMAS: Tell the audience your story, Private.

18   LIAM: What?

19   THOMAS: You can begin by telling them why you joined the

20   British Army. *(LIAM ignores this. FRIEDRICH threatens*

21   *with the rifle.)*

22   FRIEDRICH: Sprechen sie.

23   LIAM: I joined the army in Dublin.

24   THOMAS: I did not ask you to tell them where you joined, I

25   asked you to tell them why.

26   LIAM: They sent me to Templemore as a guard at the prisoner

27   of war camp.

28   THOMAS: Are you refusing?

29   LIAM: I came to Lilford Mill when the prisoners were

30   transferred from Ireland.

31   THOMAS: Very well. If you will not tell them why you joined

32   the British, tell them the reason we were transferred from

33   Ireland.

34   LIAM: They'll have to work that out for themselves.

35   THOMAS: So you will tell them nothing? *(To the audience:)*

1   **Private Mulcahey did not stay very long at Lilford Mill.**

2   **Along with the rest of his regiment he was sent to France.**

3   **He served a year in the trenches and then ...**

4 **LIAM: I was brought before a military court martial!** *(Pause)*

5 **THOMAS: You are ashamed of your actions?**

6 **LIAM: Found guilty of treason and desertion.**

7 **THOMAS: Good. That unfortunately brings us to the end of**

8   **Private Mulcahey's story. Firing party at the ready.**

9   *(FRIEDRICH presents arms.)* **Do you have anything to say?**

10 **LIAM:** *(Draws himself up to attention)* **Liam Mulcahey ...**

11   **Volunteer ... Irish Republican Army.** *(The final flag of the*

12   *four is unfurled — the Irish ticolour. The four flags remain as*

13   *a permanent part of the set for the rest of the play.)*

14 **THOMAS: Take aim!** *(FRIEDRICH aims the rifle at LIAM. LIAM*

15   *braces himself for the final shot. A pause as we wait for*

16   *THOMAS to give the order.)*

17 **THOMAS: Before the war began, you lived in Dublin, yes?**

18 **LIAM: Jesus, do you never give up!**

19 **THOMAS: It is part of the story. How else can they learn about**

20   **Lilford Mill?**

21 **MAGGIE:** *(Off-stage)* **Liam!**

22 **THOMAS: That is your mother, is it not?** *(THOMAS motions*

23   *LIAM to a different area of the set where there is a rough bed*

24   *next to a door. LIAM refuses to move.)*

25 **FRIEDRICH:** *(Threatening him with the rifle)* **Bewegen sie!**

26   *(LIAM takes off his jacket and cap as lights dim on the three*

27   *soldiers. A spotlight fades up on NUALA elsewhere on the*

28   *set. She sings unaccompanied.)*

29 **NUALA: At Boolavogue as the sun was setting**

30   **O'er the bright May meadows of Shelmalier**

31   **A rebel hand set the heather blazing**

32   **And brought the neighbours from far and near.**

33   **Then Father Murphy from old Kilcormack**

34   **Spurred up the rocks with a warning cry**

35   **"Arm, arm," he cried, "for I've come to lead you**

1   For Ireland's freedom we'll fight or die."

2   *(During the song FRIEDRICH exits. LIAM seats himself on*

3   *the bed. Lights fade down on NUALA and up on LIAM.*

4   *THOMAS watches the scene from elsewhere in half-light.*

5   *MAGGIE enters through the door. LIAM immediately*

6   *springs to attention, startling MAGGIE. LIAM sees who it is,*

7   *relaxes, sits down again. MAGGIE feels the cold of the room.)*

8 **MAGGIE:** *(Dublin accent)* **Aren't you cold sitting up here, Liam?**

9   **It's freezing.** *(He doesn't react.)* **We have the fire lit**

10   **downstairs. You could sit in the warm with myself and**

11   **Nuala.** *(Still no reaction.)* **I saw Cathal in Dublin. He looks**

12   **grand. They're a great sight alright, marching along there.**

13   **Do you not want to see them? They've even their picture**

14   **in the paper.** *(Shows it to him. He doesn't look.)* **"Irish**

15   **volunteers demand Home Rule." You'd be proud. He was**

16   **asking after you ... wondering when you'll be starting**

17   **going to the meetings again.** *(Pause)* **Would you like me to**

18   **sit with you a while?**

19 **LIAM: I'm alright, mother. Go back to Nuala.**

20 **MAGGIE: I'll make your bed before I go.** *(Moves to do it.)*

21 **LIAM:** *(Very sharply)* **No!** *(She stops, alarmed by him. He softens*

22   *a bit.)* **It's my job ... It's not time yet.**

23 **MAGGIE: Time?** *(Pause)* **I'll be downstairs with Nuala if you need**

24   **me.** *(She exits, shutting the door after her. He immediately*

25   *regrets upsetting her. After a few moments, calls out.)*

26 **LIAM: Mother ... ! Mother!** *(No response. He approaches the*

27   *door, stretches his hand nervously towards the handle. His*

28   *hand begins to shake and tremble. He touches the handle*

29   *with his whole arm and begins to shake violently. He is*

30   *unable to open the door. Gives up. Wrenches his hand away.*

31   *Returns to the bed.)*

32 **THOMAS: Why was it you could not open the door of your**

33   **bedroom?**

34 **LIAM: If you'd spent eight years in an English prison you'd not**

35   **even ask such a stupid question!**

1   **THOMAS: Of course. The English prison. We must tell the**
2   **audience about that too.** *(Takes off his jacket and cap.)*
3   **LIAM: That has nothing to do with Lilford Mill!**
4   **THOMAS:** *(Putting on prisoner's officer jacket and cap)* **On the**
5   **contrary. Lilford Mill was itself an English Prison – for**
6   **myself and Friedrich.** *(Lighting change. THOMAS enters*
7   *Liam's bedroom. Welsh accent:)* **Prisoner K561! On your feet!**
8   *(LIAM stands.)* **Stand to attention in the presence of a prison**
9   **officer!** *(LIAM straightens.)* **At the double! Quick! March!**
10   **Left right left right left right ...** *(He marches LIAM rapidly to*
11   *a different area of the set. FRIEDRICH appears dressed as a*
12   *prison governor.)* **Halt! Prisoner K561 reporting. Sir!**
13   **GOVERNOR: Mulcahey ... We never seem to see an end to you**
14   **Irish terrorists, do we.**
15   **LIAM: I'm no terror –** *(The OFFICER thumps him in the*
16   *kidneys. He doubles up in pain.)*
17   **OFFICER: Speak when you're told and stand to attention in**
18   **the presence of the governor!**
19   **GOVERNOR: I'll be brief, Mulcahey. As long as you're in this**
20   **prison you'll be subject to special rules, the most**
21   **important of which is the rule of silence. At no time will**
22   **you be permitted to speak to or communicate with any**
23   **other prisoner. Any attempt to do so will result in**
24   **punishment. If for any reason you wish to speak to a prison**
25   **officer, you will first raise your hand and wait in silence**
26   **until the officer gives his permission. Is that clear?** *(LIAM*
27   *raises his hand.)* **Permission denied. Take him to his cell.**
28   **OFFICER: Prisoner K561! Abo ... out turn! Qui ... ck march! Left**
29   **right left right left right left right ...** *(Marches LIAM back to*
30   *the bedroom.)* **Halt!** *(LIAM stands at attention. The OFFICER*
31   *relaxes. Takes stock of LIAM.)* **Well, Michael. Here we are.**
32   **This is where you spend the next eight years ... if you**
33   **manage to last that long. It's quite a pleasant little cell is**
34   **this. Too pleasant some would say. People don't like it if we**
35   **let things get too pleasant, see? If things got too pleasant**

1   we'd have every idle paddy in the country clamouring to get

2   in here, wouldn't we? That wouldn't do now, would it?

3   We've got enough of you lot already. *(LIAM'S face betrays*

4   *some interest.)* Oh, you didn't think you was the only one,

5   did you? We've had dozens like you. All as thick as pudding.

6   Do you know what happens to them – all these fellow

7   countrymen of yours – once they get in here? They lose

8   their wits ... Every one of them. Go mad as bleeding hatters.

9   *(Pause)* Do you know what it's like, Michael, not being able

10   to speak to anyone? Day after day? Week after week? Year

11   after year? 'Course you can always talk to yourself. That's

12   what they do. We've heard 'em jabbering on for hours some

13   nights. Laugh? They've had us in tears. *(Pause)* "They'll

14   never drive me insane." That's what you're thinking, isn't

15   it? "Not me. Never me." I wonder, Michael. I wonder if the

16   name Gallagher means anything to you ... ? It does so. Good.

17   You know who I'm on about then. Gallagher had this cell,

18   Michael. I can see him now, sitting on that bed snivelling

19   and whimpering, chewing on his blanket. The man

20   couldn't even pee straight. Do you know what happened to

21   him? Gallagher? We found him one day in the carpenter's

22   shop. He was kneeling on the floor and he had this little

23   wooden board there in front of him. On it was a pile of

24   something that looked like salt. There he was stuffing it

25   into his mouth. Great handfuls of it. Swallowing down into

26   his stomach. Do you know what it was, Michael ... ? Glass.

27   Crushed glass. Now I ask you, who in the world but a

28   paddy'd eat glass? "You carry on eating that and you're

29   going to kill yourself." I says to him. Do you know what he

30   turns round to me and says? *(Mimicking Irish accent:)* "A

31   pound of it'd do you no harm." *(Laughs loudly.)* A pound of

32   it'd do you no harm! *(Pause)* You'll end up the same,

33   Michael. Same as Gallagher. One year. Two if you're tough.

34   But we'll break you ... We'll break you piece by piece. *(He*

35   *exits leaving LIAM standing at attention. Lighting Change.*

1   *The door opens and NUALA enters. LIAM remains at*
2   *attention, unaware of her.)*
3 **NUALA:** **Liam.** *(He doesn't move.)* **Liam, it's alright.** *(She takes*
4   *hold of him, sits him on the bed.)* **Look around you. See**
5   **where you are.**
6 **LIAM:** **Nuala.**
7 **NUALA:** **Liam, it isn't good shutting yourself in here day in day**
8   **out. You need to get out. You need to talk to people.**
9 **LIAM:** **No.**
10 **NUALA:** **You've seen no one since you got out of prison. You're**
11   **not giving yourself chance to —**
12 **LIAM:** **I said no!**
13 **NUALA:** **There are things happening outside. Things you used**
14   **to be part of.**
15 **LIAM:** **Now is that a fact?**
16 **NUALA:** **You could at least look for work. Jobs aren't easy after**
17   **the strike but it'd get you out of the —**
18 **LIAM:** **Nuala, will you stop trying to push me around! I'm**
19   **alright. I like it here.**
20 **NUALA:** **I just don't like seeing you —**
21 **LIAM:** **Aren't you going to be late for work?**
22 **NUALA:** *(Managing to contain her impatience)* **I'm trying to help.**
23 **LIAM:** **You're a young girl, Nuala. There are things you don't**
24   **know. Things you don't understand.**
25 **NUALA:** *(Angry)* **I'll be going then. I'll see you later.** *(She exits,*
26   *leaving the door open. LIAM crosses over, carefully closes it,*
27   *lies down on the bed. Lights dim on LIAM and fade up on*
28   *NUALA as she enters a different area of the set, dressed in*
29   *maid's cap and pinny carrying a tray of tea things. She places*
30   *them on a table and pours out a cup of tea. FRIEDRICH*
31   *enters dressed as a well-heeled Anglo-Irish LADY.)*
32 **NUALA:** **Tea's all ready Ma'am.**
33 **LADY:** **Thank you, Nuala.**
34 **NUALA:** **Will that be all then, Ma'am?**
35 **LADY:** **I'd like you to wait a few moments if you will.**

1 **NUALA: Yes, Ma'am.** *(Pause. The LADY takes her time. Helps*
2   *herself to tea. NUALA stands by.)*
3 **LADY: What is your opinion of Home Rule, Nuala?**
4 **NUALA: Ma'am?**
5 **LADY: These Irish Volunteers with their green uniforms and**
6   **wooden rifles. You've seen them?**
7 **NUALA: I don't concern myself too much with political**
8   **matters, Ma'am.**
9 **LADY: Do you know what would happen, Nuala, if the**
10   **government were to allow Ireland to rule itself?**
11 **NUALA: No, Ma'am.**
12 **LADY: Every country in the Empire would want the same**
13   **thing. India, Africa, China, the West Indies. Do you**
14   **understand what I'm saying, Nuala?**
15 **NUALA: I think so, Ma'am.**
16 **LADY: I understand your brother is at liberty once more.**
17 **NUALA: He's been at home a few weeks now, Ma'am.**
18 **LADY: I'm surprised your mother tolerates him under her**
19   **roof.**
20 **NUALA: Ma'am, my brother was innocent. He did none o'**
21   **those things they said he did.**
22 **LADY: Nuala, if every criminal who professed his —**
23 **NUALA:** *(Angry)* **My brother is not a —** *(She checks herself.)*
24 **LADY: Yes?**
25 **NUALA: Nothing, Ma'am.**
26 **LADY: These are anxious times, Nuala. With talk of civil war in**
27   **the air it is hardly reassuring to find possible terrorist**
28   **connections within one's own household. I hope you**
29   **understand my meaning.** *(No reply)* **Well?**
30 **NUALA: I think I know what you're saying, Ma'am.**
31 **LADY: You may of course finish your work for today, but as**
32   **from tomorrow you may consider yourself free to look for**
33   **other employment.**
34 **NUALA: Will that be all then, Ma'am?**
35 **LADY: Clear these things away, please. I've quite finished.**

1   *(The LADY exits. NUALA clears away the tea things. Lights*
2   *crossfade back to LIAM, lying on his bed. The door opens, the*
3   *PRISON OFFICER enters. He draws his truncheon and*
4   *smashes it violently against the side of Liam's bed. LIAM*
5   *instantly leaps out.)*

6   **OFFICER: Inspection of prisoner's bedding.** *(LIAM is clearly*
7   *disoriented and desperate for sleep.)* **Stand to attention,**
8   **K561!** *(LIAM does his best.)* **You've been sleeping again,**
9   **haven't you, Michael? How many times have I told you?**
10   **Sleeping is no good for you. Makes you lazy. That's the**
11   **trouble with you lot, isn't it ... ? Nothing but sleep. Sleep**
12   **your bloody lives away if we let you, wouldn't you?** *(He*
13   *examines the bed.)* **Will you look at the state of this!** *(Hurls*
14   *it to the floor.)* **This is disgusting!** *(His movements mirror*
15   *those of LIAM in the previous scene.)* **I can see I'm going to**
16   **have to give you something of an education, Michael.**
17   **Teach you a few of the basics of civilisation. This bed**
18   **you're privileged to be using is the property of His Majesty**
19   **the King. And who knows? One day he might take into his**
20   **head to come walking in here to see how you're looking**
21   **after it. And look what he'd find if he did ...** *(He tips the bed*
22   *upside down. Kicks the bedding violently around the floor.)*
23   **Next time I come in here I want to see this bed looking**
24   **neat. Understand, Michael? Neat. I'll be back in half an**
25   **hour to make sure.**

26   *(He exits. LIAM puts the bed back in order. He does his best*
27   *to make it properly, given his exhausted state. He is about to*
28   *lie down on it again but changes his mind and lies down on*
29   *the floor at the side of it instead. Lights fade down on him*
30   *and up on MAGGIE and NUALA entering a different area of*
31   *the set together. NUALA carries a suitcase.)*

32   **MAGGIE: Will you not change your mind? You might find**
33   **something even so.**

34   **NUALA: I have no chance, mother. The old crow wouldn't even**
35   **give me a reference ... I wish I'd thrown her china tea**

1   service into the canal!

2   MAGGIE: But England, Nuala ...

3   NUALA: I'll be fine. There's work in the mills. You saw the

4   advertisement in the newspaper.

5   MAGGIE: And nowhere to live either.

6   NUALA: I'm not the first, mother. I'll find somewhere. It can't

7   be so different from Dublin. They're bound to have rooms

8   to rent.

9   MAGGIE: You'll write? You'll let me know?

10 NUALA: You know I will. And you'll let me know about Liam?

11 MAGGIE: Jesus, Mary and Joseph, I don't know what we're

12   going to do with him and that's the truth.

13 NUALA: You have to get him out of that bedroom. He'll never

14   change as long as he keeps himself shut up in there.

15 MAGGIE: When you think how he was. I hate the British,

16   Nuala. I hate them for what they've done to him.

17 NUALA: I know ... I'd better be going. *(They embrace. MAGGIE*

18   *watches her exit, then goes. Lights crossfade to LIAM still*

19   *lying on the floor of his bedroom. FRIEDRICH enters as a*

20   *smartly-dressed ENGLISHMAN.)*

21 ENGLISHMAN: Prisoner K561? *(LIAM drags himself to*

22   *attention.)* Sit down, K561. No need to stand. *(LIAM ignores*

23   *this. Remains standing.)* You may speak if you wish. *(A*

24   *pause.)* I'm here with the governor's approval. You have

25   permission to speak as much as you wish. *(LIAM hesitates*

26   *a moment.)*

27 LIAM: Who are you?

28 ENGLISHMAN: Please sit down. I understand you're on

29   punishment. Forty days solitary, isn't it?

30 LIAM: I'm not complaining.

31 ENGLISHMAN: I admire your endurance, Mr. Mulcahey. Five

32   years they tell me you've been in here. Special rules are

33   not easy. Not everyone manages to last so long.

34 LIAM: I don't know who you are, but would you stop beating

35   about the bush?

1 ENGLISHMAN: They tell me you were quite a well known
2   figure in Dublin five years ago.
3 LIAM: They seem to have told you a lot.
4 ENGLISHMAN: Home Rule by peaceful means. That's what you
5   stood for, isn't it? It's funny how things turn out, isn't it?
6 LIAM: What's that supposed to mean?
7 ENGLISHMAN: What seems anathema to one set of politicians
8   becomes acceptable to another. Personally I never trust
9   any of them.
10 LIAM: Is this some kind of game you're playing?
11 ENGLISHMAN: I'm here because the government are
12   currently discussing a bill to bring about the very thing
13   you campaigned for ... Irish Home Rule.
14 LIAM: What?
15 ENGLISHMAN: Of course, there will have to be certain
16   conditions. There's the thorny problem of the North. And
17   there's no way it can happen overnight. Negotiations will
18   be needed. These things take months. Sometimes years.
19 LIAM: So why me? Why are you telling me this?
20 ENGLISHMAN: You've always insisted you were innocent of
21   the charges against you.
22 LIAM: It's true! And there were people at my trial who knew it!
23 ENGLISHMAN: I know it.
24 LIAM: What?
25 ENGLISHMAN: You aren't naive enough to believe in natural
26   justice, are you, Mr. Mulcahey?
27 LIAM: You've got some bloody nerve.
28 ENGLISHMAN: Politics will always define justice. But political
29   climates change. And when they do, it seems a shame that
30   a man as intelligent as yourself should have to spend a
31   further three years locked in a place as grim as this. After
32   all, it would be much more useful to all concerned if you
33   were able to help influence decisions about the future
34   course of events. Don't you think?
35 LIAM: I think you'd better say exactly what you want.

1 ENGLISHMAN: Not everyone in Ireland thinks as you do.
2   There are those who have no interest in peaceful
3   discussion or legal means of any kind. They think the
4   British government is not to be trusted.
5 LIAM: Now, don't you find that truly amazing?
6 ENGLISHMAN: For these people violence is a way of life. Sadly
7   their influence is more than we would wish. There is a
8   real danger they could undermine the peace process.
9 LIAM: What's that got to do with me?
10 ENGLISHMAN: We'd like to know who they are.
11 LIAM: I think you'd better leave.
12 ENGLISHMAN: The people I'm talking about are no friends of
13   yours, Mr. Mulcahey. They're out to destroy everything
14   you ever stood for. One name. That's all I'm asking for.
15   One name.
16 MAGGIE: *(Calling from Off-stage)* Liam! *(LIAM hears her, the*
17   *ENGLISHMAN doesn't. He retires to a corner of the room.*
18   *MAGGIE enters. The rest of the scene takes place in two*
19   *realities — the scene in the bedroom and the scene in the cell.)*
20 MAGGIE: Liam, Cathal's here to see you. He's kept asking after
21   you. He's been here everyday, Liam. I didn't think it right
22   not to —
23 LIAM: I told you I didn't want to see anyone! I told you that!
24   *(CATHAL enters dressed in the uniform of the Irish*
25   *Volunteers.)*
26 CATHAL: Hello, Liam.
27 LIAM: Cathal.
28 CATHAL: It's grand seeing you again. You mother's been
29   telling us about you. *(LIAM shows no response. CATHAL*
30   *and MAGGIE share a glance.)* It was hard getting news of
31   you. The Brits'd tell us nothing. We kept the letters going
32   though. MP's. Ministers. Over to America.
33 MAGGIE: They worked hard for you, Liam. Every one of 'em.
34   The whole time you were in there. *(No reaction)* Cathal's a
35   captain in the Volunteers. Do you like the uniform?

1 LIAM: It's very grand.

2 CATHAL: There are thousands joining, Liam. All over Ireland.

3 MAGGIE: It's what I've been telling him.

4 LIAM: The Brits are giving you Home Rule. Isn't that enough
5   for you?

6 CATHAL: It's all talk, Liam. Can't you see that? They've been
7   talking of Home Rule for the last three years and not a
8   thing's been done. They're even proposing partition now —
9   leaving Ulster out of it.

10 LIAM: So you march through the park with wooden sticks on
11   your shoulders. The Brits must be shaking in their boots.

12 CATHAL: It won't be sticks much longer, Liam. There's only
13   one way we're going to get our country back and that's for
14   us to go out and fight for it.

15 ENGLISHMAN: You must know someone. You were a leader.
16   You knew people. Hot heads. You get them in any
17   organisation. A name. That's all I want. One name.

18 LIAM: Why me? Why come here to see me?

19 CATHAL: We want you with us. Leading the struggle. The way
20   you used. You're a name, Liam. People know who you are.

21 ENGLISHMAN: Five years in this place. Three more to go. Can
22   you last that long? One name could get you out now.

23 LIAM: Gallagher. Curtain. Lynch. O'Hara. They're names! I
24   had the next cell to O'Hara when he was losing his mind.
25   I'd listen to him at night, fighting against it, cursing
26   England and calling on God Almighty to strike him dead!

27 MAGGIE: Liam. All that's behind you. It's over. Let it rest.
28   Please, God, let it rest!

29 LIAM: Do you know? Do you know how I survive? How I stop
30   myself from going mad? *(Pause)* I count! *(Pause)* Bricks,
31   tiles, grills, windows, steps, shoes, knives and forks,
32   anything! Do you know how many buttons there are on
33   prisoners uniforms in this place? Five thousand seven
34   hundred and sixty four! Arrow marks on their jackets?
35   Nine thousand five hundred and twenty! Shall I tell you

1   how much hair I've had cut off in the last five years? Three
2   feet, two and a half inches! I measured the clippings and
3   worked it out! Shorthand! I've learnt shorthand! I taught
4   myself from a book they let me have from the library! Do
5   you know what I did then? I translated the Bible. Every
6   verse! Every word! Genesis to Revelations! I did it twice!
7   You want to know what else? What else I do? *(Pause)* I tame
8   spiders! *(Pause)* Don't laugh! Don't you laugh! *(Pause)* I
9   tame spiders! I teach them tricks! *(A pause. They all stand*
10   *watching him.)*
11 ENGLISHMAN: Why suffer? Why impose this on yourself — for
12   something you didn't do?
13 LIAM: Get out, will you? Just get out.
14 MAGGIE: Liam Mulcahey ... You'll not insult a friend in any
15   house o' mine!
16 CATHAL: No, Maggie ... I'd better be leaving. *(The*
17   *ENGLISHMAN exits.)*
18 LIAM: And don't bother coming back. *(CATHAL restrains*
19   *MAGGIE.)*
20 CATHAL: It's been good seeing you, Liam. I'll tell the others
21   you're looking well.
22 MAGGIE: Wait, Cathal ... I'll be coming with you. *(CATHAL and*
23   *MAGGIE exit. LIAM is left alone sitting on the bed. After a*
24   *few moments, THOMAS and FRIEDRICH enter and resume*
25   *the positions they had before the move to Ireland.*
26   *FRIEDRICH keeps the rifle.)*
27 LIAM: Satisfied? Think they've seen enough, do you?
28 THOMAS: You have still not told them why you joined the
29   British Army.
30 FRIEDRICH: Stehen sie auf. *(LIAM stands up.)*
31 LIAM: Just exactly how long do the two of you propose keeping
32   this up?
33 THOMAS: Lilford Mill is not yet built. Before they can learn
34   about the war, they must learn about your sister in
35   England. *(FRIEDRICH motions LIAM to a different area of*

1   *the set. He and THOMAS stand to one side. Spotlight upon*

2   *NUALA, singing unaccompanied.)*

3   **NUALA: As I went a-walking one morning in May**

4   **To view yon fair hills and mountains so gay**

5   **I was thinking of those flowers all doomed to decay**

6   **That bloom around ye bonny bonny Sliabh Gallion Braes.**

7   *(Song ends. Lights fade up on CISSY and NUALA, laughing*

8   *and giggling. CISSY carries a picnic basket and is wearing an*

9   *enormous and extravagant hat. Away from them a*

10 *STONEMASON [LIAM] is setting a stone plaque into the wall.*

11 *It reads: "20th January 1914. Mrs. T.D. Harrison cut the first*

12 *sod at Lilford Mill." THOMAS and FRIEDRICH watch from*

13 *the side in half-light.)*

14 **CISSY: It was right there in the middle of Whittle's window.**

15   **Eleven and six. I just couldn't resist it.**

16 **NUALA: It's enormous! It's the biggest hat I've ever seen!**

17 **CISSY: Is it silly? Does it look ridiculous?**

18 **NUALA: No! It's lovely! It's gorgeous!**

19 **CISSY: That's why you're laughing, is it?**

20 **NUALA: No ... it's just ... Well, it's the sort of chapeau you**

21   **imagine aristocratic ladies wearing to Royal Ascot.**

22 **CISSY: Oh, I see, so stuffy trade union organisers should stick**

23   **to something more in keeping with their station, that's**

24   **what you're saying? Well, let me tell you something, Miss**

25   **Mulcahey – I don't see why wealthy Tories should be the**

26   **only ones to enjoy a bit of glamour!**

27 **NUALA: Nor do I! Up the revolution! Forward to the age of**

28   **glamour!**

29 **CISSY: Here. You have a try. I bet it suits you better than me.**

30 **NUALA: *(Putting it on)* I used to dream about wearing hats like**

31   **this. Walking by the Liffey on a Sunday after mass. I'd**

32   **never summon up the nerve to buy one, though.**

33 **CISSY: You should. It'd do you good. I intend wearing this at the**

34   **Labour Party Conference. It might liven things up a bit.**

35 **NUALA: I think the gentlemen behind you might have**

1   **something to say. How does it look?**

2   **CISSY: Stunning.**

3   **NUALA:** *(Parading in the hat, posh voice)* **I think perhaps I'll**

4   **take tea outside this afternoon, Cissy. Be good enough to**

5   **serve it in the summerhouse, will you please?**

6   **CISSY: Of course, Ma'am. Would Ma'am prefer the paté de fois**

7   **or the caviar?**

8   **NUALA: Oh, the paté de fois gras. One gets quite bored with**

9   **caviar.** *(She looks across and notices the STONEMASON*

10   *watching her.)* **Get along, fellow. Get along. One's not**

11   **paying you to stand around idling.** *(The STONEMASON*

12   *refuses to share the joke. Gives NUALA a sour look and*

13   *returns to his work. The two WOMEN notice his attitude and*

14   *giggle.)* **Do you know him?**

15   **CISSY: Never seen him before. He wasn't here in the strike.**

16   **Must be new.** *(She reads the plaque.)* **"20th January 1914.**

17   **Mrs. T.D. Harrison cut the first sod."**

18   **NUALA:** *(Taking off the hat)* **I bet Mrs. T.D. Harrison never had**

19   **a hat like this.**

20   **CISSY: I bet she wasn't a trade union organiser either.** *(Puts the*

21   *hat back on her head.)*

22   **NUALA: Did you remember to bring the picnic?**

23   **CISSY: Of course. Paté de fois. As Madam ordered.** *(NUALA*

24   *stretches out on the grass as CISSY begins to unpack the*

25   *basket.)*

26   **NUALA: What a day. It's so good to get out of the noise and the**

27   **heat. I don't think I'd ever get used to working in the mills.**

28   **CISSY: Everyone says that. They do.**

29   **NUALA: I love it here by the canal. It's so peaceful. I often come**

30   **here for my dinner. Watch the men building the mill. It's**

31   **funny, after what happened I feel sort of an attraction to it.**

32   **CISSY: Why not?**

33   **NUALA: I suppose in a few months it'll be full of clattering**

34   **looms and noisy mill girls.** *(Pause)* **I used to sit like this by**

35   **the canal in Dublin. I worked as a maid for an**

1	Englishwoman. Her house was in Portobello, right next to

1   Englishwoman. Her house was in Portobello, right next to

2   the canal. On summer days I'd take out a sandwich and sit

3   on the grass, just dangling my feet in the water.

4   CISSY: You miss it, don't you?

5   NUALA: I don't miss her. *(Pause)*

6   CISSY: When are you going back?

7   NUALA: Soon ... I don't know ... Let's not talk about that.

8   CISSY: Heavens! I'm forgetting. There's a letter for you.

9   *(Searches in the basket for it.)* It came this morning after

10   you'd left for work. *(NUALA glances at the handwriting.)*

11   NUALA: It's from Liam – my brother. I never expected a letter

12   from him! *(She opens the letter. CISSY moves away to let her*

13   *read it – wanders over to the STONEMASON.)*

14   CISSY: I hope we didn't offend you. It was just a bit of fun,

15   that's all. A bit of clowning.

16   STONEMASON: The whole bloody lot of 'em's clowns if you

17   ask me.

18   CISSY: I beg your pardon.

19   STONEMASON: Come over here and want paying for doing sod

20   all.

21   CISSY: You don't know what you're talking about.

22   NUALA: *(Engrossed in the letter)* Cissy ...

23   STONEMASON: Oh I know alright. I've seen too many. Live

24   like bleedin' pigs most of 'em.

25   CISSY: Listen, you ignorant little –

26   NUALA: Cissy!

27   CISSY: No, Nuala! He's not getting away with insulting you like

28   that!

29   STONEMASON: You're Cissy Collins, aren't you? I know you.

30   You want to spend less time starting strikes and more

31   time making sure English jobs go to English workers!

32   NUALA: Cissy! *(Speechless with anger, CISSY turns, notices*

33   *NUALA's state, runs over to her.)*

34   CISSY: Nuala, don't let him upset you. He isn't worth it. He's

35   just a stupid narrow-minded little ... *(She stops, realising*

1   *it's the letter that's upset NUALA.)* **It's not him, is it ... ?**

2   **Nuala, what is it? Tell me.**

3 **NUALA: My mother ... It's my mother ... She's dead.**

4 **CISSY: Oh, my God ...** *(CISSY holds her as lights fade to black.*

5   *Heavy rumbling sound effects create an atmosphere of*

6   *threat. NUALA exits. FRIEDRICH and THOMAS take off their*

7   *jackets and become building workers along with LIAM.*

8   *Lights up on them turning a skipping rope and chanting.)*

9 **FRIEDRICH and THOMAS: World war. Revolution.**

10   **World war. Revolution.**

11   **World war. Revolution.**

12

13   *(CISSY jumps in. Starts to skip.)*

14   **In July of 1914**

15   **Austria went to war**

16   **The enemy was Serbia**

17   **But Germany wanted more.**

18   **The Russia Czar objected**

19   **And sent a note to France**

20   **Inviting them to join in**

21   **The military dance.**

22

23   **The Germans marched through Belgium**

24   **A nation not involved**

25   **And Britain had some problems**

26   **A war might help to solve.**

27   **The British claimed the Germans**

28   **Could soon be put to rout**

29   **But socialists were calling**

30   **For workers to stay out!**

31   *(CISSY tries to jump out but gets caught by the rope.*

32   *FRIEDRICH and THOMAS run around her laughing and*

33   *tangling her up. Then EACH puts his hands behind his back.)*

34 **THOMAS: Revolution or war?**

35 **CISSY:** *(Choosing one of his hands)* **Revolution.** *(THOMAS pulls*

1   *his hand from behind his back and points his finger at her*
2   *like a gun.)*
3 **THOMAS: War!** *(FRIEDRICH repeats the routine.)*
4 **FRIEDRICH: Revolution oder Krieg?**
5 **CISSY: Revolution.**
6 **FRIEDRICH: Krieg!** *(FRIEDRICH and THOMAS both laugh and*
7   *together with LIAM they start to put on their military*
8   *uniforms. CISSY untangles herself from the rope, starts to*
9   *remonstrate with them. They ignore her pleas.)*
10 **CISSY: Why do you listen to this all this talk of war? You're**
11   **building workers. You'll be fighting men the same as**
12   **yourselves. Men who carry hods and lay bricks. Men who**
13   **climb ladders and belong to a trade union ... who have to**
14   **fight for a wage they can live on just as you do. What's it**
15   **matter they speak a different language? You've more in**
16   **common with men like that than you have with the one**
17   **who owns this mill you're building. That man's never**
18   **carried a hod in his life. But he's the only one who'll**
19   **benefit from this. Can't you see? It's the army of**
20   **capitalism you're joining!** *(The three MEN finish dressing*
21   *themselves in their uniforms. They produce drums and*
22   *begin to beat a military tattoo. CISSY tries to shout above it.)*
23   **We should be organising marches! Demonstrations! We**
24   **should be calling for a general strike to stop the**
25   **government dragging us into this insane war! We can stop**
26   **it! Don't you see? We have the power to stop all this! We**
27   **can stop it ...** *(The drums continue. CISSY gives up and*
28   *backs away Off-stage. The tattoo comes to an end.*
29   *FRIEDRICH picks up the rifle.)*
30 **THOMAS: So here we are. The point at which you join the**
31   **army of the British.** *(FRIEDRICH fits a bayonet on to the*
32   *rifle and offers it to LIAM.)*
33 **LIAM:** *(Surprised)* **What's this?**
34 **THOMAS: Friedrich wishes you to show them your bayonet**
35   **drill.** *(FRIEDRICH hands the rifle to LIAM. For a moment*

1   *LIAM doesn't know whether to turn it on them or do the*
2   *drill.)* **You remember how it is done?** *(THOMAS beats out a*
3   *rhythm. Slowly and deliberately LIAM begins the bayonet*
4   *drill.)*
5   **In ... Out ... On Guard.**
6   **In ... Out ... On Guard.**
7   **In ... Out ... On Guard.**
8   **VOICE OF MAGGIE: Wait, Cathal ... I'll be coming with you.**
9   *(LIAM hears the voice, stops for a second. THOMAS starts to*
10 *increase the tempo. The voice of MAGGIE continues, repeating*
11 *the same sentence throughout the whole of the drill.)*
12 **In ... Out ... On Guard.**
13 **In ... Out ... On Guard.**
14 **In ... Out ... On Guard.**
15 *(LIAM becomes more frantic as the drumming builds and*
16 *MAGGIE's voice becomes more and more insistent.)*
17 **In ... Out ... On Guard!**
18 **In ... Out ... On Guard!**
19 **In ... Out ... On Guard!**
20 **In ... Out ... On Guard!**
21 **In ... Out ... On Guard!**
22 **In ... Out ... On Guard!**
23 *(LIAM goes berserk, losing control and becoming wildly*
24 *vicious. Eventually he screams and collapses on to the floor*
25 *of his bedroom. MAGGIE's voice and the drumming stops.*
26 *THOMAS and FRIEDRICH exit. Slowly LIAM drags himself*
27 *to his feet. He draws himself to attention, the rifle beside*
28 *him, and stands in silence. CATHAL enters through the*
29 *bedroom door, stops as he sees the uniform.)*
30 **CATHAL: You too, then?** *(LIAM makes no response.)* **Why, Liam? In**
31 **God's name why?** *(Still no response)* **You trust the British ... ?**
32 **You don't believe what they say? You don't imagine this'll**
33 **ever bring about Home Rule? They'll say anything, Liam.**
34 **Promise anything. Don't you realise that? They've used this**
35 **war to split us! The others – the others I can understand.**

1   **But you. Your own mother ...** *(He stops himself.)*

2   **LIAM: My own mother ... Go on ... My own mother ...**

3   **CATHAL: Some of us will never wear that uniform, Liam. While**

4   **you're out there fighting for the British Empire, we'll be**

5   **here, fighting against it.** *(LIAM mocks him by presenting*

6   *arms. CATHAL exits. LIAM exits as lights crossfade to CISSY*

7   *and NUALA entering. Shadowy night time light. They are in*

8   *a street. BOTH of them are drunk. NUALA is singing and*

9   *attempting to teach CISSY an Irish dance.)*

10   **NUALA: Toora loora loora loo**

11   **They're looking for monkeys in the zoo**

12   **And if I had a face like you**

13   **I'd join the British Army.**

14

15   **Watch me. It's easy.** *(Shows CISSY the steps.)*

16

17   **When I was young I used to be**

18   **As fine a man as e'er you'd see**

19   **And the Prince o' Wales he says to me**

20   **Come join the British Army.**

21   *(CISSY finds it great fun and joins the chorus. They dance*

22   *around laughing and kicking together.)*

23

24   **BOTH: Toora loora loora loo**

25   **They're looking for monkeys in the zoo**

26   **And if I had a face like you**

27   **I'd join the British Army.**

28

29   **NUALA: Sarah Curley baked a cake**

30   **Twas all for poor Kate Condon's sake**

31   **I threw myself into the lake**

32   **Pretending I was barmy.** *(By now a terrible din)*

33

34   **BOTH: Toora loora loora loo**

35   **They're looking for monkeys in the zoo**

1   And if I had a face like you —

2   *(Pin spot comes up on MR. HOLROYD — FRIEDRICH — in a*

3   *nightcap in an upstairs window.)*

4 **MR. HOLROYD:** Shut your bloody traps, the pair of you!

5   There's folks 'round here trying to get some bloody sleep!

6 **CISSY:** And a very good evening to you, Mr. Holroyd!

7 **NUALA:** Toora loora loora loo

8   They're looking for monkeys in the zoo —

9   *(Pin spot on MRS. STANDISH — LIAM — also in upstairs*

10   *window.)*

11 **MRS. STANDISH:** Is that you, Cissy Collins? You've woke my

12   Ernie up, you noisy young trollop!

13 **CISSY:** Mrs. Standish! If your Ernie had anything about him

14   he'd be down here singing with us!

15 **NUALA:** And if I had a face like you

16   I'd join the British Army.

17 **MR. HOLROYD:** If the two of you don't shut your bloody traps,

18   I sling the pair of you in the bloody flash!

19 **CISSY:** Are you sure you wouldn't sooner join us for the next

20   dance, Mr. Holroyd!

21 **BOTH:** Toora loora loora loo

22   Twas the only thing that I could do

23   To work my ticket home to you

24   And leave the British Army.

25   *(A sudden change. Spotlight up on a MAGISTRATE —*

26   *THOMAS — who bangs a gavel loudly. Spots off on MR.*

27   *HOLROYD and MRS. STANDISH. NUALA and CISSY stand*

28   *facing the MAGISTRATE.)*

29 **MAGISTRATE:** Cissy Collins and Noo-ah-la Mulcahey. You are

30   charged with being drunk and disorderly, using insulting

31   language, and disturbing the peace. How do you plead?

32 **CISSY:** I fail to see how anyone can be accused of disturbing

33   the peace when the whole of Europe is blowing itself to

34   pieces.

35 **MAGISTRATE:** This is a Court of Law. You will not use it to make

1   insolent comments. Do you plead guilty or not guilty?
2   *(Sudden switch back to the street. Spot down on*
3   *MAGISTRATE and up on MRS. STANDISH and MR.*
4   *HOLROYD.)*
5 MRS. STANDISH: You ought to be ashamed of yourself, Cissy
6   Collins – singing songs like that when there's decent lads
7   off in France!
8 CISSY: If those lads had any sense they'd still be at home
9   tucked up safe in bed like your Ernie!
10 MR. HOLROYD: You show a bit more bloody respect! Those
11   lads are fighting for their bloody country!
12 NUALA: More fool them! Up with the Germans and down with
13   the bloody English!
14 MRS. STANDISH: Did you hear that, Ernie! Did you hear what
15   the mucky little Irish taig is shouting!
16 NUALA: Can you not hear, Ernie? Is it not loud enough for you?
17   *(CISSY suddenly realises things are getting out of hand.*
18   *Tries to restrain NUALA.)*
19 CISSY: Nuala ... No ... No more.
20 NUALA: I said, "Up with the Germans and down with the
21   English!" I hope the Kaiser wins the bloody war!
22 CISSY: Nuala. That's enough. You've said enough. Let's go
23   home.
24 NUALA: *(Yelling)* I hope the Germans knock the shit out of your
25   mighty British Army!
26 CISSY: Nuala!
27 MR. HOLROYD: Right! That bloody does it! I'm bringing the
28   bloody constable to you! *(Immediate switch back to the court.)*
29 MAGISTRATE: So one of you is Irish? Well that helps to explain
30   matters a little, I suppose. I think it's time we heard what
31   you have to say for yourself, Miss Collins.
32 CISSY: If singing in the street at midnight is what it takes to
33   wake people up to the insane nature of this war then I'm
34   glad we did it.
35 MAGISTRATE: Do you admit to shouting seditious comments?

1 CISSY: I'm a socialist and a pacifist and my position on this
2   war is that –
3 MAGISTRATE: I do not wish to know your position on the war.
4   Did either you or your friend shout the comments we
5   have heard described?
6 CISSY: An argument broke out. People were shouting. A lot of
7   things were said.
8 MAGISTRATE: Did either of you shout "Up with the Germans
9   and down with the English?"
10 CISSY: Things like that might have been said. I can't
11   remember. It was in the heat of an argument. They
12   weren't meant to be taken literally.
13 NUALA: I'm not ashamed of what I said.
14 MAGISTRATE: So it was you, was it?
15 CISSY: Nuala's been very upset ... Her mother died recently and –
16 NUALA: I don't need you to make excuses for me, Cissy! *(To the*
17   *MAGISTRATE:)* I hope the Germans do win. It can't be any
18   worse for Ireland than being ruled by you British!
19 MAGISTRATE: I think I've heard quite sufficient from you,
20   young woman. Am I to assume, Miss Collins, that you
21   support these views?
22 CISSY: I've already told you. I'm a pacifist.
23 MAGISTRATE: I ask you again – do you support these views?
24 CISSY: I'm against violence of all kinds. I support neither side.
25 MAGISTRATE: Miss Collins. Let me make myself clear. I wish
26   you to state simply and unequivocally whether you
27   support the views expressed by your Irish companion ...
28   Yes or No. *(Pause. CISSY is very uncomfortable.)*
29 CISSY: No.
30 MAGISTRATE: In that case I sincerely hope you share in the
31   deep and utter contempt everyone in this court, and
32   hopefully in this country, feels towards her.
33 CISSY: Her mother's just died! Can't you understand? She's
34   upset!
35 NUALA: I meant every word, Cissy! Every last word! I'm not

1   ashamed!

2   MAGISTRATE: Cissy Collins. You appear to have played a

3   slightly less offensive part in these goings-on than your

4   friend, and for this reason I am going to fine you twenty

5   pounds and bind you over to keep the peace for a period

6   of one year. Noo-ah-la Mulcahey. You are guilty of a serious

7   offence and have demonstrated not one shred of remorse.

8   If it were in my power to do so, I would not hesitate in

9   having you deported from this country for good. As it is,

10   you will go to prison for three months. *(CISSY tries to offer*

11   *support and comfort. NUALA rejects her. They exit as lights*

12   *crossfade. FRIEDRICH and LIAM enter and THOMAS*

13   *changes from being the Magistrate as he and FRIEDRICH*

14   *sing. All three are dressed in their respective uniforms.*

15   *LIAM, on sentry duty, marches backwards and forwards*

16   *around the acting area.)*

17   FRIEDRICH and THOMAS: It's a long way to Tipperary

18   It's a long way to go

19   It's a long way to Tipperary

20   To the sweetest girl I know.

21   Goodbye Picadilly

22   Farewell Leicester Square

23   It's a long long way to Tipperary

24   But my heart's right there.

25   *(Pause. THOMAS and FRIEDRICH lounge at ease as they*

26   *watch LIAM marching.)*

27   THOMAS: *(To LIAM)* I did not know that Tipperary was a place

28   in Ireland. Even less did I think I would spend my

29   Christmas here. *(LIAM continues marching.)* Templemore

30   is a very beautiful place. You are lucky to live in such a

31   beautiful country. *(No response)* I am Thomas Bekaan ...

32   You are new here, I think. *(Still no response)* Friedrich and

33   I have been here for three months. We like it very much.

34   FRIEDRICH: Was?

35   THOMAS: Wir sind seit drei Monaten in Irland.

1 **FRIEDRICH:** *(To LIAM)* **Ja! Schon!**

2 **THOMAS: We like to be away from the war ... You have not**

3 **been yet?** *(No reply)* **They told us by now it would be over.**

4 **You live in Tipperary?** *(No reply)* **You are Irish ... ? Or**

5 **English?** *(LIAM stops marching.)*

6 **LIAM: I'm from Dublin.**

7 **THOMAS: Dublin! Then you are Irish.** *(To FRIEDRICH:)* **Er ist**

8 **aus Dublin.**

9 **FRIEDRICH: Aus Dublin! In Dublin gab es einen langen Streik!**

10 **Ich habe fur die Strikenden geld gesammelt!**

11 **THOMAS: Friedrich says he collected money to help the**

12 **workers of Dublin. He says before the war there was a long**

13 **strike ... Friedrich is a socialist, you understand.**

14 **FRIEDRICH: Haben die Arbeiter gesiegt?**

15 **THOMAS: He wishes to know if those workers won their strike.**

16 **LIAM: They lost.**

17 **THOMAS: Sie haben verloren.**

18 **FRIEDRICH: Schade! War er dabei?**

19 **THOMAS: He asks if you were in the strike yourself.**

20 **LIAM: No. No, I wasn't.** *(FRIEDRICH looks disappointed,*

21 *assumes that LIAM was not sympathetic. A pause.)* **Tell him**

22 **at the time of the strike I was in an English prison ... I'm**

23 **sure the strikers were grateful for the money he collected.**

24 **THOMAS: You were in prison?**

25 **FRIEDRICH: Was?**

26 **THOMAS: Er war im Gefangis.**

27 **FRIEDRICH: In Gefangis ... ! Wieso?**

28 **THOMAS: Friedrich wishes to know why you were in an**

29 **English prison.**

30 **LIAM: Tell him he wouldn't understand.**

31 **FRIEDRICH: Was?** *(THOMAS shrugs. A pause. FRIEDRICH*

32 *makes a decision and steps forward to hold out his hand.)*

33 **Friedrich Wilhelm Karl Schmidt. Es freut mich**

34 **kennenzulernen.** *(LIAM doesn't take FRIEDRICH's hand.*

35 *FRIEDRICH keeps it extended. To THOMAS:)* **Wie sagt man**

1   "es freut mich Sie Kennenzulernen"?

2   LIAM: What's he saying?

3   THOMAS: He wants to know how to greet you in your own
4   language.

5   LIAM: Tell him I'm not allowed to fraternise with prisoners.

6   *(Two OFFICERS enter, one English one German.)*

7   ENGLISH OFFICER: Soldier! *(LIAM jumps to attention. The*
8   *OFFICER approaches him.)* What's your name, Private?

9   LIAM: Mulcahey sir.

10 ENGLISH OFFICER: You know the rules about speaking with
11   prisoners, Mulcahey.

12 LIAM: Sir, I –

13 ENGLISH OFFICER: You're not in any rag-tag Irish Volunteers
14   here, Mulcahey. This is the British Army. When you're
15   given an order you obey it.

16 LIAM: Sir.

17 ENGLISH OFFICER: You'll take forty days loss of privileges.
18   Report to the duty officer when you're relieved.
19   Undertsand? *(Beat)* Do you understand, Private Mulcahey?

20 LIAM: I understand, sir.

21 ENGLISH OFFICER: Corporal Bekaan.

22 THOMAS: Commandant.

23 ENGLISH OFFICER: I wish to speak to Colonel Schneider. You
24   will act as interpreter. *(THOMAS glances across at the*
25   *GERMAN OFFICER.)*

26 GERMAN OFFICER: Ubersetzen Sie, Korporal.

27 THOMAS: Very well.

28 ENGLISH OFFICER: Tell your Colonel that the prison camp
29   here at Templemore is to be closed down. All prisoners
30   are to be transferred to the mainland.

31 THOMAS: We are to be moved to England?

32 ENGLISH OFFICER: Translate the message please, Corporal.

33 THOMAS: Sie wollen alle Gefangenen von Templemore nach
34   England versetzen.

35 GERMAN OFFICER: Nach England! Wieso? Fragen Sie wieso,

1   **Korporal!**
2   **THOMAS: Colonel Schneider asks to know the reason we are to**
3   **be moved.**
4   **ENGLISH OFFICER: Tell him the sanitory arrangements in**
5   **this camp are inadequate.**
6   **THOMAS: Sanitory arrangements ... I am sorry ... what are**
7   **sanitory arrangements?**
8   **ENGLISH OFFICER: Lavatories, Corporal. The lavatories are**
9   **not up to scratch.**
10 **THOMAS: Die Toiletten sind unzulanglich.**
11 **GERMAN OFFICER: Aber das ist lacherlich! Meine Manner**
12   **beschweren sich nicht, unde wollen gar nicht nach England!**
13 **THOMAS: Colonel Schneider asks me to tell you that his men**
14   **have no complaints about the lavatories and we have no**
15   **wish to move to England.**
16 **ENGLISH OFFICER: Tell him he should count himself lucky**
17   **we're taking him and his men out of this bog of a country.**
18   **All prisoners will be transferred within the next fortnight.**
19   *(ENGLISH OFFICER exits.)*
20 **GERMAN OFFICER: Korporal! Kommen Sie!** *(The GERMAN*
21   *OFFICER starts to exit with THOMAS in his wake. The*
22   *OFFICER notes FRIEDRICH's relaxed posture.)* **Achtung!**
23   **Fusilier Schmidt! Stramstehen in der Gegenwart eines**
24   **Offiziers!** *(FRIEDRICH jumps to attention. The GERMAN*
25   *OFFICER and THOMAS exeunt. FRIEDRICH relaxes.)*
26 **FRIEDRICH: Offiziere ...** *(Spits. Pause.)*
27 **LIAM: You don't speak English then?**
28 **FRIEDRICH: Englisch? Nein. Ich kann kein Englisch.**
29 **LIAM: Friedrich ... Wilhelm ... Karl ... Schmidt?**
30 **FRIEDRICH:** *(Delighted)* **Ja...! Friedrich Schmidt! Und Sie? Wie**
31   **heissen Sie ... ? Ihr Name?**
32 **LIAM: Liam ... Liam Mulcahey.**
33 **FRIEDRICH: Liam Mul ...**
34 **LIAM: ... cahey ... Liam Mulcahey.**
35 **FRIEDRICH: Liam Mulcahey ... Liam Mulcahey.**

1   **LIAM:** I'll probably get another forty days for that.

2   **FRIEDRICH:** *(Holding out his hand again)* **Es freut mich sie**

3   **kennenzulernen ... Liam Mulcahey.** *(LIAM hesitates a*

4   *moment, then takes FRIEDRICH's hand.)*

5   **LIAM:** Caed mille failte.

6   **FRIEDRICH:** Caed mille ...

7   **LIAM:** You wanted to learn hello in my language, didn't you?

8   Well, that's it ... Caed mille failte.

9   **FRIEDRICH:** Caed mille failte ... Caed mille failte! *(They shake*

10   *hands, delighted with themselves. Lights fade to black.)*

11

12   **END OF ACT ONE**

13

14

15   **ACT TWO**

16

17   *(Lights fade up on LIAM, THOMAS and FRIEDRICH sitting*

18   *around the set. THOMAS moves to pick up a broom. Holds it*

19   *out to LIAM.)*

20   **LIAM:** Not the cemetery?

21   **THOMAS:** They need to know the story.

22   **LIAM:** It's your story. You do it.

23   **THOMAS:** But you are so much better at it than I. *(Pause.*

24   *THOMAS doesn't flinch. LIAM pulls off his army cap and*

25   *jacket, snatches the broom from him and becomes a*

26   *GRAVEDIGGER. Starts to sweep. THOMAS moves away,*

27   *picks up a 60's transistor radio, places it on the ground near*

28   *LIAM, switches it on.)*

29   **THOMAS: The year is 1968.** *(THOMAS moves away to watch.*

30   *CISSY enters — now a woman in her mid-seventies. She*

31   *carries a bunch of flowers, walks straight to a certain part of*

32   *the stage where she expects to find a grave. It isn't there. She*

33   *looks puzzled, searches around for a moment or two.*

34   *Approaches the GRAVEDIGGER.)*

35   **CISSY: Excuse me.**

1   **GRAVEDIGGER:** *(Lancashire accent)* **A bit lost are you, luv?**

2   **CISSY: The grave ...**

3   **GRAVEDIGGER: Which one, my love? We've about seven**

4   **thousand in here.**

5   **CISSY: It's gone.**

6   **GRAVEDIGGER: Gone ... ? Well, let's not panic, eh? We don't get**

7   **many coffin stealers these days.** *(He laughs, she doesn't.)*

8   **CISSY: It was over there.**

9   **GRAVEDIGGER: That's the trouble with cemeteries. All the**

10   **paths look the same. We had a bloke in here last week,**

11   **swore blind we'd switched all't headstones round.**

12   **CISSY: I come every year.**

13   **GRAVEDIGGER: I'll help you find it, shall I ... ? What's the name?**

14   **CISSY: Friedrich Schmidt and Thomas Bekaan.**

15   **GRAVEDIGGER: Who?**

16   **CISSY: Soldiers.**

17   **GRAVEDIGGER: Oh, the memorial. It's right over there by the —**

18   **CISSY: German soldiers.**

19   **GRAVEDIGGER: Germans ... ? Hey, hang on a minute. I know**

20   **what you're on about — POW's. First World War.**

21   **CISSY: I'm sure it was there.**

22   **GRAVEDIGGER: Well bugger me, that's one grave I'd've laid**

23   **odds on nobody bothered with.**

24   **CISSY: Just behind the chapel.**

25   **GRAVEDIGGER: You're right. You're dead right ...** *(Suddenly*

26   *concerned)* **... Hey, you didn't have a relative or somebody**

27   **among 'em?**

28   **CISSY: No.**

29   **GRAVEDIGGER: That's alright then. You had me worried for a**

30   **moment ... They've gone.**

31   **CISSY: I beg your pardon.**

32   **GRAVEDIGGER: Been dug up. Last July thereabouts. War**

33   **Graves Commission. Transferred 'em all to Cannock Chase.**

34   **Wolverhampton way, so I believe. Central repository.**

35 **CISSY: Dug up?**

1　GRAVEDIGGER: **Oh, it went before't committee. Had to. You**
2　　　**can't just go digging up bodies. Not even Germans.**
3　CISSY: **What committee?**
4　GRAVEDIGGER: **Parks and Leisure. Funny in't it? Always**
5　　　**amuses me does that. Parks and Leisure.** *(He laughs, CISSY*
6　　　*doesn't.)* **Was it somebody you knew?**
7　CISSY: **No ... No, not really.**
8　GRAVEDIGGER: **That's alright then.** *(Pause. CISSY appears*
9　　　*confused The GRAVEDIGGER resumes his work. A YOUNG*
10　　　*WOMAN enters — NUALA in 60's dress. CISSY stares hard at*
11　　　*her. The WOMAN smiles politely as she passes, walks on.)*
12　CISSY: **Nuala?** *(The YOUNG WOMAN turns, looks puzzled,*
13　　　*smiles again. Walks to another part of the stage and stands*
14　　　*looking down at a grave. THOMAS and FRIEDRICH start to*
15　　　*pom-pom the tune from "Star of the County Down.")*
16　GRAVEDIGGER: **You're sure you're alright now?**
17　CISSY: *(To the GRAVEDIGGER)* **I'll just sit here awhile if that's**
18　　　**alright.**
19　GRAVEDIGGER: **Sit as long as you like, sweetheart ... Not too**
20　　　**long, though ... Don't want you becoming a permanent**
21　　　**resident now, do we!** *(He laughs. She sits down. THOMAS*
22　　　*and FRIEDRICH continue to pom-pom their tune. After a*
23　　　*few moments the YOUNG WOMAN starts to sing.)*
24　YOUNG WOMAN: **Near Bambridge Town in the County Down**
25　　　**One morning last July**
26　　　**Down a boreen green came a sweet colleen**
27　　　**And she smiled as she passed me by**
28　　　**She looked so sweet from her two bare feet**
29　　　**To the sheen of her nut-brown hair**
30　　　**Such a coaxing elf, sure I shook myself**
31　　　**For to see I was really there.**
32
33　　　*(CISSY mouths the words of the chorus as the YOUNG*
34　　　*WOMAN sings.)*
35　　　**From Bantry Bay up to Derry Quay**

417

1   And from Galway to Dublin Town
2   No maid I've seen like the brown colleen
3   That I met in the County Down.
4
5   As she onward sped, sure I scratched my head
6   And I looked with a feeling rare
7   And I says, says I, to a passer by
8   Who's the maid with the nut-brown hair?
9   He smiled at me and he says, says he
10   That's the gem of Old Ireland's crown
11   Young Rosie McCann from the banks of the Bann
12   She's the Star of the County Down.
13
14   From Bantry Bay up to Derry Quay
15   And from Galway to Dublin Town
16   No maid I've seen like the brown colleen
17   That I met in the County Down.
18   *(The song over, the YOUNG WOMAN exits, smiling at CISSY*
19   *as she passes.)*
20   **CISSY:** Lilford Mill. *(The GRAVEDIGGER stops his work, looks*
21   *over at her.)*
22   **GRAVEDIGGER:** What's that, luv? *(CISSY doesn't hear him. He*
23   *shrugs and turns away, returning to his work and taking no*
24   *further notice of her. THOMAS and FRIEDRICH start to pom-*
25   *pom the tune of "British Grenadiers." They continue softly*
26   *under CISSY's speech.)*
27   **CISSY:** People ask you what it was like. It never should have
28   happened, that's what I tell them. It could easily have
29   been stopped. None of them seem to realise that. They
30   look back like it was some kind of inevitable madness.
31   Human lemmings driven on by some sort of suicidal
32   impulse. We've moved on since then, they think,
33   progressed. It'd never happen today ... Wouldn't it? It was
34   our fault, you know. We were the ones who could have
35   prevented it ... should have prevented it. We gave up. Just

gave up. Swept away in all the flag waving. *(THOMAS and FRIEDRICH, wearing a blue and an orange rosette, march in front of her, waving Union Jacks and singing to the tune of "British Grenadiers.")*

THOMAS & FRIEDRICH: The Tories and the Liberals
   Are both supporting war
   (They looks towards the GRAVEDIGGER who now turns towards them. He wears a red rosette.)
   But Labour's hesitating
   He feels a bit unsure.

   But once the fighting started
   He couldn't stand the strain
   (GRAVEDIGGER hesitantly produces a Union Jack.)

   And now we politicians
   Are sounding all the same
   Are sounding all the same
   Are sounding all the same ...
   (THOMAS and FRIEDRICH retire to the side of the stage.)

THOMAS: *(Softly)* Engla ... and. Engla ... and. *(The GRAVEDIGGER limply waves his flag while CISSY looks on scornfully.)*

GRAVEDIGGER: We have to be realistic, Cissy. We can't just stick our heads in the sand and pretend the country isn't involved in a war.

CISSY: What about the resolutions we passed? "Workers stand together for peace!" "Down with the rule of brute force! Up with the peaceful rule of the people!"

GRAVEDIGGER: That was two weeks ago.

CISSY: My! Two weeks!

GRAVEDIGGER: A lot can happen in a fortnight. A nation at war has to have unity, everybody knows that. We don't want people thinking we're unpatriotic.

CISSY: God forbid. Much more sensible to encourage mass

1   slaughter.

2   GRAVEDIGGER: We did our best to stop it. You know that as

3   well as I do. We failed. Look around you. Workers are

4   enlisting in droves. What do you want us to do, tell them

5   to refuse to fight for King and Country?

6   CISSY: Yes! That's exactly what we should do!

7   GRAVEDIGGER: We'd be committing political suicide! Can't

8   you see that? Just when we're making headway. You've

9   seen the way things have been going over the last few

10   months. We're winning support right across the country —

11   places where they wouldn't even look at us before. All we

12   have to do is play things right and we stand a chance of

13   getting in come the next election.

14   CISSY: Which is obviously much more important than young

15   men being butchered.

16   GRAVEDIGGER: What is it with you? This is not some sort of

17   game we're playing — who can think up the most radical

18   slogan. It's a matter of power, Cissy. They've got it. We

19   want it. Walk out there on the streets. Listen to what

20   people are saying. You want us to fly in the face of that?

21   It'd finish us. The time for head-in-clouds idealism is over.

22   It's gone for good. We need to get rid of all that old-

23   fashioned dogma. It's a millstone round our neck. *(He*

24   *turns away, back to his work as a gravedigger.)*

25   CISSY: Socialism? Is that what you're talking about? You want

26   us to get rid of socialism now ... ? Listen. I didn't join the

27   Labour Party to end up standing on a recruiting platform

28   for the British Army! *(GRAVEDIGGER turns back to her. He*

29   *no longer wears his rosette. Stares in bewilderment. A*

30   *moment in which CISSY takes stock, then realises where she*

31   *is. She crumples in embarrassment.)* **Sorry ... I'm sorry.**

32   GRAVEDIGGER: Hey ... It's alright, luv. Here, sit down. I'll get

33   you a glass of water, shall I?

34   CISSY: No. No, it's alright, thank you.

35   GRAVEDIGGER: I think you've got yourself a bit over-excited,

1   haven't you? Losing your Germans and all that. You've got
2   to take things a bit easy at your time of life, you know.
3 CISSY: Thank you. I think I'd better be going now.
4 GRAVEDIGGER: You sure you're alright?
5 CISSY: Yes.
6 GRAVEDIGGER: Don't forget your flowers. *(Hands them to her.)*
7 CISSY: Thank you. *(She exits. Lights fade down on the*
8   *GRAVEDIGGER. He reverts to becoming LIAM, joins*
9   *THOMAS and FRIEDRICH. Lights come up on the interior of*
10   *Cissy's house. CISSY — now back to being a young woman in*
11   *her twenties — is arranging the flowers in a vase on the*
12   *table. NUALA enters.)*
13 NUALA: Flowers in January. Isn't that a bit extravagant?
14 CISSY: I wanted to have them here yesterday to welcome you
15   home. It was all such a rush it went out of my head.
16 NUALA: I didn't know if you'd want me back. I wouldn't have
17   blamed you, you know. All the trouble I created.
18 CISSY: We didn't create enough. We should have caught the
19   train to London and sung outside Buckingham Palace.
20 NUALA: They'd've probably given me life for that. *(They laugh.)*
21 CISSY: Did you find any work?
22 NUALA: *(Imitating a broad Lancashire dialect)* "I'm very sorry
23   Miss Mulcahey, but t'company does have its reputation to
24   consider, you understand."
25 CISSY: *(Laughing)* I nearly warned you. I was afraid that's what
26   they'd say.
27 NUALA: I've spent the whole afternoon walking. I must've
28   been to every mill in Leigh.
29 CISSY: Nothing?
30 NUALA: It's the same everywhere you go. There's no cotton
31   because of the German submarines. The only place
32   they're taking women on is at the munitions factory. I
33   could start there tomorrow.
34 CISSY: I wouldn't blame you, you know.
35 NUALA: I don't mind making bullets, Cissy. It's not that ... But

1   not for the British. *(Beat)*
2 CISSY: That night ... What you shouted ... I'd like to try and
3   understand.
4 NUALA: Have you seen what they've done to Lilford Mill? I only
5   managed to get half way along the street. The place is
6   covered in barbed wire.
7 CISSY: You didn't go there for a job?
8 NUALA: I thought they'd be ready for opening. I thought
9   they'd be bound to be needing girls.
10 CISSY: It'll be a good while before they need any girls at Lilford
11   Mill ... Have you not seen the paper? *(She passes a newspaper*
12   *to NUALA. NUALA begins to read. Lights crossfade to*
13   *THOMAS, FRIEDRICH and LIAM — all in uniform — in a train*
14   *on their way to Leigh. FRIEDRICH is squashed between the*
15   *other two and is scratching away at a large bone.)*
16 LIAM: *(To himself)* 63 ... 64 ... 65 ... 66 ...
17 THOMAS: Why are you counting the telegraph poles?
18 LIAM: ... 67 ... 68 ... 69 ... 70 ...
19 THOMAS: What is this place called?
20 LIAM: Wales.
21 THOMAS: Wales is part of England, yes?
22 LIAM: That's probably what the English'd tell you.
23 THOMAS: The same as Ireland.
24 LIAM: That'll change.
25 THOMAS: Ah yes ... Home Rule ... I read of it in your Irish
26   newspapers.
27 LIAM: I've lost count now.
28 THOMAS: I know nothing of Ireland. I have no quarrel with
29   anyone there. So why are Germany and Ireland at war? It
30   was a question in my mind, you understand.
31 LIAM: So now you've read a couple of articles you think you
32   know the reason, is that it?
33 THOMAS: Before the war you Irish were about to fight the
34   English, yes? You were a member of the Irish Volunteers,
35   I think.

1   LIAM: You think wrong.

2   THOMAS: You do not agree with Home Rule?

3   LIAM: Listen, Corporal. You're talking about things you don't
4   even begin to understand.

5   THOMAS: But just as it seemed you Irish would make war on
6   the English – boom! England makes war on Germany.

7   LIAM: Now isn't that strange? I always thought it was your side
8   who started it.

9   THOMAS: Do not interrupt, please ... The English are very
10   clever. They promise to give you your Home Rule if you
11   promise to join the British Army. I think the word for that
12   is "a deal," am I right? And so instead of fighting your real
13   enemy, the English, you fight us Germans instead ... That
14   is why you and I are at war ... There is just one thing I do
15   not understand. Perhaps you can explain it to me ... Why
16   did you not join with us Germans and fight the English?

17   *(Lights crossfade back to CISSY and NUALA. NUALA is still*
18   *reading the paper.)*

19   NUALA: They're bringing them from Ireland ... "The prisoners
20   are expected any day. They will sail from Dublin to
21   Holyhead and be escorted by men of the Leinster
22   Regiment."

23   CISSY: It's the talk of the town. Everybody wants to see a real
24   live Hun. Just wait till they arrive. There'll be thousands
25   turn out.

26   NUALA: "Many reasons have been adduced for the
27   transference of the Germans from Ireland, but the most
28   likely one is that the sanitary arrangements at
29   Templemore are not of the recognised standard!" Do they
30   expect us to believe that! As if no one in Ireland knows
31   how to build a lavatory! "Excellent sanitary arrangements
32   have been built at Lilford Mill, however. Being of the
33   water carriage system they are more up-to-date than at
34   any other camp in the country."

35   CISSY: No nasty smells in this town. Read on. Read the rest.

1 *(NUALA reads silently. Lighting change. CISSY addresses the*
2 *audience.)* **"It is said the prisoners have been well cared**
3 **for during their five months in Tipperary, but there is a**
4 **villainous look about these fiends, and we must not forget**
5 **that the name of Germany stinks in the nostrils of every**
6 **nation in the world. Some of the prisoners have an**
7 **impudent look that makes one feel like kicking them, and**
8 **we can quite credit that they will bite the hand that feeds**
9 **them during their internment in Leigh. We are sorry to**
10 **think that probably for the next couple of years, the pure**
11 **air of respectable Pennington will be tainted with the**
12 **breath of two thousand of these wretched specimens of**
13 **humanity. While these scrapings of hell are being fed,**
14 **housed and carefully tended at a weekly expenditure of**
15 **£1000, British prisoners in Germany are being half-**
16 **starved and treated like dogs. We English like to err on the**
17 **side of generosity."** *(Lights return to normal. NUALA throws*
18 *down the paper and exits. Lights crossfade to THOMAS,*
19 *LIAM and FRIEDRICH on the train. FRIEDRICH still*
20 *scratching away at the bone.)*
21 LIAM: What's he doing?
22 THOMAS: He is passing the time. What else is there for a
23 prisoner to do? *(Pause)* This place they are taking us to.
24 What is it like?
25 LIAM: I don't know.
26 THOMAS: Is it as beautiful as Tipperary?
27 LIAM: I don't think so.
28 THOMAS: You have never been?
29 LIAM: I have a sister there.
30 THOMAS: A sister? That is good. You will go to see her, I think.
31 LIAM: She doesn't know I'm coming.
32 THOMAS: But you will go to see her nevertheless.
33 LIAM: I don't know.
34 THOMAS: But you must. If she is your sister, you must.
35 LIAM: My family's got nothing to do with you, Corporal.

1 THOMAS: She is away from home. She will want to hear news
2   of her father and mother.
3 LIAM: My father and mother are both dead, Corporal! Now
4   will you kindly keep your mouth shut 'cos I'm sick of
5   having to listen to your constant prattle!
6 THOMAS: I am sorry. *(Silence. A tense atmosphere which*
7   *FRIEDRICH picks up. He decides to do something to break it.*
8   *He stands up and formally presents the bone to LIAM.)*
9 FRIEDRICH: Ich habe auf diesem Knochen eine Inschrift
10   gemacht ... ein Geschenk fur Sie. *(LIAM looks confused,*
11   *doesn't know what's going on.)*
12 THOMAS: It is a present. Friedrich has made it himself – for
13   you. *(LIAM is taken off guard, and takes the bone.)*
14 LIAM: Thank you.
15 FRIEDRICH: Bitte. Alles Gute. *(He sits down and LIAM*
16   *examines the bone.)*
17 LIAM: What's it say? *(THOMAS examines the bone.)*
18 THOMAS: It is a poem.
19 LIAM: A poem?
20 THOMAS: I will attempt to translate.
21   "In France we were captured
22   That was our misfortune
23   Oh, terrible was the fight
24   Against the English and the French
25   Fol de lol lol – "
26 LIAM: Fol de lol lol?
27 THOMAS: Fol de lol lol – it is a poem.
28 LIAM: Isn't it supposed to rhyme?
29 THOMAS: It is written in German. *(He continues:)*
30   "Now comes the stalwart Englishman
31   Who here is in command
32   Under his great paternal care
33   His love of exercise and ... *(With triumph:)* ... air
34   We daily in the barracks yard
35   Are ... " *(He stops, examines the bone, unable to read it.)*

1   **LIAM:** Are what?

2   **THOMAS:** Was heisst das?

3   **FRIEDRICH:** Das Gras hochziehen!

4   **THOMAS:** " ... Are pulling up the grass." *(LIAM and THOMAS*

5   *exchange blank looks. FRIEDRICH watches anxiously. A*

6   *moment that could go in several directions. Then LIAM starts*

7   *to laugh. THOMAS joins in. Their laughter grows.*

8   *FRIEDRICH assumes they like the poem and joins in too. The*

9   *three MEN roar with laughter as lights fade to black. Sound*

10   *effects of a large excited crowd. Tight enclosed light up on*

11   *CISSY and NUALA huddled together as if packed in a crowd.)*

12 **VOICES:** The Germans are coming! The Germans are coming!

13 **NUALA:** Can you see anything?

14 **CISSY:** No. Nothing.

15 **NUALA:** Do you think this is the way they'll bring them?

16 **CISSY:** They've no choice unless they intend marching them

17   through the canal.

18 **VOICE:** They're coming down Lord Street! *(Sound effects of*

19   *distant music)*

20 **CISSY:** You won't shout anything, will you?

21 **NUALA:** Up with the Germans and down with the English?

22 **CISSY:** Sssshhh!

23 **NUALA:** Don't panic. I won't shout anything.

24 **VOICE:** They're turning into Market Street! *(Music gets nearer,*

25   *also marching feet.*

26 **CISSY:** I don't know why you wanted to come. All these people

27   turning out to watch a few miserable prisoners. It's

28   ghoulish.

29 **NUALA:** I want to see them, that's all. Didn't I spend three

30   months in gaol for supporting them?

31 **CISSY:** The mills must be completely empty. The whole town's

32   here. *(Sound effects get louder. Sound of horses' hooves.*

33   *THOMAS and FRIEDRICH appear as two local lads. They*

34   *push their way in front of NUALA and CISSY.)*

35 **LAD 1:** Room for two little 'uns, is there?

1   NUALA: I can't see a thing now.

2   CISSY: Can't you stand somewhere else?

3   LAD 2: Can't move an inch, sweetheart.

4   LAD 1: Wedged in solid.

5   LAD 2: Hey look! I think they're coming! *(They all crane to see.)*

6   LAD 1: They are! I can see two coppers on horses at' front!

7   LAD 2: There! You can see tops of their hats! *(They jostle to get*

8   *a better view. Music builds to a peak. Marching music.*

9   *Horses. Crowd.)*

10   LAD 1: They're here! They're here!

11   LAD 2: Bloody hell! There's hundreds of 'em!

12   NUALA: I can't see a thing!

13   LAD 1: Look at him at' front!

14   LAD 2: Bet he's a General!

15   LAD 1: A Count maybe!

16   LAD 2: Oi, Prince Ferdinand! Thy flies are undone!

17   NUALA: Can you see anything?

18   CISSY: Heads. All I can see are people's heads.

19   LAD 1: There's two here wi' accordians!

20   LAD 2: It better than't Whit Walks this!

21   LAD 1: Look at him wi't curly moustache!

22   LAD 2: Hey, Fritz! I like thi' cap!

23   LAD 1: More like a bloody pork pie!

24   NUALA: What do they look like?

25   CISSY: I can't see.

26   LAD 2: Scruffy buggers, aren't they?

27   LAD 1: Look at all't stuff they're carrying! Where'd you think

28   you're going, Fritz? Blackpool?

29   LAD 2: One of 'em's dropped a shoe!

30   LAD 1: Somebody's grabbed it ... ! There's one here in breeches ...

31   Lost your horse have you, Fritz!

32   LAD 2: Nei ... gh!

33   LAD 1: Oi! Kaiser Bill ... It's a long way to Berlin!

34   LAD 2: What a shower! I don't think our lads'll have much

35   bother fighting this lot!

1 CISSY: Why should they fight at all! What have they ever done
2   to you!
3 LAD 1: Whose side are you on?!
4 NUALA: I can't see! I want to see them!
5 LAD 2: Hey, let's give 'em a song, eh! Make 'em feel welcome!
6   *(The two LADS start singing "It's A Long Way to Tipperary.")*
7 NUALA: They'll have gone past! I won't even have seen them!
8 CISSY: It's sickening! We've shouldn't have come!
9 NUALA: I'll put my foot on the wall and lean on your shoulder!
10   *(NUALA struggles up until she can see over the two LADS. At*
11   *the same time a spotlight comes up on LIAM elsewhere on*
12   *the set. They "see" each other.)*
13 LIAM: Nuala! ... *(Waves.)* Nuala! *(NUALA doesn't respond. Slips*
14   *back down behind CISSY. Light on LIAM fades out. The two*
15   *LADS stop singing.)*
16 CISSY: Well, now you've seen them do you mind if we go home?
17   *(NUALA edges her way out and exits.)* Nuala ... ! Nuala!
18 LAD 1: Look at this lot wi' spikes on their helmets! Oi, Fritz!
19   What's that spike on top o' your helmet for?
20 LAD 2: Maybe it's so they can stick it in't ground and shit in it!
21   *(The two LADS roar with laughter.)*
22 CISSY: Shut up, the pair of you! You're a disgrace to the
23   working class!
24 LAD 1: You some sort o' Sunday School teacher or some'at?
25 LAD 2: Happen she fancies one o' these Huns!
26 LAD 1: Is that right, luv? Fancy a bit of Hun do you?
27 LAD 2: Happen we ought to arrange an introduction, what you
28   think Harry? *(They grab CISSY's arms.)*
29 CISSY: Take your hands off me! Let me go!
30 LADS: 1 ... 2 ... 3! *(They throw her forward. Light off on the two*
31   *LADS. Tight enclosed light up on LIAM. CISSY lands at his feet.)*
32 LIAM: Look out – hey! You two!
33 LAD 1: *(From off)* Auf Wiedersehn, Frauliene! *(Laughter. LIAM*
34   *tries to help CISSY up.)*
35 LIAM: Are you alright? Did they hurt you?

1   CISSY: **Don't touch me! Don't touch me!** *(LIAM steps back,*
2   *watches as she climbs to her feet. She glares at him for a*
3   *moment, then exits. He watches her go. Lights and sound*
4   *effects fade out. Lights up on FRIEDRICH and LIAM in*
5   *Lilford Mill Camp.)*
6   LIAM: **A lot of wire.** *(FRIEDRICH looks puzzled.)* **Barbed wire ...**
7   **It's not bad, though ... A good canteen. American stoves.**
8   **You can even do your own cooking if that's what you fancy.**
9   **There's a recreation field at the back – football, skittles –**
10   **you'll have plenty to do. Baths too. One a week compulsory**
11   **... they reckon the toilets are the best in the country. You're**
12   **very privileged.** *(He laughs. FRIEDRICH joins in without*
13   *understanding.)* **Two letters a week you can write. They**
14   **have to go through the censor – that's only normal ... You**
15   **can get parcels from home, too ... from your family.**
16   FRIEDRICH: **Familie?** *(Pause)*
17   LIAM: **Look ... I won't be staying here. The English have their**
18   **own guards. They're sending us to France.** *(Not*
19   *understanding any of this, FRIEDRICH tries to respond to*
20   *the tone of LIAM's speech.)* **Ironic isn't it? Me going where**
21   **you've come from. We're leaving tomorrow. So this is the**
22   **last chance I'll have to ...** *(A jovial English SENTRY enters.*
23   *LIAM moves away from FRIEDRICH slightly.)*
24   SENTRY: **Alright there, Michael.**
25   LIAM: **My name's not Michael.**
26   SENTRY: **Oh, sorry, mate. No offence. Just trying t'be friendly.**
27   *(Holds out his hand.)* **Morris Lambert.** *(Points to a stripe on*
28   *his sleeve.)* **Lance Corporal.**
29   LIAM: *(Shaking his hand)* **How d'you do, Lance Corporal.**
30   SENTRY: **You are one o't paddies, though, aren't you – come**
31   **over wi' this lot?**
32   LIAM: **I'm Irish, yes.**
33   SENTRY: **Bit like a foreign country for you this I expect ...**
34   **Mucky hole isn't it, Leigh?**
35   LIAM: **You live here, do you?**

1   **SENTRY: What! I wouldn't live here if it were't last place on**
2   **earth ... Wigan. Born and bred. It's a bloody insult getting**
3   **sent here. Wish I were in your shoes, I'll tell you.**
4   **LIAM: My shoes?**
5   **SENTRY: Off to France ... Lucky sod! I were one o't first for't**
6   **volunteer in Wigan. First day o't war and the buggers**
7   **wouldn't have me. "Unsuitable for active service owing to**
8   **reasons of health." It's on my card. That's why I'm in't**
9   **Reserves. It isn't right, tha knows. There's nowt**
10   **undernourished about me, it doesn't matter what they say.**
11   **Anyway it shouldn't make any difference – not when you**
12   **volunteer.** *(He takes out a cigarette.)* **Got a light have you?**
13   **LIAM: I don't smoke.** *(SENTRY starts searching in his pockets.*
14   *FRIEDRICH produces a lighter, offers it.)*
15   **FRIEDRICH: Ich habe Feuer ... Hier.**
16   **SENTRY:** *(Backing away)* **No, thanks ...** *(To LIAM:)* **Never know**
17   **where it's been wi' this lot, do you? I bet he's not short o'**
18   **fags, though. It's like a flaming picnic in here. I don't**
19   **know why we bother wi' sentries. They'd not try and get**
20   **out even if we left all't gates open. You wait, they'll be**
21   **falling over each other to get captured once word gets**
22   **round about this place. You guarding 'em over there in**
23   **Ireland then, were you?**
24   **LIAM: Yes.**
25   **SENTRY: Can I ask you some'at ... ? D'you ever get used to't**
26   **stink?**
27   **LIAM: What?**
28   **SENTRY: You can smell it from th'end o't street. Must be all that**
29   **garlic sausage and black bread they stuff down 'emselves,**
30   **eh? Fair turns your stomach, dun't it? Bet you can't wait to**
31   **get over there and have a do at 'em. Mind you, we might get**
32   **a chance here. Some o't'lads are talking about fixing up a**
33   **football match. Us versus them. No rules. No ref. And't**
34   **team wi' most left alive wins ... Who knows? One of 'em**
35   **might just be daft enough to try and escape ...** *(He aims his*

1   *rifle at FRIEDRICH. FRIEDRICH, taken off guard, thinks it's*

2   *for real. He freezes.)* **Blam!!** *(SENTRY Laughs. FRIEDRICH*

3   *relaxes, angry.)* **This's my favourite ...** *(Fixes the bayonet to*

4   *his rifle and begins the same bayonet drill we saw LIAM*

5   *practicing in Act One.)* **In ... Out ... On Guard ... In ... Out ...**

6   **On Guard ... In ... Out ... On** − *(FRIEDRICH suddenly makes*

7   *a wild leap in the sentry's direction.)*

8   **FRIEDRICH: Haaaaaaaaaaaa!!!!** *(The SENTRY jumps back,*

9   *terrified. Fumbles with his weapon, trying to cock it.*

10   *Complete panic.)*

11 **SENTRY: Get back! Get back, you bloody Hun or I'll let you**

12   **have it!** *(LIAM steps smartly in front of him and lifts the*

13   *barrel of the rifle.)*

14 **LIAM: No panic, soldier ... It's Friedrich's little game. Just his**

15   **little game.**

16 **SENTRY: He's a bleedin' head case! He wants shooting!**

17 **LIAM: Oh, this one's nothing. Wait till you see the rest of 'em.**

18   **They have red eyes and blow smoke out of their ears.**

19 **SENTRY: You're mad. You're as mad as he is ... Bloody Paddy ...**

20   **Whose side are you on?** *(LIAM releases the rifle and the*

21   *SENTRY exits. LIAM and FRIEDRICH share a laugh. LIAM*

22   *holds out his hand.)*

23 **LIAM: Goodbye, Friedrich.**

24 **FRIEDRICH: Caed mille failte.**

25 **LIAM:** *(Laughing)* **You must be the only soldier in the entire**

26   **German army that speaks any Gaelic ... Gan tianga, gan tir.**

27 **FRIEDRICH: Gan tianga ... gan tir**

28 **LIAM: Don't ask me to explain that to you. Good luck, soldier.**

29   *(He exits.)*

30 **FRIEDRICH:** *(Shouting after him)* **Viel Gluck, Liam Mulcahey!**

31   *(To himself:)* **Gan tianga gan tir.** *(Lights up on the street*

32   *outside Cissy's house. Evening. LIAM enters. Examines a*

33   *piece of paper. Walks across to the door, knocks. CISSY opens*

34   *it, doesn't recognize him.)*

35 **CISSY: Yes?** *(A silence)* **Can I help you?**

1   LIAM: You're the woman in the street ... The one who was
2   pushed.
3   CISSY: Oh, I see ... You're the soldier? *(LIAM stares.)* **Well? What**
4   are you doing here ... ? Do you want something?
5   LIAM: It was my sister. I was looking for my sister. I'm sorry, I
6   must have the wrong house. *(Turns to leave.)*
7   CISSY: Not Nuala? You're not Nuala's brother, are you? *(He*
8   *stops.)* Liam?
9   LIAM: It was this address on the letter.
10 CISSY: My God, you are ... You'd better come in. *(They move*
11   *into the interior of Cissy's house.)*
12 LIAM: Does Nuala live here still?
13 CISSY: She rents a room. I'm Cissy Collins. I don't know if she
14   mentioned me.
15 LIAM: The socialist?
16 CISSY: *(Laughs.)* Yes.
17 LIAM: She's not in then?
18 CISSY: No. But you're welcome to wait ... I'm sorry I was rude
19   to you earlier ... I was blazing.
20 LIAM: I don't blame you.
21 CISSY: I appreciate you were trying to help ... You came over
22   with the prisoners then?
23 LIAM: We're here till tomorrow. Then it's up to the front.
24 CISSY: I see. You haven't seen Nuala then, since you arrived?
25 LIAM: She was there this morning, wasn't she? I saw her in the
26   crowd ... I don't think she saw me, though.
27 CISSY: I think perhaps she did.
28 LIAM: What?
29 CISSY: Do you mind if I ask you something? Did Nuala know
30   you'd joined the army?
31 LIAM: I don't think so.
32 CISSY: Well, I think perhaps it might have come as a bit of a
33   shock.
34 LIAM: Look. If you could just tell me where I'd find her ...
35 CISSY: She's been out looking for work. She goes every day.

1 LIAM: I heard there were plenty of jobs for women these days.
2 CISSY: Oh, you heard right. The thing is, Nuala refuses to do
3   them.
4 LIAM: Refuses?
5 CISSY: The sort of jobs you're talking about are all connected
6   with the war effort.
7 LIAM: I see ... Well, if you could just tell her I called ... I'll be away
8   early in the morning. *(He starts to leave, NUALA enters.)*
9 NUALA: Just leaving, are you?
10 LIAM: Your friend was just —
11 NUALA: Don't let me stop you.
12 CISSY: Nuala — He's only here for the day. He's going to France.
13 NUALA: He can go to hell for all I care.
14 CISSY: Nuala. He's your brother.
15 NUALA: Not in that uniform he's not.
16 LIAM: I'll be going.
17 CISSY: Wait! *(She prevents him.)* Nuala, I know what you think,
18   but he's still your brother. You can't let him go like this.
19 NUALA: You're defending him, are you? What's happened to all
20   the pacifist principles, Cissy? Would you like me to go along
21   to the station and wave him off with a little Union Jack?
22 CISSY: I can't believe this.
23 NUALA: He's a soldier, Cissy! A British soldier!
24 LIAM: Living in England certainly seems to have changed your
25   political outlook, Nuala. I don't remember you displaying
26   much sign of nationalism when you lived in Dublin!
27 NUALA: You wouldn't have noticed if I had! You were the hero,
28   Liam! The Great Patriot. You were the one they all talked
29   about!
30 LIAM: So now you're safely tucked away in your cosy little
31   room over here in England, you've decided to become a
32   republican, is that it?
33 NUALA: Do you think I wanted to come here! I lost my job,
34   remember! Even that was because of you!
35 LIAM: Oh, I apologise. That was most inconsiderate of me.

1   NUALA: You don't understand, do you! Not even now! Mother
2   worshipped you. She talked about nothing else. All those
3   years — wondering if you'd ever get out alive. I wasn't even
4   at her funeral.
5   LIAM: I know ... I know that.
6   NUALA: And now you come here in that uniform. They killed
7   her, Liam.
8   LIAM: You think I hadn't thought of that?
9   NUALA: I don't want to see you again. I don't want to even
10   know you. *(She exits.)*
11   LIAM: Nuala ... ! Nuala! *(He waits a moment, then starts for the*
12   *door.)*
13   CISSY: Don't go.
14   LIAM: What?
15   CISSY: You can't go ... Please ... If you go now she might never ...
16   *(She stops herself.)*
17   LIAM: I think she realises that, don't you?
18   CISSY: What did she mean ... ? About your mother?
19   LIAM: Ask her. I thought you two were friends.
20   CISSY: You're the only family she's got, Liam. She's just out of
21   prison, for God's sake!
22   LIAM: What?
23   CISSY: You didn't even know that?
24   LIAM: Prison?
25   CISSY: She served three months for shouting "Up with the
26   Germans and down with the British."
27   LIAM: Nuala?
28   CISSY: I was hoping you might be able to explain why. *(Pause)*
29   Your mother? Was it to do with your mother? *(Pause)* What
30   happened, Liam? *(Pause)*
31   LIAM: Friends of mine ... people I knew ... they were smuggling
32   guns for the Volunteers. They wanted me to help. I
33   wouldn't. So Mother went. They landed the rifles alright.
34   That wasn't a problem. But then the Brits got wind. There
35   was shooting.

1   CISSY: British soldiers.

2   LIAM: She got hit in the head. She died just before I could get

3   there.

4   CISSY: I see.

5   LIAM: Do you? She went because I wouldn't. She went along

6   instead of me. Peaceful means, you see. I always thought

7   it had to be peaceful means.

8   CISSY: It does. It does, Liam. The means and the end are not

9   separate entities. They're part of the same thing. They

10   affect each other. If we ever lose sight of that we're lost, we

11   become as bad as the other side.

12 LIAM: I expect you're wanting to know what I'm doing in this

13   uniform.

14 CISSY: Nationalism's something I don't understand, Liam.

15   English, Irish, whatever the variety. It's a disease that eats

16   the heart out of working people.

17 LIAM: We should all be brothers and sisters, is that it? The

18   international working class united against the common

19   enemy of capitalism?

20 CISSY: What other way can there be? Nationalism only pulls us

21   apart. It's nationalism that's created this war. It blinds us

22   to our humanity. Surely someone like you can see that?

23 LIAM: I see British soldiers outside my house, Cissy. I see

24   British justice sending innocent Irish people to rot in

25   British jails. I see my mother shot and killed because she's

26   simple enough to believe that Ireland belongs to the Irish

27   and the British have no right there. And tell me this – tell

28   me what the British working class have ever done to put

29   things right in Ireland? Why has your Labour Party never

30   organised demonstrations to get British troops out of my

31   country? Oh, we'll fly the red flag alright. We'll march

32   forward to socialist horizons. But right now we have

33   another nation sitting on our backs. That's the difference

34   between you and me, Cissy. Ireland has a weight on its

35   shoulders. *(Pause)* Look ... I'm sorry. I didn't mean to ... I'd

1   **better be going.**
2   **CISSY: Liam ...**
3   **LIAM: Yes?**
4   **CISSY: I'd like to keep in touch ... The odd letter now and again.**
5   **If you get the chance.** *(She watches as he moves away.*
6   *THOMAS and FRIEDRICH emerge from the shadows, pom-*
7   *pomming the tune of "Mrs. McGrath." A spotlight fades up on*
8   *NUALA on a separate area of the set. LIAM, rifle on shoulder,*
9   *begins to march around the set in time with the pom-*
10   *pomming. NUALA starts to sing. We enter Cissy's thoughts.)*
11   **NUALA: Oh, Mrs, McGrath, the Sergeant said**
12   **Would you like to make a soldier**
13   **Out of your son Ted?**
14   **With a scarlet coat and a big tall hat**
15   **Now Mrs. McGrath wouldn't you like that?**
16   **With your too-ry-ah, foddle-diddle-ah**
17   **Too-ry-oo-ry-oo-ry-ah**
18   **With your too-ry-ah, foddle-diddle-ah**
19   **Too-ry-oo-ry-oo-ry-ah**
20   *(THOMAS and FRIEDRICH follow LIAM, marching in time*
21   *but breaking up the military step with the beginnings of an*
22   *Irish step dance. After a round of this, the two GERMAN*
23   *SOLDIERS move into CISSY's space, take her by the arms,*
24   *and lead her into LIAM's space. The THREE of them then*
25   *follow LIAM dancing together in time with his marching.)*
26   **Now Mrs. McGrath lived on the sea shore**
27   **For the space of seven long years or more**
28   **Till she saw a big ship sailing in the bay**
29   **Here's my son Ted, will you clear the way?**
30   **With your too-ry-ah, foddle-diddle-ah**
31   **Too-ry-oo-ry-oo-ry-ah**
32   **With your too-ry-ah, foddle-diddle-ah**
33   **Too-ry-oo-ry-oo-ry-ah**
34   *(LIAM's own marching begins to show signs of breaking into*
35   *a step dance.)*

1

2   **Then up comes Ted without any legs**

3   **And in their place he had two wooden pegs**

4   **Well she kissed him a dozen times or two**

5   **Saying "Glory be to God, sure it wouldn't be you"**

6   **With your too-ry-ah, foddle-diddle-ah**

7   **Too-ry-oo-ry-oo-ry-ah**

8   **With your too-ry-ah, foddle-diddle-ah**

9   **Too-ry-oo-ry-oo-ry-ah**

10   *(LIAM abandons his rifle and the FOUR of them form a square,*

11   *dancing together with an increasing sense of enjoyment.)*

12

13   **Oh, were you drunk or were you blind**

14   **That you left your two fine legs behind**

15   **Or was it while walking by the sea**

16   **A fish ate your legs from the knees away**

17   **With your too-ry-ah, foddle-diddle-ah**

18   **Too-ry-oo-ry-oo-ry-ah**

19   **With your too-ry-ah, foddle-diddle-ah**

20   **Too-ry-oo-ry-oo-ry-ah**

21   *(The enjoyment takes over. The FOUR of them begin to laugh*

22   *and whoop to the music. LIAM and CISSY dance together*

23   *backwards and forwards across the floor.)*

24

25   **Well I wasn't drunk and I wasn't blind**

26   **When I left my two fine legs behind**

27   **But a cannon ball on the fifth of May**

28   **Tore my two fine legs from the knees away**

29   **With your too-ry-ah, foddle-diddle-ah**

30   **Too-ry-oo-ry-oo-ry-ah**

31   **With your too-ry-ah, foddle-diddle-ah**

32   **Too-ry-oo-ry-oo-ry-ah**

33

34   **Well foreign wars I do condemn**

35   **Between Kings and Lords and Gentlemen**

1   And I'll make fine sure that they rue the time
2   When they swept the legs from a child of mine
3   With your too-ry-ah, foddle-diddle-ah
4   Too-ry-oo-ry-oo-ry-ah
5   With your too-ry-ah, foddle-diddle-ah
6   Too-ry-oo-ry-oo-ry-ah
7   *(Light fades down on NUALA. THOMAS and FRIEDRICH*
8   *stand back, softly pom-pomming the tune. CISSY and LIAM*
9   *stand facing each other a moment. Then LIAM moves away,*
10   *picks up the rifle and marches off. THOMAS and*
11   *FRIEDRICH take CISSY by the arms and lead her back to her*
12   *original position in the house. THOMAS and FRIEDRICH*
13   *fade back into the shadows. CISSY stands alone with her*
14   *thoughts. Lights slowly fade down.*
15   *Light fades up on THOMAS and FRIEDRICH in a potato*
16   *field, each holding a bucket and picking potatos. The pom-*
17   *pomming from the previous scene continues through. A*
18   *WOMAN FARMER enters with NUALA.)*
19   **FARMER:** Well, this is it. Have you ever picked spuds before?
20   Sorry. Daft question. You're Irish aren't you … ? You'll be
21   able to show these Germans a thing or two, then. Don't get
22   me wrong, mind. They're good workers. I've no
23   complaints on that score. They work hard. They just don't
24   have much of a clue, you know what I mean? A bit simple
25   some of 'em. Slow on the up-take. Still, you've got to take
26   what you can get these days, Haven't you? You're sure
27   you're not prejudiced – about working with 'em?
28   **NUALA:** No.
29   **FARMER:** We're all God's children. That's what my good
30   husband always used to say. Strong chapel his family.
31   Never my cup o' tea really. I went back to C of E after he
32   died … You'll be Catholic, I suppose.
33   **NUALA:** Yes.
34   **FARMER:** Bit too keen for my taste. Still, it takes all types,
35   doesn't it? Live and let live, that's my motto. You'll see a

1   sentry come round every half hour just to make sure none

2   of 'em's run off. Take this whistle. Any bother, just give it

3   a blow. He'll be here in no time.

4   NUALA: Thank you.

5   FARMER: That one over there speaks English after a fashion.

6   He's a sort of interpretator for 'em. OK then, love, I'll leave

7   you to it. Dinner's at twelve thirty. You'll hear the hooter.

8   *(She hands a bucket to NUALA and exits. NUALA starts to*

9   *work, obviously unsure of how to do it. Tries watching the*

10   *Germans to find out. Eventually she approaches THOMAS.)*

11   NUALA: Excuse me ... You speak English ... ? Yes? *(A pause.*

12   *THOMAS smiles and puts down his bucket.)*

13   THOMAS: My father was a musician. He lived in England for

14   many years. He played in many orchestras. Once he even

15   played before your Queen Victoria and her husband.

16   NUALA: Oh, look I'm sorry. I didn't realise –

17   THOMAS: "Thomas." he said to me, "I will teach you how to

18   play the tuba and I will also teach you how to speak

19   English and then one day you will be able to visit England

20   like I did ... So – here I am. My English is not perfect, but

21   then neither is my tuba playing.

22   NUALA: You must think I'm stupid.

23   THOMAS: Ah! You speak English too! *(They both laugh.)*

24   NUALA: Look ... I've never picked potatoes before ... To tell you

25   the truth, it's my first time on a farm.

26   THOMAS: It is easy ... I will show you. First ... pick up the potato

27   ... Knock off the dirt ... Put the potato in the bucket ... When

28   the bucket is full, empty it over there.

29   NUALA: That's all there is to it?

30   THOMAS: It is my first time in the fields, too. *(Holds out his*

31   *hands.)* Look. Cuts. Blisters ... And never in my whole life

32   has my back ached like it does now.

33   NUALA: Then why do you do it? They can't force you, can they?

34   THOMAS: No. But the alternative is to spend each day

35   marching up and down the camp yard with officers

1   yelling their silly orders as though the war had not yet
2   begun. For them the army never stops – not even in a
3   prison. Most of us prefer to work ... And earn a little
4   money. You know about the others who were here?
5   NUALA: You mean the two who left?
6   THOMAS: It think it was because of us they left.
7   NUALA: You're right, it was. The woman told me when I took
8   the job. She said she couldn't get anyone local to work
9   with you.
10 THOMAS: But you ... you have no objections to working with us?
11 NUALA: Do you have any objections to working with me? *(He*
12   *laughs.)*
13 THOMAS: My name is Thomas Bekaan ... And this is my good
14   friend Friedrich Schmidt. *(FRIEDRICH steps forward to*
15   *shake hands.)*
16 FRIEDRICH: Caed mille failte.
17 NUALA: What ... ? What did you say?
18 THOMAS: Was sagen Sie, Friedrich?
19 FRIEDRICH: Ich sage "Es freut mich Sie kennenzulernen."
20 THOMAS: Nein! Das stimmt nicht! I am sorry. My friend was
21   trying to say that he is pleased to welcome you.
22 NUALA: That's what he did say ... Caed mille failte.
23 THOMAS: I am sorry ... ? Caed mille ... I have not come across
24   this English expression.
25 NUALA: I'm not surprised. It isn't English.
26 THOMAS: Not English?
27 NUALA: It's Gaelic – Irish.
28 FRIEDRICH: Was sagt sie?
29 THOMAS: Es ist nicht Englisch. Es ist Irisch.
30 FRIEDRICH: Irisch?
31 THOMAS: You are Irish?
32 NUALA: Guilty, your honour. *(To FRIEDRICH:)* How did you
33   come to learn that?
34 THOMAS: For three whole months we stayed in Ireland. I did
35   not even know there was an Irish language. *(FRIEDRICH is*

1   *delighted by NUALA's interest in him, and anxious to show*

2   *off his newly-learned Gaelic.)*

3   **FRIEDRICH:** *(Triumphant)* **Gan tianga, gan tir!** *(NUALA is*

4   *visibly startled.)*

5   **NUALA: What?**

6   **THOMAS:** *(Concerned)* **Was sagst du jetzt?**

7   **NUALA: Where in the name o' God did you learn that?**

8   **FRIEDRICH:** *(Apologising)* **Entschuldigen!** *(To THOMAS:)* **Ich**

9   **verstehe es nicht.**

10   **NUALA: Ask him. Ask him how he managed to learn that.**

11   **THOMAS: Friedrich did not mean to offend you ... He says he**

12   **does not know what it means.**

13   **NUALA: It's a slogan. An Irish slogan. It means "No language,**

14   **no nation." Ask him where he learnt it.**

15   **THOMAS: "No language, no nation." That is very clever.**

16   **NUALA:** *(Directly to FRIEDRICH)* **Gan tianga, gan tir. How do**

17   **you know this? Who told you? Who?** *(FRIEDRICH looks to*

18   *THOMAS for translation.)*

19   **THOMAS: Wer sagt?**

20   **FRIEDRICH:** *(To THOMAS)* **Liam ... Liam Mulcahey.** *(NUALA is*

21   *stunned by the answer. The two MEN exchange glances.)*

22   **THOMAS: You know him?** *(Pause. FRIEDRICH guesses the truth,*

23   *crosses to her.)*

24   **FRIEDRICH: Liam Mulcahey ... Ein Freund ... Ein guter**

25   **Freund. Sie ... Wie ist ihr Name?**

26   **NUALA: My name's Nuala ... Nuala Mulcahey.**

27   **FRIEDRICH: Seine Schwester! Ja! Sie sind's! Liam ist Ihr Bruder!**

28   **NUALA: He told you about me?**

29   **THOMAS: Yes ... He told us. He told us he would go to see you.**

30   **FRIEDRICH: Wie geht es ihm?**

31   **THOMAS: Friedrich asks if your brother is well.**

32   **NUALA: I don't know. I've heard nothing.**

33   **THOMAS: But it is almost a year since he left. Has he written**

34   **no letter?**

35   **NUALA: I've heard nothing.**

1   **THOMAS: They say no news is good news.** *(Awkward pause.*
2   *FRIEDRICH breaks it by thrusting a bucket at NUALA and*
3   *taking her by the arm to where he and THOMAS are working.)*
4   **FRIEDRICH: Kommen   Sie!   Zusammen!   Wir   arbeiten**
5   **zusammen! Nuala ... Freund ... Bruder ... Schwester ... Gut.**
6   *(Makes a show of formally introducing himself.)* **Mein Name ...**
7   **Friedrich ... Friedrich Wilhelm Karl Schmidt! Gan tianga,**
8   **gan tir!** *(NUALA, amazed by his display, bursts into laughter.*
9   *So does THOMAS. All THREE begin to laugh together, then*
10   *start work. NUALA begins to hum the tune of "Foggy Dew."*
11   *THOMAS and FRIEDRICH pick it up and pom-pom along with*
12   *her, working in time, all in good spirits. Lights crossfade to a*
13   *SOLDIER elsewhere on the set. He sings "Foggy Dew." Much*
14   *slower tempo, very different mood. During the song, lights*
15   *fade up on LIAM writing a letter.)*
16   **SOLDIER: As down the glen one Easter morn**
17   **To a city fair rode I**
18   **There armed lines of fighting men**
19   **In squadrons passed me by.**
20   **No pipe did hum**
21   **No battle drum**
22   **Did beat out its wild tatoo**
23   **But the Angelus bell o'er the Liffey's swell**
24   **Rang out through the foggy dew**
25
26   **Right proudly high in Dublin town**
27   **They flung out the flag of war**
28   **It was better to die neath an Irish sky**
29   **Than in Suvla or Sud el Bar.**
30   **And from the plains of Royal Meath**
31   **Strong men came hurrying through**
32   **While Brittania's huns**
33   **With their six inch guns**
34   **Sailed in through the foggy dew**
35

1	Twas England bade our Wild Geese go
2	That small nations might be free
3	But their lonely graves are by Suvla's waves
4	Or the fringes of the great North Sea.
5	Oh, had they died by Pearse's side
6	Or fallen with Cathal Brugha
7	Their names we'd keep
8	Where the Fenians sleep
9	Neath the shroud of the foggy dew.
10	*(Spotlight fades down on the SOLDIER, full light up on LIAM.*
11	*In the background, sound effects of distant artillery. France,*
12	*early May, 1919, somewhere a little way back from the front*
13	*line. Two other SOLDIERS sit separate from him. ONE of them*
14	*is engrossed in a newspaper, the OTHER is talking to him.)*
15	SOLDIER 1: So ... like I say ... there we was ... sitting in this field.
16	Just the two of us ... Like we are now. Bright sunny day.
17	Must've been fifteen miles from the line. You could barely
18	hear the artillery. He had this big chunk o' bread in his
19	hand ... cadged it off a Frog farmer ... Then these two
20	planes come over. Only low. We could see they were ours,
21	so we didn't take no notice. He had his mouth wide open –
22	just about to take a bite out o' this chunk o' bread – and
23	wham! I looks up ... and there he is, flat on his back, his
24	head smashed to a pulp. Do you know what it was? This'll
25	get you, this ... A tool box. A bleedin' tool box. Must'a fallen
26	out o' one o' them planes. *(Laughs.)* This is the best part,
27	though ... You know what the Chaplain wrote on the letter
28	to his missis? "There is something comforting about the
29	death of a gallant soldier on the field of battle" Yeah ... A
30	bleedin' tool box. *(LIAM finishes the letter, puts it in his kit*
31	*bag. SOLDIER 2 carries on reading.)* Girl friend, is it?
32	LIAM: No ... No, just someone I met in England.
33	SOLDIER 1: Paddy then, are you? *(LIAM doesn't answer.*
34	*SOLDIER 1 starts to take an interest.)* Got any grub in there?
35	LIAM: Who for?

1 SOLIDER 1: Ah, come on, Paddy. Share and share alike. We're
2   all in this together.
3 LIAM: My name's not Paddy.
4 SOLDIER 1: Bit touchy, aren't you?
5 SOLDIER 2: I don't blame him. I'd be keeping my head down
6   in your shoes too ... Paddy.
7 LIAM: Don't you think we have enough trouble out here?
8 SOLDIER 2: Oh, that's rich that is, Paddy. Maybe you should
9   tell that one to your mates back in Dublin. *(Passes the*
10   *newspaper to SOLDIER 1.)* You seen this?
11 SOLDIER 1: What? *(Starts to read.)*
12 SOLDIER 2: I know one thing, Paddy. Next time they send us
13   over the top I'm going to make sure there's none of your
14   kind anywhere at the back of me.
15 LIAM: Listen, soldier, I don't know what you're talking about
16   but —
17 SOLDIER 1: "Armed rebels declare Ireland a republic"
18 LIAM: What?
19 SOLDIER 2: Typical, ain't it? Wait till we're over here fighting
20   Fritz, then start a bleedin' war in Ireland!
21 LIAM: Let me see that! *(LIAM makes a grab for the paper,*
22   *SOLDIER 1 whisks it out of his reach.)*
23 SOLDIER 1: Oh no you don't!
24 SOLDIER 2: You're in the wrong place, Paddy. This is a real man's
25   war out here. You should've stayed back at home in Dublin.
26   You could've shot English Tommies in the back there!
27 LIAM: Let me see that paper!
28 SOLDIER 1: I'll read it to you ... "Fierce street fighting between
29   the army and Irish rebels. British casualties over three
30   hundred.".
31 SOLDIER 2: I hope they shoot every last fucking one o' the
32   bastards.
33 LIAM: You know nothing! Either of you! You know nothing
34   about Ireland!
35 SOLDIER 2: Well maybe you can explain it to us, Paddy. *(Grabs*

1   *the paper off SOLDIER 1.)* **Maybe you can explain about**
2   **this German warship off the coast of Ireland. Maybe you**
3   **can explain why it was crammed full of brand new**
4   **Mausers. Maybe you can explain what your friends in**
5   **green uniforms would've done with 'em all if our Navy**
6   **lads hadn't got there first!**

7   **SOLDIER 1: They're in with the Huns?**

8   **SOLDIER 2: Too fucking right. Fritz and Paddy. Both pissing**
9   **in the same pot.**

10   **LIAM: So why do you think me and two hundred thousand other**
11   **Irishmen came out here to get chopped up by German**
12   **machine guns! You think we did it for England! There are**
13   **four men left in my platoon! Four! Four out of thirty six!**

14   **SOLDIER 2: What's happened to the rest? Gone over to the**
15   **other side have they? I wouldn't be surprised if they've got**
16   **an whole bleedin' battalion o' Micks over there by now!**
17   *(LIAM rushes at him. SOLDIER 1 trips him. LIAM jumps to*
18   *his feet. SOLDIER 1 grabs him from behind.)* **Violence now**
19   **is it? All the same you Paddies, aren't you?**

20   **SOLDIER 1: I'll get his stuff.**

21   **LIAM: Don't you touch that!**

22   **SOLDIER 2: A bit o' grub's not much to lose, Paddy. Think of**
23   **those poor bastards in Dublin – murdered by your mates!**

24   **LIAM: Get your hands off my stuff!** *(SOLDIER 1 produces some*
25   *cans of food.)*

26   **SOLDIER 1: I knew he had some food in here. Greedy bastard.**
27   **Fucking 'ell ... what's this?** *(Pulls out the bone given to*
28   *LIAM by FRIEDRICH.)*

29   **LIAM: Put that back!**

30   **SOLDIER 2: They always say the fucking Irish live like dogs.**

31   **SOLDIER 1: It's got writing on it ...** *(Struggles to read it.)*
32   **"Schnadahupffe ... "**

33   **LIAM: I said put it back!**

34   **SOLDIER 1: Jesus fucking Christ ... it's German ... It's got fucking**
35   **Hun writing all over it ... He's sending messages to Fritz!**

1 **SOLDIER 2: You dirty stinking Irish mick! You're no different**
2 **from that lot in Dublin, are you!**
3 **LIAM: You're stupid! You're talking stupid!**
4 **SOLDIER 1: No wonder they can cut us to pieces the moment**
5 **we step out of the flaming trench!**
6 **LIAM: It's a souvenir! A souvenir, you thick Tommy!**
7 **SOLDIER 2: A souvenir is it? Well here's another one for you!**
8 *(Punches LIAM in the kidneys. LIAM doubles up. They both lay*
9 *into him. LIAM slumps to the ground. They give him a good*
10 *kicking. Finally they toss the bone on top of him.)* **That's for**
11 **our lads in Dublin.** *(They exit. Lights start to dim. LIAM crawls*
12 *a yard or so and pulls himself to a sitting position against a*
13 *wall. He stays there in half-light. Elsewhere on the set lights*
14 *fade up on NUALA and FRIEDRICH in the potato field with*
15 *their buckets. NUALA is trying to teach FRIEDRICH to juggle*
16 *with the potatoes. He can't do it. Lots of fun and laughter.)*
17 **FRIEDRICH: Dieser ... ! Eine in die luft!** *(Drops them.)* **Ahhh!**
18 **NUALA: It's easy ...** *(Takes the potatoes.)* **Watch. This one first ...**
19 **now this ... See ...** *(Juggles.)*
20 **FRIEDRICH:** *(Clapping)* **Bravo! Bravo!**
21 **NUALA: Go on ... It's not hard ... Try again.** *(He takes the potatoes.)*
22 **FRIEDRICH: Diese ... die Erste. Diese ... die Zweite ...** *(Drops*
23 *them again.)* **Ahhh...! Ich kann nicht tun!** *(They both laugh.)*
24 **NUALA: We'd better get back to work ... you'll be getting me**
25 **sacked ... Come on ... Work!** *(FRIEDRICH grins and tosses a*
26 *potato into the bucket.)*
27 **FRIEDRICH: Work!** *(Tosses the second potato in.)* **Work!** *(And*
28 *then the third)* **Work!** *(Lights fade on them, but they remain*
29 *where they are, in half-light. The door on set opens and a*
30 *BRITISH SOLDIER ushers CATHAL into a prison cell. He is*
31 *handcuffed and dirty, but still wearing the green uniform of*
32 *the Irish Volunteers. The SOLDIER closes and locks the door*
33 *on him and he settles against the wall of the cell as full light*
34 *comes back up on LIAM, still sitting against the wall in*
35 *France. The dialogue takes place in their separate realities.)*

1   LIAM: So ... you did it then ... you finally did it.

2   CATHAL: You should've been there, Liam. Felt what it was like.

3   Fought alongside us ... If only those rifles had arrived.

4   LIAM: Sounds like a total fiasco if you ask me.

5   CATHAL: Orders. Counter-orders. Nobody knew what was
6   happening. When it came to it, there were barely a
7   thousand of us in Dublin. We'd expected five times that
8   many. Oh, but I tell you, Liam, when we formed ranks in
9   Beresford Place and marched into Sackville Street, it felt
10   like nothing on earth could stop us. It felt like we were
11   marching out to set the world aflame. *(He moves out of his*
12   *own reality in the prison cell and into LIAM's in France,*
13   *addressing him directly.)* You should'a seen the looks on
14   the faces as we ran up the tricolour ... I swear to God, they
15   thought we were lunatics. We took models from the
16   waxworks on Henry Street and used 'em to barricade the
17   windows of the GPO. King George and Lord Kitchener
18   stopped a few English bullets before the week was out, I
19   can tell you. We never moved. Just held our positions and
20   waited. They positioned machine guns on the roofs so you
21   couldn't step outside. Then eventually we hear the sound
22   of artillery. "It's the Germans!" somebody shouted. "The
23   Germans are coming! The Germans are coming!" For a
24   moment we were all filled with a wild hope. "The
25   Germans are coming," we yelled. All laughing and
26   shouting. "The Germans are coming!" Then the shells
27   started smashing into the roof over our heads and we
28   knew it was British guns. By Friday it was pointless
29   continuing and all of us knew it. You remember Elisabeth
30   O'Farrell? She went out with the surrender flag. The
31   executions have started now. *(He leaves LIAM and returns*
32   *to the cell area, separate realities.)*

33   Oh, and you remember those Germans. The ones you
34   took over to Leigh. The Volunteers in Tipperary had it all
35   planned to release 'em. Think of that, Liam. Two thousand

1   **trained German troops fighting alongside us. What a**
2   **difference they would'a made. The Brits knew what they**
3   **were doing alright when they took 'em over to Lancashire.**
4   *(Lights fade slowly down on CATHAL. LIAM gets up, starts to*
5   *take off his jacket. The door opens and a SOLDIER ushers*
6   *CATHAL out of the cell. LIAM rolls up the jacket and cap and*
7   *hides them. He takes a white handkerchief and ties it round*
8   *the end of his rifle, picks up the bone, and with the white flag*
9   *held above, exits. Lights fade up on FRIEDRICH and NUALA*
10   *who are still On-stage in the potato field.)*
11 **FRIEDRICH: Nuala ... Wollen Sie eine Photo sehen?** *(Feels his*
12   *pocket.)*
13 **NUALA: A photograph ... ? What of?**
14 **FRIEDRICH: Von meine Familie.** *(Points them out to her.)* **Mein**
15   **Vater**
16 **NUALA: Look at the size of his moustache ... ! They're like**
17   **wings!** *(They laugh. FRIEDRICH mimes how his father*
18   *twists his moustache.)*
19 **FRIEDRICH: Jeden Tag, tut er Ol d'rauf!**
20 **NUALA: Is this your mother?**
21 **FRIEDRICH: Ja! Meine Mutter.**
22 **NUALA: She's very beautiful ... I love the hat she's wearing.**
23   **And look at the lace on her dress ... It's a lovely**
24   **photograph, Friedrich.** *(He puts it away.)*
25 **FRIEDRICH: Sie ... ? Mutter, Vater?**
26 **NUALA: No ... No, they're dead ... They're both dead.**
27 **FRIEDRICH:** *(Understanding)* **Tut mir leid.** *(THOMAS enters,*
28   *followed by CISSY.)*
29 **THOMAS: She is here in the field with Friedrich, I think.**
30 **NUALA: Cissy ... ! What are you doing here ... ? This is Friedrich ...**
31   **The one I told you about ... He's a Socialist, too.**
32 **CISSY: I'm pleased to meet you, Friedrich ... Nuala ... There's a**
33   **letter. It's from France.** *(Hands it to NUALA.)* **I thought I'd**
34   **better bring it straight out.** *(Waits anxiously while NUALA*
35   *opens it and reads. Pause.)* **Is it from Liam?**

1   FRIEDRICH: *(To THOMAS)* Aus Liam?

2   CISSY: Is he alright? What does he say? *(NUALA finishes*
3   *reading it.)*

4   NUALA: It isn't from Liam. *(Hands it to CISSY.)*

5   THOMAS: It isn't bad news, is it?

6   CISSY: *(Reading)* "They'll write to tell you your brother was
7   killed in action. It isn't true. He tried to cross over to
8   German lines. They court-martialled him for treason and
9   desertion. Then they made the rest of us shoot him. A lot
10   of us are beginning to wonder if we're fighting the wrong
11   enemy."

12   FRIEDRICH: *(To THOMAS)* Was ist passiert? Was steht im brief?

13   CISSY: Why, Nuala ... ? Why?

14   NUALA: Why ... ? *(She starts to laugh.)* Peaceful means ... Don't
15   you see ... ? Peaceful means. All the way to France to fight
16   Germans and he ends up getting shot by the British!

17   CISSY: *(Suddenly angry)* He's your brother. Nuala!

18   FRIEDRICH: *(To THOMAS)* Was sagt jemond nicht? Was felt Liam?

19   CISSY: Is that all that you can say? Is that all you care about —
20   who shot him!

21   NUALA: *(Switching to intense anger herself)* No! That's not all I
22   care about, Cissy! What do you want? You want tears? Is
23   that it? You want to see tears? Maybe you want me to feel
24   it's my fault he died!

25   CISSY: No ... no.

26   NUALA: Do you think I never imagined a letter like this? Never
27   thought about him getting killed? He's dead — that's all
28   there is to it as far as you're concerned, isn't it! Just one
29   more life wasted! Doesn't matter which side he was on,
30   which side killed him, they're all as bad as each other!
31   Well for me it matters! I don't expect you ever to be able to
32   understand that, Cissy, but I've been through this before
33   and tears aren't enough!

34   CISSY: I never said they were.

35   NUALA: I'm going.

1 CISSY: What do you mean? Where are you going?

2 NUALA: Back to Dublin. I should have done it months ago.

3 CISSY: I don't believe this! Your brother's just been killed! Isn't
4   one war enough for you! Haven't there been enough
5   martyrs to the cause!

6 NUALA: I used to think you were the one with the cause, Cissy.
7   What happened to the socialist revolution you thought
8   was just around the corner?

9 CISSY: That's not fair!

10 NUALA: Fair ... ? Fair!

11 CISSY: It doesn't make any sense, Nuala. None of this. You,
12   Liam, your mother, that whole miserable mess over there
13   in Ireland! It doesn't make sense!

14 NUALA: No. No. You're right. It doesn't ... So what do you
15   suggest I do? Forget about it? Wait for people like you to
16   sort it out ... ? What, Cissy? What should I do? *(She turns to*
17   *FRIEDRICH.)* I have to go ... Thomas will explain.
18   Remember me ... Gan tianga, gan tir. *(She exits.)*

19 FRIEDRICH: Nuala! Nuala, warte...! Thomas, was sagt sie? Wo
20   geht sie?

21 THOMAS: *(To CISSY)* Nuala will go to fight the British?

22 CISSY: I hope to God you can understand it. *(She exits after*
23   *NUALA.)*

24 THOMAS: Kommst du, Friedrich. *(They start to exit as lights*
25   *fade to black. Lights up on THOMAS and FRIEDRICH in the*
26   *Lilford Mill Camp. FRIEDRICH is pacing around the acting*
27   *area in an agitated manner. They are in the middle of a*
28   *heated dialogue which takes place entirely in German, the*
29   *sense being conveyed physically and by emphasizing certain*
30   *German words. English translation is in brackets.)*

31 THOMAS: Friedrich ... beruhige dich! [Friedrich, calm down,
32   will you?]

33 FRIEDRICH: Ich soll mich beruhigen? Liam is doch tot. Nuala
34   ist nach Irland gegangen. Und du sagst ich soll mich
35   beruhigen! [Calm down? Liam's dead. Nuala's gone to

450

1   Ireland. And you want me to calm down!]
2   THOMAS: Du kannst nichts dafur! [There's nothing you can do!]
3   FRIEDRICH: Ich kann von hier weg. [I can get out of this
4   place.]
5   THOMAS: Sei nicht dumm, Friedrich. [Don't talk stupid,
6   Friedrich.]
7   FRIEDRICH: Warum? Warum soll ich hier bleiben? Der Krieg
8   konnte noch funf Jahre dauern ... vielleicht sogar zehn.
9   [Why? Why should I stay here? The war could go on
10   another five years ... maybe even ten.]
11   THOMAS: Fur unst ist der Krieg zu Ende. Eines Tages gehen
12   wir heim. Denk mal, was dem Liam passiert ist. [At least
13   we're out of it. One day we'll go home. Look what
14   happened to Liam.]
15   FRIEDRICH: Jawohl! Was ist ihm passiert! Darum muss ich
16   Nuala sehen! [Yes! Look what happened to him! That's
17   why I have to see Nuala!]
18   THOMAS: Friedrich ... Nuala ist in Irland! Wie oft muss ich dir
19   sagen? Nuala is in Irland! Friedrich ... [Nuala's in Ireland!
20   How many times do I have to say it? Nuala is in Ireland!]
21   FRIEDRICH: Wenn Nuala in Irland ist, dann geh ich nach
22   Irland! [If Nuala's in Ireland, then I'll go to Ireland!]
23   THOMAS: Du bist verdeht, Friedrich! Du kannst nicht auf
24   Irland gehen! [You're out of your head, Friedrich! You
25   can't go to Ireland!]
26   FRIEDRICH: Wenn Nuala in Irland ist, dann werden ich Nuala
27   finden. Ich muss fort von hier. [If Nuala's in Ireland, then
28   I'll find her. I have to get out of here.] *(FRIEDRICH starts to*
29   *look around for some means of escape.)*
30   THOMAS: Friedrich! Halt ... ! Hor zu! Nuala ist Irin ... Du bist
31   Deutscher ... Es ist nicht dein Kampf! [Friedrich! Stop ... !
32   Listen to me! Nuala is Irish ... You are German ... It's not
33   your fight!]
34   FRIEDRICH: Warum nicht? Er ist ein bessere Kampf als der
35   wegen dem ich hier sitze. [Why not? It's a better fight than

1   the one that got me in here.]

2   **THOMAS: Du bist unmoglich! Auch wenn du weg kommst,**

3   **kannst du kein Wort Englisch sprechen! [You're impossible!**

4   **Even if you get out of here, you can't speak a word of English!]**

5   *(FRIEDRICH spots a possible escape route.)*

6   **FRIEDRICH: Ich werde also durch das Dach klettern! [I'll go**

7   **up through the roof!]**

8   **THOMAS: Du bist verruckt? Es gibt Wachtposten uberall!**

9   **Scheinwerfer! Machinengewehr! Drahtwerhau! Du hast**

10   **kein Chance! [Are you crazy? There are guards all round**

11   **this place! Searchlights! Machine guns! Barbed wire! You**

12   **don't stand a chance!]**

13   **FRIEDRICH: Du kannst hier bleiben wenn du willst, Thomas.**

14   **Ich gehen! [You stay here if that's what you want, Thomas.**

15   **I'm going!]** *(He starts to climb the set towards the roof.)*

16   **THOMAS: Freidrich! Um Gottes willen, Komm doch runter!**

17   **Die werden schiessen ... dich toten! [Freidrich! For God's**

18   **sake, come down! You're going to get yourself killed!]**

19   *(MORRIS LAMBERT, the sentry from Wigan, enters.)*

20   **SENTRY: What's going on?** *(Sees FRIEDRICH up underneath the*

21   *roof.)* **Bloody hell!** *(Pulls out a whistle, starts blowing it like*

22   *mad. Takes the rifle from his shoulder and starts to cock it.)*

23   **Escape! Prisoner escaping!**

24   **THOMAS: Don't shoot! He can't escape! He's only –**

25   **SENTRY:** *(Pushing THOMAS out of the way)* **Get away, you! Get**

26   **the fuck away!** *(Blows his whistle again. A siren starts up. He*

27   *aims his rifle at FRIEDRICH who freezes.)* **Come down out**

28   **o' that roof, Fritz, or I'll blow your fucking brains out!**

29   **THOMAS: He doesn't speak English! He doesn't understand!**

30   *(The SENTRY swings his rifle at THOMAS.)*

31   **SENTRY: Get away, you ... ! Don't come near!** *(To FRIEDRICH:)*

32   **This is your last warning, Fritz! Get down out o' that**

33   **fucking roof! I'm counting to three! One!**

34   **THOMAS: He doesn't understand you!**

35   **SENTRY: Shut up, you! Two!**

1 THOMAS: Friedrich! Komm doch h'runter! *(The SENTRY fires the*
2   *rifle, FRIEDRICH slumps down. A pause. The sirens continue.)*
3 SENTRY: I warned him ... You heard me ... I warned him.
4 THOMAS: You stupid man ... You stupid, stupid man.
5   *(Lights fade to black. Sirens fade out. Lights fade up on LIAM*
6   *and THOMAS and FRIEDRICH.)*
7 LIAM: That's it then. They've heard it all.
8 THOMAS: Not quite. There is still one part of the story they
9   need to know. *(He places a brazier On-stage and a placard*
10   *that reads "Amalgamated Engineering Union: Official*
11   *Dispute." CISSY enters, a woman in her seventies once*
12   *again, carrying the flowers from the cemetery. FRIEDRICH*
13   *produces a winter coat — 1960's — and cap which he hands*
14   *to LIAM. LIAM watches her as he puts them on and becomes*
15   *a PICKET standing by the brazier, stamping his feet and*
16   *blowing his fingers. CISSY approaches him. THOMAS and*
17   *FRIEDRICH watch from the sidelines.)*
18 PICKET: Alright there, luv.
19 CISSY: Good afternoon.
20 PICKET: Warm enough for you, is it ... ? Nice bunch o'flowers
21   you got there ... Not taking 'em in there I hope.
22 CISSY: Just to the wall.
23 PICKET: Oh ... right. That's OK then ... Just so long as it's not a
24   delivery. We're stopping deliveries, see. You wouldn't
25   want to go crossing a picket line, would you? *(CISSY*
26   *notices the placard for the first time.)*
27 CISSY: I never knew there was a strike.
28 PICKET: Been out nearly a week now, luv – you not seen our
29   photo in't Journal?
30 CISSY: No ... What's it over?
31 PICKET: Refusing to pay't union minimum ... They're all't
32   same these two bit engineering firms ... They'll do owt to
33   keep the union out.
34 CISSY: I helped organise a strike here once.
35 PICKET: No kidding? Weaver lasses was it?

1   **CISSY: No. Before that. Before Lilford Mill was ever a weaving**
2   **shed.**

3   **PICKET: I thought it'd always been a weaving shed — right up**
4   **to these lot moving in, anyway.**

5   **CISSY: Oh, no. There were German prisoners in Lilford Mill**
6   **before there were any looms.**

7   **PICKET:** *(Dubious)* **German prisoners?**

8   **CISSY: They brought them over from Ireland.**

9   **PICKET:** *(Even more dubious)* **Oh ... Right.**

10   **CISSY: They tried to tell us they'd brought them here because**
11   **the lavatories in Tipperary weren't good enough ... That**
12   **wasn't the real reason, though.**

13   **PICKET: No?**

14   **CISSY: Their grave used to be in Manchester Road Cemetery,**
15   **you see. I went every year. But the man there says they've**
16   **been dug up. Parks and Leisure. It's not right. There's not**
17   **even a headstone any more ... That's why I've come here.**

18   **PICKET: Right ... I understand ... Well ... er ... I'm not sure what**
19   **to —**

20   **CISSY: I met them, you see. One of them spoke English.**
21   **Thomas. He died of flu just after the war ended. It was an**
22   **epidemic. The other one was shot. Friedrich. Friedrich**
23   **Wilhelm Karl Schmidt. Just over there under the roof.**
24   **People say it never should have happened ... None of it**
25   **should have happened, that's what I tell 'em.** *(She*
26   *remembers something, starts rummaging in her bag.)*

27   **PICKET: Sounds like we're going to have to watch our step**
28   **when we get back in there then, luv, eh ... ? Watch out for**
29   **German ghosts.** *(He laughs good-naturedly, by now*
30   *convinced she's senile.)*

31   **CISSY: I have something ...** *(Pulls out the bone with the German*
32   *writing on it. Hands it to him.)* **One of the Germans made**
33   **it ... as a present for an Irish soldier.**

34   **PICKET: What is it ... an Irish toothpick?** *(He laughs. CISSY's*
35   *mood changes abruptly. She takes the bone away from him,*

1   *puts it back in her bag.)* **Hey, look ... I didn't mean to upset**
2   **you, luv ... It was only a joke ... It's very interesting. I**
3   **wasn't laughing at you or anything.**
4   **CISSY: I'll just put the flowers down by the wall if that's alright.**
5   **PICKET: You go ahead, luv ... Anything you like ... Nobody'll**
6   **bother you. I'll make sure o' that.** *(CISSY places the flowers*
7   *on the floor. The PICKET watches her as she stands looking*
8   *at them.)*
9   **CISSY: Thomas Bekaan. Musician. Friedrich Wilhelm Karl**
10   **Schmidt. Building Worker. Liam Mulcahey ... Volunteer ...**
11   **Irish Republican Army.** *(She turns and exits. The PICKET*
12   *watches CISSY go then strolls over to the flowers. Picks*
13   *them up.)*
14   **PICKET: I.R.A.** *(Laughs and tosses them away. Begins to whistle the*
15   *tune of "We Shall Overcome" as he takes off the Picket's coat*
16   *and becomes LIAM again. The three SOLDIERS stand in a line.)*
17   **LIAM: Atten - shun!** *(They stand to attention. Blackout.)*
18
19   **THE END**
20
21
22
23
24
25
26
27
28
29
30
31
32
33
34
35

A Single Numberless Death
by Bob Mayberry

Adapted from the book of the same title by Nora
Strejilevich, that was translated by Kathy Odgers and
Nora Strejilevich

Nora Strejilevich's memoir recounts her experiences in the late '70s when she and her brother Gerardo were abducted by the Milicos, the secret police of the Argentine military junta. Nora was released only to be re-arrested, incarcerated in a special prison for political prisoners, and repeatedly raped and tortured by her captors with electric cattle prods. She later escaped from Argentina and has lived in exile since. Nora has never located her brother; he is among the thousands of young people who were "disappeared" by the junta during its reign of terror.

This stage adaptation of her memoir — done with her approval and guidance — is really an evolving drama: a story that is ongoing and unfinished. Stage directors should seek to capture this sense of "living documentary" which, in the words of Dr. Strejilevich, "is a living history that is not yet resolved." Today in Buenos Aires — as well as in other South American and Caribbean nations — families and friends of the disappeared carry their loved ones' photos on placards as they demonstrate in their cities and before their government offices, demanding explanations.

Though the story seems to focus exclusively on the bitter experience of its central character, Naomi (the fictitious persona of the author), it is really more than that. Dr. Strejilevich remarked that it's "a collective story and a collective work" because she combined her own recollections with those of others whom she interviewed in Buenos Aires following her return from exile when she was preparing her memoir. The play voices such testimony in the form of constant dialog between Naomi and the chorus, and thus Naomi's experiences link with those of the thousands of other disappeared victims of state terror in Argentina, and with other terror victims around the world.

This stage adaptation retains the raw power and beauty of the original memoir. It is particularly challenging in the many choices it offers for staging violence and brutality. The playwright advises restraint in this regard, feeling that realistic violence "would overwhelm the play's focus on the *effect* of torture on Naomi and, by extension, on Argentina itself." Instead the playwright recommends abstraction and minimalism: "the illusion of violence is created through deliberate and precise choreography."

The play also offers numerous opportunities for music, dance and creative movement choices. There are "dance sequences" indicated in the script, masks, transformational roles for the actors, and much physical activity required — all of which should challenge the imagination of designers, directors, actors, choreographers and others. Additionally, all the roles can and probably should be portrayed by young actors, since the disappeared were mainly young Argentinians. Their photos can be integrated into the production and are readily accessible through Internet resources. And the two scenes in which older characters are called for — the letters of the loved ones and the closing demonstration — can work for a young cast with a little help from costuming and creative vocal-physical suggestions. The drama, in fact, might take on a highly-stylized, minimalist look in actual production; or it might resemble a ritualized dance; or in a documentary style the play could become high-tech, critical and modernist. And there are other choices.

Above all, however, the impact of the play's desperate and compelling message should never be lost in production, because this is what can move the spectator most strongly and powerfully engage the commitment of the young artists producing the play: "Don't forget us!" the ensemble demands of the audience during the drama's closing moments. "Don't forget us!" Indeed, this is the core idea of many plays written on the same theme by South American authors, such as *Retablo de Yumbel* by the Chilean author Isidora Aguirre, and others.

A Single Numberless Death is a powerful docudrama that celebrates and testifies to the worth as well as to the fragility of humanitarian values, despite the most shocking atrocities our contemporary world has been forced to witness.

Characters

Naomi, an Argentine Jew of indeterminate age who has experienced, and who remembers vividly, more pain and suffering than most of us will ever know
Gerardo, Naomi's brother
Narrators, a half dozen or so actors, male and female, who narrate Naomi's story, assuming minor roles as prisoners, mothers, fathers and guards as necessary
Milicos, the Argentine secret military police, 3 or 4 males, brutal and indifferent
Commander, head of the Milicos, ironic, subtle, even witty

Except for Naomi, any of the other characters might double as Narrators.

Music

The song referred to in the last scene, *El Pueblo Unido Jamas Sera Vencido*, is a popular song of revolution from South America, although not necessarily Argentinian in its source, nor factually based on what political demonstrators have sung and chanted in Argentina. Numerous recorded versions can be found, with the help of which the cast can easily learn it. The version used for the world premiere can be found on CD, and was done by the composer/performers Sergio Ortega & Quilapayun.

Setting

The stage is empty except for the shell of a '60s Ford Falcon, green, without doors or windows, conspicuously missing its license plate, sitting on blocks or perhaps suspended from above, but arranged so actors can climb in and out of it, even on it, and so the audience can see them beneath the green bug-like shell.

A Single Numberless Death was first produced in November, 2001, at Grand Valley State University, Michigan, with the following cast and crew:

Stage Director: Michael Page
Lighting Design: Andrew Dorland
Set Design: Alfred Sheffield
Costume Design: Jill Dole Hamilton
Stage Manager: Jeff Williams
Technical Direction: Paul Collins
Choreography & Combatives: Erin Merritt
Original Music: Alex Hamel & Gregory Secor
NAOMI: Heather Hartnett
GERARDO: Rodel Salazar
MILICOS: Jayme Wooster, Matt Wilson, Eddie Kleinfeld
COMMANDER: Scott Rosendall
NARRATORS, MOTHERS, FATHERS, RELATIVES, FRIENDS, PRISONERS, GUARDS: Dan Kennedy, Becky Black, Nick Randall, Carolyn Ratkowski, Justin Fournier, Tamira A. Henry, Rachel Roos, Jennifer L. Rashleigh, Megan Lynette Staples, Christina Hoffman, Michael L. Houser, Nathan Bauer

1	**SCENE 1: GERARDO'S ARREST**
2	
3	**VOICES OFF-STAGE: Bring the knife, ring the bell, when you**
4	**die you'll go to hell.**
5	*(Whispered:)* **Step on a crack ...**
6	**Bring the knife, ring the bell, when you die you'll go to hell.**
7	*(Whispered:)* **Step on a crack ...**
8	**Bring the knife, ring the bell, when you die you'll go to hell.**
9	*(Whispered:)* **Step on a crack ...**
10	**Break your mother's back.**
11	*(The NARRATORS enter, speaking as they come, gathering*
12	*casually around the Ford Falcon, leaning on it, exploring it,*
13	*etc. NARRATORS speak individually, one speaker per unit of*
14	*text [units are marked by ellipses or end punctuation] except*
15	*when it's indicated they speak together.)*
16	**NARRATORS: It's not everyday that you open the door and**
17	**four rooms are wrecked by a gale that murders the past**
18	**and tears the hands off the clock.**
19	**It's not every day that mirrors shatter and garments shred.**
20	**It's not every day that you try to escape and the clock has**
21	**moved ...**
22	**the door unhinged ...**
23	**the windows jammed.**
24	**Cornered, you cry.**
25	**Minutes do not tick by.**
26	**It's not every day that you stumble and fall with hands**
27	**behind your back.**
28	**Trapped in a night so dark ...**
29	**lost amid overturned chairs ...**
30	**emptied drawers ...**
31	**opened suitcases ...**
32	**torn maps ...**
33	**severed roads.**
34	**You barely make out the reverberating echoes –**
35	*(Enter MILICOS, in uniforms; they stand like soldiers*

1	*Upstage and shout.)*
2	**MILICOS: You thought you could escape!**
3	**NARATORS: An enormous mouth opens up.**
4	**An enormous mouth devours you.**
5	*(MILICOS pull NAOMI and GERARDO out of the crowd.)*
6	**MILICOS: Bitch!**
7	**Bastard!**
8	**NARRATORS: What's happening?**
9	**Who are these —**
10	**Why me? Why us?**
11	**Familiar voices whisper —**
12	**NAOMI & GERARDO: We haven't done anything.**
13	**We haven't.** *(MILICOS pull NAOMI and GERARDO*
14	*Downstage. The NARRATORS move away to separate*
15	*themselves from the victims. They leer at the fate of their*
16	*friends.)*
17	**NARRATORS: Yet, here you are, on this side, in this body.**
18	**If you haven't done anything ...**
19	**Soles tattooed onto your skin ...**
20	**Why else are you here? Why else would the police ...**
21	**Boots on your back ...**
22	**Unless you ...**
23	**A gun at the nape of your neck.**
24	**Unless.**
25	**MILICOS: On your feet!**
26	**NARRATORS: You stand meekly ...**
27	**confused ...**
28	**bewildered ...**
29	**beaten ...**
30	**NAOMI: They're taking me, they're taking me!** *(MILICOS*
31	*blindfold first GERARDO, then NAOMI. She resists.)*
32	**NARRATORS: We watch as they blindfold you ...**
33	**Stuff you into the elevator ...**
34	**Drag you out of the building ...**
35	**Two in the afternoon!**

1   Space vanishes under your feet.

2   You scream at the top of your lungs ...

3   With your legs ...

4   Arms ...

5   **Guts.** *(NAOMI screams silently.)*

6 **NARRATORS:** On the sidewalk you kick and scream against a

7   nameless fate in some mass grave.

8   You flail untamed on the edge of obliteration.

9   They push you.

10   You land on the floor of a car.

11   Blows rain on you. *(GERARDO is pushed onto his knees in*

12   *front of the Ford Falcon. NAOMI is shoved into the Ford*

13   *Falcon.)*

14 **MILICOS:** *(Kicking)* Take this for screaming, you piece of shit.

15   This for kicking us.

16   And this and this.

17 **NARRATORS:** One moment you're here, the next ...

18   Gone.

19   Only the fading sound of the car to remind us

20   That you lived and died here,

21   In this neighborhood,

22   Your neighborhood ...

23   Gone.

24   The car that snatched you from among us

25   Now offers you up to them,

26   In their neighborhood.

27 **VOICE:** *(Calling out)* Where?

28 **NARRATORS:** Only the distant sound of the car ...

29   The Ford Falcon

30 **MILICOS:** You stink! Both of you.

31   We're gonna clean you up, alright.

32   Clean you good.

33   Won't recognize yourselves.

34   We're gonna turn you into soap.

35 **NARRATORS:** *(Retreating Upstage, whispering together)* **Bring**

1   the knife, ring the bell, when you die you'll go to hell.

2   **Step on a crack ...** *(MILICOS remove GERARDO's gag, then*

3   *mime beating him in a stylized fashion.)*

4 **MILICOS: Confess!**

5   **Spill your guts, pukehead.**

6   *(GERARDO speaks rapidly, fearful of being hit.)*

7 **GERARDO: The lock to the front door, as if by some perverse**

8   **magic, turns itself, steps rush in, three pairs of shoes,**

9   **practice their disjointed tap-dance on the floor, the**

10   **clothes, the books, an arm, a hip, an ankle, a hand. My**

11   **body. I am the trophy of the day. A hide with hollow head,**

12   **glass eyes. The make-believe hunters step on me ...**

13 **NARRATORS:** *(Whispered from Upstage together)* **Step on a**

14   **crack, break your mother's back.**

15 **GERARDO: My sins are exorcised in a ritual inside the temple**

16   **of the Ford Falcon bearing no license plates: a green-**

17   **colored temple speeding through traffic lights down**

18   **Corrientes Street on the wrong side of the road. No one**

19   **bats an eye.**

20 **NARRATORS: Business as usual.**

21   *(Whispered:)* **Bring the knife, ring the bell ...**

22   **Nothing unusual.**

23   *(Whispered:)* **When you die ...**

24   **Anybody see anything?** *(Heads shaken, SEVERAL turn away.)*

25 **GERARDO: They came looking several times, closing in**

26   **gradually until one dawn they took me away from here**

27   **forever. Were there warnings, signs, hints of what was to**

28   **come? Sure. The first was when the hooded men came to**

29   **our workplace. Several friends had already been**

30   **kidnapped, and yet ... You persist in believing ... can't**

31   **happen ... Even as their clubs ... their fists ... the heavy**

32   **cords ... swung like lariats ... even then ... even then, no ... I**

33   **could not ... Mistake ... mistake ... I cried out ... please ...**

34   *(GERARDO collapses from the beating. MILICOS stop*

35   *beating, study their victim, prod him.)*

1   **NAOMI:** Don't, don't, please, no more, you're going to kill me,

2   you're killing me.

3   **MILICOS:** Step on a crack ...

4   Break your mother's back.

5   **NAOMI:** That smell. A blue smell. Gerardo. That's Gerardo. It's

6   his voice. I don't know anything, stop, stop, oh please stop.

7   It's him. I know it's him. Please don't hurt him, please.

8   **MILICOS:** Bring the knife, ring the bell ...

9   **NAOMI:** He must be in the next room, or is it just a recording

10   to make me talk? I bite my tongue so that I won't scream.

11   *(Screams from NARRATORS Upstage.)*

12   **MILICOS:** Hey, look. She's got a scar exactly like his.

13   They must stamp them like that at the factory.

14   We got her brother. Toss her out with the garbage.

15   *(MILICOS shove NAOMI aside, then drag GERARDO's*

16   *beaten body Off-stage. Silence. NARRATORS approach*

17   *NAOMI, comforting her as they speak.)*

18   **NARRATORS:** Our infected vaccination marks we wore so

19   proudly ...

20   Little soldiers with our war wounds ...

21   Binding us together ...

22   Setting us apart.

23   **NAOMI:** They got me.

24   **MILICOS:** *(Off-stage)* Bring the knife, ring the bell, when you

25   die you'll go to hell.

26   Step on a crack! *(A sudden, loud, jarring noise. Blackout.)*

27

28

29   **SCENE 2: REMEMBERING**

30

31   *(NAOMI in a spotlight. NARRATORS in the shadows.)*

32   **NAOMI:** I've seen you on the sidewalks ...

33   **NARRATORS:** I've seen you on the walls ...

34   **NAOMI:** In the silhouettes that remember you,

35   between the paint and the bricks.

1   I've found you multiplied a thousandfold,
2   filling the streets, in the voices.
3   NARRATORS: *(Together)* In the thousands of voices.
4   NAOMI: Gerardo!
5   NAOMI and NARRATORS: Gerardito!
6   NAOMI: They left me in the street. Alone. Hurting. *(Faint*
7   *screams heard Off-stage.)* Eyes blind with tears, ears deaf
8   from the sound of your voice. It was you, wasn't it? Wasn't
9   it? It smelled like you. Blue like you, Gerardo. I drown in
10   the memories.
11 NARRATORS: *(Swapping tales like gossips, trying to cheer*
12   *NAOMI)* Gerardo competes in the relay race in first grade.
13   "On your mark, get set ... go!" He is one of the fastest.
14   Suddenly he stops short and turns his head 90 degrees; he
15   smiles, he waves!
16   His mama is there.
17   Then he runs again, as fast as he can.
18   But Gerardo is the last to cross the finish line; he cries.
19   Gerardo is in high school but still doesn't wear long pants.
20   Gerardito wants to be an orchestra conductor.
21   But his parents convinced him otherwise.
22   Gerardo makes mischief and always gets caught.
23   He is smart but does not apply himself.
24   He has to change schools after being expelled, more
25   demerits than hairs on his head.
26   Gerardo has knee surgery to avoid the draft.
27   Gerardo talks too much about politics.
28   He speaks out at those damn political rallies at the
29   university.
30   Gerardito has a girlfriend he sneaks into the house to
31   spend the night.
32   Gerardo draws up political pamphlets using his papa's
33   typewriter.
34   He is clever, he is daring.
35   No, he is loco.

1   Gerardito is smart. *(To NAOMI:)* You remember when

2   he wrote about the music, yes?

3 GERARDO'S VOICE: *(Amplified)* We have in our country an

4   orchestra composed of: The Great Orchestrator, Señor

5   Bourgeois; the Conductor, John D. Repressive; the

6   Musicians, field and factory workers; and the Music,

7   composed in Buenos Aires, in 3 movements: economic

8   (imperialism *vivace*), social (jailhouse *andante* with *molto*

9   state of siege), and political (*fugue* in fraud major). Music

10   so lovely it hurts to listen to.

11 NARRATORS: Brilliant, no?

12   Dangerous, that's what.

13   Gerardo is under surveillance; he does not sleep at home.

14   Even his love letters are written in code. *(To NAOMI:)* You

15   have one, yes?

16   Read it.

17 NAOMI: Dear Miss Isabel, I regret to inform you that our firm

18   requires, in lieu of payment for your entrance to the

19   cinema last evening, the following services:

20   Quotations from Marx and Hegel ... 4

21   Caresses ... 8

22   Smiles ... 16

23   Kisses ... 3

24   Total ... 31

25   Please be good enough to remit this amount immediately.

26 NARRATORS: Romantic, no?

27   He writes too much.

28   He lives in fear because he's being followed.

29 GERARDO'S VOICE: Like becoming conscious, seeing oneself

30   as suddenly not indestructible, as if they had stolen a

31   chunk of you, as if, craftily, patronizingly, they had told

32   you, "Watch it, kid," implying that in the end, whether you

33   know it or not, they will continue to steal bits of you, little

34   by little, until there's nothing but ashes left.

35 NARRATORS: Gerardo certainly never killed or kidnapped

1   anyone.

2   But Gerardo will be kidnapped. *(Pause.)*

3   And almost certainly killed.

4 NAOMI: I never saw you again. Gerardito!

5 NARRATORS: *(Whispering)* They came looking several times,

6   closing in gradually until one dawn ...

7   Were there warnings, signs, hints of what was to come?

8   When the hooded men came to your workplace ...

9   Friends had been kidnapped ...

10   You persist in believing it can't happen to you.

11   Even as they beat you ...

12   Clubs ...

13   Fists ...

14   Even then ...

15 NAOMI: It must be a mistake. I cried out –

16 NARRATORS: We all cried out –

17 ALL: Gerardo! *(Silence. Slowly, GERARDO appears Upstage,*

18   *ghostlike. He wears a black mask or blindfold. His voice is*

19   *amplified, unreal, perhaps on tape. He speaks slowly,*

20   *dispassionately.)*

21 GERARDO: When they stole my name

22   I was one ... I was hundreds ... I was thousands ...

23   and I was no one.

24   My face stripped of gesture ...

25   of look ... of sound

26   *(The NARRATORS don identical black masks and move*

27   *slowly in a line across stage, compelling NAOMI to move*

28   *with them.)*

29   My numbered nakedness

30   walked in line ... without eyes ...

31   with them ... alone.

32   My alphabet bled dry

33   by guttural chains ...

34   by the moans of citizens in a country

35   without initials.

1   *(The NARRATORS tie a bright red blindfold over NAOMI's*

2   *eyes, tie her hands behind her back, and silence her by using*

3   *their hands as gags. Her muffled moans are heard as the*

4   *NARRATORS drag her Downstage to face the audience.)*

5   **Eyelid and blindfold**

6   **my horizon**

7   **all silence and echo**

8   **all iron grid ... all nightness**

9   **all wall without mirror**

10   **wherein to copy a wrinkle**

11   **a grimace ... a perhaps**

12   *(NAOMI stops moaning, submits to her fate.)*

13   **All dead end.**

14   *(One by one the NARRATORS remove their hands and exit,*

15   *leaving NAOMI alone Downstage. GERARDO exits Upstage,*

16   *but his amplified voice continues.)*

17   **Silence and echo**

18   **Wall without mirror**

19   **A grimace**

20   **A perhaps**

21   **All dead end.**

22   *(Silence. NAOMI tries to look around, to see through or*

23   *above the blindfold, but she cannot. She turns, listening,*

24   *hearing nothing. Then she hears the sound of military boots*

25   *marching, softly at first, rising in volume until they threaten*

26   *to deafen the audience. Most of NAOMI's following speech*

27   *can hardly be heard above the noise, except her name, which*

28   *the audience must hear clearly ringing above the bootfalls.)*

29 **NAOMI: No, wait! Stop! I'm not the one! It's not me! You're**

30   **mistaken, please! We've already done this part.** *(To*

31   *audience:)* **Oh my god, they're taking me. Me! Naomi!**

32   **Remember me! Naomi! Remember!**

33   *(The sound of the boots overwhelms her voice. MILICOS enter*

34   *marching doubletime, much faster than the sound of boots. In*

35   *great haste, looking over their shoulders as if they fear being*

1　*observed, they grab NAOMI and carry her to the Ford Falcon,*
2　*where they leave her alone, inside the shell of the car. ONE OF*
3　*THE MILICOS, armed with an automatic weapon, remains*
4　*momentarily behind, brandishing the weapon at the*
5　*audience, securing their silence and complicity. Exit as the*
6　*sound of marching boots fades with the lights.)*
7
8
9　　　　　　　　**SCENE 3: RECAPTURED**
10
11　*(NAOMI, alone inside the Ford Falcon. NARRATORS gather*
12　*slowly On-stage.)*
13　**NARRATORS: Of course this ritual takes place in the temple of**
14　　　　**a Ford Falcon.**
15　**Of course.**
16　**A Falcon without plates.**
17　**Of course.**
18　**Accelerating down the street and through the red lights**
19　　　　**without the bystanders batting an eye.**
20　**Business as usual.**
21　**Same old same old.**
22　**Stories we have heard more times than we care to**
23　　　　**remember.**
24　**Of course.**
25　**NAOMI: But it's not every day that the laws of gravity are broken.**
26　**NARRATORS: Heard it before.**
27　**NAOMI: It's not every day you open the door to a tornado.**
28　**NARRATORS: Old hat.**
29　**NAOMI: It's not every day you try to escape and the lock has**
30　　　　**moved, the door unhinged, the window stuck. That's not**
31　　　　**just any day!**
32　**NARRATORS: Of course it is.**
33　　　　**Where do you think you are?**
34　　　　**This is Argentina, remember?**
35　　　　**Land of the disappeared.**

1   The unannounced knock on the door.

2   Boot in the face.

3   Cattle prod to the privates.

4

5   What did you think, you could escape?

6   Run away to Israel or Canada?

7   The junta will always find you, you know.

8   Always.

9

10   And you will be "invited" to rejoin your friends, your

11   comrades, the thousands –

12   No, tens of thousands.

13   Numberless others lost.

14   Who knows where.

15   You think yours is a new story?

16   A different story?

17   It's an everyday occurrence.

18   Every day.

19   And it inevitably begins ...

20

21   *(In unison:)* In a Ford Falcon.

22

23   A green Ford Falcon.

24   Sometimes new ...

25   Sometimes old ...

26   But always a Ford.

27   *(NARRATORS assemble on edge of stage to tell stories to the*

28   *audience, ignoring NAOMI.)*

29 **NARRATORS:** My cousin Olga leaves the university – she's

30   studying psychology – and is about to get onto the bus she

31   takes to go home when this Ford Falcon without license

32   plates pulls up to the curb facing the wrong way and two

33   huge goons pull her down off the bottom step of the bus

34   and shove her into the car – at 6 p.m. – right in the center

35   of town!

1 Were there witnesses?

2 *(In unison:)* **Of course not!**

3 The car disappears without any trace of the young

4 woman and everything continues at its normal pace, until

5 they get on their radios to confirm the suspect, who's

6 supposed to be a blond, but the one they've picked up is

7 brunette, so they start pulling her hair to see if it was

8 really blond or if she'd dyed it!

9 They spent two hours driving around the city not

10 knowing what to do with her.

11 Either the dye was excellent or she really did have dark

12 hair.

13 In which case they had the wrong person.

14 In the end they got an order to let her go and they drove

15 her to the front door of her house.

16 How gallant!

17 She could never decipher the mystery of that day, there

18 was nowhere in her mind to put it, so she left the university,

19 dropped her friends, lost all interest in the carefree life of a

20 student, and shut herself away from the world.

21 She had never taken part in political activities, she

22 didn't have the slightest idea why they had chosen her,

23 nor whether the incident would happen again.

24 *(In unison:)* **Business as usual.**

25 I remember they came at about five in the morning,

26 jumped over the garden wall and stared through the

27 window – their knocking woke me up – they weren't the

28 slightest bit concerned about waking the neighbors – they

29 were gesturing me to open up, but I couldn't find the keys

30 anywhere, not that they need anyone to open the door for

31 them, but they waited, and I realized I'd left them in the

32 lock, the keys, remember? I hesitated before opening the

33 door because my brother wasn't going to have time to

34 escape, but I realized it was already too late, so I let them in,

35 and they threw me to the floor, made me close my eyes, held

1   my hands against the wall while they swore at me and beat
2   me up. They took us away, but some of them stayed behind
3   to trash the house. The neighbors say there were three cars
4   in the operation and that they had cleared the area.
5   Ford Falcons?
6   *(In unison:)* **Of course.**
7   The police didn't intervene.
8   Probably had orders *not* to intervene.
9   *(In unison:)* **Business as usual.**
10   They spun the Ford Falcon around to make us dizzy,
11   then they accelerated towards the center of town, and it
12   must have taken about twenty minutes to cover the
13   distance from my place to the detention center, where we
14   were separated. That's the last I heard ... you know.
15   Always the same story.
16   How many times have we heard it?
17   How many stories can we forget?
18   Each time gets a little more difficult.
19   Each telling another reminder.
20   You don't want to know.
21   You want to forget it all. *(Beat)*
22   Remember Gerardo's girlfriend?
23   Isabel?
24   Yes, I saw her, in a green Falcon, alone with three
25   uniformed men, coming home from studying with my
26   brother and some friends. They welcomed her with an
27   impressive display of force: the house wired with
28   explosives, her parents and sister taken hostage, the whole
29   block patrolled by Fords without license plates. "They
30   arrived at about 10 at night," her father told me later. He's a
31   retired military man, said he thought at first they were
32   guerillas and was getting ready to resist, but then he
33   realized they were his own men, fellow servicemen – and
34   they were waiting for his daughter! They said they'd let her
35   go afterwards, that it wasn't her they wanted.

1   Right!

2   She didn't have time to say anything when they took

3 her, just screamed when they put her in the Ford and she

4 was never heard from again. Her father thought it would

5 be easier for him than for other people to find out where

6 she was, but ...

7   Nothing?

8   *Nada.*

9   Same old same old.

10   I remember when they came we opened the door —

11   First mistake.

12   Never open the door.

13   They just kick it down.

14   But we asked them to identify themselves —

15   Lotta good that'll do!

16   We had no choice but to come out with our hands up: I

17 saw that the windows in the back were smashed, and they

18 had planted explosives along the front of the house and

19 threatened to set them off if the family did not comply, so

20 what choice do you have?

21   The men were all in civilian clothes, eight of them,

22 armed with automatic weapons, carrying hand grenades,

23 and handcuffs. We were blindfolded, my youngest

24 daughter and I, put in different rooms and interrogated

25 about the habits of our family. They thought our house was

26 a hideout for terrorists. Why? Why did they think that?

27   That's what they want to think.

28   They believe we're all terrorists armed to the teeth.

29   Maybe we should be.

30   Get a grip.

31   Why not?

32   Because they'd kill us all.

33   They're doing that now.

34 *(Silence. NAOMI raises herself up into the window of the*

35 *Ford Falcon to make herself heard.)*

1   NAOMI: I didn't think it was real, at first. The noise and
2   confusion, the blindfold. Then the engine starts and I
3   hear the sound of the car rolling over the gravel in front
4   of our house, and I realize where I am. The Ford Falcon!
5   I've seen them everywhere, on my way to school, at the
6   store, downtown, kicking dust up on dirt roads,
7   everywhere you go there's a green Ford Falcon.
8   NARRATORS: Following you.
9   Or waiting for you.
10   NAOMI: And now I'm inside one. The trip from my house to
11   the place of detention can't last more than fifteen
12   minutes. *(MILICOS enter unobtrusively, lift NAOMI gently*
13   *from the Ford Falcon and assist her moving Downstage*
14   *where she stands with guards at her elbows, propping her*
15   *up during the interrogation. None of the action she*
16   *describes is mimed. Two MILICOS stand almost at attention.*
17   *NAOMI stands between them, occasionally requiring their*
18   *assistance to remain standing. The remaining MILICOS try*
19   *to disperse the crowd of NARRATORS, slowly pushing them*
20   *away from NAOMI until they leave the stage.)*
21   NARRATORS: It's right in town?
22   Where'd you think it was?
23   This hellhole is right in our town?
24   We walk past it every day.
25   No way!
26   Where?
27   Hidden.
28   Underground.
29   You're making it up.
30   In an empty warehouse.
31   Behind metal doors and security cameras.
32   Oh, come on!
33   NAOMI: It isn't like that. The room is ... normal, old, almost
34   empty. They drag me down some stairs and leave me. They
35   tell me I'm supposed to undress before a group of men

1   who will proceed according to their usual routine. Which
2   means they are going to torture me. One of them asks
3   what words I was yelling in Jewish. I tell him: my name.
4 MILICOS: Lie down and we'll see how much you feel like
5   making jokes.
6 NAOMI: I lie on a table where they bind my feet and hands. I turn
7   into a chronometer, each stroke to my feet another moment
8   passed, another moment I've survived. No more weakness,
9   no more pleading. I just keep time. Take it as it comes.
10 NARRATORS: How could you bear it?
11   I couldn't.
12 NAOMI: "Even if you don't know anything," he tells me,
13   "you'll pay for being Jewish."
14 NARRATORS: She's Jewish?
15   I thought she was one of us, you know, Argentine.
16   She is.
17   She's both.
18 NAOMI: We hardly knew what it was to be Jewish. My
19   grandparents knew, they came to America, to Argentina,
20   because religion didn't matter. What mattered was a good
21   education. How naive they were – how they would cry if
22   they knew what happened to me and my brother.
23   *(MILICOS have herded the crowd of NARRATORS Off-stage*
24   *– except for one MAN who lingers to hear what NAOMI has*
25   *to say.)*
26   The man who beat my feet with a metal rod, he assured
27   me their only concern was finding subversives, not Jews.
28   But the other one, the one who made me lie naked on the
29   table, he wanted to know the names of my Jewish friends.
30   He said they'd punish me for speaking Jewish in public.
31   When I told him it was only my name, he spit in my face.
32   It all happened so fast, I hardly remember it. One minute
33   they're talking, the next ... I try to ignore their presence.
34   Except when they talk to me. When they bark their orders.
35   I tried to think of dogs, packs of barking dogs.

1   **MILICOS:** **Take off your clothes!**

2   **Lie on your back!**

3   **Turn over.**

4   **Now!** *(No one moves. A long beat. Sweetly:)*

5   **The kid misbehaves, does she? Looks like we'll have to**

6   **give her a little spanking. Pat, pat on the fanny. Would you**

7   **like that?** *(Pause)* **Bitch!** *(MILICOS laugh.)*

8   **NAOMI: There was this girl in prison, she told me they asked**

9   **her which torture she wanted: cattle prod or rape. At first**

10   **she chose the prod, but soon, very soon, she asked to be**

11   **raped. The very next day a guard asked her what they did**

12   **to her the night before. "They raped me, sir," she said. He**

13   **slapped her. "Liar," he said, "no one did anything to you.**

14   **Understand?" "Yessir," she said. "What happened to you**

15   **last night?" he asked again. "Nothing, sir. They did**

16   **nothing to me."**

17   **MAN: I remember they were interrogating me, fully clothed.**

18   **Since I wouldn't talk, they made me undress for the cattle**

19   **prod. At the first charge of voltage I swore like an idiot and**

20   **then, realizing that would get me nowhere, I bit my tongue.**

21   **I assured them I didn't know anything about politics or**

22   **about my friends' politics: a complete moron, just a regular**

23   **guy who works during the day and studies at night, too busy**

24   **supporting my family to get mixed up in politics. They used**

25   **the cattle prod on me twice. When they finished they took a**

26   **declaration from me in a place that looked like a police**

27   **station, full of typewriters. That's where I saw your brother.**

28   **NAOMI: You saw Gerardo?**

29   **MAN: They bound my feet and put me in a big room divided by**

30   **partitions into smaller cells. They brought your brother in**

31   **and left us alone together for a while. I don't know if it was**

32   **a mistake on their part or whether they wanted to**

33   **eavesdrop on us.**

34   **NAOMI: How was he?**

35   **MAN: We only exchanged a few words, that he hadn't said**

1   anything about me, that I hadn't said anything about him.
2   NAOMI: How did he look?
3   MAN: What do you expect? He'd been beaten just like me.
4   Some guards realized that we knew each other and took
5   him out. I never saw him again. Maybe they transferred
6   him to another camp, maybe they put him in solitary
7   confinement. They left me there in that room, a kind of
8   lobby to the main prison, where I could overhear all kinds
9   of conversations. The guards would talk in front of us as if
10   we didn't exist. I heard about a girl they'd trained to
11   undress as soon as a guard called out her code number. If
12   she didn't have her clothes off and get down on all fours in
13   a couple of seconds, they started hitting her with sticks
14   and the rubber truncheon. She was raped. In that way it
15   was lucky being a man. *(MAN is led off by MILICOS.)*
16   NAOMI: But Gerardo, did you ... was he ... You saw him.
17   Perhaps that's enough. Wait! What was his number, his
18   prisoner number?
19   MAN: *(Shouting back to her)* I don't know.
20   NAOMI: But without his number ...
21   MILICOS: *(Calling out)* K-48. K-48.
22   NAOMI: Perhaps he whispered it to you or wrote it on
23   something or —
24   MILICOS: K-48. K-48.
25   NAOMI: He'd have to remember that, it was the code number
26   for the combination of the lock around your ankles and
27   the lock on the door to your cell and ...
28   MILICOS: *(To NAOMI)* Heh! You're K-48, right? When you hear
29   your number, you answer up, got it? *(Pause)* Got it?!
30   NAOMI: K-48.
31   MILICOS: Sir!
32   NAOMI : Sir.
33   MILICOS: If you forget your number, you can forget about ever
34   getting out of here. Understand, K-48? Understand?!
35   NAOMI: Yes. Sir. K-48, Sir. I understand. Sir. K-48. Did you forget

1 **your number, Gerardo, is that why? Too much to remember.**
2 **Forgetting ... Forgetting ... Where are you, Mama?** *(MILICOS*
3 *exit. Beat. NAOMI screams, then sobs. Enter GUARDS. As*
4 *they approach her, she attacks them. They quickly subdue*
5 *her, take the pen away, gag her and tie her to the chair.*
6 *GUARDS exit.)*
7
8
9   **SCENE 4: INTERRGOATION, MILITARY STYLE**
10
11 *(NARRATORS enter whispering; they stand behind NAOMI.)*
12 **NARRATORS:** *(In unison)* **Bring the knife, ring the bell, when**
13   **you die you'll go to hell.**
14 *(Whispered:)* **Step on a crack ...**
15 **Bring the knife, ring the bell, when you die you'll go to hell.**
16 *(Whispered:)* **Step on a crack ...**
17 **Bring the knife, ring the bell, when you die you'll go to hell.**
18 *(Whispered:)* **Step on a crack ...**
19 **Break your mother's back.**
20 *(NAOMI is gagged, seated, surrounded by MILICOS and*
21 *NARRATORS. She does not speak or struggle; she is mute,*
22 *motionless, expressionless. By contrast, the faces of various*
23 *NARRATORS silently mime the pain she must be feeling.*
24 *However, when the NARRATORS speak, their voices are*
25 *dispassionate, clinical, precise. The MILICOS run through a*
26 *gamut of emotions, from frustration to sexual release. They are*
27 *totally engaged in the horror they wreak upon NAOMI. The*
28 *COMMANDER steps forward and addresses the audience.)*
29 **COMMANDER:** **You're wondering how we go about**
30   **interrogating a person. We don't diddle around with all**
31   **that psychological mumbo-jumbo. We rely on technology.**
32   **The pace of questioning is determined by how rushed we**
33   **feel, by the time of day the subject was brought in. For**
34   **instance, if it was two in the afternoon, the questioning**
35   **would have to be done swiftly ... because we might have a**

1   meeting in an hour and a half and, in order not to miss
2   that meeting, the interrogation would have to be hastened
3   through the scientific application of electric shocks. You
4   understand, I'm sure.
5 NARRATORS: It all happens so fast I remember nothing, how
6   or where I get out of my clothes, even though I'm not in
7   the habit of undressing in public. I do it in a split second
8   but I still get prodded with their rifle butts.
9 MILICOS: The kid misbehaved, did she?
10   Looks like we'll have to give her a spanking.
11   A little pat-pat on the fanny.
12 NARRATORS: Unable to see, I ignore their presence, unless
13   they talk to me.
14   And oh do they talk.
15   No, they bark, sort of.
16 MILICOS: Strip naked, bitch!
17 NARRATORS: Bark, bark.
18 MILICOS: Lie on your back!
19 NARRATORS: Bark. *(Beat)*
20   It's a cold metal table.
21   They tie me up.
22 MILICOS: Even if you don't know a thing ...
23   You're going to pay ...
24   Just for being a Jew.
25 COMMANDER: We assured the subject that our main concern
26   was subversives —
27 MILICOS: And Jews!
28 COMMANDER: — followed closely by the Jewish problem. We
29   were simply gathering facts.
30 MILICOS: What was that you were screaming back there, huh?
31   That wasn't Spanish. Was it?
32 NARRATORS: My name.
33 MILICOS: There's laws against saying Jewish words in public ...
34 NARRATORS: My last name.
35 MILICOS: ... and for being a Jewish shit!

1   **COMMANDER: There'll be no Jewish names in the new**
2   **Argentina.** *(MILICOS laugh.)* **Were you planning a trip to**
3   **Israel? Getting out of the country? Why would anyone**
4   **want to leave Argentina?**
5   **MILICOS: Unless they're a traitor.**
6   **COMMANDER: We are required to learn who was planning to**
7   **travel with you, where you were going, who your contacts**
8   **were. Understand? You are required to tell us.**
9   **NARRATORS: I lie face up on a metal table ...**
10 **COMMANDER: There are no options, no choices.**
11 **NARRATORS: ... naked, spread-eagled, bound hand and foot,**
12   **blindfolded.**
13 **COMMANDER: You** *will* **tell us.**
14 **NAOMI: Music plays somewhere.**
15 **COMMANDER: Put the Chopin on!** *(To audience:)* **This is the**
16   **technology I spoke of before, the most up-to-date. The**
17   **interrogator's bible. The cattle prod.** *(MILICOS show cattle*
18   *prod to audience, demonstrate.)*
19 **NARRATORS: They fire electricity through the end of a cable.**
20 **MILICOS: Confess!**
21 **NARRATORS: The charge penetrates my brain, my teeth, my**
22   **gums, my breasts –**
23 **COMMANDER: Names, if you please.**
24 **NARRATORS: – my ovaries, my nails, my ears, my skull.**
25 **COMMANDER: Your code name?**
26 **NARRATORS: The pores of my skin smell burnt.**
27 **COMMANDER: You cannot help but tell us.**
28 **NARRATORS: They turn me over, laughing, and go up and**
29   **down over my back until the voltage drives me crazy and**
30   **I yell out ...**
31 **COMMANDER: Spare yourself.**
32 **NARRATORS: But then I control myself.**
33 **COMMANDER: Brother's code name, his friends' code names,**
34   **his friends' friends' code names.**
35 **NARRATORS: I won't give this gentleman the pleasure of my**

1   tears.
2   COMMANDER: What are the names of your university
3   classmates ...
4   NARRATORS: Electrodes on my teeth ...
5   COMMANDER: Your cousin's wife ...
6   NARRATORS: Each lightning bolt cracking my head open ...
7   COMMANDER: Your traveling companions?
8   NARRATORS: A thin cord with tiny little balls, each ball an
9   electrode ...
10   COMMANDER: Names.
11   NARRATORS: A thousand pieces of glass shattered ...
12   MILICOS: Namesssss.
13   NARRATORS: Spraying my insides with exploding shards that
14   rip through ...
15   COMMANDER: Name names.
16   NARRATORS: I couldn't shout or moan or move.
17   MILICOS: Name names, name names.
18   NARRATORS: Just a convulsive shaking. *(As NAOMI begins to*
19   *shake with each electric charge, only a twitch at first,*
20   *building to a convulsive dance, the MILICOS are chanting*
21   *beneath the NARRATORS.)*
22   MILICOS: Name names.
23   Name names.
24   Namename.
25   Namename.
26   NARRATORS: Voices whispering ...
27   Questions in a strange language ...
28   Sickening, dizzy music ...
29   A concert of nonsense lyrics, spasmodic rhythms and a
30   strange percussion that jolts my skin ...
31   I feel no blows ...
32   But something brushes past without stinging or burning
33   or shaking or hurting or drilling ...
34   MILICOS: Nnnnnaaaaaammmmmmeeeeeesssss!
35   NARRATORS: It kills me.

1   That humming ...

2   That agony ...

3   That precarious fraction of a second that precedes the

4   shocks ...

5   The sharp point that explodes on contact with the skin ...

6   Vibrating ...

7   Cutting ...

8   Piercing ...

9   *(Voices overlapping:)* **Destroying my brain my teeth my**

10   **gums my ears my breasts my eyelids my ovaries my**

11   **nails the soles of my feet.**

12   My skin gives off a burnt smell.

13   A blue smell.

14   *That* blue smell.

15   **Gerardo!** *(NAOMI screams, then begins spewing made-up*

16   *names as fast as she can.)*

17 **NAOMI: John Doe, Joe Blow. Marcus and Aurelius. Romeo**

18   **Jones, Juliette Garcia. Uncle Jorge, Granpapa Borges.**

19   **Franco Kafko, Eduardo Muncho ...**

20 **NARRATORS: My screams and the music merge with voices**

21   asking me questions until I am naming names because I

22   can't help it ...

23   Can't stop it ...

24   Have to do something ...

25   Anything!

26 **NAOMI: Gabriela, Isabela, Consuela, Tinkerbell-a, Donuella ...**

27 **NARRATORS: I don't know what to invent without**

28   contradicting myself.

29   Luckily my memory is bad.

30   I can hardly remember anyone.

31 **NAOMI:** *(Running out of names, slower)* **Señora Freud. Señorita**

32   **Jung ...**

33 **COMMANDER:** *(To audience)* **Sometimes even the best**

34   **application of technology produces less than the desired**

35   **results. In such cases, we've found that patience and the**

1 resolute re-application of technology is usually successful.

2 *(To NAOMI)* **You're gonna pay for this!** *(Exeunt*

3 *COMMANDER and all but one of the MILICOS. Silence.)*

4 **NAOMI: Gerardo ... and ... Norita ... and ... and ... nobody's left.**

5 *(As they speak, the NARRATORS untie NAOMI, help her to*

6 *her feet, escort her to the Ford Falcon.)*

7 **NAOMI: After the first session with the cattle prod they throw**

8 **me into a cell.**

9 **I take off my blindfold, but I can't see anything.**

10 **I'm in a dark cubicle so small I can't stand up.**

11 **They want me to think it over until I decide to**

12 **cooperate.**

13 **NARRATORS: Think it over! I can't think.**

14 **NAOMI: I don't know any words to think with.**

15 **There are vacant lots between me and my memories.**

16 **I've already forgotten myself ...**

17 **NARRATORS: Who I was ...**

18 **Where I lived ...**

19 **Where I was born ...**

20 **How it felt to be alive ...**

21 **When I died.**

22 **I have nothing to say, nothing to add, nothing to understand.**

23 **NAOMI: They come back.**

24 **Boots echoing in my brain.**

25 **I cover my eyes and the door opens.**

26 **Once again they drag me and I fall.**

27 **We reach another room and I feel a white light through**

28 **the blindfold.**

29 **MILICOS: You're gonna remember this just like you**

30 **remember your mama.**

31 **NARRATORS: I don't understand a word.**

32 **More voices. More music.**

33 **I don't care.**

34 **Don't feel a thing.**

35 **Dead already.**

1   (*Exeunt all but NAOMI.*)

2

3

4   **SCENE FIVE: INTERROGATION AND SEX**

5

6   (*NAOMI alone in Ford Falcon, silent and motionless at first.*

7   *Then slowly she begins to exercise: simple movements of her*

8   *arms, then legs, and finally her torso.*)

9   **NAOMI: Fingers open, fingers close. Open. Close. Just when**

10   **you thought you were dead. Hands reach, hands return.**

11   **Just when you thought they were lost forever. Arms up,**

12   **arms down. Up, down. Like flying.**

13   **And you thought there was no getting out. Just flap**

14   **hard enough, girl, just keep flapping. Look: legs. Move**

15   **one, move the other. A simple miracle to keep hope alive.**

16   **Will there be no end to it, to all of it? How can these**

17   **muscles, these tissues and nerves and synapses keep**

18   **working after that? How?**

19   **What did granmama used to say? Keep moving, always**

20   **moving, and let the bastards try to catch up with you.**

21   (*Laughs.*) **The bastards** *have* **caught up, and still arms**

22   **work, legs work, body stretches, stands, continues moving**

23   **in spite of all. In spite of them. If I'm not careful I'll be**

24   **dancing in a moment.** (*NAOMI uses the frame of the Ford*

25   *Falcon to exercise, stretching arms and legs outside of the car,*

26   *beginning to develop a rhythm to her movements. Bootsteps*

27   *approaching.*)

28   **Concentrating on my exercises, I don't hear the**

29   **footsteps approaching down the corridor to my cell. The**

30   **massive metal door opens without giving me time to cover**

31   **my eyes.**

32   **MILICOS: Put on your blindfold!**

33   **Keep still!** (*They drag her Downstage to the chair, toss her in*

34   *it. No attempt is made to tie or gag her this time. Each of the*

35   *MILICOS produces a cattle prod.*)

1 I am a son of a bitch!

2 They pay me to torture and be a son of a bitch!

3 Let's have a quick electrical fondling of this one. *(They taunt*

4 *NAOMI with rapid-fire questions they never expect answers*

5 *to, pointing the cattle prods at her on each question.)*

6 What's it like, eh?

7 Where?

8 When?

9 How?

10 Do you understand you died the moment you came here?

11 You're ours, got it?

12 'Cuz you're gonna get it! *(NAOMI stands, oblivious to the*

13 *burlesque behind her. She moves away from the chair.*

14 *MILICOS surround the chair, as if she's still in it, and*

15 *continue their taunting interrogation. NAOMI points back at*

16 *the empty chair.)*

17 NAOMI: Why don't I remember anything? I was there, wasn't I?

18 That was me they did that to, wasn't it?

19 MILICOS: Do you like this?

20 Or this?

21 Do you?

22 NAOMI: What's wrong with me?

23 MILICOS: What's your pleasure, baby?

24 NAOMI: I don't remember if I was standing or lying, if I

25 screamed or not. I don't remember.

26 MILICOS: You're ours, got it?

27 'Cuz you're gonna get it!

28 NAOMI: I must have gone away, far far away, so far away that

29 what was happening wasn't happening. I wanted to

30 scream but could not. I hoped I'd die. Death is the only

31 way out, I kept telling myself. It happened in broad

32 daylight. Coming home from school, I get into the elevator

33 with a stranger. He's fat and traps me between his

34 stomach and the mirror. "How old are you?" he asks

35 between clenched teeth, so that his soft fat has an excuse

1   to move closer to me. An anxious hand rubs against my
2   body, hurries through the pleats of my smock, touches
3   me, pinches me. I go tense. I smell a blue smell. A glove
4   covers my mouth. A voice promises me pleasures I don't
5   understand. On the third floor I push him aside, I open
6   the door and run away. The blue smell stays there.
7 MILICOS: Do you understand you died the moment you came
8   here?
9 NAOMI: I free myself from one ordeal to find myself in the
10   grip of another. I am afraid to go out and afraid to stay
11   home, afraid to move, afraid to feel afraid. Tomorrow he'll
12   be there at school. Tomorrow must not come. I hide in the
13   present tense within the walls of our apartment, spying
14   down on the menacing street. Girls, women, young
15   people, walking alone along the sidewalk. Around the
16   corner, something will happen to them and then bars will
17   grow on their windows.
18 MILICOS: I am a son of a bitch!
19   They pay me to be a son of a bitch!
20 NAOMI: That obsessive throbbing stays with me. Endless days
21   and months. An endless year of watching bodies glide
22   down the street with their heavy sexual cargo. I go to
23   school holding my father's hand. I undress the teacher
24   and she looks ridiculous with her grey pubic hair and her
25   flaccid breasts. During history class I imagine armies of
26   rapists. *(Whispered:)* **And now, here they are.** *(She points*
27   *back at MILICOS. They've finished their rape, the cattle*
28   *prods hang loose at their sides as they begin their noisy exit.)*
29 MILICOS: You bitches, how dare you provoke us right here.
30   Under our very noses.
31   In our house.
32   And we even let you.
33   You're all a bunch of communists.
34   Mothers of subversives.
35   Still you dare to march and make demands.

1	**Women should stay at home.**
2	**Off the streets.**
3	**None of this damn marching**
4	**This pathetic protesting.**
5	**What do you think you'll accomplish?**
6	**You can't bring back the dead with your slogans**
7	**Your pictures**
8	**Your morbid dancing.**
9	**Why do you think they call them "the disappeared," huh?**
10	*(ONE member hangs back to deliver a final threat to the*
11	*audience before exiting:)* **If only I could, I'd make a clean**
12	**sweep of the Plaza with machine gun fire.** *(Waving the*
13	*cattle prod like an automatic weapon and making the*
14	*appropriate sounds of gunning down a crowd, he exits.)* **You**
15	**would not come back.**
16	
17	
18	**SCENE 6: INTERROGATION AND DEATH**
19	
20	*(GUARDS enter bringing NAOMI old clothes.)*
21	**NAOMI:** *(As she dresses)* **The guards give me someone else's**
22	**clothes – the pants, shirt, shoes, and underwear of**
23	**someone who won't be needing them any more. Cold,**
24	**sweaty hands drag me to an office where I have to repeat**
25	**my testimony in front of a typewriter, my official version**
26	**of the facts, so official that I sign it without seeing what it**
27	**says, without knowing who will be made guilty by my**
28	**name signed blindly at the bottom of the page. Then they**
29	**drag me back to my cell. Suddenly I hear voices.**
30	**GUARDS: Attention!**
31	**NAOMI: I don't know what is all about, but I stand in front of**
32	**the door to my cell, which is open. I don't know what I'm**
33	**supposed to do about the chain I hear dragging along the**
34	**corridor. I think I've been left alone in my section, that**
35	**the other cells are empty and that they're going to punish**

1   me for not following the invisible group of prisoners I
2   belong to. I remain at attention, defying the darkness, the
3   fear of possible reprisals. The voice of a woman comes to
4   rescue me. *(NARRATORS enter in a line, each with a hand*
5   *on the shoulder of the person in front of them. They are*
6   *choo-chooing along like a train at the GUARD's insistence. A*
7   *WOMAN steps out of line to explain to NAOMI.)*
8 WOMAN: That order was to go to the bathroom. When they
9   open the door, you have to wait for the signal to turn right,
10   put your hand on the shoulder of the person in front of
11   you and start moving. I'll take you this time so they won't
12   know you stayed behind. When you hear them call out
13   number one, you turn. When they say two, you put hands
14   on the shoulders of the one in front of you. On three, you
15   march. Like a train. Sometimes they want us to make
16   sounds. *(She demonstrates.)* Don't let them notice we're
17   falling behind. You march on command, squat on
18   command, return on command.
19 NAOMI: What if I can't – you know – on command?
20 WOMAN: You'll learn. You have to.
21 NAOMI: And if you need to go some other time?
22 WOMAN: You can't. If you foul yourself, they beat you. If you
23   continue shitting your pants, they beat you to death.
24   *(The line of NARRATORS circles back to pick up NAOMI and*
25   *the WOMAN.)*
26 NAOMI: I come back coupled to the train of bodies I had lost. A
27   half-turn, my hand on a shoulder, one, two, one, two ... a
28   centipede going to its hole, an insect with twenty, thirty,
29   forty pairs of legs, crawling blindly along.
30 NARRATORS: The rules of the game: bait the victim to show
31   him his impotence ...
32   Transform him into a sniveling weakling ...
33   Beat a new language into him ...
34   A nice simple one with no past or future tense ...
35   No first person singular.

1
2 You soon forget who you are, what you think, what day it is.
3 You can't remember your birthday, even though you know
4 you're getting old.
5 But you damn well remember your place in line, eh?
6
7 They take us to the showers in single file, up to a huge
8 room with pipes spewing out water ...
9 Plenty for everyone.
10 We undress in front of a group of men.
11 GUARDS: How do you like the ass on the second one on the
12 right?
13 NARRATORS: You have to shower looking at the floor ...
14 GUARDS: Look at the tits on that fourth one!
15 NARRATORS: Pick up the soap without shifting your gaze ...
16 GUARDS: The one in the middle's too fat.
17 NARRATORS: Pretend you can't hear their jeers and their
18 laughter ...
19 GUARDS: Hey, baby!
20 NARRATORS: Not react to the icy water that condenses the
21 cold of the walls and the body ...
22 GUARDS: Get ready!
23 NARRATORS: Forget there are no towels.
24 NAOMI: I was filled with dread every time a guard's footsteps
25 echoed in the corridor. Everyone was afraid to be taken
26 back for more torture.
27 GUARDS: I'm saving it for you!
28 NARRATORS: Sometimes you wanted to go out just to stretch
29 your legs or use the bathroom ... But at the same time you
30 didn't because that exposed you to their glances ... To
31 anything and everything that popped into the minds of
32 your captors.
33 GUARDS: Heh, you! Come here. Let's look you over.
34 We could make it easier for you. Whadda you say?
35 NARRATORS: You grew progressively smaller, limiting your

1   world.

2   When they open the door, when they close it ...

3   What you eat today, what you eat tomorrow ...

4   When you are punished, when not.

5   Life gets so small you forget where you are, who you are.

6   You're grateful for a friendly gesture, for a plate of decent

7   food.

8   Happy to be out for a bit.

9

10   You're not allowed to speak ...

11   Couldn't look ...

12   Couldn't walk.

13   Codes tapped on cell walls ...

14   Whispers squatting over the hole.

15

16   The cells had a peep-hole on the outside.

17   They'd approach suddenly and look in ...

18   And if they found you –

19   Even in the darkness –

20   With your blindfold off ...

21   Or walking about ...

22   Or exercising ...

23   Or giving the least sign of being human in any way ...

24   Or showing any sign of resistance ...

25   GUARDS: Put your blindfold back on, bitch! You're gonna pay

26   for this!

27   NARRATORS: At least they remembered to bring us food.

28   Yeah, food the other prisoners didn't want.

29   Heh, I'd eat whatever I could.

30   Never knew when you'd get another chance.

31   NAOMI: Soup is my clock. It marks my nights and dawns until

32   I lose track and enter an unrelieved twilight. The massive

33   door of the cell opens three times a day. Once to go to the

34   bathroom, twice to provide the concoction they call soup.

35   I grope for a place for the bowl on top of the mattress and

1   I try to place the spoon in the liquid. It's scalding. I blow
2   on each spoonful so I won't burn my mouth. But I'm not
3   used to it. I take too long for their liking. At the fifth
4   spoonful, they take it away.
5 NARRATORS: Time has gotten sick.
6   Lost in a labyrinth where tomorrow, yesterday and today
7   search for each other without ever meeting ...
8   Time flickers and goes out.
9
10   Those who lead us to and from the bathroom ...
11   Those who drag us to the cattle prod ...
12   Those who quietly hand a cigarette to someone desperate ...
13   Those we know only by their voices echoing in the hollow
14   silence of our cells ...
15   They locked us up every night ...
16   Locked us out for bathroom and shower ...
17   Locked us back in after each.
18   So we called them "locks."
19   Which meant there was one lock on the door to your cell ...
20   And another one outside to guard you.
21   And you were called out by your lock number.
22
23   The guards are prisoners as much as we are.
24   Rubbish!
25   They too are among the disappeared.
26   Come on!
27   They end up collaborating just to be without a blindfold ...
28   Willing to exchange anything for the hope of survival ...
29   Exchanging even their selves for a certain satisfaction in
30   doing a job ...
31   Whatever it might be.
32
33   Remember their names?
34   You mean the names they told us to call them by?
35   Shark ...

1   **Viper ...**

2   **Tiger ...**

3   **Blondie ...**

4   **Turk ...**

5   **Bell ...**

6   **Light bulb ...**

7   **Pacifier ...**

8   **Angel ...**

9   **Scorpion.**

10

11   **They were better than the regular police —**

12   **Part of the Special Forces.**

13   **Better than Milicos, that's for sure.**

14   *(Spits.)* **Milicos!**

15

16   **Death is better than Milicos.**

17

18 **NAOMI:** How do you remember so much? The only thing I

19   recall is a window, but not whether the beds were metal or

20   wood. I remember the toilet and how the prison felt like a

21   vault. I remember a kind of storage closet and not much

22   more. I remember very little else. The need and the

23   urgency of forgetting situations, of forgetting partners, of

24   forgetting faces was such that I really did forget them. For

25   nothing, right?

26 **NARRATORS:** Don't forget to forget the forgetting.

27   *(Whispered:)* **Bring the knife, ring the bell ...**

28

29   **Where are we?**

30   **In a hell hole.**

31   **Top security.**

32   **For how long?**

33   **I been here six months.**

34   **All my friends have been killed.**

35

1	*(Whispered:)* **When you die ...**
2	
3	**NAOMI: What keeps you going?**
4	**NARRATORS: Step on a crack!**
5	*(Enter MILICOS, shouting both the questions and the*
6	*answers, rapid-fire, almost to the point of incomprehension.*
7	*They gather NAOMI up in a white sheet and carry her*
8	*offstage, like a corpse. At the same time, in the rhythmic*
9	*intervals of the MILICOS' lines, the NARRATORS begin*
10	*whispering, building slowly in volume.)*
11	**MILICOS: Name?**
12	**Naomi.**
13	
14	**Residence?**
15	**Buenos Aires.**
16	
17	**Nationality?**
18	**Argentine.**
19	
20	**Ethnicity?**
21	**Jewish.**
22	
23	**Politics?**
24	**Marxist.**
25	
26	**Sexual preference?** *(Guffaws.)*
27	
28	**Associates?**
29	**Gerardo, Juan, José, Raul, Manuel ...**
30	
31	**Charges?**
32	**Violating curfew,**
33	**interfering with activities of the Armed Forces,**
34	**tarnishing image of Security Police, associating with**
35	**known subversives, and circulating anti-Argentine**

1   materials.

2

3   How do you plead?

4

5   **GUILTY!** *(MILICOS exeunt. Silence.)*

6 **NARRATORS:** *(Whispering simultaneously)*

7   **The shocks came faster than before, more powerful.**

8

9   **Spasmodic rhythms ...**

10   **strange percussion ...**

11   **jolts to my skin.**

12

13   **Something brushes past ...**

14   **stinging ...**

15   **burning ...**

16   **shaking ...**

17   **drilling.**

18

19   *(Louder:)* **All that humming ...**

20   **the hatred ...**

21   **the agony ...**

22   **the sharp point −**

23

24   **Everything explodes on contact with the skin ...**

25   **vibrating ...**

26   **cutting ...**

27   **slashing ...**

28   **piercing ...**

29

30   **destroying my brain ...**

31   **my teeth ...**

32   **my gums ...**

33   **my ears ...**

34   **my breasts ...**

35   **my toes ...**

1 my lips ...

2 my eyelids ...

3 my ovaries ...

4 my nails ...

5

6 even the soles of my feet.

7

8 *(Shouting together:)* **The soles of my feet!** *(Silence. MILICOS*

9 *exeunt.)*

10

11 *(Whispered:)* **My skin gives off a burnt smell.**

12 **Blue!**

13 NARRATORS: The charges are so fast, so persistent, that it

14   doesn't seem like I'm going to die ...

15 I am already dying.

16 I only want to finish dying.

17 But no, they stop and I'm still alive.

18 They untie me and take me along stinking corridors to a

19   wider place they call the infirmary.

20 I try to orient myself by using my ears, the only sense

21   available to me.

22 The voice of the male nurse ...

23 Or doctor ...

24 Or paramedic ...

25 Echoes in a space big enough for twelve hospital beds.

26 They are well-equipped and they treat my infected wounds.

27

28 The cattle prod opens them ...

29 And, with great care, they close them ...

30 So they can be opened again.

31

32 I am being bandaged by soft, delicate hands.

33 It's the first time I've been touched without being beaten ...

34 Spoken to without being sworn at.

35

1 **Perhaps it's because of this that words bubble up ...**

2 **I don't know anything!**

3 **They have to release me!**

4 **I've got nothing to do with it!**

5

6 *(One by one, NARRATORS hide behind blank white masks.*

7 *They gather Center Stage in a tight group. Those who speak*

8 *are hidden behind those in the front. During the following,*

9 *NAOMI sneaks On-stage, unseen, to hide behind the*

10 *NARRATORS.)*

11 **I know nothing, yet ...**

12 **If I speak, I condemn myself.**

13 **If I don't speak, they condemn me.**

14 **I will be liquidated, either way.**

15

16 **No more fresh air ...**

17 **No more friends ...**

18 **No more books ...**

19

20 **No kisses ...**

21 **No letters ...**

22 **No more.**

23

24 **I would love to submerge myself in tears.**

25 **But what for?**

26 **NAOMI'S VOICE: Tears don't open padlocks, my grandmother**

27 **used to say.** *(The NARRATORS part to reveal NAOMI, still*

28 *wrapped in the white sheet.)*

29 **NARRATORS: Don't forget to forget the forgetting.**

30 **NAOMI: I am nothing. Everything is erased.**

31 **NARRATORS:** *(In unison)* **Don't forget.**

32 **NAOMI: I am invisible.** *(Blackout.)*

33

34

35

1 **SCENE 7: THE DIARIES**

2

3 *(The MOTHERS and FATHERS appear one at a time to share*

4 *their diaries and journals with the audience. SOME read*

5 *what they've written, OTHERS speak their thoughts aloud.*

6 *After each has spoken, she or he joins the others Upstage*

7 *swaying to soft music. As the final diary is read, the*

8 *MOTHERS and FATHERS begin the formal Dance of the*

9 *Disappeared — in silence.)*

10 **MOTHER 1:** I always wanted to keep a diary, but I've never done

11 it because I don't feel capable of writing down sensations,

12 thoughts, ideas, and the hardest thing of all — feelings. That

13 is a word much used and yet for each person it has a

14 different meaning. Some people call their emotions or

15 passions feelings, but I think feeling is higher than just

16 impulse, or those passions which make us wound even

17 those dearest to us. Why? That is the mystery. But I know at

18 those moments real feelings don't play a part — they would

19 not permit us to wound the people we love most.

20 **MOTHER 2:** Why did I choose today to sit down and pour out my

21 feelings in this unfinished notebook, half-filled with the

22 algebraic calculations that I've never understood and will

23 never understand? Simply because they were written by my

24 son whom I don't know if I will ever see again, who is today

25 entering the twenty-ninth year of his life, if he's still alive.

26 **FATHER 1:** I feel too much despair to go out or to talk about it;

27 I don't want to keep acting so aggressively towards my

28 wife who has suffered as much as I have but who has the

29 courage to overcome it and not to show it in front of me. I

30 don't want to complain because people avoid people who

31 complain, for whatever reasons they feel justification.

32 That's why I'm writing in this little notebook. It belongs to

33 my daughter and brings me closer to her.

34 **MOTHER 3:** If the day should come I'd like to tell her all this in

35 person. If that is not to be, I want her at least to know that

1   we've missed her. I don't want to dwell on our suffering,

2   she must have suffered much more. And, if at some point

3   she has been able to think about us, she must have

4   suffered thinking of our pain, since she knew we didn't

5   know what might have happened to her. I think that

6   whenever we dream of her it's because she's concentrating

7   her thoughts on us. I know she wouldn't want me hidden

8   away, crying. *(Pause, fighting off tears)* I hope she'll forgive

9   me for not doing what she'd want me to.

10 FATHER 2: Today is sunny and warm; I've closed the shutters

11   and turned on the lamp. Daylight bothers me. If only it

12   had been overcast. But we can't choose these things

13   either. Where are you, *mi hijo*? Do you know that today is

14   the day of your birth twenty years ago? Are you anywhere

15   that lets you know this? What thoughts, memories,

16   images, must be passing through your mind today? Have

17   you been able to find a balance since you ceased to belong

18   to the world of people who move to and fro without

19   thinking that it can all suddenly end, that something can

20   happen so casually and then we are no more? It's the not

21   knowing that's terrible.

22 MOTHER 2: Not knowing, yes, that's the worst possible thing,

23   worse than death. There you have certainty, here we have

24   permanent doubt, no rest, no peace.

25 MOTHER 1: We live, we speak, we eat, we walk, but we are not;

26   we are empty of the knowledge of what has happened, we

27   lack the presence of that one human being. His things are

28   here, his books, his writing, his clothes, but he is not.

29 MOTHER 3: Only those who've lived through this can know it.

30   Imagining it is not the same.

31 FATHER 1: At times, the emptiness is so great that I don't know

32   how I reach the end of the day having accomplished

33   things, walked along the streets, talked to people,

34   carrying on what would be called a normal life. All that is

35   an appearance, inside I am empty. How can I be cured?

Only with your return. When will that be?

MOTHER 1: There is no answer. It is terrible to realize that we are anonymous numbers, that we don't count. We disappear, our place is filled by someone else and life goes on.

MOTHER 3: I hope this won't last very much longer. It would kill too many parents. It's too cruel.

FATHER 2: I'll go on another day, if I have something more to tell you.

MOTHER 2: Perhaps this will be useful in some way, otherwise it serves as my confession. *(One FATHER has struggled to compose this letter/diary while the OTHERS have spoken and danced.)*

FATHER 3: Your mother and I miss you more than words can say. *(Long pause)* That is all? One measly sentence? Ahhhhh! What more? The rest is silence. *(They dance, in silence. Lights fade to black.)*

SCENE 8: DANCE OF THE DISAPPEARED

(Music in the dark, perhaps the dance music of the previous scene. Lights up slowly to reveal NAOMI inside the Ford Falcon. GUARDS lounge about the shell of the car, ignoring her.)

NAOMI: "A woman without hands, without feet, without a head. Death is just eyes," my grandmother used to say. "If she comes ahead of her time, she leaves a pair of eyes and scurries away before we can catch even a glimpse of her. Do not be afraid! Those eyes can see wonders that you never imagined. When the right time comes, though, not a minute before or after, she comes back and you follow along in silence." *(GUARDS laugh to themselves.)* I long for those eyes, to see a way out of here, any way, the only way. They don't let me sleep, so I dream of those eyes while they torture me. Far, far away, my body just a shell lying

1   on that table, jerking with each new electric charge, but I
2   am gone, somewhere they can't find me.
3   Yesterday one of the guards let slip that the President
4   had been kidnapped. Kidnapped! The president of
5   Argentina! I felt wonderful, I don't know why, like I had
6   company. As if the others weren't enough.
7   Last night, he was waiting for me in my cell, *el*
8   *Presidente*. A sweet old man with a rosary in his hands. "I
9   have just finished my prayers," he stated. "Perhaps these
10   will help you," and he offered me his rosary. I asked about
11   Gerardo, if he knew anything. Why *el Presidente* should
12   know about everyone who's been disappeared, I don't
13   know. But he was here! So I asked. He said — and I got this
14   right, because I asked him to repeat it — he said, "His
15   disappearance might be an instance of self-kidnapping."
16   Self-kidnapping! Why hadn't I thought of that? And what
17   about me? I asked. If Gerardo kidnapped himself, why am
18   I here? "Oh, my dear," he said, "you're not here because of
19   him. No. You have your own sins to absolve." Then he
20   called for a guard and left me alone to wonder what sins I
21   have to answer for.
22   My sin was staying in Argentina; my sin was believing a
23   government would not dare to execute its own citizens on
24   the streets in broad daylight. My sin was naïveté, and I am
25   paying for it. Never again will I sleep in peace. Never again
26   believe a political promise, never see a soldier without
27   wondering how many he's disappeared, never see a
28   policeman without imagining the victims he's tortured.
29   Never, never be touched by a man without hearing the
30   laughter of the Milicos. *(GUARDS laugh again. After a*
31   *moment, NAOMI laughs too. They hear her.)*
32   GUARDS: What's so funny?
33   NAOMI: I was just complaining about all the ways my life is
34   changed ... as if I had a life to return to. As if ...
35   GUARDS: You never know.

1   Tomorrow may be your day.
2   Yeah, you'll win the lottery! *(GUARDS laugh.)*
3   NAOMI: Excuse me, sirs, could I please move around a little?
4   *(GUARDS are astounded.)*
5   GUARDS: What!?
6   NAOMI: I'm cold. *(Pause)*
7   GUARDS: All right.
8   Why not?
9   *(For a moment, NAOMI doesn't believe what they've said.)*
10   We said okay.
11   Move.
12   *(NAOMI eases herself out of the Ford Falcon, half expecting
13   to be punished, and starts moving her body, flexing her
14   arms and going up on tiptoe.)*
15   Bravo!
16   Let's see it again!
17   Look, guys, it's "The Death of a Swan."
18   Keep it up!
19   *(GUARDS watch as NAOMI continues, growing more
20   confident and more dancelike with each passing moment.
21   The music rises to greet her.)*
22   Let's have the Nutcracker!
23   That same rhythm, and a one and a two —
24   The "Tarantela"!
25   *(Dancing now for herself, not the GUARDS, NAOMI moves
26   Downstage joyously.)*
27   NAOMI: *(To audience)* And a three and a four, I forget the
28   chorus harassing me — and down and up — because
29   somewhere from deep down inside where they can't
30   touch an unknown warmth flows over me — and two and
31   three — down my arms and hands and reaching my neck
32   and "Yes!" comes out my mouth and "Good!" and I laugh
33   and laugh, and it's the first time that I've been warm and
34   happy, and I laugh inside not outside, and I dance the
35   dance of Blind Woman's Bluff and I laugh inside not

1   **outside, inside not out** – **two, three, and** ... *(She finishes*
2   *with the music. Silence. The GUARDS are astonished,*
3   *appreciative, but quiet. Blackout.)*
4
5
6   **SCENE 9: THE FORD FALCON AGAIN**
7
8   *(MILICOS usher blindfolded NARRATORS and NAOMI On-*
9   *stage, herding them towards the Ford Falcon. The*
10   *NARRATORS mutter among themselves.)*
11 **NARRATORS: What's happening?**
12   **Where are we going?**
13   **Can you see anything?**
14   **Are they going to kill us?**
15   **If you get transferred, then they kill you.**
16   **If you spend a night on the first floor, they let you go.**
17   **Is this a transfer?**
18   **I've never been on the first floor!**
19   **It's all lies.**
20   **Happened to my first cellmate that way.**
21   **Hush!** *(MILICOS frisk them, shove them into the Ford*
22   *Falcon. They stick out of the windows and doors in every*
23   *which way. Then MILICOS stand next to the Falcon, holding*
24   *on to doors or windows or whatever is available, as if they*
25   *were riding on the running boards. Sound of the Falcon*
26   *starting up and driving off. MILICOS stare ahead as if*
27   *watching the road.)*
28   **Where're we going?**
29   **Can anybody see?**
30   **What is it? What is it?** *(NAOMI peeks beneath her blindfold*
31   *and narrates what she sees.)*
32
33 **NAOMI: We're downtown, I don't recognize it. My god, the**
34   **buildings, they cast such shadows! I'd forgotten about**
35   **sunlight and shadows.**

1   **NARRATORS:** Cut the poetry, where're we going?

2   **NAOMI:** I don't know, away from town. Smaller houses, dirt

3   streets, empty, it's all empty. Like an empty movie lot, far

4   from town.

5   **NARRATORS:** They're going to execute us, I knew it.

6   Shut up!

7   They could have done that a hundred times already.

8   Wait!

9   What're we stopping for? *(MILICOS dismount the Ford.)*

10 **NAOMI:** It's an intersection.

11 **MILICOS:** *(To NAOMI)* You! Back in! *(MILICOS pull one male out*

12   *of Falcon.)* Move it! *(The MAN does not understand. Perhaps*

13   *he thinks he is standing before a firing squad.)* Don't try to be

14   clever, asshole. *(He walks a few steps forward, blindfolded,*

15   *lost.)* Start walking, you moron, or do you want to stay with

16   us forever? *(He is paralyzed by doubt, by fear.)*

17   Give me that gun and I'll blow him away for being such

18   a jerk.

19   C'mon, hurry up, we got lots more cargo to dump off.

20   All right, buddy, count to a hundred and then take off

21   the blindfold.

22   If you do it before then, you're dead meat, you hear?

23   *(MILICOS remount and the Ford Falcon roars away.)*

24 **NARRATORS:** They just left him.

25   They're releasing us!

26   *(A wave of excitement passes through the NARRATORS.)*

27   Don't jinx it!

28   Shh.

29   Hush! *(In silence the act is repeated — MILICOS dismount,*

30   *pull someone from Falcon, push them away, remount and*

31   *the sound of the car pulling away is all we hear. The released*

32   *PRISONERS stagger Off-stage. The procedure is repeated*

33   *until only NAOMI remains in the Ford Falcon. She has put*

34   *the blindfold back on, but leans her head out to breathe the*

35   *fresh air.)*

1   NAOMI: **Finally it's my turn. I feel the air on my face for the**
2   **first time. It's like being born again. I don't believe it – I**
3   **keep waiting for the electricity, the gunshot, the sound**
4   **and wind to disappear forever.** *(Once more, MILICOS*
5   *dismount. They pull NAOMI from Ford, push her Center*
6   *Stage, remount and stare straight ahead as sound of Ford*
7   *Falcon departing fills the theatre. It takes a long time to fade*
8   *to silence.)*
9   **The door opened and the street rescued me. The howl**
10   **of the engine trails off and I start counting out loud,**
11   **gulping in breaths of fresh air. I follow the instructions**
12   **scrupulously. 98, 99, 100.** *(She removes the blindfold, looks*
13   *about in both fear and wonder.)*
14
15   **Balconies hide whispers and shadows,**
16   **Secret pulsings throng the porches.**
17
18   **Three messages slice the streets:**
19   **Forbidden.**
20   **Will die.**
21   **From now on.**
22
23   **Clocks are set, peepholes spy, corners tremble.**
24   **Solemn and armed, bloody honors march by.**
25   **Meanwhile in secret and fleeting encounters, shy**
26   **crannies raise their voices.**
27   **The mercury street lamps blind me. I have to open my**
28   **eyes slowly to get used to the glare. I'm in an old**
29   **neighborhood, not my own, but it looks familiar. High**
30   **sidewalks as a precaution against floods, cobblestone**
31   **streets, a little sidestreet celebrated in tangos, and the**
32   **river. It's La Boca. La Boca. Mouth of the river, mouth of**
33   **hope and freedom, my mouth, daring me to speak.**
34
35   **I am Naomi!**

1   Can you hear me?

2   **NAOMI!**

3   *(A POLICEMAN enters.)*

4   **POLICE:** Heh! *(NAOMI starts to panic.)*

5   **NAOMI:** Oh god no, I just – you can't!

6   **POLICE:** Your ID.

7   **NAOMI:** I don't have it.

8   **POLICE:** Don't you know it's forbidden to go without it?

9   **NAOMI:** Yessir, but ... they kept it.

10 **POLICE:** Someone took your ID?

11 **NAOMI:** Yes – no – I mean ...

12 **POLICE:** Do you want to report it stolen? If you do, you have to

13   pay.

14 **NAOMI:** No, no. I know I should have it. I just ...

15 **POLICE:** Forgot it? Don't worry, just don't do it again. Okay?

16   You might end up at the station. *(POLICE exits. Other*

17   *NARRATORS enter and move about stage like residents of*

18   *the neighborhood. They cross paths with NAOMI, perhaps*

19   *even bump into her in their haste. She studies their faces.)*

20

21

22   **SCENE 10: FORGET THE FORGETTING**

23

24 **NAOMI:** I dreamed that one day, a sunny day preferably –

25   though fog would be more fitting – one day I would step

26   outside, into the light again, onto the street, without

27   shackles or blindfold, no armed escort, and I would see ...

28   everything, everybody, the Argentina I thought I'd lost.

29   *(Moving among the NARRATORS.)* I would walk the

30   streets and greet strangers like lost brothers until, quite

31   by chance, I found you, Gerardo. Why you? Why not me? I

32   feel guilty to be alive. Half of me is missing. Mothers of the

33   disappeared march each day around the Plaza. I want to

34   join them, but I am afraid. I will go out one day with your

35   picture in my purse.

1   *(She shows his picture to passersby.)* **I will take you**
2   **around the city to show you to whoever holds the key, the**
3   **clue to putting you into a conventional narrative with a**
4   **beginning, a middle, and an end. You will pass from hand**
5   **to hand, wander among ex-prisoners, survivors, the**
6   **reappeared, strangers, acquaintances.** *(The MOTHERS*
7   *unfurl handwritten banners and posters and pictures held*
8   *on sticks. They process in silence.)*
9   **I spot the corner where the marchers are gathering, but**
10   **before I take a step in that direction you cut in front of me.**
11   **I bump into your name, scrawled across a worn strip of**
12   **white cloth. Your black letters sting my memory and my**
13   **legs take on a will of their own. I stand there, rooted**
14   **before your one-dimensional scream.** *(A banner with*
15   *"GERARDO" written across it appears behind her.)*
16   **Someone knows. Someone misses you. Someone**
17   **marches for you, Gerardo. You are counted, among the**
18   **disappeared. They won't tell me how long you survived,**
19   **only that someone had seen you in another prison, only**
20   **that you'd been shot. I already knew — knew from the**
21   **moment I smelled you in the adjoining interrogation**
22   **room, smelled your blueness — but it's not the same as**
23   **hearing it. I almost cry. I almost scream. Almost. Still,**
24   **each day I go in search of you.** *(She holds aloft the picture*
25   *of Gerardo.)*
26   **Ladies and gentlemen, the one I'm looking for likes to**
27   **strum the guitar, has a weakness for coffee, plays soccer**
28   **and other sports, has been known to watch TV, and cooks**
29   **much better than mama ever did.** *(She is joined by other*
30   *MOTHERS who hold aloft their child's name or picture*
31   *while speaking.)*
32 **MOTHERS: She's fond of camping and staying up all night ...**
33   **Has friends in many different languages ...**
34   **Travels the length of the continent ...**
35   **Writes poems at dawn.**

1   NAOMI: He's about to finish his thesis on the permanence of
2   matter, but he can't endure even the metal of the scissors
3   that I threw at him when I was four years old.
4   MOTHERS: She is thinking about getting married.
5   He is accepted at university.
6   She passed the bar exam.
7
8   The one I'm looking for has eyes that speak ...
9   Untamed hair ...
10   Imposing height ...
11   Wavy voice.
12
13   NAOMI: The one I'm looking for has never grown old, his brow
14   is not wilted nor his temples graying.
15   MOTHERS: He delights in playing hide-and-seek ...
16   Cowboys and Indians ...
17   Hopscotch ...
18   Chess.
19   He's great at math but incapable of drawing a cow.
20   As a kid she locked herself in the bathroom.
21   As an adolescent, in his bedroom.
22
23   MOTHERS: *(Together)* Now they lock them in a camp.
24   NAOMI: He lives yet in a black and white photo ID.
25   MOTHERS: In a color slide, her T-shirt in a knot showing her
26   navel.
27   In a math notebook filled with formulas.
28   In a pair of shoes.
29   NAOMI: Why not go backwards, you used to say, remember,
30   Gerardo? When we played as kids? Backwards, like in fairy
31   tales, why not? Why don't you come back? *(Pause)* Say
32   something to me. *(Silence. NARRATORS gather on edge of*
33   *stage to address audience. NAOMI is left alone.)*
34   NARRATORS: From 1976 to 1983, the military junta
35   disappeared thousands of Argentine citizens.

1   How many?
2   Too many.
3   Numberless many.
4
5   Roberto Viola, second president of the regime, said the
6   miltary coup was an unavoidable act supported by
7   practically all Argentine citizens.
8
9   Yeah, right!
10
11   Despite having been found guilty of grave human rights
12   violations and sentenced to 16 years in prison —
13   Even that was cut short by the amnesty granted
14   military leaders —
15   Viola still claimed there was no governmental terrorism.
16
17   Amazing!
18   Is he blind?
19   He's an idiot.
20
21   Quote, the expression *governmental terrorism* simply
22   does not fly, unquote.
23   Viola said that?
24   "Does not fly"?
25   *Idiota!*
26
27   In 1994, the kidnapped and disappeared were legally
28   recognized by the new regime and were therefore eligible
29   for indemnity payments.
30 NAOMI: Gerardo, say something.
31 NARRATORS: Naomi went to the Office of Human Rights.
32   From the third floor she was sent to the first ...
33   And from there back to the third ...
34   Where they said what they already said before ...
35   In the exact same tone of voice ...

1   That tone of official indifference that drives you crazy ...

2

3   "A person who claims to have been one of the disappeared

4   must be named in some official document."

5

6   See? Their reasoning is perfectly logical. You cannot be

7   catalogued with any precision if there are no records of

8   your booking or release.

9   *(Pause. Consternation.)*

10

11   But ...

12   No records were kept of the disappeared.

13   That's how they were disappeared.

14

15   Get it?

16

17   In the end it's still unclear whether the disappeared

18   *legally* exist or not, but one thing is certain. We will have

19   to prove it.

20

21 NAOMI: Gerardo!

22 NARRATIORS: Naomi decides to see a psychologist for the

23   usual reasons.

24   Sleepless nights ...

25   Bad dreams ...

26   Voices from the interrogations ...

27   Strange pains your doctor cannot explain ...

28   Flashbacks.

29

30   She spends a long time in the waiting room rehearsing

31   her speech, before she is ushered in. The psychologist

32   asks the standard question ...

33

34   "What brings you here?"

35

1 She answers with a summary description of her situation,

2 an outline of what happened to her.

3

4 She is unaware of his reaction until, at the end of her

5 summary, she sees his eyes.

6

7 NAOMI: Are you crying? I ask.

8 NARRATORS: Yes, the doctor is crying. He has to take his

9 glasses off to dry the tears which smear his face.

10 NAOMI: It's not that bad, doctor, others had it worse.

11 NARRATORS: She offers him a tissue.

12 He cannot stop sobbing.

13 She moves closer and dries his cheeks, then holds his head.

14 After a moment, he composes himself ...

15 Thanks to her first-aid.

16 He makes an appointment to see her again another day ...

17

18 But Naomi doesn't wait for his diagnosis.

19 She marches out of his office and declares herself cured.

20 Cured!

21 NAOMI: He cried more in those few minutes than I have cried

22 in ten years. What is it, Gerardo, that keeps me from

23 crying, keeps me from letting go? Why do I search for you

24 in every face I pass when I already know — ? I hear your

25 laughter at the cinema, your voice in every stranger

26 shouting on the street. Why can't I say goodbye to you?

27 NARRATORS: *(To audience)* Compañeros ...

28 We came today to tell you a story ...

29 Because they never succeeded in vanquishing our minds ...

30 Or our souls ...

31 Or our memories.

32 It was 25 years ago today ...

33 On a dark and stormy night ...

34 That the dictatorship began.

35 NAOMI: *(As if in a trance)* The key to the front door turns as if

1   by some perverse magic steps rush in three pairs of shoes
2   practice their disjointed tap dance on the floor the clothes
3   the books an arm a hip an ankle a hand.
4   **NARRATORS:** Step on a crack ...
5   **NAOMI:** I look around me, surprised by a voice.
6   **NARRATORS:** Break your mother's back.
7   **NAOMI:** I turn the page, paper rustles between fingers
8   inventing the figure of a circle, incredulous amid images
9   that are and are not. The secret road between my house
10   and the city is filled with Ford Falcons – green Falcons
11   with no license plates. The floodgates have opened. Voices
12   from the past take over my body. I am – we are – a song, a
13   poem, a memory, one voice.
14 **NARRATORS:** *(Quickly)* They murdered my brother ...
15   Her son ...
16   His grandson ...
17   Her mother ...
18   His girlfriend ...
19   Her aunt ...
20   Her grandfather ...
21   His cousin ...
22   Her neighbor.
23 **CAST:** *(In one voice)* **Ours** ...
24   Yours ...
25   All of us. *(GERARDO enters Upstage singing softly, "El*
26   *Pueblo Unido Jamas Sera Vencido." He continues to sing*
27   *beneath the NARRATORS' voices.)*
28 **NARRATORS:** We were injected with their emptiness ...
29   Our dreams haunted by their fears ...
30   Our ears infected with their insults ...
31   Our bodies wracked by their cruelties ...
32
33   We all lost a version of ourselves ...
34   And we tell our stories in order to survive.
35   *(GERARDO's voice rises to finish the song.)*

1   **NAOMI: Don't forget the forgetting!**

2   *(ENSEMBLE sings the song together. Song builds to a chant.)*

3   **CAST: El pueblo unido jamas sera vencido!**

4   **El pueblo unido jamas sera vencido!**

5   *(Beat.)*

6   ***Remember us!***

7

8

9   **THE END**

10

11

12

13

14

15

16

17

18

19

20

21

22

23

24

25

26

27

28

29

30

31

32

33

34

35

Roimata
by Riwia Brown

The action of *Roimata* revolves around the axis of city versus country. In this drama, the new and evolving values of urban youth stand in sharp contrast to traditional standards — largely religious and family-based — that co-exist and occasionally come into conflict with them.

In this engaging contemporary story about coming-of-age in New Zealand, the young heroine Roimata leaves her rural home on the east coast of the North Island of New Zealand and travels to the city of Wellington to visit her half-sister, Girlie. Once there, however, she encounters more than just a new and exciting social circle into which she seeks admittance. She also discovers both her personal vulnerabilities and true strengths, and these discoveries cause a radical life change in her by the time the drama concludes.

One of the noteworthy features of this piece that makes it distinct in this collection, is that the playwright, Riwia Brown, engages head-on two of the most critical challenges facing young people today: substance abuse and sexuality. Both these issues seem woven inextricably into the fabric of modern youth culture, and the heroine confronts them early in the action. The play, in fact, may seem controversial because of this: its depiction of Roimata drinking in bars or involved in sexual situations. But it is this very realism in its style that makes the discussion both compelling and authentic for young readers, audiences and players.

A second noteworthy feature of the play is the way in which Riwia Brown introduces the note of evangelical Christianity, partially in response to the dangers facing young people who are finding their way in urban settings. The playwright never becomes mawkish and sentimental, however, about the potential of Christianity to "rescue" at-risk youth. Just when spectators begin to feel that Roimata will "find Jesus," marry Kevin and live happily ever after, the author twists the action to reveal yet another side to her heroine. Instead of religion, she offers us a definition of "female empowerment" that both embraces and understands, yet remains fiercely independent of social supports like religion and traditional married life. In this regard, the play seems uniquely modern, relevant, and a refreshing surprise to readers and audiences alike.

Although somewhat challenging in its dramaturgy that seems to require numerous cinematic settings, the play can be staged very sparingly and effectively with a versatile unit set, a good sound track and plenty of inventive "add-ons" for establishing locales. The action must flow smoothly and seamlessly from one situation to the next; and thus the play poses interesting challenges to directors, designers, players and stage technicians.

Characters

Roimata — Maori, 22. She has been brought up on the East Coast of the North Island.

Girlie — Maori, 24. She has been brought up in the city.

Eddy — Maori gang member, 25. He was brought up in the city.

Kevin — Maori, 23. He was adopted at birth by Salvation Army Pakeha parents. This is his first year as a Salvation Army cadet.

Blue Boy — Maori gang member, 19. He has spent his life in foster homes and different institutions.

Mouse — Pakeha, 18. She was brought up by her mother. Her father left them when she was very young.

Nan — A kuia. She was brought up on the East Coast and has lived there all her life.

Major — Major Barnes. Pakeha woman, early 40s.

ROIMATA was first produced by Te Ohu Whakaari at the Depot Theatre, Wellington, from July 27 — August 7, 1988. It was directed by Rangimoana Taylor with the following cast:

ROIMATA	Arihia Tania Bristowe
NAN/GIRLIE	Poto Stephens
MOUSE	Angela Heffernan
EDDY	Peter Kaa
KEVIN	Apirana Taylor
MAJOR	Katherine McLuskie

SCENE ONE

(The living room of NAN's home on the coast.)

NAN: Roimata!

ROIMATA: What's wrong?

NAN: What are you doing with your boots on? Want to dirty your nice clean floor? Take those off. I want to talk to you.

ROIMATA: *(Takes her shoes off)* Nan, you're supposed to be in bed.

NAN: Plenty of time for sleep! You've made the bread?

ROIMATA: Ae.

NAN: Where's that kite? I want to finish it.

ROIMATA: You have to stay in bed. *(NAN gets petty.)* Otherwise you'll have to go to hospital. Go on, I'll bring you your medicine and your weaving.

NAN: Twenty years of living with me, when have you seen me weave in bed? Medicine! What use is that to me? Do what I want. Plenty of time for sleep. I had a dream. I saw Papa, he was handsome, even when he was old he was a fine looking man. Handsome, kind, and gentle. Lucky to get him. Dolly, she wanted him, too. *(NAN and ROIMATA laugh.)* We laugh about it now, back then it was serious business. Dolly, well, she worked on her cooking and weaving, I worked on my smile. I had a lovely smile then. Plenty of time for those ... other things. Dolly got nine kids. I always wondered about that. We wanted a big family. Papa said, "Ne'a min', we got our girl." I saw Papa, his arms reached out to me, we almost touched, then his arms went to his sides, his face looked troubled. What is it? Then I knew what troubled his heart. Who will look after our moko? What about that then?

ROIMATA: I'm twenty-two.

NAN: We all need looking after, we all need family. Twenty two, you're pretty enough, aren't you? You're skinny, but your cooking would put Dolly's to shame. Let me see you smile.

1 **ROIMATA: Don't be silly, Nan.**

2 **NAN: Go on, show me your stuff. You got the young fellas after**

3   **you. I'd frighten them off. Throw things at them.**

4 **ROIMATA: I grew up with the boys here.**

5 **NAN: They're all settled with kids now. Mothers were keeping**

6   **their girls away from the dances. I had to chase you there**

7   **with a stick. Except that young fella, Kevin. He was a good**

8   **fella. I liked him. His father, Captain Phillips, was an**

9   **alright preacher, too. Looked smart in his uniform. He**

10   **used to throw people out of the pub. Used to make us**

11   **laugh.** *(ROIMATA has had this conversation many times*

12   *before. She wants to change the subject.)*

13 **ROIMATA: You tired? I'll get your medicine.**

14 **NAN: No! What use is that to me? When that young fella Kevin**

15   **left with his parents, that sparkle went out of your eyes.**

16   **You should've followed him. Never mind that taretare job**

17   **of yours at the shop. All the way to the seventh form and**

18   **that's what you do.**

19 **ROIMATA: That was seven years ago. I was still at school.**

20 **NAN: Just like your mother, too independent. I didn't want her**

21   **to go with your father.** *(ROIMATA is more interested in*

22   *pursuing this conversation about her father.)*

23 **ROIMATA: Why not?**

24 **NAN: They were different, he was a pakeha.**

25 **ROIMATA: Because he was a pakeha?** *(Pause. NAN senses her*

26   *interest, tries to make light of it.)*

27 **NAN: No. He wasn't Maori. He couldn't live here. He took her to**

28   **the city. You know what I think about the city.**

29 **ROIMATA: What about Dad?**

30 **NAN: No mountains, no rivers, no trees.**

31 **ROIMATA: Nan, what about my father?**

32 **NAN: No God.**

33 **ROIMATA: Nan.**

34 **NAN: They went to the city and got married.**

35 **ROIMATA: Then what?**

1   NAN: Then you. I went to get you to bring you home. Your
2   mother, she argued but she wasn't very well. The city is no
3   place for a child or anyone.
4   ROIMATA: When did she come home? *(NAN begins to*
5   *reminisce.)*
6   NAN: Papa and I were working in the garden. You were being
7   hoha. The bus pulls up blowing dust all over the show. A
8   letter, we thought. Your mother stood by the gate so
9   helpless looking. There were a lot of tears that day.
10 ROIMATA: The letter was written ages ago. I won't leave you.
11 NAN: We all need family. You will go to the city. I should have
12   given you the letter before. I was waiting for the right
13   time. Sit with me awhile.
14
15
16   **SCENE TWO**
17
18 *(Four months later. GIRLIE's flat in Wellington. MOUSE*
19   *enters.)*
20 MOUSE: Girlie? Are you in?
21 GIRLIE: Yeah.
22 MOUSE: I saw your car outside. Taking the day off?
23 GIRLIE: I've taken a couple of weeks off, about time I had a
24   break.
25 MOUSE: What are you doing? A bit of cleaning?
26 GIRLIE: Sort of. Want to help?
27 MOUSE: I've just finished cleaning the pad.
28 GIRLIE: Well, leave that, go and make us a coffee. Have you got
29   any gear?
30 MOUSE: No, but I should score by the weekend.
31 GIRLIE: Hell. I'm all out, too. Never mind, best I stay straight,
32   give a good impression.
33 MOUSE: What's up?
34 GIRLIE: I've got someone coming to stay.
35 MOUSE: New man in your life?

1   GIRLIE: Hardly. What do I want one of those for? They're only
2   good for one thing, and not always that. My sister's
3   coming. I got a letter from her last week.
4   MOUSE: Really! I didn't know you had a sister. I always
5   thought you were the only one.
6   GIRLIE: You don't know everything about me, do you?
7   Roimata. Nice name, aye? She's my half-sister. Roimata
8   was to Dad's first wife, not that he married Mum.
9   MOUSE: So, she's older than you?
10 GIRLIE: Nope. They had me before Dad married Roimata's
11   mother. So I'm his bastard. Not as big a one as that father
12   of mine. When he died, he explained it all in his will. My
13   mum knew all about it, but she didn't say anything. When
14   she did talk, she said Roimata's mother was a sick woman
15   and it would only be time before Dad would come back.
16 MOUSE: So Roimata's younger? Where's she been?
17 GIRLIE: She was brought up by her grandmother who died a
18   few months back. Before she died she gave Roimata a letter
19   I wrote ages ago. Apart from wanting to meet her I'd've like
20   to have seen the house and property Dad left her.
21 MOUSE: Hell, you father must've been loaded. He left you
22   heaps.
23 GIRLIE: Yeah, a few bucks. Anyway, now she's coming to meet
24   her sister. God! I hope she's not one of those country hicks.
25 MOUSE: Na, she's bound to be cool. I'd better go. When's she
26   coming?
27 GIRLIE: Tonight, on the bus.
28 MOUSE: Why don't you bring her to the pub on Friday?
29 GIRLIE: Might come down. Where are you off to?
30 MOUSE: I'm going to see Charlie up the Mount. Ya' know,
31   breaking and entry, bad buzz aye?
32 GIRLIE: Same old Charlie. Boys looking after you?
33 MOUSE: Yeah, not bad. Well, we might see you Friday. Things
34   aren't the same without you around. The girls are real
35   bitchy.

1 GIRLIE: Same old girls. Might see you Friday.

2

3

4 **SCENE THREE**

5

6 *(A few days later. Girlie's flat.)*

7 ROIMATA: Who's going to be there?

8 GIRLIE: Just some mates. Don't worry about it. They'll know

9 all about you by now. They'll be wanting to meet you, Roi.

10 Hurry up and get dressed.

11 ROIMATA: I am.

12 GIRLIE: You're going like that? At least put some makeup on.

13 Come on, help yourself. Hey! Grab my brush for me,

14 will you?

15 ROIMATA: Where is it?

16 GIRLIE: On the kitchen table.

17 ROIMATA: Girlie, I've told you about that. The table is for kai.

18 You're either parking your bum or your brush on the

19 table. Don't know about city Maoris.

20 GIRLIE: Don't nag. It doesn't matter here. I'll brush my hair

21 while you put some makeup on.

22 ROIMATA: No. Nan used to say people who wear makeup had

23 something to hide.

24 GIRLIE: Nan this. Nan that. *(Laughs.)* She's not wrong this

25 time. I've got plenty to hide, besides all these bloody

26 pimples. You must have been close to her.

27 ROIMATA: After Papa died we only had each other.

28 GIRLIE: Which earrings do you like?

29 ROIMATA: Those ones.

30 GIRLIE: Well, you can wear the other ones.

31 ROIMATA: I haven't got my ears pierced.

32 GIRLIE: What? I thought women were born with holes in their

33 ears. The next time we go shopping I'll get them pierced

34 for you. At least put some lipstick on. Try a couple.

35 ROIMATA: If I don't like it, I won't wear it.

1   **GIRLIE:** You have a play. I'll go and get us a drink to put us in
2   the mood. *(GIRLIE leaves the room. ROIMATA is left to try*
3   *the lipsticks. GIRLIE comes back with two glasses of wine.*
4   *She watches ROIMATA.)* You're quite good looking, you
5   know. You must have taken after your mother. Here, let
6   me have a go. Can't see much of Dad in you. Although he
7   was quite a looker. Me, I take after my mum.
8   **ROIMATA:** No, from all the photos you showed me, I think you
9   look a lot like your father. That's enough.
10   **GIRLIE:** Dad? He talked about you all the time to my mum.
11   Used to really piss her off.
12   **ROIMATA:** He never tried to see me.
13   **GIRLIE:** He probably did, but that Nan of yours wouldn't let
14   him, I bet. Look at that letter I wrote, she held on to that
15   for a couple of years at least.
16   **ROIMATA:** She would have done what she thought best. She
17   gave me a good home.
18   **GIRLIE:** The one Dad left you? What's it like?
19   **ROIMATA:** It's not flash, but it's a home. You should come and
20   see it sometime.
21   **GIRLIE:** Maybe I should come and suss it out. Now, it's just the
22   lips. There, how's that? You haven't touched your wine. I'll
23   finish it. Are you sure you don't want to borrow anything?
24   I've got this sexy little number.
25
26
27   **SCENE FOUR**
28
29   *(The pub. GIRLIE and ROIMATA enter. EDDIE, BLUE BOY*
30   *and MOUSE are already there.)*
31   **ROIMATA:** Are we going to stay here? The hotel at home is
32   flashier than this.
33   **GIRLIE:** I just want to show you off. We won't be staying long.
34   There they are, come on. You fellas been here all day?
35   **EDDY:** *(To ROIMATA)* Want a seat? I'm Eddy. Mouse told us

1   about you.

2 MOUSE: Yeah, gidday, I'm Mouse.

3 BLUE BOY: I'm Blue Boy.

4 GIRLIE: This is Roimata. How about getting us a drink?

5 BLUE BOY: What are you drinking?

6 GIRLIE: My usual. What about you, Roi?

7 ROIMATA: I'll have a Coke.

8 GIRLIE: She drinks heaps of Coke and juice.

9 BLUE BOY: You can't be serious. What about a beer? Hell,
10   they'll throw us out. What about a bourbon and Coke?

11 MOUSE: Not into drinking, aye? Like me. I prefer a good
12   smoke, aye? Want to come outside? I'll blow you away.

13 ROIMATA: Pardon? No, I don't smoke, but thanks all the same.

14 MOUSE: What've you been doing? Girlie been showing you all
15   the sights? Has she taken you to her work? Real cool
16   saunas, plunge pools. Maybe she could get you a job there,
17   she earns heaps.

18 GIRLIE: My sister has six School Certificate Subjects, five
19   University Entrances, and seventh form certificate, so she
20   doesn't want to listen to all your crap. *(GIRLIE takes*
21   *MOUSE aside. EDDY is pleased to be left alone with*
22   *ROIMATA.)*

23 EDDY: So, Princess, having a bit of a rage?

24 ROIMATA: Sorry?

25 EDDY: Out to have a good time?

26 ROIMATA: Oh, well I hope so.

27 EDDY: I know so. Finish that and I'll get you a real drink.

28 ROIMATA: Coke's fine. Where's the bathroom?

29 EDDY: Just through those doors. Mouse better go with you.

30   *(EDDY indicates to MOUSE, who runs after ROIMATA. Enter*
31   *KEVIN from the opposite direction.)*

32 KEVIN: Hello, folks.

33 BLUE BOY: Shit, man, what are you up to, selling raffle tickets?

34 KEVIN: No, we don't gamble. I'm just handing out "The War
35   Cry," and if you can spare it, we ask for a small donation.

1   BLUE BOY: What about a drink? Yeah, man, I'll buy you one.

2   KEVIN: No, I don't drink, but I could use the money for a

3   donation.

4   BLUE BOY: What about a smoke?

5   KEVIN: No, I don't smoke either, but the price of a packet

6   could go a long way to helping.

7   BLUE BOY: Do you shit, man, or do you just hustle?

8   GIRLIE: You must have some small vice? A nice-looking guy

9   like you?

10 BLUE BOY: I know, man, you must be one of those band fellas.

11 KEVIN: Yes, we do have a band, you should come and hear it

12   one Sunday.

13 GIRLIE: Do you need any singers?

14 KEVIN: Yes, come along, you'd be welcome.

15 GIRLIE: Yeah, like a snake in the grass.

16 KEVIN: That's very good, but honestly you'd be welcome.

17 GIRLIE: The Salvation Army? That's a Pakeha religion, isn't it?

18   Don't you feel a bit out of place? *(MOUSE enters from the*

19   *direction of the pub toilets.)*

20 MOUSE: Here, I'll take one of those. Is a dollar enough? Good

21   for loo paper. *(EDDY turns to MOUSE.)*

22 EDDY: Where's Girlie's sister? You're supposed to be looking

23   after her.

24 GIRLIE: Go and get her, Mouse. *(MOUSE takes one of the*

25   *magazines and exits.)*

26 KEVIN: Well, thanks, folks, for your time.

27 EDDY: Is that it? So you're going to take the money and run? I

28   don't think we've had our money's worth.

29 KEVIN: No? Well, I could stay and tell you what we're about. In

30   fact, I'd like to.

31 EDDY: No, not tonight, mate, you might spoil my night.

32 KEVIN: Have a good evening, folks.

33 GIRLIE: Name the place, I'll make sure you have a good one.

34   *(KEVIN exits from the direction he came. Moments later*

35   *MOUSE and ROIMATA enter from the opposite direction.)*

1   Where have you been?

2 MOUSE: She was gassing to some bird in the piss house. I told

3   her she missed out on seeing the spunk.

4 ROIMATA: I thought I'd seen her face before. We used to play

5   basketball against their school ages ago. *(Music)*

6 EDDY: Yeah, you look pretty sporting.

7 BLUE BOY: Yous coming to the party tonight? Should be a good

8   rage.

9 GIRLIE: You want to?

10 EDDY: Go on.

11 GIRLIE: Come on, Roi, just relax and enjoy yourself. Let's not

12   waste these sounds.

13 ROIMATA: No, wait, Girlie, I don't like dancing.

14 EDDY: Go on, Princess, don't let your sister show you up. I'll

15   get us a drink. *(BLUE BOY follows EDDY to the bar, the*

16   *GIRLS are left chatting.)*

17 BLUE BOY: New blood, aye, Ed, wouldn't mind getting into that.

18 EDDY: It's mine and you can spread that around.

19 BLUE BOY: Yeah, okay. Next week my turn, aye, Ed? *(BLUE BOY*

20   *turns and goes back to the table.)*

21 GIRLIE: *(To ROIMATA)* At least try and look like you're having

22   a good time. Here, Blue, come and dance with Roi. Keep

23   your hands in your pockets. *(BLUE BOY and ROIMATA*

24   *move onto the dance floor. EDDY returns with the drinks.)*

25 EDDY: *(To GIRLIE)* What's going on here?

26 GIRLIE: Just give us a drink.

27 EDDY: You into drinking Coke?

28 GIRLIE: Coke, aye? What's the matter, Eddy, don't want me any

29   more? I remember a time when you would've kissed my

30   arse.

31 EDDY: Yeah, and what did you used to say? Never run after a

32   bus once you've caught it. *(MOUSE cuts in.)*

33 MOUSE: Girlie, I've got some real good herb, want to come

34   outside for a blow?

35 GIRLIE: I've seen the way those bitches are eyeing Roi. You tell

1   them if they so much as lay a finger on her they'll have me

2   to deal with. I need a drink.

3 **EDDY:** Mouse, go and dance with Blue Boy.

4 **MOUSE:** I'd better go and tell those girls what Girlie said. Blue

5   Boy is already dancing.

6 **EDDY:** I didn't ask you, I'm telling you. Let me worry about

7   them. *(MOUSE moves onto the dance floor.)*

8 **MOUSE:** This is our dance, aye, Blue?

9 **BLUE BOY:** Piss off, Mouse. We're having a good time. Aren't

10   we, sweetie?

11 **MOUSE:** Just one dance.

12 **BLUE BOY:** If I wanted to dance with you it'd be in the back of

13   the car.

14 **ROIMATA:** You dance. *(ROIMATA returns to the table. EDDY*

15   *offers ROIMATA her drink.)*

16 **EDDY:** Enjoy your dance?

17 **ROIMATA:** No, I don't like dancing. I feel stupid.

18 **EDDY:** Ha, you looked beautiful. You made Blue Boy look stupid.

19 **ROIMATA:** Is Mouse his girlfriend?

20 **EDDY:** No. Why, you interested?

21 **ROIMATA:** No. Girlie asked him to dance with me. I don't

22   think Mouse liked it very much.

23 **EDDY:** Sorry, Princess, I'm just a jealous bastard. Bet Blue

24   thought all his birthdays had come at once. You've got a

25   boyfriend, someone from your home town? No? Hell, they

26   must be all sheep up your way. You've got a real pretty

27   smile. Don't turn away. Look me in the eye and say, "You

28   silly bastard." I've heard that line a thousand times.

29   *(On the dance floor:)*

30 **BLUE BOY:** Come on, Mouse, you wanted to dance with me so

31   much, let's go outside, I'll put a bit of Maori in you since

32   you want it so much.

33 **MOUSE:** Settle down, Blue, Charlie wouldn't like it.

34 **BLUE BOY:** Charlie wouldn't give a damn, so long as the boys

35   are kept happy. You liked it the other night, didn't you?

1   You bloody enjoyed it. Come on, we're going outside.

2 MOUSE: Blue! You're hurting me.

3 BLUE BOY: I'll bloody hurt you all right. I'll rape you.

4   *(EDDY sees what's going on.)*

5 EDDY: *(To ROIMATA)* **You stay here.** *(He goes over to BLUE BOY*

6   *and MOUSE and says to MOUSE:)* **Go and sit with Roi.**

7   *(MOUSE goes back to table. Turns to BLUE BOY.)* **Give her a**

8   **break.**

9 BLUE BOY: Ah, what the hell? You're trying to score Girlie's

10   sister, aye, man. Bet you twenty you don't, she's not our

11   type. Get Tania and Joe to come outside. We'll have a little

12   party.

13 EDDY: Yeah, man, later. Let's go. *(As EDDY escorts BLUE BOY*

14   *out of the pub:)*

15 BLUE BOY: Twenty bucks.

16   *(At the table:)*

17 MOUSE: I'm sick of being treated like that. I'll get a good

18   hiding when Charlie hears about this.

19 ROIMATA: Why do you put up with it? Why do you let him treat

20   you like that?

21 MOUSE: You're okay, Roi. Well, you must be, you're Girlie's

22   sister and she's tops. The boys don't mess with her. You

23   don't know nothing about us. We're like a family, the boys

24   take care of me most of the time. *(GIRLIE comes back with a*

25   *drink. Overhears the conversation.)* Sure, we all get hidings,

26   but if you didn't that would mean they didn't care.

27 GIRLIE: Yes, and Charlie cares about you one hell of a lot.

28   You've always got black eyes and bruises. What happened?

29   Got Blue a little hot?

30 MOUSE: You know Blue, he doesn't mean anything. I think I'll

31   get another drink. How about yous?

32 GIRLIE: Hang about, wait for Eddy, then we'll go for that

33   smoke. How's Eddy treating you, Roi? He's already spread

34   it around that it's hands off. Hell! Some of the women

35   would kill for that guy. Take it from one who knows, he's

1   great in the sack. Now where's he got to? *(EDDY enters.)*

2   Loosen up, Eddy will take care of you. Here he comes. I'll

3   leave you to it.

4 EDDY: Blue's okay, he's had a bit too much to drink. Talking

5   about drinks, would you like another?

6 ROIMATA: No, thanks. I've had enough. I'd —

7 EDDY: Yeah, I suppose there's only so much Coke you can

8   drink in one night.

9 ROIMATA: Is there a phone here? I'd like to call a taxi.

10 EDDY: What about the party? You're not going because of

11   Blue? Don't worry about it. I haven't done anything, have

12   I? *(ROIMATA stands to leave.)*

13 ROIMATA: Of course not, I'm just tired.

14 EDDY: Why didn't you say so, I'll call us a cab. *(EDDY goes to*

15   *leave. ROIMATA calls after him.)*

16 ROIMATA: No! I'm going by myself. *(EDDY turns.)*

17 EDDY: I thought ... Never mind what I thought. Do you feel like

18   a walk? *(ROIMATA walks past him. EDDY follows after her.)*

19   Come on, I'll walk you to the stand.

20

21

22   **SCENE FIVE**

23

24   *(GIRLIE's flat the following evening. GIRLIE has arrived*

25   *home after staying out all night.)*

26 ROIMATA: Where have you been?

27 GIRLIE: Oh, you're still home. Didn't Eddy ask you to the pub

28   tonight? He said he did.

29 ROIMATA: I was worried about you.

30 GIRLIE: Worried about me? I had a fantastic night. You should

31   worry about yourself.

32 ROIMATA: Me?

33 GIRLIE: Yes, you spend half the night chatting to some bird in

34   the club loo, then you pass up an opportunity to get it on

35   with Eddy! Don't look at me like that, I'm only joking.

1	Poor Eddy, couldn't have been good for his ego, you taking
2	off. Hell, I cracked up, we all did. There's a good band
3	playing tonight, you coming?
4	ROIMATA: No!
5	GIRLIE: Why not? Eddy's okay, just use him. Men are just after
6	one thing, so get in first, then kiss his arse goodbye.
7	ROIMATA: Don't you like him? He's better than some of those
8	mates of his.
9	GIRLIE: He's worse. I can't stand around chatting all night. I'd
10	better finish getting dressed. If you want to come you'd
11	better get ready. I had a stunning night. After you left the
12	pub I went clubbing. I met this real spunk. Not only good
13	looking but loaded. We partied all night. No, you don't
14	want to take Eddy seriously, he'll probably pick someone
15	else up tonight, you're the type that could get hurt. Just
16	enjoy yourself, live for the moment. What are you looking
17	at me like that for?
18	ROIMATA: How could you spend the night with someone you
19	just met?
20	GIRLIE: I'm going out with him later tonight, if that makes it
21	any better. Don't tell me you haven't had a man? What
22	about that bloke – Kevin – you were telling me about?
23	And don't spare the details.
24	ROIMATA: We were friends. We spent hours by the river.
25	GIRLIE: Yes?
26	ROIMATA: We could talk about anything.
27	GIRLIE: Boring, boring, boring. Where is he now?
28	ROIMATA: I don't really know, we just lost contact.
29	GIRLIE: Now I am really worried about you. What did your
30	mother do? She was stuck on one guy, Dad. What a piss poor
31	time she must have had. I bet she never lived. I mean really
32	lived. You're scared, aren't you? Too scared to enjoy yourself.
33	ROIMATA: That's a cruel thing to say. Mum was dying from
34	cancer. Dad couldn't stand to see her suffer, so she sent
35	him away.

1 GIRLIE: Do you believe that? I bet I know who told you, your
2   Nan. Maybe the truth hurts. Think about it. I'll be in the
3   pub for a few hours, so if you change your mind. Oh, I see
4   you've been cooking. Enjoy yourself with the meat and
5   veggies. *(GIRLIE goes to leave. There is a knock at the door.)*
6   Well, Eddy, fancy you being here.
7 EDDY: Where's your sister?
8 GIRLIE: Sorry, she's not interested. She's having an early
9   night. You can drive me, though. Save me taking my car.
10   Oh, well, I'll wait in the car. *(GIRLIE leaves. EDDY sees*
11   *ROIMATA sitting on the couch.)*
12 EDDY: There goes the wicked sister. Cinderella, your carriage
13   is waiting. *(ROIMATA is surprised and confused.)*
14 ROIMATA: What?
15 EDDY: *(Playing along)* Don't you recognize me? It's your fairy
16   God-brother.
17 ROIMATA: You're mad.
18 EDDY: Not as mad as the others will be when they find
19   themselves sitting in a pumpkin. Actually, maybe a quiet
20   night wouldn't be such a bad idea. I'll tell Blue Boy to take
21   the car. Trouble is he's a bit of a maniac behind the wheel,
22   I couldn't guarantee anyone's safety. *(ROIMATA thinks for*
23   *a moment.)*
24 ROIMATA: Hold it, Eddy, I'll come. Give me five minutes.
25 EDDY: Oh, okay. I'll just go and check on the horses.
26
27
28   SCENE SIX
29
30   *(Eddy's bedroom the next morning. EDDY is sitting on the*
31   *bed having a beer and watching ROIMATA sleep. She begins*
32   *to stir.)*
33 EDDY: Good morning, beautiful. You okay? Oh, got a bit of a
34   sore head?
35 ROIMATA: Oh, no.

1   **EDDY: Don't worry, you're with me. I looked after you last**
2   **night. You were beautiful. You had a bit too much to**
3   **drink, that's all. Showed your sister a thing or two!**
4   **ROIMATA: Where is she?**
5   **EDDY: I don't know. She left quite early with some bloke.**
6   **ROIMATA: Yes, I remember now.** *(BLUE BOY enters the room.*
7   *He is still drunk from the previous night. He circles the bed*
8   *then stands beside EDDY.)*
9   **BLUE BOY: You dirty bastard! Duchess, wouldn't be right to**
10   **call you Princess. Here's the twenty, mate. Come and buy**
11   **us a drink.** *(EDDY is furious with BLUE BOY.)*
12   **EDDY: In a minute. Don't stand there. Piss off.** *(Turns to*
13   *ROIMATA, calls after BLUE BOY:)* **You know Blue, if he had**
14   **half a brain it would be lonely.**
15   **ROIMATA: Where are my clothes?**
16   **EDDY: Folded neatly at the end of the bed.**
17   **ROIMATA: Can you pass them to me?** *(EDDY stands up.)*
18   **EDDY: I don't want you to get up, just let me check on the boys.**
19   **I'll come back. Don't look at me like that. I'll be back.**
20   **ROIMATA: Is there somewhere I can wash?**
21   **EDDY: I'll make sure it's clean.** *(EDDY moves into the other room.)*
22   **BLUE BOY: Have a drink, mate. Was it good? Was she as good as**
23   **her sister?**
24   **EDDY: She's the best, better than her sister. Where's Mouse?**
25   **BLUE BOY: Wasn't she enough, you want Mouse, too?** *(EDDY*
26   *goes over to MOUSE.)*
27   **EDDY: Mouse! Wake up, go and clean the shithouse.**
28   **MOUSE: What?**
29   **EDDY: Get up, clean the bathroom.**
30   **MOUSE: What for?**
31   **EDDY: Because I said. When it's clean, tell Roimata, she's out**
32   **the back.** *(EDDY moves in the direction of the bedroom.)*
33   **BLUE BOY: Where are you going to? Finish your beer, bro.**
34   **EDDY: I'm going to, in prettier company.** *(EDDY comes back*
35   *into the living room. He is angry.)* **Where is she? She**

1   **must've gone out the back door.** *(BLUE thinks it's a bit of a*
2   *laugh.)*
3   **BLUE BOY: Taken off, aye, bro? Don't worry about it. You got**
4   **your twenty. Come and finish your beer.** *(EDDY turns,*
5   *looks at BLUE BOY. Heads back into the bedroom with BLUE*
6   *BOY following close behind.)*
7   **EDDY: Ah, shut up.**
8   **BLUE BOY: If you're that worried about it, I'll go and have a**
9   **look she might be hiding under the bed.** *(MOUSE enters*
10   *looking tired and confused.)*
11   **EDDY: Where the hell are you going, Mouse?**
12   **MOUSE:** *(Sleepily)* **To get Roimata. The bathroom's clean.**
13   **EDDY: Use it!** *(MOUSE leaves, still in a confused state. BLUE BOY*
14   *is gloating.)*
15   **BLUE BOY: Was she a virgin? A virgin, you lucky bastard. Did**
16   **she scream?**
17   **EDDY: Get out!** *(BLUE BOY leaves in a hurry. ROIMATA comes*
18   *into the room from the opposite direction.)*
19   **ROIMATA: I've lost my bag.**
20   **EDDY: Is this it?** *(EDDY kicks ROIMATA's bag, she grabs it off him.)*
21   **ROIMATA: What are you staring at?**
22   **EDDY: I'm just checking you've got both shoes. What's the**
23   **story, Cinderella? Why pull the disappearing act?**
24   **ROIMATA: I wanted to go home.**
25   **EDDY: I was only gone for a minute. I'll drive you home if you**
26   **want to go. Why make me look stupid in front of Blue?**
27   **ROIMATA: What about how I feel?**
28   **EDDY: What's the problem? You didn't mind getting into bed**
29   **with me last night?**
30   **ROIMATA: I must have been drunk.** *(EDDY'S ego is hurt.)*
31   **EDDY: Thanks very much. I've never had to get a woman**
32   **drunk before.**
33   **ROIMATA: I didn't mean it like that.** *(EDDY tries again.)*
34   **EDDY: You want to go for a walk?**
35   **ROIMATA: Where? I can't go like this.**

1   EDDY: Well, I'll have to take you to Girlie's so you can change
2   into something more comfortable.
3
4
5   **SCENE SEVEN**
6
7   *(Girlie's flat later that day. ROIMATA and EDDY have*
8   *returned from a day and are sitting at the kitchen table*
9   *having just finished a meal.)*
10   ROIMATA: I like the way you cleared the beach. It was so
11   funny. One minute there were people, the next all gone.
12   EDDY: Yeah, people do tend to freak out. *(Indicates his gear.)*
13   This can work wonders. I was on the bus the other day,
14   amazing how all the seats clear. I never have any trouble
15   getting a seat. *(Laughs.)*
16   ROIMATA: Is that why you do it? To freak people out?
17   EDDY: Na. Oh, maybe when I first joined up, but not now.
18   ROIMATA: Why did you join up?
19   EDDY: My older brother. I used to drink with him and the boys.
20   I suppose I just drifted in. Been with them since.
21   ROIMATA: Is your brother still around?
22   EDDY: Na. He and his missus were killed in a car accident.
23   Wrapped themselves around a lamp post. *(ROIMATA is*
24   *shocked.)* Oh, what the hell, he went out happy, pissed as a
25   skunk. He escaped. They were planning to go to Aussie.
26   Things will be different for me. I know what I want. I'll give
27   myself another year or so, then I'll put "Plan B" into action.
28   ROIMATA: What's "Plan B?"
29   EDDY: Get myself a place, a bit of land. Somewhere to grow
30   dope, have a few kids. *(Silence)* I haven't had rewana bread
31   in ages. On top of everything else you're a great cook. I'm
32   a bit of a master chef myself. You got any eggs, bacon?
33   ROIMATA: You still hungry?
34   EDDY: Na, I was thinking of breakfast. I'll bring it to you in
35   bed. *(Silence)*

1 ROIMATA: I don't think that's a good idea.

2 EDDY: What?

3 ROIMATA: You staying.

4 EDDY: You want to stay here on your own?

5 ROIMATA: I'll be all right.

6 EDDY: What did Girlie say when she rang?

7 ROIMATA: She said she'd be away for a couple of days.

8 EDDY: She means when she's got rid of the fella's bank
9   balance. What about last night?

10 ROIMATA: I told you I don't want to talk about it.

11 EDDY: Okay, if that's what you want, I'll go. *(EDDY stands to*
12   *leave.)*

13 ROIMATA: I don't want you to go. But –

14 EDDY: But what? You're tying me up in knots here, woman.

15 ROIMATA: I'd like you to stay, but I don't want to sleep with
16   you. Would you mind?

17 EDDY: Yes. It would bloody kill me. Na, stuff it. See ya round.
18   *(EDDY leaves. Moments later he returns.)* If that's what you
19   want. I can hack it. But you can make breakfast.

20

21

22 **SCENE EIGHT**

23

24 *(Major Barnes' office at the Salvation Army the next day.*
25 *KEVIN knocks on the office door and enters.)*

26 MAJOR: Ah, Kevin, sit down. I expect you know why I want to
27   speak to you?

28 KEVIN: You've made a decision on the youth group?

29 MAJOR: That's not a decision I can make. I don't intend to take
30   the matter any further. No, I –

31 KEVIN: Why not?

32 MAJOR: Do you honestly believe I'm going to let you take our
33   young people into hotels to socialize? How do you think
34   that would reflect on the Army?

35 KEVIN: Very well. I don't expect to be in uniform.

1   MAJOR: Oh, I see, you'd be undercover as it were. What about
2   the temptation to drink and what it can lead to?
3   KEVIN: We could recite The Lord's Prayer.
4   MAJOR: Pardon?
5   KEVIN: They do serve non-alcoholic drinks.
6   MAJOR: I'm perfectly aware of that.
7   KEVIN: A building isn't evil, only some of the people that
8   congregate there. A lot are lonely. I'm thinking mainly of
9   the young. We could change that, invite them to our
10   activities, to our homes. It wouldn't happen overnight.
11   MAJOR: In the meantime we may lose some of ours to the
12   other side. *(KEVIN looks at her.)* Don't you think that's a
13   possibility?
14   KEVIN: Even the best armies lose a few in battle.
15   MAJOR: No. I'm sorry, Kevin. The risk is too great.
16   KEVIN: It would test our faith.
17   MAJOR: I've already given you my answer. Trust my judgment.
18   That's not the reason I asked you here. Although it does
19   come into it. I believe there was a bit of trouble the other
20   night. I've heard disturbing reports. Am I right in
21   believing you were nearly arrested?
22   KEVIN: I wouldn't be the first Salvationist to be arrested.
23   MAJOR: You are not allowed to obstruct the public during the
24   open air. Almost getting involved in a street brawl. You're
25   working too hard, I want you to have a break. The training
26   college can be a lonely place for a single person. I've
27   already sent a letter to your father. Have a holiday. I
28   believe your mother has been unwell, go and spend some
29   time with her. Think carefully about your future. We have
30   such high hopes for you. I'm sure your father will be a
31   tremendous help to you. *(KEVIN stands to leave.)* Where
32   are you going?
33   KEVIN: I have to prepare for my hotel visit. Unless you want
34   me to go tonight?
35   MAJOR: Of course not. Monday will be soon enough.

1   **SCENE NINE**

2

3   *(Later, in the lounge bar. MOUSE is a little tipsy.)*

4   **MOUSE:** Tell me you won't ever finish with Eddy. Hell, he's

5   been sweet as. We haven't seen much of him this week,

6   been shacking up at Girlie's, have you? Blue's been a bit

7   pissed off, not seeing his main man. Look at the way

8   Eddy's dressed, he looks spunky.

9   **ROIMATA:** He does, aye. I haven't seen you in a dress before.

10   *(MOUSE is pleased that ROIMATA has noticed her dress.)*

11 **MOUSE:** Don't think Eddy wanted us to come, so he said we had

12   to dress up. No slumming tonight. Look at Blue, even he's

13   made an effort. What a laugh. Have you heard from Girlie?

14 **ROIMATA:** Yes, the other night. She went to Auckland with this

15   fella, said she'd be back soon.

16 **MOUSE:** Yeah, that's her, cool as. *(EDDY and BLUE BOY join the*

17   *girls.)*

18 **EDDY:** You okay, Princess, can I get you anything?

19 **BLUE BOY:** Want a drink? You're not drinking Coke again!

20 **EDDY:** She doesn't drink, okay? If she wants one, I'll get it. So

21   leave off. *(BLUE BOY is hurt but tries to cover it up.)*

22 **BLUE BOY:** Well, it's boring in here, all the action's in the

23   public, Manu's down, and some of the boys are next door.

24   They told me to come and get you for a game. They know

25   of a good rage tonight.

26 **EDDY:** Ah, that old bastard's here. If you want to go, go. I didn't

27   ask you to come with us.

28 **BLUE BOY:** No, I'm coming with you, but at least come and

29   have one drink with your mates.

30 **EDDY:** Do you mind, Princess?

31 **ROIMATA:** No. *(EDDY stands to leave, BLUE BOY follows closely*

32   *behind.)*

33 **EDDY:** I won't be long. I'll just clean them up on the pool table

34   then they'll be begging me to leave.

35 **MOUSE:** Did you see Blue's face? Eddy's never put a woman

1 before the boys.
2 **ROIMATA:** Eddy's been good to me while Girlie's been away.
3 **MOUSE:** Tell me about it. *(KEVIN is seen in the background.)*
4 **ROIMATA:** It's nothing like that, he's sleeping in Girlie's room.
5 **MOUSE:** You must be joking? *(KEVIN comes up to ROIMATA*
6 *and MOUSE's table.)*
7 **KEVIN:** Good evening, ladies. Roimata? *(Great excitement)*
8 **ROIMATA:** Kevin!
9 **KEVIN:** You look fantastic, all grown up. It's good to see you.
10 What are you doing here?
11 **ROIMATA:** I'm here with some friends. This is Mouse.
12 **KEVIN:** Hello. Have we met before? *(MOUSE thinks KEVIN is*
13 *quite spunky and she's impressed that ROIMATA knows him.)*
14 **MOUSE:** Yeah, gidday.
15 **ROIMATA:** It's great to see you. You're still in the Army?
16 **KEVIN:** Yes. Only just.
17 **ROIMATA:** What?
18 **KEVIN:** It's a long story.
19 **ROIMATA:** Can you sit and talk?
20 **KEVIN:** Yes, I'd like to. So what are you doing in the big city? I
21 thought you'd never leave the coast.
22 **ROIMATA:** Nan died earlier this year.
23 **KEVIN:** I'm sorry, I didn't know that. I'm leaving on Monday to
24 see the folks. Mum hasn't been well. They'll be very sad
25 when I tell them the news. Was she very sick?
26 **ROIMATA:** After Papa died she went downhill. I think I'm what
27 kept her going. Before she died she gave me a letter written
28 by my half-sister, Girlie, so I'm staying here with her.
29 **KEVIN:** That must have been a bit of a shock. I thought you were
30 an only child. *(MOUSE can't wait to tell the boys about KEVIN.)*
31 **MOUSE:** I need a piss, you fellas want a drink?
32 **ROIMATA:** No, I'm fine.
33 **KEVIN:** No, thanks.
34 **MOUSE:** I'm going to see what the boys are up to. *(MOUSE*
35 *leaves. KEVIN continues his conversation with ROIMATA.)*

1 KEVIN: Are you working?

2 ROIMATA: No. I had a bit saved so I'm having a holiday.

3 KEVIN: That's what I need, a break. It will be good to get away.

4 ROIMATA: Where are you going?

5 KEVIN: Auckland. Mum and Dad have retired there.

6 ROIMATA: I hope your mother's not too sick.

7 KEVIN: Actually, I think it's a ploy to get me home.

8 ROIMATA: Why is that?

9 KEVIN: Our Corps Officer thinks I'm straying from the flock.

10   She wants me to have a think about my future in the Army.

11 ROIMATA: So you did go to training college? *(Enter EDDY*

12   *followed by BLUE BOY.)*

13 KEVIN: Yes. *(EDDY is uneasy. He talks to ROIMATA but looks at*

14   *KEVIN.)*

15 EDDY: Are you ready to go?

16 ROIMATA: Eddy, this is Kevin. Kevin and his parents lived

17   back home for awhile.

18 KEVIN: We've met before.

19 EDDY: I've seen you about.

20 ROIMATA: Kevin's at the Salvation Army training college. *(EDDY*

21   *is unimpressed. BLUE BOY is enjoying the whole conflict.)*

22 EDDY: Training to be what? An arsehole? *(ROIMATA is shocked.)*

23 ROIMATA: Eddy!

24 KEVIN: Eddy's entitled to his opinion.

25 EDDY: I don't need you to defend me. I don't like you and I

26   don't like what you stand for. *(KEVIN tries to witness. He is*

27   *not afraid of EDDY.)*

28 KEVIN: You don't like "Jesus Christ?" *(EDDY is enjoying himself.)*

29 EDDY: I didn't say that. He's a cool dude. He helped me a lot

30   when I was inside.

31 KEVIN: I'm pleased to hear it. *(EDDY is getting more angry.)*

32 EDDY: Don't patronize me. I know one thing. He didn't die for

33   do-gooders like you, who think you're a cut above

34   everyone else. Look at you, can't you read, "NO PATCHES

35   ALLOWED." I bet it's harder to get into your mob than into

1   a woman wearing a chastity belt.

2   KEVIN: Have you ever tried?

3   EDDY: What? Getting into a woman wearing a chastity belt?

4   You should try and get into one of ours. At least we don't

5   grease up to the system. *(ROIMATA is embarrassed by*

6   *EDDY's behaviour.)*

7   ROIMATA: That's enough, Eddy. *(EDDY is standing over KEVIN*

8   *in an imposing manner.)*

9   EDDY: Bloke comes in here imposing on people. I want to

10   know what he wants. What's that crap you carry around?

11   KEVIN: A Salvation Army magazine. "The War Cry." *(KEVIN*

12   *offers EDDY a copy. EDDY snatches at it.)*

13   EDDY: Like at haka?

14   KEVIN: Yes, in a way.

15   EDDY: Bullshit. Give us a look. Will it cost me an arm and a

16   leg?

17   KEVIN: It won't cost you anything.

18   EDDY: You were charging the other week.

19   KEVIN: No, not charging. Just asking for a small donation.

20   EDDY: For what? To pay for the Mercedes parked outside?

21   KEVIN: I don't have a car.

22   EDDY: What's the matter, sales down? What is this shit,

23   Brigadier Hill promoted to Glory. Look around. Do people

24   here look like they might be interested? *(Again KEVIN*

25   *tried to witness.)*

26   KEVIN: There is a message. Like when you were in prison.

27   Some people might be in their own personal prison, the

28   message might help.

29   EDDY: What's this little bit here? What a rip-off. What do you

30   know about life on the street? Or is it just what you've

31   learnt at that college of yours? For a start, you don't just

32   move in on someone else's woman, not here.

33   ROIMATA: I'm not your woman. Kevin and I are just friends.

34   EDDY: Friends don't look at you the way he has. Do you think

35   I'm blind?

1   **ROIMATA: I don't want to hear any more. Let's go, Kevin.**

2   *(EDDY goes to stop KEVIN leaving.)*

3   **EDDY: You're not going anywhere.**

4   **BLUE BOY: Soldier Boy's found himself a real fight.** *(BLUE BOY*

5   *takes KEVIN's hat.)* **Give us a try of your hat.** *(KEVIN is*

6   *getting annoyed.)*

7   **KEVIN: Give the hat back.**

8   **EDDY: Give it here, Blue.** *(BLUE BOY gives the hat to EDDY.*

9   *EDDY challenges KEVIN.)* **Let's see if you've got any balls.**

10   **You want it, you come and get it.** *(KEVIN rises to the*

11   *occasion, a scuffle develops.)*

12   **ROIMATA: Give it back, Eddy. You're making a fool of yourself.**

13   **EDDY: Take the hat then.** *(Shoves the hat at KEVIN. To*

14   *ROIMATA:)* **If you prefer a gutless wonder like that.** *(To*

15   *KEVIN:)* **Next time I see you, you better be with your army.**

16   *(He storms out of the bar. BLUE BOY is close behind.)*

17   **ROIMATA: Kevin, I'm so sorry.**

18   **KEVIN: Come on, I'll take you home. So, how is Uncle Stan and**

19   **all those East Coast Maoris?**

20

21

22   **SCENE TEN**

23

24   *(Later that evening. KEVIN has returned with ROIMATA to*

25   *Girlie's flat. He is about to leave.)*

26   **KEVIN: Well, thanks for the food and company. You make me**

27   **laugh.**

28   **ROIMATA: Why?** *(KEVIN places his hands on ROIMATA's*

29   *shoulders.)*

30   **KEVIN: You're just like your grandmother, always kai in the**

31   **pot. Well, I'd better go.** *(ROIMATA looks up at KEVIN.)*

32   **ROIMATA: Kei te pai.**

33

34

35

1	**SCENE ELEVEN**
2	
3	*(Girlie's place the next morning. ROIMATA is sitting with a*
4	*cup of coffee. There is another cup on the table. KEVIN*
5	*enters, straightening his tie and putting on his jacket.)*
6	**KEVIN:** You okay?
7	**ROIMATA:** *(Smiles.)* Yes.
8	**KEVIN:** Roimata, I never needed anyone so much. You know
9	what the worst thing is?
10	**ROIMATA:** What? *(KEVIN gets up and stands behind ROIMATA*
11	*who is seated on the couch.)*
12	**KEVIN:** I should feel guilty. Perhaps we should have done this
13	years ago. I should have come back for you. I'll be back as
14	soon as I can this time. I suppose I should go. *(ROIMATA*
15	*turns towards KEVIN.)*
16	**ROIMATA:** Yeah, your mates will be wondering where you are.
17	*(KEVIN, more light-hearted, kneels behind ROIMATA and*
18	*puts his arms around her.)*
19	**KEVIN:** It doesn't matter. I've been given my marching orders.
20	They've probably been down to Taranaki Street to check
21	the cells.
22	**ROIMATA:** You're being too hard on yourself, and them. It
23	sounds like you've been overdoing it. Your father will be
24	able to help.
25	**KEVIN:** Come with me. Tomorrow, to the meeting.
26	
27	
28	**SCENE TWELVE**
29	
30	*(Later that morning at the Salvation Army office.)*
31	**MAJOR:** I thought it might be you. I've had several calls from
32	the college. It's very late.
33	**KEVIN:** *(Head down)* I need to talk.
34	**MAJOR:** Of course. I could prepare us breakfast, or would a hot
35	drink do?

1   **KEVIN:** No, nothing.

2   **MAJOR:** *(Indicating that KEVIN should sit)* **Okay, let's talk.**

3   **KEVIN:** I've been walking.

4   **MAJOR:** Is that how you got here?

5   **KEVIN:** Yes. I met a friend last night. Someone very special to
6   me I hadn't seen since we moved from the coast. We
7   talked for a long time.

8   **MAJOR:** *(Thinking for a moment)* That was a very special time
9   for you.

10 **KEVIN:** Yes. It was there I was first made aware of my Taha
11   Maori. After tonight I am more determined to learn.

12 **MAJOR:** So you've been with him all this time? You could at
13   least have let us know.

14 **KEVIN:** Not with him. Her.

15 **MAJOR:** I see.

16 **KEVIN:** It does make a difference. That's why I need to talk to
17   you.

18 **MAJOR:** Oh, Kevin, I know you've been under a lot of pressure
19   lately.

20 **KEVIN:** I love her.

21 **MAJOR:** I can't dispute the fact that you may have strong
22   feelings for this woman and I hope that you do. What is
23   her name?

24 **KEVIN:** Roimata.

25 **MAJOR:** Yes, strong feelings for Roimata. If you love her as you
26   say you do, don't you think you have done her a great
27   injustice? She wouldn't know you as well as I do at this
28   time. What you have done, Kevin, is to impose your own
29   insecurities on her. By doing so you have let yourself down
30   and the Army you have sworn to serve. I know how
31   disappointed you were when we were unable to locate
32   your birth mother. But from your birth I believe that you
33   were called to serve Christ. Our Maori Mission is weak
34   and we look to people like you. We could support you with
35   your Maori studies. When you do these studies, which I

have faith you will, you will have to choose how best to
serve your people ... The Army is not for everyone, Kevin;
our discipline is hard but whatever road you choose the
going will be tough. You have grown up in the Army; you
are only a baby in your own culture. I'm going to take you
out of the training college, Kevin, until you are more sure
of yourself. It is a decision that saddens me greatly. You
have always been a good soldier, Kevin, not afraid to fight.
You have frightened me many times with the strength of
your commitment. I hope you will again. I pray for you as
I hope you pray for guidance. It's time we both got some
sleep before the meeting.

SCENE THIRTEEN

(Later that day. ROIMATA and KEVIN are having a picnic.)

ROIMATA: *(Looks around.)* This place is just like home, not a
sign of life anywhere except for the sheep and cows. Nan
would have liked it. *(KEVIN is stretched out, hands behind
his head. He props himself up.)*

KEVIN: I come here to think. It reminds me of the coast, too.
Brings back good memories. Remember that time your
uncle took us up that mountain, Whitu Matarou?

ROIMATA: Yeah, he spent the entire time on the way up telling
us if we got caught at the top after dark the kehuas would
come out and get us.

KEVIN: That's why we had to start out so early.

ROIMATA: He still managed to get us lost.

KEVIN: Yeah, when the sun set I thought he was going to jump
over the side of the cliff. He went as white as a sheet.

ROIMATA: Yeah, he was the first kehua out that night.

KEVIN: Did you enjoy the service?

ROIMATA: It was neat. I enjoyed the singing, I even recognized
some of the tunes.

1   KEVIN: I liked you being there. You made a few heads turn.

2   ROIMATA: Yeah, especially from those girls with their

3   tambourines. Why did you go to the front and kneel with

4   those other people?

5   KEVIN: The mercy seat? You go up to acknowledge your faith.

6   Sometimes for forgiveness or renewed strength in God.

7   Like a public confession.

8   ROIMATA: Why did you?

9   KEVIN: It had to do with last night. *(KEVIN sits up.)* Do you

10   know what my father was before he was a Salvationist?

11   ROIMATA: I thought he always was.

12   KEVIN: An alcoholic. When my father marched up to the mercy

13   seat, knelt, he was transformed. Filled with the holy spirit.

14   A soldier with a sharpened sword. His past life turned to

15   his advantage. He understood. Like your friend said, what

16   do I know about street life? In fact, I don't know anyone in

17   our corps that does among the younger ones. We've been

18   so well protected. Sometimes in the meetings I don't know

19   whether I'm among soldiers or just a congregation in

20   uniform. And the gossip. I've seen good Salvationists

21   forced out because of gossip. *(ROIMATA looks at him.)* Yes,

22   you have to be squeaky clean. We've put ourselves on

23   pedestals. Christ himself had to get amongst it.

24   ROIMATA: It's not just what Eddy said, is it?

25   KEVIN: No. Although a lot of what he said was the truth, with

26   a hint of jealousy.

27   ROIMATA: What do you mean?

28   KEVIN: Why didn't you reply to any of my letters?

29   ROIMATA: What letters? *(KEVIN looks at her.)* Honestly, Kevin.

30   KEVIN: I must have written you half a dozen. I said I'd write.

31   *(ROIMATA is thoughtful.)*

32   ROIMATA: Myra! *(KEVIN is confused.)*

33   KEVIN: Myra?

34   ROIMATA: You remember her, don't you?

35   KEVIN: How could I forget?

1 ROIMAYA: How she got a job in the post office I don't know. I
2   thought she was giving me funny looks when I went to call
3   for the mail.
4 KEVIN: What do you mean?
5 ROIMATA: She used to take mail home, the interesting stuff,
6   and have a good read before burning it. *(ROIMATA and*
7   *KEVIN laugh.)* It's funny now.
8 KEVIN: What happened to her?
9 ROIMATA: She got the sack. I thought you'd forgotten about us.
10 KEVIN: How could I forget you or your grandmother? She
11   helped me a lot. Learning about things Maori, and marae
12   etiquette (although I never felt comfortable on the marae).
13   And you, the first time I saw you riding across the
14   paddock on your horse. I thought, Kevin, there must
15   surely be a God in heaven. *(KEVIN helps ROIMATA to her*
16   *feet.)* I'm going to hate leaving tomorrow. I'll write to you.
17   Let's hope Myra hasn't gotten a job down here.
18
19
20   SCENE FOURTEEN
21
22   *(Two months later. Girlie's flat. GIRLIE calls out to ROIMATA.)*
23 GIRLIE: There's another letter for you. That's about the eighth
24   one this week. How did you get on at the doctor's? I was
25   expecting you an hour ago.
26 ROIMATA: I've been walking.
27 GIRLIE: You had things to think about then? It just didn't
28   occur to me that you weren't on the pill. I'm late for work
29   already. Don't worry. I know this doctor, won't cost you
30   anything. In and out all on the same day. All the girls use
31   him. *(ROIMATA has no idea what GIRLIE is talking about.)*
32 ROIMATA: I like the doctor I saw today.
33 GIRLIE: Does she do them? When do you go in?
34 ROIMATA: In about seven months.
35 GIRLIE: What are you talking about?

1   ROIMATA: What are you?

2   GIRLIE: Abortion. What else? You spend one lousy night in the
3   sack, one lousy screw, which was so good you can't
4   remember anything about it. You can't throw your life
5   away, and for what? A screaming kid, spend the next few
6   years changing dirty nappies. What about money, how
7   will you support it?

8   ROIMATA: I'll manage. Nan did.

9   GIRLIE: Is that what you want, just to manage?

10 ROIMATA: I made one mistake.

11 GIRLIE: What do you think I'm talking about? Do you think
12   Eddy's good father material?

13 ROIMATA: I need to talk to him.

14 GIRLIE: What about? He's already got a kid he never sees. What
15   about him spreading it around, he took your virginity?

16 ROIMATA: I need to see him before Kevin arrives.

17 GIRLIE: Of course, that fella, Kevin. He nearly proposed to you
18   in one of his letters.

19 ROIMATA: You shouldn't read my mail.

20 GIRLIE: You left it lying about.

21 ROIMATA: In my room. Anyway, I thought you and Mouse
22   thought it was a great joke.

23 GIRLIE: Well, he is a bit of a poet. That's it, marry him and tell
24   him about the kid later. Can't be worse than bringing up a
25   baby on your own. I'd go for the abortion. Hey, can you
26   imagine Mouse a bridesmaid at a church wedding? That's
27   what she's been hinting at.

28 ROIMATA: Go to work.

29

30

31   **SCENE FIFTEEN**

32

33   (*The next morning. Blue Boy's bedroom. BLUE BOY and*
34   *MOUSE are in bed.*)

35 BLUE BOY: When did you see Girlie?

1   MOUSE: Last night. I went for a sauna and that's what she told
2   me, she reckons that Roimata is up the duff.
3   BLUE BOY: That'll put her in her place. Does Eddy know?
4   MOUSE: Na, I don't think so. *(BLUE BOY smiles to himself and*
5   *then grabs MOUSE.)*
6   BLUE BOY: Come here, you.
7
8
9   **SCENE SIXTEEN**
10
11   *(Eddy's flat later that morning. BLUE BOY arrives and*
12   *surprises ROIMATA who is already there.)*
13   ROIMATA: *(Startled)* **You gave me a fright.**
14   BLUE BOY: What are you doing sneaking around here?
15   ROIMATA: I'm not sneaking. Is Eddy in?
16   BLUE BOY: Can you see him? You're out of luck. Hey! Where do
17   you think you're going? Won't I do?
18   ROIMATA: Get out of my way, Blue. I want to talk to Eddy.
19   BLUE BOY: What about, you being up the duff? Do you think
20   he wants your sprog?
21   ROIMATA: Get your hands off me.
22   BLUE BOY: Don't play hard to get. Eddy told us all about you,
23   said you screamed.
24   ROIMATA: Stop it. *(EDDY enters from the back.)*
25   BLUE BOY: You know that night you stayed here? I drugged
26   your drinks.
27   EDDY: You lousy bastard. I'll kill you. *(BLUE BOY and EDDY*
28   *fight. BLUE BOY succumbs.)*
29   BLUE BOY: I did it for you. I did it for you.
30   EDDY: When have I needed that kind of help? Get out.
31   *(BLUE BOY exits. Silence, then EDDY turns to ROIMATA.)*
32   EDDY: What are you doing here?
33   ROIMATA: I came to see you.
34   EDDY: Why didn't you call first?
35   ROIMATA: Back home you don't have to call.

1 EDDY: You're not back home now. I tried calling you. Seeing
2   you, but you'd have nothing to do with me. Last I heard
3   was a soldier boy wanted to marry you.
4 ROIMATA: I came to ask —
5 EDDY: For my blessing?
6 ROIMATA: I wanted to ask you about that night I stayed here.
7 EDDY: I didn't know he spiked your drinks. That's not my style.
8 ROIMATA: Did anything happen between us?
9 EDDY: I thought there was a lot between us. What? The bastard
10   doesn't want second-hand goods? Don't you know?
11 ROIMATA: I can't remember.
12 EDDY: You think I'm some kind of lousy screw. What does he
13   want, a written note? I wasted all that time sleeping in
14   Girlie's room like some kind of wanker. What a laugh! So
15   write to soldier boy, you've got the all-clear. I hate pricks
16   like him.
17 ROIMATA: Why?
18 EDDY: I told you from the beginning. I'm a jealous bastard.
19 ROIMATA: It's not just me.
20 EDDY: He's had it easy.
21 ROIMATA: He was abandoned at birth.
22 EDDY: What do you want me to do, hand out tissues? So now it
23   makes him feel good to visit pubs, see how the other half
24   lives?
25 ROIMATA: What about you? Does it make you feel good to be
26   the main man? What about all your plans and dreams?
27   What are you afraid of?
28 EDDY: I'm not afraid of anything. Not like that bloody Pakeha
29   in brown skin.
30 ROIMATA: What's that supposed to mean? At least he turns his
31   dreams into reality. I've grown up with our people and
32   most of them are hard-working, good family people. They
33   would identify more with Kevin than you.
34 EDDY: You don't know what you're talking about. You'd better
35   go before I do something I'll regret. *(ROIMATA goes to leave.)*

1	Roimata, those days at Girlie's were the best. Nothing good
2	stays here. I didn't want this for you. I could have made
3	things good for us. *(ROIMATA leaves. BLUE BOY enters.)*
4	EDDY: So you're back.
5	BLUE BOY: I had nowhere to go.
6	EDDY: You poor bastard.
7	BLUE BOY: This is our home, man.
8	EDDY: What am I feeling sorry for you for? Wall-to-wall carpet,
9	swimming pool out the back or did we fill in the hangi pit?
10	Bloody marvelous.
11	BLUE BOY: What's bugging you? I'm sorry about the drinks.
12	EDDY: You were wrong, man. You were way out of line. How do
13	you think that made me feel? Do you think I can't get my
14	own women?
15	BLUE BOY: You're the best. I didn't think.
16	EDDY: You never think. What do you think of Manu?
17	BLUE BOY: He's the best. He's one of us.
18	EDDY: He's fifty. Didn't you notice? I don't know whether to
19	hate the bastard or love him. The only difference between
20	you two is he's running around with grey hair. He's got
21	nothing. What have you got?
22	BLUE BOY: We've got each other.
23	EDDY: He's got kids. They don't want anything to do with him.
24	His youngest beat him up one night, did you know that?
25	BLUE BOY: You want your kid?
26	EDDY: Then what? What can I give him? No, he doesn't need
27	me.
28	BLUE BOY: It's always been us.
29	EDDY: You're not thinking. You don't need me. I don't need
30	you bastards. Do you think I want to be bouncing you on
31	my knee when I'm fifty? This is shit. I should go.
32	BLUE BOY: Well, go, then, if that's what you think, but leave
33	the patch behind. *(EDDY grabs BLUE BOY by the throat.)*
34	EDDY: Who's going to stop me? You? You think you're a big
35	man? I've had my patch for ten years, you've had yours for

1   five minutes.

2   BLUE BOY: I don't want to fight you, man. I just don't want you

3   to leave.

4   EDDY: *(Releasing BLUE BOY)* Get us another beer. You spiked

5   her drink, ay?

6   BLUE BOY: I said I'm sorry and I am.

7   EDDY: She fell asleep on me. Bloody hell, I tried everything.

8   BLUE BOY: But you said —

9   EDDY: No, that's what you thought. Here's your twenty.

10   BLUE BOY: I don't want the money.

11   EDDY: Take it.

12   BLUE BOY: Come on, man, what about all that time you spent

13   at Girlie's?

14   EDDY: I slept in the other room. I didn't have to prove anything.

15   BLUE BOY: Then it must be bullshit, aye?

16   EDDY: What?

17   BLUE BOY: Mouse reckons she's up the duff.

18   EDDY: Who, Mouse?

19   BLUE BOY: Na, Roimata.

20

21

22   **SCENE SEVENTEEN**

23

24   *(Girlie's living room the next day. ROIMATA has been*

25   *shopping and goes straight into the living room with her*

26   *parcels, including some books on motherhood. She looks*

27   *through them. Meanwhile, KEVIN has been waiting for her*

28   *in the kitchen. He comes through.)*

29   KEVIN: Guess who?

30   ROIMATA: Kevin, don't do that!

31   KEVIN: I didn't mean to frighten you. Pleased to see me?

32   ROIMATA: Of course I am. I'll put the jug on.

33   KEVIN: I've had a cup. Your sister let me in, she's quite a

34   character. She went out for something. You go ahead. You

35   were expecting me? You got my letter?

1   **ROIMATA:** *(Calling from the other room)* **Yes, yesterday.** *(She*
2   *returns with a pack of cigarettes.)*
3   **KEVIN: I didn't know you smoked.**
4   **ROIMATA:** *(Taking one from the packet and playing with it)* **I**
5   **don't really, just the odd one.**
6   **KEVIN: Is something wrong?**
7   **ROIMATA: No, nothing. Tell me about your trip.**
8   **KEVIN: I told you most of it in my letters. I'm going back to**
9   **training college. I hope to re-enter the next intake. I have**
10   **a meeting with the Major tomorrow.**
11   **ROIMATA: And your mum's fit and well?**
12   **KEVIN: Yes, she's fine. Both mum and Dad. They send their love.**
13   **ROIMATA:** *(Putting the cigarette back into the packet)* **I got your**
14   **mother's letter.**
15   **KEVIN: They want you to go for a holiday. I thought we could**
16   **go together next time.**
17   **ROIMATA: I'll be going home soon.**
18   **KEVIN: You're what?**
19   **ROIMATA: I'm thinking of going back to the coast.**
20   **KEVIN: I thought you were going to look for work here.**
21   **ROIMATA: I did think about it. But I don't want to stay here.**
22   **KEVIN: What happened, Roi? You seemed so positive in your**
23   **last letter. Have you fallen out with your sister?**
24   **ROIMATA: No. I don't know why. I suppose I'm homesick.**
25   **KEVIN: But I don't want you to go. I want to marry you.**
26   **ROIMATA: What?**
27   **KEVIN: Does that come as a surprise? I want you to have my**
28   **children.**
29   **ROIMATA: You want kids?**
30   **KEVIN: Yes, lots, but not right away. We need to spend some**
31   **time together. We have to get you into the training college.**
32   **ROIMATA: What?**
33   **KEVIN: The training college. You'll have to become an officer,**
34   **too. You'll be great. We'll make a good team.**
35   **ROIMATA: No. I can't.**

1 KEVIN: What?

2 ROIMATA: I don't want to. It wouldn't be right.

3 KEVIN: I'm rushing you. Let's take it one step at a time. Do you
4   want to marry me? Do you?

5 ROIMATA: I don't know.

6 KEVIN: What about your letters?

7 ROIMATA: I'm pleased that you're staying in the Army.

8 KEVIN: You just don't want to be a part of it?

9 ROIMATA: I'm not suited. That's where you feel comfortable. I
10   wouldn't. Just like the marae for you. Relationships don't
11   last because of those differences.

12 KEVIN: They can be strengthened by those differences. It
13   depends on the couple and how much they're willing to
14   put into the relationship. Didn't that night we spent
15   together mean anything to you?

16 ROIMATA: It shouldn't have happened.

17 KEVIN: No, it shouldn't have. I was weak, but I loved you then
18   and I love you now.

19 ROIMATA: One night doesn't mean you have to throw your
20   whole life away.

21 KEVIN: Is that what you think you'd be doing? You've changed.
22   Just give me a yes or a no.

23 ROIMATA: No. Believe me, it wouldn't work, not now. *(GIRLIE*
24   *enters, unnoticed.)*

25 KEVIN: I don't understand. Is there someone else?

26 ROIMATA: No.

27 KEVIN: When are you planning to go?

28 ROIMATA: Soon.

29 KEVIN: So that's it, then? You've made up your mind?

30 ROIMATA: Yes.

31 KEVIN: I've always loved you. I only realized that when I saw
32   you again. Tell me something, what if I had decided to
33   leave the Army?

34 ROIMATA: That would be a mistake. I wouldn't be a part of it.

35 KEVIN: You know where you can get hold of me. Take care of

1   **yourself.** *(KEVIN goes to leave. ROIMATA stands for a*

2   *moment before flopping into a seat. She is near tears.)*

3   **ROIMATA: You too, Kevin.** *(KEVIN leaves.)*

4   **GIRLIE: I came in the back. Why didn't you tell Kevin?**

5   **ROIMATA: You wouldn't understand.**

6   **GIRLIE: Is he the father?**

7   **ROIMATA: I don't know.**

8   **GIRLIE: What did Eddy say?**

9   **ROIMATA: He said nothing happened between us.**

10   **GIRLIE: Bastard! But if he's telling the truth, Kevin must be**

11   **the father.**

12   **ROIMATA: Girlie, it doesn't matter whose baby it is.** *(GIRLIE*

13   *sits beside ROIMATA.)*

14   **GIRLIE: Stay. I'll help. We can manage.**

15   **ROIMATA: I thought you said you didn't want a screaming kid**

16   **around.**

17   **GIRLIE: I still think abortion is your best option. I had a baby**

18   **once. I adopted him out. I should have got rid of him. It**

19   **would have been easier. I think about him all the time.**

20   **He'd be nearly school age now.**

21   **ROIMATA: Why didn't you tell me before?**

22   **GIRLIE: What for? What's done is done. What's the use of**

23   **talking about it?**

24   **ROIMATA: Where is he, can you see him?**

25   **GIRLIE: No, I don't want to. You make one mistake and you pay**

26   **for it the rest of your life. I learnt to live with it. Please don't**

27   **go, Roimata. Give me a chance. I thought you liked it here?**

28   **ROIMATA: It would be too difficult.**

29   **GIRLIE: Things could work out for you and Kevin.**

30   **ROIMATA: No! Kevin knows exactly what he wants. Eddy**

31   **doesn't know what he wants.**

32   **GIRLIE: Look, I know I'm not the easiest person to live with,**

33   **but I'll make a real effort. I'd even help with the odd meal.**

34   **ROIMATA: Na, things wouldn't be the same if you went all tidy**

35   **on me.**

1   GIRLIE: Yeah, you're right. Probably wouldn't last a day. But we
2   got on okay, didn't we? I've got used to having you around.
3   ROIMATA: Why don't you come with me?
4   GIRLIE: What?
5   ROIMATA: Come with me, you might like it.
6   GIRLIE: Na.
7   ROIMATA: When I read your letter to Nan, she said you should
8   come back home.
9   GIRLIE: Did she?
10   ROIMATA: Yes, she did.
11   GIRLIE: She was a wise old lady. She brought you up okay.
12   ROIMATA: Why don't you? You said you wanted to. Just for a
13   look?
14   GIRLIE: Maybe I should. There's nothing keeping me here.
15   ROIMATA: Do you think you could stand the quiet?
16   GIRLIE: How quiet do you think a kid would be? Let's have a
17   drink to celebrate. *(ROIMATA looks at GIRLIE.)* We'll crack
18   open a bottle of Coke. *(They both laugh. GIRLIE gets up.)*
19   Roimata?
20   ROIMATA: Yeah?
21   GIRLIE: Any rich single fellas up there?
22
23
24   **THE END**
25
26
27
28
29
30
31
32
33
34
35

About the Playwrights

DONNA ABELA has been continuously involved with Powerhouse Youth Theatre, a company she co-founded in South-West Sydney in 1987. Since writing a number of their early works, she has written over twenty plays, many of them in a youth theatre or community development context. She has been a writer-in-residence a number of times, including with the Sydney Theatre Company, where she was also an affiliate writer in 1992–1993. She also has extensive experience as a dramaturge, script assessor and scriptwriting teacher. She completed her Master of Arts (Theatre Studies) at University of New South Wales in 1998 and has also studied at the New South Wales Institute of Technology and the National Institute of Dramatic Arts. In 1992, her play *HIGHEST MOUTAIN, FASTEST RIVER*, created with Salamanca Theatre Company, won the Human Rights and Equal Opportunities Award for Drama. Some of her other titles include *CIRCUS CARAVAN, QUEST, THE ROOD SCREEN* and the *DAPHNE MASSACRE*.

SHIRLEY BARRIE co-founded and was Associate Director of the Tricycle Theatre in London, England from 1972 to 1984 where she began writing plays for young audiences. In Toronto, she co-founded Straight Stitching Productions in 1989 and won two Chalmers awards and a Dora for *STRAIGHT STITCHING* and *CARRYING THE CALF*. Her most recent play for young audiences, *BRIGHT BONDFAST: SPACE SCIENTIST*, has been produced in Canada and the U.S.A. She has been writing a series of plays about fascinating women from the past: *MARGUERITE DE ROBERVAL* was produced in Newfoundland in 1997, and *THE PEAR IS RIPE* was staged at the Alumnae Theatre in Toronto in 2001. Her one-act, *REVELATION*, won the Drama Workshop Playwriting Competition in Des Moines, Iowa in 2000 and was produced in Toronto in 2001.

SUSAN BATTYE is Head of Drama at Epsom Girls Grammar School in Auckland, New Zealand, and President of the New Zealand Association for Drama in Education. She is currently the association's Australasian delegate on the International Drama and Education Association General Council. Susan has worked for many years as a writer of resources and workshop designer for the renown Maori Theatre in Education company, Te Rakau Hua O Te

Wao Rapu. In 2000 Susan co-authored and staged with Tim Bray an adult play, *PONSONBY ROAD*, which has been staged in Auckland. Her published plays include *THE SHADOW OF THE VALLEY* with Thelma Eakin, *EASY AS PIE* and *RADIO WAVES.*

WILLIAM BORDEN is a core alumnus playwright at The Playwrights' Center in Minneapolis, Playwright In Residence with Listening Winds Theatre, Fiction Editor of *THE NORTH DAKOTA QUARTERLY* and Chester Fritz Distinguished Professor of English Emeritus at the University of North Dakota. His plays have won 22 national playwriting competitions and have been widely published in such collections as *THE BEST STAGE SCENES OF 1998, ONE-ACT PLAYS FOR ACTING STUDENTS, THE PRAGUE REVIEW*, and other books and journals. His plays have had over 200 productions in New York, Los Angeles, Canada, Germany, the Actors Theatre of Louisville and elsewhere. The film adaptation of his play, *THE LAST PROSTITUTE*, starring Sonia Braga, was produced by Universal and shown on Lifetime television. In 1992, *TURTLE ISLAND BLUES* won the Deep South Playwriting Competition and the Great Platte River Playwriting Competition, and in 1993 it received a staged reading at the Phoenix Theatre Ensemble in New York. It has been widely produced in professional and community theatres, on Indian reservations, in community arts centers, schools and universities throughout Minnesota since then. Mr. Borden lives on a lake in northern Minnesota with his wife of 40 years.

RIWIA BROWN is a Maori writer, whose tribal affiliations are Ngati Porou, Te Whanau-A-Apanui and Taranaki. She received her education at St. Joseph's Maori Girls College in Napier, and she worked in London for several years before returning to New Zealand where she began work as an actor in Wellington with the group, Te Ohu Whaakari ("Young Maori in Performance"). *ROIMATA* was her first play, and following its production in 1988, it was published in 1991. Since then she has been a prolific playwright and a screenwriter for television and motion pictures. She has received commissions from the Queen Elizabeth Arts Council, has written the screenplays for prize-winning films at the Berlin Film Festival and other competitions, and since 1998 has been a member of the New Zealand Film Council. She is best known nationally and internationally for her screen adaptation of Alan Duff's novel, *ONCE THERE WERE WARRIORS*. She lives and works in New Zealand and currently serves as a member of the

New Zealand Film Commission.

MIRJANA BULJAN is a Croatian writer whose plays, books, films and other work have been widely published and produced in Europe. She has written six books, including *DUGO PUTONAJE U BIJELO (THE LONG VOYAGE IN THE WHITENESS — PLAYS FOR RADIO, TELEVISION AND THE THEATER, 1989), LUDI DANI U LUDOLANDIJI (CRAZY DAYS IN THE CRAZYLAND, 1990)* and *KOŠUTA JESEN I DRUGE BAJKE (THE ROE AUTUMN AND OTHER FAIRY TALES, 1995)*. Her teleplays include *PIJESAK (THE SAND*, produced in Sarajevo in 1974), *DOBA RASTA (TIME OF GROWING UP*, produced by RTV Zagreb in 1975); and some of her films include *PRED ODLAZAK (BEFORE GOING AWAY, 1976)*, and *RODENDAN (BIRTHDAY*, unproduced). Her plays have been translated into English, Italian, Slovenian, German, Hebrew and Hungarian, and she is also active as translator of works by James Joyce, Günter Grass, Strindberg, Horvath and others into her native Croatian. She has received the Grand Prix Ohrid from the Yugoslav Radio Festival and the Silver Medal in Italy's Giorgio La Pirra International Competition. Ms. Buljan lives and works in Zagreb, and is an active member of PEN, the Croatian Writers Association, the Croatian Journalists Association, Europäische Autorvereinigung "Kogge", and Women Playwrights International.

NEIL DUFFIELD has written over fifty plays for young audiences which have been produced widely throughout the United Kingdom and overseas. Recent work includes *THE FIREBIRD* (Dukes Theatre, Lancaster), *THE SNOW QUEEN* (Octagon Theatre, Bolton), *TALKING WITH ANGELS* (Quicksilver Theatre, London), *THE SECRET GARDEN* (Nottingham Playhouse), *NANNA'S NIGHTINGALE* (Action Transport Theatre, Cheshire) and *THE JUNGLE BOOK* (Arden Theatre, Philadelphia).

PATRICIA FRASER is a writer, actor and director who works primarily in the creation of original material for the stage, video and CBC radio. In 2000 she worked on a languages initiative project with the Little Salmon Carmacks First Nation, acted as guest Artistic Director of Nakai Theatre in Whitehorse, dramaturged New Theatre North, toured the high schools with a specially commissioned theatre piece, performed in the Leaky Heaven Circus and wrote Mortal Coil's *TREMENDOUS JOURNEY*. Currently she is working as a script mentor for Pacific Cinematheque on a youth and video project. Patti has been writing for the theatre in collaboration with other artists for the past twenty years.

ROSALIND GARDNER is an actor, director and author who lives and works in Auckland, New Zealand. A tutor on the Bachelor of Performing and Screen Arts at Unitec, she teaches acting technique and directs and writes for the program. For the past five years she has been Artistic Director of the "Out Loud" Youth Theatre Company for the Performing Arts School of New Zealand. For this company she has written and directed *AFTER TROY, MAP FOR RUNNING, THIS THING CALLED LOVE, CRYING FOR TIME* and most recently *DREAM IT [my life as it is.co.nz]*. Rosalind is currently working on a collection of three Theatre in Education plays for teenagers entitled *WHAT ARE YOU LOOKING AT?*

CLAUDIA MARINELLI is an Italian author who writes novels, short stories and poetry. She is a graduate of the Università de La Sapienza in Rome and has taught both in Italy and in the U.S. She has won numerous Italian literary prizes on a national and international level, and published an autobiographical novel about her experience in New York entitled *950 49th STREET BROOKLYN NEW YORK — A WOMAN'S INSIGHT INTO AMERICA*, that won two international Italian prizes in 1999 and has since been translated into English. *A LITTLE MONSTER'S JOURNAL* is her first attempt to write for the stage in order to realize her unfulfilled dream to become a playwright.

BOB MAYBERRY is co-founder of Attention Deficit Drama, a theatre group in West Michigan committed to short, experimental forms. Their most recent production was *KNEELING FOR THE BUTCHER*. Bob also teaches composition and playwriting at Grand Valley State University. His play *DISAPPEARING IN NEPAL* won the White Bird Annual Playwriting Contest in 1998. Other plays include *ASSIGNATION, THE CATECHISM OF PATTY REED, EATING MEMORY, RAGTOWN, THE THREE-MINUTE GODOT* and *CRISTOFINA SETS SAIL FOR THE NEW WORLD.*

JULIE SALVERSON is a playwright and the co-director of Flying Blind Theatre Events, producing community arts projects with professional artists, and based in Toronto, Canada. She is also a theatre professor who teaches acting, playwriting and performance classes at Queen's University in Kingston. She is widely published in scholarly presses as an expert in "performance testimony:" exploring through performance the relationship between aesthetics and ethics. *BOOM* has been frequently produced across Canada in schools and on community stages and was recently published in the *Canadian Theatre Review*.

R.N. SANDBERG's plays include *A WOMAN OF MEANS, CONVIVENCIA, DONE, IN BETWEEN, JARPEETZA/THE FIREBIRD, ROBINSWOOD, THIS LAND, EVENINGS IN/EVENINGS OUT* and adaptations of *ANNE OF GREEN GABLES, FRANKENSTEIN, THE MOONSTONE* and *SARA CREWE*. His work has been presented by theaters such as the Dallas Children's Theatre, The Empty Space, Fulton Opera House, George Street Playhouse, Houston's Stages Rep, Idaho Shakespeare Festival, Intiman Theatre, Laguna Playhouse, Louisville's Stage One, New City Theatre, Pennsylvania Stage Company, Seattle Children's Theatre, Seattle Public Theater, Seattle Rep and Yale Cabaret. He is currently writing *FRANKENSTEIN'S CHILDREN* for Metro Theater Company and *TRUE* for the McCarter Theatre. Since 1995, he has taught at Princeton University. He is a member of the Philadelphia Dramatists Center and the Dramatists Guild.

Credits

BACK WHERE YOU BELONG by Susan Battye. Copyright © 2000 by Susan Battye, all rights reserved. Reprinted by permission. All inquiries concerning rights should be directed to the author's agent: Playmarket, P.O. Box 9767, Te Aro, Wellington, NEW ZEALAND. E-mail: info@playmarket.org.nz, www.playmarket.org.nz.

BOOM by Julie Salverson and Patti Fraser. Copyright ©1998 by Julie Salverson and Patti Fraser, all rights reserved. Reprinted by permission. Information concerning rights should be addressed to the author: Julie Salverson, Dept. Of Drama, Queens University, Kingston, Ontario, CANADA. E-mail: salverson@oise.utoronto.ca.

CARRYING THE CALF by Shirley Barrie. Copyright © 1999 by Shirley Barrie. All rights reserved. Reprinted by permission. Information concerning rights should be addressed to the author: Shirley Barrie, 462 Clendenan Avenue, Toronto, Ontario M6P 2X6, CANADA. E-mail: sbarrie.kchubb@sympatico.ca.

CRYING FOR TIME by Ros Gardner. Copyright ©1998 by Rosalind Gardner, all rights reserved. Reprinted by permission. Information concerning rights should be addressed to the author: Ros Gardner, 180 Cliff View Drive, Green Bay, Auckland, NEW ZEALAND. E-mail: easton@ihug.co.nz.

HIGHEST MOUNTAIN, FASTEST RIVER by Donna Abela with Salamanca Theatre Company. Copyright © 1993 by Donna Abela, Annette Downs, Lian Tanner, Kym Tonkin, David Williamson and Salamanca Theatre Company. All rights reserved. Reprinted by permission. Information concerning rights should be addressed to the author: Donna Abela, 3/41 Shaw Street, Petersham NSW 2049, AUSTRALIA. E-mail: dabela@aol.com. Or to Salamanca Theatre Company, 77 Salamanca Place, Hobart, Tasmania 7000, AUSTRALIA. E-mail: stc@salamancatheatre.com.au.

LILFORD MILL by Neil Duffield. Copyright © 1999 by Neil Duffield. All rights reserved. Reprinted by permission. Information concerning rights should be addressed to the author: Neil Duffield, 2 Gorses Mount, Darcy Lever, Bolton BL2 1PQ, UNITED KINGDOM

A LITTLE MONSTER'S JOURNAL by Claudia Marinelli, Copyright © 2000 by Claudia Marinelli, all rights reserved. Reprinted by permission. Information concerning rights should be addressed

About the Editor

Roger Ellis is a theatre director, university professor and author living in Michigan. He earned his M.A. in Theatre from the University of Santa Clara, and his Ph.D. in Dramatic Art from the University of California at Berkeley. He trained as an actor under Michael Shurtleff, Carlo Mazzone-Clementi of Dell'Arte, Robert Goldsby of the Berkeley Repertory Theatre and James Roose-Evans of Great Britain's National Theatre. He has also spent nine seasons as an actor-director with repertory, summer stock, Festival, and dinner theatres in California and Michigan; he frequently conducts workshops in the Great Lakes region and abroad on acting and auditioning skills. He has authored or edited twelve books for the stage, including anthologies, critical works and acting texts. In 1991 he initiated an ethnic theatre program at Grand Valley State University in Michigan, creating guest artist residencies and presenting new international plays dealing with cultural diversity; in 1993 he established that University's Shakespeare Festival, currently the oldest and largest in Michigan; and in 1997 he established Grand Valley's annual New Plays-in-Process program, bringing national playwrights to Michigan for extended rehearsals and staged reading productions of their new work. He is currently the President of the Theatre Alliance of Michigan, editor of the international theatre journal *IDEACTION* and a Professor of Theatre Arts at Grand Valley State University.

Order Form

Meriwether Publishing Ltd.
PO Box 7710
Colorado Springs CO 80933-7710
Phone: 800-937-5297 Fax: 719-594-9916
Website: www.meriwether.com

Please send me the following books:

_____	**New International Plays for Young Audiences** #BK-B257	**$19.95**
	edited by Roger Ellis	
	Plays of cultural conflict	
_____	**International Plays for Young Audiences** #BK-B240	**$16.95**
	edited by Roger Ellis	
	Contemporary works from leading playwrights	
_____	**Multicultural Theatre** #BK-B205	**$15.95**
	edited by Roger Ellis	
	Scenes and monologs by multicultural writers	
_____	**Multicultural Theatre II** #BK-B223	**$15.95**
	edited by Roger Ellis	
	Contemporary Hispanic, Asian, and African-American plays	
_____	**Plays for Young Audiences by Max Bush** #BK-B131	**$16.95**
	edited by Roger Ellis	
	An anthology of widely produced plays for youth	
_____	**Scenes and Monologs from the Best New Plays** #BK-B140	**$15.95**
	edited by Roger Ellis	
	An anthology of new American plays	
_____	**One-Act Plays for Acting Students** #BK-B159	**$17.95**
	by Dr. Norman A. Bert	
	An anthology of complete one-act plays	

These and other fine Meriwether Publishing books are available at your local bookstore or direct from the publisher. Prices subject to change without notice. Check our website or call for current prices.

Name: _____

Organization name: _____

Address: _____

City: _____ State: _____

Zip: _____ Phone: _____

❏ **Check enclosed**

❏ **Visa / MasterCard / Discover #** _____

Expiration

Signature: _____ *date:* _____

(required for credit card orders)

Colorado residents: Please add 3% sales tax.
Shipping: Include $3.75 for the first book and 75¢ for each additional book ordered.

❏ *Please send me a copy of your complete catalog of books and plays.*

DATE DUE

PRINTED IN U.S.A.

GAYLORD